June 30–July 4, 2014
Marcq-en-Baroeul, France

Association for
Computing Machinery

Advancing Computing as a Science & Profession

CBSE'14

Proceedings of the 17th International ACM SIGSOFT Symposium on

Component-Based Software Engineering

(part of CompArch 2014)

Sponsored by:

ACM SIGSOFT

Advancing Computing as a Science & Profession

The Association for Computing Machinery
2 Penn Plaza, Suite 701
New York, New York 10121-0701

Notice to Past Authors of ACM-Published Articles

ACM intends to create a complete electronic archive of all articles and/or other material previously published by ACM. If you have written a work that has been previously published by ACM in any journal or conference proceedings prior to 1978, or any SIG Newsletter at any time, and you do NOT want this work to appear in the ACM Digital Library, please inform permissions@acm.org, stating the title of the work, the author(s), and where and when published.

ISBN: 978-1-4503-2577-6 (Digital)

ISBN: 978-1-4503-3116-6 (Print)

Additional copies may be ordered prepaid from:

ACM Order Department
PO Box 30777
New York, NY 10087-0777, USA

Phone: 1-800-342-6626 (USA and Canada)
+1-212-626-0500 (Global)
Fax: +1-212-944-1318
E-mail: acmhelp@acm.org
Hours of Operation: 8:30 am – 4:30 pm ET

Printed in the USA

CompArch 2014 General Chair's Welcome

Welcome to CompArch 2014, the Federated Events on Component-Based Software Engineering and Software Architecture, held in Lille, France, from 30 June to 3 July 2014.

The three main events composing CompArch are:

* CBSE 2014: the 17th ACM SIGSOFT Symposium on Component Based Software Engineering

* QoSA 2014: the 10th International ACM SIGSOFT Conference on Quality of Software Architectures

* WCOP 2014: the 19th International Doctoral Symposium on Components and Architecture

We would like to thank those who helped us organize CompArch this year. In particular, we thank Lisa Tolles, Cindy Edwards and her associates at Sheridan Communications who assembled the proceedings you are reading; Romain Rouvoy, who took care with maestro of the event publicity; Laurence Duchien and Martin Monperrus, who provided their assistance, support and enthusiasm for organizing the event; Sophie Lefebvre and Pauline Bachelard from Perspectives & Organisation, who mastered all the details of the organization.

At ACM and ACM SIGSOFT, we want to thank for her support Adrienne Griscti, and Will Tracz, chair of SIGSOFT, for his backing. A special thanks also to Clemens Szyperski, Ivica Crnkovic, Ralf Reussner, Raffaela Mirandola, and all the members of the CompArch steering committee for selecting Lille as the host of the 2014 edition and their continuous support.

At the University of Lille (Lille 1), I want to thank the research council, Sophie Tison, director of the Computer Science Laboratory, and Marc Douay, director of the Ambiant Intelligence Campus program, for their support in organizing this event.

We hope that you'll find the overall program interesting, inspiring and that you will return home with plenty of new insights and connections into our community, that will lead you to further successes.

Lionel Seinturier
CompArch 2014 General Chair
Université Lille 1
France

Welcome to CBSE'14

It is a great pleasure to welcome you to the 17th International ACM SIGSOFT Symposium on Component-Based Software Engineering – CBSE'14. Although component-based development is stabilizing as a more mature field, in academia as well as in industry, it is still an active and expanding research domain with plenty of challenges remaining, both in terms of fundamentals and concerning how to efficiently apply the concepts in practice. Recently, component-based approaches have also gained momentum in the domains of embedded and cyber-physical systems, where resource limitations and safety concerns give rise to new challenges. Reflecting this, the special theme for 2014 is "Dependable and Predictable Components".

The call for papers attracted 62 submissions from Europe (France, Germany, Czech Republic, United Kingdom, Spain, Sweden, Austria, Belgium, Luxembourg, Switzerland and Cyprus); Asia (India, Pakistan, Lebanon and Korea); America (Brazil, United States, Canada and Colombia); Africa (Algeria and Tunisia); and Australia. Each paper was assigned three reviewers, and after extensive discussions the Program Committee decided to accept 21 papers (14 regular papers and 7 short papers). The topics of the accepted papers range from testing and monitoring, over connector classification, to formal reasoning and model checking. A clear trend among the accepted papers this year is that many of them address different aspects of reconfigurable and adaptive component-based systems.

CBSE 2014 is part of the federated event CompArch 2014 together with the 10th International ACM SIGSOFT Conference on the Quality of Software Architectures (QoSA) and the 19th International Doctoral Symposium on Components and Architecture (WCOP). We thank the CompArch general chair Lionel Seinturier and the CompArch organization team for coordinating and setting up the various events.

Special thanks go to all authors who submitted papers for their valuable contributions that allowed the CBSE 2014 program committee to put in place an exciting program. We are also very grateful to the program committee members who worked actively on paper reviewing and discussions, and provided the authors with detailed comments for improving the scientific content and quality of their papers. Finally, we also want to thank Cindy Edwards and Lisa Tolles at Sheridan Communications, for coordinating the proceedings, and of course our sponsor, ACM SIGSOFT.

We hope that you will find the CBSE 2014 program interesting and relevant to your own research activities, and that your participation in the event will give you new contacts, and hopefully trigger new collaborations, with researchers and practitioners in the international CBSE community.

Eduardo Almeida
CBSE'14 Program Chair
Federal University of Bahia, Brazil

Jan Carlson
CBSE'14 Program Chair
Mälardalen University, Sweden

Table of Contents

CBSE 4: Analysis and Monitoring

CBSE 5: Connecting Components

CBSE 6: Formal Approaches to CBSE

Tutorials

CBSE 2014 Conference Organization

General Chair: Lionel Seinturier *(Université Lille 1, France)*

Program Co-Chairs: Eduardo Almeida *(Federal University of Bahia, Brazil)*
Jan Carlson *(Mälardalen University, Sweden)*

Publicity Chair: Romain Rouvoy *(Université Lille 1, France)*

Organizing Committee: Laurence Duchien *(Université Lille 1, France)*
Martin Monperrus *(Université Lille 1, France)*

Steering Committee: Ivica Crnkovic *(Mälardalen University, Sweden)*
Ian Gorton *(Software Engineering Institute, USA)*
George Heineman *(Worcester Polytechnic Institute, USA)*
Grace A. Lewis *(CMU Software Engineering Institute, USA)*
Raffaela Mirandola *(Politecnico di Milano, Italy)*
Ralf Reussner *(Karlsruhe Institute of Technology, Germany)*
Heinz Schmidt *(RMIT University, Australia)*
Judith Stafford *(University of Colorado, USA)*
Clemens Szyperski *(Microsoft Research, USA)*

Program Committee: Franck Barbier *(University of Pau, France)*
Steffen Becker *(University of Paderborn, Germany)*
Domenico Bianculli *(University of Luxembourg, Luxembourg)*
Etienne Borde *(Telecom ParisTech, France)*
Premek Brada *(University of West Bohemia, Czech Republic)*
Radu Calinescu *(University of York, UK)*
Carlos Canal *(University of Málaga, Spain)*
Alessandro Garcia *(PUC-Rio, Brazil)*
Gregor Goessler *(INRIA, France)*
Ian Gorton *(CMU Software Engineering Institute, USA)*
Lars Grunske *(University of Stuttgart, Germany)*
George Heineman *(Worcester Polytechnic Institute, USA)*
Petr Hnetynka *(Charles University in Prague, Czech Republic)*
Gang Huang *(Peking University, China)*
Oliver Hummel *(Karlsruhe Institute of Technology, Germany)*
Valerie Issarny *(INRIA, France)*
Fabrice Kordon *(LIP6/UPMC, France)*
Anne Koziolek *(Karlsruhe Institute of Technology, Germany)*
Magnus Larsson *(ABB, India)*
Kung-Kiu Lau *(University of Manchester, UK)*
Grace A. Lewis *(CMU Software Engineering Institute, USA)*
Frédéric Loiret *(Institute für Informatik, Germany)*

Program Committee (continued):

Patricia López Martínez *(University of Cantabria, Spain)*
Raffaela Mirandola *(Politecnico di Milano, Italy)*
Henry Muccini *(University of L'Aquila, Italy)*
Rob van Ommering *(Philips Research, Netherlands)*
Noel Plouzeau *(IRISA/University of Rennes 1, France)*
Sanjai Rayadurgam *(University of Minnesota, USA)*
Ralf Reussner *(Karlsruhe Institute of Technology, Germany)*
Salah Sadou *(IRISA/University of South Brittany, France)*
Séverine Sentilles *(Mälardalen University, Sweden)*
Judith Stafford *(University of Colorado, USA)*
Clemens Szyperski *(Microsoft Research, USA)*
Massimo Tivoli *(University of L'Aquila, Italy)*
Michael Wahler *(ABB Corporate Research, Switzerland)*
Claudia Maria Lima Werner *(Federal University of Rio de Janeiro, Brazil)*

Additional reviewers:

Asmaa Alayed
Fahad Albogamy
Mauricio Alferez
Olivier Barais
Johann Bourcier
Eric Cariou
Vasileios Christou
Marco Di Beneditto
Simone Di Cola
Didier Donsez
Lucia Happe
Robert Heinrich
Christian Heinzemann
Lom Messan Hillah
Kamil Jezek
Kenneth Johnson
Shinji Kikuchi
Max Kramer
Olivier Le Goaer
Andrea Magdaleno
Ivano Malavolta
Aurelien Monot
Qais Noorshams
Richard Parker
Alina Patelli
Samson Pierre
Teerat Pitakrat
Marie Christin Platenius
Claudia Prieserjahn
Misha Strittmatter
Chouki Tibermacine
Tewfik Ziadi

Sponsor:

Principles and Methods for Elastic Computing

Schahram Dustdar
Vienna University of Technology
Distributed Systems Group
dustdar@dsg.tuwien.ac.at

Abstract

In this talk I will address one of the most relevant challenges for a decade to come: How to design, model, and execute distributed systems utilizing the Internet of Things, software services, as well as human based services, considering modern Cloud Computing and Elasticity principles. Elasticity is seen as one of the main characteristics of Cloud Computing today. Is elasticity simply scalability on steroids? In this talk I will discuss the main principles of elasticity, present a fresh look at this problem, and examine how to integrate people, software services, and things into one composite system, which can be modeled, programmed, and deployed on a large scale in an elastic way.

Categories and Subject Descriptors

C.2.4 Distributed Systems; H.3.4 Systems and Software

Keywords

Cloud Computing; Elasticity; Internet of Things; Human-based services

CBSE'14, June 30–July 4, 2014, Marcq-en-Baroeul, France.
ACM 978-1-4503-2577-6/14/06.
http://dx.doi.org/10.1145/2602458.2611455

Short Bio

Schahram Dustdar is Full Professor of Computer Science with a focus on Internet Technologies heading the Distributed Systems Group, Institute of Information Systems, Vienna University of Technology (TU Wien). From 2004-2010 he was Honorary Professor of Information Systems at the Dept. of Computing Science at the University of Groningen (RuG), The Netherlands. Since 2009 he is an ACM Distinguished Scientist. At this time his h-index is 46.

He is a member of the Academia Europaea: The Academy of Europe, Informatics Section (since 2013), recipient of the ACM Distinguished Scientist award (2009), and the IBM Faculty Award (2012). He is an Associate Editor of IEEE Transactions on Services Computing, ACM Transactions on the Web, and ACM Transactions on Internet Technology and on the editorial board of IEEE Internet Computing. He is the Editor-in-Chief of Computing (an SCI-ranked journal of Springer).

His past work experience includes several years as the founding head of the Center for Informatics (ZID) at the University of Art and Industrial Design in Linz (1991-1999), Austrian project manager of the MICE EU-project (1993 - 97), and director of Coordination Technologies at the Design Transfer Center in Linz (1999 - 2000). He was a post-doctoral research scholar (Erwin-Schrödinger scholarship) at the London School of Economics (Information Systems Department) (1993 and 1994), and a visiting research scientist at NTT Multimedia Communications Labs in Palo Alto, USA during 1998. From 1999 - 2007 he worked as the co-founder and chief scientist of Caramba Labs Software AG (CarambaLabs.com) in Vienna.

His research interests include Distributed Systems, Internet Technologies, Service-oriented Computing, Cloud Computing, Social Computing.

Modular Coordination of Multiple Autonomic Managers *

Gwenaël Delaval, Soguy Mak-Karé Gueye, Noël De Palma
Univ. Grenoble Alpes, LIG
Grenoble, France
gwenael.delaval@inria.fr,
soguy-mak-kare.gueye@inria.fr,
noel.depalma@imag.fr

Eric Rutten
INRIA
Grenoble, France
eric.rutten@inria.fr

ABSTRACT

Complex computing systems are increasingly self-adaptive, with an autonomic computing approach for their administration. Real systems require the co-existence of multiple autonomic management loops, each complex to design. However their uncoordinated co-existence leads to performance degradation and possibly to inconsistency. There is a need for methodological supports facilitating the coordination of multiple autonomic managers. In this paper we propose a method focusing on the discrete control of the interactions of managers. We follow a component-based approach and explore modular discrete control, allowing to break down the combinatorial complexity inherent to the state-space exploration technique. This improves scalability of the approach and allows constructing a hierarchical control. It also allows re-using complex managers in different contexts without modifying their control specifications. We build a component-based coordination of managers, with introspection, adaptivity and reconfiguration. We validate our method on a multiple-loop multi-tier system.

Categories and Subject Descriptors

K.6 [**Management of Computing and Information Systems**]: System Management; D.2.2 [**Software Engineering**]: Design Tools and Techniques—*Computer-aided software engineering, State diagrams*; D.2.11 [**Software Engineering**]: Software Architectures—*Domain-specific architectures, languages, patterns*

Keywords

Autonomic computing; Component dynamic adaptation; Automated management; Control loops; Formal methods; Self-adaptive systems; Software reuse

*This research is partly supported by the FSN Datalyse project and ANR INFRA (ANR-11-INFR 012 11) under a grant for the project Gtrl-Green.

CBSE'14, June 30–July 4, 2014, Marcq-en-Baroeul, France.

http://dx.doi.org/10.1145/2602458.2602465 .

1. INTRODUCTION

1.1 Context

Complex computing systems are increasingly designed to be self-adaptive, and therefore adopt the autonomic computing approach for the management of their administration [18]. Computing infrastructures are equipped with Autonomic Managers (AM), where monitors or sensors gather relevant information on the state and events of the Managed Elements (ME). Execution of administration actions, offered by the system API, implements regulation of the ME's activities. In between, the loop is closed by a decision component. An AM is a component that continuously reacts to flows of input information by flows of output actions, it can therefore be considered as a reactive system [11]. Self-management issues include self-configuration, self-optimization, self-healing (fault tolerance and repair), and self-protection. Typical examples are found in data-centers, with managers for resources, dependability, and energetic efficiency, as we consider in the Ctrl-Green project[1]. Usually, the automation of such administration issues is approached by building efficient and robust AMs, such as self-sizing, self-repair [21], robust reconfiguration [4] or consolidation [16].

1.2 Coordination of managers

Real systems have multiple dimensions to be managed. They do require the co-existence of multiple autonomic managers. However their uncoordinated execution can lead to interferences that could cause performance degradation or even inconsistency [1]. This is still an open problem in autonomic computing [17]. One solution consists in re-designing a new global loop taking into account combined effects, but this is even more complex than for individual loops, and is contrary to the benefits of modularity and re-usability of the AMs. Therefore, there is a deep need for methodological supports facilitating the coordination of multiple autonomic managers. Many approaches have been proposed for coordinating managers. For instance in the presence of quantitative metrics, like energy and performance, it is possible to define composition functions [6], for example involving notions of utility. Here, we consider the case of event-based coordination focusing on qualitative aspects. The coordination strategy can be ensured by an upper-level AM. This latter AM, above the individual AMs considered as MEs themselves, constitutes a coordination controller.
Some component-based frameworks, e.g., Fractal [5], provide

[1]`http://www.en.ctrlgreen.org/`

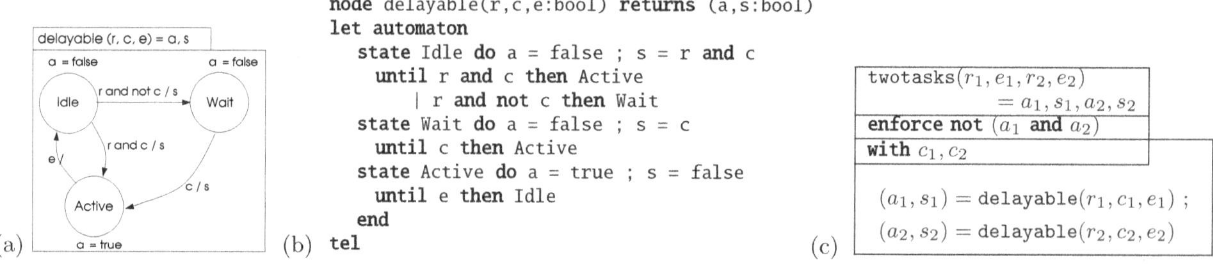
delayable (r, c, e) = a, s
a = false
a = false
Idle
r and not c / s
Wait
r and c / s
e
c / s
Active
a = true
(a)
node delayable(r,c,e:bool) returns (a,s:bool)
let automaton
state Idle do a = false ; s = r and c
until r and c then Active
| r and not c then Wait
state Wait do a = false ; s = c
until c then Active
state Active do a = true ; s = false
until e then Idle
end
(b) tel
twotasks(r_1, e_1, r_2, e_2)
$= a_1, s_1, a_2, s_2$
enforce not (a_1 and a_2)
with c_1, c_2
$(a_1, s_1) =$ delayable(r_1, c_1, e_1) ;
$(a_2, s_2) =$ delayable(r_2, c_2, e_2)
(c)

Figure 1: Heptagon/BZR example: delayable task control(a) graphical / (b) textual ; (c) exclusion contract.

a structural hierarchical framework, associating a control behavior locally to a component, where the problem of coordination can be addressed. AM components are equipped with notions of observability and controllability. However, hand-made methodologies remain complex and error-prone, and hard to re-use. The difficulty in designing coordinators is in the combinatorial complexity of cases of interferences, for which there is a need for support models and tools. Another way to look at it is to consider actions invocations and their firing conditions as events, and to enforce a control logic that prevents malfunction, based on states of the AMs. Coordinating AMs can then be seen as the problem of synchronization and logical control of administration operations which can be applied by AMs on the MEs in response to observed events. The combinatorial complexity of formal techniques at compilation time calls for methods explicitly considering scalability issues, e.g., through modularity.

1.3 Our approach and contribution

In previous work [7, 9], we have defined the notion of controllable autonomic manager components, and proposed the reactive control of their coordinated assemblies in a hierarchical, systematic structure. Our approach involves formal models and techniques originally designed for reactive embedded systems. We adopt the so-called "synchronous" languages which are specially well-fit for the specification, validation and implementation of reactive kernels [11], which makes them relevant for the problem domain of autonomic loops. Additionally, we benefit from the Discrete Control Synthesis (DCS) technique, stemming from Control Theory [20] and integrated in the synchronous languages and tools [19] : it enforces coordination logic between concurrent activities, in terms of events and states, with automated algorithms used off-line, at compilation time. However, in [9], our hierarchical proposal remained monolithic.

In this paper, our contribution is to leverage the approach with a method stressing modularity, with benefits for the design of multiple-loop managers: (i) re-use of complex managers and their control specifications without modification, in different contexts, (ii) scalability for the state-space-based control technique, by breaking down its combinatorial complexity. Another contribution is the validation of our method in the coordination of a multi-loop autonomic multi-tier system, supporting multiple applications.

The principle of our approach is to identify design constraints on AMs : observability and controllability, and to construct a component-based structure where they are explicit, in a way not involving modifying the AMs. Section 2 introduces background ; Section 3 defines the modular specification and formalization of behaviors and coordination control objectives ; Section 4 validates our approach on a class of multi-tier autonomic systems ; Section 5 discusses related work ; Section 6 concludes and draws perspectives.

2. BACKGROUND: REACTIVE CONTROL

2.1 Reactive languages and Mode Automata

Reactive systems are characterized by their continuous interaction with their environment, reacting to flows of inputs by producing flows of outputs. They are classically modeled as transition systems or automata, with languages like StateCharts [13]. We adopt the approach of synchronous languages [11], because we then have access to the control tools used further. The synchronous paradigm refer to the automata parallel composition that we use in these languages, allowing for clear formal semantics, while supporting modelling asynchronous computations [12]: actions can be asynchronously started, and their completion is waited for, without blocking other activity continuing in parallel. The Heptagon/BZR language [8] supports programming of mixed synchronous data-flow equations and automata, called Mode Automata, with parallel and hierarchical composition. The basic behavior is that at each reaction step, values in the input flows are used, as well as local and memory values, in order to compute the next state and the values of the output flows for that step. Inside the nodes, this is expressed as a set of equations defining, for each output and local, the value of the flow, in terms of an expression on other flows, possibly using local flows and state values from past steps.

Figure 1(a,b) shows a small Heptagon/BZR program. The node `delayable` programs the control of a task, which can either be idle, waiting or active. When it is in the initial Idle state, the occurrence of the **`true`** value on input `r` *requests* the starting of the task. Another input `c` can either allow the activation, or temporarily block the request and make the automaton go to a waiting state. Input `e` notifies termination. The outputs represent, resp., `a`: activity of the task, and `s`: triggering the concrete task start in the system's API. Such automata and data-flow reactive nodes can be reused by instantiation, and composed in parallel (noted "`;`") and in a hierarchical way, as illustrated in the body of the node in Figure 1(c), with two instances of the `delayable` node. They run in parallel, in a synchronous way: one global step corresponds to one local step for every node.

The compiler produces executable code in target languages such as C or Java, in the form of an initialisation function *reset*, and a *step* function implementing the transition function of the resulting automaton. It takes incoming values of

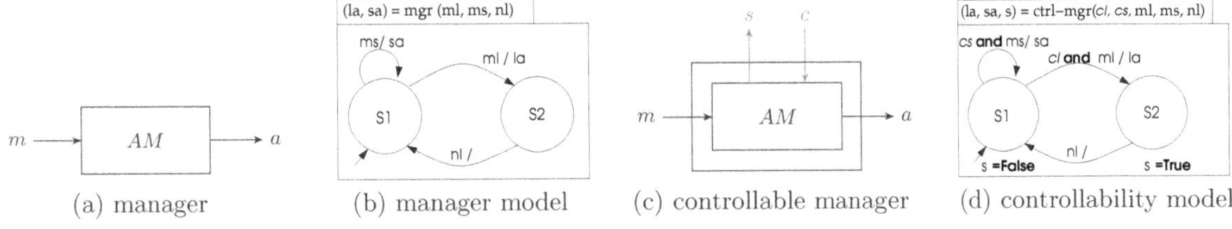

(a) manager (b) manager model (c) controllable manager (d) controllability model

Figure 2: Modelling managers control

input flows gathered in the environment, computes the next state on internal variables, and returns values for the output flows. This function is called at relevant instants from the infrastructure where the controller is used.

2.2 Discrete control and Heptagon/BZR

Using a reactive language gives all the support of the the classical formal framework of Labelled Transition Systems (LTS), not formally described here due to space limitations. In this work, we focus on software engineering and methodology; formal techniques are not in the scope of this paper [8]. Particularly, we benefit from state-space exploration techniques, like Model-Checking or, more originally, Discrete Controller Synthesis (DCS). Initially defined in the framework of language theory [20], DCS has been adapted to symbolic LTS and implemented in tools within the synchronous technology [19]. It is applied on an FSM representing possible behaviors of a system, its variables being partitioned into controllable ones and uncontrollable ones. For a given control objective (e.g., staying invariantly inside a given subset of states, considered "good"), the DCS algorithm automatically computes, by exploration of the state space, the constraint on controllable variables, depending on the current state, for any value of the uncontrollables, so that remaining behaviors satisfy the objective. This constraint is inhibiting the minimum possible behaviors, therefore it is called *maximally permissive*. Algorithms are related to model checking techniques for state space exploration. If no solution is found, because the problem is over constrained, then DCS plays the role of a verification.

The Heptagon/BZR language[2] includes a behavioral contract syntax [8]. It allows for the declaration, using the **with** statement, of *controllable variables*, the value of which being not defined by the programmer. These free variables can be used in the program to describe choices between several transitions. They are defined, in the final executable program, by the controller computed off-line by DCS, according to the expression given in the **enforce** statement. Knowledge about the environment such as, for instance event occurrence order can be declared in an **assume** statement. This is taken into account during the computation of the controller with DCS. Heptagon/BZR compilation invokes a DCS tool, and inserts the synthesized controller in the generated executable code, which has the same structure as above: *reset* and *step* functions. Figure 1(c) shows an example of contract coordinating two instances of the `delayable` node of Figure 1(a). The `twotasks` node has a **with** part declaring controllable variables c_1 and c_2, and the **enforce** part asserts the property to be enforced by DCS. Here, we want to ensure that the two tasks running in parallel will not be both active at the same time: **not** (a_1 **and** a_2). Thus, c_1 and c_2 will be used by the synthesized controller to delay some requests, leading automata of tasks to the waiting state whenever the other task is active. The constraint produced by DCS can have several solutions: the Heptagon/BZR compiler generates deterministic executable code by favoring, for each controllable, value **true** over **false**, in the order of declaration.

[2]`http://bzr.inria.fr`

3. MODULAR COORDINATION

In this section, we first introduce the basic elements of modeling for coordination by discrete control in Section 3.1: the notions explored in previous work [9] are redefined in a new way, so that given the need for modularity detailed in Section 3.2, it allows for their re-use to build up the method for modular coordination in Section 3.3.

3.1 Basic AMs coordination

3.1.1 Behavior of managers

We model an autonomic manager as a reactive data-flow component. As shown in Figure 2(a), it receives a flow m of monitor inputs that it analyses in a decision process based on a representation of the managed system status. It appropriately emits a flow a of actions according to a management policy or strategy AM. Figure 2(b) shows a simple example of a manager behavior's model. It has two execution states represented by $S1$ which is the initial state, and $S2$. In $S1$ when it receives the input ms, it emits sa and stays in $S1$. We distinguish between such simple, short actions (instantaneous in the particular sense that they are completed within the execution of a step of the automaton) and long actions (asynchronous), as can be done classically with synchronous models [3]. Thus, when the automaton receives ml, it emits la and goes to $S2$ representing the processing of the action la. It returns back to $S1$ at the reception of nl notifying the completion of the asynchronous execution of la. In general, FSMs distinguish states useful for the coordination, as illustrated by concrete cases further in Section 4.

3.1.2 Controllability of managers

The controllability of the managers is considered here only at large-grain and consists in allowing or inhibiting the trigger of the management processes inherent to their management decisions. In the models, the control is represented by control variables, however its real implementation can be done in several different ways: for example the manager can be suspended and re-activated, or it can have an event interception mechanism. As shown in Figure 2(c), we exhibit the controllability of the manager by adding additional control variables c that allow to inhibit the actions a the manager can trigger. Without loss of generality, we consider one Boolean input for each action which we want to be controllable. If some actions are not controllable due to their nature (e.g., urgent recovery), or if the coordination problem does not require all of them to be controllable, then only the relevant ones can be associated with such a control condition. In general, additional outputs are also needed to exhibit an internal state s of AM, necessary for the outside controller to compute c e.g., in the case of a long action, informing that a notification nl has not arrived yet. Figure 2(d) shows how we integrate control in the previous model. We add in **ctrl-mgr** Boolean inputs cl, cs for each corresponding action, to condition transitions firing, in conjunction with the monitoring, hence giving the possibility of inhibiting actions. Output s exhibits the current state of the manager, typically the fact that a long action is executed. Note that the long action, once started, cannot be prevented or interrupted here.

3.1.3 Coordination of managers by control

The coordination of several managers is defined by the composition of the models exhibiting the controllability of their behaviors to which we associate a behavioral contract specifying the coordination policy. Figure 3(a) shows a composite node **coord-mgrs**, its body corresponds to the parallel composition of the control models **ctrl-m**$_i$ of the managers to coordinate. The associated contract for their coordination consists of three statements. The `with` statement is where their control variables c_i are declared to be local to **coord-mgrs**, and to be controllable in terms of DCS, as introduced in Section 2.2. The `enforce` statement gives the contract in the form of a Boolean expression *Obj* on variables from the nodes inputs or internal state s_i. The **`assume`** statement is where knowledge about the environment is defined. For simplicity we do not use it.

For example a coordination objective between two manager components, AM_1 and AM_2, can be to prevent AM_2 from triggering an action a_2 when AM_1 is in some state given by s_1. This is encoded by the following expression, to be made invariant by control: **`not`** (s_1 **`and`** a_2). The generated controller enforcing the coordination policy, as in Figure 3(b), is in charge of producing appropriate values for the c_i control inputs to the managers. The coordination logic acts as an additional component. It enforces a policy defined in the contract for managing the interactions between the AM_i based on their inputs m_i, n_i and state s_i. At this level, the DCS problem formally encoding the coordination problem can be solved using monolithic DCS. In case of a hierarchical structure, the main Heptagon/BZR node is constructed with the contract enforcing the conjunction of all the local objectives, declaring the union of all local controllable variables, and with a body composing all manager control automata in parallel. Hence the control is centralized since only one controller is in charge of enforcing the overall objectives, if the synthesis succeeds.

3.2 The need and means for modularity

3.2.1 Limitations and need for modularity

Advantages of our DCS-based approach are manifold: (i) high-level language support for controller design (tedious and error-prone to code manually at lower level) ; (ii) automated formal synthesis of controllers, correct by design (hard to guarantee manually) ; (iii) maximal permissiveness of controllers : they are minimally constraining, and in that sense optimal (even more difficult to obtain manually). However, until now the approach had not been leveraged to hierarchical modularity, and remained monolithic.

This produces a unique controller enforcing the overall control objectives. However, when considering a large number of managers, this monolithic approach might not succeed, because exploring the large state space would be very time consuming. This can take several days and can fail due to computing resource limits. This limits the scalability of the approach. Furthermore, a modification, even partial, leads to a recompilation of the overall coordinated composition invalidating previous generated codes which limits the re-usability of management components.

To address this issue, we want to exploit modular DCS, where the control objectives can be decomposed in several parts, each part managed by a controller. Each controller manages a limited number of components. This decreases the state space to explore for the synthesis of each controller. The recompilation of a controller that has no impact on other controllers does not require the recompilation of the latter. This makes possible the re-use of controllers generated codes. Not only autonomic managers are available for re-use but coordinated assemblies of managers can also be made available for further re-use. In the following Sections we detail how modular DCS is used to obtain this scalability and re-usability of management components.

3.2.2 Modular contracts in Heptagon/BZR

Modular DCS consists in taking advantage of the modular structure of the system to control locally some subparts of this system [19]. The benefits of this technique is firstly, to allow computing the controller only once for specific components, independently of the context where this component is used, hence being able to reuse the computed controller in other contexts. Secondly, as DCS itself is performed on a subpart of the system, the model from which the controller is synthesized can be much smaller than the global model of the system. Therefore, as DCS is of practical exponential complexity, the gain in synthesis time can be high and it can be applied on larger and more complex systems.

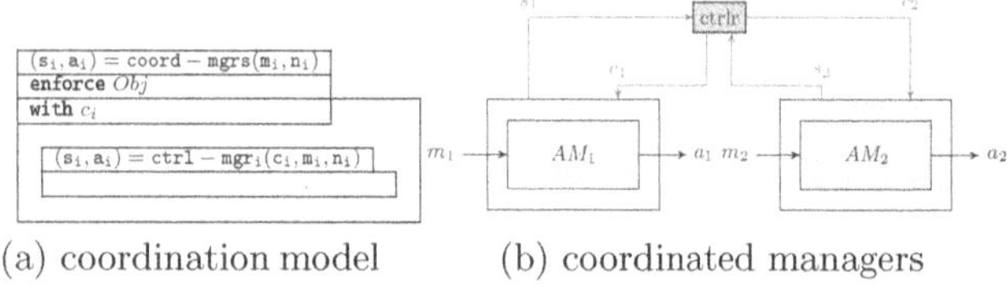

Figure 3: Single-level coordination of managers

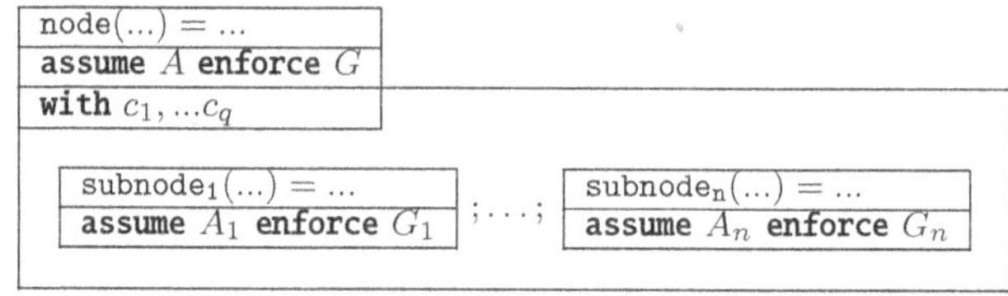

Figure 4: Modular contracts in Heptagon/BZR.

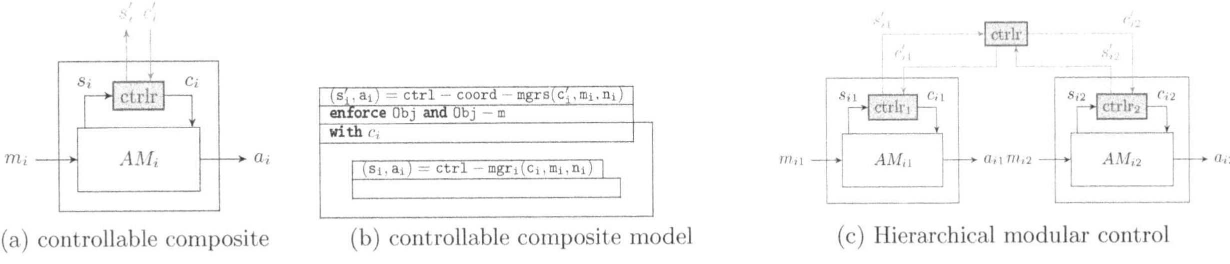

(a) controllable composite (b) controllable composite model (c) Hierarchical modular control

Figure 5: Modular coordination of managers

Heptagon/BZR benefits from the modular compilation of the nodes: each node is compiled towards one sequential function, regardless of its calling context, the inside called nodes being abstracted. Thus, modular DCS is performed by using the contracts as abstraction of the sub-nodes. One controller is synthesized for each node supplied with local controllable variables. The contracts of the sub-nodes are used as environment model, as abstraction of the contents of these nodes, to synthesize the local controller. As shown in Figure 4, the objective is to control the body and coordinate sub-nodes, using controllable variables $c_1, ..., c_q$, given as inputs to the sub-nodes, so that G is true, assuming that A is true. Here, we have information on sub-nodes, so that we can assume not only A, but also that the n sub-nodes each do enforce their contract : $\bigwedge_{i=1}^{n}(A_i \implies G_i)$. Accordingly, the problem becomes that: assuming the above, we want to enforce G as well as $\bigwedge_{i=1}^{n} A_i$. Control at composite level takes care of enforcing assumptions of the sub-nodes. This synthesis considers the outputs of local abstracted nodes as uncontrollable variables, constrained by the nodes' contracts. A formal description, out of our scope here, is available [8].

3.3 Modular coordination principle

With modularity, we can decompose the coordination policy in several parts structured in a hierarchical way. This involves to make coordinated assemblies themselves controllable. In contrast to the monolithic DCS, the modular DCS allows to construct local controllers so that they can be re-used in an assembly composite to form a global control. These local controllers can also be the composition of sub-controllers themselves. The control is decentralized in the sense that each part of the assembly handles part of the control. The first step to achieve a modular control is to make a coordinated assembly composite controllable. This can be seen as making the latter expose their controllability (like AMs before) in order to allow to enforce further additional coordination policy for a global management.

3.3.1 Controllable coordinated managers

In order for a controller to be controllable, it must enforce local objectives defining the local control strategy, as well as outside objectives. The enforcement of the outside objectives is required to allow the re-use of the controller in different contexts in which additional control strategies have to be enforced beside the predefined local one. Hence the outside objectives describe the guarantee of a control strategy received from elsewhere. This must be explicitly part of the contract of the controller. Starting from a coordinated composite as before, making the latter controllable is achieved by first equipping it with controllable Boolean inputs c'_i for each of the actions to be controlled. The second step is to install a way for the node to exhibit information about its state to outside. It can be done by outputting state information s'_i directly as suggested informally in Figure 5(a). Alternately, in order to formalize things in a way enabling modular DCS, we transform the **enforce** part of the contract, so that it can be used in an upper-level contract as environment model, as explained above and in Section 3.2.2. We modify the objective into the conjunction of the previously seen local objective Obj, **and** a term Obj_m, formalizing the fact that when the new control variable c'_i is **false**, it does inhibit its associated action a_i, i.e., it implies that it is **false**. For each action, its associated outside control objective for its inhibition is formulated as follows: $(\neg c'_i \Rightarrow \neg a_i)$. However depending on the type (short or long) of the action the objective is translated differently. For short action it is translated directly to: $Obj_m = (c'_i$ **or not** $a_i)$.

Long actions must be handled differently, because once a_i is triggered, c'_i can no longer prevent or interrupt it. Therefore, in order to make this explicit in the local contract, to be used by upper-level contracts, we must link the values of a_i (triggering of the action) and s_i (current state of the action). This is done by saying that, if the action was not active at the previous instant, i.e., that s_i was false (**not** (**false fby** s_i) [3], and a_i is not true at the current instant, then s_i will remain false. As before, c'_i can prevent the triggering of the action, i.e., that a_i becomes true. Hence, $Obj_m = \text{LongActions}(c'_i, a_i, s_i)$ defined by:

$$\text{LongActions}(c'_i, a_i, s_i) \stackrel{\text{def}}{=} (c'_i \textbf{ or not } a_i) \textbf{ and } \Big((\textbf{not } (\textbf{false fby } s_i) \textbf{ and not } a_i) \Rightarrow \textbf{not } s_i\Big)$$

As illustrated in Figure 5(b), in the node **ctrl-coord-mgrs** a DCS problem will be solved, by taking as control objective to be made invariant: $Obj \wedge Obj_m$, where Obj_m of this level of contract is defined as previously explained. The sub-nodes M_i each exhibit their contract Obj_i, which includes the local modularity term as above. Hence, the DCS problem at this level will make the assumption that $\bigwedge_i Obj_i$ is enforced by lower-level contracts and coordination controllers, as explained in Section 3.2.2.

3.3.2 Modular coordination of managers

As composites have been made controllable in the same way as managers, they can be used to construct coordinated assemblies modularly. Re-use of instances of composites is made seamless in new assemblies. For example, the previous

[3] **fby** is an Heptagon operator introducing an initialized delay: v **fby** x denotes the previous value of x, initialized with v at the first instant.

c_i' variables will be used as controllable variables w.r.t. a policy at the upper-level composite (in Figure 5(c)), possibly combined with a controllable manager with its corresponding c_i variables.
Note that transformations above, adding modularity terms, concern only the interface and contract, i.e., the signature of the node, and not at all the internals of the managers. This is ensuring modularity in that nodes can be re-used, and combined in different contexts without modification.
The other, even more important impact of modularity is to break down the algorithmic complexity of DCS, from exponential on the global system, i.e., the parallel composition of all automata, down to a sum of DCS problems, local to much smaller models. This is enabling the scalability of the approach: comparative evaluations on the case-study are given below in section 4.3.2.

4. MULTI-LOOP MULTI-TIER SYSTEMS

We apply and validate our approach to multi-loop multi-tier systems, typical of the domain of data centers administration. This work is done in the framework of the Ctrl-Green project, in cooperation with Eolas, who make a business in providing Cloud services.

4.1 Datacenter management

4.1.1 Multi-tier replication based system

The JEE multi-tier applications we consider, as shown in Figure 6, consists of: an apache web server[4] receiving incoming requests, and distributing them with load balancing to a tier of replicated tomcat servers[5]. The latter access to the database through a mysql-proxy server[6] which distributes the sql queries, with load balancing, to a tier of replicated mysql servers[7]. The global system running in the data-center consists of a set of such applications in parallel.

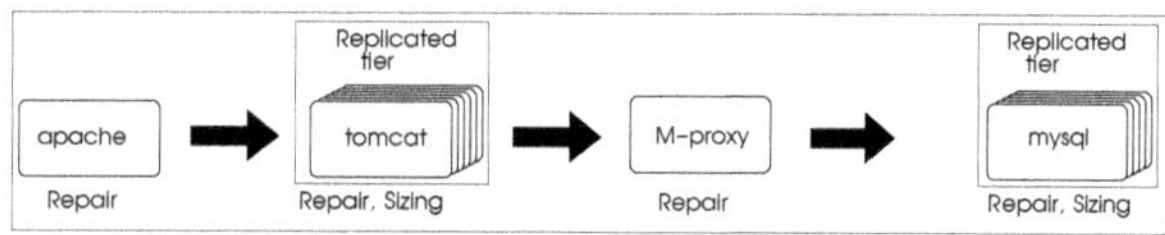

Figure 6: Multi-loop JEE Multi-tiers application.

4.1.2 Autonomic managers

For each AM, we describe its target, aim, input sensors, output actions (short or long), and controllability.

Self-sizing targets replicated servers. It aims at lowering the resources usage while preserving the performance. It automates the process of adapting the degree of replication depending of the system load measured through the CPU usage of the servers hosts. The desired state is delimited by thresholds, `minimum` and `maximum`. Periodically, an exponentially weighted moving average (EWMA), `cpu_Avg`, is computed. When `cpu_Avg` is higher than the `maximum` threshold (i.e., `overload`), it triggers size-up (a long action) for the provision of a new replica. When `cpu_Avg` is lower than the `minimum` threshold (i.e., `underload`), it triggers size-down (short action) for the removal of a replica. Each of these two actions can be inhibited.

Self-repair targets a server as well as replicated servers. It aims at preserving the availability of the server service. It manages `fail-stop` failure detected through `heartbeat`, and automates the process of restoring a server when it fails. It triggers the repair (long action, can be inhibited) of a failed server which consists in deploying the server on a new host, configuring it, and launching it. For replicated servers, the degree of redundancy is restored to tolerate up to *m-1* failures of m servers during the mean time to repair.

Consolidation targets the global virtualized data-center. It aims at optimizing global resource usage while preserving system performance. It automates the process of adapting the computing capacity made available in a virtualized data-center. It periodically evaluates the resources allocated to the virtual machines (`VM`) and the available computing capacity, and plans long actions to either reduce (`Decr`) or increase (`Incr`) the capacity. In this work, we use `VMWare DPM` for power management in a virtualized data-center. It plans migration actions to deliver more resources to the overloaded `VMs`, which can require to turn physical servers on. When the physical servers are under-utilized, it plans migration actions to turn some servers off. It can be controlled by delaying or cancelling the actions. Controllability of the consolidation manager is considered here only at large-grain: an interesting perspective is finer-grain control, between the sequential phases of this complex operation, but it requires difficult determination of appropriate synchronization points.

4.1.3 Coordination problems

As seen in Figure 6, within a multi-tier application, the failure of a server in a replicated tier can cause a saturation (hence temporary overload) of the remaining servers due to the fail-over mechanism. Furthermore, each tier depends on its predecessor (e.g., load balancer) since its service is requested by the latter. An increase of the requests received from its predecessor increases its activity and reciprocally. However the decrease of the requests can be caused by a failure, which can cause a temporary underload, and useless sizing operations. At the global level of the data-center, the uncoordinated execution of instances of self-sizing and self-repair at the same time as consolidation can lead to failures of actions triggered by the managers. The execution of a consolidation plan can take a long time to complete and its success as well as its efficiency depends on the consistency of the state of the data-center along the process. The adding, repair and removal actions, occurring at any time, can invalidate a consolidation plan being executed, which did not anticipate them. This can cause failure of migration operations or inefficiency of the consolidation. Consolidation can also cause failure of adding and repair actions e.g., it can reduce the computing capacity of the VMs.

4.1.4 Coordination policy

To avoid the above interferences, policies are defined, to be enforced by inhibiting some managers accordingly.

1. Within a replicated tier, avoid size-up when repairing.

[4] http://httpd.apache.org/
[5] http://tomcat.apache.org/
[6] http://dev.mysql.com/doc/refman/5.1/en/mysql-proxy.html
[7] http://www.mysql.com/

2. Within a load-balanced replicated tier, avoid size-down when repairing the load-balancer.
3. In multi-tiers, more generally, avoid size-down in a successor replicated tier when repairing in a predecessor.
4. At global data-center level, when consolidating, avoid self-sizing or repairing.
5. Wait until repairs or add finish before consolidation decreasing, and until removals finish before increasing.

4.2 Modular control model

In this Section we formalize the previous description, by modelling the behaviors of individual managers, and their coordination policy, in the form of a DCS problem, following the method of Section 3.3.

4.2.1 *Modelling the managers control behaviors*

Self-sizing control is actually an instance of the general pattern of Figure 2(d), node `ctrl-mgr`, with outputs : long action `add`, short action `rem` and busy state `adding` ; with inputs : controls `ca` and `crm` for the actions, monitoring overload `o` and underload `u`, and adding notification `na`:
`(add, rem, adding) = self-sizing(ca, crm, o, u, na)`

Self-repair control is a simpler case, with only a long action of repairing. This can also be defined as an instance of the node `ctrl-mgr` of Figure 2(d) with outputs : long action `rep`, and busy state `repairing` ; and inputs : control `ca` , monitoring failure `fail` , and notification of repair done `nr`. Unused parameters for short actions of the `ctrl-mgr` node can be, for inputs, given the constant value `false`, and for outputs be left unused. This defines the new node:
`(rep, repairing) = self-repair(cr, fail, nr)`

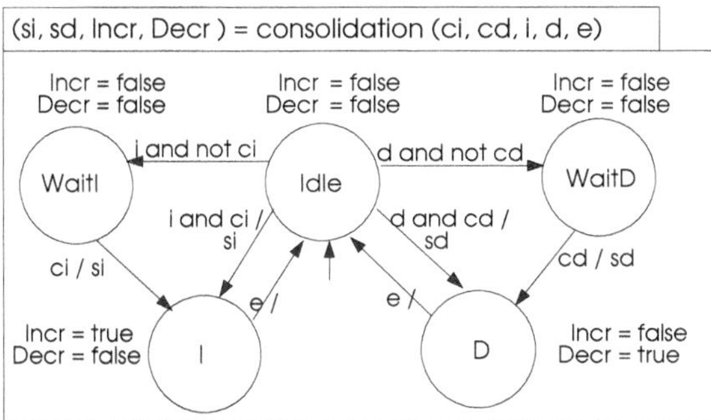

Figure 7: Consolidation control behavior model.

Consolidation control is an example showing that different control patterns can be modelled in our approach, according to specific managers behaviors, and also depending on the relevant states to be exhibited for different control purposes. In Figure 7, its automaton presents essentially the waiting mechanism of the delayable action, as in Figure 1(a), for each of its two long actions, the activity of which is given by `Incr` and `Decr`. In the initial Idle state, when i is **true** (increase of the computing capacity is required), if ci is **true** it goes to I and emits si to start the increasing plan, otherwise it goes to WaitI. There, it awaits ci to be **true** to go to Incr and emits si. When in Incr, it awaits until the completion of the execution (e is **true**) then returns back to the Idle state. The case for decrease is similar.

4.2.2 *Coordination objectives*

The parallel composition of instantiations of the above automata describes the coexistence of the instances of the corresponding managers. The control is specified on this composed behavior. We formalize the strategy of Section 4.1.4.

1. Within each replicated tier, avoid size-up when repairing: **not** (repairing **and** add)
2. Avoid size-down when repairing the load-balancer: **not** (repairingL **and** rem)
3. In multi-tiers, more generally, between predecessors and successors: **not** (repairing$_{pred}$ **and** rem$_{succ}$)
4. When consolidating, avoid repair and sizing: **not** ((Incr **or** Decr) **and** (repairing* **or** adding* **or** rem*))
5. Wait for consolidation decreasing until repairs or add finish: **not** ((repairing* **or** or adding*) **and** sd) and for increasing when removals: **not** (rem* **and** si)

4.3 Exploiting the models with DCS

4.3.1 *Monolithic synthesis*

In order to evaluate the benefit of modularity, we make the exercise of performing DCS the classical way.

```
(...) = Main_node (...)
enforce all contracts
with all controllable variables
  (rep_1, repairing_1)   = self-repair (c'_1, fail_1, nr_1);
  ...
  (rep_N, repairing_N)   = self-repair (c'_N, fail_N, nr_N);
  (add_1, rem_1, adding_1) = self-sizing (ca_1, ...);
  ...
  (add_M, rem_M, adding_M) = self-sizing (ca_M, ...);
  (si, sd, Incr, Decr) = consolidation (ci, cd, i, d, e);
```

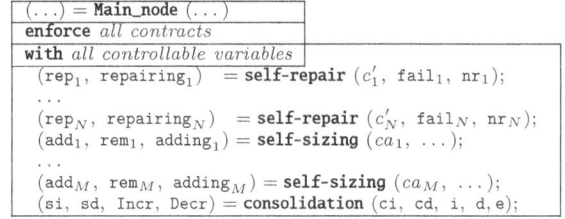

Figure 8: Monolithic node.

The specification of the monolithic control is encoded in a single composite node, shown in Figure 8, grouping all instances of involved managers composed in parallel in its body, and a conjunction of all control objectives in its contracts. This can be tedious and complex when a huge number of managers are considered. It does not allow a decentralized control because the overall control objectives are grouped in the single upper-level node. The structure of this coordination is shown in Figure 14.

4.3.2 *Modular synthesis*

We present reusable nodes bottom-up, as shown in Figure 9 from left to right: we first build the coordination controller for `self-sizing` and `self-repair` in a replicated tier. The latter controller is re-used for the coordination of managers in two consecutive tiers, the front tier being a load balancer for the second tier constituted of replicated servers. The resulting controller is re-used for the coordination of a mult-tier system.

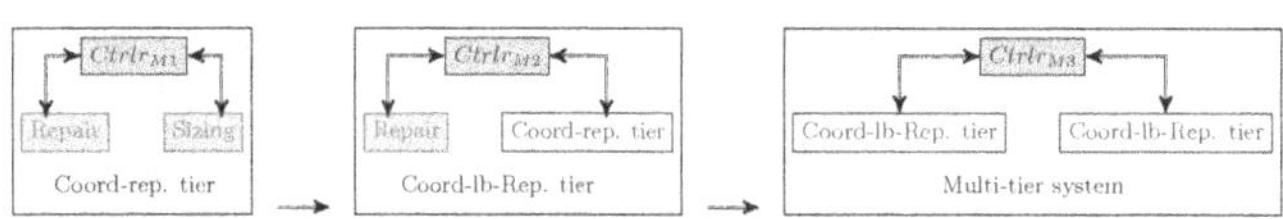

Figure 9: Bottom-up re-use of nodes.

Replicated servers tier. The composite node shown in Figure 10, specifies the control of instances of `self-sizing` and `self-repair` managing the same replicated tier. Its contract is composed of four objectives, one for the local coordination: (**not** (`repairing` **and** `add`)), while the rest concerns the guarantee of the enforcement of a coordination strategy from outside the node. The control from outside is received through the input variables `cr'`, `ca'` and `crm'`. As can be seen here, the modularity objective is very systematic and could easily be covered in syntactic sugar.

```
(...) = coord_repl-tier (cr', fail, nr, ca', crm', o, u, na)
enforce (not (repairing and add))
        and LongActions(cr', rep, repairing)
        and LongActions(ca', add, adding)
        and (crm' or not rem)
with cr, ca, crm
  (rep, repairing)      = self-repair (cr, fail, nr);
  (add, rem, adding) = self-sizing (ca, crm, o, u, na);
```

Figure 10: Replicated tier node.

Load balancer and replicated servers tier. In this node, shown in Figure 11, we re-use an instance of the above composite node from Figure 10, and an instance of self-repair, dedicated to the management of a load balancer in front of the replicated servers which distributes the incoming load to them. Here also, the local coordination strategy to be enforced : **not** (`repairingL` **and** `remove`), is complemented with modularity objectives.

```
(...) = coord_lb-repl-tier (cL', failL, nrL,
                            c', fail, nr,
                            ca', crm', o, u, na)
enforce (not (repairingL and rem))
        and LongActions(cL', repL, repairingL)
        and LongActions(c', rep, repairing)
        and LongActions(ca', add, adding)
        and (crm' or not rem)
with cL, c, ca, crm

  (repL, repairingL)  = self-repair (cL, failL, nrL);
  (rep, repairing, add, rem, adding)
     = coord_repl-tier (c, fail, nr, ca, crm, o, u, na);
```

Figure 11: Load-balanced replicated tiers node.

Application. The node of Figure 12 coordinates two instances of the previous node from Figure 11, for the control of instances of self-sizing and self-repair managing two consecutive load-balanced replicated tiers. The coordination strategy consists in preventing size-down in the back-end load-balanced replicated tier ("successor") when a failure is being repaired in the front. This is expressed as follows:
(**not** ((`repairingL`$_1$ **or** `repairing`$_1$) **and** `rem`$_2$))

```
(...) = coord_appli (cL'_1, failL_1, nrL_1,
                     c'_1, fail_1, nr_1, ca'_1, crm'_1, o_1, u_1, na_1)
                     cL'_2, failL_2, nrL_2,
                     c'_2, fail_2, nr_2, ca'_2, crm'_2, o_2, u_2, na_2)
enforce (not ((repairingL_i or repairing_i) and rem_2))
        and LongActions(cL'_i, repL_i, repairingL_i)
        and LongActions(c'_i, rep_i, repairing_i)
        and LongActions(ca'_i, add_i, adding_i)
        and (crm'_i or not rem_i)     i = 1,2
with cL_1, c_1, ca_1, crm_1, cL_2, c_2, ca_2, crm_2

 (repL_1, repairingL_1, rep_1, repairing_1, add_1, rem_1, adding_1)
   = coord_lb-repl-tier (cL_1, failL_1, nrL_1, c_1, fail_1, nr_1,
                         ca_1, crm_1, o_1, u_1, na_1);
 (repL_2, repairingL_2, rep_2, repairing_2, add_2, rem_2, adding_2)
   = coord_lb-repl-tier (cL_2, failL_2, nrL_2, c_2, fail_2, nr_2,
                         ca_2, crm_2, o_2, u_2, na_2);
```

Figure 12: Multi-tier application node.

Global system: data center. The whole multi-application system will be constructed progressively, by first considering the two-application case. Figure 13 shows the node and contract instantiating the previous node for each of them,

```
(...) = two-data-center (...)
enforce (not ((Incr or Decr) and
              (repairing_ij or adding_ij or rem_ij))
        and (not ((repairing_ij or adding_ij) and sd)
              and not (rem_ij and si))
        and LongActions(cL'_ij, repL_ij, repairingL_ij)
        and LongActions(c'_ij, rep_ij, repairing_ij)
        and LongActions(ca'_ij, add_ij, adding_ij)
        and (crm'_ij or not rem_ij)      i = 1, 2; j = 1..2  )
with cL_11, c_11, ..., crm_22, ci, cd

 (...) = coord_appli (cL_11, c_11, ca_11, crm_11, ...,
                      cL_21, c_21, ca_21, crm_21, ...)
 (...) = coord_appli (cL_12, c_12, ca_12, crm_12, ...,
                      cL_22, c_22, ca_22, crm_22, ...)
 (si, sd, Incr, Decr) = consolidation (ci, cd, i, d, e);
```

Figure 13: Two-application data-center.

as well as a consolidation manager. At this level of control, only the coordination strategy between the multi-tiers applications and the consolidation manager is specified, the control within multi-tier applications being delegated to the instance of the previous node modelling it. Having more applications in a data-center is done by composing an instantiation re-using the previous node, with a new instantiation re-using the application node. The contract of this new composition is similar to the one in Figure 13. This enables a hierarchical construction of the control of an N-application.

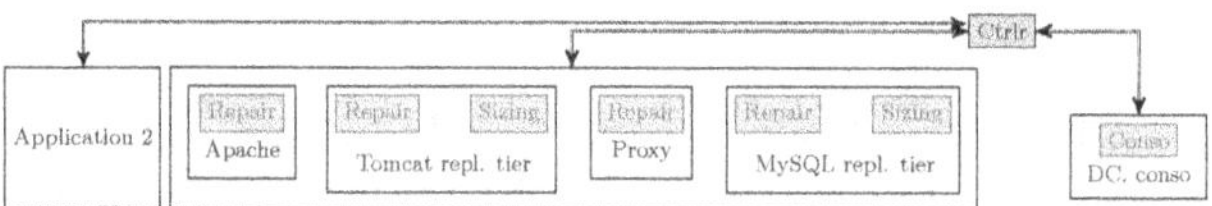

Figure 14: Monolithic coordination design

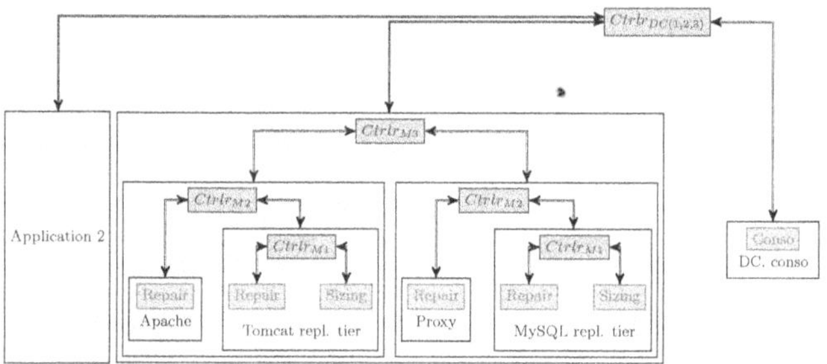

Figure 15: Modular coordination design

Comparisons and discussion.

Advantages of modularity can be seen here, in terms of the objectives of Section 1.3. Regarding the specification aspect (objective (i) of Section 1.3): tiers and groups of tiers are described locally, including their control, and assembled hierarchically, as shown in Figure 15; instead of having all automata on one side, and all contracts on the other side, in the monolithic case as shown in Figure 14. This favors the re-use of Heptagon/BZR nodes in different contexts. In particular, the repair manager is re-used in the replicated tier and for the load balancer. More significantly, because it has a contract and controller, the coordinated load-balanced and replicated tier is used twice in an application, with a difference in the controls, in that the downstream one is submitted to more constraints than the upstream one.

On the other aspect, the combinatorial complexity of DCS and the cost of compilation of the controllers (objective (ii) of Section 1.3): for various sizes of the system (i.e, various number of applications), we have performed Heptagon/BZR compilations and synthesis, the results of which are shown in Table 1. Comparative costs of DCS, monolithic and modular, for the different cases varying in number of applications in the data-center, are given in terms of compilation CPU time, and memory usage. For small numbers of applications, values are not significant for memory; at 4 applications, the monolithic approach reaches the limits of the natural combinatorial explosion of the state-space exploration techniques : the computation was not finished after more than two days, and no values were sought for larger systems. The other approach, benefiting from modularity, goes significantly further, even if still presenting growing costs. In brief, we can see that monolithic DCS is exponentially costly in the size on the system, whereas modular DCS keeps producing results, showing scalability.

nb.	Synthesis time		Memory usage	
app.	monolithic	modular	monolithic	modular
1	0s	5s	-	-
2	49s	11s	-	-
3	42m24s	24s	34.81MB	-
4	> 2 days	1m22s	>149,56MB	-
5	-	4m30s	-	20,37MB
6	-	13m24s	-	53,31MB
7	-	25m57s	-	77,50MB
8	-	50m36s	-	115,59MB
9	-	2h11m	-	236,59MB
10	-	9h4m	-	479,15MB

Table 1: DCS : duration and memory usage.

Although we show the total compilation time in Table 1, the synthesis of the control logic of each node equipped with a contract is performed independently. A composite node which is the assembly of sub-nodes equipped with a contract, requires just the contract defined in the sub-nodes at compilation for the synthesis of its control logic. Therefore the compilations can be run in parallel. Furthermore, the recompilation of the composite node is necessary only when their interface (inputs, outputs) and their contract are modified, otherwise it can be re-used as such.

4.4 Implementation

The system we described has been implemented on our experimental data-center. Figure 16 shows uncoordinated executions in which failures occur in 16(b) at 17 min (Apache server fails), and in 16(b) at 19 min (Tomcat server fails). In 16(b), the failure leads to an underload in `Tomcat` and `Mysql` tier causing the removal of a replicated server in each tier. In 16(b) the failure causes an underload in Mysql tier which leads to the removal of a replica., as seen in the square-edged curve (numbers of replica) going down. However, the degree of replication is restored after the repair of the failed server, by re-adding the uselessly removed server as shown in 16(a) at 21 min and 28 min, and in 16(b) at 25 min.

By contrast, in Figure 17 for executions coordinated by the controllers as expected, reaction to the underloads during the failure repair (in 17(a): 20min, and in 17(b): 17min) is inhibited, square-edged curves remaining flat, hence the system administration saves unnecessary operations.

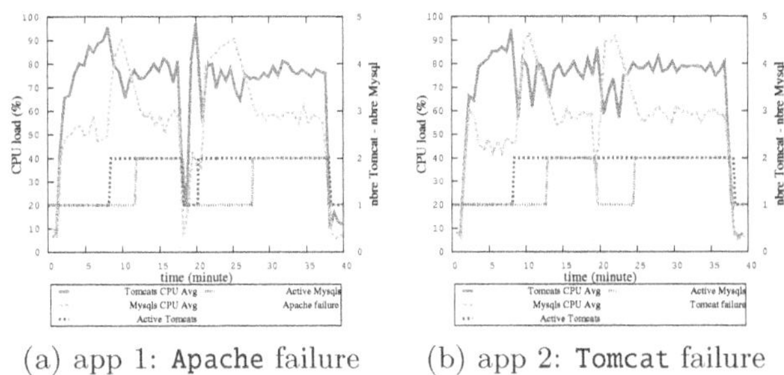

(a) app 1: `Apache` failure (b) app 2: `Tomcat` failure

Figure 16: Uncoordinated execution

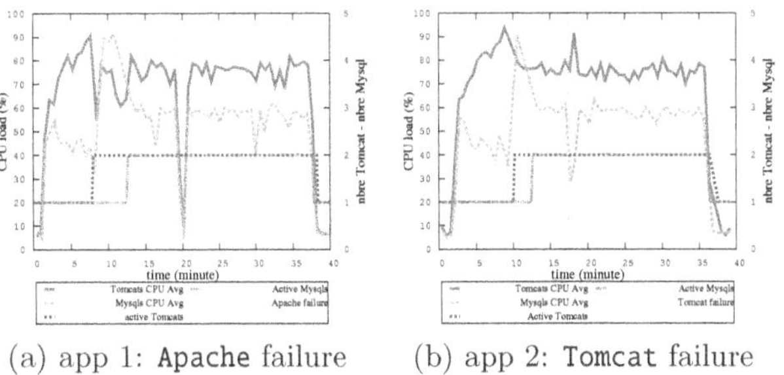

(a) app 1: `Apache` failure (b) app 2: `Tomcat` failure

Figure 17: Coordinated execution

5. RELATED WORK

The general question of coordinating autonomic managers remains an important challenge in Autonomic Computing [17] although it is made necessary in complete systems with multiple loops, combining dimensions and criteria. Some works propose extensions of the MAPE-K framework in order to allow for synchronization [23], which can be e.g., through the access to a common knowledge [2]. A distinctive aspect of our approach is to rely on explicit automata-based behavioral models, amenable to formal techniques like verification or the more constructive DCS. Coordination of multiple energy management loops is done in various ways, e.g., by defining power vs. performance trade-offs based on a multi-criteria utility function in a non-virtualized environment [6], or also tuning mechanisms as in OptiTuner [15]. These approaches seem to require modifying AMs for their interaction, and to define the resulting behavior by quantitative integration of the measure and utilities, which relies on intuitive tuning values, not handling logical synchronization aspects. We coordinate AMs by controlling their logical activity state, rather than modifying them.

Concerning decision and control of autonomic systems, some approaches rely upon Artificial Intelligence and planning [22] which has the advantage of managing situation where configurations are not all known in advance, but the corresponding drawback of costly run-time exploration of possible behaviors, and lack of insured safety of resulting behaviors. Our work adheres to the methodology of control theory, and in particular Discrete Event Systems, applied to computing systems [14]. Compared to traditional error-prone programming followed by verification and debugging, such methods bring correctness by design of the control. Particularly, DCS offers automated generation of the coordination controller, facilitating design effort compared to hand-writing, and modification and re-use. Also, maximal permissivity of synthesized controllers is an advantage compared to over-constrained manual control, impairing performance even if correct. Applications of DCS to computing systems have not been many until now; it has been applied to address the problem of deadlock avoidance [24]. Compared to this, we consider more user-defined objectives.

Works on compositional verification have brought some issues which can be related to modular controller synthesis. As instance, a method for automatic assumption generation have been proposed [10]. It relies on algorithms for the generation of automata based on language equivalence, in order to generate intermediary assumptions for compositional verification. Compared with modular controller synthesis, the generated automata do not act upon the system, and only helps its verification. Nevertheless, an interesting perspective would be to consider mixing the two techniques, in order to facilitate the controller synthesis, and relieve the programmer from the burden of writing intermediary assumptions. Though, this technique cannot be applied as is, as assumptions cannot be inferred from properties to be enforced, without knowledge about the generated controller.

6. CONCLUSIONS

We put the principle of modularity in practice for the problem of coordination in multiple-loop autonomic management, in a component-based approach. Instead of redesigning a global combined loop, we benefit from the advantages of modularity, by defining a new method. We propose a general design methodology based on formal modelling with automata, and the application of DCS to obtain automatically correct controllers. We leverage modularity in this approach, and confront it to commensurate experiment on a real-world multi-tier, multi-service-level system. We achieve our objectives of Section 1.3 by:

1. enabling re-use and coordination of complex administration managers, through their control specifications,
2. modularizing the DCS, thereby breaking down the exponential complexity of the basic algorithms

On the latter point, the gain in compilation-time synthesis opens new perspectives on the scalability of our method, and its applicability to larger systems.

Perspectives are at different levels. The general method is systematic enough to form the basis of an administration management-level Domain Specific Language (DSL), allowing for a designer to construct systems for which the formal automata models and control objectives can be generated automatically. Improvement of the DCS technique is ongoing to integrate not only logical but also quantitative aspects in the synthesis algorithms, like consumption or load. Also the compilation using modular DCS produces a modular code which opens perspectives for a distributed execution which is an ongoing work.

7. REFERENCES

[1] T. Abdelzaher. Research challenges in feedback computing: An interdisciplinary agenda. In *Proc. Workshop Feedback Computing*, 2013.

[2] F. Alvares de Oliveira Jr., R. Sharrock, and T. Ledoux. Synchronization of multiple autonomic control loops: Application to cloud computing. In *Proc. Conf. Coordination*, 2012.

[3] T. Bouhadiba, Q. Sabah, G. Delaval, and E. Rutten. Synchronous control of reconfiguration in Fractal component-based systems – a case study. In *Proc. Conf. EMSOFT*, 2011.

[4] F. Boyer, O. Gruber, and D. Pous. Robust reconfigurations of component assemblies. In *Proc. Conf. ICSE*, 2013.

[5] E. Bruneton, T. Coupaye, M. Leclercq, V. Quema, and J.-B. Stefani. The Fractal component model and its support in java. *Software – Practice and Experience (SP&E)*, 36(11-12), sep 2006.

[6] R. Das, J. Kephart, C. Lefurgy, G. Tesauro, D. Levine, and H. Chan. Autonomic multi-agent management of power and performance in data centers. In *Proc. Conf. AAMAS*, 2008.

[7] G. Delaval and E. Rutten. Reactive model-based control of reconfiguration in the Fractal component-based model. In *Proc. Symp. CBSE*, 2010.

[8] G. Delaval, E. Rutten, and H. Marchand. Integrating discrete controller synthesis into a reactive programming language compiler. *Discrete Event Dynamic Systems*, 23(4):385–418, Dec. 2013.

[9] S. M.-K. Gueye, N. de Palma, and E. Rutten. Coordination control of component-based autonomic administration loops. In *Proc. Conf. Coordination*, 2013.

[10] A. Gupta, K. McMillan, and Z. Fu. Automated assumption generation for compositional verification. In W. Damm and H. Hermanns, editors, *Computer Aided Verification*, volume 4590 of *Lecture Notes in Computer Science*, pages 420–432. Springer Berlin Heidelberg, 2007.

[11] N. Halbwachs. Synchronous programming of reactive systems, a tutorial and commented bibliography. In *Proc. Conf. CAV*, 1998.

[12] N. Halbwachs and S. Baghdadi. Synchronous modeling of asynchronous systems. In *Proc. Conf. EMSOFT*, Grenoble, Oct. 2002.

[13] D. Harel and A. Naamad. The statemate semantics of statecharts. *ACM Trans. Softw. Eng. Methodol.*, 5(4):293–333, Oct. 1996.

[14] J. Hellerstein, Y. Diao, S. Parekh, and D. Tilbury. *Feedback Control of Computing Systems*. Wiley-IEEE, 2004.

[15] J. Heo, P. Jayachandran, I. Shin, D. Wang, T. Abdelzaher, and X. Liu. Optituner: On performance composition and server farm energy minimization application. *IEEE Trans. Parallel Distrib. Syst.*, 22(11), 2011.

[16] F. Hermenier, X. Lorca, J.-M. Menaud, G. Muller, and J. Lawall. Entropy: A consolidation manager for clusters. In *Proceedings of the 2009 ACM SIGPLAN/SIGOPS International Conference on Virtual Execution Environments*, VEE '09, pages 41–50, New York, NY, USA, 2009. ACM.

[17] J. Kephart. Autonomic computing: The first decade. In *Proc. Conf. ICAC*, 2011.

[18] J. O. Kephart and D. M. Chess. The vision of autonomic computing. *IEEE Computer*, 36(1), 2003.

[19] H. Marchand and M. Samaan. Incremental design of a power transformer station controller using a controller synthesis methodology. *IEEE Trans. on Soft. Eng.*, 26(8):729 –741, 2000.

[20] P. Ramadge and W. Wonham. On the supervisory control of discrete event systems. *Proc. IEEE*, 77(1), Jan. 1989.

[21] S. Sicard, F. Boyer, and N. De Palma. Using components for architecture-based management: the self-repair case. In *Proc. Conf. ICSE*, 2008.

[22] D. Sykes, W. Heaven, J. Magee, and J. Kramer. Plan-directed architectural change for autonomous systems. In *Proc. Workshop SAVCBS*, 2007.

[23] P. Vromant, D. Weyns, S. Malek, and J. Andersson. On interacting control loops in self-adaptive systems. In *Proc. Conf. SEAMS*, 2011.

[24] Y. Wang, S. Lafortune, T. Kelly, M. Kudlur, and S. Mahlke. The theory of deadlock avoidance via discrete control. In *Proc. ACM Conf. POPL*, 2009.

A Component-based Meta-level Architecture and Prototypical Implementation of a Reflective Component-based Programming and Modeling Language

Petr Spacek
LIRMM, CNRS and Montpellier II University
161, rue Ada, 34392 Montpellier Cedex 5 France
co-affiliation
Faculty of Information Technology
Czech Technical University in Prague
Thakurova 9 16000 Prague 6 Czech Republic
spacepe2@fit.cvut.cz

Christophe Dony and Chouki Tibermacine
LIRMM, CNRS and Montpellier II University
161, rue Ada
34392 Montpellier Cedex 5 France
{dony,tibermacin}@lirmm.fr

ABSTRACT

Component-based Software Engineering studies the design, development and maintenance of software constructed upon sets of connected components. Using existing standard solutions, component-based models are frequently transformed into non-component-based programs, most of the time object-oriented, for run-time execution. As a consequence many component-level descriptions (part of code), e.g. explicit architectures or ports declarations, vanish at the implementation stage, making debugging, transformations or reverse-engineering difficult. It has been shown that component-based programming languages contribute to bridge this gap between design and implementation and to provide a conceptual and practical continuum to fully develop applications with components. In this paper we go one step further in this direction by making a component-oriented programming and modeling language truly reflective, thus making verification, evolution or transformation stages of software development part of this new continuum. The gained reflection capabilities indeed make it possible to perform architecture checking, code refactoring, model transformations or even to implement new languages constructs with and for components. The paper presents an original executable meta-level architecture achieving the vision that "*everything is a component*" and an operational implementation demonstrating its feasibility and effectiveness. Our system revisits some standard solutions for reification in the component's context and also handles new cases, such as ports reification, to allow for runtime introspection and intercession on components and on their descriptors. We validate these ideas in the context of an executable prototypical and minimal component-based language, named Compo, whose first goal is to help imagining the future.

CBSE'14, June 30–July 4, 2014, Marcq-en-Baroeul, France.

http://dx.doi.org/10.1145/2602458.2602476 .

1. INTRODUCTION

Component-based software engineering studies the production of reusable components and their combination into connection architectures. It appears that component-orientation has been more studied from the design stage point of view, with modeling languages and ADLs [18, 10] than from the implementation stage one. As stated in [10] "most component models use standard programming languages ... for the implementation stage"; and most of today's solutions [13] use object-oriented languages. Such a choice is somehow natural because object-oriented languages provide means to capture quite easily some of component-based concepts (encapsulation or provisions) and has practical advantages related to the availability and maturity of object-oriented programming languages, tools and practices. However this choice raises the issue that there is no conceptual continuum between models and their implementation (at least it is incomplete). Many concepts used during design (component descriptors, required services, ports, architectures, components themselves) vanish (are not represented as such, i.e. are not explicit) in the implementation.

This is a source of various issues. It makes debugging or reverse-engineering (e.g. from implementations to models) complex. It can entail some loss of information or some inconsistencies when implementing a model, such as the violation of the communication integrity [13, 1]. Different languages have to be learned and mastered to write an application e.g. an ADL for the architecture, a programming language for the implementation (model transformations only generate skeleton implementations), a language for expressing architecture constraints (such as OCL) and possibly a language for model transformations. Some pieces of code, working at the meta level such as a constraint checking [32], may have to be written twice; once using elements of the design world meta-model and once using the implementation world meta-model. Dynamic (runtime) constraints checking is only possible if the implementation language has an executable meta-model that allows for introspection (for example if the implementation language is Java, constraints-checking expressions can be written using the *Reflect* package). Runtime model transformations, are only possible if the implementation language has an executable meta-model that allows for intercession; furthermore, after such a transformation, a reverse-engineering is needed to update the model.

Facing these issues, component-based programming languages [1, 27, 13] propose a first global solution towards a continuum for component-based development. Modeling and programming languages [30, 31] extend the idea by making it possible to describe as well components, their connection architectures and their implementations in a unified component-based context. We aim at going further in this new work by suggesting that this continuum principle can also encompass all kinds of model-driven activities. This globally means to allow software engineers to define, using the same language described by a unique meta-model M, not only standard applications (architectures and code) having the same description of architecture at design-time and at run-time, but also all those meta-programs, e.g. constraint-checking or model transformation or program transformation programs, that use or manipulate M constitutive elements and their instances, either statically or at runtime[1].

We can rephrase this as defining a reflective modeling and programming component-based language (only structural reflection is considered). Two global approaches can be considered to achieve this goal : to extend a reflective modeling language with programming support (as done for example with KerMeta [21]), or to extend a reflective programming language with modeling support [12]. Both are interesting, the former provides a richer modeling context while the latter benefits from the efficiency of existing virtual machines. This paper describes a language named COMPO, that applies the second approach in the component-based context, proposing an original "*everything is a component*" solution to build up an executable meta-model, allowing introspection and intercession. It can be used at all stages of component development to manipulate standard and "meta"-components as first-class entities. Various alternative solutions do exist for component-based application runtime adaptation (see the related works section) but we do not know of such a reflective solution being at the same time component-based, usable at all development stage and allowing for full intercession.

The paper is organized as follows. Section 2 presents COMPO's standard syntax, constructs and use, necessary to the understanding of later examples. Section 3 presents several examples of COMPO's reflection capabilities including constraints checking and model transformation. Section 4 presents the meta-model and how potential infinite regressions while interpreting it are solved. Section 5 describes COMPO's prototype implementation in Smalltalk. Comparison with related works is presented in Section 6 and we conclude in Section 7 by discussing future work.

2. COMPO'S BASIC CONSTRUCTS

Our solution for reflection can be adapted to any component-based language. We present it in the context of our experimental solution COMPO, a component-based language making services, provisions, requirements and internal architectures explicit. Thanks to this last point it is an ADL. As described in this section it is somehow a minimal ADL, but it is to be considered that the base presented here firstly is a partial view (see [29] for a complete presentation) and secondly should be augmented with newer solutions provided by advanced ADLs [18]. Before discussing and describing COMPO's reflective version, it is needed that we give an overview of its basic constructs and syntax.

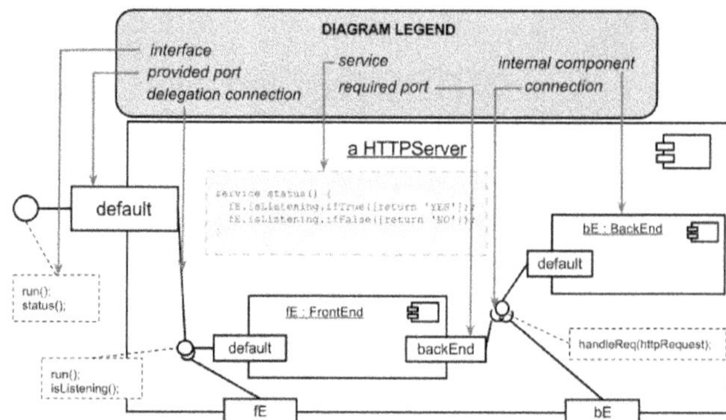

Figure 1: a component, instance of the HTTPServer descriptor

```
Descriptor HTTPServer {
    provides {
        default : { run(); status() }
    }
    internally requires {
        fE : FrontEnd;
        bE : BackEnd;
    }
    architecture {
        connect fE to default@(FrontEnd.new());
        connect bE to default@(BackEnd.new());
        delegate default@self to default@fE;
        connect backEnd@fE to default@bE;
    }
    service status() {
         if(fE.isListening())
              { [return name.asstr() + ' is running'] }
         else { [return name.asstr() + ' is stopped'] };
    }
    service run() { ... }
}
```

Listing 1: An example of a component Descriptor : **HTTPServer**.

An excerpt of COMPO component's model is described by the MOF meta-model in Figure 2 (only those concepts attributes and operations useful for this paper are shown in the figure and presented in the section). The language is based on a descriptor/instance dichotomy; components are instances of descriptors. Listing 1 shows an example of a descriptor named **HTTPServer** and Figure 1 an informal graphical representation of a component, instance of the **HTTPServer** descriptor. A descriptor describes the *structure* (ports and internal architecture descriptions) and *behavior* (service definitions) of its instances. For example, an **HTTPServer**'s behavior is defined with the **status** and **run** service definitions. External provided (vs. required) ports descriptions define the external *contract* (vs. *requirements*) of components. An **HTTPServer**'s external contract

[1]Using such a solution of course does not imply to abandon those ideas brought by the component approach (e.g. the separation of development of architectures and implementations or transformation-based automatic deployment of components, etc). It simply opens the possibility that architectures, implementations and transformations can all be written at the component level and possibly (but not mandatorily) using a unique language.

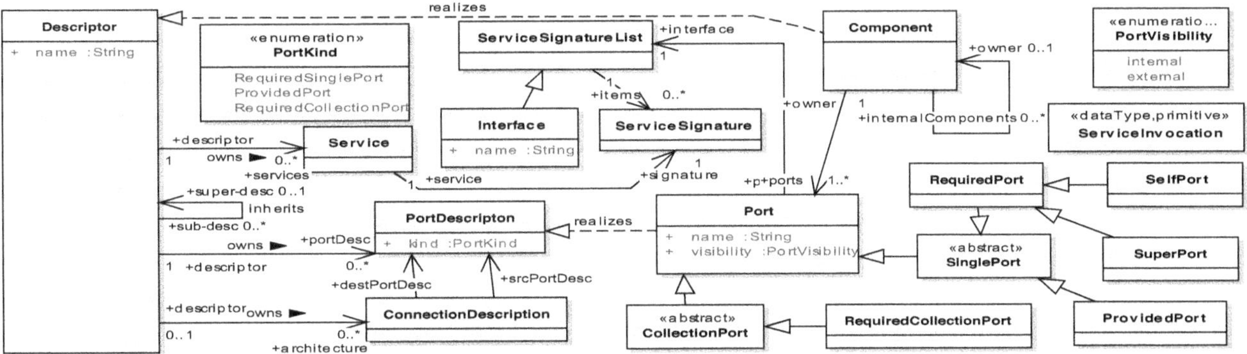

Figure 2: COMPO's meta-model, before the integration of reflection

is to provide, as defined by its `default` provided port, the services `run` and `status`; and it has no external requirement[2]. A composite component has "*internal*" components, i.e. components to which it is connected via its internal required ports and unaccessible to the outside world. An HTTPServer is a composite with two internals, one instance of `FrontEnd` accessible via the internal required port `fE` and an instance of `BackEnd` accessible via `bE`. The architecture description of a composite define its *internal architecture* i.e. the way its internal components are accessible and how they are interconnected. The `architecture` of an `HTTPServer` is thus composed of an instance of `FrontEnd` connected to an instance of `BackEnd` via their ports as explained below.

Ports realize port descriptions (similarly to slots realizing classes' attributes in UML [23]). A port has a role (provided or required), a visibility (external or internal), a name and an interface. An interface is a list of service signatures which can be given either in extension (as for the `default` port of an `HTTPServer`) or via a descriptor name as a shortcut for the list of service signatures of its default provided port. Any component has at least 3 ports named: *default*, *self* and *super* (the semantics of these is explained in paragraph First-Class Component of Section 4.) Ports are connection points; components are connected through their ports (to say that components are connected is an admitted shortcut to say that one port of the former is connected to one port of the later). A connection establishes a communication channel between two ports. A regular connection connects a required port to a provided one, allowing for standard service invocation. An example of an expression establishing a regular connection is: `connect backEnd@fE to default@bE;` in `HTTPServer`'s architecture[3]. A delegation connection connects two ports having the same role and is used to delegate (or redirect) information from the outside to the inside of a component (or the opposite). An example of a "provided to provided" delegation connection is `delegate default@self to default@fE;` in `HTTPServer`'s architecture. Ports also are communication channels; any service invocation (e.g. `fE.isListening()` in service `status` in listing 1) is made via a required port and transmitted to the port it is connected to.

Finally COMPO has an inheritance system [30] making it possible to define a descriptor as an extension of an existing one (`extends` keyword), to extend requirements and to extend or specialize architectures which has proven useful to our integration of reflection as it will be explained in the following sections (see the "inherits" reflexive association of `Descriptor` in Figure 2).

[2]An example with an external requirement is given later.

[3]The expression `backEnd@fE` should be read: "the port `backEnd` of the component that will be connected to `fE` internal port of the current instance of `HTTPServer` (self)"

3. COMPO'S REFLECTION CAPABILITIES

In this section we present reflection capabilities of COMPO. The MOF meta-model presented in Figure 3 shows COMPO elements, representing the main component-level concepts, on which we apply the *component-oriented reification*[4]. Reification can be seen as a process that makes meta-model elements accessible (read access in the case of introspection or read/write in the case of intercession) at the model level (or programming level). The component-oriented reification means that for each element we create a descriptor, i.e. we define component-oriented representation of the elements, to turn these elements into first-class entities accessible in COMPO's programs. Component-oriented reification supposes to solve various potential infinite regressions related to the definition of descriptors representing descriptors, ports and connectors (or connections). We detail these issues in the "Integrating reflection" section (Section 4.) In the following we present how these component-oriented representations can be used to achieve meta-programming, i.e. to design new kinds of descriptors and ports; to design and perform transformations and to verify architecture constraints.

An introspection example.

The following code snippet shows a basic use of introspection. The expression returns the descriptions of ports named `default`, `self` and `super`, which are defined by the descriptor `Component`, see Listing 4.

```
Component.getPortNamed('default').getDescribedPorts();
```

An intercession example.

The following code snippet shows the descriptor (named `ServiceMover`) of a refactoring component, which combines *get*, *remove* and *add* services to move a service from one descriptor to another.

[4]This is an excerpt of the complete meta-model that only presents its central "interesting" parts.

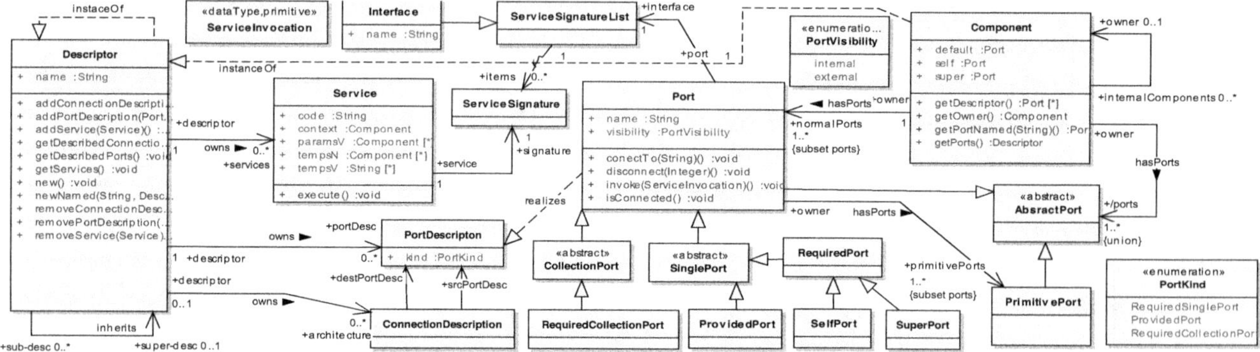

Figure 3: An Excerpt of the meta-model of Compo showing the integration of reflection

```
Descriptor ServiceMover {
  requires {
    srcDesc : Descriptor;
    destDesc : Descriptor
  }
  service move(serviceName) {
    |srv|
    srv := srcDesc.getService(serviceName);
    destDesc.addService(srv);
    srcDesc.removeService(serviceName);
  }
}
```

An example of defining a meta-descriptor.

`Descriptor` is a meta-descriptor, i.e. an entity whose instances are standard descriptors. A new meta-descriptor can be defined by extending it. As an example, consider the following issue. Having an inheritance system, it is possible for a sub-descriptor SD to define new required ports, thus adding requirements to the contract defined by its super-descriptor D. In such a case, the substitution of an instance of D by an instance of SD needs specific checking (child-parent incompatibility problem of inheritance systems in CBSE [30]). It may be wanted to define some descriptors that do not allow their sub-descriptors to add new requirements. Such a semantic restriction is achieved by the `DescriptorForSafeSubstitution` definition shown in the following code snippet. The meta-descriptor extends the meta-descriptor `Descriptor` and specializes its service `addPortDescription`, which implements the capability to add a port description. The service is redefined in a way that it signals an exception each time it is tried to add a description of an external required port.

```
Descriptor DescriptorForSafeSubstitution
  extends Descriptor
{
  service addPortDescription(portDesc) {
    | req ext |
    req := portDesc.isRequired();
    ext := portDesc.isExternal();
    if (reg & ext)
    { [self.error('no new reqs. allowed')] }
    else { [super.addPortDescription(portDesc)] };
  }
  ...
}
```

An instance (a new descriptor) of the `DescriptorForSafeSubstitution` meta-descriptor named `TestDescriptor` extending descriptor `Component` could then be created by the following expressions:

- Run-time creation:

```
DescriptorForSafeSubstitution
    .newNamed('TestDescriptor', Component);
```

- Static creation:

```
DescriptorForSafeSubstitution TestDescriptor
  extends Component
{ ... }
```

An Example of a new kind of port: a read-only port.

The following code snippet shows the `ReadOnlyProvidedPort` descriptor realizing a new kind of provided ports through which only services without side effect, i.e. services not affecting the state of the component, could be invoked. It redefines the standard service invocation to check whenever it is correct or not to invoke the requested service and it also redefines the standard connecting service in a way, that a provided port of kind read-only can be delegated only to another read-only provided port.

```
Descriptor ReadOnlyProvidedPort
  extends ProvidedPort
{
  service invoke(service) {
    |bool1 bool2|
    bool1 := owner.implements(service);
    bool2 := owner.isConstantService(service);
    if(bool1.and([bool2]))
    { super.invoke(service); }
    else { ... }
  }
  service connectTo(port) {
    if(port.getDescriptor().isKindOf(ReadOnlyPort))
    { super.connectTo(port); }
  }
}
```

To conclude this part on ports, we can say that their explicit status is a way to further control references between entities. For example, the read-only example illustrates the fact that using different kinds of provided ports can facilitate different view-points on a component, in this case the read-only view-point.

An Example of a transformation design and constraint verification.

Examples of introspection, intercession and meta-modeling applications have already been given in previous paragraphs. Here we present two larger applications[5] of these features, which were our main motivation to develop this work: a runtime component-based model transformation, and an architecture constraint checking.

The first application deals with a transformation scenario performed on COMPO's implementation of the simple HTTP server, described in Section 2. This transformation migrates this component-based application from classic front-end/back-end architecture into a bus-oriented architecture. The transformation (sketched in Fig. 4) was motivated by a use-case when a customer (already running the server) needs to turn the server with multiple fronts-ends and back-ends.

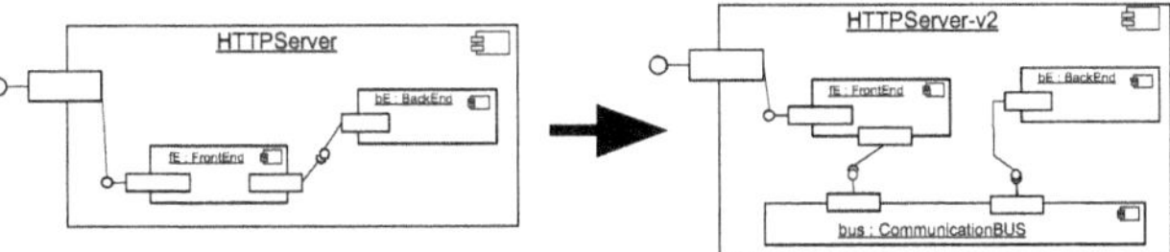

Figure 4: Simplified diagram illustrating the transformation from classic front-end back-end architecture into bus-oriented architecture.

A bus-oriented architecture reduces the number of point-to-point connections between communicating components. This, in turn, makes impact analysis for major software changes simpler and more straightforward. This makes easier monitoring for failure and misbehavior in highly complex systems, and allows easier modifications on components.

```
Descriptor ToBusTransformer {
 requires { context : IDescriptor }
 service stepOne-AddBus() {
  |pd cd|
  pd := PortDescription.new('bus','required'
                         ,'internal',IBus);
  context.addPortDescription(pd);
  cd := ConnectionDescription
         .new('bus'
             ,'default@(Bus.new())');
  context.addConnectionDescription(cd);
 }
 service stepTwo-ConnectAllToBus() {...}
 service stepThree-RemOldConns() {...}
}
```

Listing 2: A code-snippet of the **ToBusTransformer** descriptor.

The results of the transformation are checked using architecture constraints also implemented as COMPO components [32].

The transformation is modeled as a descriptor named **ToBusTransformer**. An instance was connected to the **HTTPServer** descriptor (COMPO's code in Listing 1) and it performs the following transformation steps: (i) introduce a new internal required port named **bus** to which an instance of a **Bus** descriptor (not specified here) will be connected; (ii) extends the original architecture with new connections from front-end and back-end to bus; (iii) removes the original connection from front-end to back-end. Finally, a constraint component, an instance of the **VerifyBusArch** descriptor will be connected to the server to perform post-transformation verification. The constraint component executes a service

```
Descriptor VerifyBusArch extends Constraint
{
 service verify() {...}
 service stepOne-IsBusPresent() {...}
 service stepTwo-HasBusIOPorts(busPD){...}
 service stepThree-AreAllConnsToBus(busPD){
  |conns|
  conns := context.getConnsDescs();
  conns.remove([:cd|cd.getSrcPort()
               .getInterface()==IBus]);

  if((conns.remove([:cd|
     cd.isDelegation()]))
  {} else { return false };

  if(conns.forEach([:cd|
   (cd.srcPortDesc()==busPD)
   .or([cd.destPortDesc()==busPD])
  ]) {return true } else { return false };
 }
}
```

Listing 3: A code-snippet of the **VerifyBusArch** descriptor.

verify which does the following steps: (i) verifies the presence of the bus component; (ii) verifies that the bus component has one input and one output port; (iii) verifies that all the other components are connected to the bus only and the original delegation connection is preserved.

Listings 2 and 3 show snippets of COMPO code of the **ToBusTransformer** descriptor and the **VerifyBusArch** descriptor. The following code snippet shows the use of the transformation and verification components:

```
transformer := ToBusTransformer.new();
constraint := VerifyBusArch.new();

connect context@transformer to default@HTTPServer;
connect context@constraint to default@HTTPServer;

transformer.transform();
constraint.verify();
```

4. INTEGRATING REFLECTION

This section describes the integration of structural reflection[6] capabilities into COMPO, i.e. "to provide a complete reification of both a program currently executed as well as a complete reification of its abstract data types." [11]. The integration is based on the new version of the meta-model presented in Figure 3. The following sub-sections explain it, present the COMPO's reflective description of its essential elements, discuss the issues it eventually raises and give clues on how the associated interpretation processes, that makes the meta-model executable, cope, when necessary, with infinite regressions potentially induced by cycles it contains.

First-Class Components.

Our "*everything is a component*" requirement is achieved via the transposition of the Smalltalk [14] original solution (also re-introduced for the same purpose in MOF reflection [22]) that any entity is an instance of a descriptor and that *Component* (conceptually conforming to

[5]Actually we present code snippets because of the space limit.

[6]Our solution makes it possible to define new kind of ports (e.g. aspect ports, see [29]) in which service invocation can be altered, this is a very limited form of behavioral reflection; we offer no way to control or modify basic services invocation and execution.

MOF::Reflection::Object) is the root of the descriptor inheritance hierarchy; this makes, together with the classical set theoretic interpretation of inheritance, any instance of any descriptor a component.

The Component descriptor then defines the basic structure and behavior shared by all components. Its reflective definition in COMPO (cf. Listing 4) shows that any component has at least one provided port named default through which all public services it defines (* notation) can be invoked. Any component also has two internal provided ports named self and super[7] allowing a component to send service invocations to itself via these ports. Component also defines different services of global interest, like getDescriptor() which returns the receiver's descriptor.

```
Descriptor Component {
  provides { default : * }
  internally requires {
    super : * ofKind SuperPort;
    self : * ofKind SelfPort;
  }
  service getPorts() {...}
  service getPortNamed(name) {...}
  service getDescriptor() {...}
  service getOwner() {...}
}
```

Listing 4: The Component descriptor.

First-class descriptors.

Components as we see and propose them with COMPO differ from objects mainly by their explicit requirements, explicit architectures, their connections and their communication via ports[8]. Concerning the question of seeing and manipulating descriptors as components, these differences do not prevent from reusing standard meta-classes solutions to manipulate classes as objects. Among existing solutions, we have chosen the ObjVlisp one [8], because (i) it solves in the simplest way the problem that each component, including descriptors, should be an instance of a descriptor, and (ii) it is perfectly adapted to our requirements of allowing for new explicit meta-descriptors (e.g. independent from the descriptors inheritance hierarchy.

Translated in our context, it leads to the COMPO's recursive definition given in Listing 5 where Descriptor is instance of itself and extends Component. Of course it needs a bootstrapped implementation to become executable. This is presented in Section 5. It defines the new service to create instances and newNamed(name, super-desc) to create new descriptors and some base services for using introspection (various read-accessors such as getDescribedPorts()) and for intercession (such as addService(service)). These services, together with those inherited from Component, set the basis for creating more complex reflective operations. In addition to what is defined in Component, a descriptor has four internal required ports: name, ports (a collection of instances of PortDescription according to which ports of its instances are), architecture (a collection of instances of ConnectionDescription[9] representing its instances architecture description), and services (its services dictionary).

```
Descriptor Descriptor extends Component {
  internally requires {
    name : IString;
    ports[] : { getName(); getRole();...};
    architecture[] : { getSrc(); getDest();...};
    services[] : { execute();...};
  }
  service new() {...}
  service newNamed(name, super-desc) {...}
  service getDescribedPorts() {...}
  service getDescribedConnections() {...}
  service addService(service) {...}
  ...
}
```

Listing 5: The Descriptor descriptor.

First-class ports.

Unlike the case for descriptors, seeing and manipulating ports as components raises an interesting open issue. Ports are high-level abstractions to represent connections and the capacity for architects to disconnect and reconnect other components, whatever form they can take, either possibly physical connections of physical devices or references to addresses in memory. Reifying ports resembles to handling first-class references [2], but looks at them at a higher abstraction level. This also allows do deal with the problem in a simple way (and obviously without handling efficiency considerations). Ports abstract connection points and communication channels. Reifying them opens the door to the creation of various kinds of connections or to various ways to send, transmit, interpret or control services invocations (read-only ports described in section 3 is one example, aspect-ports would be another one (see [29]).

The problem that we should tackle in this case is the following: Reified ports should have ports: i) internal required ports to hold some internal data, for example their name or the name of the interface that describe them, ii) one external provided ports to which other components could connect to invoke their services. Using the base level, it should be possible to use ports in a standard way as a communication channel to transmit services invocations as for example with the expression printer.print('hello') (see Figure 5), where printer is a port of a component c, will invoke the service print of the component connected to c via printer. Using the meta-level, it should be possible to use ports as standard components, i.e. for example to invoke, in a way that conforms to COMPO's meta-model and semantics, the isConnected() service (see Listing 6) for port printer, which

[7]The statement ofKind in the definition states that the self and super ports are created as instances of specific descriptors SelfPort and SuperPort respectively.

[8]This vision is compatible with other components models, including those that consider components as packaging entities. If it were to be considered how to pack one COMPO component and put it on a shelves, as for javabeans, we would consider putting in the pack its descriptor, or its descriptor with this particular instance, or its descriptor together with all the descriptors of its internal components, etc.

[9]PortDescriptions and ConnectionDescriptions are used at instantiation time and also during static or runtime architecture checking or transformation. In the case of a runtime transformation implementation it should be ensured that descriptor level descriptions and instances internal representations are still causally connected, when the description changes.

should return true. The above requirements induce an infinite regression as soon as it is tried to invoke a service of a port seen as a component. To build a usable system, we have altered them by denying the component status to ports of ports. This alters in a very marginal way the reflective possibilities of the system. All examples presented in the previous section, and all applications we can think of, stay achievable.

Our complete solution comes as follows. All standard ports can be used as components on demand. All Standard ports conform to the COMPO reflective definition of the `Port` descriptor shown in listing 6. A primitive port is not a component and cannot be used as such. Any port of any standard port is automatically created as a primitive port by the virtual machine. The attachment of a primitive port to its port is primitive and done by the virtual machine. The special `&` operator (the Semantics of which bears some resemblance with the C `&` operator's one) is introduced such that, for any port `p`, `&p` is, and behaves as such, a primitive internal required port automatically connected to the **`default`** port (all components have it), itself a primitive port, of `p`. Used in the context of our previous example, it is then possible to write `&printer.isConnected()`, where `&printer` is a port of the current component connected to a primitive port of `printer`. The invocation is then transmitted to `printer` seen as a component thus invoking the **`isConnected()`** service of `Port` descriptor. Because primitive ports are not components, they cannot be used as such and the`&` operator is made idempotent, `&printer == &&printer`, etc.

It is to be noted that to have ports made explicit is a way to abstract connections between components. Having first class ports also opens the door to introspection and experimentation with various kinds of connections [19]. The read-only ports defined in section 3 can also be seen as implementing read-only connectors. Together with this capability our model makes it possible to define adapter components and interconnect them between any components.

```
Descriptor Port extends Component {
  requires {
    owner : IComponent
    connectedPorts[] : IPort
  }
  internally requires {
    name : IString;
    interface : IInterface
  }
  service getName(){...}
  service getIterface(){...}
  service invoke(service){...}
  service isConnected(){...}
  service connectTo(port){...}
  service disconnect(index){...}
}
```

Listing 6: The `Port` descriptor.

First-class services.

Reifying services as components does not raise new issues compared to their reification as objects, and it is shortly given to complete the presentation. Listing 7 shows the COMPO implementation of the `Service` descriptor. Each service has a signature (port `serviceSign`) to which an instance

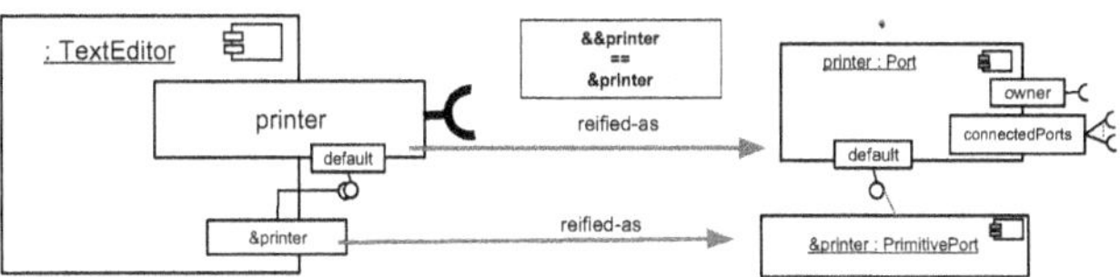

Figure 5: The & operator for accessing the component-oriented reification of the `printer` port of component `TextEditor`

of `ServiceSignature`[10] descriptor will be connected), temporary variables names and values (collection ports `tempsN` and `tempsV`), a program text (port `code`), actual parameters (collection port `paramsV`), an execution context (port `context`, to be connected at run-time to a component representing an execution context). To shorten, the architecture section and implementation of the `execute()` service are omitted.

```
Descriptor Service extends Component {
  requires {
    context : IComponent;
    paramsV[] : *;
  }
  internally requires {
    serviceSign : ServiceSignature;
    tempsN[] : IString;
    tempsV[] : *;
    code : IString;
  }
  ...
  service execute() {...}
}
```

Listing 7: The `Service` descriptor.

Next section gives insights into the implementation that makes this meta-model and these COMPO definitions of COMPO descriptors executable.

5. BOOTSTRAP IMPLEMENTATION

COMPO could be implemented from scratch, e.g. with a new virtual machine, but our first solution to validate our ideas more rapidly has been to implement it on top of an existing language having objects and a reflective level offering intercession on structures. Among various possible alternatives (CLOS could have been used), we have chosen Smalltalk, because it has been shown that its meta-model is extensible enough [4, 12] to support another meta-class system.

Our meta-model is based on the two core concepts (captured in Figure 3): `Component` and `Descriptor`. Both are implemented as sub-classes of Smalltalk-classes: `Object` and `Class`, respectively. Figure 7 shows their integration into the Smalltalk meta-model. This integration makes COMPO components and descriptors manageable inside Pharo Smalltalk environment. For example, one can use basic inspecting tool, the *Inspector*. `Descriptor` being defined as a sub-class of Smalltalk-class `Class` enables us to benefit from class management and maintenance capabilities provided by the environment. For example, all descriptors are "browsable" with

[10]Due to space reasons we omit the `ServiceSignature` descriptor definition. To give a hint, it provides a service to store and access names and parameters names of services.

the standard *SystemBrowser* tool. We benefit from such a deep integration and provide COMPO also its own tool to support descriptors' design process, see Figure 6. By the way, the tool is also an example of reflection usage.

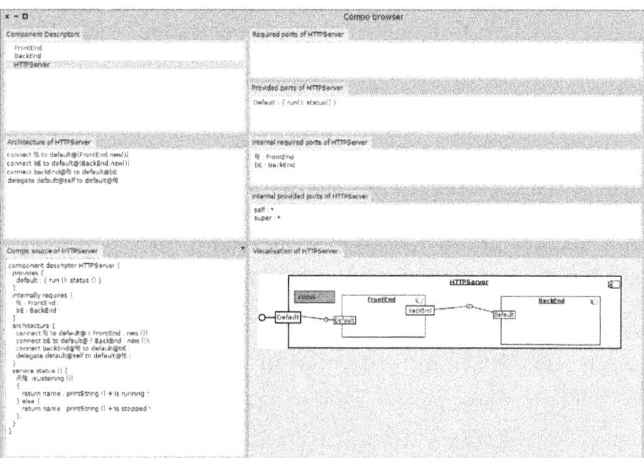

Figure 6: Screenshot of the COMPO's HTTPServer implementation in the descriptor's development tool.

One of the problems we challenged during the implementation is the fact that Smalltalk supports single-inheritance only. The meta-model shown in Figure 3 says that `Descriptor` inherits from `Component`, but as it is said above, we implement `Descriptor` as a sub-class of Smalltalk-classes (`Class`). Consequently `Descriptor` should have two parents and multiple-inheritance is needed[11]. Concretely, there are two critical points, where multiple-inheritance is needed, marked with red ellipses in Figure 7: (i) `Descriptor` should inherit from Smalltalk-class `Class` and from Compo-class `Component` (ii) the automatically created Smalltalk-meta-class `Component class` should inherit from Smalltalk-meta-class `Object class` and from Compo-class `Descriptor`. To solve this we simulate the multiple inheritance by automated copying attributes and methods from `Component` to `Descriptor` and from `Object class` to `Component class`, when one of the parents evolves.

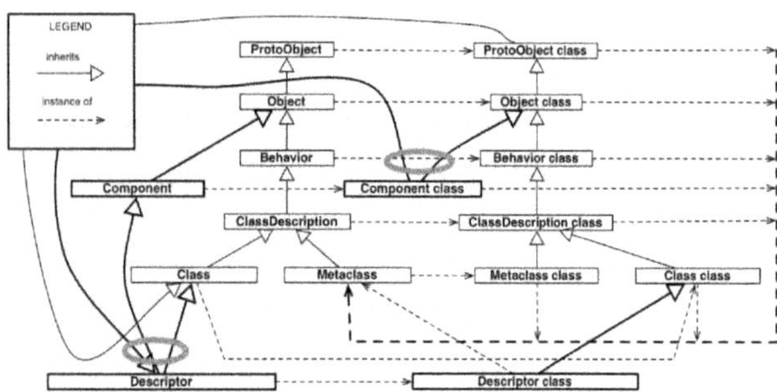

Figure 7: Integration of basic COMPO classes into Smalltalk meta-model

Another problem we encountered is the implementation of `Descriptor` as an instance of itself. Smalltalk-class `Descriptor` is a unique instance of Smalltalk-meta-class `Descriptor class`, which is automatically created as a sub-class of Smalltalk-meta-class `Class class` (parallel hierarchy rule of Smalltalk) and therefore it does not have the same structure as `Descriptor` class. To solve this problem we have extended Smalltalk-meta-class `Descriptor class` in a way that it has the same attributes and provides the same methods as Smalltalk-class `Descriptor`.

Additionally, we have extented `Object` to behave as a primitive component providing all methods defined by `Object` (seen as compo services) through a unique provided port. Thus Smalltalk-objects can be seen as primitive COMPO-components and they are usable in COMPO. This makes it possible to reuse Smalltalk class library. For example, the `PrimitivePort` Smalltalk-class can be used as rock-bottom primitive component used to implement primitive ports.

[11]Although there is a solution based on single-inheritance, the solution introduces a unsuitable issue when distinguishing components/descriptors from objects/classes in the implementation level.

6. RELATED WORK

In this section we compare reflection capabilities and solutions offered by COMPO with those provided by other component-based systems. For that purpose we classify existing systems into three categories: Modeling languages, Middleware component models and Component-oriented programming languages.

Modeling languages.

UML 2 provides support for component-based software modeling. Although UML itself is not a reflective language, its meta-model (defined with MOF [22]) is. Reflection capabilities (manipulation of properties, instance creation, etc.) provided by MOF are specifications only, i.e. there is no support for run-time reflection capabilities as we introduced in COMPO.

A specific category of modeling languages are Architecture Description Languages (ADLs). The static nature of ADLs also do not match well with reflection [18]. Reflection or at least introspection capabilities depend on the code which is generated from architectures that these ADLs describe. For example, reflection is partially supported in C2 [17] through *context reflective interfaces*. Each C2 connector is capable of supporting arbitrary addition, removal, and reconnection of any number of C2 components.

Middleware component models.

Existing middleware technologies and standards provide limited support for platform openness, usually restricted to high-level services, while the underlying platform is considered as a black box.

CORBA Component Model (CCM) [24], Enterprise Java Beans (EJBs) [25] or Component Object Model (COM) [20] do not provide support for explicit architecture definition. The black-box approach they support does not fit with reflection very well. Introspection interfaces (like `IUnknown` interface in COM), which can be used to discover the capabilities of components, are the only reflection capability they offer.

Only few solutions consider reflection as a general approach which can be used as an overall framework that encompasses platform customization and dynamic reconfiguration. These models try to overcome the limitations of the black-box approach by providing components with meta-information about their internal structure. Projects like OpenCOM [7] (a lightweight and efficient component model based on COM), OpenCORBA [16] and DynamicTAO [15] adopt reflection as a principled way to build flexible middleware platforms. In opposite to COMPO, reflection capabilities of these are usually limited to coarse-grained components, without the possibility to control more detailed structures of platforms.

Many reflection capabilities are supported in Fractal component model [5], but the capabilities vary depending on kinds of *Controllers* a Fractal component membrane contains. Controllers can be combined and extended to yield components with different introspection and intercession features as shown by FRASCATI model [28] for the development of highly configurable SCA solutions. In COMPO, reflection capabilities are the same for all components (an orthogonal model). In addition, we go further in the reification of component-level concepts: services, ports and descriptors are components.

Furthermore, middleware component models are often designed to be platform independent by providing tools for generating code skeletons to be filled later. Consequently, and in opposite to COMPO, run-time transformations on components and their internal structure are performed through objects and not components. as it is for example in SOFA [26] and its reification of connectors which has to be mapped by developers to some (object-oriented) code.

Meta-ORB [9] as a representant of the Models@runtime stream [3] pushes the idea of reflection one step further by considering the reflection layer as a real model that can be uncoupled from the running architecture (e.g. for reasoning, validation, and simulation purposes) and later automatically re-synchronized with its running instance. In contrast to COMPO's orthogonal model where a change to a descriptor is propagated to all its instances, Meta-ORB reflection is based on per-object meta-objects, enabling to isolate the effects of reflection.

Component-based programming languages, CBPLs.

The big advantage of CBPLs is that they do not separate architectures from implementation and so they have potential to manipulate reified concepts. In opposite to COMPO, component-level concepts are often reified as objects, instead of components. This leads to a mixed use of component and object concepts. For example reflection package of ArchJava [1] specifies a class (not a component class) named `Port` which represents a port instance. Often the representations are not causally connected to concepts they represent. In case of ArchJava, which relies on Java reflection, the reason is that reflection in Java is mostly read-only, i.e. introspection support only.

Reflection is not explicitly advocated in ComponentJ [27]. It however appears that a running system certainly has a partial representation of itself to allow for dynamic reconfiguration of internal architectures of components as described in [27] but it seems to be a localized and ad-hoc capability, the reification process being neither explicited nor generalized as in our proposal.

7. CONCLUSION

We have described an operational original reflective modeling and programming component-based language allowing for the development of component-based models (architectural part at this point), applications and of static or runtime model and program transformations. It offers developers an effective conceptual continuum to use components at all stages of software development with no conceptual loss between stages. It opens the essential possibility that architectures, implementations and transformations can all be written at the component level and using a unique language. As a reflective language giving a model access (via meta-components) to elements of a uniform component-based meta-model, COMPO also makes it possible to design and implement new component-based construct (as exemplified with achieving a new kind of ports).

We have described a full component-based meta-model and a reflective description in COMPO of its main component descriptors made executable via a concrete implementation. We have proposed some concrete, adapted from existing works (first-class descriptors) or new (first-class ports), solutions for a component-based reification of concepts leading to a uniform "*everything is a component*" operational development paradigm.

COMPO in its today's state is an operational prototype mainly designed as a research laboratory to experiment new ideas. Here are the main ones we intend to follow on. (1) COMPO does not yet embed all new capabilities offered by existing ADLs and modeling languages, but its reflexive architecture is especially designed to integrate them and to rapidly experience the impact of their integration. (2) Using the same reflective capabilities, we aim at integrating generalized bound properties (primarily exemplified by JavaBeans), aspects components, an more powerful solutions to express requirements and provisions. (3) The global idea that objects plus explicit requirements and explicit architectures are components is already largely present in this paper, we aim at experiment its full generalization. (4) To improve COMPO's program efficiency can be done in various ways; firstly known optimization for reflexive language [6] but following previous point 3 we can imagine updating existing virtual machines for reflective object-oriented languages to components-based ones.

Acknowlegments.

The authors would like to thank Roland Ducournau, Luc Fabresse and Marianne Huchard for fruitful discussions.

8. REFERENCES

[1] J. Aldrich, C. Chambers, and D. Notkin. Archjava: connecting software architecture to implementation. In *Proceedings of the 24th International Conference on Software Engineering*, ICSE '02, pages 187–197, New York, NY, USA, 2002. ACM.

[2] J.-B. Arnaud, M. Denker, S. Ducasse, D. Pollet, A. Bergel, and M. Suen. Read-only execution for dynamic languages. In *Proceedings of the 48th international conference on Objects, models, components, patterns*, TOOLS'10, pages 117–136, Berlin, Heidelberg, 2010. Springer-Verlag.

[3] G. Blair, N. Bencomo, and R. France. Models@ run.time. *Computer*, 42(10):22–27, 2009.

[4] J.-P. Briot and P. Cointe. Programming with explicit metaclasses in smalltalk-80. *SIGPLAN Not.*, 24(10):419–431, Sept. 1989.

[5] E. Bruneton, T. Coupaye, M. Leclercq, V. Quéma, and J.-B. Stefani. The fractal component model and its support in java: Experiences with auto-adaptive and reconfigurable systems. *Softw. Pract. Exper.*, 36(11-12):1257–1284, Sept. 2006.

[6] S. Chiba. Implementation techniques for efficient reflective languages. Technical report, Departement of Information Science, The University of Tokyo, 1997.

[7] M. Clarke, G. S. Blair, G. Coulson, and N. Parlavantzas. An efficient component model for the construction of adaptive middleware. In *Proceedings of the IFIP/ACM International Conference on Distributed Systems Platforms Heidelberg*, Middleware '01, pages 160–178, London, UK, UK, 2001. Springer-Verlag.

[8] P. Cointe. Metaclasses are first class: The objvlisp model. *SIGPLAN Not.*, 22(12):156–162, Dec. 1987.

[9] F. M. Costa, L. L. Provensi, and F. F. Vaz. Using runtime models to unify and structure the handling of meta-information in reflective middleware. In *Proceedings of the 2006 international conference on Models in software engineering*, MoDELS'06, pages 232–241, Berlin, Heidelberg, 2006. Springer-Verlag.

[10] I. Crnkovic, S. Sentilles, A. Vulgarakis, and M. Chaudron. A classification framework for software component models. *Software Engineering, IEEE Transactions on*, 37(5):593 –615, sept.-oct. 2011.

[11] F.-N. Demers and J. Malenfant. Reflection in logic, functional and object-oriented programming: a short comparative study. In *In IJCAI '95 Workshop on Reflection and Metalevel Architectures and their Applications in AI*, pages 29–38, 1995.

[12] S. Ducasse and T. Gîrba. Using smalltalk as a reflective executable meta-language. In *Proceedings of the 9th international conference on Model Driven Engineering Languages and Systems*, MoDELS'06, pages 604–618, Berlin, Heidelberg, 2006. Springer-Verlag.

[13] L. Fabresse, N. Bouraqadi, C. Dony, and M. Huchard. A language to bridge the gap between component-based design and implementation. *COMLAN : Journal on Computer Languages, Systems and Structures*, 38(1):29–43, Apr. 2012.

[14] A. Goldberg and D. Robson. *Smalltalk-80: The Language and Its Implementation.* Addison-Wesley Longman Publishing Co., Inc., Boston, MA, USA, 1983.

[15] F. Kon, M. Román, P. Liu, J. Mao, T. Yamane, C. Magalhã, and R. H. Campbell. Monitoring, security, and dynamic configuration with the dynamictao reflective orb. In *IFIP/ACM International Conference on Distributed systems platforms*, Middleware '00, pages 121–143, Secaucus, NJ, USA, 2000. Springer-Verlag New York, Inc.

[16] T. Ledoux. Opencorba: A reflective open broker. In *Proceedings of the Second International Conference on Meta-Level Architectures and Reflection*, Reflection '99, pages 197–214, London, UK, UK, 1999. Springer-Verlag.

[17] N. Medvidovic, P. Oreizy, J. E. Robbins, and R. N. Taylor. Using object-oriented typing to support architectural design in the c2 style. *SIGSOFT Softw. Eng. Notes*, 21(6):24–32, Oct. 1996.

[18] N. Medvidovic and R. N. Taylor. A classification and comparison framework for software architecture description languages. *IEEE Trans. Softw. Eng.*, 26(1):70–93, Jan. 2000.

[19] N. R. Mehta, N. Medvidovic, and S. Phadke. Towards a taxonomy of software connectors. In *Proceedings of the 22nd international conference on Software engineering*, ICSE '00, pages 178–187, New York, NY, USA, 2000. ACM.

[20] Microsoft. *COM: Component Object Model Technologies.* Microsoft, 2012.

[21] P.-A. Muller, F. Fleurey, and J.-M. JeÃŇÂĄzeÃŇÂĄquel. Weaving executability into object-oriented meta-languages. In *Proceedings of the 8th international conference on Model Driven Engineering Languages and Systems*, MoDELS'05, Berlin, Heidelberg, 2005. Springer-Verlag.

[22] OMG. *Meta Object Facility (MOF) Core Specification Version 2.4.1*, 2011.

[23] OMG. *Unified Modeling Language (UML), V2.4.1.* OMG, August 2011.

[24] OMG. *CORBA Component Model (CCM).* OMG, 2012.

[25] Oracle. *Enterprise JavaBeans Specification Version 3.* Oracle, 2012.

[26] F. Plášil, D. Bálek, and R. Janecek. Sofa/dcup: Architecture for component trading and dynamic updating. In *procs. of CDS*, Washington, DC, USA, 1998. IEEE Computer Society.

[27] J. C. Seco, R. Silva, and M. Piriquito. Componentj: A component-based programming language with dynamic reconfiguration. *Computer Science and Information Systems*, 05(02):65–86, 12 2008.

[28] L. Seinturier, P. Merle, R. Rouvoy, D. Romero, V. Schiavoni, and J.-B. Stefani. A component-based middleware platform for reconfigurable service-oriented architectures. *Softw. Pract. Exper.*, 42(5):559–583, May 2012.

[29] P. Spacek. *Design and Implementation of a Reflective Component-Oriented Programming and Modeling Language.* PhD thesis, Montpellier II University, Montpellier, France, December 2013.

[30] P. Spacek, C. Dony, C. Tibermacine, and L. Fabresse. An inheritance system for structural & behavioral reuse in component-based software programming. In *Proceedings of the 11th GPCE*, pages 60–69. ACM, 2012.

[31] P. Spacek, C. Dony, C. Tibermacine, and L. Fabresse. Wringing out objects for programming and modeling component-based systems. In *procs. of the 2nd Int. Workshop on Combined Object-Oriented Modeling and Programming Languages (COOMPL'13) - co-located with ECOOP.* ACM Digital Library, July 2013.

[32] C. Tibermacine, S. Sadou, C. Dony, and L. Fabresse. Component-based specification of software architecture constraints. In *Proceedings of the 14th CBSE*, pages 31–40, New York, NY, USA, 2011. ACM.

Towards a Meta-Model for Dynamic Applications

Sahar Smaali, Aïcha Choutri, Faïza Belala
LIRE Laboratory, Constantine 2 University, Algeria
sahar.smaali@gmail.com, aichachoutri@gmail.com, belalafaiza@hotmail.com

ABSTRACT

Interfaces are the key architectural elements able to offer a better behavior or evolution view of software system architecture and components interactions. In this paper, we propose a single software architecture description meta-model based on MDA approach to deal with both static and dynamic aspects. It is particularly centered on the interface concept considered as a first class entity. This has the advantage to allow a loose coupling of basic constructing blocks. Moreover, it will ensure facilities for software maintainability and flexibility. Our high-level architecture behavior and dynamics definition is illustrated and evaluated through a realistic example of a ubiquitous system.

Categories and Subject Descriptors

D.2.11 **[Software Engineering]**: Software Architectures—*domain-specific architectures, languages, patterns.*

Keywords

Dynamic software architecture description, Meta-model, MDA, Interface.

1. INTRODUCTION

The increasing size and complexity of current software systems has led the computing community to acknowledge the importance of software's evolution as a challenge [10]. In fact, the dynamic evolution is an important feature in the field of software engineering as it extends the software life and ensures its viability. This system feature covers changes not only in its source code, but in its Software Architecture (SA) as well. Evolving the architecture description provides a higher level of abstraction and reasoning, that shifts the developer's focus away from lines-of-code to components and their overall interconnection structure [7]. This can affect software architecture structure or behavior. It also can be planned or unplanned, and occur before or during the execution phase [19]. In each of these cases, any part of the software architecture may evolve or change. Therefore, it is necessary to identify what can evolve, how does it evolve, and how do these changes affect the architecture [19].

Furthermore, meta-modeling is the key technology that ensures precise model manipulations, model evolution and model behavior. In this paper, we consider the above challenges in the meta-modeling context to provide an alternative definition of SA in terms of a complete meta-model that promotes the use of interfaces as the primary artifact to be specified and maintained.

CBSE'14, June 30–July 4, 2014, Marcq-en-Baroeul, France.

http://dx.doi.org/10.1145/2602458.2602469

This simplified meta-model called DySAM (Dynamic Software Architecture Meta-model) maintains both structure and dynamic behavior of SA. The model elements are not only structure constructs comparable to those of architecture description languages (ADL), but also:

- The interfaces' behavior as a state transition System. An interface may be either active or passive allowing shutting down a part of the system in order to perform some architectural changes without altering its consistency.
- The interactions between the architectural elements in terms of information exchange, in order to analyze and verify the system behavior in the early phases of the software development cycle.
- The architecture dynamic evolution as a set of strategy rules that allow adding, destroying, or even replacing architectural entities. An evolution manager is responsible of applying this rules and maintaining the coherence of the system.

The obtained meta-model is precise, analyzable and transformable to be executable. Its well-defined transformations may support rigorous model evolution and refinement. Thus, the main advantages of the DySAM model are:

- The loose coupling of software architectural entities since, we focus on architecture's interfaces rather than components and connectors, the description of their evolution in terms of state transition, and the concise specification of their interactions.
- The MDA (Model Driven Architecture) approach [8], adopted to define DySAM and the model transformations thereafter, offers a good tool support to reason about SA. In particular, we show how basic operations on model elements, such as subtyping, cardinalities calculus, and type inference, may be used to design dynamic software systems at a high abstraction level rather than that of conventional programming languages.
- With increasing adoption of MDE (Model Driven Engineering), model transformation supporting code generation from a SA is becoming essential in system development and evolution processes. Indeed, we may use a given source meta-model (DySAM in our case), as the foundation for building a model transformation based framework and generate a chain of various target models to implement or analyze the SA model.

The remainder of the paper is organized as follow:
In section 2, we discuss some works on meta-modeling dynamic software architecture to situate ours among them. Section 3 presents the proposed DySAM model for dynamic SA description. In section 4, we illustrate and evaluate our meta-model through its instantiation with a ubiquitous system example. Finally, the paper is concluded in Section 5 by drawing some comments and outlining some perspectives for future work.

2. RELATED WORK

We are currently witnessing how the software engineering community is embracing the SA description initiative with increasing interest. So far, most of the efforts have been focused on defining models, meta-models and transformations between them. For instance, some ADL provide their meta-models such as COSA

[16], AADL [15], SOFA.2 [6]. Even if these languages definitions support dynamic aspects, their models focus on the static architectural description elements. Their behavior and dynamic features are generally modeled separately with either UML profiles (case of AADL and SOFA) or other meta-models (case of COSA). Indeed the authors in [1] define a multi-view meta-modeling approach to describe the behavior of SA denoted in COSA, considering the interface concept as the core of all behaviors views. However, the Fractal [5] meta-model is more complete since it introduces the controller concept to manage component configuration and evolution through its membrane concept containing the interfaces but, interactions between components are partially modeled.

UML 2.0 [13] has the advantage to provide a unified notation with many constructs to describe a SA. However, its meta-model has to be instantiated by different models (different diagrams) for modeling the structural, behavioral and evolution aspects of SA, without any constraints for their coherence.

Authors in [14] propose a model called SAEV (Software Architecture Evolution Model) that serves not to model structural or behavioral aspects, but to manage architectural elements evolution using strategies and rules. In [17], authors present a language called MADL (Meta Architecture Description Language) to abstract the notions of architectures (components, connectors, architectures), in order to facilitate their manipulation, reuse, and evolution. The meta-model proposed in [18] defines common architectural structures abstraction of both architecture description languages and components technologies. It allows the definition of some evolution contracts, neglecting the behavior and the evolution aspects.

We deduce that the most cited works focus on giving a precise description of the architecture structure in terms of components, connectors and an assembly topology, while they do not pay attention to the SA dynamic modeling, although some of them propose separate models for defining dynamic evolution of SA.

Our proposed meta-model DySAM is quite similar, since it is designed to describe SA. However, it is different, as it gives a complete view of dynamic software architecture and covers its main aspects using the interfaces as fundamental description elements. Moreover, it provides at once the description of the structure and the dynamic evolution, as well as the specification of the architecture behavior in terms of well-defined interactions.

3. META MODELING DYNAMIC SA

Meta modeling is a critical part of our SA specification approach. It provides a mechanism to define unambiguously architecture description languages for dynamic systems. It is the prerequisite for a model transformation tool to access and use models. We will now look into the design of our Dynamic Software Architecture Meta-model.

3.1 Principle

Components are developed as reusable entities, they must be general enough but also sufficiently specific to be easily identified, understood and used. However, in all proposed SA description definitions (namely those given by ADL or related to component based models); the interface concept is the key element characterizing or even identifying an architectural element [9]. In fact, components are composed only through their interfaces and connector interfaces specify participant roles in an interaction. Interfaces support a part of architectural elements semantics and behavior allowing the description of dynamic aspects as well as constraints that may be attached to them.

Our findings led us to suggest a new definition of architectural description, primarily based on the interface concept (figure 1). Thus, this later is considered in DySAM as first class entity while leaving components and connectors as grey boxes. In what follows, we explain DySAM (figure 2) for dynamic and evolutionary SA specification, which is described in Ecore [4], a meta-modeling language similar to the MOF standard [12], having a graphical representation (based on a subset of UML class diagrams) in Eclipse environment.

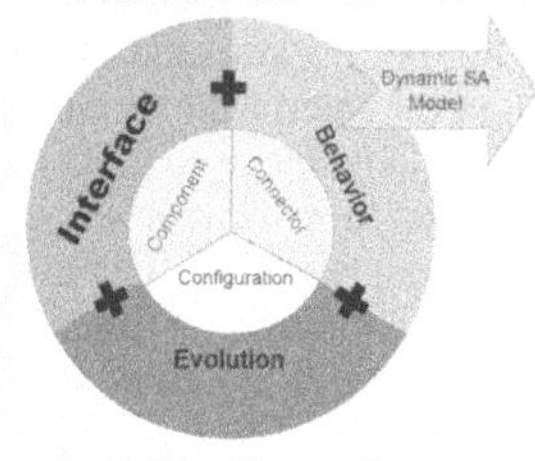

Figure 1. DySAM model motivation

3.2 Architectural elements

As shown in figure 2, DySAM model defines SA as a set of interfaces and attachments. The class Interface is the core of the proposed meta-model. It has two subclasses **Component Interface** and **ConnectorInterface**. The basic definition of each sub-class is related to the associated element (component or connector) when it is primitive. An instance structure of the first (respectively second) one contains a set of the class **Port (**respectively **Role**) instances.

Provided or required services through a port (association **uses)** are represented by the class **Service** related to the class **Parameter**, since a service is generally a procedure call which may need arguments. The **Role** class defines the connection category in term of a particular class that may be **Communication**, **Coordination**, **Facilitation**, or **Conversion.** It depends on the connector type. The **Attachment** class relates the Port and Role classes to build a given structure of SA.

A Component/ Connector interface may be primitive or composite allowing a hierarchical definition of SA. A **Composite Component interface** may contain a whole system architecture, while a **Composite Connector interface** may contain sub- connector interfaces. The **Port-binding** and **Role-binding** classes represent the link between a port/role of an interface and a port/role of a sub-interface.

The interface abstract behavior is defined by a state transition system (**State** and **Transition** classes).The **State** class models the interface state at a given time. We consider two kinds of state: **Active** (e.g. sending or receiving a message or an event) and **Passive** (e.g. nothing happen).The **Transition** class models the possible state changes. The **source** and **target** associations represent respectively both initial and final states of a transition, while **triggers** associations define its trigger event. The same cardinality **0..*** assigned to the ends of these associations is due to the fact that any trigger type may cause (zero or more) interface state changes. The super-class **ArchitecturalElement** is a generalization of different element classes (SystemArchitecture, Interface, Attachement, PortBinding, RoleBinding). It is associated to the classes **Property** and **Constraint** with multiplicity 0..* since any architectural element could have properties and constraints.

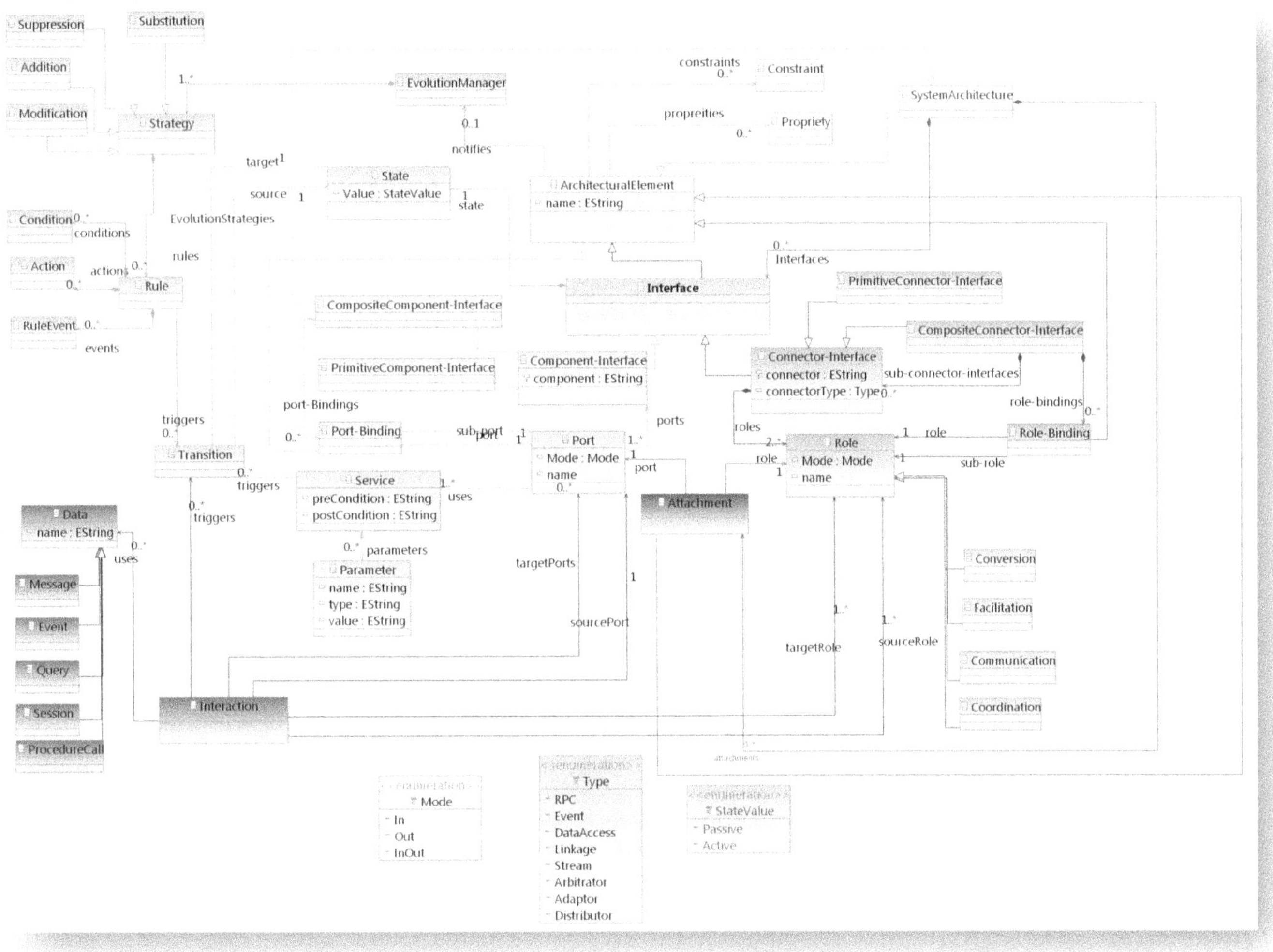

Figure 2. DySAM model for dynamic software architecture

3.3 Interactions

We use the added classes to better define architectural elements interactions. The **Interaction** class models data exchanges between interfaces. **SourcePort** association indicates the port that initiates the interaction (output port); while the **targetPorts** designates one or more receiving ports (input port). The fact that an interaction has only one trigger port and zero or more target ports, explains the cardinalities assigned to the ends of these associations. The **Source/Target Roles** relations specify the possible interactions of roles. An interaction depends on the connector type and needs at least two roles to be achieved. Furthermore, the interaction uses the **Data** class to represent exchanged information between interfaces that may be a **message**, an **event**, a **session**, or even a **database access**. The **triggers** association allows an interface state change according to the architecture behavior.

3.4 Dynamic Evolution

A SA configuration can change dynamically by creating or destroying the SA elements and their interactions during the system execution. This evolution must be identified and managed to maintain the coherence and the correct running of the system. The **Evolution Manager** class is responsible of any architectural element change; that is why it is related to **Architectural Element** class. It represents an autonomic entity, which supervises the architecture and ensures the system consistency avoiding its long interruption. The **Evolution Strategy** class models a set of evolution manager politics to determine when and how architectural elements will change. The association **notifies** alerts the evolution manager to choose an evolution strategy to be applied. An evolution strategy is a set of rules represented by the **Evolution Rule** class. This former is defined by a set of change **Actions**, resulting **Events**, and **Conditions**. A rule can also change an active interface state to a passive one, in order to shut down a part of the system. This will allow the rules execution without altering the architecture.

4. CASE STUDY

A real-life example of a ubiquitous system is chosen to highlight the ability of meta-modeling dynamic software architecture in a single model specifying all dynamic aspects of such systems. This considered case study, a Call forwarding System (figure 3), will demonstrate in next work how a dynamic software application is transformed automatically into executable models and code, and fulfils real-life needs.

This adaptive system has to redirect a phone call to the desk room where an employee is currently located because, a busy employee may lose an important phone call while he is constantly moving around the company building or having a meeting in another office. Sensors distributed in the company's offices detect an employee tag or device (e.g. a cell phone). If the employee receives a call while he is not in his office, a virtual phone will transfer the call to the office where currently he is, indicating his name on the phone's screen.

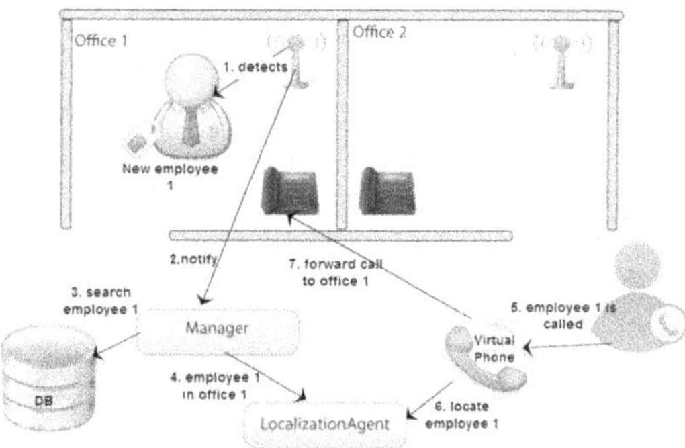

Figure 3. Forwarding Call System

We can elaborate the model of this system according to DySAM while instantiating all the meta-model elements. In particular, we are able to define dynamic aspects. For instance, we may naturally specify the communication and the coordination between different interfaces, as well as susceptible architectural changes.

4.1 Call forwarding System Architecture

The first task of developing the model of Call forwarding system is its architectural structure instantiation from DySAM (figure 4). This important step is achieved with respect to the deduced correspondences summarized in table 1. Obviously, the model contains a collection of component-interface classes:

- ✓**Presence** with three ports, one manages the detection of employees locations, another one provides access to the database contents, and the last one controls employees presence.
- ✓**Localization** with one port requiring an employee presence and a second one offering a mapping service between identifier and current office of the employee.
- ✓**Audio** with two ports to establish a call session between two phones.
- ✓**Virtual Audio** with two ports to establish an audio session and a third one that requests an employee location.
- ✓**DBInfo** with one port to provide employees information taken from the database storing association between employee and their identifiers.

These component interfaces are respectively implemented by **Sensor, Manager, Localization Agent, Phone, Virtual Phone, DB** components defined as attributes. Other classes are also defined to specify a set of connector-interfaces:

- ✓**Access** with two communication roles to extract information from the database
- ✓**Publish** with four communication roles that distribute interaction events among components interfaces.
- ✓**RPC** with two coordination roles that connect a virtual phone to the localization agent.
- ✓**Stream** with four communication roles that open a data flow between two phones to establish a call.

These connector interfaces are respectively implemented by **DB Access, Event Publisher, Procedure Call, Call Session** connectors defined as attributes.

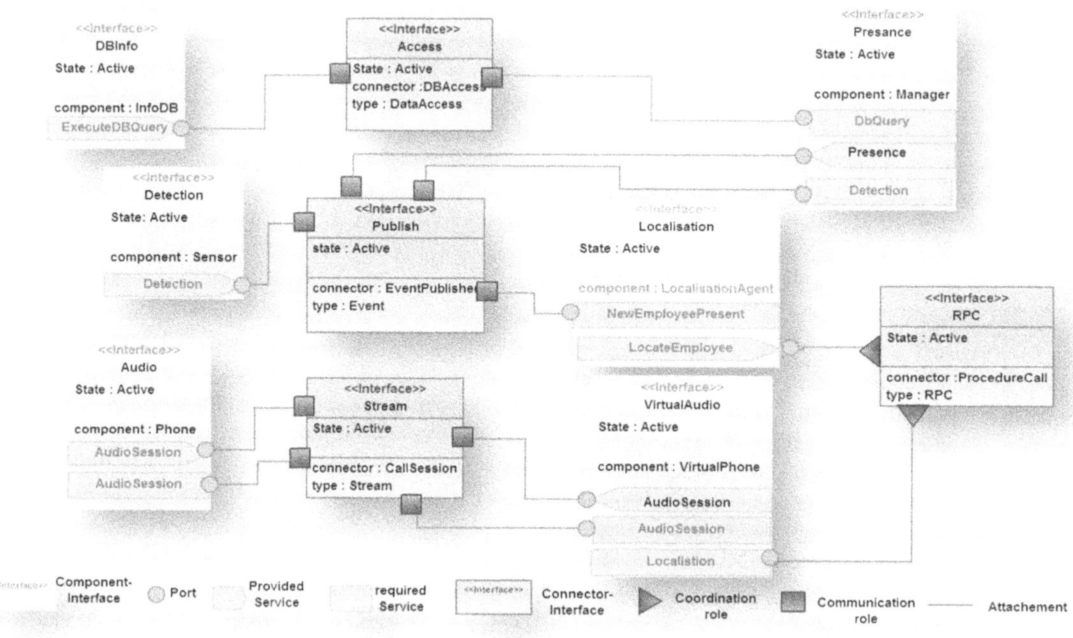

Figure 4. SA model of the call forwarding System

Table1. Architectural elements definition in DySAM

Architectural element	DySAM entity
Detection, Presence, Localization, Audio, VirtualAudio, DBInfo	Component-Interface class
Detection, DBQuery, Presence, NewEmployeePresent, LocateEmployee, AudioSession, Localisation, ExecuteDBQuery,	Service class
Access, Publish, RPC, Stream	Connector-Interface class
State : Active	State Class
	Port, Communication, Coordination classes
	Attachment class

4.2 System Architecture Dynamics

We use our meta-model to capture more complicated modeling aspects in SA (see table 2). A typical case is explained through a precise description (figure 5) of the architectural elements interactions and dynamic evolution related to the following scenario: When a sensor detects a new employee entering the office, its **Detection** interface will send an event via the **publish** interface to the **Presence** interface. This later will look up the identifier of the device owner in the database and stores the current office as the owner's location. If the employee (not in his office) is called, the component interface **Audio** will notify the **Evolution manager** by sending a trigger event "**Call Employee**" indicating the name of the called employee. Then, the Evolution manger selects the strategy **AddVirtualPhone** of the interface Virtual Audio invoked by the event. Within this strategy, it selects the evolution rule R1 having its conditions satisfied, and triggers the execution of its actions. R1 actions will create a new Virtual Audio interface and attaches it to a new Virtual phone component.

R1 changes **Stream** interface to passive making the rule **R2** conditions satisfied. **R2** actions will so be executed adding two new attachments between component interface **VirtualAudio** and connector interface **Stream**. **R2** will activate the **Stream** interface and set the **RPC** interface into passive state. By the same way, the rule **R3** connects the audio interface with **RPC** interface. The interface state changing should block all incoming transactions to maintain the architecture in a coherent state without intercepting the system too long.

When no further transaction is executed, the corresponding interface may be handled by the ongoing evolution strategy. Once no further evolution strategy rule has to be applied, interfaces set to passive state or added, are (re) activated in order to (re) accept incoming interactions. Thus, the new **VirtualAudio** will request the **LocateEmployee** service provided by the **Localization** interface, which will return a message containing the employee localization (current office). The **VirtualAudio** will then open an audio session between the phone in the employee current office and that providing the call.

The DySAM model gives a precise specification of SA dynamic aspects. Indeed, thanks to its well exploitation to model the call forwarding system, we have defined interaction between architectural elements as data exchange among interfaces, along with their evolution strategies as rules to manage the dynamic architecture reconfiguration.

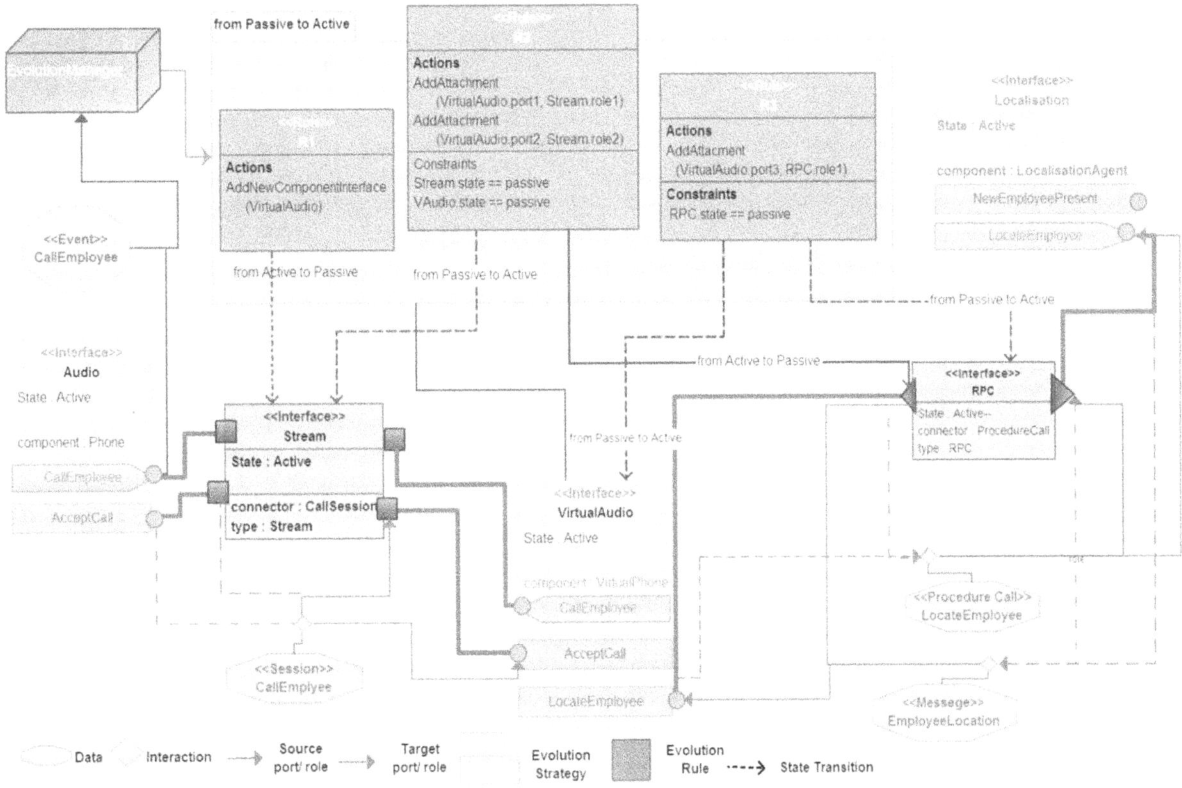

Figure5. Modeling interactions and dynamic evolution of the call forwarding System

Table 2. Dynamic aspects definition in DySAM

Architectural element	DySAM entity
Evolution Maneger	EvolutionManager class
AddVirtualPhone	Addition Strategy class
CallEmployee	notify evolution manager association
R1	Rule class
Actions: AddNewComponentInterface(VirtualPhone)	Action class
R2	Rule class
Actions: AddAttachment (VirtualAudio.port1, Stream.role1) AddAttachment (VirtualAudio.port2, Stream.role2)	Action class
Conditions : Stream.state == passive VirtualPhone.state == passive	Condition class
R3	Rule class
Actions: AddAttachment(VirtualAudio.port3, RPC.role1)	Action class
Conditions : RPC.state == passive	Condition class
callEmployee, EmployeeLocation, LocateEmployee	Session, Message, ProcedureCall class
From Passive to Active/ From Active to Passive Arrows	Transition class
- - - -➔ ——➔	Source/Target association
◇	Interaction class

5. CONCLUSION

As SA dynamic evolution becomes more and more important feature in the field of software engineering, we have proposed a meta-model called DySAM in order to cope with all principal features of dynamic software architecture. It is based on interface concept since it is the key element to identify behavior and evolution of the SA. In fact, DySAM model, designed according to the MDA approach, shows how to define the interactions between architectural elements in terms of data transactions as well as their evolution strategies in terms of evolution rules. Through its instantiation, we have shown that it is effectively easier and more flexible to build architecture description models of complex and dynamic systems.

In a model driven development, an application is developed as a chain of models. Therefore, we propose for our ongoing work a typical approach for dynamic application life cycle starting with DySAM, a platform independent model to be transformed in a transparent manner to a meta model in Maude [2] using MDA artifacts (meta transformation). This will provide facilities for automatic generation of executable and analyzable realistic dynamic system models. To achieve the goal of this perspective, we plan to: (1) Enrich our proposed meta-model with some OCL [11] constraints to get a more precise SA description. Such enrichment allows preserving certain non-functional properties during the application evolution or defining adaptation contracts (based on reflective property) for any dynamic architecture reconfiguration occurrence. (2) Integrate the meta-model into modeling tools based on Eclipse Modeling Framework [3].

6. REFERENCES

[1] Bessam, A., Kimour, M. T. 2009. Multi-view Metamodeling of Software Architecture Behavior. Journal of Software, 4(5), 478-486.

[2] Clavel, M., Duràn, F., Eker, S., Lincoln, P., Marti-Oliet, N., Meseguer, J., and Talcott, C. L. 2007. "All about Maude", A High-Performance Logical Framework, volume 4350 of lecture Notes in Computer Science. Springer.

[3] Eclipse. Eclipse modeling framework (emf). http://www.eclipse.org/modeling/emf/

[4] Ecore Tools. http:/projects.eclipse.org/projects/modeling.emft.ecoretools

[5] Fractal Technical Documentation. 2009. Object Web Consortium. http://fractal.ow2.org/f4e/technical-documentation.html.

[6] Hnetynka, P., Plasil, F., Bures, T., Mencl, V., Kapova, L. 2005. SOFA 2.0 meta-model. Technical report, *11*.

[7] Hongzhen, X., Guosun, Z. 2010. Specification and verification of dynamic evolution of software architectures. Journal of Systems Architecture 56, 523–533.

[8] MDA - The Architecture Of Choice For A Changing World. http://www.omg.org/mda/.

[9] Medvidovic, N., Taylor, R.N. 2000. A Classification and Comparison Framework for Software Architecture Description Languages. IEEE Transactions on Software Engineering (26): 70-93.

[10] Mens, T., Wermelinger, M., Ducasse, S., Demeyer, S., Hirschfeld, R., Jazayeri, M. 5-6 September 2005. Challenges in Software Evolution. 8th International Workshop on Principles of Software Evolution, Lisbon, Portugal.

[11] Object Management Group (OMG). (2006, Mai). Object constraint language. Internet. (http ://www.uml.org/)

[12] OMG Meta Object Facility (MOF) Core Specification version 2.4.1., 2003. http://www.omg.org/spec/MOF/2.4.1/

[13] OMG Unified Modeling LanguageTM (OMG UML), Superstructure, 2011. http://www.omg.org/spec/UML/2.4.1

[14] Oussalah, M., Sadou, N., Tamzalit, D. 2006. SAEV: A model to face evolution problem in software architecture. Proceedings of the International ERCIM Workshop on Software Evolution.

[15] SAE AADL META MODEL AND XML/XMI, 2011. http://www.aadl.info/aadl/currentsite/tool/metamod.html

[16] Smeda, A., Alti, A., Boukerram, A. 2009. An environment for describing software systems. WSEAS Transactions on Computers 8, no. 9: 1610-1619.

[17] Smeda, A., Khammaci, T., Oussalah. M., 2005. Meta architecting: Toward a new generation of architecture description languages. Journal of Computer Science 1.4: 454.

[18] Tibermacine C. March 2005. Un méta-modèle pour la description de contraintes architecturales sur l'évolution des composants. In Proceedings of SE'05 workshop (Software Evolution), held in conjunction with LMO'05, Bern, Switzerland.

[19] Verjus H., Cîmpan S., Alloui I. (2012). An Architecture-Centric Approach for Information System Architecture Modeling, Enactement and Evolution, Innovative Information Systems Modelling Techniques, ISBN: 978-953-51-0644-9, InTech, DOI: 10.5772/36808.

Runtime Modularity in Complex Structures: A Component Model for Fine Grained Runtime Adaptation

Barry Porter
School of Computing and Communications
Lancaster University
Lancaster, UK
b.f.porter@lancaster.ac.uk

ABSTRACT

Online modular adaptation and self-adaptation techniques have demonstrated significant benefits in coarse-grained software, enabling agile and high-performance deployments. We are studying the same kinds of runtime adaptation applied to fine-grained software such as graphical user interfaces and web server implementations. However, this kind of software is defined by pervasive use of *behaviourally-driven structure*. Existing runtime component models fail to capture this necessity due to their exclusive reliance on externally-driven structural composition. In this paper we present a novel runtime component model that both satisfies the need to externally manage software structure, enabling runtime adaptation and self-adaptation, while also satisfying the need for fine-grained software to create elements of its own structure based on application-specific system behaviour. We present the key details of our model along with an initial evaluation.

Categories and Subject Descriptors

D.2.3 [**Software Engineering**] Coding Tools and Techniques – *Component models*

1. INTRODUCTION

Online modular adaptation and self-adaptation methods, in which software can evolve its composition at runtime, have demonstrated significant benefits in coarse-grained software [4, 13, 8, 16, 12]. In detail, these approaches propose that software continually observes its external environment, while also measuring its own behaviour and performance, to constantly adapt itself towards optimal compositions.

We are studying the use of online component-based adaptation and self-adaptation in *fine-grained* software systems. By fine-grained we refer to software such as graphical user interfaces, web server implementations, and database implementations. We are interested in decomposing this kind of software into its smallest re-usable units and making those units into strongly separated components, the composition of which we can then reason about and adapt at runtime. By doing this we are able to investigate similar levels of performance enhancement, agility, and complexity management to that seen in the application of runtime adaptation to coarser-grained modular software as mentioned above.

The current crop of runtime component models, however, fails to apply to fine-grained software. In particular, all runtime component models that we are aware of strictly enforce and manipulate software structure *externally to* the components that make up a system's behaviour [6]. The composition of system structure is therefore the exclusive domain of a 'meta-level' or 'composition level' which lies outside the application-specific behaviour of the software system. This approach works well at coarse software granularity and indeed is an important enabler of modular runtime adaptation.

Unfortunately, at fine software granularity, it is very difficult to design systems whose structures are entirely defined by such an external entity. This is because (i) 'instances' must often be created *as a direct result of* system behaviour; and (ii) these instances must interact with each other using (correspondingly) *behaviourally-driven structure*. Examples of behaviour-based instance cardinality include populating a window with graphical widgets such as file or directory entries in a file browser; and instance-per-client architectures in network server implementations. Example inter-instance structures include observer patterns in event-based logic or polymorphic iterators in centralised control dispatch logic.

In this paper we present a novel runtime component model that both satisfies the need to externally manage software structure, supporting runtime software adaptation and self-adaptation, while also satisfying the need for fine-grained software to create elements of its *own* structure based on its application-specific system behaviour. Our model links these two distinct structural levels (externally-imposed and internally-driven) together into a fully generalised runtime adaptable paradigm for fine-grained software.

In detail, we propose a runtime component model with:

1. A traditional **macro-level** of strongly-separated software components. Each component exports provided and required interfaces that are wired / re-wired by an external meta-level to drive runtime adaptation.
2. A novel **micro-level** in which components freely create *micro-component* instances from each required interface based on their application-specific behaviour.
3. A concept of **gateways** to support *referential persistence* for micro-components, linking freeform micro-structure to meta-level adaptation of macro-structure.

In the remainder of this paper we first present our component model in Sec. 2. We then present an initial evaluation of the key aspects of our model in Sec. 3, followed by a survey of the literature in Sec. 4. We offer conclusions in Sec. 5.

CBSE'14, June 30–July 4, 2014, Marcq-en-Baroeul, France.

ACM 978-1-4503-2577-6/14/06 ...$15.00.
http://dx.doi.org/10.1145/2602458.2602471.

2. THE DANA COMPONENT MODEL

Our component model is realised within a full-featured, purpose-built programming language called *Dana* [1]. In the majority of this paper we focus on the runtime component model on which Dana is founded, enabling runtime adaptation in fine-grained software structures. At a language level all functionality in Dana is expressed within strongly-separated components that are independently deployable. It is an imperative, procedural, interpreted language, is multi-threaded, and features only interface, record and primitive types. It is syntactically similar to contemporary languages like Java and its source code library includes over 100 components from networking and data manipulation to graphics and system-level APIs. In the remainder of this section we first describe the Dana component model in detail, then we provide an example of its use in fine-grained structures, and finally we describe its runtime adaptation mechanics.

2.1 Component model details

A software component in our model is defined as a unit of functionality that expresses one or more 'provided' interfaces and zero or more 'required' interfaces. An interface is a list of function prototypes and each interface type may inherit from one other interface type. Interfaces that do not explicitly inherit from another type automatically inherit from a common base type which includes the functions `equal()`, `clone()` and `toString()`. Each component may only use external functionality via its required interfaces.

A system is constructed from a composition of components, created by loading each desired component into memory and interconnecting each required interface of each component to a type-compatible provided interface on another component. This composition is performed by a third-party 'meta-program' outside the behaviour of the components that make up the system itself. Aside from interface inheritance, this core design is similar to classic runtime component models (e.g. [3, 5]) and enables a meta-program to compose systems from the desired units of functionality and later adapt those systems online to meet changing needs.

Beyond these fundamentals however our component model diverges significantly from its contemporaries as follows.

Firstly, we introduce the concept of a 'micro-component'. In detail, each provided interface that a component advertises actually represents an *instantiable micro-component* (or 'microcom'). Each such microcom has one primary interface, which maps to a component's advertised provided interface as described above, and zero or more secondary interfaces. Each microcom may also have its own per-instance state. These structural elements are illustrated in Fig. 1. Secondary interfaces, and any per-instance state, used by a microcom are a part of its implementation detail. Two components can thus provide the same interface type which internally maps to two different microcom implementations with different secondary interfaces and different instance state. The syntax with which components declare provided interfaces is exemplified in Fig. 3(a); this component provides an instantiable microcom with a primary interface of type `FileBrowser` (i.e. a provided interface of the component) and a secondary interface of type `ClickListener`.

Symmetrically, each required interface that a component declares in fact therefore represents an instantiable microcom sourced from the component to which that required interface is currently connected.

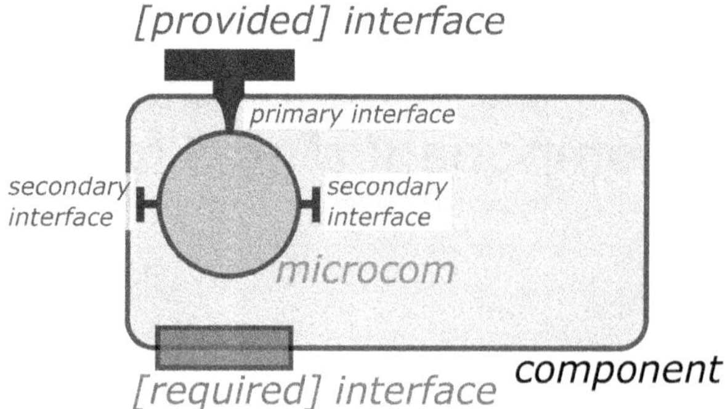

Figure 1: The main structural elements of our component model. Secondary interfaces of microcoms, and any per-instance state fields, are internal implementation details that are not outwardly visible.

Microcoms can be instantiated in a completely freeform manner (such as instantiating many graphical, clickable file representations) according to the particular behaviour of a given component. Furthermore, references to microcoms (specifically to one of their interfaces) can be handed around to other microcoms in a similarly freeform fashion by passing them as parameters to functions. Complete micro-structures (such as a observer patterns or polymorphic collections) of microcom instances and inter-instance references can thus be formed as a result of system behaviour.

The second novel feature of our model is then the way in which macro-structure (components and inter-component wiring) is linked to micro-structure (microcoms and inter-microcom reference graphs) in the face of externally-driven runtime adaptations in the former.

This is achieved with the concept of *gateways*. In detail, whenever a component C uses one of its required interfaces to create a new microcom in another component, a gateway is created in C which serves as an indirection to that microcom. A gateway adopts the interface type of the corresponding required interface (which is respectively the provided interface type to which it is connected, and is by extension the primary interface of the microcom) and so serves as a gateway to a microcom whose primary interface is of that type. Whenever a component C hands out a reference to a microcom that it created, it actually hands out a reference to its gateway for that microcom. When a required interface of C is being re-wired to a different provider component, all of C's gateways from that required interface stay in place, while the microcoms behind it are switched to instances from the new provider component. We return to runtime adaptation mechanics in more detail in Sec. 2.3.

At the macro level our components exhibit all the features of traditional runtime component models [15, 10]. They are independently deployable, using only explicitly-declared dependencies, making them highly re-usable and their compositions highly re-configurable. They also offer the strong discretisation of software that makes component-based compositions particularly conducive to introspection, self-analysis and self-adaptation [10]. At the micro-level, meanwhile, components can freely create microcom instances and can freely pass around references to them, knowing that these instances and inter-instance reference graphs will remain in place despite implementation changes caused by runtime adaptation at the macro level. In the next section we use an example GUI system to demonstrate these concepts.

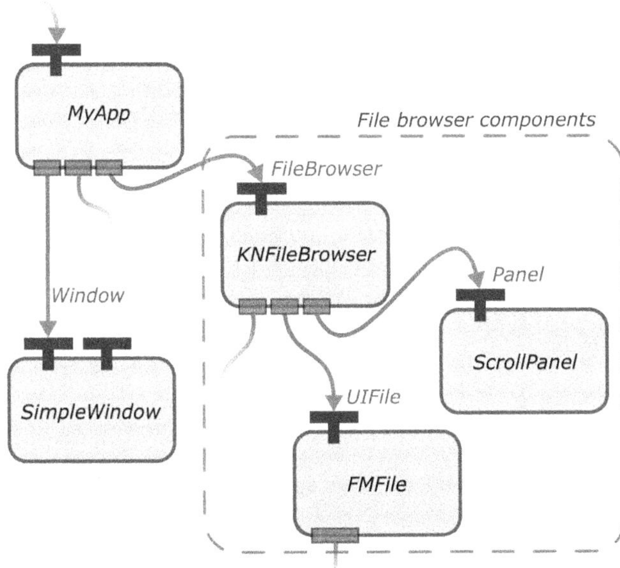

Figure 2: Component architecture of our example system. As shown in Fig. 1, note that an instantiable microcom implementation lies behind each provided interface (not shown here to simplify the diagram).

2.2 Example system

To better illustrate our component model we now present a simple example using part of a file browser dialog. This is taken from one of our graphical user interface systems and demonstrates both behaviourally-driven microcom instance populations and inter-instance reference graphs (via an observer pattern and a polymorphic collection).

The functionality of the file browser is simply to be given a directory D and to display each directory and file that D contains. The user can click on a displayed directory D' to move into it, thereby showing the contents of D' instead.

At the macro level the file browser is composed of a file browser component, a panel component which arranges the file display artefacts, and a graphical file representation component which provides the visual appearance of files and directories. The composition can be reconfigured online to change the way in which files are displayed (as a simple scrolling list or as a variety of alternatives) depending on user preferences, accessibility considerations, and the number and types of files in a particular directory.

The macro architecture is illustrated in Fig. 2 and source code extracts of the components are shown in Fig. 3.

Within the outer macro level is a complex, behaviourally-driven population of microcom instances and inter-instance references forming a dynamic micro-structure. Aided by the use of gateways as detailed earlier, this micro-structure stays in place despite runtime adaptations affecting the macro-structure when required interfaces are re-wired to alternative components. These forms of micro-structure pervade the kinds of fine-grained software that we target and demonstrate the novel abilities of our component model.

For example, in Fig. 3(a) we see a function `setDir()` which needs to instantiate many 'UIFile' microcoms (line 8), each representing one directory or file in the current directory. Similar patterns are found in other kinds of systems software such as instance-per-client patterns and worker pools.

```
1  component provides FileBrowser(ClickListener)
           requires UIFile, Panel, FileSystem fs{
2     Panel myPanel;
3
4     void FileBrowser:setDir(char path[]){
5        myPanel.clear();
6        FileEntry files[] = fs.getFiles(path);
7        for (int i; i < files.arrayLength; i++){
8           UIFile nf = new UIFile(files[i].path);
9           nf.addListener(this);
10          myPanel.addObject(nf);
11          }
12       }
13
14    void ClickListener:click(Object o){
15       UIFile f = o;
16       if (f.isDirectory())
17          setDir(f.getPath());
18       }
19    }
```
KNFileBrowser

(a)

```
1  component provides Panel{
2     GraphicsObject objects[];
3
4     void Panel:addObject(GraphicsObject go){
5        objects += go;
6        /* ... position the object ... */
7        }
8
9     void Panel:paint(Canvas c){
10       c.drawRect(...);
11       /* ... now draw my objects ... */
12       }
13    }
```
ScrollPanel

(b)

Figure 3: Source code extracts from our example system. We do not have space to show the interfaces used here; note however that the `UIFile` interface for example inherits from `ClickableObject` which in turn inherits from `GraphicsObject`. All source code from this example system is available online [2].

The same function drives two other kinds of common micro-structure in the form of an observer pattern and a polymorphic collection. The observer pattern is used on line 9 of Fig. 3(a). Here the `FileBrowser` microcom registers itself, using its internal secondary interface of type `ClickListener`, as a callback target with each `UIFile` microcom. Similar fine-grained software patterns include system up-calls and dynamic event-condition-action logic.

The polymorphic collection is used on line 10 of Fig. 3(a). Here the 'panel' microcom is provided with a reference to each file microcom created by the file browser. As shown in Fig. 3(b) (line 4) the panel component accepts as a parameter to this function any microcom with an interface that is a subtype of `GraphicsObject`. Key to our model is that even if the implementation of the UIFile microcoms is changed at runtime, gateways ensure that all references to those microcoms held by the panel *will still be valid* (and will have been automatically routed to equivalent microcoms of the new implementation). Similar polymorphic collection patterns are found in other kinds of systems software like queueing modules and centrally-orchestrated task execution managers.

2.3 Runtime adaptation mechanics

Runtime adaptation allows us to adjust software to its current deployment environment by selecting between different components that are judged to be best suited to current conditions. *Self*-adaptation occurs when a software system analyses its own behaviour and performance and uses runtime adaptation to optimise that performance without human intervention. This approach fosters agile and high-performance systems in changing environments such as variable client workloads or fluctuations in system resources.

In this section we present Dana's runtime adaptation mechanics. Runtime adaptation in general has two important elements: the mechanism(s) by which adaptation is achieved; and the way in which continuity of overall system integrity (or state) is maintained when adaptation occurs.

2.3.1 Adaptation mechanics

The single mechanism by which Dana supports runtime adaptation is by allowing a meta program to re-wire a selected required interface of a component C from its current resolution against component D to instead be resolved against a different component E. This is illustrated below. Wider architectural change occurs when component E itself has a different set of required interfaces than D. Component E could for example be a completely different implementation of D, implying different behaviour and performance characteristics; or could be an interceptor component that is actually itself connected to D through one if its own required interfaces and which simply performs some pre-processing before calls arrive at D; or could even be acting as a proxy to a remote version of D running on a different host.

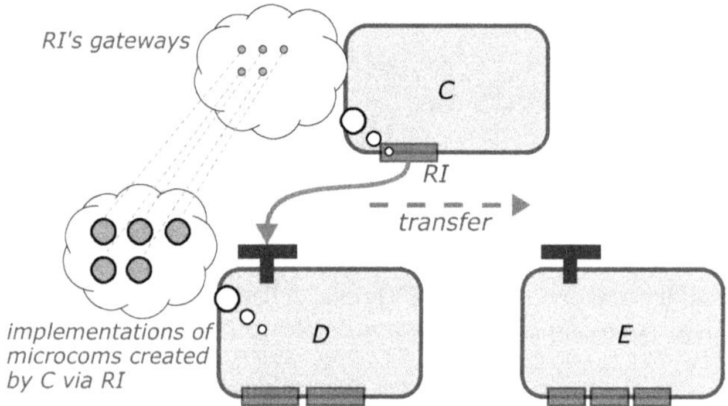

Unlike contemporary runtime component models, Dana uses each required interface as a source of microcom instances, created and destroyed as needed by the component declaring that required interface. Many microcom instances sourced from that interface may thus be active at any time.

The runtime adaptation procedure therefore works in the following stages. First, we isolate (or 'pause') the required interface, stopping further interaction through it and so preventing further externally-driven state transitions in the associated microcoms. This works simply by waiting for any existing function calls passing through a required interface to complete, and holding any new function calls at the required interface boundary. Once paused we then iterate over *each* microcom that is active over that required interface, sourced from component D, and transfer each such microcom to instead be sourced from component E (including state transfer). Once this is complete the selected required interface is finally 'resumed', re-enabling interaction through it (and allowing any calls held at the required interface to proceed).

```
void UIFile:clone(Object o) {
    UIFile prev = o;  UIFile(prev.getFile());
    Point p = prev.getPosition();
    setPosition(p.x, p.y);
    listeners = prev.getClickListeners();
    }
```

2.3.2 System integrity across adaptation

The way that we maintain continuity of overall system integrity (or state) across adaptations is then as follows. As part of the process of iterating over each microcom active over a required interface, we perform *state transfer* to microcom instances from the new implementing component. In detail, for each microcom instance i active over RI of component C we use Dana's 'transfer' procedure to migrate $microcom_i$ to its new implementation in component E. This transfer procedure first creates a new microcom instance using the corresponding provided interface of component E and then invokes the `clone()` function (from the common interface base type mentioned in Sec. 2.1) on that new microcom, passing in a reference to the existing microcom instance sourced from component D. From within its `clone()` function, the new microcom instance sourced from component E is then able to use the functions from the microcom's *primary interface* (which both the existing and new microcom must necessarily have in common) to manually extract any necessary state from the existing instance (i.e. using 'getter' functions) and apply that state to itself.

It is important to note that the actual implementation of `clone()` functions is left entirely to the programmer to write as appropriate, including designing necessary 'getter' functions in interfaces. An example is shown above. We are not therefore concerned with any semantic or structural issues of inter-component state compatibility that occur with many automated or transparent state transfer mechanisms.

Finally, as detailed in Sec. 2.1, our component model uses *gateways* to provide sufficient indirection to ensure that any *references* to microcoms that are migrated to a new implementation remain valid despite the fact that their implementation (and internal state representation) has changed. After each state transfer operation, the Dana runtime thus completes the overall transfer procedure by updating the gateway for that particular microcom instance so that it points at the new instance in the new component (component E). It is this mechanism that links freeform micro-structure to externally-controlled and adapted macro-structure.

In detail, recall that whenever a microcom is instantiated, a gateway for that microcom is made in its creator. Any references to a microcom that are then handed out by its creator are actually references to that gateway, which lies in the creator's internal state rather than in the implementing component of the microcom. As described above, these gateways stay in place despite changes to the component that is implementing the microcoms behind those gateways.

Not *all* forms of microcom reference enjoy persistence across adaptation, however. In detail we say that microcom references that are handed out *by the creator* of a microcom will persist across evolutions of that microcom's implementation, since the creator is not the subject of the evolution (i.e. it is staying in the system) and as such any effects of its implementation logic should persist. This applies for example to the references to `UIFile` instances (via `nf`) that are handed out to the `Panel` instance on line 10 of Fig. 3(a).

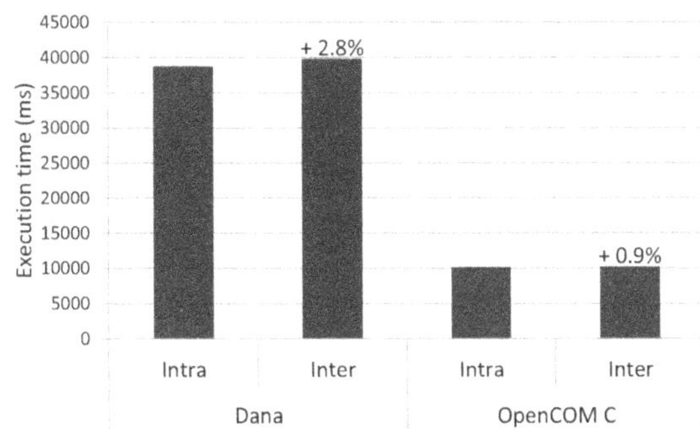

Figure 4: Differences in execution speed for 1 million calls when using internal component (local/intra) calls versus inter-component calls.

In contrast, microcom references that are handed out *by a microcom instance itself* (i.e. self-references derived using the 'this' notation) do not persist across runtime evolutions of that microcom's implementation. Instead such references are removed from the system after transfer is complete. This is done to avoid the need to make any assumptions between two different components implementing the same interface. Specifically, the incoming implementation can safely assume that it is starting from a 'clean slate' when state is transferred into microcom instances that it implements. It can then choose when and to whom any self-references should be handed out according only to the logic of its own implementation, safe in the knowledge that no other self-passed references to its microcoms are left over from the logic performed by other implementations. In this way components can be designed as black boxes and will operate in a consistent way with respect to runtime adaptation procedures.

3. INITIAL EVALUATION

In this section we provide an initial evaluation of the main elements of our component model's baseline performance characteristics. Our aim is to demonstrate a capable level of performance primarily in terms of execution speed (we consider program size less important for modern computers).

The main factor involved is the extra level of indirection that gateways create for any references used by, and given out by, the creators of microcoms. In addition to this there is a minor added overhead in making inter-component calls due to the need for our runtime to check whether or not a required interface is currently paused. All experiments were conducted on a 1.8Ghz Intel Atom Z2760 with Windows 8.1.

Fig. 4 shows the differences in call speed between local function calls (within a component) and inter-component calls. This experiment was performed both with Dana and, as a point of comparison, for the C implementation of OpenCOM [5], a traditional runtime component model that does not support fine-grained sub-structure. The results demonstrate the expected performance delta between local and inter-component calls. As noted above, we expect that the difference is greater in Dana due to the extra gateway indirection along with checks on required interface paused status. OpenCOM, by comparison, does not use gateway-like mechanics because it lacks support for fine-grained behaviourally driven structures, and has no in-built 'pause' feature to aid with seamless runtime adaptation.

Examining the ratio of local to inter-component microcom calls, our simple GUI file browser example performs 2164 local calls during startup and 25999 inter-component microcom calls; 92.3% of all calls in this example are therefore microcom calls. Such a ratio is expected due to the finer granularity of component in our model, though in more complex systems we might tend to find lower ratios when individual functions carry out more work. Inter-component calls in this kind of model may therefore be a particular target for some form of just-in-time compilation.

On a qualitative level, our graphical user interface systems demonstrate sufficiently high levels of execution speed to provide an interactive user experience. The above overheads do not therefore appear to noticeably harm overall system performance impressions on modern commodity hardware.

In future we expect the performance figures reported here to improve further in successive iterations of our implementation. In future work we also intend to perform a more extensive evaluation in multiple different kinds of example system to provide a more complete picture.

4. RELATED WORK

In this section we examine related work in three categories. First, in Sec. 4.1, we discuss existing runtime component models. In Sec. 4.2 we then examine runtime update approaches in the Java platform in particular. Finally in Sec. 4.3 we discuss the rationale for using a new language.

4.1 Runtime component models

All existing runtime component models that we are aware of lack support for the behaviourally-driven sub-structural relationships that we have described throughout this paper and which pervade fine-grained software. Examples of such component models include [5, 11, 3]; see [6] for a recent survey of work in this field. Specifically, these models focus on wiring components together as instances and have no feature for those components to then go on to create sub-structural constructs as a factor of their behaviour (and pass sub-structural references around to create entire micro-structural graphs driven by that behaviour).

Because these behavioural factors are far too application-specific for a runtime meta-model to describe, these models are therefore limited either to relatively simple software structures or else tend towards coarse-grained components.

Our aim to apply runtime component-based adaptation to finer-grained, structurally complex systems functionality therefore required a rethink of the component paradigm. This has resulted in the model described in this paper in which traditional macro-level components can create micro-components on demand as a factor of their behaviour.

4.2 Runtime update approaches in Java

The popularity of the Java language platform has created significant interest in approaches to increase the reconfigurability of Java programs. There are two main bodies of work in this area: component models like OSGi and EJB, and runtime update approaches like Javeleon and JRebel.

The component models were designed with very different requirements to ours and so work in correspondingly different ways. EJB is a server-side technology for client/server interactions with the intention of separating 'container' concerns (like security and access/interaction technology) from functional behaviour. Components in EJB sit in tightly defined categories such as 'stateful' and 'message-driven' and have corresponding constraints on their interactions. It is not therefore a general-purpose system building technology. OSGi, meanwhile, is primarily designed to support plug-in architectures. It works at a coarse granularity by arranging Java classes into jar 'bundles' and using the concept of a 'bundle scope' – a private classloader scope which hides internal classes of the bundle aside from selected exceptions that form the exported services of a component. While the amount of inter-bundle micro-structure is unbounded (as all of the usual Java features are available) there is no link from this micro-structure to a meta-level controlled macro-structure. This effectively prevents post-initialisation online architecture adaptation over a system's execution.

The runtime update approaches (like JRebel [9], Javeleon [7] and JavAdaptor [14]) are designed to transparently support dynamic differential patching of Java programs while they execute. As input they take the current system architecture (often examining its source code) along with the updated system architecture's source code and calculate a way to transform the former to the latter without taking the program offline. These approaches work for some difference patterns but will fail if the scale of difference is too great, for example with major changes to the internal member fields of a particular class. In addition to these limitations, the main drawback of these approaches in terms of our requirements is that they are designed only for administratively-instructed updates. This makes them unsuitable for self-adaptation approaches which require strong discretisation of software into 'components' and 'connections' as first-class concepts [10].

4.3 Language comparison

Developing a new language as part of a component model is a larger undertaking than developing a language-targeted runtime component model of the kind mentioned in Sec. 4.1. We took this route to provide a clean and simple programming model and also to avoid some of the pitfalls of using popular languages like C and Java. For C, these limitations include a lack of desirable constructs like 'instances' and 'interfaces' as well as the difficulty of intercepting multi-threaded inter-component interactions when runtime adaptation takes place. Other drawbacks include robustness (one faulty component can bring down the entire system) and multi-platform portability / interaction. In Java, while many drawbacks of C are improved, the introduction of typed classes makes fully generalised runtime loading and unloading of classes very difficult (see [7, 14]), and the unconstrained mixing of data and behaviour in 'objects' significantly hinders well-structured runtime adaptation.

5. CONCLUSION AND OUTLOOK

In this paper a novel runtime component model is proposed that supports the expression of behaviourally-driven micro-structural relationships. This is achieved by introducing the concept of a 'micro-component' for freeform instantiation and inter-instance referencing. At the same time our model supports unconstrained adaptation of the macro-level component graph and uses a new concept of 'gateways' to link the micro- and macro-levels together across adaptation.

Our model is highly adept at implementing finer-grained software in which this kind of micro-structure is pervasive. This in turn supports our study of runtime adaptation and self-adaptation in such systems to examine the performance improvements and higher-level reasoning that can be gained.

In future work we intend to provide a more extensive evaluation, both quantitative and qualitative, of our component model, as well as continue to explore the benefits of runtime adaptation in fine-grained software such as web server implementations, databases and graphical user interfaces.

6. REFERENCES

[1] Dana language: http://www.projectdana.com/.

[2] Demos and code from this paper with instructions: http://research.projectdana.com/cbse2014porter.

[3] E. Bruneton, T. Coupaye, M. Leclercq, V. Quema, and J.-B. Stefani. An open component model and its support in java. In *Component-Based Software Engineering*, volume 3054 of *LNCS*, pages 7–22. Springer Berlin Heidelberg, 2004.

[4] S. Chaitanya, D. Vijayakumar, B. Urgaonkar, and A. Sivasubramaniam. Middleware for a re-configurable distributed archival store based on secret sharing. In *Proceedings of the ACM 11th International Conference on Middleware*, Middleware '10, pages 107–127, Berlin, Heidelberg, 2010. Springer-Verlag.

[5] G. Coulson, G. Blair, P. Grace, F. Taiani, A. Joolia, K. Lee, J. Ueyama, and T. Sivaharan. A generic component model for building systems software. *ACM Trans. on Comp. Systems*, 26(1):1:1–1:42, Mar. 2008.

[6] I. Crnković, S. Sentilles, A. Vulgarakis, and M. R. V. Chaudron. A classification framework for software component models. *Software Engineering, IEEE Transactions on*, 37(5):593–615, 2011.

[7] A. R. Gregersen and B. N. Jørgensen. Dynamic update of java applications: Balancing change flexibility vs programming transparency. *Journal of Software Maintenance and Evolution*, 21(2):81–112, Mar. 2009.

[8] D. Hughes, P. Greenwood, G. Blair, G. Coulson, P. Grace, F. Pappenberger, P. Smith, and K. Beven. An experiment with reflective middleware to support grid-based flood monitoring. *Concurrency and Compututation: Practice and Experience*, 20(11):1303–1316, Aug. 2008.

[9] J. Kabanov. JRebel tool demo. *Electron. Notes Theor. Comput. Sci.*, 264(4):51–57, Feb. 2011.

[10] F. Kon, F. Costa, G. Blair, and R. H. Campbell. The case for reflective middleware. *Communications of the ACM*, 45(6):33–38, June 2002.

[11] J. Magee, J. Kramer, and M. Sloman. Constructing distributed systems in conic. *Software Engineering, IEEE Transactions on*, 15(6):663–675, 1989.

[12] D. A. Menasce, J. a. P. Sousa, S. Malek, and H. Gomaa. Qos architectural patterns for self-architecting software systems. In *Proc. of the 7th Int. Conf. on Autonomic computing*, ICAC '10, pages 195–204, New York, NY, USA, 2010. ACM.

[13] J. Philippe, N. De Palma, F. Boyer, and O. Gruber. Self-adapting service level in java enterprise edition. In *Proceedings of the 10th ACM International Conference on Middleware*, Middleware '09, pages 8:1–8:20, New York, NY, USA, 2009. Springer-Verlag New York, Inc.

[14] M. Pukall, C. Kästner, W. Cazzola, S. Götz, A. Grebhahn, R. Schröter, and G. Saake. Javadaptor : flexible runtime updates of java applications. *Software, practice and experience*, 43(2):153 – 185, 02 2013.

[15] C. Szyperski, D. Gruntz, and S. Murer. *Component Software: Beyond Object-Oriented Programming*. Acm Press Series. ACM Press, 2002.

[16] W. Wang and G. Huang. Pattern-driven performance optimization at runtime: experiment on JEE systems. In *Proc. of the 9th Workshop on Adaptive and Reflective Middleware*, pages 39–45. ACM, 2010.

Injecting Quality Attributes into Software Architectures with the Common Variability Language

Jose-Miguel Horcas
Universidad de Málaga,
Andalucía Tech, Spain
horcas@lcc.uma.es

Mónica Pinto
Universidad de Málaga,
Andalucía Tech, Spain
pinto@lcc.uma.es

Lidia Fuentes
Universidad de Málaga,
Andalucía Tech, Spain
lff@lcc.uma.es

ABSTRACT

Quality attributes that add new behavior to the functional software architecture are known as functional quality attributes (FQAs). These FQAs are applied to pieces of software from small components to entire systems, usually crosscutting some of them. Due to this crosscutting nature, modeling them separately from the base application has many advantages (e.g. reusability, less coupled architectures). However, different applications may require different configurations of an FQA (e.g. different levels of security), so we need a language that: (i) easily expresses the variability of the FQAs at the architectural level; and that (ii) also facilitates the automatic generation of architectural configurations with custom-made FQAs. In this sense, the Common Variability Language (CVL) is extremely suited for use at the architectural level, not requiring the use of a particular architectural language to model base functional requirements. In this paper we propose a method based on CVL to: (i) model separately and generate FQAs customized to the application requirements; (ii) automatically inject customized FQA components into the architecture of the applications. We quantitatively evaluate our approach and discuss its benefits with a case study.

Categories and Subject Descriptors

D.2.11 [**Software Architectures**]: Languages; D.2.13 [**Reusable Software**]: Reuse models

Keywords

CVL, quality attributes, SPL, variability, weaving

1. INTRODUCTION

The quality of a software system is measured by the extent to which it possesses a desired combination of quality attributes (QAs) [2] such as usability, reliability, security and scalability. Whether or not a system will be able to exhibit its desired (or required) QAs is substantially determined by its software architecture, through the use of different architectural tactics [3]. For some QAs, the architectural tactic to be followed consists in the injection (i.e. introduction) of specialized elements into the architecture (e.g. an authorization mechanism to satisfy the security QA) [3]. These QAs are normally known as functional quality attributes (FQAs) [12], and are different from other QAs such as cost or efficiency that can be mapped to architectural or implementation decisions, but not directly to functional components. Examples of FQAs are error handling, security, context awareness, usability, persistence, recovery, etc.

Our main idea is to give priority to the FQAs that are required by an application from the early stages of the software development, based on three main contributions: (1) the specialized elements required for satisfying the FQAs are modeled separately from the base software architecture; (2) these elements are then semi-automatically injected into the application architecture; and (3) the approach is implemented using the Common Variability Language (CVL) [10].

The motivation for modeling FQAs separately from the base architecture is that FQAs are normally required by several applications — i.e. they are recurrent, and most of them crosscut the system architecture. So, modeling them separately from the base application has many advantages (e.g. reusability, less coupled architectures, etc.). For instance, an encryption algorithm used to encrypt the information does not depend on the application that needs it. Also, different applications may require different levels of an FQA (e.g. security). For example, a specific application may require access control and anonymity while another may require only encryption, or may require a different kind of encryption algorithm. In other words, there is much variability in FQAs, and the Software Architect (SA) should be able to select the set of specialized architectural elements that need to be injected to fulfill the application requirements regarding a particular FQA, which is not a trivial task.

Regarding the second part of our approach, once we have generated custom models of the FQAs for a given application, these models need to be injected into the base model of the application. Being inspired by Aspect-Oriented Modeling (AOM)[1], in our approach, first we identify and select the points in the base model where the custom FQA models have to be injected, and then automatically generate the application architecture woven with the customized FQAs.

Finally, our third contribution is the technical details of our approach. In order to define a family of FQAs, a language to model the variability of FQAs is needed. Although most of the variability approaches use Feature Models (FMs), their main shortcoming is that an additional process is re-

[1] `http://www.aspect-modeling.org/`

CBSE '14 Lille, France

http://dx.doi.org/10.1145/2602458.2602460.

quired to generate an architectural configuration that meets an FM configuration. CVL is more suitable for use at the architectural level, since it defines links between the variability specification and the product line architecture (PLA). The advantages of using CVL are: (i) it is an MOF-based variability language and this means that any MOF-based architectural language can be used with the variability information of CVL; (ii) the links between the variability and base architectural models make it possible to automatically generate software architecture configurations, ensuring that they fulfill the variability specification, (iii) the semantic of the CVL variation points can be extended, and (iv) CVL includes the most important characteristics of similar variability models (e.g. FM) such as cardinality of variation points, cross-tree constraints, etc. Due to all these advantages there is a great interest in the SPL community in adopting CVL in their proposals [5, 6]. But, since both the CVL language and its tool support are novel, the effort of using CVL is currently considerable.

Summarizing, in this paper we present an SPL approach based on the use of CVL to automatically generate, from a family of reusable FQAs, software architecture configurations that include custom made FQAs. As discussed further on, in Section 3, this approach is an extension of our previous work [11] and defines a more generic, integrated and extensible approach. One important contribution is that the custom made FQAs are automatically woven with the base application by extending the semantic of the CVL variation points. We quantitatively evaluate our approach by using appropriate metrics to assess the benefits of our approach, and illustrate it with an Intelligent Transportation System case study. Also, we discuss the benefits of using CVL in achieving the goals posed in this paper.

Besides this introduction, Section 2 presents the CVL, and describes the case study used throughout the paper. Section 3 overviews our approach and highlights its main novelties in comparison with our previous work [11]. In Section 4 we explain in detail how we model FQAs by using CVL. The customization and injection of the FQAs into the base application of our case study is explained in Sections 5 and 6, respectively. In Section 7 we evaluate our proposal. Section 8 discusses the related work. Finally, Section 9 concludes the paper and presents further work.

2. BACKGROUND INFORMATION

In this section we briefly summarize CVL.[2] Then, the case study followed throughout the paper is described.

2.1 CVL

The CVL is a domain-independent language for specifying and resolving variability over MOF-compliant models.

CVL provides an executable engine to automatically produce a *resolved model* from three main models: (1) the *base model* over which the variability is specified and resolved. (2) The *variability model* that specificies the variability in an abstract level with *variability specifications* (*VSpecs*) and in a concrete level through *variation points*. VSpecs are tree structures representing choices ("features" in most SPL terminologies) and can include logical constraints defined in a subset of the Object Constraint Language (OCL). Variation points define specific modifications to be applied to the base model during *materialization* — i.e. the process of transforming a base model into a configured product model. (3) A *resolution model* that provides resolutions for the VSpecs in order to materialize a base model with a variability model. The main characteristics of CVL that we will use are:

Configurable unit (CU). Set of variation points that hides the internal of a base model, exposing a *VInterface*.

Variability interface (VInterface). Group of VSpecs that have to be resolved to materialize a CU.

Composite VSpec (CVSpec). VSpec that is resolved by resolving other VSpecs that are *variability interfaces*.

Opaque Variation Point (OVP). It allows customizing the semantic of the existing CVL variation points through a model transformation language.

2.2 Case Study

We motivate our proposal presenting a case study based on Intelligent Transportation Systems (ITSs) [1]. In this context, there is a set of services (e.g. road safety, weather conditions,...) that all require communication between vehicles (V2V) and via roadside access points (V2I).

An ITS application requires specific **security** services: *privacy*, to protect the personal information of drivers such as the route followed; *integrity*, to ensure the data authenticity exchanged over the network; and *confidentiality* and *authentication*, to allow the drivers to use certain services of V2I (e.g. payment at electronic toll). **Context awareness** and **usability** FQAs are also required in order to obtain *context information* of the user (e.g. license detector, weariness) or of the car (e.g. GPS, proximity sensors) and to provide *contextual help* according to the users needs, respectively.

3. OUR PROPOSAL

This section presents a general overview of our approach (Figure 1). We distinguish three main stages with two different actors: (1) FQAs modeling, performed by a domain expert in quality attributes; (2) FQAs customization to the requirements of a particular application, and (3) FQAs weaving. Steps (2) and (3) are performed by the SA.

Stage 1: FQAs modeling.

In this stage, an expert in the domain of the QAs models the variability of FQAs following the CVL approach. To do this, he/she first builds the software architecture of the FQAs by using any MOF-compliant language (`FQAs Base Model` in Figure 1), and then defines a variability model of the FQAs in CVL (`FQAs Variability Model`). This supposes a novelty in comparison with our previous work [11] in which the FQAs had to be obligatorily modeled with aspect-oriented software architectures, making use of a propietary ADL and of propietary tools.

Most of the FQAs are composed by many concerns. The security FQA, for example, is composed by access control, authentication, privacy, integrity, and encryption, among other concerns. However, not all of the concerns of an FQA are required by all the systems. For example, an application may require only authentication and access control. Also, the domain expert needs to consider that some of the concerns of an FQA have dependencies between them, such as the confidentiality concern that depends on the encryption concern to ensure that all the information is encrypted and cannot be obtained by third persons. We call these dependency relationships between the concerns of the same FQA,

[2]Complete description in `http://www.omgwiki.org/variability/`

intraFQA-dependencies. Furthermore, FQAs affect each other, so dependency relationships between different FQAs must also be considered. For instance, the contextual help concern of the usability FQA depends on the authentication concern of the security FQA in order to provide customized help based on the previous experience of the user. We call these dependency relationships between concerns of different FQAs, **interFQA-dependencies**.

This supposes a difference between our approach and other proposals that address FQAs' variability (e.g. QADA [13], RiPLE-DE [4]), basically because they model these FQAs as part of the domain analysis of an SPL, and not separately as we propose.

An important thing that is worth highlighting is that this stage is performed only once. This means that the FQAs base model and the FQAs variability model will be completely reused by any application that wants to incorporate these FQAs into its software architecture, just by following stages 2 and 3 of our approach.

Stage 2: FQAs customization.

In the second stage of our approach, the SA creates a configuration of the FQAs (`FQAs Resolution Model`) according to the requirements of a particular application. This means that those variable concerns that are not required by the base application will not be incorporated into the final application. This stage is automated by using the execution engine of CVL (`CVL Execution`) that resolves the variability of the FQAs variation points. This is another novelty of this approach. Previously, in [11], an additional language had to be used to link the FQAs variability model with the FQAs base model. Moreover, the customization of the FQAs depended on the definition and instantiation of aspect-oriented architectural templates, which were defined using our proprietary ADL. The CVL engine takes as inputs the `FQAs Resolution Model`, the `FQAs Variability Model` and the `FQAs Base Model`, and automatically derives (materializes) the resolved model of the FQAs (`FQAs Resolved Model`). This model only contains the software elements of the FQAs that are needed according to the requirements of the application.

Stage 3: FQAs weaving.

Once the FQA resolved model has been generated in the previous stage, the next step consists of "weaving", or composing, it with the software architecture of the base application (`Application Base Model` in Figure 1). The output of this weaving process is an application architecture that also incorporates the FQAs (`Application Resolved Model (application architecture + FQAs)`). This weaving is not a straightforward task since each FQA will have to be woven at different points of the base applications (join points) and, furthermore, each FQA's concerns will be woven according to a different weaving pattern, depending on the semantic of the concern. Moreover, this should be done automatically, without manually modifying the application architecture.

Thus, the challenge here is to define a process that systematically integrates high-level quality solutions into the base architecture of a given application, but without having to understand the inner workings of the quality solutions. In order to do that, we need to adapt the CVL approach (see Section 6). Firstly, our based model is formed by two models, the `FQAs Resolved Model` and the `Application Architectural Model`. Secondly, during the `CVL Execution` the control must be delegated to a Model-2-Model engine (`M2M Engine`) such as QVT, in charge of performing the weaving of these two models. The weaving is performed according to the weaving information provided by the `Application Weaving Model`. This model uses the OVPs of CVL, which are the mechanism provided by CVL to extend the semantic of the CVL variation points. Using the OVPs the weaving rules that indicate where the FQAs must be incorporated into the core software architecture are specified as user-defined M2M transformations (`Weaving Rules (M2M transformations)`). The weaving process introduced here, and detailed in Section 6, is a new contribution of this paper and was not part of the proposal presented in [11].

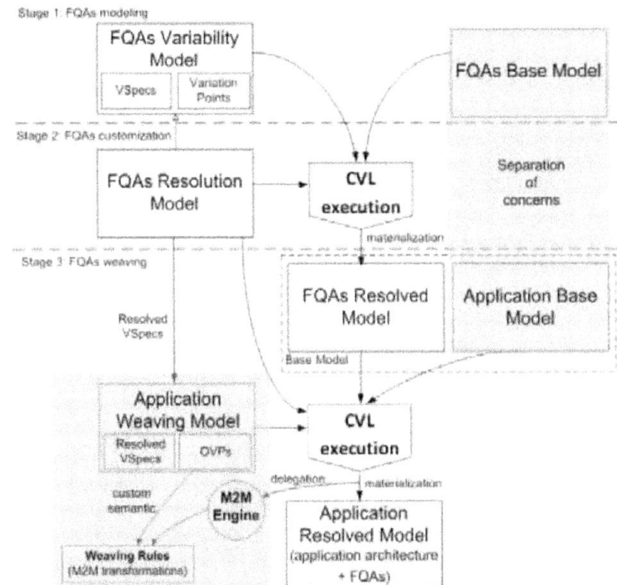

Figure 1: Our approach for modeling FQAs.

The rest of the paper describes each stage in more detail, using the case study described in the previous section.

4. MODELING FQAS WITH CVL

This section describes the first stage of our approach, in which the FQAs (security, context awareness, and usability), their commonalities and variabilities, and the dependencies between them are modeled.

4.1 FQAs base model

In our approach the `FQAs Base Model` specifies the software architecture of the FQAs. For instance, the UML software architecture modeling the functionality of the different concerns of the security FQA is shown at the bottom of Figure 2. This architectural model should include the complete functionality of the security FQA. In order to simplify the model, we only include here the `Integrity`, `Confidentiality`, `Encryption`, `Authentication`, and `Hash` components. These are composite components that include other necessary components to implement the functionality of each concern. For instance, `Encryption` includes components to encrypt and decrypt information using different encryption algorithms.

In order to achieve a better modularization we model each FQA independently of each other and then we model the dependencies and interactions between them. Thus, the bottom of Figure 3 shows the high-level architectural model of all the FQAs together. Although not included due to

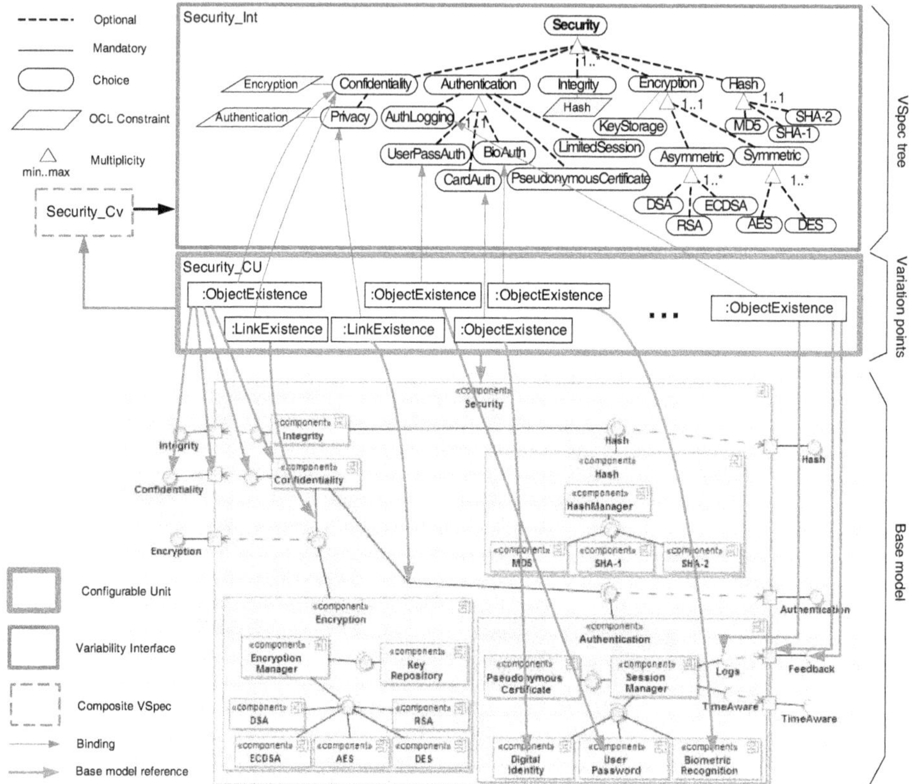

Figure 2: Modeling security FQA in CVL.

the lack of space, the software architectures of the context awareness and the usability FQAs are modeled in a similar way as for the security FQA.

4.2 FQAs variability model

Once the FQAs base model has been specified, the next step is to model the `FQAs Variability Model`. This CVL variability model includes the VSpecs, the variation points, the bindings between the variation points and the VSpecs, and the references from the variation points to the base model.

As an example, the variability model of the security FQA is shown in Figure 2. We distinguish three parts: (1) the VSpec tree of the security FQA (top of Figure 2), (2) the base model of the security FQA (bottom of Figure 2), and (3) the variation points (middle of Figure 2). The variation points are grouped into the security configurable unit (`Security_CU`). Then, the `Security_CU` is bound to a composite VSpec (`Security_Cv`) which refers to the variability interface `Security_Int` — i.e. the VSpec tree.

In the `Security_Int` VSpec we identify all the concerns that are part of the security attribute, model them by choices whose later resolution requires a yes/no decision, indicate which are optional and which are mandatory, and what the intraFQA-dependencies between them are. As stated, in this VSpec tree we only show a subset of the security concerns. These concerns are also composed by other concerns. For instance, there are different kinds of authentication: user + password (`UserPassAuth`), intelligent card (`CardAuth`), and biometric (`BioAuth`).

The kind of variability that we need to express is that "not all of the concerns of an FQA are required by an application and thus, not all of the components of that FQA base model need to be incorporated into the application architecture". In CVL this kind of variability is expressed by using the "existence" variation point that indicates the existence of a particular object, link, or value in the base model. Finally, in CVL, the variation points need to be bound to elements of the VSpec tree and need to refer to elements of the FQA base model. This is how the relationship between the variability model and the base model is specified in CVL. Moreover, these links are used by the CVL execution engine to automate the generation of a product configuration. For instance, the variation point bound to the `Confidentiality` concern in the `Security_Int` VSpec (`:ObjectExistence`) indicates that if confidentiality is decided positively (marked as "True" in the resolution model) in a configuration, the related elements (the `Confidentiality` component and the associated interfaces and ports with their attachments) in the base model will exist in the final application and if confidentiality is decided negatively (marked as "False" in the resolution model) those related elements will be removed from the FQA resolved model.

In order to maintain the consistency and to achieve a good modularization of the design, we specify the variability model at the same abstraction level as we did for the FQA base model. This means that the variability of each FQA is specified independently from the variability of the other FQAs. This can be done in CVL by using composite VSpecs and configurable units. Then, we relate the different variability models defining a "complete" variability model including all the FQAs with their relationships (Figure 3). We apply the conceptual integrity principle[3] to compose the different FQAs configurable units. As Figure 3 shows, the FQAs VSpec includes the three FQAs by including the three

[3]The overall design pattern of a system is reflected in any part of the system.

composite VSpecs previously created (Security_Cv, Usability_Cv, and ContextAwareness_Cv). These VSpecs refer to the interfaces of the configurable unit of each FQA (Security_CU, Usability_CU, and ContextAwareness_CU). Each configurable unit refers to its own composite component in the FQAs base model (bottom of Figure 3). Each of these components have inner variability that we have previously modeled for each FQA.

4.2.1 *Dependency modeling*

Our approach models the dependencies by using the CVL constraints. CVL constraints express relationships between elements of the VSpec that cannot be directly defined by hierarchical relations. We define the intraFQA- and the interFQA-dependencies at a different level of abstraction: intraFQA-dependencies are defined in the context of each FQA configurable unit while interFQA-dependencies are defined in the context of the complete FQAs variability model.

IntraFQA-dependencies. In Figure 2, each intraFQA-dependency is represented by a prepositional constraint (expressed in OCL) in a parallelogram that captures a condition in a choice. For instance, the dependency 'confidentiality requires encryption' is modeled by attaching the constraint Encryption to the choice Confidentiality. Thus, the choice Encryption has to be positively decided whenever Confidentiality is positively decided.

Dependencies are also presented in the security base model. For instance, although confidentiality affects data in general and only requires encryption, privacy also affects people's information and requires the authentication of the user. So, there is a dependency between the *privacy* concern and the *authentication* concern. In Figure 2, the variation point (:LinkExistence) bound to the Privacy choice refers to a required interface of the Confidentiality component in the UML security base model. This link represents the dependency relationship between the *privacy* and the *authentication* concerns. The variation point indicates the existence of that particular link. If Privacy is decided positively in a resolution model the link will exist in the resolved model, and if Privacy is decided negatively, the link will be removed.

InterFQA-dependencies. The FQAs_Int VSpec of Figure 3 includes the CVL constraints that specify the interFQA-dependencies. For instance, the constraint AuthLogging implies HistoryLog represents the dependency between the *authentication logging* concern of the security FQA and the *history log* concern of the usability FQA, and means that if the AuthLogging choice is decided positively, the HistoryLog choice has to be positively decided too. InterFQA-dependencies are also presented in the FQAs base model. It shows how the Security component relates with the Context-Awareness and Usability components due to the existing dependencies between them. For instance, Authentication is required by Usability in order to provide contextual help. Also, Security requires Feedback from Usability and TimeAware from Context-Awareness in order to allow the authentication logs and the control of the session time respectively. Finally, Context-Awareness requires Feedback to provide alerts when the information context demands it.

5. CUSTOMIZATION OF THE FQAS

In the second stage of our approach a valid configuration (customization) of the FQAs variability model is generated, taken as input the requirements of the application under development, which in our case is the ITS case study.

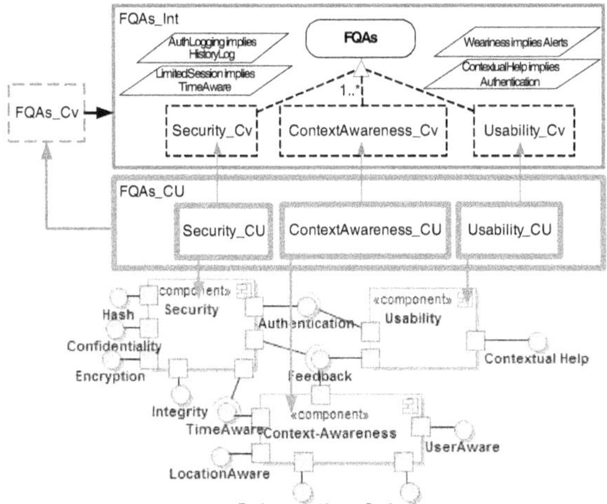

Figure 3: FQAs variability model.

As shown in Figure 1, the customization of the FQAs implies the definition of a FQAs Resolution Model. A resolution model is created by deciding which choices of the VSpec tree are positively decided and which ones are negatively decided. The VSpec at the top of Figure 4[4] shows a valid configuration of the FQAs (a resolution model) that satisfies the requirements of our ITS application. Some of the choices shown in Figure 4 have been selected because the application requirements explicitly identified them as needed, such as privacy, integrity, confidentiality, authentication, location aware, user aware and contextual help. Other concerns, such as encryption, hash, feedback, and time aware, had to be selected in order to obtain a valid configuration due to the existing dependencies between those concerns and those that were originally required.

For instance, there are concerns that had to be selected due to the parent-child relationship in the VSpec (e.g. the Confidentiality and the Privacy choices). Other concerns had to be selected because of the intraFQA-dependencies between concerns of the same FQA (e.g. Confidentiality and Encryption). Finally, other concerns had to be selected due to the interFQA-dependencies between concerns of different FQAs (e.g. AuthLogging of the Authentication concern in the security FQA and Log of the usability FQA).

Thus, in our case study, there are concerns, as is the case of the encryption or the hash concerns, that are required by other concerns but had not explicitly specified as part of the application requirements. This occurs basically because these dependencies are not always obvious to the application requirements engineer or the SA. By having a domain expert specifying the intraFQA- and interFQA-dependences as part of the definition of the FQAs variability in the first stage of our approach, in this second stage our approach helps the SAs to specify software architectures that are more accurate regarding the specification and customization of the FQAs to the necessities of the applications.

Once the resolution model has been created, the CVL Execution engine is executed to automatically generate the FQAs Resolved Model, which is shown in Figure 5. Only the necessary functional components are included in the resulting FQAs software architecture.

[4] Middle and bottom of Figure 4 are described in the next section. We show only one figure for reasons of space.

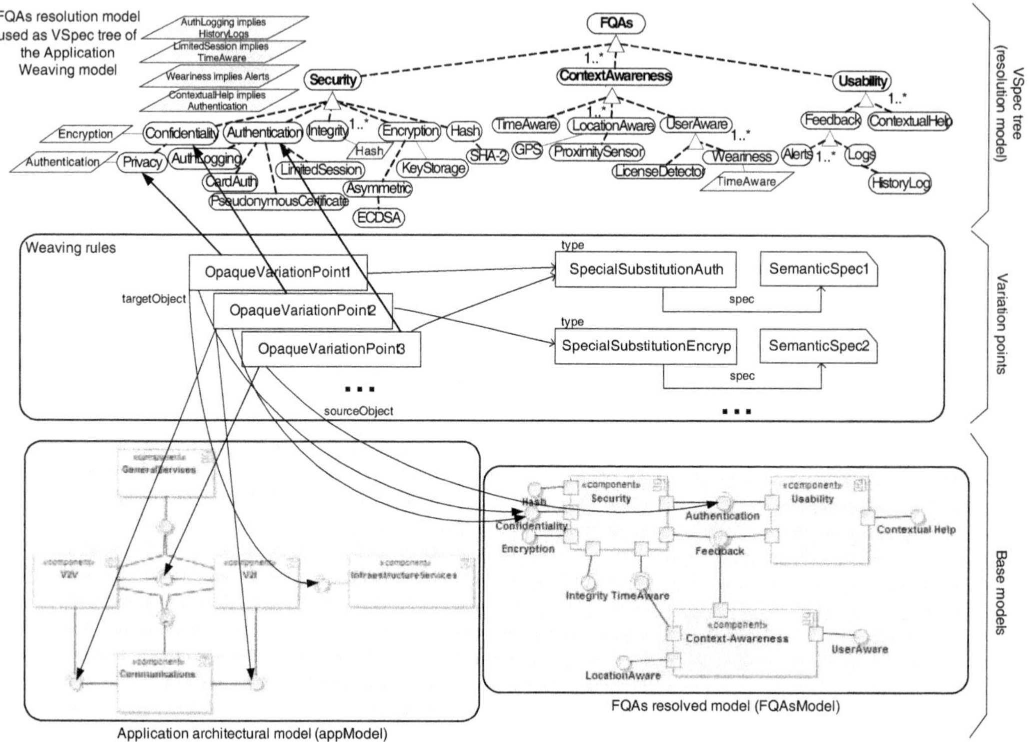

Figure 4: CVL model for the injection of the FQAs inside the application architecture.

6. WEAVING THE CUSTOMIZED FQAS

At this point, an architectural model customized with the required FQAs and concerns has been generated (high level view in the `FQAsModel` in Figure 4 and low level view in Figure 5). Now, in the third stage of our approach this FQAs resolved model has to be incorporated into the software architecture of the core application (`appModel` in Figure 4).

As previously stated, each concern of the FQAs needs a particular transformation because it is woven with the application in a different way. The `Application Weaving Model` (Figure 4) uses the OVPs of CVL to define a new semantic of a variation point using model transformation rules. The steps are: (1) binding an OVP to each of the concerns of the FQAs in the resolution model (e.g. encryption, contextual help); (2) specifying a reference to the specific architectural elements that model that concern in the FQAs resolved model, and (3) indicating how the concern will be woven with the application base model. OVPs are also bound to an OVPType, where this type explicitly defines the semantic of a special substitution. A special substitution implies the combination of a standard substitution and user defined transformations. In our case the special substitution is done from the "source object" to the "target object" referenced by the OVP as we show in Figure 4. Based on this special substitution the SA needs to refer to one or more join points (target objects) in the application model where the behavior of the selected concern (source object) will be incorporated.

We have identified a set of weaving patterns (Table 1) that fulfil our needs to incorporate the FQAs concerns based on how the functionality of the concerns (advices) needs to be applied into the different points of the application (join points). The special substitution needed by each concern is mapped to one weaving pattern presented in Table 1.[5] For instance, the privacy and the authentication concerns have the same special substitution that indicates that only one advice (e.g. `authenticate()`) of the selected concern (e.g. authentication) is woven into the selected join point (e.g. an interface of the base application).

Continuing with our example, to simplify Figure 4, we only show three OVPs bound to three concerns: confidentiality, which is achieved using encryption, privacy, and authentication. For instance, the **`OpaqueVariationPoint1`** is bound to the **`Privacy`** concern in the VSpec tree and it is also bound to the OVPType **`SpecialSubstitutionAuth`**[6] (OVPType 1 in Table 1). This in turn specifies the semantics of the special substitution with the necessary transformations (weaving rules) to incorporate the related element (**`Confidentiality`** that contains the **`Privacy`** functionality) of the FQAs resolved model (FQAsModel in Figure 4) into the application base model (AppModel in Figure 4).

Algorithm 1 shows the weaving process during the variability resolution performed by the CVL engine. It takes the set of OVPs defined (S_{OVP}) and for each OVP the semantic of the special substitution associated (OVPType) is executed by the M2M transformation engine (line 4). $S_{joinpoints}$ is the set of join points referenced by the OVP. When CVL is executed taking as inputs the application weaving model, the application base model (appModel) and the FQAs resolved model, the output is an automatically generated model representing the complete application software architecture (Figure 6), which includes the custom FQAs.

Note that the configuration of the architecture (the components and their relationships) is clearly visible in the static part of the design. Additionally, stereotyped dependencies

[5] Implementation in ATL of the M2M transformations are available in http://caosd.lcc.uma.es/spl/cvl/CVL-models-transformations.zip

[6] In our approach privacy is achieved using authentication.

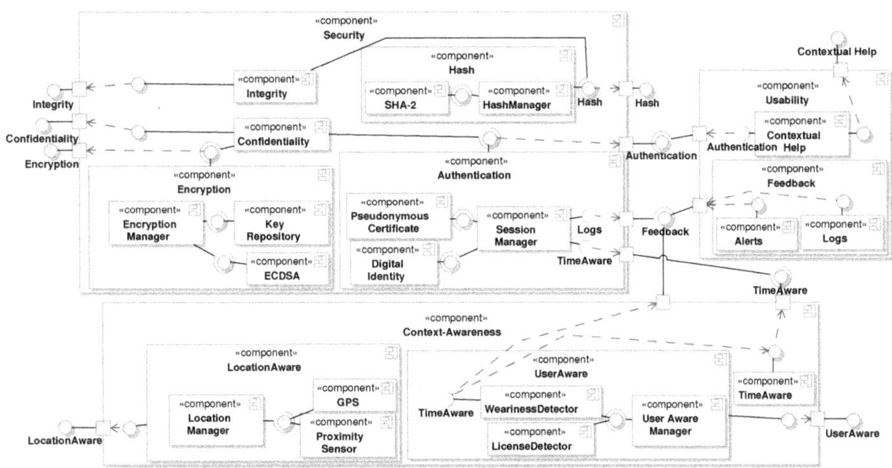

Figure 5: FQAs resolved model.

Table 1: Special substitutions.

OVPType	Description	Example
1	Only one advice of a concern is woven into a join point.	**Authentication**: the `authenticate()` advice is performed *around* the join point.
2	The same advice is woven multiple times into a join point.	**Time aware**: `currentTime()` is applied twice (*before* and *after*) to measure the time session of the user.
3	The same advice is woven into different join points.	**Location aware**: the `acquirePosition()` advice needs to be applied on the client and on the server side to establish locations.
4	Multiple advices of the same concern are woven into a join point.	**Feedback**: `log()` advices are invoked *before* and *after* the join point.
5	Multiple advices of the same concern are woven into different join points.	**Encryption**: encrypt the information (`encrypt(Object)`) *before* sending it and decrypt it (`decrypt(Object)`) *after* receiving it.
6	Advices of different concerns are woven into a join point.	**Contextual help**: first check whether the user is authenticated (`isAuthenticated()`) and then show information (`showHelp()`) based on the preferences of the user.
7	Advices of different concerns are woven into different join points.	**Integrity**: `hash(Object)` is applied *before* sending information to the server and `checkIntegrity(Object)` is applied *before* use the information in the server.

Algorithm 1 Weaving process using CVL.

Require: S_{OVP}
Ensure: ResolvedModel
for all vp in S_{OVP} **do**
  $c \leftarrow vp$.sourceObject
  $S_{joinpoints} \leftarrow vp$.targetObjects
  ResolvedModel $\leftarrow$ specialSubstitution(c, $S_{joinpoints}$, vp.type)
end for
return ResolvedModel

between components of the FQAs and components of the base application make explicit that the sources of the relationships crosscuts the architectural level, and the targets are the point of the application where they take place (i.e. the join points in the AOM terminology). However, this is insufficient because the interactions between the components are not represented. In order to solve this limitation, in our approach the interactions between the components are represented in a set of sequence diagrams that are also automatically generated [14] by the transformation rules of the special substitutions. For instance, the behavior of the crosscutting relationship of the authentication concern is represented in the sequence diagram in Figure 6 (b). This diagram shows how the `V2V` component invokes the `paymentToll()` method of the `InfraService` interface, and that before the call is effective the `authenticate()` method of the `Authentication` component is invoked. Similarly, the sequence diagram of Figure 6 (c) shows the behavior of the encryption concern when the `V2V` component transmits information; that is, before sending the message to the `Communication` component the `encrypt()` method of the `Encryption` component is invoked.

7. EVALUATION

We evaluate our work both quantitatively, by using metrics to quantify the benefits provided by our approach, and qualitatively, when the use of a metric does not make sense.

Table 2 describes the metrics suite that have been used to evaluate our approach. Using these metrics we have identified that there is: (1) a *degree of dependency* between FQAs (metrics 1–3). This means that there is a significant number of concerns whose inclusion in a particular solution depends on the correct identification of these dependencies, which are not always straightforwardly derived from the requirements of the system. Consequently, these dependencies may go unnoticed by the SA even if they should be taken into account to satisfy the requirements of a system; (2) a high *degree of variability* (metrics 4–6), since modeling the FQAs as a "family" of products, and the automatic materialization of the FQAs base model considerably increases the number of "valid" resolutions of a FQA that can be generated; (3) a high *degree of automation*, due to the high number of architectural elements that are automatically generated in comparison with the manual effort that needs to be made in order to include the FQAs inside the software architectures of the applications. This degree of automation implies a lower development effort and gains in productivity; and (4) a high *degree of separation of concerns* (metrics 7–8), which is improved due to splitting our approach into three stages.

We present the results of modeling the three FQAs described in this paper: security, context awareness and usability.

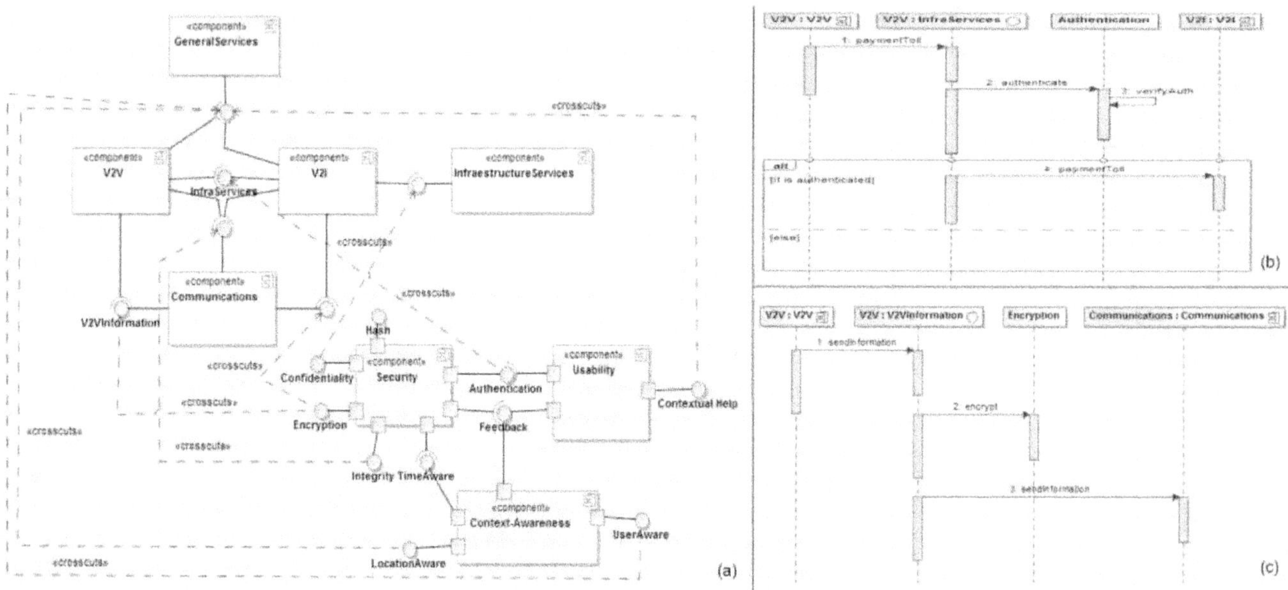

Figure 6: Complete application architecture (a); authentication (b) and encryption (c) sequence diagrams.

Table 2: Metric Suite

Dependency Metrics	**1. #intraFQA-dependencies:** It measures the number of dependencies (tree-constraints and OCL constraints) between the concerns of a FQA. **2. #interFQA-dependencies:** It measures the number of dependencies (cross tree-constraints and OCL constraints) between different FQAs. **3. #dependent-elements:** It measures the minimum number of architectural elements (components, interfaces, relationships,...) that need to be defined due to the existence of a dependency.
Variability Metrics	**4. #choices:** It measures the total number of choices in a VSpec. **5. #resolutions:** It measures the total number of valid resolutions that can be generated from a VSpec. **6. Variability level:** Expressed as the ratio `#choices:#valid resolutions`.
Separation of Concerns Metrics	**7. Lack of concern-based cohesion (LCC):** It measures the number of concerns tangled in a particular component. **8. Concern diffusion over architectural components (CDAC):** It measures the number of components in which a concern is scattered.

Degree of Dependency.

The degree of dependency of the FQAs is shown in Table 3. By applying the dependency metrics (see Table 2), we count the number of intraFQA- and interFQA- dependencies, as well as the number of architectural elements that are needed in order to satisfy those dependencies. Note that these numbers correspond only with the concerns of the three FQAs presented in this paper.

At this point, we would like to highlight that each FQA dependency can imply the incorporation of a considerable number of architectural elements into the software architecture. For instance, the security FQA has only four intraFQA-dependencies but, in order to satisfy these four dependencies, the SA needs to define at least 33 architectural elements. InterFQA-dependencies are even more difficult to satisfy because they involve concerns of the other FQAs. For instance, to satisfy the interFQA-dependency of the usability FQA with the security FQA, the SA needs to define at least 13 architectural elements.

The relevant issue here is that, using our approach, this complexity is not managed directly by the SA. Basically, because we make those dependencies explicit to make sure he/she is made aware of them and must only select the desired concerns that satisfy the dependencies. Then, the required architectural elements are automatically incorporated into the architecture. Note that this is certain only by assuming that the domain experts correctly do their job of modeling the FQAs and the dependencies between them.

Table 3: Degree of dependency

Dependencies	Security	Context awareness	Usability
#intraFQA	4	3	1
#elements	33	12	3
#interFQA	2	1	1
#elements	21	11	13

Table 4: Degree of variability

	Security	Context awareness	Usability	Total
#choices	23	15	10	48
#components	21	19	7	47
#resolutions	5354	575	79	313784

Degree of Variability.

Table 4 shows the number of choices that were specified in the VSpec of the security, the context awareness, and the usability FQAs, the number of components that were defined in the software architecture of each FQA and the number of different "valid" resolutions (configurations) that can be generated using our approach.

The number of possible resolutions will depend on the number of initial choices and on the number of dependencies between choices in the VSpec. In Table 4, we see that, for security, the domain expert will only once have to make, the effort of defining a VSpec with 23 choices and of specifying an architectural model with 21 components. Then the CVL engine automatically generates one of the 5354 valid security configurations based on the selections in the VSpecs done by the SA. The correctness of the generated software architectures will depend on the correct specification of the variability model. The variability level is lower for context

Table 5: Degree of automation

Case study	Specified elements manually	automatically	Degree of automation
ITS	27	25	48.08%
HW	42	38	47.50%
TS	115	16	12.20%
CS	43	34	44.20%

awareness (15 choices: 575 resolutions) and usability (10 choices: 79 resolutions) than for security.

These numbers indicate that some FQAs have a high degree of variability — i.e. there are many different configurations of security that can be created to satisfy the security requirements of different applications, and the manual specification of these configurations by the SA (5354 in the case of security) is a hard and error-prone task. So, this metric indicates that the use of an SPL approach makes sense.

Degree of Automation.

Defining the architectural model of the FQAs and the variability model with the VSpecs and the variation points is a difficult and specialized task. However, in our approach, this effort only needs to be made once and then the FQA models can be reused in the development of many systems. Therefore, the main effort consists of modeling the core architecture of the application. Thus, in order to specify the degree of automation of our approach, we compare the number of architectural elements (i.e. components, provided and required interfaces, and relationships) that are manually created in the specification of the core software architecture with the number of architectural elements that are automatically generated, as defined in Equation 1. This is an adaptation of the degree of automation defined in [8], to be able to use this metric at the architectural level. Basically, at the architectural level, the complexity of defining a software architecture is measured by the complexity of designing their components, interfaces, and the relationships between those components; and it does not depend on the complexity of the particular implementation of the components.

$$\text{Degree of Automation} = \frac{\#elements\_FQAs}{\#elements\_core + \#elements\_FQAs} \quad (1)$$

We have applied the degree of automation in our approach when: (1) security, context awareness and usability are added to the ITS case study, and (2) security and usability are added to a health watcher (HW) industrial case study, a toll (TS) case study and a crisis management (CS) case study (see Table 5). We note that, in the case study of this paper, the core application is composed by 27 architectural elements, and when the FQAs are incorporated, 25 new elements are added to the architecture, obtaining a degree of automation of 48.08%. This value is higher than in other case studies because the ITS requires more QAs concerns, and those concerns have many dependencies between them. Thus, the results obtained by applying this metric indicates that our approach can be useful. However, an empirical study that imply SAs developing projects of different complexities using our approach needs to be performed to confirm the benefits suggested by this metric.

Degree of Separation of Concerns.

In our approach, the separated modeling of the FQAs from the core application architecture and the subsequent combination with the use of CVL and the crosscuts relationships all contribute to improve the separation of concerns. On the one hand, we have modeled each FQA separately from each other in order to (1) identify the concerns and their dependencies, and (2) avoid the duplication of concerns in different FQAs. The result is that the concerns of the FQAs are well-encapsulated only in those components that were part of the security, the context awareness, and the usability composite components (the CDAC metric for all of them is 1). The LCC metric has also been applied to the same components, and the results show that they only contain security, context awareness, or usability concerns, respectively, and the information of the required concerns of the other FQAs to satisfy their dependencies. On the other hand, this good degree of separation is kept after the incorporation of the FQAs into the application architecture due to the use of the crosscuts relationships at the architectural level.

7.1 Discussion

The evaluation results obtained indicate that the effort of separately defining FQAs forming an SPL family presents the following advantages: (i) helps the SA to identify the dependencies, take them into account and resolve them; (ii) helps the SA to create different configurations of the FQAs; (iii) helps the SA to incorporate the customized FQAs into the architecture; (iv) there is a better degree of separation of concerns due to the encapsulation of the crosscutting behavior of the FQAs in separate software components. This facilitates the subsequent modification of the application and/or the FQAs. The initial results obtained by some of the metrics (degree of dependency and degree of variability) support our decision to use techniques and tools of SPLs for modeling the FQAs. Others (separation of concerns) support our decision to model them separately from the base application. Finally, the degree of automation suggests that it is worth using our approach with regard to the effort required to generate and introduce the customized FQAs models into a software architecture. However, we need to complete the evaluation with empirical studies in order to evidence the benefits and usefulness of our approach.

Despite the benefits of using the techniques and tools of SPLs and CVL in particular, we have also identified some shortcomings to our approach. A possible disadvantage is that the SA has to deal with many models. However, we need to take into account that some of these models are just configurations of the others (e.g. the resolution models), others are automatically generated by CVL (e.g. the resolved models), and others are defined only once and are reusable in other applications (e.g. the FQAs base model and the FQAs variability model).

Another disadvantage of our approach is that the weaving rules implemented as model-to-model transformations in the last stage of our approach depend on the meta-model used to specify the core software architecture. This means that these rules will need to be adapted or redefined if the SA decides to use a software architectural model that, in spite of being MOF-dependent, does not incorporate the same meta-model constructors that we used to define the weaving rules. This is however a minor limitation in the sense that our approach enables the integration of different model-to-model transformations as part of the weaving step, by using the extension mechanism provided by CVL (i.e. the OVPs). Also note that even if the weaving rules need to be adapted, this is the last step of our approach and all the previous steps remain without changes — i.e. the definition and the variability modeling of the FQAs as well as the configuration of them do not change.

Finally, another limitation of our approach is that we have modeled only the dependencies between the concerns of the FQAs, but there can also be dependencies between the concerns of the FQAs and the base application (e.g. the feedback concern of the usability FQA may require introducing a new panel into the graphical interface of the base application in order to show the feedback information). So, as part of our on-going work, we plan to extend the variability model to include these kinds of dependencies.

8. RELATED WORK

Most of the approaches that model QAs variability principally focus on the analysis of the QAs as non-functional requirements (e.g. cost, maintenance) in the final product of an SPL, and/or how the variations in the functional components of the application affect those QAs. For example, in [15, 16], Tawhid and Petriu propose a technique to model the commonality and variability in structural and behavioral SPL views using MDD. They add generic annotations related to a QA (e.g. performance) in a UML model that represents the set of core reusable SPL assets. Then, through model transformations, the UML model of a specific product with concrete annotations (e.g. UML profiles with stereotypes [7]) of the QA is derived, and a model for the given product is generated. Annotating the base model makes this highly related to variability specifications and prevents the reuse of both the base model of the application and the variability model of the QAs.

QADA [13] is a specific method to design PLAs by transforming systematic functionality and QAs into architectures, but this proposal do not take into account the quality requirements explicitly. RiPLE-DE [4] is a domain design process for SPL that models the FQAs variability by using FMs complemented with numerical values from the base application to evaluate and achieve the desired quality levels. However, the variability of the FQAs directly depends on the base application, avoiding the reuse of the FQAs.

In [5], the authors adopt the CVL approach to specify and resolve the variability of workflows. Then, they compose the detailed structural and behavioral design models of the chosen variants by using a Reusable Aspect Models (RAM) weaver. However, this external weaver is responsible for composing the reusable aspects instead of implementing the weaving process by using CVL as we do. Additionally, they apply the CVL approach at the design level while we focus at the architectural level (e.g. component diagrams).

Architectural patterns are also used to integrate QAs into software architectures [9]. This approach uses patterns for architectural partitioning in order to help the SA satisfies non-functional characteristics of the system. The main limitation of this approach is that a specific implementation of a pattern for a QA cannot be directly re-used in other different application architecture, and the pattern needs to be applied from the scratch.

9. CONCLUSIONS AND FUTURE WORK

We have proposed a generic, integrated and extensible approach for modeling FQAs separately from the base application architecture. By separating the modeling of the FQAs from the application architecture we have improved the modularization and the reusability of models. CVL makes our approach suitable for any MOF-compliant language and allows us to automatically generate architectural configurations of the FQAs and inject them into the application architecture by extending the semantic of the CVL variation points.

In our follow-up work, we plan to evaluate our approach with empirical studies in order to evidence its benefits and usefulness. For example, we need to quantify the problem of using many models in order to save effort for the SAs. We also plan to extend the variability model in order to include those FQAs' concerns that have dependencies with the base application.

10. ACKNOWLEDGMENTS

Work supported by the European INTER-TRUST FP7-317731 and the Spanish TIN2012-34840, FamiWare P09-TIC-5231, and MAGIC P12-TIC1814 projects.

11. REFERENCES

[1] INTER-TRUST: Interoperable Trust Assurance Infrastructure. `http://www.inter-trust.eu`.

[2] M. Barbacci, M. Klein, T. Longstaff, and C. Weinstock. Quality Attributes. Technical report, 1995. `http://resources.sei.cmu.edu/asset_files/TechnicalReport/1995_005_001_16427.pdf`.

[3] L. Bass, P. Clements, and R. Kazman. *Software Architecture in Practice*. Addison-Wesley Professional, 3rd edition, 2012.

[4] R. d. O. Cavalcanti, E. S. de Almeida, and S. R. Meira. Extending the RiPLE-DE process with quality attribute variability realization. In *QoSA-ISARCS*, 2011.

[5] B. Combemale, O. Barais, O. Alam, and J. Kienzle. Using CVL to operationalize product line development with reusable aspect models. In *VARY*, 2012.

[6] J. B. F. Filho, O. Barais, J. Le Noir, and J.-M. Jézéquel. Customizing the common variability language semantics for your domain models. In *VARY*, 2012.

[7] M. Fontoura, W. Pree, and B. Rumpe. *The UML profile for framework architectures*. Addison-Wesley Longman Publishing Co., Inc., 2000.

[8] A. Harrington and V. Cahill. Model-driven engineering of planning and optimisation algorithms for pervasive computing environments. In *PerCom*, pages 172–180, 2011.

[9] N. Harrison and P. Avgeriou. Leveraging architecture patterns to satisfy quality attributes. In *Software Architecture*, volume 4758 of *LNCS*, pages 263–270. 2007.

[10] O. Haugen, A. Wąsowski, and K. Czarnecki. CVL: Common Variability Language. In *SPLC*, 2012.

[11] J. M. Horcas, M. Pinto, and L. Fuentes. Variability and dependency modeling of quality attributes. In *SEAA*, 2013.

[12] N. Juristo, A. Moreno, and M.-I. Sanchez-Segura. Guidelines for eliciting usability functionalities. *IEEE TSE*, 33(11):744–758, 2007.

[13] M. Matinlassi, E. Niemelä, and L. Dobrica. *Quality-driven Architecture Design and Quality Analysis Method: A Revolutionary Initiation Approach to a Product Line Architecture*. VTT publications. Technical Research Centre of Finland, 2002.

[14] M. Pinto, L. Fuentes, L. Fernández, and J. Valenzuela. Using AOSD and MDD to enhance the architectural design phase. In *On the Move to Meaningful Internet Systems: OTM Workshops*. 2009.

[15] R. Tawhid and D. Petriu. Integrating performance analysis in the Model Driven Development of Software Product Lines. In *MoDELS*. 2008.

[16] R. Tawhid and D. Petriu. Automatic derivation of a product performance model from a software product line model. In *SPLC*, 2011.

Enriching Software Architecture Models with Statistical Models for Performance Prediction in Modern Storage Environments

Qais Noorshams, Roland Reeb, Andreas Rentschler, Samuel Kounev, Ralf Reussner
Chair for Software Design and Quality
Karlsruhe Institute of Technology
Karlsruhe, Germany
[firstname.lastname]@kit.edu

ABSTRACT

Model-based performance prediction approaches on the software architecture-level provide a powerful tool for capacity planning due to their high abstraction level. To process the increasing amount of data produced by today's applications, modern storage systems are becoming increasingly complex having multiple tiers and intricate optimization strategies. Current software architecture-level modeling approaches, however, struggle to account for this development and are not well-suited in complex storage environments due to overly simplistic storage assumptions, which consequently leads to inaccurate performance predictions. To address this problem, in this paper we present a novel approach to combine software architecture-level performance models with statistical models that capture the complex behavior of modern storage systems. More specifically, we first propose a general methodology for enriching software architecture modeling approaches with statistical I/O performance models. Then, we present how we realize the modeling concepts as well as model solving to obtain performance results. Finally, we evaluate our approach extensively in the context of three case studies with two state-of-the-art environments based on Sun Fire and IBM System z server hardware. Using our approach, we are able to successfully predict the application performance within 20 % prediction error in almost all cases.

Categories and Subject Descriptors

C.4 [**Performance of Systems**]: Modeling techniques, Performance attributes; D.2.11 [**Software Engineering**]: Software Architectures

Keywords

I/O, Statistical Model, Storage, Software Architecture, Performance, Prediction

CBSE'14, June 30–July 4, 2014, Marcq-en-Baroeul, France.

ACM 978-1-4503-2577-6/14/06 ...$15.00.
http://dx.doi.org/10.1145/2602458.2602475.

1. INTRODUCTION

Over the past couple of decades, the I/O resource demands of modern IT systems have grown exponentially [28]. Until the year 2020, the amount of digital data is expected to double every two years [9]. As a consequence of this development, storage systems have evolved significantly from simple disks to sophisticated tiered systems employing intricate caching and optimization algorithms.

With the increasing amount of I/O-intensive applications, however, performance modeling and evaluation techniques are required for capacity planning at deployment time as well as to guarantee the continuous compliance to Service-Level Agreements (SLAs) during operation as application workloads evolve. Component-based software architecture-level performance modeling techniques are popular approaches to address capacity planning issues at design time and during operation. It is clear and well-understood that the execution environment has a significant impact on the performance of a software system [15]. Current software architecture-level performance modeling approaches, however, struggle to account for the increasingly complex storage infrastructures and only provide rudimentary support for I/O performance prediction.

Existing approaches model the storage performance of I/O-intensive applications on a low abstraction level, e.g., [10, 16], however, it is difficult to include such models into software architecture models, because the required information between the two modeling abstraction levels needs to be synchronized. Such a synchronization is not straightforward and multiple questions arise, such as, for instance: i) What system information is required to enable fine-granular performance analysis? ii) What information needs to be part of the component interfaces? iii) How can the information be analyzed to reason about the end-to-end system performance?

To address this issue, in this paper we propose a novel approach for performance modeling of modern storage systems combining high-level component-based software architecture models with low-level statistical I/O models. More specifically, we first propose a general methodology for enriching software architecture modeling approaches with statistical I/O performance models. Statistical models are a powerful approach to capture the complex behavior of storage systems and they can be typically obtained in a fully automated manner. Then, we present how we realize the modeling concepts as well as model solving to obtain performance results. We

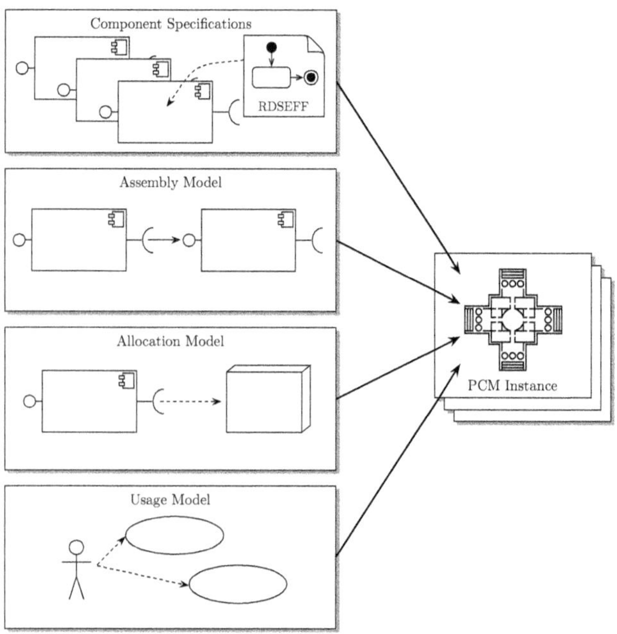

Figure 1: PCM Model Instance (Source: [3])

show how we model I/O requests on the architecture-level and how we map the requests to the required information on the storage level. Finally, we extensively evaluate our approach in the context of three case studies with two state-of-the-art environments based on Sun Fire and IBM System z server hardware. Using our approach, we are able to successfully predict the application performance within 20 % prediction error for both end-to-end response time as well as I/O response time in almost all cases.

In summary, the contribution of this paper is two-fold: i) We present a novel approach to integrate statistical I/O models into software architecture-level performance models allowing to predict the performance in modern storage environments. ii) We validate our approach in two state-of-the-art real-world environments based on Sun Fire and IBM System z server hardware.

The remainder of this paper is organized as follows: Next, we introduce the background of our approach in Section 2. In Section 3, we present our general methodology. Section 4 presents the realization of our approach. We evaluate our approach in Section 5. Finally, Section 6 reviews related work and Section 7 summarizes and concludes the paper.

2. BACKGROUND

In general, our approach can be applied to any software architecture modeling approach supporting a model-based performance prediction. We apply our approach to the Palladio Component Model (PCM) [4], a modeling language for component-based software architectures, since it is a mature approach with a significant amount of validation case studies, e.g., [3, 4, 11, 12, 17, 19]. The PCM is aligned with the component-based software engineering (CBSE) development process and provides modeling constructs to describe the i) software components, ii) system architecture, iii) resource allocations, and iv) usage profile of a component-based software system in respective sub-models, cf. Figure 1:

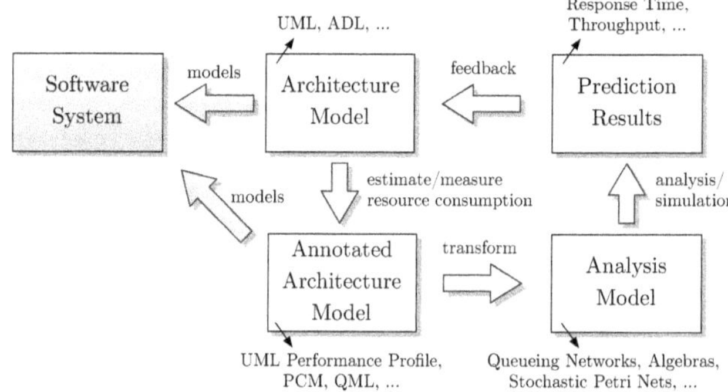

Figure 2: Model-based Performance Prediction (Source: [3])

- *Component specifications* contain an abstract, parametric description of components. Furthermore, the behavior of a component as well as its resource demands can be specified in *RDSEFFs* (short for *Resource Demanding Service EFFect specification*) in a UML activity diagram-like syntax.
- An *assembly model* defines the software architecture, i.e., which components are used and how they are connected.
- The resource environment and the allocation of components to resources are specified in an *allocation model*.
- The *usage model* specifies the usage of the system, i.e., a description of the sequence and frequency of users accessing the system operations.

Using model transformations, e.g., to simulation code or to queueing networks, a PCM model instance can be simulated or analytically solved to predict the system performance. The performance prediction serves as feedback and enables a model-based quality assessment of software systems. The model-based performance prediction process is illustrated in Figure 2.

In the PCM, I/O resources are represented as a single-/ multi-server queue with FCFS (First-Come-First-Serve) or processor sharing service policy and I/O requests are represented merely by their demands, which need to be estimated by the modeler manually. While this has been shown to be a reasonable abstraction for basic hardware environments [3], modern storage systems are much more complex and have many influencing factors [26, 27]. Therefore, we focus on enhancing the PCM with statistical I/O models, especially since their creation can be fully automated and does not require additional expert knowledge [24, 25].

3. METHODOLOGY

In this section, we show how we extend the model-based performance prediction process to allow performance predictions in modern storage environments. An overview of our approach is given in Figure 3 (the upper elements are analog to the corresponding elements in Figure 2). First, we present an analysis of the factors that need to be considered when modeling I/O performance using a storage analysis model. Based on the factors, we design a storage interface that is integrated into the software architecture model. Finally, we propose a combination approach of the software architecture model with the storage analysis model.

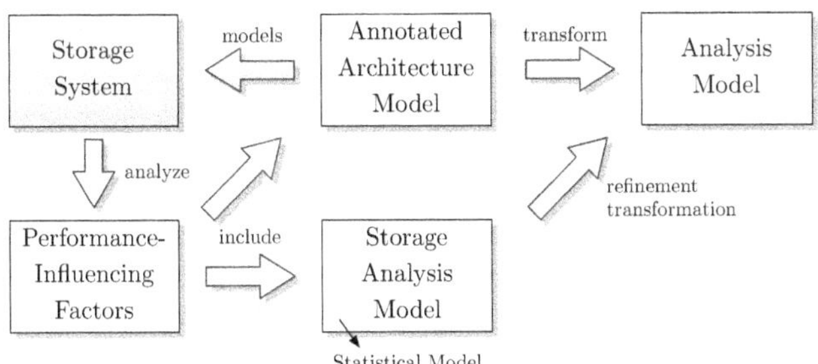

Figure 3: Proposed Approach

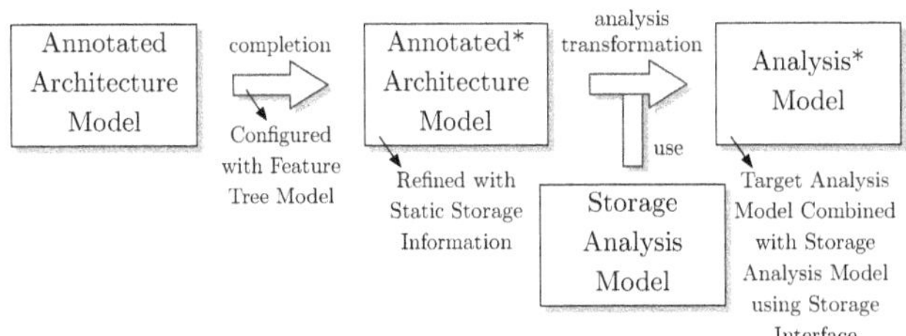

Figure 4: Refinement Transformation Approach

3.1 Performance-Influencing Factors

Starting point for creating a performance model of a storage system is analyzing the performance-influencing factors. In [26], we identified and evaluated the performance-influencing factors of applications deployed in a sophisticated environment with a complex storage system. We categorized the factors into workload-specific characteristics and system-specific configuration parameters.

It is important to find an appropriate abstraction level for the factors. On the one hand, too coarse-grained factors lead to inaccuracies in the performance models. On the other hand, too fine-grained factors cannot be specified by software developers and deployers. The performance-influencing factors are included into the architecture model and the storage analysis model. While the system-specific factors are specified once in the architecture model, the workload-specific factors need to be specified for every I/O request in the modeled application.

3.2 Storage Analysis Model

Based on the systematic evaluation of the performance-influencing factors, we create storage analysis models by applying multiple statistical regression techniques. Regression-based models are powerful techniques to capture and learn the influence of multiple *independent variables*, e.g., requests size and request type, on a *dependent variable*, e.g., request response time. The models are especially suited as they can be obtained in a fully automated manner, thus, lifting the burden for performance engineers to manually develop the models.

We have automated the storage model building process as part of our *Storage Performance Analyzer (SPA)* [23] framework. We specify the workload factors (i.e., the independent variables) that should be analyzed and the performance metric (i.e., the dependent variable) we want to characterize. Using the specified workload factors, a system profile is created by exploring the possible workload values with systematic measurements. The measurements are then used to optimally tune and build a *statistical I/O model*, i.e., a specific I/O model using a statistical regression technique, which in turn can be integrated into the software architecture model.

3.3 Storage Interface Design

The goal is to combine the low-level storage analysis model with the high-level software architecture model. A prerequisite for the combination of the two modeling abstractions is the design of a *storage interface* at the software architecture-level. The storage interface determines the well-defined use of the storage analysis model in the software architecture. The storage interface includes the required dynamic information (i.e., the workload-related performance-influencing factors) in the software architecture model that is passed as input to the storage analysis model (e.g., the distinction between read and write requests and their access patterns). Furthermore, the set of static storage-relevant information (i.e., the system-related performance-influencing factors) is used to configure or choose the appropriate storage analysis model. While the static information needs to be passed only once, e.g., when initializing the storage analysis model, the dynamic information needs to be passed with every I/O request.

3.4 Refinement Transformations

For the combination of the software architecture model with the statistical I/O model, we propose to use *refinement transformations*. As illustrated in Figure 4, the transformations may include both i) a *completion* [33] as well as ii) an *analysis transformation*.

The completion refines the architecture model with the static storage-relevant information and is configured, e.g., using feature tree models, cf. [13]. Depending on the context, the completion may be realized using a full-blown higher-order transformation (HOT) [13] or by simply adding the required static information where required. The analysis transformation uses the architecture model and creates the target analysis model to predict the system performance, cf. Figure 2. This transformation is extended to combine the target analysis model with the storage analysis model over the storage interface using a bridge or adapter. Finally, the combined analysis model is solved to obtain the performance results of the modeled software architecture.

4. REALIZATION

In this section, we present how we realize our approach presented in the previous section in the PCM and how we combine the software architecture model with the statistical I/O model. We start by presenting the modeling concept. Then, we detail how we obtain our I/O model and we show how the software model is solved to obtain the performance results. Finally, we outline the process how to use our approach for performance prediction.

4.1 Modeling Concept

For the models, we use the modeling concept of *layered execution environments* of the PCM introduced in [11] and illustrated in Figure 5.

We distinguish *business components* running at the application layer and *resources* running at the infrastructure layer. The interface of one or more business components may

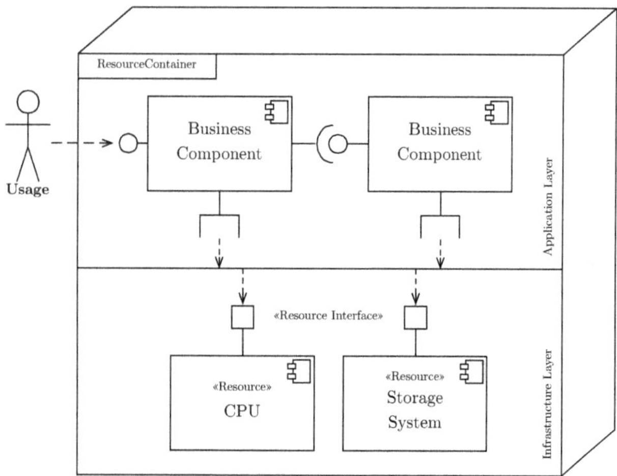

Figure 5: Modeling Concept Overview (derived from [11])

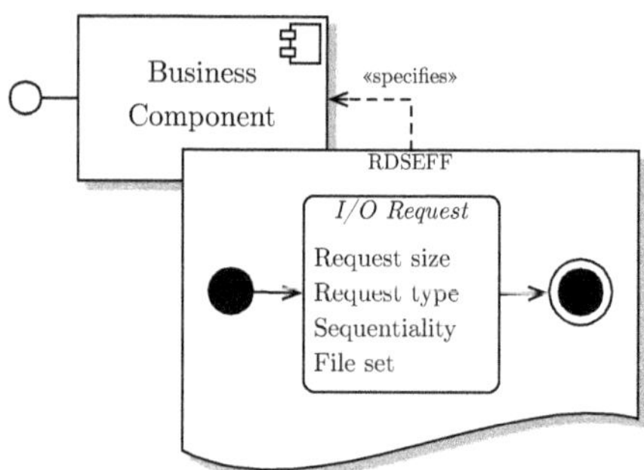

Figure 6: Realization I/O Request

be exposed to users. The business components access the CPU and I/O resources using so-called *resource interfaces*. We use this concept to model our storage system as an I/O resource enabling to realize our storage interface introduced in Section 3.3.

To use the storage interface, the I/O requests of the business components are modeled in the RDSEFF as illustrated in Figure 6. The storage interface is comprised of the following four parameters:

- *Request size*: specifies the I/O demand
- *Request type*: read or write request
- *Sequentiality*: percentage (or probability) of a sequential request
- *File set*: name and size of the file set the request is operating on

The need for former two parameters is apparent, e.g., to distinguish between small read requests and big write requests. The latter two parameters are required to estimate the impact on the caching hierarchy at the storage system, e.g., if the file set is too large to fit in the caches or if the requests are sufficiently sequential such that the requests can be reasonably anticipated and pre-fetched by the storage system.

The storage resource encapsulates the statistical I/O model. The exact model depends on a number of static parameters,

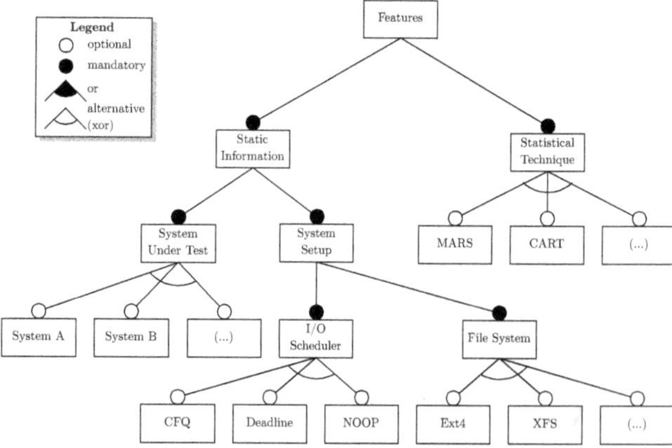

Figure 7: Feature Tree of Statistical I/O Model (cf. [26])

e.g., which target environment is used. The feature tree we employ leading to the fitting I/O model is shown in Figure 7. The *system under study* and its *setup*, i.e., *I/O scheduler* and *file system*, are captured by separate models. While it would be possible to use all the information in one big statistical model, we chose to integrate only the information that is necessarily required as part of the model for a clear conceptual separation and reduced model building effort (e.g., required measurements). Moreover, for given measurements, the model can be extracted with different *statistical techniques* with different strengths and weaknesses (cf. [24]).

4.2 Statistical I/O Model

In our previous work [24], we showed how to effectively create I/O performance models in complex environments with statistical regression techniques. Our approach is briefly summarized in the following for the sake of completeness. For more details, the reader can refer to [24]. As previously mentioned, the process is fully automated.

We first identify the independent variables, we need to capture in the models. The space spanned by the independent variables is then explored to extract a system profile with systematic measurements. The independent variables we use for I/O performance modeling are:

- Number of clients (concurrent requests)
- Request type (read or write)
- Mean read request size
- Mean write request size
- Read access pattern (random or sequential)
- Write access pattern (random or sequential)
- Read/write ratio
- File set size

The dependent variables are read response time and write response time.

Since regression techniques usually have configuration parameters (e.g., the maximum number of modeling terms) that influence their effectiveness in a certain application scenario, we apply a heuristic search algorithm (introduced in [24])

Figure 8: Transformation of the PCM Model

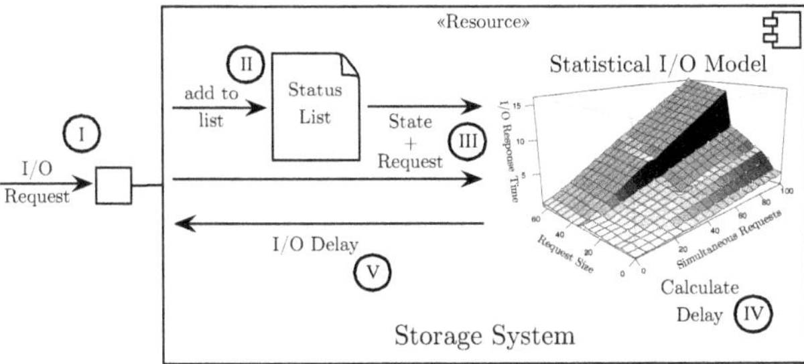

Figure 9: Storage Component Simulation

to optimally tune the regression techniques. For given measurements, we iteratively search for best fitting regression parameters that minimize the average root mean square error of a 10-fold cross-validation.

In this paper, we use *Multivariate Adaptive Regressions Splines (MARS)* [8] for the statistical models. However, other popular methods, e.g., binary decision trees such as *Classification and Regression Trees (CART)* [5], could be used as well. MARS models consist of piecewise linear functions, so-called *hinge functions* h_i. Thus, MARS constructs a model f of the form $f(\vec{x}) = \beta_0 + \sum_{i=1}^{n} \beta_i h_i(\vec{x})$ with coefficients $\beta_0, \ldots, \beta_n$. Furthermore, we consider MARS models with *interaction terms*, which includes terms that are a product of one or more hinge functions.

4.3 Simulation for Model Solving

We use a simulation approach to solve the PCM model and to obtain the performance results. We transform the annotated PCM Model to the target analysis model, which is simulation code, as indicated in Figure 4 and realized as schematically shown in Figure 8. In the simulation, we integrated the statistical I/O model that is used over the storage interface. More specifically, we have extended the PCM simulator SimuCom [3] by a storage system scheduler as illustrated in Figure 9 to simulate the I/O delay at the storage system. The simulation is comprised of the following five steps:

I. Initially, the I/O requests of the business components, which are modeled as shown in Figure 6, are passed to the storage resource.

II. The arriving request is added to an internal *status list*, where the last n requests are stored in order to determine and derive the current state of the I/O workload at the storage system, e.g., the current read/write ratio of requests accessing the storage system, since such information is not given by the request itself. The choice of n determines the *memory length* and can be estimated from the workload using the average I/O delay and the number of I/O requests arriving per time $delay_{I/O}^{avg} \cdot requests_{I/O}^{Intensity}$. While this may not always be the best choice, the memory length n can also be calibrated for a given model.

III. The workload state information is calculated and passed together with the request information to the statistical I/O model. The exact information (i.e., the independent variables) required by the statistical model is given in Section 4.2.

IV. The statistical I/O model, which is encapsulated by the resource component, uses the independent variables to calculate the actual I/O delay. Since the model is a mathematical function, the calculation is fast and does not introduce significant simulation overhead.

V. By using the workload state information of the storage resource including the number of concurrent requests, the statistical model inherently captures the contention at the resource. Thus, the calculated response time is assigned to the arriving request such that the request is delayed by this calculated value.

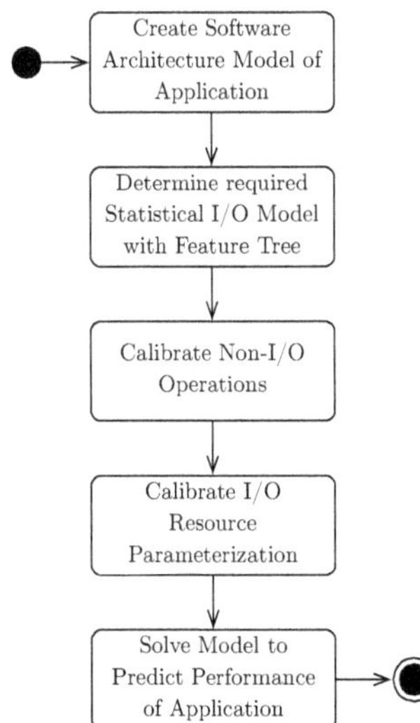

Figure 10: Performance Prediction Steps

4.4 Prediction Process

Figure 10 illustrates the process to obtain performance predictions of an application with our approach. The process is comprised of the following five steps:

1. The starting point is creating the PCM model instance of an application whose performance should be evaluated. The model instance is comprised of the submodels as before our extension (cf. Figure 1) with the added information on the I/O requests, which are the parameters of the storage interface (cf. Figure 6).

2. Using a feature configuration of the feature tree model shown in Figure 7, the required statistical I/O model is chosen. The feature tree is used by simply choosing the statistical technique and evaluating the appropriate system configurations. The statistical models can be stored in a repository or created with measurements when they are needed, e.g., for a new environment. If a new model is created, it can be created incrementally by

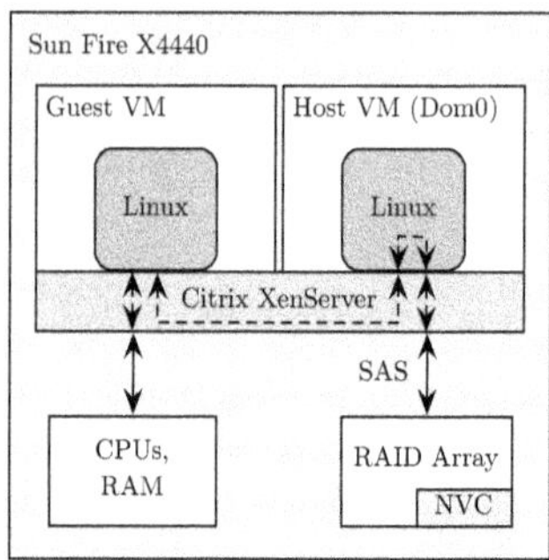

Figure 11: Schematic Illustration of Sun Fire X4440

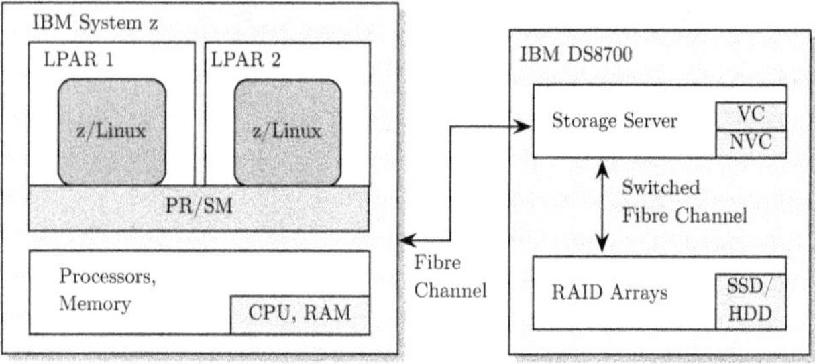

Figure 12: Schematic Illustration of IBM System z and DS8700

fixing some independent variables when measuring the environment, e.g., if an application is known to access a file set of a certain size, this independent variable is not needed to be fully evaluated and its exploration can be postponed to save time.

3. If the structural and behavioral model of the application is created, the resource demands of the non-I/O operations of the model need to be estimated and calibrated, e.g., for CPU resources.

4. Additionally, the parameters used for the storage component as illustrated in Figure 9 might be calibrated for the application model, e.g., the memory length can be adapted if required.

5. After the model creation and calibration steps have been completed, the solution of the model, which is fully automated, can be triggered and the performance results can be used to predict the performance of the application, e.g, to predict the performance for an increasing number of users.

5. EVALUATION

In this section, we present three case studies to evaluate our approach. We start by introducing our system environments and conclude with a summary and discussion of the results after the case studies.

5.1 System Environments

For the evaluation of our approach, we use two representative, state-of-the-art server environments.

5.1.1 Sun Fire

Our first environment is a *Sun Fire* X4440 x64 server system and is illustrated in Figure 11. It contains four 6-core processors and 128 GB of memory. The storage back end is a RAID array with 8 Serial Attached SCSI (SAS) hard disks. The array contains a battery-backed, non-volatile write cache (NVC).

The application runs in a guest Linux virtual machine (VM) virtualized using a Citrix XenServer hypervisor. The scheduler of the hypervisor manages the access of the guest VMs to the CPUs. For I/O requests, XenServer uses a privileged host VM (Dom0) able to access the physical devices.

The guest VM is equipped with 4 cores and 2 GB of memory and we focus the measurements on the storage performance using POSIX configuration. The file system is configured to the de facto standard *EXT4* and as I/O scheduler, we use the default scheduler in virtualized environments [22].

5.1.2 IBM System z

Our second environment is based on the IBM mainframe *System z* and the storage system *DS8700*. As illustrated in Figure 12, the System z provides processors and memory, whereas the DS8700 provides storage space. The resources are managed by the *Processor Resource/System Manager (PR/SM)*, which is basically a hypervisor creating logical partitions (*LPARs*) of the machine.

The System z supports special Linux ports for System z commonly denoted as *z/Linux*. The System z is connected to the DS8700 via fibre channel. In the DS8700, storage requests are handled by a storage server containing a volatile cache (VC) and a non-volatile cache (NVC). The storage server is connected via switched fibre channel to SSD- or HDD-based RAID arrays. Furthermore, the storage server applies several pre-fetching and destaging algorithms for optimal performance [7]. When possible, read requests are served from the volatile cache, otherwise, they are served from the RAID arrays and stored together with pre-fetched data in the volatile cache for future accesses. Write-requests are propagated both to the volatile and non-volatile cache and are destaged to the RAID arrays asynchronously.

In our experimental environment, the DS8700 contains 2 GB NVC and 50 GB VC with a RAID5 array containing seven HDDs and measurements are obtained in a z/Linux LPAR. The I/O-related operating system configuration is as in our previous environment.

5.2 Case Study I

In our first case study, we model a *file server* application in the Sun Fire environment. The file server application is emulated using the popular *Filebench*[1] framework. Filebench has a workload definition language used to describe and emulate typical I/O-intensive applications. The application workload is comprised of a sequence of file system operations that is repeatedly executed by a number of clients (threads), e.g., a file in a file set is opened, read, and then closed. Filebench uses the following operations to define the workload:

- *openfile:* Opens a randomly chosen file returning the file handle.
- *closefile:* Closes an opened file.

[1] `https://github.com/Filebench-Revise/Filebench-Revise` (version with fixes from `http://sourceforge.net/projects/filebench/`)

Listing 1: File Server Workload

```
File set:
  - number of files = 10000
  - mean file size = 128 KB
  - file preallocation = 80%
Threads:
  - 50 (default)
Operations:
  - createfile
  - writewholefile
  - closefile
  - openfile
  - appendfilerand, mean size = 16 KB
  - closefile
  - openfile
  - readwholefile
  - closefile
  - deletefile
  - statfile
```

- *createfile:* Creates an empty file.
- *deletefile:* Deletes a randomly chosen file.
- *statfile:* Requests the meta information of a file.
- *readwholefile/writewholefile:* Read or write a file in one request.
- *appendfilerand:* Appends a random amount of data (with specified mean size) to a file.

Using these operations, the *file server* application is defined as shown in Listing 1. During the application runtime, the operations are executed in a sequence repeatedly by the clients.

We run the file server application three times with one minute warm up time and five minutes measurement time and averaged the measurements across the three runs. We modeled the create and delete operations as requests to the CPU resource. We modeled the open, close and stat operations as requests to a so-called DELAY resource (infinite server resource). We modeled the I/O operations read, write, and append as requests to our new storage system resource.

We calibrate the PCM model of the file server with 40 clients (a value below the default value to also predict the default number of clients), where we calibrate the operations using the CPU and Delay resource as well as the memory length for the statistical model and the passed parameters. We increase the number of clients and evaluate both the mean I/O response time prediction as well as the end-to-end response time prediction. The mean I/O response time prediction error $err^{I/O}$ and the end-to-end response time prediction error err^{E2E} are defined as

$$err^{I/O} = \frac{1}{n}\sum_{i}^{n}\left|\frac{opsIO_i^M - opsIO_i^P}{opsIO_i^M}\right| \quad (1)$$

and

$$err^{E2E} = \left|\frac{\sum_i ops_i^M - \sum_i ops_i^P}{\sum_i ops_i^M}\right|, \quad (2)$$

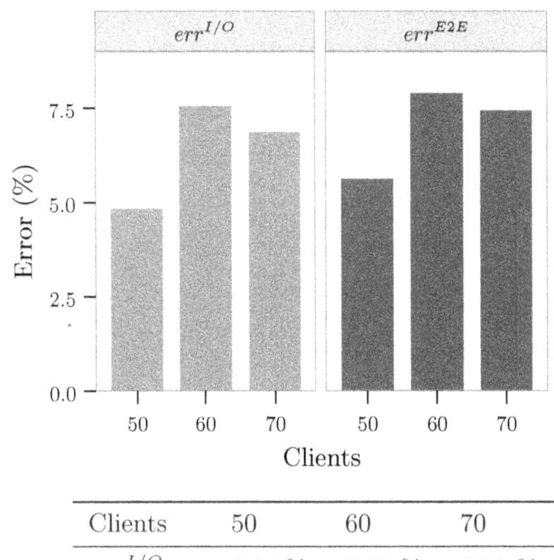

Clients	50	60	70
$err^{I/O}$	4.84 %	7.56 %	6.86 %
err^{E2E}	5.62 %	7.90 %	7.43 %

Figure 13: Prediction Error in Case Study I

respectively, where $opsIO_i^M$ and $opsIO_i^P$ is the measured and predicted response time of the i-th I/O operation (i.e., read, write, or append), respectively, and ops_i^M and ops_i^P is the measured and predicted response time of the i-th operation, respectively.

For the prediction, we increase the number of clients up to 70, while the end-to-end response time measurements increase from 103.09 ms (40 clients) to 188.51 ms (70 clients). Figure 13 summarizes the prediction error with the simulation model. Overall, the prediction accuracy in this case study is very high with a prediction error between 5 % and 8% for both the I/O response time and the end-to-end response time. The prediction accuracy is significantly high especially considering the fact that two different types of write operations (128 KB write and 16 KB append) are predicted using the same statistical model in the simulation.

5.3 Case Study II

In this case study, we model a *mail server* application in the Sun Fire environment. The mail server application is emulated using Filebench similar as the file server application in the previous case study. The mail server application is defined as shown in Listing 2. Similar to the previous application, the operations are executed in a sequence repeatedly by the clients during the runtime of the application.

We also run the mail server application three times with one minute warm up time and five minutes measurement time and averaged the measurements across the three runs. The operations were modeled as in our previous case study.

We calibrate the PCM model of the mail server with 10 clients (a value below the default value to also predict a number of clients close to the default value), where we calibrate the operations using the CPU and Delay resource as well as the memory length for the statistical model and the passed parameters. We increase the number of clients and evaluate both the mean I/O response time prediction $err^{I/O}$ as well as the end-to-end response time prediction err^{E2E}.

Listing 2: Mail Server Workload

```
File set:
  - number of files = 50000
  - mean file size = 16 KB
  - file preallocation = 80%
Threads:
  - 16 (default)
Operations:
  - deletefile
  - createfile
  - appendfilerand, mean size = 16 KB
  - closefile
  - openfile
  - readwholefile
  - closefile
  - openfile
  - appendfilerand, mean size = 16 KB
  - closefile
  - openfile
  - readwholefile
  - closefile
```

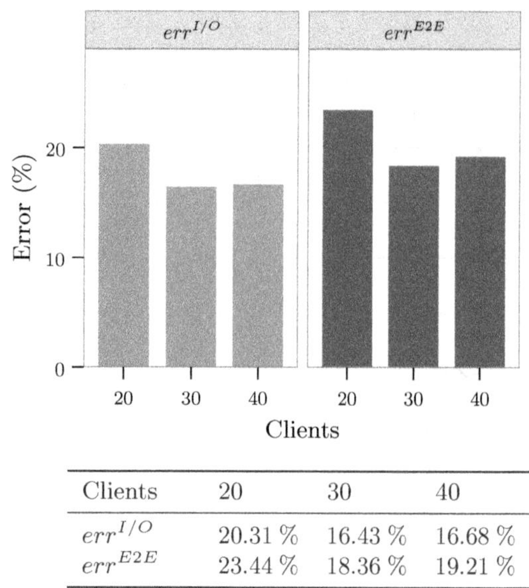

Clients	20	30	40
$err^{I/O}$	20.31 %	16.43 %	16.68 %
err^{E2E}	23.44 %	18.36 %	19.21 %

Figure 14: Prediction Error in Case Study II

For the prediction, we increase the number of clients up to 40, while the end-to-end response time measurements increase from 24.98 ms (10 clients) to 56.40 ms (40 clients). Figure 14 summarizes the prediction error with the simulation model. Compared to our previous case study, the prediction error is slightly higher, however, the accuracy with an I/O prediction error between 16 % and 20 % and an end-to-end prediction error between 18 % and 23 % is still very good.

5.4 Case Study III

In our final case study, we model the file server application introduced in our first case study (cf. Listing 1) in the IBM System z environment. We again calibrate the PCM model of the file server with 40 clients and increase the number of clients to evaluate both the mean I/O response time prediction error $err^{I/O}$ and the end-to-end response time prediction error err^{E2E}.

For the prediction, we increase the number of clients up to 70, while the end-to-end response time measurements increase from 37.46 ms (40 clients) to 47.04 ms (70 clients). Figure 15 summarizes the prediction error with the simulation model. The prediction error in this case study is also very encouraging with a prediction error between 15 % and 21% for the I/O response time and a prediction error between 2 % and 10% for the end-to-end response time.

5.5 Summary and Discussion

In the three case studies, we modeled a file server and a mail server application in two sufficiently complex environments that are not easily modeled or simulated. We demonstrated that the combination approach can be used to predict the performance of the considered applications when the number of users increases with a mean end-to-end prediction error across the prediction scenarios of 6.98 %, 20.34 %, and 7.34 % in the three case studies, respectively. This increases the applicability of such software architecture performance models where the I/O-intensive operations can be captured by the statistical I/O model since, e.g., in our final case study, only the statistical I/O model needed to be exchanged when changing the environment and the structural and behavioral model of the application could be reused.

In addition to the prediction results, the case studies also revealed some considerations. First, the prediction quality might also depend on the calibration of the I/O resource parameterization. For example, the produced I/O load on the system in our IBM System z environment was reduced due to a software bottleneck in the file server application during the measuring of response times because of very fast I/O request processing by the storage system. We accounted for this observation by reducing the calculated *concurrent request* parameter by 25% when passed to the statistical I/O model during simulation. Consequently, a more tailored calibration might increase prediction accuracy locally, however, with the possible sacrifice of extrapolation quality due to "overfitting" if the prediction configuration is more beyond the calibrated configuration. In our case studies, we reasonably limited the calibration process to obtain a sufficiently accurate prediction model. Another consideration is that the statistical I/O models employed in the case studies – as every model and modeling formalism – have an inherent potential for inaccuracies as they are created at a certain abstraction level with the goal to predict mean response times. To capture response time distributions, for example, the approach could be extended by further statistical I/O models, which are used during simulation, to capture important response time quantiles. Finally, to obtain a statistical I/O model, a potentially large number of measurements might be needed to cover all configuration combinations. As indicated in Section 4.4, we reduced the number of required measurements in the case studies by first testing the parameter ranges produced by the application and then explored the region around those ranges with measurements for the statistical I/O model.

6. RELATED WORK

Our approach is based on performance prediction of component-based software architectures [3, 4], modeling of layered

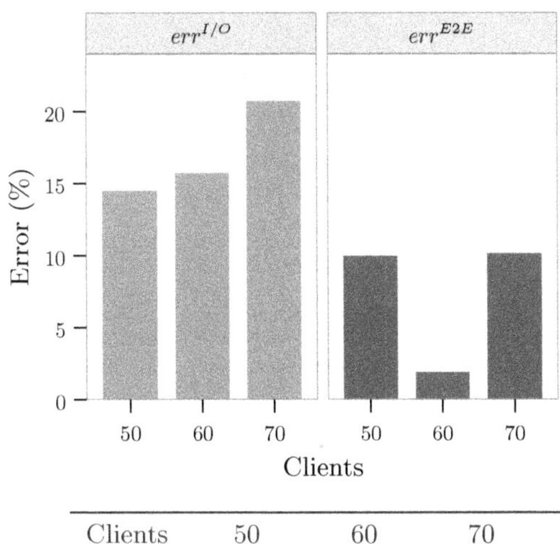

Clients	50	60	70
$err^{I/O}$	14.50 %	15.72 %	20.73 %
err^{E2E}	9.98 %	1.90 %	10.15 %

Figure 15: Prediction Error in Case Study III

component execution environments [11], and statistical I/O performance modeling of storage systems [24].

In general, Balsamo et al. [2] and Koziolek [15] present extensive surveys on approaches for performance modeling and evaluation of software systems without explicit focus on storage systems as in this paper.

More specifically, multiple performance modeling approaches of complex storage systems in native and virtualized environments have been proposed, e.g., [10, 20, 21, 30, 31] and [1, 6, 14, 16, 18], however, none of these approaches considers the system performance at the software architecture-level as presented in this paper. Closest to our work among those approaches, Kundu et al. [18] use artificial neural networks and support vector machines for dynamic capacity planning to answer which CPU and memory limits and I/O latency should be assigned to an application to meet performance limits. In [31], Wang et al. use CART models to predict disk device performance. They use an interesting set of workload parameters, however, it is unclear if the parameters can be used for more complex storage systems and whether the parameters can be used in software architecture-level approaches. Furthermore, Chiang et al. [6] use linear and second degree polynomials to model I/O performance interference of data-intensive applications. They use the models for scheduling algorithms to manage task assignments in XEN-based virtualized environments. As input to their model, they use read and write request arrival rates as well as local and global CPU utilization within the guest and the host VM, respectively. However, they do not distinguish between request sizes or sequential and random requests, for instance. Our measurements have shown that these and more factors have a significant impact on I/O performance.

The general approach closest to the work presented in this paper, Wert et al. [32] outline a general concept to combine software architecture models with domain-independent, measurement-based statistical models. They focus on the technical realization of the approach, but they show no evaluation of the combination. Thus, it is unclear what information needs to be exchanged when performing such a combination, whereas we propose a specific design of I/O-relevant parameters in the storage interface and in the statistical I/O models.

In [34], Woodside et al. present a workbench for statistical resource demand models of software components and subsystems. They outline that the resource models could be used in a performance model of the software environment without going into specific details how the combination could be realized.

Further, Shanthikumar et al. [29] present a classification scheme for hybrid analytic/simulation models and present several case studies including ones modeling simple disks as queues. As this was possible with the PCM before, our approach allows to model and predict the performance when using more complex storage systems.

7. CONCLUSION

In summary, we presented a novel approach for performance modeling and analysis of a) I/O-intensive applications in b) modern storage environments at the c) software architecture-level. To the best of our knowledge, there are no other approaches that combine these three aspects to our extent.

To realize our approach, we applied the model-based performance prediction process and extended the Palladio Component Model, a model-based performance prediction approach for component-based software architectures. We introduced a storage system scheduler that uses a statistical I/O model that was created in a fully automated manner to capture the behavior of the storage system. We used the concept of layered execution environments and encapsulated our storage system scheduler in a resource component that can be used over its resource interface. We described the required parameters at the resource interface and for the statistical I/O model. To solve the model and obtain performance data, we use a simulation approach where we calculate state information of the I/O workload (e.g., read/write mix) from the I/O requests. The state and I/O request information is then used to determine the delay at the storage resource with the statistical I/O model for a given I/O request.

The evaluation of our approach showed very promising results. We modeled a file server and a mail server application and used two modern environments based on Sun Fire and IBM System z server hardware. For the models, we evaluated the mean I/O response time error and the end-to-end response time error when predicting the application performance if the number of users increases. Modeling the file and mail server application in the Sun Fire environment, we obtained a mean I/O response time error of 6.42 % and 17.81 %, respectively, and a mean end-to-end response time error of 6.98 % and 20.34 %, respectively. Modeling the file server application in the IBM System z environment, we obtained a mean I/O response time error of 16.98 % and a mean end-to-end response time error of 7.34 %. Thus, the software architecture models were able to capture the performance characteristics in the respective environments.

The main lessons learned can be summarized as follows. i) We designed the component interface of a storage component specifying the required information for I/O modeling of storage systems with statistical regression techniques to use it in software architecture modeling approaches. ii) We modeled the I/O requests in a form that they can be easily expressed by software architects, i.e., the I/O requests are specified without requiring to estimate their resource demands, and the required information for statistical I/O models can be derived. iii) We could easily transfer the existing software architecture model of an application from one environment to another by recalibrating after replacing the statistical I/O model. iv) Overall, we successfully predicted the performance in sufficiently complex storage environments with reduced manual effort due to the automated statistical I/O model creation, which is integrated in our approach.

Our approach enables multiple application scenarios. Generally, our approach is targeted at reducing the effort for the analysis and evaluation of data-intensive applications running on modern storage systems by allowing to analyze the application performance on a software architecture-level. Our approach is especially beneficial in cases that prohibit applying explicit, fine-grained performance models due to, e.g., time constraints for the manual performance model creation, calibration, and validation. Our automated performance modeling approach can aid (e.g., the system developer) to create a performance profile of the storage system once and tailor the configuration and resource allocation as needed using the software architecture model. This model can be used in different scenarios to assess the system capacity limits when the number of users increases and evaluate deployment and trade-off decisions when using different system environments.

Acknowledgements

This work was partially supported by the German Research Foundation (DFG) under grant No. KO 3445/6-1, and the German Federal Ministry of Economics and Energy (BMWI), grant No. 01MD11005 (PeerEnergyCloud). We especially thank the Informatics Innovation Center (IIC) – `http://www.iic.kit.edu/` – for providing the system environment of the IBM System z and the IBM DS8700.

8. REFERENCES

[1] I. Ahmad, J. Anderson, A. Holler, R. Kambo, and V. Makhija. An Analysis of Disk Performance in VMware ESX Server Virtual Machines. In *WWC-6*, 2003.

[2] S. Balsamo, A. Di Marco, P. Inverardi, and M. Simeoni. Model-based performance prediction in software development: A survey. *IEEE TSE*, 2004.

[3] S. Becker. *Coupled model transformations for QoS enabled component-based software design*. PhD thesis, Universität Oldenburg, 2008.

[4] S. Becker, H. Koziolek, and R. Reussner. The palladio component model for model-driven performance prediction. *J. of Systems and Software*, 82(1), 2009.

[5] L. Breiman, J. Friedman, C. J. Stone, and R. Olshen. *Classification and Regression Trees*. The Wadsworth and Brooks-Cole statistics-probability series. Chapman & Hall, 1984.

[6] R. C. Chiang and H. H. Huang. TRACON: Interference-aware Scheduling for Data-intensive Applications in Virtualized Environments. In *SC '11*.

[7] B. Dufrasne, W. Bauer, B. Careaga, J. Myyrrylainen, A. Rainero, and P. Usong. IBM System Storage DS8700 Architecture and Implementation. `http://www.redbooks.ibm.com/abstracts/sg248786.html`, 2010.

[8] J. H. Friedman. Multivariate Adaptive Regression Splines. *Annals of Statistics*, 19(1):1–141, 1991.

[9] J. Gantz and D. Reinsel (IDC). THE DIGITAL UNIVERSE IN 2020: Big Data, Bigger Digital Shadows, and Biggest Growth in the Far East. `http://idcdocserv.com/1414`, 2012. Last accessed: Jan 2014.

[10] P. Harrison and S. Zertal. Queueing models of RAID systems with maxima of waiting times. *Performance Evaluation*, 64:664–689, 2007.

[11] M. Hauck, M. Kuperberg, K. Krogmann, and R. Reussner. Modelling Layered Component Execution Environments for Performance Prediction. In *CBSE '09*.

[12] N. Huber, S. Becker, C. Rathfelder, J. Schweflinghaus, and R. Reussner. Performance Modeling in Industry: A Case Study on Storage Virtualization. In *ICSE '10, Software Engineering in Practice Track*.

[13] L. Kapova and T. Goldschmidt. Automated feature model-based generation of refinement transformations. In *SEAA '09*.

[14] Y. Koh, R. Knauerhase, P. Brett, M. Bowman, Z. Wen, and C. Pu. An Analysis of Performance Interference Effects in Virtual Environments. In *ISPASS '07*.

[15] H. Koziolek. Performance evaluation of component-based software systems: A survey. *Perform. Eval.*, 2010.

[16] S. Kraft, G. Casale, D. Krishnamurthy, D. Greer, and P. Kilpatrick. Performance Models of Storage Contention in Cloud Environments. *SoSyM*, 2012.

[17] K. Krogmann. *Reconstruction of Software Component Architectures and Behaviour Models using Static and Dynamic Analysis*. PhD thesis, Karlsruhe Institute of Technology (KIT), 2010.

[18] S. Kundu, R. Rangaswami, A. Gulati, M. Zhao, and K. Dutta. Modeling Virtualized Applications using Machine Learning Techniques. In *VEE '12*.

[19] M. Kuperberg, K. Krogmann, and R. Reussner. Performance Prediction for Black-Box Components using Reengineered Parametric Behaviour Models. In *CBSE '08*.

[20] A. S. Lebrecht, N. J. Dingle, and W. J. Knottenbelt. Analytical and Simulation Modelling of Zoned RAID Systems. *The Computer Journal*, 54:691–707, 2011.

[21] E. K. Lee and R. H. Katz. An analytic performance model of disk arrays. *SIGMETRICS Perform. Eval. Rev.*, 21(1), 1993.

[22] X. Ling, S. Ibrahim, H. Jin, S. Wu, and T. Songqiao. Exploiting Spatial Locality to Improve Disk Efficiency in Virtualized Environments. In *MASCOTS '13*.

[23] Q. Noorshams, D. Bruhn, A. Busch, S. Kounev, and R. Reussner. The Storage Performance Analyzer (SPA), 2014. `http://sdqweb.ipd.kit.edu/wiki/SPA`.

[24] Q. Noorshams, D. Bruhn, S. Kounev, and R. Reussner. Predictive Performance Modeling of Virtualized Storage Systems using Optimized Statistical Regression Techniques. In *ICPE '13*.

[25] Q. Noorshams, A. Busch, A. Rentschler, D. Bruhn, S. Kounev, P. Tůma, and R. Reussner. Automated Modeling of I/O Performance and Interference Effects in Virtualized Storage Systems. In *DCPerf '14*.

[26] Q. Noorshams, S. Kounev, and R. Reussner. Experimental Evaluation of the Performance-Influencing Factors of Virtualized Storage Systems. In *EPEW '12*.

[27] Q. Noorshams, K. Rostami, S. Kounev, P. Tůma, and R. Reussner. I/O Performance Modeling of Virtualized Storage Systems. In *MASCOTS '13*.

[28] S. Oliveira, K. Furlinger, and D. Kranzlmuller. Trends in Computation, Communication and Storage and the Consequences for Data-intensive Science. In *HPCC-ICESS'12*.

[29] J. G. Shanthikumar and R. G. Sargent. A unifying view of hybrid simulation/analytic models and modeling. *Operations Research*, 31(6):pp. 1030–1052, 1983.

[30] E. Varki and S. X. Wang. A performance model of disk array storage systems. In *Int. CMG Conference*, 2000.

[31] M. Wang, K. Au, A. Ailamaki, A. Brockwell, C. Faloutsos, and G. R. Ganger. Storage Device Performance Prediction with CART Models. In *MASCOTS '04*.

[32] A. Wert, J. Happe, and D. Westermann. Integrating Software Performance Curves with the Palladio Component Model. In *ICPE '12*.

[33] M. Woodside, D. Petriu, and K. Siddiqui. Performance-related completions for software specifications. In *ICSE '02*.

[34] M. Woodside, V. Vetland, M. Courtois, and S. Bayarov. Resource Function Capture for Performance Aspects of Software Components and Sub-systems. In R. Dumke, C. Rautenstrauch, A. Scholz, and A. Schmietendorf, editors, *Performance Engineering, State of the Art and Current Trends*. 2001.

Enabling Collaborative Testing Across Shared Software Components

Teng Long[1], Ilchul Yoon[2], Atif Memon[1], Adam Porter[1] and Alan Sussman[1]
[1]UMIACS and Department of Computer Science, University of Maryland
College Park, MD, USA
[2]Department of Computer Science, State University of New York
Incheon, South Korea
[1]{tlong,atif,aporter,als}@cs.umd.edu, [2]icyoon@sunykorea.ac.kr

ABSTRACT

Components of numerous software systems are developed and maintained by multiple stakeholders, and there is significant overlap and synergy in the process of testing systems with shared components. We have designed and implemented infrastructure that enables testers of different components to share their test results and artifacts so that they can collaborate in testing shared components. We also develop an example collaborative testing process that leverages our infrastructure to save effort for regression testing of systems with shared components. Our empirical study of this process shows that collaborative testing of component-based software systems can not only save significant effort by sharing test results and artifacts, but also improve test quality of individual components by utilizing synergistic data shared among component testers.

Keywords

component-based software, software integration

1. INTRODUCTION

The "old school" of testing advocated "test everything on your own." This go-it-alone approach worked well for developer groups and organizations that implemented much of their software from scratch in isolation. Over the years, the practice of software development has changed; so too must the practices of testing. Rarely does a developer group or an organization develop software from scratch anymore. Instead, they rely on third-party software components, knitting them together to implement their system. However, when it comes to testing these systems, they continue to follow the old school approach.

In this paper, we posit that the paradigm shift to component-based software development has created numerous opportunities for sharing test effort. We exploit these opportunities in the context of an important software maintenance activity, *regression testing*. Our supposition is based on two characteristics of component-based systems that we discuss via the example shown in Figure 1 (we will discuss the nomenclature of the figure later in Section 2).

The first characteristic is that components in component-based software systems have relationships between them, i.e., some components *use* or depend on other components. Consider the top-level right-most shaded node in Figure 1 labeled *Subversion*, which relies on other "lower-level" components, in this case *APR-util*, *SQLite*, *APR*, *Neon*, and *BerkeleyDB*, also shown as nodes connected directly to *subversion* via "$*$" connector boxes. **Opportunity 1: Exploit such provider-user relationships to share test effort and improve local tests of individual components.** More specifically, the higher-level components can inform the lower-level components about the context in which they are being used. Similarly, the lower-level components can inform the higher-level components relying on them of the latest code changes and the latest test efforts and results. This bi-directional flow of information can help to avoid overlaps in testing and also enables testers to focus their efforts where it can do the most good.

The second characteristic is that many components are commonly used by multiple software systems. Consider, for example, that the *Apache Portable Runtime* library (*APR*) in Figure 1 is used not only by *Subversion*, but also by other systems, such as *Serf* and *Flood*. Building and testing any of these systems necessarily involves building *APR*, and therefore exercises *APR* as well. **Opportunity 2: Distribute test effort and share results for common components to lower cost and improve test quality.** More specifically, when two or more component-based systems use at least one common component, developers of the systems can collaborate in the testing of the common component, for instance, when pooling their test cases would help to achieve some desired coverage criteria. Alternatively, in the case where two or more low-level components implement the same interface and functionality, and could therefore be used interchangeably by the same high-level component [15], tests run on one low-level component could be extracted and applied to the other low-level components.

Our preliminary results [13] showed that testing top-level components such as *Subversion* induced line coverage of the lower-level components beyond that achieved by running the lower-level components' own unit tests. This implies that top-level components exercise lower-level components

CBSE'14, June 30–July 4, 2014, Marcq-en-Baroeul, France.
Copyright 2014 ACM 978-1-4503-2577-6/14/06 ...$15.00.
http://dx.doi.org/10.1145/2602458.2602468.

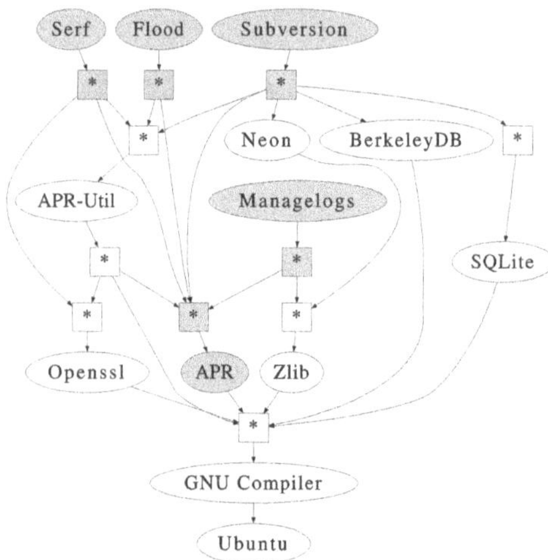

Figure 1: Systems with Common Components

in ways not anticipated by the testers of the lower-level components. We also saw substantial overlap in the line coverage induced by each individual top-level component. Moreover, despite the overlaps, each top-level component induced line coverage that was not induced by the other top-level component. Such observations and prior results suggest that **collaborative testing** of multiple component-based systems may provide benefits beyond that offered by individual component unit testing and beyond that provided by testing any single top-level component. Eliminating redundancies in testing across different components may also reduce costs without affecting test quality.

While the collaborative test processes we envision appear to be promising, current test approaches cannot support them effectively. First, there lacks a formal model of test environment of component-based systems that testers can use to describe their test environment, nor can testers exchange their test environment efficiently, which prevents testers from sharing and reusing their test results at all. Second, current tools lack methods and algorithms to guide the sharing of test efforts between provider-user pairs, or to improve local tests of components from test data generated by others. Third, collaborative testing will require efficient and easy-to-use mechanisms to automatically coordinate the test processes of different systems, for sharing and reusing test artifacts, and for comparing and merging independent test results.

As a step towards realizing collaborative test processes, this paper proposed a formal model for a test environment, presents a test process and support infrastructure for collaborative testing, and empirically explores the two opportunities we described within this process. The results of our study demonstrate that i) significant time spent on build and functional testing of component-based systems can be saved by reusing test results and leveraging pre-built environments shared from testing of other components; ii) hidden faults in both ends of the user-provider pair are discovered by analyzing shared test results, and local unit tests of provider components can be created from tests of user components; and iii) the size of the regression test suite to run can be greatly reduced when changes to a subcomponent only affect parts of the test suite.

The contributions of our work include:

1. Formal modeling of the environment that a component is to be built and tested in.
2. A web-service based data sharing repository that enables effective and efficient test data and environment sharing between testers.
3. Initial implementation of a collaborative test process over the support infrastructure we developed.
4. Empirical evaluation of the test processes over multiple component collections to explore the benefits of collaboration.

The rest of the paper is organized as follows. Section 2 presents background that forms the foundation for our current work. Section 3 describes our test data sharing infrastructure, and Section 4 explores the processes of collaborative testing using our infrastructure. We present experimental results of evaluating the benefits of such collaboration in Section 5, address related work in Section 6 and conclude in Section 7.

2. BACKGROUND

We now discuss our prior work on modeling component-based systems and efficiently build testing them across a large configuration space. We also summarize an initial empirical study that demonstrated the potential utility of collaborative testing.

2.1 Modeling Component-based Systems

We model component-based systems using a representation [21] that contains two parts: a directed acyclic graph called the *Component Dependency Graph(CDG)* and a set of *Annotations*. As shown in Figure 2, each node in the CDG represents a unique component, and inter-component dependencies are specified by connecting nodes with **AND(*)** or **XOR(+)** relationships. For example, in Figure 2 component A "depends on" component D and either one of B or C. Here dependency means that one component requires another component at build-time, runtime, or both. *Annotations* in this example include version identifiers for components, and constraints between different components and component versions, written in first-order logic.

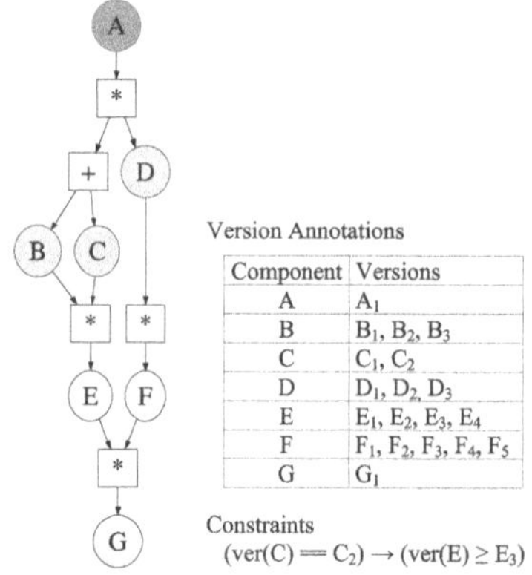

Component	Versions
A	A_1
B	B_1, B_2, B_3
C	C_1, C_2
D	D_1, D_2, D_3
E	E_1, E_2, E_3, E_4
F	F_1, F_2, F_3, F_4, F_5
G	G_1

Figure 2: An Example System Model

When different systems share components, the relationships between these systems can be represented by an integrated CDG with overlapping regions. In the example

CDG in Figure 1, the top-level components (*Serf, Flood, Subversion* and *Managelogs*) depend on different provider components. There are overlaps between the set of required provider components, and the *APR* component is required by all top-level user components. This suggests that each top-level component developer will use his/her test resources to build the components contained in the shared sub-graph, starting from the *APR* node to the bottom node, and then test the behavior of those components to ensure a functioning build of the top-level component. In this scenario, those developers are likely spending redundant test effort that could be eliminated or advantageously redirected if all of these components were able to share their test data and artifacts.

2.2 Automatic Build Testing Framework

One concern that component developers have is to make sure that their components build correctly. This activity has typically been performed by manually checking component builds on a handful of popular user configurations. However, this is time-consuming, error-prone and limited in scope given the large number of combinations of platforms, components, and versions in which components might be built. In our prior work we designed a process and infrastructure called *Rachet* [21] to address this challenge.

Rachet tackles this problem in several ways. First, it reduces the number of configurations that must be tested, by applying a sampling strategy called *DD-coverage*. With this coverage criteria, all *direct dependencies* between components are covered at least once by sampled configurations. Second, *Rachet* generates a schedule to test sampled configurations, and then performs build testing in parallel using multiple nodes in a cluster or cloud computing environment. Each configuration is tested in a virtual machine (VM) environment hosted on a physical node. *Rachet* further reduces test effort by reusing virtual machine environments that instantiate partially-constructed configurations. Because building components is time-consuming and because multiple configurations often share common partial configurations, *Rachet* builds systems inside virtual machines and then reuses the virtual machines across different physical cluster nodes.

Even though *Rachet* utilizes distributed resources to conduct build testing, its test plans and associated test tasks are still managed and assigned in a centralized way locally by the tester. In other words, this infrastructure is currently designed to be used to test a single software system at a time. In addition, the virtual machine instances that *Rachet* currently employs are quite large, which will be problematic in a collaborative test situation. In order to share build test results and cached virtual machine artifacts among multiple testers, an external collaborative framework is needed, a set of APIs must be provided to *Rachet* to interact with that framework, and *Rachet*'s virtual machine artifacts must be compact for efficient sharing.

2.3 Overlap and Synergy in Collaborative Functional Testing

In our previous work [13], we studied overlap and synergy achievable from sharing test data across multiple component-based systems. More specifically, we measured the line and branch coverage of a shared component and the spectrum of parameter values used to invoke methods of this component, both for executing the test suite of the shared component and for executing multiple test suites of components that depend on the shared component. Our analysis of the resulting test data showed that test cases designed and run by the higher-level components were individually less comprehensive than those of the shared component, but in some cases exhibited new behaviors or used unexpected test inputs not covered by the shared component's test cases. The results suggest that test data collected by component developers can be complementary. However, sharing such test data is only possible when the data to be shared is well-defined, and when a systematic way to share that data is available to component developers. In the remainder of this paper, we describe ways to define the desired test data and also discuss techniques and tools for sharing the data across multiple component-based systems.

3. DATA SHARING INFRASTRUCTURE

To support collaborative testing we have developed an automated data sharing infrastructure that provides support for creating test environments, for storing and sharing test data, and for efficiently managing and sharing test environments.

3.1 Environment Model

Collaborative activities work when individual efforts can be leveraged in a common group activity or used as artifacts. For instance, configuration management systems allow individual developers to modify source code independently and then merge their changes into a common version. In order to leverage independent testing of component-based software systems, it is necessary to control the test *environment* in which a component is built and tested so that test results will be comparable across different test efforts. Thus, we provide a notional definition of a test *environment* as follows:

Definition 1: An *environment* for a component to be built and tested in includes all **pre-built component** instances in a system, the **tools** to be used to build the new component, all **source code** needed by the build, and **all other controllable factors** known to determine the result of the component's build process and the correct functioning of the component.

Controlling the environment in this way maximizes the likelihood that two testers building and testing the same component can share and combine their test results. That is, any differences in results should be attributable only to differences in how the components were tested, not in where or by whom they were tested. To gain this control, we attempt to standardize the test *environment* used by each tester. We have identified several factors that may affect the build and functional testing of components, and therefore must be captured by the test *environment*. These factors include:

- Hardware parameters (processor type, memory system, etc.)
- Operating system (architecture, kernel version, system core libraries, etc.)
- Build environment (compiler, compiler options, extra instrumentation inserted, etc.)
- Provider components (versions, their build settings and installation options, etc.)

Component	
name	sqlite3-1.3.5
compiler-used	gcc-4.4.6
build-flag	with-apr="/usr/local/apr"
build-flag	CFLAGS="-O0"
Component	
name	apr-1.4.5
compiler-used	gcc-4.4.6
build-flag	CFLAGS="-O0"
Component	
name	bdb-6.0.20
status	system-prebuilt
Component	
name	neon-1.6
status	system-prebuilt
Compiler	
name	gcc-4.4.6
status	system-prebuilt
OS	
name	Ubunt-12.04
archtecture	X86_64
Hardware	
cpu_cores	2
cpu_frequency	2.8GHz
RAM	1024M

Figure 3: Simplified example environment description for a VM

Of course, this approach is not bullet-proof. We cannot, for example, account for **unknowable or random** factors, such as transient hardware faults in one tester's computing device, which surely affect how a component behaves.

A *Virtual Machine*(VM) with an installed operating system and pre-built core components is an intuitive way to encapsulate an environment, and sharing of pre-built environments then becomes sharing of VM images. In order to describe the *environment* encapsulated in a VM image, we associate an XML description file with each shared VM image. The description contains information about the hardware parameters of the VM, operating system information, pre-built components and their build options, and other information that may affect the test results. When accessing the repository, test tools search for VM images instantiating specific *environments* based on the description files.

The information contained in a typical description file is shown in Figure 3. In this *environment* there are six components, including the operating system and a compiler. Two of them (*SQLite* and *APR*) are built from source code, and their build flags are shown. The other components, except the operating system, are pre-built binary packages provided in the Ubuntu 12.04 software distribution. Three hardware parameters are also included in this *environment.*

3.2 Data Sharing Repository via Web Services

To facilitate data sharing among testers and their tools, we have designed and implemented a web-service based data repository called *Conch.* The structure of *Conch* is shown in Figure 4. The repository uses a MySQL database as the back-end, and provides a set of data query and management methods wrapped as web services. The web services are described using WSDL [19] and can be accessed via standard SOAP [17] protocols. Using the protocols, testers or other third-parties can easily write tools and plug-ins that allow their automated test systems to access the repository, to analyze repository data, and to coordinate their test processes with those of other testers.

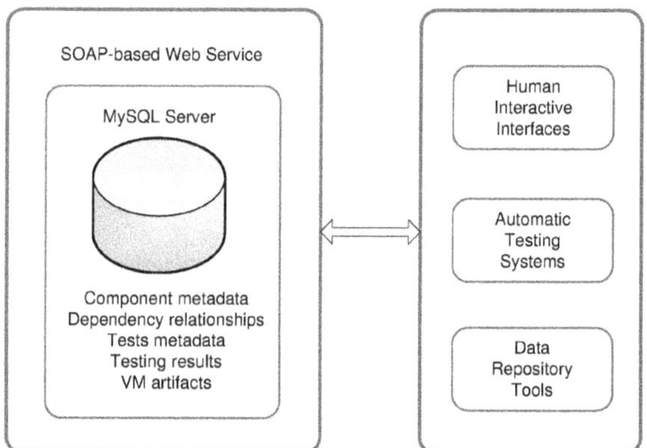

Figure 4: The Conch Data Sharing Repository

Conch Request	
command_name	getCDG
command_session	001
component	SQLite

Figure 5: Request for *SQLite* dependency data

Depending on the type of collaborations between automated test tools, the data types shared in the repository can be different, thus the data schema for the repository can be customized too. For the sharing scenarios we consider in this paper, the data stored in *Conch* has five major types: (1) component metadata, (2) component dependency relationships, (3) test case metadata, (4) test results, and (5) virtual machine artifacts (environments).

When an automated test tool submits test results to the repository, a unique test data record is created for each result. Each test data record is associated with the *environment* in which the test activity was performed, and with an outcome or test result, such as test success or failure. Other information regarding the tests (e.g., the raw output of running such tests) can also be stored in the repository for other test tools to interpret. Testers and their tools can retrieve existing test results by searching through the *environment* descriptions of existing test results. Users can submit or query test data by sending and receiving messages to the repository via Web service interfaces.

A response from the *Conch* server may contain links to access data, instead of actual data. For example, a response may contain a URL that points to a virtual machine image file. The information shown in Figure 5 and Figure 6 illustrates the content of example message exchanges for a user's request for dependency information for the *SQLite* component. The dependency data is returned back to the requester as a string in the server's response. The data request is initiated by a user-side automatic testing system that provides *Conch* with the information in Figure 5, and the response is in the form of an XML file that contains the information in Figure 6.

3.3 Sharing Virtual Machines with Environment Differencing

Before building and testing a component, an *environment* that contains all its provider components must be prepared.

Conch Response	
command_name	getCDG
command_session	001
component	SQLite
CDG	[+ gcc pgcc intelc] ncurses tclsh

Figure 6: *Conch* response with *SQLite* dependency data

Such an *environment* can be encapsulated as a virtual machine (VM) image. However, unlike test results or component metadata, the size of a VM image can be very large[1]. Moreover, the sheer number of potential pre-built *environments* that could be shared among testers and their tools makes it difficult to store the VM images in the repository, and limited network bandwidth makes it challenging to transfer the environments over a wide-area network, if they are cached locally at individual testers' sites.

To overcome these challenges, we have developed a tool called *Ede* (**E**nvironment **D**ifferencing **E**ngine) that supports automated *Environment Differencing*. Whenever a new *environment* containing a pristine operating system is prepared, *Ede* creates a signature file for the whole operating system, which includes the state of all existing files. After building and installing additional components in this environment, *Ede* inspects all files and records all changes as a *delta* file. A *delta* file records file deletions and creations, permission changes, etc., and can be automatically applied to another VM that has the **same** pristine operating system installed. More details about our work on *Ede* are described in [14].

With help from *Ede*, test tools that target at systems with common components can share their pre-built *environments* by storing only *delta* files, along with *environment* descriptions, in the repository. Sharing pre-built *environments* will save time for provisioning a new environment, compared to building an environment from scratch. Consider the components illustrated in the CDG of Figure 2. Testing components D and F requires an environment where G is installed. However, a tool that tests component D can save test effort and focus on testing only component D if the tool can reuse a pre-built *environment* in which F is already built. In this case, the tool testing component F will first retrieve from the *Conch* repository a *delta* file for a VM that has G installed. The tool can then restore the full VM locally by invoking *Ede*, build and test F in the VM, then create yet another *delta* file that contains both G and F in the corresponding VM. This *delta* file and its description file are then stored into the repository for later sharing.

Environment Differencing requires individual test tools to locally store root virtual machine images, which encapsulate environments with a pristine operating system installed on a specific hardware platform. Whenever a tester needs a pre-built environment that is available in the *Conch* repository, the test tool can download the desired *delta* file and automatically apply it using *Ede*. Storing delta files and transferring them over a wide area network is not too expensive. The size of a typical *delta* file is small (often between 10MB and 100MB), and the patch process does not take long (usually less than one minute). This enables the repository to store many environments created during test sessions. This approach is more cost effective than our previous approach of transferring whole virtual machine images [21]. In Section 5, we describe the performance benefits from sharing pre-built environments.

[1]The size of a virtual machine image that encapsulates just a Linux operating system can easily be greater than 1 GB, even with only a minimal installation.

4. COLLABORATIVE TEST PROCESS

In this section we describe a collaborative test process for component-based software systems implemented upon the data sharing infrastructure we introduced in Section 3. In this process, pre-built *environments* and functional test results are shared by different testers, as well as coverage information for provider components induced from testing their user components. Testers of different components collaborate by accessing test data stored in the *Conch* repository and do not need to directly communicate with each other in order to benefit from the collaboration.

4.1 Testing Procedures for Component-based Systems

A component-based system can be considered as a top-level user component plus all the provider components where it depends. Thus whenever a provider component is updated, part or the whole of this component-based system needs to be rebuilt and tested to validate whether the newer version of the modified component still works in the system correctly. Three steps should be followed for the system validation activity at such changes:

1. Build and run functional tests of the new version of the provider component in desired environments.
2. Build and run functional tests of all other provider components dependent upon the modified component directly or indirectly.
3. Build and run functional tests of the user component.

Consider, for instance, the *Subversion* system in Figure 7. If a new *APR* version is available for the *Subversion* system, *Subversion* testers will first need to build the *APR* version on system configurations they support, and then run the test suite of *APR* to make sure it functions correctly on the configurations. Afterward, all other components that directly and indirectly depend on the *APR* component need to be rebuilt and functionally tested with the new *APR* version. If everything works correctly, testers will build and test *Subversion* last to make sure it behaves correctly.

Since components are developed and maintained by separate groups, when *APR* is updated, testers of not only *Subversion* but also all other components in Figure 7 that use *APR* may be interested in the effects of the update. Thus part of the building and testing work conducted by testers of *Subversion* may also be repeated by testers of other components. In addition, as seen in Figure 1, *APR* is used by multiple other systems as well. It is very likely that testers of those components repeat the identical build and test activity that may have already been conducted by other testers. Hence the opportunity to reuse existing pre-built *environments* and functional test results generated by other testers does exist if component-based systems are tested collaboratively. In Section 4.2, we will discuss how to use *Conch* to share pre-built environments and functional test results and save test time by avoiding redundant work.

A component typically accesses only a subset of code regions in its provider components when its test cases are executed. In the example of testing *Subversion* upon a newer version of *APR*, testers would run the whole test suite of *Subversion*. However by sharing code coverage data, a regression test tool for *Subversion* can keep the mapping between individual test cases and the code regions in *APR* covered by executing the test cases. Thus the regression test tools for *Subversion* and for all other user components of *APR* should be notified when the *APR* code is changed. Then, the tools can execute only the selected test cases relevant to the change by analyzing the coverage data, and this will contribute to reducing the test workload further.

If a regression test fails for a revision of a provider component when it used to pass with a previous revision of the provider component, it means either the newer version introduces a new fault that makes the test fail, or there are problems in the failed test itself. In the former case, testers may provide feedback to the developer of the provider component, so that the fault can get fixed in later revisions. In the latter case, the testers can fix the erroneous test. In either case, the developers and testers benefit from receiving regression test results promptly.

4.2 Collaborative Build and Functional Testing

In a component-based software system, build testing of a specific component can be considered as a part of its functional testing, because the component can be functionally tested only if it can be successfully built in an *environment* (or *configuration*). In addition, all the components on which it depends (i.e., its provider components) must also be built and function correctly.

Assuming that an operating system deployed on a hardware platform provides hardware independence, one of the primary interests of component testers will be to test the correct build and behavior of their components on a large set of heterogeneous *environments*. Note that an *environment* on which a component is to be built and tested is an instantiated subgraph of a CDG – i.e., all its provider components are assigned a specific version already.

Given a component and an *environment*, a test tool can use Algorithm 1 to provision the *environment*. The algorithm is designed to reuse existing pre-built *environments* in *Conch* as much as possible to rapidly provision the environment before building and testing the component.

In this algorithm, ***C*** is the subject component to be tested, ***Env*** is the desired *environment* in which ***C*** will be tested, and ***Repo*** is the data sharing repository that stores pre-built *environments* as VM artifacts. If the desired *environment* ***Env*** is already instantiated (by this tester or a different tester) and available in the repository, the test tool can simply retrieve the VM that encapsulates the environment, and build and test ***C*** (line 1–3). Otherwise, the tool retrieves all provider components and their versions contained in ***Env*** (line 5), finds a pre-built *environment* from ***Repo*** that requires the minimum extra build effort to create the desired *environment* (line 6). The tool can then build the extra components required by ***C*** (line 7–8), and finally build and test ***C*** (line 9).

The procedure *findBestMatch()* can be implemented using either historical records or heuristics to find a partial *environment* that a test tool can modify to meet its requirements. In the special case that no pre-built *environment* is found and ***subEnv*** is empty, the test tool will have to start from scratch – i.e., all components contained in the *environment* ***Env*** (except the operating system) must be built and tested.

Algorithm 1: RapidTest(*C*, *Env*, *Repo*)

```
Data:
C: subject component
Env: target environment
Repo: repository that includes pre-built environments
1  if Env exists in Repo then
2  |  Retrieve Env from Repo;
3  |  Build and test component C in Env;
4  else
5  |  P ← getProviders(Env);
6  |  subEnv ← findBestMatch(Env, Repo);
7  |  P' ← getProviders(subEnv);
8  |  Build and test P – P' on subEnv;
9  |  Build and test component C on subEnv;
10 end
```

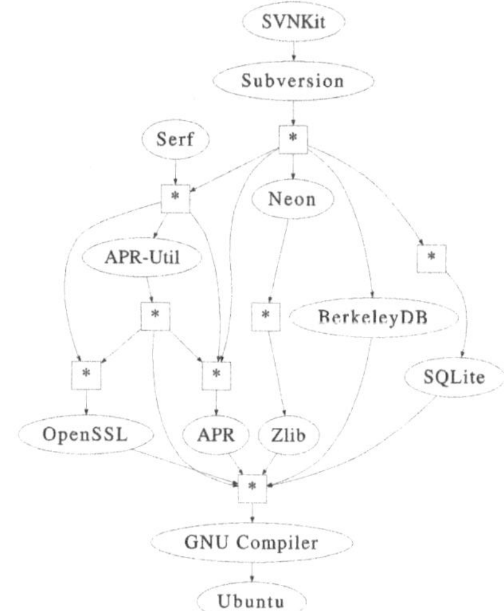

Figure 7: Subject Systems on Ubuntu for Collaborative Testing

5. EXPERIMENTAL RESULTS

In this section we evaluate the benefits of applying the collaborative test process described in the previous sections to test components with overlapping regions in their CDGs, compared to testing the components in isolation.

In Section 5.1, we evaluate the benefits of the collaborative test process with two sets of top-level components that share provider components, as shown in Figure 7 and 8. While replaying the version release history of the components contained in the CDGs over a period of time, we conducted compatibility testing using *Rachet* [21] at each component version release, and measured the building and testing time that could be saved when different sharing strategies supported by *Conch* are applied.

In Section 5.2 we demonstrate the value of collaborative regression testing in the development process. We ran the regression tests of user components at new provider com-

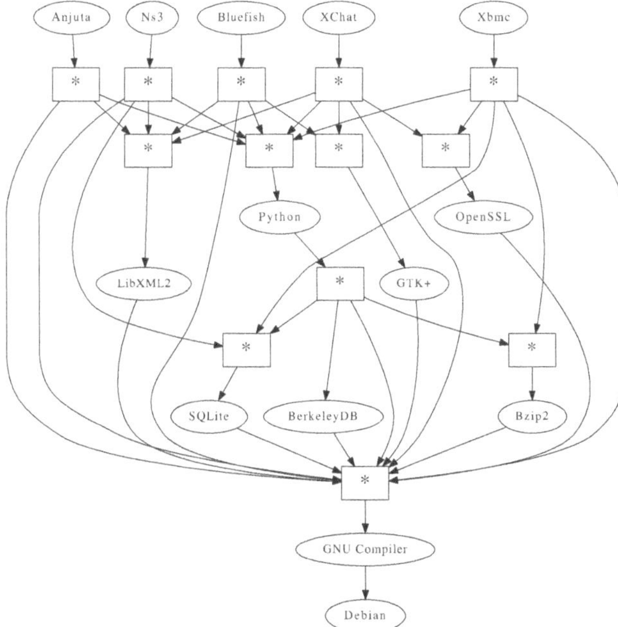

Figure 8: Subject Systems on Debian for Collaborative Testing

Table 1: Subject Components

Component	Description
SVNKit	Open Source pure Java Subversion library
Subversion	version control system
Neon	HTTP and WebDAV client library
Zlib	compression library
BerkeleyDB	library for embedded database
APR	supporting library for Apache projects
APR-util	support library for *APR*
SQLite	SQL database engine
Openssl	open source toolkit for SSL/TLS
Gcc	GNU C compiler
Ubuntu	Ubuntu Operating System
Anjuta	GNOME Integrated Development Environment
Ns3	discrete-event network simulator
Bluefish	editor targeted towards programmers
XChat	multi-platform IRC chat program
XBMC	open Source Home Theater Software
Python	object-oriented programming language
LibXML2	XML C parser and toolkit of Gnome
GTK+	toolkit for creating GUI on multiple platforms
Bzip2	high-quality, open-source data compressor
Debian	operating system

ponent version releases, and found bugs in both provider components and user components' test cases. That is, developers can discover problems caused by the changes in their provider components quickly after the problems are introduced, as well as can find previously undiscovered problems in users' tests. We also have developed a tool that uses regression test data stored in *Conch*, selects test cases that have to be rerun when a provider component changes, and then triggers the regression tests with the selected test cases. The tool uses *Jenkins* [11] as the automatic regression test client. We evaluate the collaborative test process with the version release history of the components in Figure 7 over one year.

5.1 Collaborative Build and Functional Testing

In order to evaluate the benefits of collaborative testing, we first recorded the wall-clock time required for building and testing the components in the CDGs shown in Figure 7 and 8 on an environment (i.e., a VM image) sandboxed with VirtualBox. For each component, the recorded time includes only the time required for building and testing the component itself, assuming that all its provider components are already built in the environment. Only default test suites supplied with the component source code are executed and the running times are measured. In Figure 7, the top-level components are *SVNKit* and *Serf*. *SVNKit* is an Open Source Pure Java Subversion Library, and *Serf* is a high performance C-based HTTP client library. In Figure 8, the top-level components are *Anjuta*, *Ns3*, *Bluefish*, *Xchat* and *XBMC*, all of which are user applications in the Debian Linux system. The CDGs also show the components on which the top-level components depend (i.e. their provider components). Brief descriptions of the components are given in Table 1.

For each component, we replayed all its version releases over one year (between 8/3/2012 and 8/3/2013). At each version release, we test the compatibility of the version with existing versions of its provider components, and also trigger compatibility testing of all its user components. For the existing provider component versions, we used the versions released between 8/3/2011 and 8/3/2012. The direct-dependency coverage (DD coverage [21]) criterion is used to compute configurations newly introduced because of the version releases. The recorded times required for building and testing components are then used to simulate the total test time using the following three sharing strategies. We used the time cost of successfully building each component and executing all its tests for the simulation, so that the simulated time cost reflects the worst scenario.

Strategy 1: No sharing. This is the baseline strategy, which is the most time-consuming, because testing any component in a CDG requires both building and functionally testing of *all* its provider components (i.e., all the components in the CDG sub-graph rooted at the component being tested), before building and testing the target component. In this strategy, there is no test data sharing between testers at all. **Strategy 2: Sharing test results only.** Test tools share functional test results for each component tested. Provider components still must be built, but their functional tests will not be run if the results are available in the *Conch* repository. That is, the tools execute functional tests of the provider components only when there has been no previous test session that contains the test result. **Strategy 3: Sharing test results and pre-built environments.** Test tools share not only functional test results, but also pre-built *environments*. In this strategy, a test tool can select a pre-built *environment* in the format of a Virtual Machine delta file from the repository, and only build and test the components missing from the retrieved environment.

For Strategies 2 and 3, when a new component version is released, we expect that different developer groups will start testing their components with the new version at different times. Then the group that starts its testing later will have more opportunities to reuse test results and artifacts pro-

Table 2: Configuration Preparation Cost(hours) and Benefits(%)

Comp.	Strategy 1	Strategy 2	Strategy 3	Save-2	Save-3
SVNKit	2194.4	1863.9	1050.0	15.1	52.2
Serf	12.1	9.6	5.0	20.7	58.7
total	2206.5	1873.5	1055.0	15.1	52.2
Anjuta	2311.1	2036.1	327.8	11.9	85.8
Ns3	2330.6	2055.6	438.9	11.8	81.2
Bluefish	2500.0	2219.4	591.7	11.2	76.3
XChat	2972.2	2700.0	1072.2	9.2	63.9
XBMC	2344.4	2080.6	411.1	11.3	82.5
total	12458.3	11091.7	2841.7	11.0	77.2

duced during the test sessions performed by other groups. For a fair evaluation, we have the repository notify the different developer groups in random orders for Strategies 2 and 3, and we repeated each simulation 100 times and computed the average times. We assume a bandwidth of 4MB/s for transferring VM delta files over the Internet.

To better understand the amount of work that can be saved by sharing test information via the *Conch* repository, we added up the times required for building and testing newly introduced configurations at each version release of the provider components of the top-level components. We call the sum the **total configuration preparation cost**. Table 2 shows the total configuration preparation cost for each top-level component shown in Figures 7 and 8.

In Table 2, the first column shows the names of the top-level components in both CDGs, the next three columns present the average configuration preparation cost (in hours) for each component in our simulation for the different strategies, and the last two columns show the configuration preparation cost saving in percent for Strategy 2 and 3, respectively, compared to Strategy 1. The table shows that sharing functional test results alone reduces the preparation cost by 10% to 15% for most components. We see huge time savings when testers start sharing test results and pre-built test environments. The total cost was reduced by 52.2% for testing *SVNKit* and *Serf*, and by 77.2% for testing the top-level Debian components. These results clearly show that testers can significantly reduce their testing workload by sharing their test results and pre-built environments with other testers though *Conch*.

5.2 Continuous Collaborative Regression Test

In this section we replay the continuous development of three provider components, *APR*, *Openssl* and *SQLite*, contained in the combined CDG in Figure 7 using their version release history between 8/3/2012 and 8/3/2013. Our tool monitors the code repositories of the three components. Whenever there are source code changes in any of the components, the tool (1) identifies all user components whose regression tests could be affected, (2) automatically builds the affected user component(s) as well as all other required components relying on the new provider components, and (3) reruns the selected regression tests whose result could be affected by the code changes. Pre-built environments are reused to reduce the component build times.

We considered two user components, *Subversion* and *Serf*, from Figure 7. The components rely on the three provider components described above and also have regression test suites with reasonable sizes. The regression tests were performed for fixed versions of the user components (*Subversion 1.8.1* and *Serf 1.3.0*) on the days when there were code changes for at least one of the provider components.

During the one year time period, there were 80 *APR* revisions, 148 *Openssl* revisions and 221 *SQLite* revisions. From all those revisions, we had to build and test *Subversion* 241 times and *Serf* 148 times. We now demonstrate four observed benefits from running regression tests of user components when a provider component changes.

Detecting faults in provider components: Regression tests for user components can reveal faults in provider components, and the fault-revealing test cases of the user components can be carved as new test cases of provider components. Techniques have been developed that potentially enable automatic carving of such test cases [8].

One example we found was that the test case `wc-queries-test` of the *Subversion* failed when it was built with *SQLite* revision `d7a25cc797`. The error occurred because a series of valid queries to *SQLite* returned errors.

We manually carved out the queries and created a unit test for *SQLite* and confirmed that the test case exposes the identical fault. Even though the fault was fixed in later releases, this example suggests that our automatic regression test process can be used to detect faults relevant to provider components quickly, and also to produce new test cases that can detect the faults, thereby contributing to enriching the test suites of the provider components. Moreover, developers of other user components can also benefit from finding such faults because they are informed of the faults and can avoid spending time to find out the causes.

Discovering problems in accessing provider components: When changes in a provider component cause problems in building and testing user components, the collaborative test process can be used to notify the provider component developers of the problems, so that they can use the information to pinpoint the origins of the problems.

In our experiment we found that multiple test cases of *Serf* and *Subversion* failed with the error message: `Couldn't perform atomic initialization`, when they were built and tested with some revisions of *SQLite* – for example, revision `62225b4a4c`). A simple Web search result revealed that many *SQLite* users experienced the same problem. The problem occurred when the *SQLite* library was linked in an obsolete way that was no longer supported. If *SQLite* developers had been informed of the problem quickly, they could have fixed the problem, or at least could have updated user documentation so that users could be made aware of the problem.

Discovering faults in user components or in their test suites: When user components are built with a new provider component version, running regression tests for the user components can often reveal faults in their own test cases.

For example, *Subversion*'s test cases written in Python encountered unhandled exception errors, when *Subversion* was built and tested with specific *SQLite* revisions (e.g. revision `6f21d9cbf5`). This example suggests that the quality of user components and their test suites can be improved if and when our collaborative test process is adopted by provider and user component developers.

Reducing the number of regression tests to run: We also observed that maintaining a mapping between the individual test cases of user components and code coverage

Table 3: Regression Test Selection Results

	Subversion		Serf	
	APR	SQLite	APR	Openssl
Rerun-Required Updates	29%	72%	9%	55%
Reduced Test Suite Size	80%	59%	98%	30%

information for provider components can greatly reduce the number of test cases that must be rerun when a provider component changes. When the changed part of the provider component is not previously covered by a regression test, we don't necessarily need to rerun that test. With help from *Conch*, it is feasible for user component testers to share their unit-test coverage data for provider components, and such a mapping can be easily obtained by analyzing the coverage data.

Our experimental result is presented in Table 3. The "Rerun-Required Updates" row in the table shows the percentage of provider component revisions that caused rerunning the regression tests of its user components, compared to the number of revisions that contain source code changes. As we can see, when the source code of *APR* changes, the regression tests are triggered in only 29% of such changes. The "Reduced Test Suite Size" row shows the average percentage of selected regression tests that must be rerun, compared to the total number of regression tests. In the 29% cases when changes in *APR* triggered regression tests of *Subversion*, we don't need to return the whole regression test suite of *Subversion* either. On average, only 80% of the regression tests need to be rerun. From Table 3, this trend also exists for other evaluated components. It is evident that testers can save considerable effort on regression testing if they share the coverage information across components and properly use them for regression test selection.

6. RELATED WORK

Our work focuses on component-based software systems that share components. The components are developed by different groups; i.e., there is no central control over the component development. We maintain the information in a shared repository but in a distributed manner.

Researchers have emphasized the importance of tool support for collaboration between distributed teams [3, 4]. Bird et al. [4] reported that globally distributed software development within a single company may not perform worse (in terms of failures) than centralized development. In [3], Begel et al. developed tools based on news-feeds to support developer teams collaborating with each other, because the teams should be aware of what other teams are doing for managing risk in their development.

Software researchers have also begun to examine the notion of self-organizing software development teams. For example, as social media gain increasing popularity, researchers have started to discuss the impact that social media has on software development, especially on enabling new ways for software teams to form and work together [2].

Distributed continuous quality assurance (QA) environments such as Dart [16] and CruiseControl [6] are systems for conducting continuous integration testing, which involves executing build and test processes whenever check-ins to a repository occur. Users install agents that automatically check out software from a repository, build the software, execute functional tests, and submit the results to the server. However, the underlying QA process is hard-wired in Dart and CruiseControl and therefore other QA processes or implementations of the build and test process are not easily supported.

Web services are another example of component-based systems where each service may be developed by different developer groups. Bai [1] developed a tool to test Web services by coordinating distributed test agents for conducting decomposed testing tasks, and Dallmeier [7] developed a tool to test the compatibility of Web applications on multiple browsers by identifying all functionally different states of the services at runtime. However, these approaches are designed for a single developer group. Our approach is focused on reducing the overall test cost and on deriving synergy from the collaborative testing across developer groups.

An important aspect of our approach is the shared repository of software and test artifacts. As software gets larger and more complex, many researchers have focused on analyzing and leveraging software repositories. For example, Zeller [18] has worked on analyzing repositories to better understand the reason systems fail. Xie has also studied the wide variety of information largely unused even though the information is stored in software repositories [10]. Researchers have also developed new data mining techniques that make use of software repositories to extract error patterns [12] or to understand correct API usage from code examples [20]. Such techniques could be used to analyze test results that are accumulated in the *Conch* repository.

Our work is broadly related to prioritization and selection of regression test cases. Elbaum et al. introduced different techniques for test case prioritization [9], with some of them based on code coverage information, which is similar to our regression test case selection technique. But those techniques are not for component-based software systems developed independently by multiple developer groups. Berries et al. have developed a tool called ProxiScientia [5] that helps to visualize the dependencies among collaborating software development teams, but that system does not provide functionality to facilitate collaboration.

7. CONCLUSIONS

Our work is based on the hypothesis that when two or more component-based systems use one or more common components, testers of such systems can lower test cost and improve test effectiveness by sharing test artifacts.

As a step toward making collaboration between testers of such systems easier, we have developed infrastructure and support tools, which include a model to specify test *environments*, a sharing repository for exchanging test data, an initial implementation of a collaborative test process, and an empirical evaluation of the process. The model for test *environments* can accurately capture the hardware, system and inter-component relationships for build and test processes, so that test data shared between testers are compatible. The data sharing repository enables test tools to easily store or retrieve test data by querying the repository. We have shown that the example test process not only saves significant time for build and functional testing, but also improves regression test effectiveness.

The ultimate goal of our research is to enable collaborative testing across different testers and their test tools to avoid redundant work, as well as to improve test quality for all component-based software developers. In order to accomplish the goal, we will continue to develop collaborative test processes that utilize the repository for testing component-based systems, and extend the repository to accommodate those processes. We will also design algorithms and methods to conduct deeper analyses of test data stored in the repository. Modifying existing frameworks such as *Rachet* to use the infrastructure is also a short-term goal for better coordination of test tasks across multiple components.

Acknowledgments

This work was partially supported by the US National Science Foundation (ATM-0120950, CCF-0811284, CNS-1205 501, CNS-0855055), the National Research Foundation of Korea (NRF-2013010695), and the MSIP of Korea (NIPA-2013-H0203-13-1001).

8. REFERENCES

[1] X. Bai, G. Dai, D. Xu, and W.-T. Tsai. A multi-agent based framework for collaborative testing on web services. In *Proceedings of the The 4th IEEE Workshop on Software Technologies for Future Embedded and Ubiquitous Systems, and the 2nd International Workshop on Collaborative Computing, Integration, and Assurance*, pages 205–210, 2006.

[2] A. Begel, R. DeLine, and T. Zimmermann. Social media for software engineering. In *Proceedings of the FSE/SDP Workshop on the Future of Software Engineering Research*, November 2010.

[3] A. Begel and T. Zimmermann. Keeping up with your friends: Function foo, library bar.dll, and work item 24. In *Proc. of the First Workshop on Web2.0 for Software Engineering*, May 2010.

[4] C. Bird, N. Nagappan, P. Devanbu, H. Gall, and B. Murphy. Does distributed development affect software quality? an empirical case study of windows vista. In *Proceedings of the 31st International Conference on Software Engineering (ICSE)*, pages 518–528, 2009.

[5] A. Borici, K. Blincoe, A. Schroter, G. Valetto, and D. Damian. Proxiscientia: Toward real-time visualization of task and developer dependencies in collaborating software development teams. In *Proceedings of the 5th International Workshop on Cooperative and Human Aspects of Software Engineering*, pages 5–11, June 2012.

[6] Cruisecontrol. *cruisecontrol.sourceforge.net/*, 2010.

[7] V. Dallmeier, M. Burger, T. Orth, and A. Zeller. Webmate: A tool for testing web 2.0 applications. In *Proceedings of the Workshop on JavaScript Tools*, pages 11–15, 2012.

[8] S. Elbaum, H. N. Chin, M. Dwyer, and M. Jorde. Carving and replaying differential unit test cases from system test cases. *IEEE Transactions on Software Engineering*, 35(1):29–45, Jan 2009.

[9] S. Elbaum, A. G. Malishevsky, and G. Rothermel. Test case prioritization: A family of empirical studies. *IEEE Transactions on Software Engineering*, 28(2):159–182, Feb. 2002.

[10] A. E. Hassan and T. Xie. Software intelligence: the future of mining software engineering data. In *Proceedings of the FSE/SDP workshop on Future of software engineering research*, pages 161–166, 2010.

[11] Jenkins: an extendable open source continuous integration server. *http://jenkins-ci.org/*, 2013.

[12] B. Livshits and T. Zimmermann. *Mining Software Specifications: Methodologies and Applications*, chapter DynaMine: Finding Usage Patterns and Their Violations by Mining Software Repositories. CRC Press, May 2011.

[13] T. Long, I. Yoon, A. Porter, A. Sussman, and A. Memon. Overlap and synergy in testing software components across loosely-coupled communities. In *Proceedings of the 23rd IEEE International Symposium on Software Reliability Engineering (ISSRE)*, pages 171–180, November 2012.

[14] T. Long, I. Yoon, A. Sussman, A. Porter, and A. Memon. Scalable system environment caching and sharing for distributed virtual machines. In *Proceedings of the IPDPS Workshop on High-Performance Grid and Cloud Computing*, 2014.

[15] L. Mariani, S. Papagiannakis, and M. Pezze. Compatibility and regression testing of COTS-component-based software. In *Proceedings of the 29th International Conference on Software Engineering*, pages 85–95, 2007.

[16] A. M. Memon, I. Banerjee, N. Hashmi, and A. Nagarajan. DART: A framework for regression testing nightly/daily builds of GUI applications. In *Proceedings of the 19th International Conference on Software Maintenance*, pages 410–419, Sep. 2003.

[17] SOAP Ver. 1.2. *www.w3.org/TR/soap12-part1/*, 2007.

[18] W. Tichy. An interview with Prof. Andreas Zeller: Mining your way to software reliability. *Ubiquity*, 2010.

[19] Web Services Description Language (WSDL) 1.1. *www.w3.org/TR/wsdl*, 2001.

[20] T. Xie and J. Pei. MAPO: Mining API usages from open source repositories. In *Proceedings of the 3rd International Workshop on Mining Software Repositories*, pages 54–57, May 2006.

[21] I.-C. Yoon, A. Sussman, A. Memon, and A. Porter. Effective and scalable software compatibility testing. In *Proceedings of the ACM/SIGSOFT International Symposium on Software Testing and Analysis*, pages 63–74, 2008.

Using a Model to Generate Reconfiguration Plans at Runtime

Marco Eugênio Madeira Di Beneditto
Universidade Federal do Rio de Janeiro
Centro de Análises de Sistemas Navais
Rio de Janeiro - RJ, Brazil
dibene@cos.ufrj.br,
dibeneditto@casnav.mar.mil.br

Cláudia Maria Lima Werner
Universidade Federal do Rio de Janeiro
Cidade Universitária 21945-970
Rio de Janeiro - RJ, Brazil
werner@cos.ufrj.br

ABSTRACT

In this paper, we present a reconfiguration procedure that generates a software reconfiguration sequence at runtime, being architecturally-consistent in respect to the components, compositions and connections provided by the underlying component model. Besides this, the procedure also regards the state for reconfiguration. Our procedure is based on the concept of Automated Planning, an Artificial Intelligence area. Given two architectural configurations, the procedure generates, if existing, a sequence of reconfigurations actions that will drive the architectural evolution among the configurations. The procedure can also generate an initialization sequence when the current configuration is empty, and the goal configuration represents a functional application. We generated the procedure for the FRACTAL component model and applied it to a publish/subscribe communications software developed in FRACTAL, as a proof of concept.

Categories and Subject Descriptors

D.2.11 [**Software Engineering**]: Software Architectures; I.2.8 [**Artificial Intelligence**]: Problem Solving, Control Methods, and Search—*Plan execution, formation, and generation*

Keywords

dynamic update; reconfiguration; software architecture; planning; component-based software

1. INTRODUCTION

In some systems, to deploy a new version or adjust a small part of it, stopping all application, evolving and then starting it all over again, may result in an unacceptable system downtime. In these cases, the ability to be dynamically reconfigured, where only the parts that must be adjusted are affected, rather than the whole application, becomes a desired attribute. In component-based software systems, applications are built as compositions of components and the connections between them. A *compositional reconfiguration* means the addition or removal of a set of components, the modification of its connections and compositions. Among the dynamic reconfiguration techniques, like those mentioned in [15], the reflection capability provided by some component models is a good answer to the previous kind of reconfiguration.

CBSE'14, June 30–July 4, 2014, Marcq-en-Baroeul, France.

ACM 978-1-4503-2577-6/14/06 ...$15.00.
http://dx.doi.org/10.1145/2602458.2602466.

The traditional software reconfiguration at runtime executes a previously defined and fixed sequence of reconfiguration actions, like the set of rules encoded in an expert system. This solution cannot treat unexpected situations and opportunities because the reconfiguration was previously established and fixed by the rules set. So, if the generation of the sequence of reconfiguration actions, called *reconfiguration plan*, is made at runtime, instead of in a fixed way, the context can be considered, and new solutions may be generated.

For this, the long established accepted reconfiguration plan is derived from the protocol described in [8], where this protocol first defines a region of *quiescence* - a component safe-state for reconfiguration - altering the component life cycle and then describing the partial order relation between the reconfiguration actions. Current hierarchical and reflective component models, like FRACTAL [3] and iPOJO [6], have order relations similar to those described in the protocol, but both models have new concepts like composition between components, optional and mandatory interfaces, different constraints for the reconfiguration actions and a different view about the safe-state for reconfiguration. The consequence of this is the extension of invariants and reconfiguration actions and the evolution of the order relations, which directly impact the component lifecycle - a component start or stop.

A current challenge is to generate a reconfiguration plan consistent with the protocol derived from the component model used to develop the application. For this, a *reconfiguration model*, which represents the underlying component model and its reflective capabilities, will be used to build this plan.

In this paper, we propose a solution to generate a reconfiguration plan automatically. Briefly, given a target software architecture, or goal, the solution employs a *reconfiguration model* to generate the plan, which execution at runtime over the software will adjust it in order to achieve the goal. The target software architecture can be obtained by an engineer or an autonomic manager. With a description of the software architecture, they introspects the architecture and can decide the target.

The contributions of our work are the following. We build a reconfiguration model, derived from the reflective component model, to be used in the generation of the reconfiguration plan at runtime. The generation employs the Automated Planning technique from Artificial Intelligence that allows the division of the problem into decoupled parts. We show that this model generates correct plans in relation to the component model used, that is, every plan respects the relations orders and the architectural invariants from the reflective component model used. The remainder of this paper is divided as follows: Section 2 describes the theory behind the problem, Section 3 shows the proposed solution, and in Section 4 the results of a case study are presented. Section 5 discusses related works and finally, Section 6 presents the conclusions and some future work.

2. BACKGROUND

In this section, we discuss the theory of the problem and proposed solution. First, we describe the problem of this research and give a graphically interpretation of a software reconfiguration and respective formalization. Then, the automated planning technique is introduced and the employment to generate the reconfiguration plan is present. Finally, the reflective component model used is described and its constraints are shown.

2.1 A Model for Dynamic Reconfiguration

A reconfiguration can be viewed as a transition between two vertices (or nodes) in a graph, where each vertex, or state, represent a software configuration and each edge, or transition, represent a reconfiguration action between the two states that an edge joins. Figure 1 illustrates it, where: $Config_{ini}$ is the initial software configuration or initial state, $Config_{goal}$ is the target software configuration or goal state, and C_2 and C_3 are intermediate software configurations. The previous mentioned *reconfiguration plan* is the sequence of actions between $Config_{ini}$ and $Config_{goal}$ and, in Figure 1, this plan is $\pi = \langle action_a, action_b, action_c \rangle$.

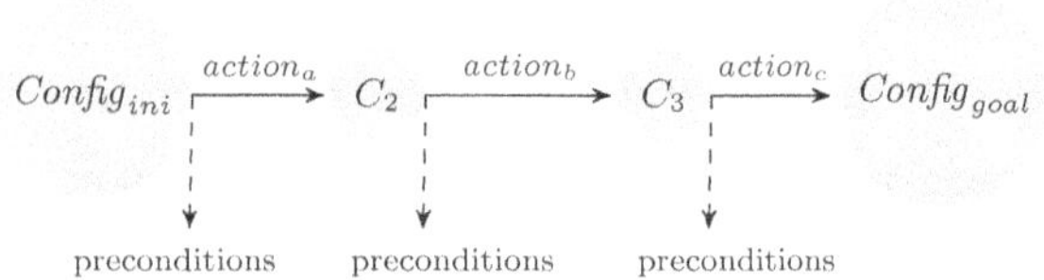

Figure 1: A reconfiguration as a State Transition System (STS).

In this STS, a state is described by a set of propositions, informing which propositions currently hold in this state. Given a goal software configuration, the problem of this research is to generate the plan π at runtime and consistent with the component model and dynamic reconfiguration aspects. As previously mentioned, this generation will be based on a *reconfiguration model*, that will be formalized as a state model. It can be specified as follows: let $L = \{p_1, p_2, \ldots, p_n\}$ be a finite set of proposition symbols. A basic state model is $\Sigma = (S, A, \gamma)$, where:

- $S = \{s_1, s_2, \ldots\}$ a finite and discrete state space, where $S \subseteq 2^L$, i.e., a state s is a subset of L.
- $A = \{a_1, a_2, \ldots\}$ a finite set of actions.
- $\gamma : S \times A \rightarrow 2^S$ a transition function.

Note that Σ captures the fact that the effects of certain actions in the environment may be non-deterministic. The transition function γ is generically specified through a set of operators, where an operator is the triple $o = (name(o), precond(o), effects(o))$, where:

- $name(o)$: the name of the operator in the form $n(x_1, \ldots, x_n)$, where n is a symbol called operator, and $x_1, ..., x_n$ are all of the variable symbols that are used inside o. In addition, n is unique, that is, there are no two operators with the same operator symbol.
- $precond(o)$: are the preconditions that must be true to make an action applicable at some state s.
- $effects(o)$: these effects are defined with two subsets: $effects^+(o)$, the propositions to be added to state s, and $effects^-(o)$, the propositions to be removed from s.

An *action* is any ground instance of an operator o, which is instantiated in action a in state s. This instantiation can occur if this action is applicable in s, that is, if $precond(a) \subseteq s$, and the result of applying a to state s is the state $\gamma(s, a) = s \cup effects(a)$.

2.2 Automated Planning

The solution to the problem of reconfiguration plan generation, proposed in this paper, is inspired by the intelligent agent view, described in [14], in which an agent decides the next action to be executed. In our case, given two architectures or states in the previous transition system, the decision is to find a path between them, if it exists. In other words, decide the sequence of reconfiguration actions that transforms the current architecture in the goal one.

According to [7], three approaches have been used to select the next action: i) the *programming-based approach*, where the agent controller is given by a human in a program, that is, in a prescriptive way; ii) the *learning-based approach*, where the controller is induced from experience via a learning algorithm, and iii) the *model-based approach*, where the controller is derived from a model of the problem, in a declarative way. Learning methods have the greatest promise and potential, but tend to be limited in scope since the agent needs to learn the model before being able to generate the plan. The programming-based approach puts all the burden on the developer and, in general, it is supported by an expert system and a respective rule-set. In this kind of agent, the developer should know: 1) the goal, i.e., the new software configuration to be obtained; and 2) how to obtain it. The first question is implicit in the rule set and only the second question is explicitly described by the rules. On the other hand, the model-based approach requires a model of the actions, sensors, and goals, and faces the computational problem of solving the model, that is, a solution to the model is the reconfiguration plan which represents a path between the initial and goal states, that in our case, represents the two given architectures.

With the model described in Section 2.1, a procedure chooses an action in a state if, in this state, the preconditions of the action are true and the postconditions contribute to reach the goal state. This procedure is called Automated Planning, its purpose is to find the appropriate sequence of actions to reach some goal when starting from some given state [12]. Given the previous basic state model Σ, also called *Planning Domain*, the planning problem is $\mathcal{P} = (\Sigma, s_0, S_g)$, where: $s_0 \in S$ is the initial state; and $S_g \in S$ is a set of goal states.

The solution of this problem is a *plan* $\pi = \langle a_1, a_2, \ldots, a_k \rangle$, a sequence of applicable actions that corresponds to a state transition sequence $\langle s_0, s_1, \ldots, s_k \rangle$ such that, $s_1 \in \gamma(s_0, a_1)$, $s_2 \in \gamma(s_1, a_2)$, ..., $s_k \in \gamma(s_{k-1}, a_k)$ and $s_k \in S_g$.

A planning algorithm usually has to consider many possible actions and this makes the search space very big, with exponential computational complexity. To cope with this complexity, instead of looking at every possible action, some planners employ a specific *Planning Domain* description, such as the Hierarchical Task Network (HTN) Planners. In this work, this kind of planner is used because it is a domain independent planner, the semantic of the planning domain is very rich, widely used, shows good performance on different domains and there are correct algorithms implementations. The last feature is important for reliability and means that the plan is correct in relation to the planning domain.

The hierarchical planning provides a particular form of domain representation, controlling the search and reducing the search space. In this kind of planner, the domain is a set of *methods*. A *method* is a prescription of how to solve a small problem by means of a sub task decomposition and it is applicable if preconditions are true. In order to clarify what a method is, in Figure 2, the method **destroySingle** is described in the JSHOP2[1] domain language notation.

```
(:method (destroySingle)

  _0destroySingle
  ; PRECONDITIONS single component to be removed
  (
    (component ?comp single)
    (active ?comp)
    (not (to-active ?comp))
  )
  ; TASK DECOMPOSITION
  (
    (removeBindingTo ?comp)
    (removeBindingFrom ?comp)
    (removeSingleFromAllParent ?comp)
    (!removeComponent ?comp)
    (destroySingle)
  )

  _9destroySingle
  ; PRECONDITIONS no more components to be removed
  (
    (not (
      (component ?comp single)
      (active ?comp)
      (not (to-active ?comp))
    ))
  )
  ; TASK DECOMPOSITION
  ()
); END (:method (destroySingle)
```

Figure 2: The textual description of method **destroySingle**.

A method represents a means of decomposing a task, expanding it into a set of subtasks (smaller tasks). A task can be composite or primitive. A composite task can be expanded by another method of task decomposition and a primitive task is represented by an operator planning. The simplest version of a method has three parts: the task for which the method is to be used, the precondition that the current state must satisfy for the method to be applicable, and the subtasks that need to be accomplished in order to achieve that task. A method can be decomposed in different ways and the planner chooses an applicable decomposition for the method, that is, it checks if the precondition for a decomposition holds in the current state and then chooses it.

At Figure 2, the **destroySingle** method decomposes the removal of a single component (non-composite component) in two decomposition ways. In the first way, named **_0destroySingle**, the precondition means a component present in the $Config_{ini}$ and not present in $Config_{goal}$ - represented by logical expression: **(component ?comp single)** $\wedge$ **(active ?comp)** $\wedge$ **(not (to-active ?comp))**. So, the component represented by the variable `?comp` should be removed. In the second way, named **_9destroySingle**, the precondition means that there not is a single component to be removed. If the precondition is true, thus the removal is done and no decompositions should be made.

The decomposition named **_0destroySingle** contains five subtasks:

1. `(removeBindingTo ?comp)`
2. `(removeBindingFrom ?comp)`
3. `(removeSingleFromAllParent ?comp)`
4. `(!removeComponent ?comp)`
5. `(destroySingle)`

During the task decomposition, the planner algorithm follows the sub task order. First, task **1** removes all binding directed to component `?comp`. Then, task **2** removes all binding from `?comp`. After all bindings removed, in task **3** the component is removed from all parents, that is, the composite components which contain it. This is a precondition for FRACTAL: a component can only be removed from a parent if it does not have more bindings in the parent space, that is, bindings between siblings or the parent. After that, task **4** removes the component from the application and this task is a primitive one, representing the planning operator **(!removeComponent ?comp)** - the preceding **!** means a planning operator. Finally, the method is recursively called in task **5**. If no more components need to be removed, the precondition **_0destroySingle** is false and the planner tries the next decomposition. Now, the task decomposition **_9destroySingle** is used - the precondition is true - and there is no subtasks else to be done.

The network of tasks is being built during the task decomposition. The method decompositions are being made until a primitive task - a planning operator - is reached, and an example of this network can be viewed in Figure 6, where the **removeBindFrom** method is decomposed by the subtask **removeBindFromComp**. A plan is a sequence of primitive tasks instantiated into actions and, if a plan is found, the sequence of actions is the list of leaf nodes in the network, read from left to right.

In [13], the authors demonstrate that HTN planner SHOP2, that uses the same algorithm as the JSHOP2 used in this work, is sound and complete. However, the sound proof means that the planning algorithm should work correctly if the domain description is correct [11]. Then, in order to generate plans that are sound, we have to demonstrate the soundness of the planning domain, which will be shown in Section 3.1.

[1]http://sourceforge.net/projects/shop/files/JSHOP2/

2.3 Reflective Component Model

We choose FRACTAL [3] for the reflective component model used to build an application that will be dynamically reconfigured. FRACTAL is an off-the-shelf hierarchical component model and provides a mature base to build adaptable systems. It is based on the classic concepts of: component (a runtime entity), interface (an interaction point between components) and binding (a communication channel between component interfaces). A component consists of a membrane which can show and control its encapsulated content. In that component model, the reflective capability is obtained by a set of controllers, which provides the reflection API. Besides this, there is a Domain Specific Language (DSL) called FScript/FPath [4], which simplifies the use of this reflection API. In this work, we are concerned with compositional reconfiguration and, for this task, the FRACTAL controllers used and respective FScript primitive actions are:

1. *Binding Controller*: to manage the binding between component client interfaces to server interfaces and intra composite interfaces. FScript: `unbind`, `bind` and `cbind`. The action `cbind` is used to bind a required collection/multiple interface;
2. *Content Controller*: to manage the composition between the components. FScript: `add` and `remove`; and
3. *Lifecycle Controller*: start and stop the execution of the component. FScript: `start` and `stop`.

In order to execute a reconfiguration action, its preconditions or transition constraints must be respected. In FRACTAL, every component must be inside a component that is its parent, and a component cannot be a parent or child of itself. In relation to a bind, there is the concept of *Local Binding*, which can be of three types and are illustrated in Figure 3: a) bind **1**, **3** and **5** are binds between sibling components, where both have the same direct parent; b) bind **2** is a bind between a child required interface with a parent provided internal interface; and c) bind **4** is a bind between a parent required internal interface with a child provided interface.

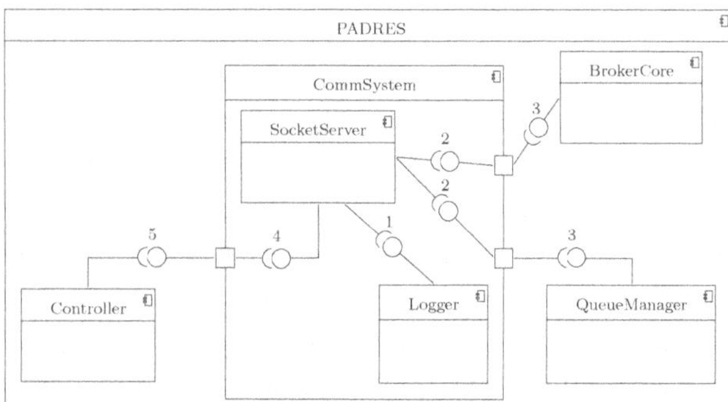

Figure 3: An excerpt showing the possible binding between a required (client) interface and a provided (server) interface in FRACTAL.

During bind and unbind actions the lifecycle control is also necessary to reach a correct state where preconditions are true. Again, in Figure 3, for bind **1** the component `SocketServer` must be stopped before the bind removal. For **2**, `SocketServer` must be stopped before the bind removal. For **4**, `CommSystem` should be stopped before the bind removal. The interfaces from a composite component are, in fact, served by interfaces from its subcomponents that are promoted to the composite ones. The internal interface is like an *inverse* interface in the sense that a composite provided interface will generate an internal required interface, and a composite required interface will generate an internal provided interface. For the parent removal actions, if `SocketServer` should be removed, the parent `CommSystem` should be stopped before it.

In order to define a safe state to perform a reconfiguration, we must describe the execution and the communication model. In FRACTAL, the execution is thread based, where the component activity corresponds to a thread's execution and, in the case of JULIA implementation, a Java thread. In relation to the communication between components, they are Java method synchronous invocations. A started FRACTAL component can:

a. accept operations invocation from other components that require a provided interface from it;
b. serve operations invocation from a component through its required interface to another component;
c. start operations invocation from its required interfaces;
d. execute internal activity without external invocation.

In order to reach a quiescent state, a component in FRACTAL has to be stopped using the *Lifecycle Controller* interface. A stopped component in JULIA using the default Lifecycle Controller does not receive new requisitions but can emit new ones, that is, a component does not receive previous **a** and **b**, but can emit **c** and **d**. To solve **c** and **d**, stopping all activities, the developer should put his own Java code, and the API provides an easy way to do that employing a specific Java annotation. In the JULIA implementation, the solution to stop the component activity is a counter of the number of threads that call a provided (or server in FRACTAL nomenclature) interface. Every time a provided interface is called, a counter is incremented and when that thread ends, the counter is decremented. When there is a request to stop a component, it will enter an intermediate state called **stopping**. In this state, the component does not receive new invocations like items **a** and **b**. However, if it is serving an invocation, that is, a thread is active, it waits until all threads are finished - thread counter value is 0 - and then goes to state **stopped**.

In relation to the bind removal action, some observations must be done. In order to avoid a livelock, first remove *binding to* a component and then remove *binding from* that component. The livelock comes from the execution and the communication model. In Figure 3, suppose that component `SocketServer` should be removed and an invocation in bind **5** generates a invocation in bind **1**, i.e., a thread path across **5**, **4** and **1**. If `SocketServer` is stopped before `CommSystem`, a new thread issued by `Controller` will be intercepted and put in a wait state. When there is a request to stop `CommSystem`, in order to remove bind **4**, the previous thread is alive but will not be finished because `SocketServer` is stopped. So, `CommSystem` will remain in state **stopping**, never reaching the desired state **stopped**, avoiding the execution of unbind action.

3. A PLAN GENERATION FOR FRACTAL

In this Section, the planning domain $\Sigma = (S, A, \gamma)$, mentioned in Section 2.1, and planning problem $\mathcal{P} = (\Sigma, s_0, S_g)$ for FRACTAL will be discussed. The first set to be described is L, the finite set of proposition symbols used to describe a state in S. In Table 1 the set L is enumerated and the last four propositions in this table: g_1, g_2, g_3 and g_4, are only used in the goal state. The values preceded by *?* represent variables that should be replaced to typify a real subject. For example, the propositions described in Figure 4, represent an initial configuration s_0 and part of it is illustrated in Figure 3. These propositions are also used to describe a task decomposition precondition.

```
(component padres composite)
(component commsystem composite)
(component socketserver single)
(component brokercore single)
(interface iface1 BrokerIface)
(interface iface2 BrokerIface)
(interface iface3 BrokerIface)
(reference socketserver iface1 collection)
(reference commsystem iface2 collection)
(service brokercore iface3)
(active padres)
(active commsystem)
(active socketserver)
(active brokercore)
(contain padres commsystem)
(contain padres brokercore)
(contain commsystem socketserver)
(bindinternal socketserver iface1 commsystem iface2)
(bind commsystem iface2 brokercore iface3)
(started padres)
(started commsystem)
(started socketserver)
(started brokercore)
```

Figure 4: A textual description of an initial configuration s_0.

Some observations are necessary for the comprehension of problem description. A composite component configuration is fully described, that is, in the initial configuration, all components and sub components are declared and if a composite is not present in the goal configuration, the respective subcomponents will not be either. One assumption made in the reconfigurations for this work is that the highest composite component in the hierarchy, named **PADRES** in Figure 4, is never removed, that is, if it exists in the initial configuration, it will be present in the goal. The propositions g_1, g_2, g_3 and g_4 describe the components to be created, the bind - external and internal - to be made and the parent relationship. The component name is unique, identifying a component and although it is possible to alter it in FRACTAL, we do not consider the component name modification. Other non-modifiable aspects are an interface type - represented by p_5 - and the component interface required and provided - represented by p_6 and p_7, respectively. The proposition p_9 represents a bind between a subcomponent and its parent. We chose this proposition because in FRACTAL there is a very clear separation between external and internal interfaces.

As mentioned in Section 2.2, for an HTN planner, the planning domain consists of a set of methods, operators and axioms. We did not identify any axiom for the domain, so we will describe the methods and operators. We used 15 methods and the first method to be called is `configure`, illustrated in Figure 5.

```
(:method (configure)
    ; PRECONDITIONS
    (
      (component ?comp ?var1)
    )
    ; SUBTASKS
    (
      (destroySingle)
      (removeBindingFrom)
      (reconfigureComposite)
      (reconfigureSingle)
      (reconfigureBindFrom)
      (destroyComposite)
      (startComponent)
    )
)
```

Figure 5: The textual description of method `configure`.

This method provides a way of configuring an application if any component `?comp` exists. For the planner, the subtasks decomposition is totally ordered, for example, **destroySingle** is called before `removeBindingFrom`. However, in relation to the component model to be reconfigured, some tasks can be reordered, as will be shown later. The semantic of each subtask decomposition is:

1. `destroySingle`: all single (non-composite) components not present in goal configuration should be removed from the application;
2. `removeBindingFrom`: the bindings from required interfaces in the initial configuration but not present in the goal should be removed. The removals also include a bind between components that exists in the goal configuration but under a different parent.
3. `reconfigureComposite`: create the composite components that are new - only existing in the goal - and reconfigure those that will remain - existing in the initial and in the goal configuration. This reconfiguration means the positioning of these composites in the hierarchy.
4. `reconfigureSingle`: create the single components that are new - only existing in the goal - and reconfigure those that will remain - existing in the initial and in the goal configuration. It also solves the positioning of these components in the hierarchy. A single component should be in its parent before the binding of its interfaces. The creation of composite components is treated in sub task `reconfigureComposite`, so a father already exists.
5. `reconfigureBindFrom`: the bindings in the goal configuration are made. This task should be executed after the component is positioned in the component hierarchy.
6. `destroyComposite`: the composite components not present in the goal configuration should be removed.
7. `startComponent`: after the components are inside its parent and the binds are fulfilled, the stopped components should be started, in order to leave the application running.

For each task above, there is a decomposition by another sub task set. Due to space limitations, the complete set of decompositions will not be treated here. Some issues from the component model should be explained in order to clar-

Nr	Proposition	Semantic
p_1	(component ?name composite)	The *composite* component called *?name*.
p_2	(component ?name single)	The *non-composite* component called *?name*.
p_3	(active ?name)	The component called *?name* is created.
p_4	(contain ?parent ?child)	The *?child* component is a sub-component of *composite* component *?parent*.
p_5	(interface ?name ?typeIface)	An interface name and type. The interface *?name* has type *?typeIface*.
p_6	(reference ?name ?iface single)	A required interface. The component *?name* requires the interface named *?iface* which is *single*. The word *multiple* is used instead of *single* if the cardinality of the required interface is a collection.
p_7	(service ?name ?iface)	A provided interface. The component *?name* provides the interface named *?iface*.
p_8	(bind ?compReq ?ifaceReq ?compProv ?ifaceProv)	A bind between interfaces. The component *?compReq* required interface *?ifaceReq* is bound with the component *?compProv* provided interface *?ifaceProv*. The name of interfaces can be different because the interface type is represented by the proposition *interface*.
p_9	(bindInternal ?compReq ?ifaceReq ?compProv ?ifaceProv)	A bind between a parent composite component interface and its subcomponents interfaces. The component *?compReq* required interface *?ifaceReq* is internally bound with the parent component *?compProv* provided interface *?ifaceProv*.
p_{10}	(started ?name)	The component called *?name* is *started*, that is, in a state where it can emit or accept operations invocations.
g_1	(to-active ?name)	The component called *?name* should be created in the goal state.
g_2	(to-contain ?parent ?child)	The component called *?parent* should be the parent of component *?child* in the goal state.
g_3	(to-bind ?compReq ?ifaceReq ?compProv ?ifaceProv)	The *?ifaceReq* interface required by *?compReq* should be bound with *?ifaceProv* interface provided by *?compProv* in the goal state.
g_4	(to-bindInternal ?compReq ?ifaceReq ?compProv ?ifaceProvr)	The *?ifaceReq* interface required by *?compReq* subcomponent should be bound to the *?ifaceProvr* interface provided by its parent *?compProv* in the goal state.

Table 1: The propositions used in Σ for FRACTAL.

ify this order. A composite removal implies its sub components removal in case are not inside another composite, once FRACTAL supports component sharing across a different parent component. So, a component that exists in the initial and the goal configuration should be reconfigured before any composite removal and this implies that the method `destroyComposite` should be after a component has been reconfigured by `reconfigureComposite` and `reconfigureSingle`. An external bind among component interface can be made if both components are in the same parent. If a bind pre-exists and a component is moved to a different parent, this bind should be removed first, in order to avoid a non-local binding (remember Section 2.3 for local binding concept).

For example, using the notation from Section 2.1, the operator *!bind* that performs a binding between two components, using their interfaces, can be described as:

1. **name**: *!bind(x, i_c, y, i_s)* - binds the components x and y with interface i_c from x and interface i_s from y;
2. **precond**: *(component x ?varX), (component y ?varY), (active x), (active y), (reference x i_c ?card), (service y i_s), (interface i_c typeIface), (interface i_s typeIface), (not bind(x, i_c, y, i_s)) (stopped x)* - x and y are components, both are active, y provides the interface i_s, x requires the interface i_c, interfaces i_c and i_s have the same type, the interfaces are not bound and x is stopped;
3. **effects**: *effects*$^+$ = *bind(x, i_c, y, i_s)*; *effects*$^-$ = $\varnothing$ - the components x and y are bound.

The *?varX* and *?varY*, in propositions *(component x ?varX)* and *(component y ?varY)*, represent the type of component, which can be composite or single. The *?card* in *(reference x i_c ?card)* represents the cardinality of the required interface. The operators that are instantiated in actions are described below using the planner domain syntax, where the name of

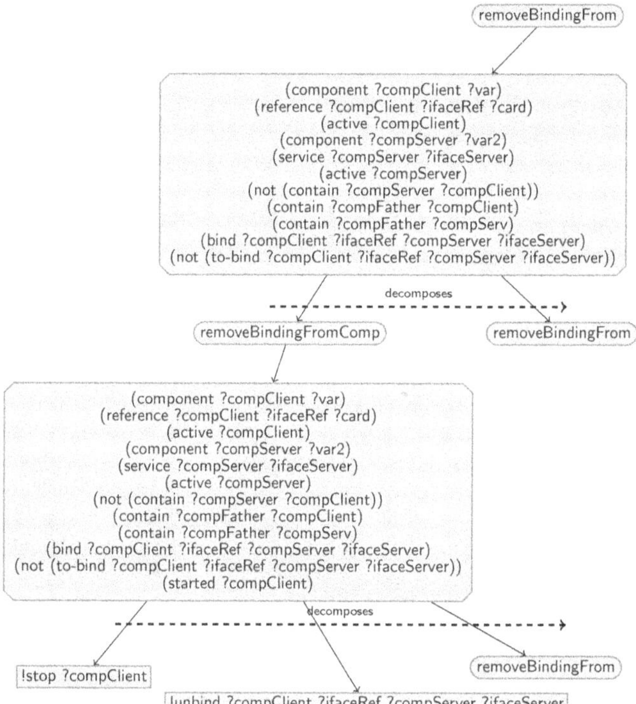

Figure 6: A graphical representation of the method `removeBindingFrom`.

the operator is preceded by an exclamation mark (!) and each variable symbol is preceded by a question mark (?).

o_1 - (`!instantiateNew ?comp`): Creates a new component present in the goal configuration.

o_2 - (`!bindNew ?compRef ?ifaceRef ?compSrv ?ifaceSrv`): Binding between interfaces. It takes as arguments the client and server interfaces to connect, in this order. The client component must be inside a composite, stopped and the interface is not bound. The client component must be stopped, the interface must not be bound if single and both components are siblings.

o_3 - (`!bindInternalNew ?cmpRef ?ifRef ?cmpSrv ?ifSrv`): Binding between internal interfaces. It takes as arguments the client and server interfaces to connect, in this order, where one of them is an internal interface from the parent composite component. The client component must be stopped and the interface is not bound if it is single (not a collection).

o_4 - (`!unbind ?cmpRef ?ifRef ?cmpSrv ?ifSrv`): Unbind between interface. It takes only the client interface to disconnect as an argument. The client component must be stopped. It takes as arguments the client and server interfaces to disconnect, in this order. The client component must be stopped.

o_5 - (`!unbindInternal ?cmpRef ?ifRef ?cmpSrv ?ifSrv`): Unbind an internal interface. It takes as arguments the client and server interfaces to disconnect, in this order. The client component must be stopped.

o_6 - (`!addChildNew ?compFather ?comp`): Adds the component denoted by `?comp` into the composite denoted by `?compFather`. For FRACTAL, a component cannot be parent of itself or be parent and child of the same component.

o_7 - (`!removeChild ?compFather ?comp`): Removes the component denoted by `?comp` from the composite denoted by `?compFather`. The parent component must be stopped.

o_8 - (`!start ?comp`): Component life-cycle control. It takes a single argument denoting the component to start.

o_9 - (`!stop ?comp`): Component life-cycle control. It takes a single argument denoting the component to stop.

For each operator above, with suffix `New`, there is an operator with suffix `Old`, that is, `!instantiateOld`, `!bindOld`, `!bindInternalOld` and `!addChildOld`. An operator with suffix `Old` is to be removed from the final plan, and they are not translated to `Fractal` reflective API. These `Old` operators are used for the components, connections and parent relations that exist in the initial and goal configurations, that is, do not change between them.

3.1 Verifying the Planning Domain

The correctness of the planning domain will be verified considering two aspects.

1. the operators will be checked if the preconditions are in accordance to the component model and if the effects of its execution - postconditions - don't violate any constraint from the component model.

2. the order relation provided by the method decomposition represents other constraints derived from the reconfiguration execution.

The reference to build logical expressions that form the pre and post conditions in item **1** is the work in [10], where the authors formalize in first-order logic the pre and post conditions of FRACTAL architectural elements and the reconfiguration actions. The formalization in that work is used to check a software configuration and a reconfiguration plan, that is, after a software configuration is determined or a reconfiguration plan is generated, both can be checked using a model described in Alloy[2] model checker. This kind of check guarantees that neither the configuration, nor the plans are inconsistent with the model derived from FRACTAL. They do not treat the plan generation, and we used it to elicit the pre and postconditions for the planning operators in the planning domain. However, that work can be used in our approach to check $Config_{goal}$ and the plan generated by JSHOP2 planner. The correctness of $Config_{goal}$ in relation to the component model is important not to compromise the search for a plan, because a precondition can never be true and no action is applicable in some state.

[2]http://alloy.mit.edu/alloy/

During the search for a plan, the methods are being decomposed by the subtask set until primitive tasks are instantiated into actions, as illustrated in Figure 6. If these actions, when executed from left to right, reach the goal, then a plan is found. An action is reached from the main method, forming a path, and the union of each precondition set along each decomposition path - in Figure 6 this set is the union of the chamfered rectangle propositions - gives the preconditions set to be checked for an operator. One exception to this precondition set must be highlighted. Using Figure 6, the method `removeBindingFromComp` is decomposed in three tasks. The first and second are primitive and the last is a composite. The path until the second task, named `!unbind ?compClient ?ifaceRef ?compServer ?ifaceServer`, is not enough to make true the preconditions for this action. However, the first task, `!stop ?compClient`, changes the state so that `!unbind` is applicable.

For FRACTAL, 15 methods were identified in the planning domain, resulting in 102 different paths that end in a leaf node that can be a planning operator or an empty task. For the item **2**, remember that the task decomposition is totally ordered, that is, they are executed in the given order. So, some actions are performed before others. This feature will meet the order relations identified for FRACTAL which are:

- a parent component should be created or reconfigured before its subcomponents.
- a unbind between interfaces should be made before a component is moved to another parent.
- a bind between interfaces should be made after the component is inside the parent of the goal configuration.

This order relation is respected in the main method `configure` illustrated in Figure 5.

4. CASE STUDY

The planning algorithm JSHOP2 is a Java implementation of planner SHOP2. In Figure 7, the sequence of activities that produces a reconfiguration plan is illustrated.

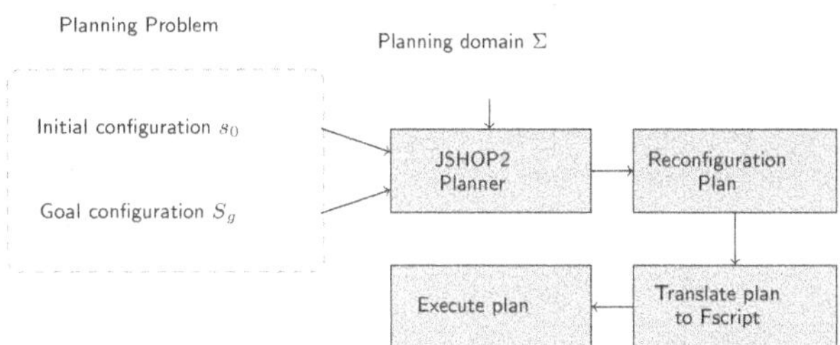

Figure 7: Sequence of activities to plan generation.

Nr	Action	FScript - FPath
1	(!stop CommSystem)	stop($commsystem)
2	(!unbindInternal CommSystem rx SocketServer rx)	unbind($commsystem/internal-interface::rx, $socketserver/interface::rx)
3	(!stop SocketServer)	stop($socketserver)
4	(!unbind SocketServer logIface Logger logIface)	unbind($socketserver/interface::logiface, $logger/interface::logiface)
5	(!unbindInternal SocketServer brokerIface CommSystem brokerIface)	unbind($socketserver/interface::brokeriface, $commsystem/internal-interface::brokeriface)
6	(!unbindInternal SocketServer queue CommSystem queue)	unbind($socketserver/interface::queue, $commsystem/internal-interface::queue)
7	(!removechild CommSystem SocketServer)	remove($commsystem, $socketserver)
8	(!addNew SocketListener)	socketList = adl-new('file:///src/resources/socketList')
9	(!addNew SOAPServer)	soapSrv = adl-new('file:///src/resources/soapSrv')
10	(!addNew PADRESMsgServer)	padresSrv = adl-new('file:///src/resources/padresSrv')
11	(!addChildNew CommSystem SocketListener)	add($commsystem, $socketList)
12	(!addChildNew CommSystem SOAPServer)	add($commsystem, $soapSrv)
13	(!addChildNew CommSystem PADRESMsgServer)	add($commsystem, $padresSrv)
14	(!bindInternalNew CommSystem rx SocketListener rx)	bind($commsystem/internal-interface::rx, $socketList/interface::rx)
15	(!bindInternalNew SocketListener brokerIface CommSystem brokerIface)	bind($socketList/interface::brokerIface, $commsystem/internal-interface::brokerIface)
16	(!bindNew SocketListener logIface Logger logIface)	bind($socketList/interface::logIface, $logger/interface::logIface)
17	(!bindNew SocketListener transIface SOAPServer transIface)	bind($socketList/interface::transIface, $soapSrv/interface::transIface)
18	(!bindNew SocketListener transIface PADRESMsgServer transIface)	bind($socketList/interface::transIface, $padresSrv/interface::transIface)
19	(!bindInternalNew SOAPServer queue CommSystem queue)	bind($soapSrv/interface::queue, $commsystem/internal-interface::queue)
20	(!bindInternalNew PADRESMsgServer queue CommSystem queue)	bind($padresSrv/interface::queue, $commsystem/internal-interface::queue)
21	(!start SOAPServer)	start($soapSrv)
22	(!start PADRESMsgServer)	start($padresSrv)
23	(!start SocketListener)	start($socketList)
24	(!start CommSystem)	start($commsystem)

Table 2: The **PADRES** reconfiguration plan in operators and FSCRIPT.

Given the planning domain Σ for FRACTAL, the initial configuration s_0 and goal configuration S_g are the input to generate a plan. Both initial configuration s_0 and goal configuration S_g are described in the same file. The software application to be reconfigured is a component based version of a content-based publish and subscribe middleware named **PADRES**[3]. We refactored the original application and created an application with 14 components.

PADRES was used as a middleware for data exchange during a runtime execution of a maneuvering simulator developed to serve the professional maritime in the Brazilian Navy. This simulator is composed by a set of clients that should exchange messages to interact during a simulation. This simulator is being integrated to other simulators and systems that will be **PADRES** clients. We identified different technologies used in the systems to be integrated and in some cases, this integration should be made at runtime, where the maneuvering simulator will be part of a bigger software simulation already in execution. So, a pub/sub middleware that has the ability to be dynamically reconfigured is a good way to deal with this kind of requirement.

A reconfiguration example is the ability to process client messages in different protocols. Considering this new requirement and Figure 3 as the initial configuration, a new component `SOAPServer`, that is used to process messages in SOAP format, will be added to the `CommSystem`. The previous `SocketServer`, that designed to listen in a socket port and process messages in the custom grammar from PADRES, will be split in two: `SocketListener` and `PADRESMsgServer`. The first will listen in the port and the second will process messages in the original PADRES format. The messages in the SOAP format will be sent to component `SOAPServer`. After a message has been processed by the respective component, it will be delivered to `QueueManager`. This goal configuration is illustrated in Figure 8 and the generated reconfiguration plan is illustrated in Table 2.

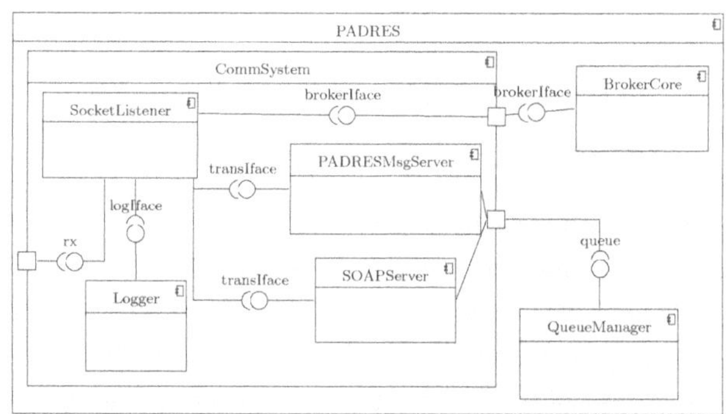

Figure 8: An excerpt showing the goal configuration.

In the plan, actions with suffix Old are not shown, but the action `(!addChildNew CommSystem SOAPServer)` should occur after `(!addChildOld Padres CommSystem)`, inserting the `CommSystem` in the hierarchy. Sometimes the planner can find more than one plan and the difference between these plans is the variable substitution. For example, actions 11 and 12 can have their order changed.

The component start sequence obeys a child to parent direction and the dependency relation. A parent is only started after its sub components are. For the dependency relation, first start component that do not have dependen-

[3]http://www.msrg.utoronto.ca/projects/padres/

cies, like `QueueManager` in Figure 8. Then the components which dependecies are already started or are parent internal-interfaces, like `brokerIface` bind. The problem will occur with a circular dependency and, in case there isn't some specific data about the application, it becomes impossible to know which component should be started first. Our solution to this includes a proposition that describes the dependency at the start of a component. Two components depending on another, at start time, is forbidden.

Another test is the initialization of an application. If the initial configuration is empty, the planner will try to find a plan to build the application. In this case, the plan will not contain any action with suffix `Old`.

4.1 Discussion

The case study shows how a reconfiguration task can be solved at runtime. The reconfiguration was not a simple component swap, which could be previously encoded and stored in a procedure, using the FSCRIPT language like proposed in [4]. Certainly, some reconfiguration can be very similar to a swap, but will be very difficult to encode all possibilities and use them when necessary.

The traditionally-accepted ordering for the reconfiguration actions is derived from the protocol proposed in [8]. In that work, the authors propose a strong property, called *quiescence*, which must be reached by the components involved in the reconfiguration of a distributed system. The *quiescent* state is defined as a property where a component is not within a transaction and will neither receive nor initiate any new transaction. This property is obtained putting a set of components in a state called *passive* state. A component is *passive* if it is not engaged in transactions it initiated and if it will not start new ones. However, in this same state, it must accept and service transactions in order to let other nodes become passive. So, to put a component C in a quiescent state, node C and all components with connection arcs towards C must be in the passive state and this set is called the passive set $PS(C)$.

The proposed protocol establishes an order relation between the following reconfiguration actions: **create** a component, **unlink** two components, **remove** a component and **link** two components. After determining the set of components that must be placed in a quiescence state, the sequence of actions is: 1) put the set of components in the passive state; 2) unlink; 3) remove; 4) create; 5) link; and 6) activate the components. The order is a partial order relation because the action **create** could be performed at any time before the **link** action.

However, as shown in Section 3, this protocol cannot be applied to modern reflective component models. Clearly, FRACTAL introduces new constraints derived from its concepts evolving the previous reconfiguration protocol, in special, those derived from the composition between components not considered in [8].

For FRACTAL, the subtask decomposition for method *configure* illustrated in Figure 5 can be changed, if the previous order relations were respected. So, the order relation is a partial order. For example, *destroySingle* can be decomposed just before *destroyComposite*.

In a *model-based approach* the model is used like a *predictor*, that is, the model is an abstraction of reality, and its purpose is to support the search for a solution to the problem, without using the real environment. So, an engineer can use this model to evaluate a plan before its execution. Depending on the extent of reconfiguration, a plan can stop a considerable part of the application, making it unacceptable. Thus, the engineer can try different goal software configuration - goal state - in order to generate reconfiguration plans that cover small parts instead of a complete one. Another possible use, for the approach proposed here, is the generation of plans that will be encoded in a rule-set. As a predictor, the engineer can try different kinds of reconfigurations and, after that, choose the one that will form the rule set.

The hierarchical feature from FRACTAL opens the possibility to execute reconfigurations in parallel because a parent component encapsulates its sub components. Considering this, the plan could be post processed in order to organize the actions inside a composite component and allow a parallel plan execution. However, this kind of reconfiguration execution is impossible using the default FSCRIPT engine retrieved by the method `getFScriptEngine(Component fscript)`, because the class returned by this method is a Singleton. To do that, the user should use the reflection API.

5. RELATED WORK

One of the first works to employ AI planning techniques was described in [1], where a planner was used to find an optimal deploy plan for a distributed application. Another example is in [16], where the author proposes analyzing different component assembly choices and assist the user in making cost-effective decisions, using automated planning for this analysis. Other approaches that use planning techniques to reconfigure a component based application, as [17] and [18], generate an application build plan but don't consider the dynamic reconfiguration aspects, like lifecycle control and order relation between reconfiguration actions. One reason for this is the component model used in these works - both employ a robotic system - where the reflection capabilities are not treated at the planning generation, abstracting it and delegating this issue to the component model. In order not to violate the consistency from complex component models like FRACTAL, [10] and [9] propose formal methods and tools to guarantee that a reconfiguration plan will not violate any constraint from the component model. However, they do not treat the problem of reconfiguration plan generation with these aspects.

More recently, [2] proposes an algorithm to generate a reconfiguration plan that can handle any number of failures during a reconfiguration, always producing an architecturally consistent assembly of components that can be safely introspected. This work solves a problem very similar to ours, but the component model used to build an application is a proposal and not a real one, it has features much simpler than FRACTAL, does not support compositions, and the proposed solution is coupled to that component model.

6. CONCLUSIONS AND FUTURE WORKS

The research presented in this paper is the continuation of [5]. This work extends the previous one to show the correctness of the planning domain and a real application to be reconfigured at runtime. The assumption for this work is the use of an off-the-self reflective component model that considers the composition concept between components (hierarchy). This work shows how to generate a reconfiguration plan at runtime, employing a model-based solution that considers the constraints related to the component model. More specifically, these constraints are closely related to the correctness of the reconfiguration execution and are responsible for the application reliability.

The automated planning view decouples the reconfiguration in two parts: the model and the problem. The search for a plan is made by the independent domain planner JSHOP2. This decoupling opens the possibility to represent different component models, without changing the planner procedure, like iPOJO and compare the differences between the planning domains. One of them is the life cycle control, which is made by iPOJO. For example, let `compRef`, `compServer1` and `compServer2` be iPOJO components. If `compRef` requires an interface, and it is bound in the initial configuration with `compServer1`, but in the goal configuration, the provided interface will be fulfilled by another component `compServer2`, `compServer2` should be active before bind removal, because the iPOJO middleware makes the bind automatically.

A simple reconfiguration like the case study presented shows how a plan can be complex and hard to be created manually. Another point is the goal software architecture to be reached, as it unfeasible to predict what will be the goal until it is needed, and some resources will not be available until they are necessary.

One of the application of this work is in the area of self-adaptive systems. Due to the intrinsic uncertainties around the execution environment, the large number of potential configurations that an application can assume and the constraints from the reflexive component model, it is very difficult to predict all the possible contexts of adaptation and generate all reconfiguration plans before deploy time. So, a plan must be generated at the moment it is necessary and consider the environment at the same time.

7. REFERENCES

[1] N. Arshad, D. Heimbigner, and A. L. Wolf. Deployment and dynamic reconfiguration planning for distributed software systems. In *Proceedings of the 15th IEEE International Conference on Tools with Artificial Intelligence*, ICTAI '03, pages 39–, Washington, DC, USA, 2003. IEEE Computer Society.

[2] F. Boyer, O. Gruber, and D. Pous. Robust reconfigurations of component assemblies. In *Proceedings of the 2013 International Conference on Software Engineering*, ICSE '13, pages 13–22, Piscataway, NJ, USA, 2013. IEEE Press.

[3] E. Bruneton, T. Coupaye, M. Leclercq, V. Quéma, and J.-B. Stefani. The FRACTAL component model and its support in Java. *Softw. Pract. Exper.*, 36:1257–1284, September 2006.

[4] P.-C. David, T. Ledoux, M. Léger, and T. Coupaye. FPath and FScript: Language support for navigation and reliable reconfiguration of Fractal architectures. *Annals of Telecommunications*, 64:45–63, 2009. 10.1007/s12243-008-0073-y.

[5] M. E. M. Di Beneditto and C. M. L. Werner. A declarative approach for software compositional reconfiguration. In *Proceedings of the 11th International Workshop on Adaptive and Reflective Middleware*, ARM '12, pages 7:1–7:6, New York, NY, USA, 2012. ACM.

[6] C. Escoffier, R. Hall, and P. Lalanda. iPOJO: an extensible service-oriented component framework. In *Services Computing, 2007. SCC 2007. IEEE International Conference on*, pages 474–481, 2007.

[7] H. Geffner. The model-based approach to autonomous behavior: A personal view. In M. Fox and D. Poole, editors, *Proceedings of the Twenty-Fourth Conference on Artificial Intelligence, AAAI, Atlanta, Georgia, USA*. AAAI Press, July 2010.

[8] J. Kramer and J. Magee. The evolving philosophers problem: dynamic change management. *Software Engineering, IEEE Transactions on*, 16(11):1293 –1306, nov 1990.

[9] A. Lanoix, J. Dormoy, and O. Kouchnarenko. Combining proof and model-checking to validate reconfigurable architectures. *Electronic Notes in Theoretical Computer Science*, 279(2):43 – 57, 2011. Proceedings of the 8th International Workshop on Formal Engineering approaches to Software Components and Architectures (FESCA).

[10] M. Léger, T. Ledoux, and T. Coupaye. Reliable dynamic reconfigurations in a reflective component model. In *CBSE*, pages 74–92, 2010.

[11] D. Nau, T.-C. Au, O. Ilghami, U. Kuter, J. W. Murdock, D. Wu, and F. Yaman. Shop2: An htn planning system. *J. Artif. Int. Res.*, 20(1):379–404, Dec. 2003.

[12] D. Nau, M. Ghallab, and P. Traverso. *Automated Planning: Theory & Practice.* Morgan Kaufmann Publishers Inc., San Francisco, CA, USA, 2004.

[13] D. Nau, H. M. noz avila, Y. Cao, A. Lotem, and S. Mitchell. Total-order planning with partially ordered subtasks. In *In Proceedings of the Seventeenth International Joint Conference on Artificial Intelligence*, pages 425–430, 2001.

[14] S. J. Russell and P. Norvig. *Artificial Intelligence - A Modern Approach.* Pearson Education, 3 edition, 2010.

[15] M. Salehie and L. Tahvildari. Self-Adaptive Software: Landscape and Research Challenges. *ACM Trans. Auton. Adapt. Syst.*, 4(2):1–42, 2009.

[16] B. Srivastava. A decision-support framework for component reuse and maintenance in software project management. In *Software Maintenance and Reengineering, 2004. CSMR 2004. Proceedings. Eighth European Conference on*, pages 125–134, March 2004.

[17] D. Sykes, W. Heaven, J. Magee, and J. Kramer. From goals to components: a combined approach to self-management. In *Proceedings of the 2008 international workshop on Software engineering for adaptive and self-managing systems*, SEAMS '08, pages 1–8, New York, NY, USA, 2008. ACM.

[18] H. Tajalli, J. Garcia, G. Edwards, and N. Medvidovic. Plasma: a plan-based layered architecture for software model-driven adaptation. In *Proceedings of the IEEE/ACM international conference on Automated software engineering*, ASE '10, pages 467–476, New York, NY, USA, 2010. ACM.

AO-OpenCom: An AO-Middleware Architecture Supporting Flexible Dynamic Reconfiguration

Bholanathsingh Surajbali
Smart Research and Development
CAS Software AG
Karlsruhe, Germany
b.surajbali@cas.de

Paul Grace
IT Innovation
University of Southampton
Southampton, UK
pjg@it-innovation.soton.ac.uk

Geoff Coulson
School of Computing
Lancaster University
Lancaster, UK
geoff@comp.lancs.ac.uk

ABSTRACT

Middleware has emerged as a key technology in the construction of distributed systems. As a consequence, middleware is increasingly required to be highly modular and configurable, to support separation of concerns between services, and, crucially, to support *dynamic reconfiguration*: i.e. to be capable of being changed while running. Aspect-oriented middleware is a promising technology for the realisation of distributed reconfiguration in distributed systems. In this paper we propose an aspect-oriented middleware platform called AO-OpenCom that builds AO-based reconfiguration on top of a dynamic component approach to middleware system composition. The goal is to support extremely flexible dynamic reconfiguration that can be applied at all levels of the system and uniformly across the distributed environment. We evaluate our platform by the capability in meeting flexible reconfiguration and the impact of these overheads.

Categories and Subject Descriptors

C.2.4 [**Computer-Communication Networks**]: Distributed Systems – Distributed applications; D.2.11 [**Software Engineering**]: Software Architectures – Doman-specific architectures; D2.13 [Software engineering]: Reusable Software – Reusable libraries

Keywords

Aspect Oriented; Middleware; Dynamic Reconfiguration

1. INTRODUCTION

Dynamic reconfiguration in aspect-oriented (AO) based middleware is very promising, but under-developed. AOP addresses these two problems by encapsulating logically independent pieces of functionality into separate modules known as *aspects*. The aspects are then *woven* into the system (this weaving process can be performed at compile-time, load-time or runtime) to build the required behaviour. An aspect defines both *behaviour* and *composition logic*, the latter describing both where and when the behaviour is executed. The compositional logical associated with an aspect is often referred to as a *pointcut*. The points in a program at which composition occurs, as directed by a pointcut, are referred to as *join points*. The declarative approach of aspect-oriented programming (AOP) is of considerable help to the developer in terms of facilitating the description and enactment of dynamic reconfiguration. However, most current AOP middleware systems [3, 5, 6, 8, 9, 11, 12, 15] are evolutions of earlier systems that lack reconfiguration *flexibility* and are focused primarily on *local* reconfiguration with limited dynamic reconfiguration capabilities. The lack of flexibility of AO-middleware can be categorised in terms of *five* different dynamic reconfiguration variability of distributed system such as granular scope reconfigurability, vertical scope, horizontal scope, performance and resource overhead. First, granular scope of reconfigurability is important because it defines the extent to which reconfiguration can be applied and can be classified in terms of fine-grained and coarse-grained reconfiguration support. Coarse-grained composition allows entire system functionality to be added or removed, while fine-grained composition relates to smaller changes (e.g. changing protocols from Wi-Fi to Bluetooth technology when there is a drop in power and vice-versa [4]). Second, vertical scope is an important issue because many systems allow only application level reconfigurability and this is insufficient in many cases, where system infrastructures need to change. For example, reconfiguration may also be required at the infrastructure level to add new functionality such as the support for new group communication or apply updates such as correcting anomalies from existing infrastructure services. Third, horizontal scope reconfigurability is crucial as both local and distributed nodes should be reconfigurable to ensure consistent view of the middleware service. Finally, performance and resource overhead are important criteria because if a system is highly reconfigurable but it runs too slowly or consumes too much resource it is not acceptable. In particular the platform must allow aspects to be dynamically woven as needed and unwoven when no longer necessary. This decreases the resource overhead and performance of invoking aspects at a join point.

In this paper, we present a novel *dynamically reconfigurable AO-middleware architecture, AO-OpenCom* providing a principled way of dynamic reconfiguration with degrees of flexibility that go beyond the state of the art by following a component-based, reflection and AOP design approach. In particular, the architecture will address the *five* main areas of deficiency as discussed above and the design is evaluated by its flexibility and expressiveness in specifying a range of types of dynamic reconfiguration. In particular, the platform offers four flexible distributed reconfiguration operation in terms of support for: i) local pointcut – local advice; ii) local pointcut- remote aspect; iii), remote pointcut – local aspect; and iv) remote pointcut and remote aspect.

The remainder of this paper is structured as follows. First, Section 2 presents the aspect composition model of AO-OpenCom. Next, Section 3 presents the concepts and implementation of the AO-OpenCom middleware architecture

CBSE'14, June 30 - July 4, 2014, Marcq-en-Bareul, France.

http://dx.doi.org/10.1145/2602458.2602472

which is then evaluated in Section 5. Then, Section 6 provides a discussion on how the AO-Opencom meets the requirements based on the experimental results, as well as an analysis against related work. Finally, Section 7 draws concluding remarks.

2. AO-CONNECTOR MODEL

Aspects in AO-OpenCom are composed with the base components (hereafter termed components) within component interfaces/ receptacles using connectors. The AO-OpenCom connector model have two variants: the Default-Connector which contains the direct reference of a receptacle to an interface of components (no aspectual composition); and the AO-Connector is the architectural element offering aspectual composition (weaving) of aspects between a receptacle and a provided interface of components.

2.1 Interface/Receptacle AO-Connector

The runtime composition of aspects using an interface/receptacle AO-Connector is achieved using a proxy that redirects the call or execution through the chain of advices on the interface or receptacle as illustrated in Figure 1. A key benefit of the interface/receptacle aspect composition approach is that it allows aspects to be composed even when no binding is present.

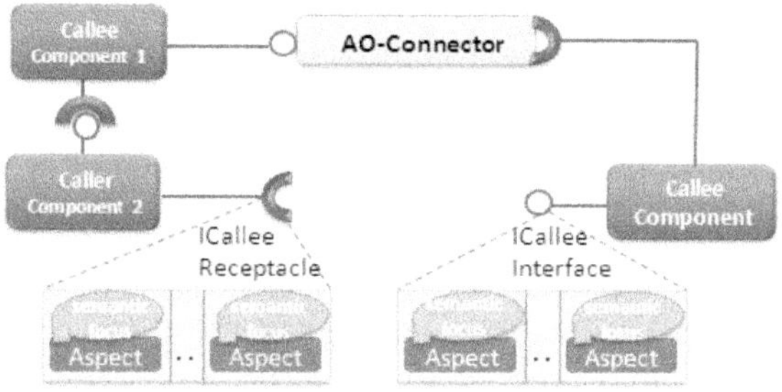

Figure 1. Aspect Composition execution chain with Semantic Locus using Interface/Receptacle AO-Connector

2.2 AO-Connector Binder Composition

The AO-Connector composition differs from component to component connectors by maintaining the metadata containing references to aspects instances in an advice chain. For example, it maintains details of all advised aspects and their types and allows these to be queried to determine the operations they support and the aspects currently advising them. It also supports the runtime manipulation of the chain to add new advices, or remove or reorder aspects in the chain of advices. Figure 2 shows the AO-Connector connecting two components, the Caller component receptacle to the Callee component provided interface, containing the advice chain with advice$_1$ to advice$_n$. The AO-Connector also supports the inspection and reconfiguration of the woven aspects in the advice chain. The inspection mechanism allows type checking of the aspect before it is woven in the advice chain. Furthermore, the introspection capability allows the detection of conflicts between the hosting aspects or the CF they belong to.

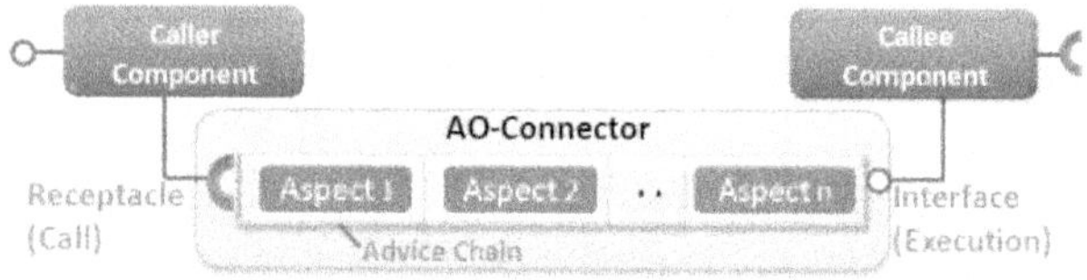

Figure 2. Aspect Composition execution chain with Semantic Locus at AO-Connector

2.3 Local Aspect Composition

Each AO-Connector is responsible for generating at runtime the appropriate advice chain for the set of possible join points that can occur at its bound interfaces. Figure 3 illustrates a local AO composition whereby the Callee Component has a *methodCallee()* method attached to the AO-Connector aspects with the respective locus semantics. It should be noted that the around advice is different to that used in AspectJ. The order follows the similar semantics as in DyMAC [5] and AspectOpenCom [3], that is:

> *before* advices or *around$_{before}$* advices are executed in the order in which they are encountered within the chain followed by the *method execution*, then followed by *after* advices or *around$_{after}$* advices in the order in which they are encountered within the chain.

For example from Figure 3, a call from the Caller component to the Callee component, results in the aspect chain to be invoked in the following order:

[before0 from Aspect A_1] → [around $_{before}$ from Aspect A_2] → [before1 from Aspect A_4] → [before2 from Aspect A_5] → [methodCallee()]→ [after0 from Aspect A_3] → [around $_{after}$ from Aspect A_2].

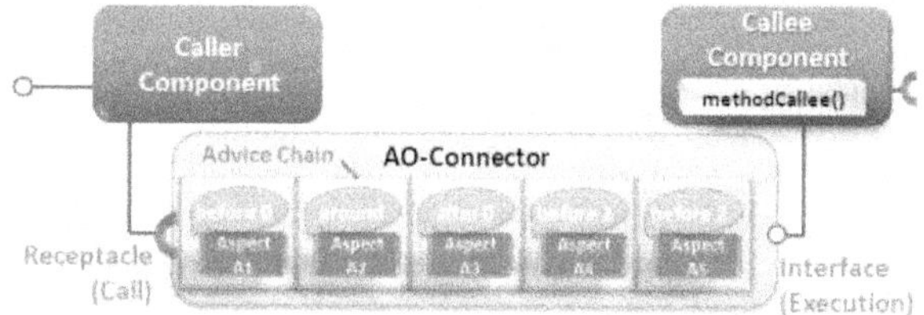

Figure 3. Aspect Composition execution chain

In the absence of the locus semantics, then each interface (execution join point) and receptacle (call join point) call gets redirected through a chain of advices attached through the AO-Connector as illustrated in Figure 4. When a call takes place from the Caller Component the execution follows the following order:

[Aspect 1] → [Aspect 2] → [Aspect 3] → [methodCallee()]

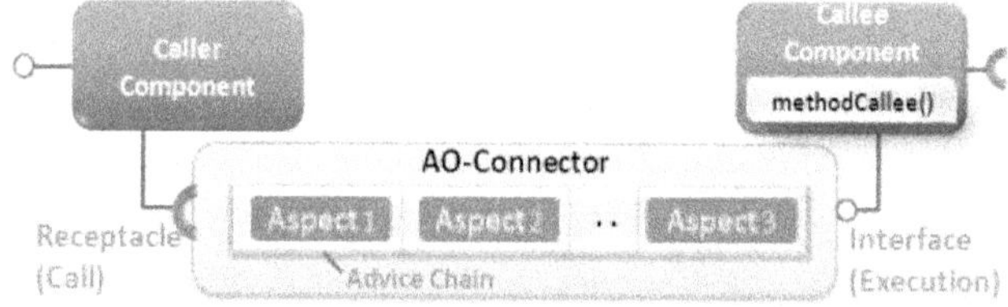

Figure 4. Aspect Composition without Semantic Locus

2.4 Remote Aspect Composition

Aspects can also specify and implement remote method invocations and are classified in terms of remote advices. These aspects can be used to provide distributed remote AO compositions. Similar to local aspect composition, remote aspects support the three locus semantics (before, after and around) of aspect execution and their references can be attached to the AO-Connector. A key difference between remote and local advice is that remote advices implement the Serialisable mechanism, e.g. Java Serialisable interface such that their method calls and return values can be used on remote CFs. A remote aspect is advisable like any other method invocation, and can capture both call and execution of components.

3. AO-OpenCom

AO-OpenCom is an extension of the OpenCom component model and its associated reflective meta-models and component framework CF architectures. The extension introduces a novel AO-meta framework layer on top of the existing underlying component-based reflective middleware substrate. This approach follows from the need of the AO-meta framework to cover the crosscutting functionality, and to ensure it preserves the separation concern [7]; that is, to ensure the middleware platform keeps separate views for better understanding and preservation of modularity within the middleware platform. The meta-layer and base-layer of each node crosscuts multiple address-spaces, and thus a top-level view provides separate viewpoint coverage of the crosscutting concerns across multiple address-spaces. This hides the complexity of the underlying reflective meta-layer from programmers. Moreover, the AO-meta framework is built as an independently-deployable service using components throughout the architecture (the AO-meta framework layer is constructed from components like the rest of the underlying reflective component-based middleware substrate). This means that the AO-meta framework can advise not only distributed applications, but also the underlying middleware services and the AO-meta framework layer itself. Being independent from the rest of the framework allows the AO-meta framework to be dynamically deployed when required and un-deployed when further reconfiguration is not required in the foreseeable future (thus avoiding any overhead when not in use). The AO-OpenCom architecture consists of the following main entities (see Figure 5): i) Base Framework; ii) Reflective-meta Framework; iii) AO-meta Framework; iv) Aspect Repository Framework; v) Distribution Framework; and vi) Configurator.

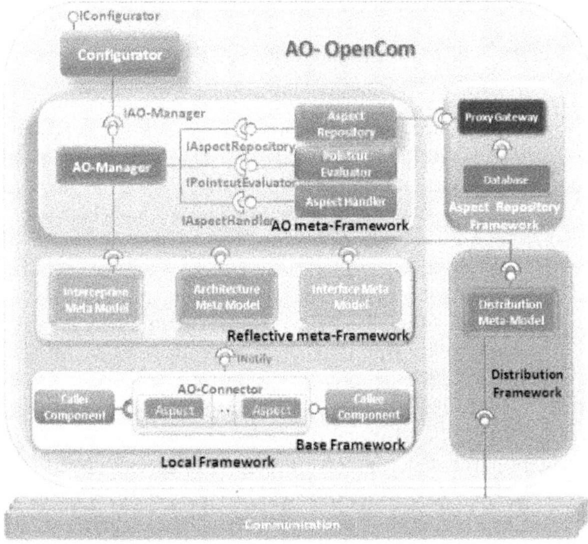

Figure 5. The AO-OpenCom Middleware

3.1 Base Framework

The base framework consists of the kernel which provides an API allowing new components and aspect-components together with the AO-Connectors to be instantiated, loaded, unloaded and destroyed. Furthermore, the kernel maintains a causal connection with the three meta-models in terms of the *distribution meta-model*, *AO meta-model* and the *reflective meta-model* such that any changes in the base runtime are reflected to the respective meta-model. Components, reflection and AO are at the core of this architecture, providing a principled approach to dynamic reconfiguration. At the base, *components* are encapsulated units of functionality and deployment that interact with other components exclusively through *interfaces* and *receptacles*. AO-Connectors represent the bindings between a single interface and a receptacle. Reflection technologies through the meta-models provide information about the current system state to inform about reconfiguration decisions; next a component-based approach allows the composition among components' provided and required interfaces. Next, AOP provides a declarative approach to support local and distributed quantification as well as local and remote aspect reconfiguration capabilities.

3.2 Reflective-meta Framework

The AO-OpenCom reflective-meta framework consists of the OpenCom reflective meta-models that provide the inspection, reconfiguration and extension of component and aspect-component composition with a local CF (e.g. of a component composition that represents a middleware platform instance). Each of the three meta-models can be optionally (and dynamically) deployed whenever required, and un-deployed when no longer required.

3.3 AO-meta Framework

The AO-meta framework internal architecture comprises a set of components that are instantiated into the host DCF. The set of components is as follows:

AO-Manager. This component is responsible for accepting and handling the configurator requests that will apply to the host DCF. Instances of the AO-Manager may run on more than one node in the DCF if desired. The AO-Manager interacts with Pointcut Evaluator and Aspect Handler components (see below) to perform the requested AO compositions within the DCF. It also caches join point information it receives from Pointcut Evaluators in case similar behaviour needs be applied in the future.

Aspect Repository. The Aspect Repository holds a set of instantiable aspect-components. Actually, the Aspect Repository is itself a (sub) CF which supports the configuration of repository functionality in a variety of ways. The sub-CF consists of a Front End component and a back-end Database component. This simple architecture enables a wide range of configurations; e.g. different Front Ends can apply different load balancing strategies and some Database components can be simple proxies to other Front Ends.

Pointcut Evaluator. The Pointcut Evaluator supports the parsing of pointcut expressions provided by the AO-Manager component and to return to the latter a list of all the matching join points found within the local address space. The supporting quantification by the Pointcut Evaluator component are DCF signatures, operation signatures, interface and receptacle signatures, component types and instances as well as dynamic properties of the CF runtime instances. Moreover, the Pointcut Evaluator component also supports the remote pointcut functionality to evaluate join points located in remote address spaces. To do so, it connects to the distribution framework to locate the appropriate join points in remote CFs. The inclusion of CFs in the list of quantifiable entities means that distribution is inherently supported in a network-independent manner. In addition, it can evaluate dynamic context properties associated for corresponding component instances that are stored in the AO-OpenCom runtime kernel and aspect-components by evaluating their dynamic properties from the Aspect Repository. Finally, the Pointcut Evaluator evaluates pointcuts and returns a list of matching join points within the local node in case it is a local pointcut, and for remote pointcuts, the lists of matching join points in each DCF.

Aspect Handler. This is also present in each address space. Its role is to act on instructions from the AO-Manager to weave advice at join points in its address space. The weaving is accomplished using the above-mentioned AO-Connector connector type which enables advices (i.e. an operation supported by an aspect) to be inserted between a pair of bound components. As well as purely address-space-local AO-Connectors, distributed AO-Connectors are also supported that can use distributed framework endpoints as well as local receptacle and interface pointers. This enables the AO-Connector to support the invocation of aspects that are resident in other address spaces. Finally, the Aspect Handler on receiving the join points and advice instances, performs advice weaving at specified join points in its CF, according to the advice specification.

3.4 Distribution Framework

The AO-OpenCom DCF architecture is illustrated in Figure 6 following a generic component approach to support various communication protocols (e.g. TCP, UDP, Multicast, JGroups, Broadcast, group protocols such as SCAMP [4]).

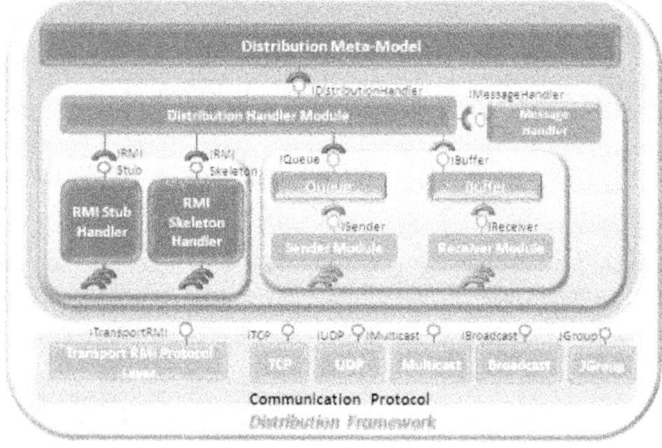

Figure 6. AO-OpenCom Distribution Framework

Each CF maintains a basic architecture of the distribution framework, as well as a distribution meta-model containing contents of the CF as well as other instances of the DCF. The distribution module functions as a hub to the communication protocol choosing the desired communication protocol required to ensure reliable communication among the CFs'. For non-remote method invocation, based on the chosen communication protocol, the Distribution module component translates the outgoing messages using a message handler and then stores in the Queue component. The sender module extracts queued messages and sends them according to the outgoing protocol. On the receiving side the Receiver module component is responsible for receiving messages. Received messages are placed in the buffer component, which is then read by the Distribution module to update the distribution meta-model accordingly. Importantly, this communications service of the AO-OpenCom DCF is realised as a pluggable component, meaning that the service can replace the basic service (which is unreliable and does not support any ordering semantics) with a range of alternative communications services chosen according to the reliability and scalability requirements under which the DCF is deployed.

3.5 Configurator

Each Configurator interacts with its local Pointcut Evaluator and Advice Handler to carry out either a *reconfigure* or a *reorder* reconfiguration on its local node. The reconfigure operation provides the coarse-grained reconfiguration of aspects (add, remove and replace) at a join point and the reorder operation provides fine-grained reconfiguration, that is allowing aspects to be reordered at a join point. Consequently, AO-OpenCom provides granularity scope of reconfigurability requirements. Furthermore, the Configurator also interacts with other peer Configurators, for a distributed reconfiguration across multiple DCFs'. This allows the platform to provide for horizontal scope reconfigurability.

4. AO-OpenCom PROGRAMMING MODEL

4.1 AO-OpenCom Kernel API

The AO-OpenCom platform is supported using the minimal kernel API that is offered by each DCF. These operations provide the minimum functionality required to create instances and connect them. The key operations supported by the kernel API consists of eight main operations (as shown in Figure 7).

```
interface IAOOpenCom{
    //loads a new aspect / component and inserts it into the AO-Opencom runtime
    long load(String componentType);
    //creates a new instance of a component/aspect type
    long instantiate(long componentTypeId);
    //deletes a component/aspect instance which has been previously created in the
    runtime
    boolean destroy(long ComponentID);
    //connects a receptacle with an interface
    long connect(long ReceptacleId, long InterfaceId, AOConnector connectorType);
    //a particular property is inserted into the runtime registry
    boolean putprop(long entity, String key, Object value);
    //a particular property is retrieved from the runtime registry
    Object getprop(long entity, String key);
    //unloads an existing component/aspect type from the AO-OpenCom runtime
    boolean unload(long componentTypeId);
    //registers a callback to receive kernel events notifications
    void notifyCall(NotifyCallback c);
}
```

Figure 7. AO-OpenCom Kernel Base-level operations

The *load()* method loads a named component type from the component repository and aspects from the Aspect Repository, and the *unload()* method unloads an existing component type and aspect type from the runtime respectively. The *instantiate()* method provides the instantiation of aspects and component. Furthermore, a component or aspect can be instantiated multiple times if desired, with each having a different unique identifier. The *connect()* method connects a provided interface with a required interface of another. The *getprop()* returns a reference of associated entities (aspect types, component types, aspects, components, interfaces and receptacles) dynamic properties in the form of <name, value> tuples. The *putprop()* method writes into the registry the respective entities tuples. Finally, the *notifyCall()* method provides the callback operations whenever one of the methods in the kernel base-level system gets called causing call to be updated in the meta-model layers. It should be noted that the reconfiguration does not need to use the lower level AO-OpenCom base-level operations to reconfigure the platform. The base-level operations are available and can be used by the middleware developer. To perform any reconfiguration, the reconfiguration developer makes use of the configuration API that is described in the next section.

4.2 Configurator API

Aspect configuration and reconfiguration in AO-OpenCom can be specified in terms of an XML-based independent pointcut languages as well as programmatically which enables pointcuts signatures to be defined in terms of: i) capsules/hosts/DCF address expression; ii) a component type expression; iii) a component instance expression; iv) an interface/ receptacle type expression; v) a method type expression; and vi) metadata that can be attached to any of the foregoing. The main API provided by the AO-OpenCom enabled CF and DCF for AO composition and reconfiguration are shown in Table 1. The configuration specification containing the pointcut and advice specification is passed to AO-OpenCom Configurator. The configurator supports both programmatic and XML specifications to be sent to it following the BNF specification [12]. Note, that the Configurator API protects the reconfiguration developer from the low level details of actually managing and weaving the aspects among distributed nodes. Hence, facilitating the usability of the platform to support reconfiguration and to deploy new aspects, the programmer can use a deployment script similar to components deployment.

Table1. API AO-OpenCom Reconfiguration protocol

Configurator Methods	Configurator Methods Description
+ **long** reconfigure(String pointcutSpec, CommandAction cAct, String aspectSpec, Locus lc);	*Reconfigure from xml pointcut and advice specification*
+ **long** reconfigureDyn (Pointcut pc, CommandAction cAct, AspectList aspectlist, Locus lc);	*Reconfigure from dynamic pointcut and advice properties*
+ **long** reorder(String pointcutSpec, String aspectSpec);	*Reorder from xml pointcut and advice specification*
+ **long** reorderDyn (DynamicPointcut pc, DynamicAspect aspectSpec);	*Reorder from dynamic pointcut and advice properties*
+ **boolean** getreconfInfo (long reconfUID);	Retrieve reconfiguration with reconfUID

4.2.1 Local Reconfiguration

The local reconfiguration using the AO-OpenCom meta-layer is split into four main stages:

1. Stage I: Reconfiguration Setup

When a user issues a local reconfiguration request, the reconfiguration is initially handled by the Configurator component. This component forwards the aspect reconfiguration to the AO-Manager component. The latter, then checks if a similar reconfiguration request has not been performed. If a similar reconfiguration request is present, then the cached join point information is retrieved and reconfiguration proceeds to Stage IV (Aspect Weaving Stage). The AO-Manager maintains a time-out cache period, after which any cached reconfiguration from the AO-Repository is removed. Furthermore, using the base runtime notify() operation, any changes made to the runtime are notified to the AO-Manager, so that cached requests are removed. Additionally, after performing an update, the updated reconfiguration is cached by removing the old cached entry. If the reconfiguration is not present in the cached repository, then the AO-Manager component, first submits the pointcut specification to the Pointcut Evaluator component (Stage II) followed by submitting the advice specification and the join point (received from Stage III) to the Aspect Handler component.

2. Stage II : Join point Lookup

Next, in case the reconfiguration is a new request that is not present in the cache, the AO-Manager component submits to the Pointcut Evaluator component the pointcut specification in order to retrieve the required join points.

Stage IIa: Pointcut Specification Parsing. The Pointcut Evaluator first uses the Parser CFs components to parse each of the pointcut signatures and expressions. If the pointcut specification contains dynamic properties signatures, the Dynamic Property Parser component is used to parse and extract the associated pointcut expressions. Otherwise, the specification is parsed by the Expression Parser component to retrieve the appropriate names associated for the aspect/component and interface/receptacle pointcut signature and the Method Parser component to extract the associated operations signatures. The Parser CF then returns the parsed signatures back to the Pointcut Evaluator component.

Stage IIb: Join point Lookup. The Pointcut Evaluator translates the respective parsed signatures/expressions whereby the aspects / component expressions are inspected using the Architecture meta-model component, followed by the interface and operation expressions. For the identified entities in the runtime, the respective connectors are returned to the Pointcut Evaluator component. In case the connector does not have an aspect then the default connector is returned to the AO-Manager component. Conversely, the AO-Connectors are returned to the AO-Manager in case of already woven aspects-components at the join points.

3. Stage III : Aspect Instance Retrieval

On receiving the list of connectors (either default-connector or AO-Connector), the AO-Manager component then submits the aspect specification and the connectors list to the Aspect Handler component. On the other hand, if the list of connectors is empty, the reconfiguration is not applicable and the reconfiguration is aborted. For *add* or *replace*, this may involve obtaining the aspect from an Aspect Repository. It will also involve weaving the aspect according to the specified scope and locus.

4. Stage IV: Aspect Weaving

The aspect weaving interaction varies according to the reconfiguration command-action.

1.) Add reconfiguration command-action.

Before the aspect weaving is performed, the AO-Handler ensures the aspects are type compatible by performing type-safety checking using the TypeValidator component. That is, it checks if the aspect exposes a matching interface and receptacle and its methods operations at the *callee* and *caller* components. Then, if at the join point there is no AO-Connector present, then the default-connector must first be replaced by an AO-Connector capable one. To do so, the Aspect Handler component, instructs the Quiescent Handler component to set the components under reconfiguration as well as the default connector to a quiescent state before the connector replacement is initiated. That is, the Aspect Handler component ensures that the associated components on the default connector are in a steady state before any reconfiguration can proceed. For this purpose, a read/write lock mechanism is used, such that every non-reconfigure operation can access the lock as a reader (there can be *n* readers using the lock at any one time) and for any reconfiguration calls an exclusive writer lock is used. Once in a quiescent state, the Aspect Handler component then calls the AO-Connector-Factory (In the simplest form of bindings between components, the default-connector-factory component is used to instantiate connectors without any interception capability) component via the CF load() and instantiate() methods respectively. Subsequently, the interface-receptacle pair of the reconfigured components are connected by using the CF *connect()* method and parsing the instantiated AO-Connector-Factory factory as one of its arguments. Once created, a success message is returned to the AO-Manager component. In the case of failure the *fail_created_AOConnector_Timeout* failure message is sent to the AO-Manager. The error message signifies that the AO-Connector creation reached the reconfiguration timeout. If the AO-Connector has successfully been created, then the AO-Manager instructs the Aspect Handler to weave the aspects. By default for the *add* reconfiguration command-action the aspect is added in an ordered manner in the AO-Connector chain. If the order of the aspect order is specified, then based on the specified order the aspect is woven in the AO-Connector chain.

2.) Replace reconfiguration command-action.
The reconfiguration to replace an aspect takes place in four interaction stages. Similar to the add command-action reconfiguration, the reconfiguration is first checked if they are type compatible with the interface-receptacles at the join point components, followed by placing the join point list of components and the AO-Connector aspect components to the quiescent state. Next, the Aspect Handler component extracts the execution state from the existing reconfigured aspect. This state extraction mechanism is optionally supported by aspects, the capability being dynamically discovered by the CF member using reflection. Then, the old aspect reference is removed and the new-aspect component reference added at the AO-Connector chain state is restored to the newly replaced aspect. If the old aspect state was extracted the state is restored to the newly updated aspect using the State Handler component *restore-state()* method operation.

3.) Remove reconfiguration command-action.
The remove reconfiguration command-action takes place in a three stage interaction, with the first stage consisting of setting the reconfiguration join point to quiescent. Then, in Stage II, the aspect reference is removed from the AO-Connector. In the final stage, Stage III the quiescence on the AO-Connector is removed, after completing the reconfiguration. Moreover, if there is no other aspect attached to the AO-Connector, then the AO-Connector is replaced by a default-connector. Once the weaving/un-weaving has been completed the Aspect Handler returns an acknowledgment message to the AO-Manager component. If the reconfiguration is successful the updated reconfiguration join point is cached. Finally, a reconfiguration *ack()* message is returned to the Configurator informing that the reconfiguration has been completed and the lock on the Configurator can be removed, such that the Configurator component can accept new reconfiguration requests.

4.) Reorder reconfiguration command-action.
The Aspect Reorder Reconfiguration involves the Stage I, II and III of the reconfiguration interaction. Stage IV is similar to the aspect removal reconfiguration action. However, instead of removing the aspect reference, the aspect references are reordered according to the specified advice specification.

4.2.2 Distributed Reconfiguration
The *Configurator.reconfigure()* reconfiguration protocol in AO-OpenCom is as follows:

1. *Configurator.reconfigure()* is called on the Configurator of one of the nodes supporting the DCF to be reconfigured; in the following this node is referred to as the 'initiator'.
2. The initiator determines how the specified aspect is to be applied. In the case of a per-DCF scope, it instantiates the aspect at a suitable node and sends a remote reference to the nodes where it is to be woven. Otherwise, the initiator decides if it has the specified aspect available locally (or can get it from an Aspect Repository) and wants to send it 'by value' to the nodes where it is to be woven, or if it wants to send the aspect 'by reference' and implicitly instruct the other DCF members to obtain the aspect from an Aspect Repository.
3. The initiator sends a 'reconfigure' message to all DCF member nodes. This essentially contains the parameters originally passed to *reconfigure()*. By default, the initiator employs the DCF's default communications service for this.
4. When it receives a 'reconfigure' message, each DCF member node's Pointcut Evaluator applies the specified pointcut and thereby locates all the target join points within its scope.
5. If the command is 'replace', the Aspect Handler extracts execution state from the existing aspect. Similar to local aspect reconfiguration, the state extraction mechanism is optionally supported by distributed aspects, with the capability being dynamically discovered by the DCF member using reflection.
6. Each member node's Aspect Handler then actions the 'add', 'remove' or 'replace' command as appropriate. For 'add' or 'replace', this may involve obtaining the aspect from an Aspect Repository. It will also involve weaving the aspect according to the specified scope and locus (a remote binding per-DCF scope may be created if needed).
7. Each node replies to the initiator that it has completed the reconfiguration locally.
8. When all nodes have reported completion the initiator node returns control to the caller of *reconfigure()*.

Note in passing that there is considerable scope for optimising this protocol in terms of performance. For example, the configuration of aspect repositories in the system, and the corresponding choice of whether to pass aspects by value or by reference, can have a significant influence on performance, as can the use of, and location of, remotely accessible per-DCF aspects.

5. EVALUATION
To evaluate AO-OpenCom approach to offer flexible dynamic reconfiguration requirements we use a case-study based methodology which is described in Section 5.1. Then, in Section 5.2 we describe the AO-OpenCom use case solution. Finally, in Section 5.3 the reconfiguration performance is evaluated.

5.1 Airport Crisis Management Scenario
The use-case scenario is inspired by an *airport crisis management* scenario taken from the EU DiVA FP7 STREP project [2]. This was chosen because it offers a realistic scenario taken from a real project and because it offers sufficient opportunities for dynamic reconfiguration. The architecture of the crisis management scenario consists of four different domains: the Main Control Room, Administration, Sales, and Terminal. The Main Control Room centralises all phases of the management of the other three domains by determining the different types of dynamic reconfiguration necessary to maintain their optimal operation. More specifically, the Main Control Room is responsible for identifying any crisis, building appropriate crisis management strategies according to the nature of the incident, collecting crisis information and providing it to all the domains dealing with crisis management. The Main Control Room contains human crisis actors and a crisis management system offering a messaging system for crisis actors so that they can communicate through the exchange of text messages. The Main Control Room dynamically reconfigures the crisis management system configuration according to the crisis type and context. The Administration domain hosts the key stakeholders (CEO, Operation Manager, CIO) representing the airport's decision making authority. In case of any crisis they need to be notified immediately. In crisis situations, the Sales and Terminal domains are notified about incidents and, based on the gravity of the incident, the Terminal operations (such as boarding) are stopped or delayed.

As a crisis situation is initiated from the Main Control Room, alerts sent to the different crisis actors within the airport are logged to keep track of events and can be studied later on for service improvement. Alerts are logged during both crisis and non-crisis situations. In a non-crisis situation, all crisis actors send their logs to the main control room. Under a crisis situation only crisis actors involved in the crisis are logged.

5.2 AO-OpenCom based solution

From the use-case scenario, the MessageHandler and the Communication modules as shown in Figure 8a are two main entities responsible for the transmission of messages among nodes before reconfiguration and after reconfiguration in Figure 8b.

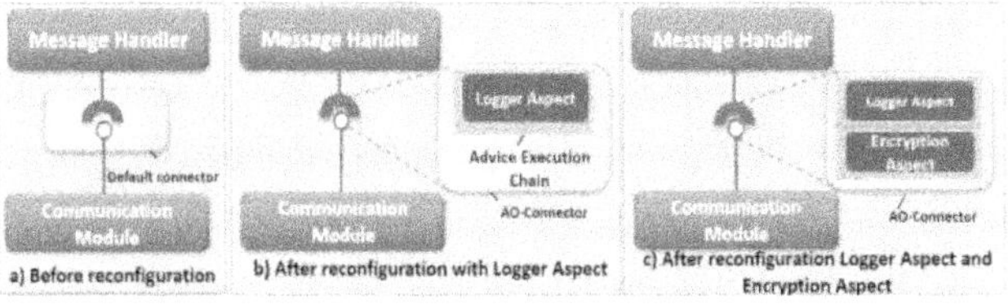

Figure 8. Reconfiguration for use case scenario.

The Messager module is responsible to transmit messages based and requires an IMesageHandler interface which takes as parameters the MessageType, DCF, port id and communication mode. Figure 9 illustrates the MessageHandler code fragment implementation.

```
1  public class MessageHandler implements IMessageHandler  {
2      public OCM_SingleReceptacle<ICommunication> m_PSR_ICommunication;
3      public OCM_SingleReceptacle<IAOOpenCom> m_PSR_IAOOpenCom;
4      public MessageHandler() {
5          m_PSR_ICommunication = new OCM_SingleReceptacle<ICommunication>(ICommunication.class);
6          m_PSR_IIAOOpenCom =  new OCM_SingleReceptacle<IAOOpenCom>(IAOOpenCom.class);
7      }
8      public void sendMsg(MessageType msgType, String DCF,
9                          int portid, CommunicationType, commType){
10             ((ICommunication) m_PSR_ICommunication.m_pIntf).sendMsg( msgType, DCF,
11                         portid, commType);
12     }
13     ...
14 }
```

Figure 9. Code extract of the Message Handler

From Figure 9, Line 1 implements the IMessageHandler interface to handle the message communication to the Communication component. Line 2 specifies the receptacle reference of the MessageHandler component to the Communication component and Line 3 details the reference to the AO-OpenCom runtime base-level kernel. Lines 4-7 contain the constructor for the MessageHandler component. Lines 8-12 detail the call to the sendMsg operation of the Communication component. In the use-case scenario, the alert logging is a crosscutting concern that is tangled across multiple nodes. In order to facilitate the reconfigurability the application developer needs to untangle this functionality from the component implementation. Another requirement from the use-case scenario is the need to provide secure transmission of the logs. To do so an encryption module is needed and since the encryption module is crosscutting similar to the alert logging module, it needs to be applied as an aspect (as shown in Figure 8c). The code-fragment of the local Logger aspect implementation is illustrated in Figure 10 and that of the remote Logger aspect in Figure 11.

5.3 Evaluating Reconfiguration Protocol

To measure the reconfiguration protocol a small network of five standalone workstations has been employed: a 1.8 GHz Core Duo 2 PC with 3GB RAM; a 3.4 GHz Pentium IV PC with 1GB of RAM; a 2.8GHz Pentium IV PC with 1 GB of RAM; a 1.33 GHz Core Duo 2 laptop with 2GB of RAM; and a MacBook 2.4 GHz Core Duo 2 laptop with 4GB RAM. Two of the machines ran Ubuntu 12.04, two ran Windows XP with service pack 3, one ran Windows 7 SP1 and the other ran OS X. All of these are connected via a 100Mbps local area network. While this network is small in terms of physical nodes, each physical node is used to host multiple instances of the framework and in this way the evaluation environment was able to scale to support the equivalent of 100 nodes (frameworks) under four Java VMs per machine. Each evaluation machine was installed with the AO-OpenCom framework which was executed on a Java 1.7 virtual machine (VM). Note that the different machines used to perform the experimental setup demonstrate the capability of AO-OpenCom of being deployed independently in various operating system environments and with different hardware resources as long as these machines support the Java VM. Each machine was able to scale to support 100 of these configurations as virtual nodes.

```
public class LoggerAspect implements ILogger{
    public OCM_SingleReceptacle<IAOOpenCom> m_PSR_IAOOpenCom;
    public OCM_SingleReceptacle<ICommunication> m_PSR_ICommunication;

    public LoggerAspect(Properties properties, int IPM_PORT){
        public OCM_SingleReceptacle<ICommunication> m_PSR_ICommunication;
        m_PSR_IOpenCOM =  new OCM_SingleReceptacle<IOpenCOM>(IOpenCOM.class);
        this.properties = properties;
    }
    public sendMsg(MessageType msgType, String DCF,
                   int portid, CommunicationType, commType){
        //... implementation details
        LogMessageHandler();
    }

    public void LogMessageHandler(){
        try{
            FileOutputStream fos = new FileOutpuStream(
                           properties.get(LoggerAspect));
            fos.write(alertLog.message);
            fos.close();
        } catch(Exception e){}
    }
}
```

Figure 10. Code extract of the Local Logger Aspect

```
public class LoggerAspect extends UnicastRemoteObject implements ILogger, Serializable {
    public OCM_SingleReceptacle<IAOOpenCom> m_PSR_IAOOpenCom;
    public OCM_SingleReceptacle<ICommunication> m_PSR_ICommunication;

    public LoggerAspect(Properties properties, int IPM_PORT)
                throws RemoteException{
        super();
        public OCM_SingleReceptacle<ICommunication> m_PSR_ICommunication;
        m_PSR_IOpenCOM =  new OCM_SingleReceptacle<IOpenCOM>(IOpenCOM.class);
        this.properties = properties;
    }
    public sendMsg(MessageType msgType, String DCF,
                   int portid, CommunicationType, commType){
        //... implementation details
        LogMessageHandler();
    }

    public void LogMessageHandler() throws RemoteException{
        try{
            FileOutputStream fos = new FileOutpuStream(
                       properties.get(LoggerAspect)+currentDCFNode);
            fos.write(alertLog.message);
            fos.close();
        } catch(Exception e){}
    }
}
```

Figure 11: Code extract of the Remote Logger Aspect

5.3.1 Add command-action

To evaluate the performance overhead of the reconfiguration protocol add-command-action, the logger aspect is woven at the communication stack. The reconfiguration involves weaving the logger aspect at the AO-Connector connecting the Message Handler and the Communication Module. To perform this reconfiguration, the reconfiguration developer needs to specify the reconfiguration request by writing code along the lines of Figure 12 (the code is simplified for presentational purposes).

```
Pointcut pc = new Pointcut( "*", "MessageHandler*", "ICommunication","msg*");
Aspect aspectlist = new Aspect(Logger);
Configurator.reconfigure(pc, add, aspectlist, perDCF, before);
```

Figure 12. Reconfiguration specification

The *Configurator.reconfigure()* call takes the given pointcut and aspect specifications which are as follows: the aspects that need to be "added"; the scope of the reconfiguration, stating that this reconfiguration need to be applied for all nodes; and that the weaving locus should be a *before* advice weaving. The results of the experiment are illustrated in Figure 13. The results confirm the expected outcome that as the number of reconfigured nodes increases, the amount of time required to perform reconfiguration increases linearly. The result shows that on a single node (as would be expected) the reconfiguration using the local pointcut and local aspect is similar to that of using remote pointcut and local aspect, and the reconfiguration using local pointcut and remote aspect is similar to that of remote pointcut and remote aspect. The differences between LL, RL and LR and RR lie in the remote aspect instantiation for LR and RR. This instantiation is an out-of-band overhead on the initiator node and if the aspect is already instantiated in the aspect repository, then the reconfiguration time is decreased, with the overhead comparable to that of LL and RL. The results also show that:

i) For less than 170 nodes LL offers significantly better reconfiguration performance than LR. This means the instantiation of the local aspect across each node is expensive as the number of reconfigured nodes gets above 170 nodes.
ii) Above 160 reconfigured nodes LL reconfiguration overhead gets worse compared to RR. The difference at 10 nodes between LR and RR when compared to LL, is due to the remote pointcut offering less reconfiguration overhead in RR.
iii) For less than 220 reconfigured nodes RL offers better reconfiguration time compared to RR. This is explained by the instantiation of the remote aspect being expensive, and the reconfiguration cost offset the instantiation time as more than 220 nodes are reconfigured.
iv) When reconfiguring more than 220 nodes RR reconfiguration is better compared to LL, LR and RL. This is mainly attributed to the instantiation cost while weaving remote aspects as well as the method *Lookup()* operation to ensure remote aspect interface compatibility as the remote aspect is woven to the AO-Connector chain.

Overall, the experimental results show that there is a large overhead while reconfiguring on a single node using LR and RR compared to LL and RL. As the number of reconfigured nodes increases, reconfiguration using RL and RR offers better performance compared to LL and LR. The higher reconfiguration time using LR and RR is mainly due to the remote aspect instantiation on the initiator node which is on average 147ms. Having the remote aspect instantiated will amortise the reconfiguration time as shown in the dotted lines in Figure 13 for both LR and RR making RR better for large scale reconfiguration.

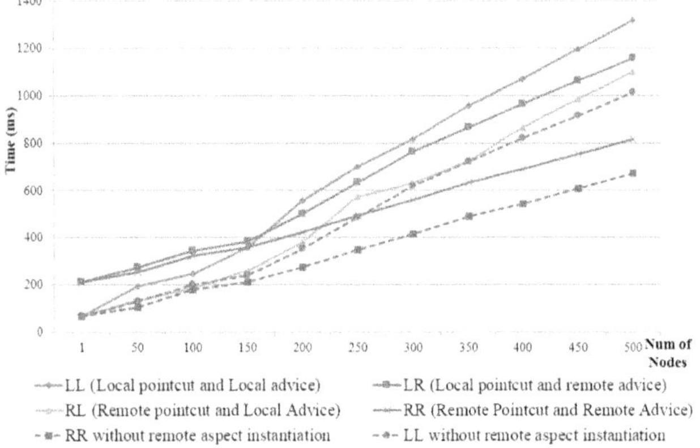

Figure 13. Add reconfiguration command-action

5.3.2 Replace command-action

Here the Logger aspect is replaced by the Multicast Logger aspect. This operation involves a *replace* operation of the existing Logger aspect at the message handler AO-Connector by the Alert Logger and the resulting reconfiguration. To measure the reconfiguration overhead of the replace command-action the same environmental setup as in Section 5.3.1 is used, whereby the woven Logger aspect is replaced by a Multicast Logger aspect. The results from Figure 14 show an increase in the reconfiguration time to perform the *replace* command-action compared to the *add* command-action. This is due to the fact that the replace command-action requires the un-weaving of the old aspect component followed by the weaving of the new aspect component, while that of the add command-action involves only the aspect weaving. The results show:

i) RL offers better reconfiguration compared to LL, RL and RR to reconfigure up to 160 nodes. This is explained by the quantification of the pointcut being performed only on the initiator node and the instantiation remote aspect on smaller number of nodes offers better reconfiguration overhead compared to remote aspect instantiation.
ii) A steeper gradient to reconfigure LR compared to RR as the number of reconfigured nodes increases shows that pointcut quantification on each reconfigured node is expensive.
iii) RR setup offers better reconfiguration time compared to LL, LR and RR, similar to the add command-action.

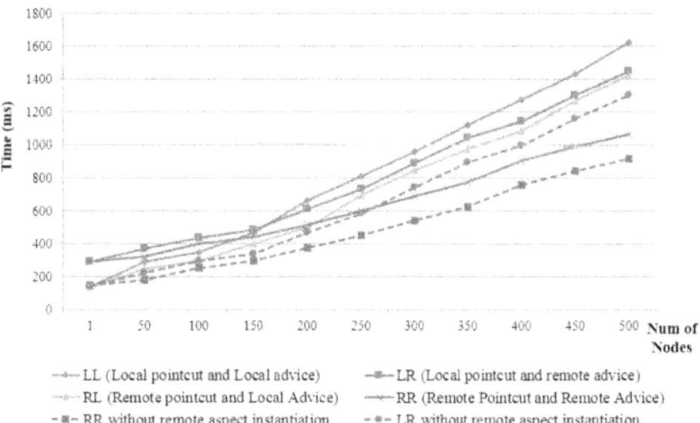

Figure 14. Replace reconfiguration command-action

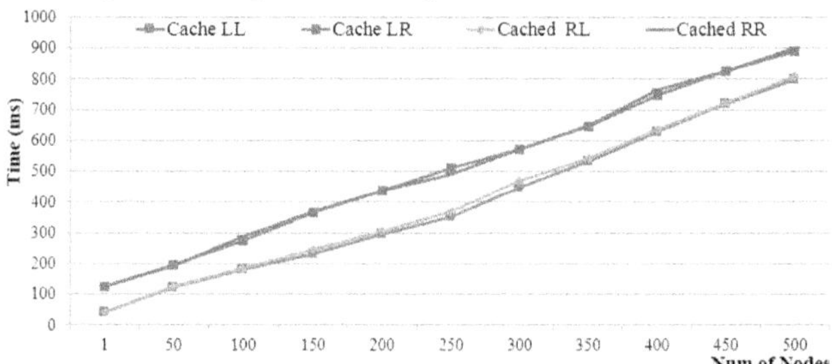

Figure 15. Replace command-action using cached pointcut

An additional experiment was performed to measure reconfiguration overhead while updating the aspect using cached pointcuts by retrieving the pointcut from the AO Repository. The measurements of the experiment are shown in Figure 15. The results show a significant decrease in the reconfiguration time for all the four reconfiguration operations. The decrease in overhead is on average by 30% per reconfigured node. It should be noted that the cached pointcut still requires the parsing of the XML specification to check if the required reconfiguration request matches the ones previously retrieved and cached. The results also show that the time needed to perform remote aspect is lower than that of local aspect. This is explained by the fact that the remote aspect is instantiated only once on the initiator node compared to local instantiation on each Aspect Repository in the case of LL and RL.

5.3.3 Remove command-action

Finally, the Logger aspect may no longer be necessary, and can be removed. The reasons behind a remove reconfiguration command include: removing the Logger aspect as the policy associated to it has been deleted, or being incompatible (such as semantic inconsistencies) and needs to be removed to allow a reconfiguration to be completed. This involves a remove reconfiguration command, such that the reconfiguration leaves an empty advice chain at the join point. As discussed earlier, an AO-Connector is woven to support the advice chain at the appropriate join point. The AO-Connector component should be removed when no aspect is present at the join point. This is because leaving an empty AO-Connector will result in an in-band overhead that negatively affects the system performance. The results from Figure 16 show a lower reconfiguration overhead for un-weaving an aspect compared to the weaving or replacing of an aspect. This is because, the un-weaving of aspects involves the parsing of the reconfiguration operations from the script, locating the join point and setting the reconfigured join point to quiescent mode and removing the references of the aspect from the AO-Connector. It can also be observed that the un-weaving of an aspect is faster for LL and RL compared to LR and RR. This is explained by the reflective calls needed to get the aspect operations before its methods are removed at the AO-Connector. For the remote aspect, the reflective call involves the *Lookup()* method for the remote aspect causing higher performance penalty. The next measurement involved measuring the amount of time required to remove an aspect and then remove the AO-Connector by reinstalling the default connector. The additional reconfiguration time per node is about 10ms for all the setup reconfigurations (LL, LR, RL and RR). This lower increase is mainly due to the fact no reflective calls are needed with an *Unload()* followed by a *Connect()* method call executed.

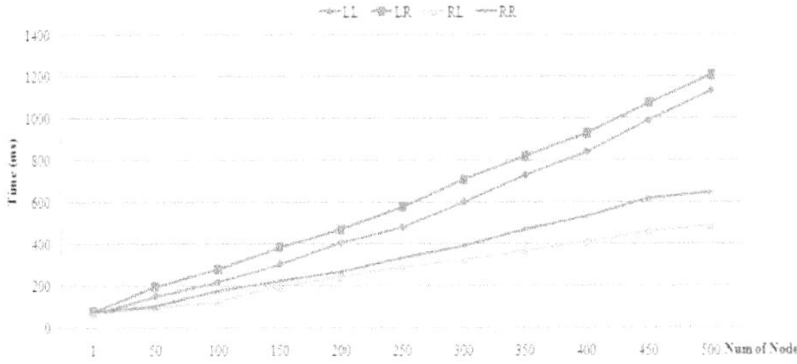

Figure 16. Remove command-action reconfiguration

5.3.4 Reorder reconfiguration protocol

A reorder command action may be applied when more than one aspect is woven at a join point. To measure the overhead of the reorder command action all messages sent are encrypted and then logged. This reconfiguration involves the reorder operation which reorders the advice chain.

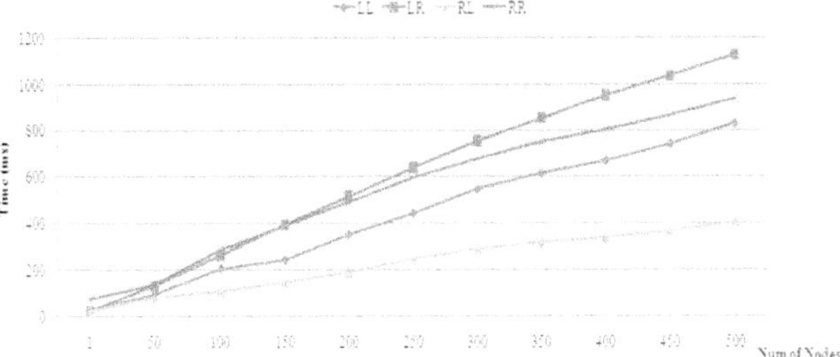

Figure 17. Reorder command-action reconfiguration

The results of Figure 17 show that the reorder command-action has a significantly lower reconfiguration cost than the coarse-grained operations. Additionally, it can be observed that the cost of using LR and RR to perform the reorder reconfiguration is significantly higher (by 50%) compared to LL and RL. The higher overhead is explained by the *Lookup()* reflective method call for remote aspects having higher overhead.

5.3.5 Evaluating resource overhead

This section examines the resource costs (in terms of memory) in reconfiguring the middleware platform using a reliable and an unreliable communication protocol. Figure 18 shows the resource overhead on the initiator node of AO-OpenCom using first a reliable communication protocol (JGroups) and then an unreliable multicast protocol. The measures represent the resource overhead of the Distributed Meta Architecture: i.e. configurations for the binding of the case study application and the base elements of the AO-OpenCom platform. Furthermore, it can be observed that there is an extra memory overhead from the use of reliable communications. The additional cost ranges between 3.9% to 119.2% increase in the amount of memory consumed by each node. Additionally, it can be observed there is a linear increase in resource overhead as the number of nodes increases. This measure demonstrates that a large part of resource overhead is incurred to ensure reliable communication and is representative of the increase in overhead as applications are reconfigured across a distributed system.

Figure 18. Reconfiguration resource overhead

6. DISCUSSION AND RELATED WORK

The experiments results demonstrate the flexibility of AO-OpenCom to robustly support a wide range of dynamic reconfiguration variability in terms of i) *granular scope reconfigurability* supporting coarse-grained reconfiguration using the reconfiguration command-actions (add, replace and remove and operations) provide coarse-grained and fine-grained reconfiguration (reorder operation); ii) *vertical scope reconfigurability* allowing both infrastructure services reconfigurability as demonstrated and measured in Section 5.3.5 and application services reconfigurability as the demonstrated in Section 5.3.1 to Section 5.3.4; iii) *horizontal scope reconfigurability* supporting both local and distributed reconfiguration as demonstrated in Section 5.3.1 to Section 5.3.4; and iv) *performance;* and v) *resource overhead* with the main resource overhead within the AO-OpenCom being from the distributed framework which is influenced by the choice of the communication protocol. The resource overhead on each node can be minimised by creating group nodes and having one node hosting the distributed framework of the group of nodes.

Turning to related work, a number of AO-middleware platforms have emerged. Most of the AO-middleware platforms offer only coarse-grained reconfiguration. However, AspectOpenCom [3] and JAC [8] provide support for fine-grained reconfigurability, by allowing the reordering of aspects at a join point. Regarding application-level vertical scope of reconfigurability most middleware platforms provide support to weave and un-weave aspects that are applied to an application at runtime. However, with the exception of FAC [9], none of the AO-middleware platforms supports infrastructure-level evolution, but FAC is limited to local infrastructure-level only. With respect to horizontal scope reconfiguration, AO-middleware platforms support three types of aspect composition. First *aspect composition being separate from the distribution model*, such that the middleware architectures use their own distribution specific technologies to provide distribution. Most of the AO-middleware platforms (PROSE [11], JBoss-AOP [15], Lasagne [14], DyReS [15] and CAM/DAOP [10]) have aspect being separate from the distribution model. These AO-middleware platforms use distribution technologies to provide distribution. Second, *aspects abstractions are used with the distribution model*, such that the middleware architectures use aspect technology to provide reconfiguration. DJasCo [1], JAC [8] and ReflexD [13] platforms use aspects abstractions with the distribution model by offering the remote pointcut functionality. Third, *aspect form an integral part (i.e. as a first class entity) of the distribution model*, such that the middleware platforms (DyMAC [5] and Damon [6]) use aspects to provide reconfiguration and build the distribution models. The DyMAC platform supports both remote advice and remote pointcut functionality but the platform only allows remote aspect deployment (aspects are non-reconfigurable in the platform). In the case of Damon the explicit connector defined for each composition makes the composition of distributed aspects non-transparent. However, none of the AO-middleware platforms provide for flexible distributed reconfiguration with the support of local pointcut - local advice; remote pointcut - local advice; local pointcut – remote advice; and remote pointcut – remote advice.

Finally, with respect to performance and resource overhead, AO-middleware platforms using byte-code instrumentation weaving (DJasCo, JBoss AOP, JAC, Damon, ReflexD) usually introduce some level of overhead in the system while performing reconfiguration, while CAM/DAOP and Lasagne which use a message interception mechanism to invoke aspects introduce significant overhead. PROSE uses a two-way weaving mechanism such that alternate weaving mechanism can be chosen based on the performance need. In DyMAC, since the weaving is done on all possible join points at load-time the runtime weaving of aspects is not significant. However, similar to AspectOpenCom the use of proxy-based interceptors on all join points even those not having any aspects behaviour bound to them, introduce an indirection in the call invocation for all component communications as the calls need to pass through the proxy. In our approach, the use of default-connector and AO-connector at runtime diminishes the indirection when no aspects are present.

7. CONCLUSIONS

In this paper we have presented an aspect-oriented component framework architecture that offers comprehensive AOP support for both local and distributed reconfiguration. The AO meta-framework can be independently deployed such that it imposes no overhead when it is not used and can be dynamically deployed/un-deployed where and when required. In addition, the AO meta-framework is built using the same programming language independent component-based principles as the underlying reflective middleware layer, and the overlying application.

The AO-OpenCom platform provides the development of a fully distributed realisation of dynamic aspects. This is achieved by layering our AO provision on top of the distribution framework and by providing a pointcut language that is inherently distributed in nature (i.e. it supports quantification over capsules). In addition, the AO-OpenCom middleware supports in a natural way the composition of advices that is remote from the advised join points. Furthermore, the AO-OpenCom approach significantly decreases the complexity of deploying new functionality in a distributed environment as compared to the reflective middleware approach. Nevertheless, the lower-level reflective APIs are still available to the developer should they be required.

Additionally, the experimental results show that AO-OpenCom is scalable and achieves flexibility providing an important step towards the path of enhancing dynamic reconfiguration in AO-middleware for real-world critical distributed applications.

8. REFERENCES

[1] Benavides, et al. Explicitly distributed AOP using AWED. RR INRIA 5882 Technical Report March 2006.

[2] DiVA. 2009 - Diva-dynamic variability in complex, adaptive systems.ftp://ftp.cordis.europa.eu/pub/fp7/ict/docs/ssai/project-diva_en.pdf.

[3] Grace, P., Truyen, E., Lagaisse, B. & Joosen, W. 'The Case for Aspect-Oriented Reflective Middleware'. In Proc. of the 6th Workshop on Adaptive and Reflective Middleware 2007.

[4] Grace, P. 2009. 'Dynamic Adaptation'. In Middleware for Network Eccentric and Mobile Applications, B. Garbinato, H. Miranda and L. Rodrigues (Eds.), pp. 285-304, Springer.

[5] Lagaisse, B. 'A Comprehensive Integration of AOSD and CBSD concepts in Middleware'. Ph.D. Thesis, Department of Computer Science, K.U.Leuven, Belgium, Dec 2009.

[6] Mondejar, R., García, P., Pairot, C., Urso, P. & Molli, P. 'Designing a Distributed AOP Runtime Composition Model'. In 24th ACM Applied Computing, USA 2009.

[7] Parnas, L. 1972. 'On the Criteria to be Used in Decomposing Systems into Modules'. In Proc. ACM, Vol 15.

[8] Pawlak, R., Seinturier, L., Duchien, L. & Florin, G. 2001. 'JAC: A Flexible Solution for AOP in Java'. In Proceedings of the Third International Conference on Metalevel Architectures and Separation of Crosscutting Concerns.

[9] Pessemier, N. 2007. 'Unification des approaches par aspects et a composants'. PhD Thesis, University of Lilles.

[10] Pinto, M., Fuentes, L. & Troya, J.M. 2005. 'A Component And Aspect based Dynamic Platform'. The Computer Journal, Volume 48, Issue 4, 401-420, 2005.

[11] Popovici, A., Gross, T. & Alonso, G. 2001. Dynamic Homogenous AOP with PROSE. Technical Report, Dept. of Computer Science, March 2001.

[12] Surajbali, B., Coulson, G., Greenwood, P., and Grace, P.. Augmenting reflective middleware with an aspect orientation support layer. In Proc. of the 6th ARM 2007.

[13] Tanter, E. & Toledo, R. 'A Versatile Kernel for Distributed AOP'. In Proceedings of the IFIP Conference on DAIS 2006.

[14] Truyen, E. 2004. Dynamic and context-sensitive composition in distributed systems. Ph.D. Thesis, Department of Computer Science, K.U.Leuven, Belgium.

[15] Truyen, E., Janssens, N., Sanen, F., & Joosen W. 2008. 'Support for distributed adaptations in aspect-oriented middleware'. In Proc. of the 7th Conference on AOSD, 2008.

Coqcots & Pycots: Non-stopping Components for Safe Dynamic Reconfiguration

Jérémy Buisson[1,3], Everton Cavalcante[1,2,4], Fabien Dagnat[1,5], Elena Leroux[1,2], Sébastien Martinez[1,5]

[1]IRISA, Brest – Rennes – Vannes, France
[2]University of South Brittany, Vannes, France
[3]St-Cyr Coëtquidan Schools, Guer, France
[4]DIMAp, Federal University of Rio Grande do Norte, Natal, Brazil
[5]Télécom Bretagne, Brest, France

jeremy.buisson@irisa.fr, evertonrsc@ppgsc.ufrn.br, fabien.dagnat@irisa.fr, elena.leroux@irisa.fr, sebatien.martinez@telecom-bretagne.eu

ABSTRACT

Software systems have to face evolutions of their running context and users. Therefore, the so-called *dynamic reconfiguration* has been commonly adopted for modifying some components and/or the architecture at runtime. Traditional approaches typically stop the needed components, apply the changes, and restart the components. However, this scheme is not suitable for critical systems and degrades user experience. This paper proposes to switch from the stop/restart scheme to *dynamic software updating* (DSU) techniques. Instead of stopping a component, its implementation is replaced by another one specifically built to apply the modifications while maintaining the best quality of service possible. The major contributions of this work are: (i) the integration of DSU techniques in a component model, and; (ii) a reconfiguration development process including specification, proof of correctness using Coq, and a systematic method to produce the executable script. In this perspective, the use of DSU techniques brings higher quality of service when reconfiguring component-based software and the formalization allows ensuring the safety and consistency of the reconfiguration process.

Categories and Subject Descriptors

D.2.11 [**Software Engineering**]: Software Architectures

Keywords

Dynamic reconfiguration, component model, dynamic software updating, DSU, Python, Coq, runtime evolution

CBSE'14, June 30–July 4, 2014, Marcq-en-Baroeul, France.
Copyright 2014 ACM 978-1-4503-2577-6/14/06 ...$15.00.
http://dx.doi.org/10.1145/2602458.2602459.

1. INTRODUCTION

Software systems need to be highly available and should be built using secure, safe, performant, and robust components. These components must be regularly modified to fix vulnerabilities and bugs, to face new environments, and to offer new services. Enabling these evolutions, while maintaining a high level of availability, requires changing the architecture of such a system during its execution. This capability is especially important for critical systems such as air-traffic control systems and networks, in which stopping systems is not an option due to financial or human costs. It also improves user experience as a user can continue to use a software system being updated without noticing the update, *i.e.*, the updating process is transparent to the users.

In software engineering, *dynamic reconfiguration* was introduced to build component-based software systems that can be modified during their execution, with minimal or no interruption. In this approach, components and connectors of a system can be inserted, removed or replaced at runtime, thus fostering the continuity of the services it provides.

Since the proposition of the *quiescence* concept [9], reconfiguring a system typically requires the suspension of a set of components that will be affected by the reconfiguration. Maintaining the system in an operational status while stopping part of its components leads to a visible degradation of its quality of service [6, 10] due to component dependencies. Another essential issue to be considered is to preserve the consistency of the component assembly throughout the reconfiguration process. Some works in the literature have faced these challenges by minimizing the set of suspended components and/or decreasing the duration of their suspension [7, 18]. Focusing on consistency, Boyer et al. [2] propose a scheme in which an invariant requires to stop any component that depends on a stopped component. However, such dependencies often propagate until the user frontend, and then the system may be almost entirely stopped.

To maintain service continuity, we must refrain from stopping components when reconfiguring a system. In this paper, we propose to use *dynamic software updating* (DSU) techniques [14, 16] instead of suspending components. The main idea is to mitigate the effect of any reconfiguration action by dynamically updating the implementation of directly and in-

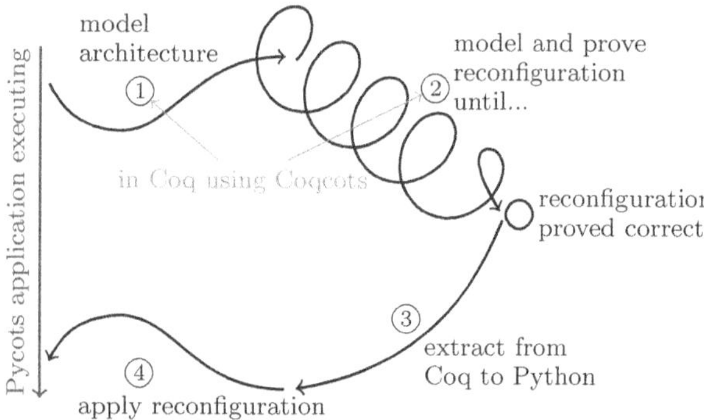

Figure 1: Overview of the proposed approach.

directly affected components. For example, if a component B used by a component A needs to be reconfigured, then the component A can be updated with a new implementation that no longer uses B before reconfiguring B.

The two major contributions of this paper are: (i) integration of DSU techniques in a component model named Coqcots/Pycots, and (ii) a reconfiguration development process. In Figure 1, which depicts the process, the left-hand side arrow represents the execution flow of the target application. During execution, if a reconfiguration is needed, its design and execution follow the four steps on the right of the figure. The two first steps of this process are performed in Coq using Coqots: ① the current architecture of the target software system is modeled as a Coqcots architecture, and ② this model is used as an input to develop the reconfiguration using the Coq proof assistant. Once the reconfiguration is valid: ③ the reconfiguration script is translated to Python and ④ the Python script is submitted to the Pycots manager, which is a platform component that receives and applies reconfiguration scripts.

The remainder of this paper covers steps ①, ② and ④ of the process. Section 2 outlines the DSU techniques. Section 3 presents Coqcots, our component model for dynamic reconfiguration, while Section 4 covers Pycots, the Python framework that implements it. Section 5 is dedicated to the validation of our approach with a case study. Section 6 briefly discusses some relevant work related to the dynamic reconfiguration of component-based systems. Finally, Section 7 contains final remarks and directions for future work. All the material described in this paper is available online at http://coqcots.gforge.inria.fr.

2. DYNAMIC SOFTWARE UPDATING

Dynamic software updating (DSU) gathers several mechanisms whose goal is to update software at runtime. Whereas dynamic reconfiguration affects the architectural structure, DSU modifies the software at procedural or object-oriented level. Most classical DSU mechanisms replace a function by its newer version when it is not being called (*i.e.*, when it is not in the call stack) and convert instances of a given class to a new structure by using a transformer function.

Surveys [14, 16] list several platforms that provide DSU mechanisms. Each of these platforms offers a different perspective on DSU among the following aspects: How and when shall the update be triggered? How and when shall data be converted? How shall the execution flow of the application be modified? In this work we use Pymoult [13], a Python-based platform that provides several of the existing DSU mechanisms and well addresses all of the previously mentioned aspects.

In the current state-of-the-art, two triggering mechanisms are proposed. With *active* triggering, the program signals to the platform that it can be updated by calling a specific function placed in the code by the program developer. With *passive* triggering, the platform detects when the program can be updated. In both cases, detecting this moment requires being able to monitor the program (*e.g.*, detect if a function is in the stack), especially when using passive triggering. Pymoult provides the two triggering mechanisms as well as tools for monitoring the program.

Data is usually converted by the combination of an access strategy (*eager* or *lazy*) and a conversion method. For the eager strategy, Pymoult intercepts the creation of each object in order to store a weak reference to this object. The created pool is then used to access all objects at a given time. For the lazy strategy, Pymoult uses the Python metaobject protocol to access objects whenever their fields are used (read or written). Regarding conversion, Pymoult provides tools such as the usage of *mixins* or *proxies*.

Several ways of modifying the execution flow (*e.g.*, changing the code of a function, altering the stack) are used in the literature. Pymoult supports *safe redefinition* for modifying a function or method code when it is not in the stack as well as more sophisticated techniques such as *stack reconstruction* [11] and *thread rebooting* [5, 13]. The two latter mechanisms allow to change the behavior of a function even if it is in the stack. In order to initialize the new behavior, it is possible to capture the runtime stack and read values from it thanks to the Python introspection tools.

3. THE COQCOTS COMPONENT MODEL

In this section we introduce our component model named Coqcots, formally defined by using the Coq formalism. The design of Coqcots follows the consensual component model described by Boyer et al. [2], except for the following points. In [2], each component follows a definite lifecycle: components can be started or stopped, and for each state of the lifecycle, a specific behavior is defined and embedded in the component. Instead of the predefined collection of behavior variants, Coqcots uses DSU techniques to dynamically change the behavior as needed by each reconfiguration. Moreover, changing the behavior of a component implies a change of its type. For example, a port may be added or removed when a new behavior implements a different set of functionalities. This change of type is explicit in Coqcots.

In the following, we first introduce our component model and explain how to specify a system architecture. Next, we define five operations used to reconfigure a system. Finally, we introduce a set of invariants whose role is to ensure a correct definition of a system architecture.

3.1 Specification of an architecture

As illustrated in Figure 2, a component (client) has an associated implementation (i) that uses a set of *used services* (U, which contains only the srv_port service in the case of the client component) to provide a set of *provided services* (P, which is empty for the client component). The architecture instance contains components (client and server) and defines

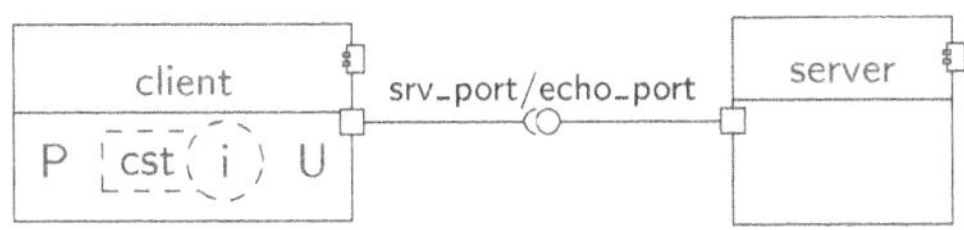

Figure 2: Anatomy of a Coqcots architecture.

the bindings between a used service of one of its components and a provided service of another of its components (srv_port/echo_port). When a used service of a component is not bound, the implementation of that component cannot use this unbound service.

In our approach, the implementation of a component may come with a precondition that specifies its assumption on the architecture in which the component is instantiated. This *architectural constraint* (cst for the client component) is an invariant that ensures that the implementation will only run in the expected situation. For example, a given component may require that some of its used services must be bound (the *mandatory services*), while the other services are allowed to remain unbound (the *optional services*). The component implementation can then assume that only optional services may be unbound. Using architectural constraints enables the designer to assume the mandatory semantics discussed by Boyer et al. [2] and Bruneton et al. [4].

Formally, Coqcots comes with two predicates, *contains* and *binds*, which respectively state that an architecture contains a given component and a given binding. The *contains* predicate takes as first argument an architecture a, followed by the five elements of a component: (1) the name of the component c, (2) the set[1] of its used services U, (3) the set of its provided services P, (4) its architectural constraint cst, and (5) its implementation i. The definition of *contains* is:

```
Parameter contains:
  ∀ (a: arch) (c: comp) (U: facet) (P: facet)
    (cst: arch → comp → Prop)
    (i: ∀ (u: facet_record U),
          cst a c → no_exc_if_bound a c u → facet_record P),
    Prop.
```

The architectural constraint is defined as a function that maps an architecture a and a component c to a proposition. It is used by the implementation as a precondition to provide the component's services (term cst a c). The other precondition no_exc_if_bound relieves the implementation from defensively checking for availability when a used service is guaranteed to be bound according to the constraint cst.

The *binds* predicate formally states that a binding exists in an architecture a. The binding is represented by six values: three for the client component (the user of the binding) and three for the server component (the provider of the binding). Both components are represented by (1) their identity respectively clt and srv, (2) the set of their involved services clt_U and srv_P, and (3) the ports clt_port and srv_port bound by the predicate. The definition of *binds* is:

```
Parameter binds:
  ∀ (a: arch)
    (clt: comp) (clt_U: Type) (clt_port: namedport clt_U)
    (srv: comp) (srv_P: Type) (srv_port: namedport srv_P),
    Prop.
```

Using these two predicates, the designer can define an architecture. For example, the architecture represented in Figure 2 is an element of the following type:

```
Definition client_server :=
  { a | ∃ client server,
      contains a client client_use_facet client_provide_facet
          client_constraint (client_implementation a client)
    ∧ contains a server server_use_facet server_provide_facet
          server_constraint (server_implementation a server)
    ∧ binds a client _ srv_port server _ echo_port }.
Definition client_constraint (self_arch: arch) (self: comp) :=
  ∃ s provs port, binds self_arch self _ srv_port s provs port.
Definition server_constraint (self_arch: arch) (self: comp) :=True.
```

In this exemple, the client srv_port must be bound as it is a mandatory dependency, and the server has no constraint. For the binding, the set of used and provided ports (third and sixth arguments elided as _) are inferred by Coq.

3.2 Reconfiguration operations

In this subsection, we formally define five primitive reconfiguration operations:

1. *create* adds a new component to the current architecture by taking its used and provided ports, constraint and implementation.
2. *destroy* removes an existing component from the current architecture by taking the name of the component.
3. *link* creates a binding from a provided ports of a component to a used ports of another component by taking the requiring component and its used port and the providing component and its provided port.
4. *unlink* destroys a binding from the current architecture by using the same parameters as *link*.
5. *hotswap* changes the behavior of an existing component by taking the component's name, the four new elements of the component, and two functions mapping respectively the used ports and the provided ports of previous version to the ones of the new version.

For sake of space, we only explain in details the *create* operation, whose Coq code is quite compact and easy to understand. All the other operations follow a similar scheme.

The *create* operation is a function that returns a pair r composed of the new architecture new_a and the newly created component new_c. They satisfy the create_post postcondition informally described later in this section. The *create* function takes seven parameters: (1) the current architecture a, (2) the set of used services of the new component U, (3) a proof U_all_opt that the used services are all of the type **optional**[2], (4) the set of provided services P, (5) the constraint cst, (6) the implementation i, and (7) a proof cst_all_hold that in the resulting architecture the architectural constraints of all the components (including the created one) are satisfied. The *create* operation is defined by:

```
Parameter create:
  ∀ (a: arch) (U: facet)
    (U_all_opt: List.Forall (fun p ⇒ ∃ t, p = optional t)
                            (ports_of _ (facet_spec U)))
    (P: facet) (cst: arch → comp → Prop)
    (i: ∀ self_arch self u, cst self_arch self
          → no_exc_if_bound self_arch self u → facet_record P)
    (cst_all_hold: ∀ new_a new_c,
```

[1]In our model, we define a set of ports as a **facet**.

[2]The **optional** type models that used services can be unbound, thus having no value.

```
create_post a U U_all_opt P cst i new_a new_c
  → ∀ c' U' P' (cst': arch → comp → Prop)
      (i': ∀ a'' c'' u, cst' a'' c''
            → no_exc_if_bound a'' c'' u → _),
    contains new_a c' U' P' cst' (i' new_a c')
      → cst' new_a c'),
  { r: arch × comp | let (new_a, new_c) := r in
    create_post a U U_all_opt P cst i new_a new_c }.
```

The postcondition of the *create* operation is the conjunction of six parts: (1) The previous architecture a does not contain the newly created component new_c. (2) The new component new_c exists in the new architecture new_a with the given elements (used U and provided P services, constraint cst and implementation i). (3) The new architecture new_a contains all the components of the previous architecture a. (4) The new architecture new_a contains only the components contained by the previous architecture a and the new component new_c. (5) In the new architecture new_a, the new component new_c is well-defined, *i.e.* it has unique elements (U, P, cst and i). (6) The previous a and new new_a architectures contain exactly the same bindings.

It is important to notice that a reconfiguration operation should preserve constraints and bindings of unaffected components. We address this point with the so-called *frame axiom* approach [8] in postcondition of reconfiguration operations. For example, regarding the *create* operation, postconditions 3, 4 and 6 above are the frame axioms.

The *hotswap* operation is the key point of Coqcots. The goal of this operation is to replace ports, constraints and implementation of a given component. It is important to notice that all of these replacements must be done at once. This constraint of our model comes from the fact that the type of an implementation depends on ports and constraints. For example, changing a port while keeping the implementation unchanged, is not well-typed. For the same reason, the bindings must also be adjusted. To do so, the *hotswap* operation takes two additional parameters, which map bound ports of the old set of ports to the new set of ports. As these mappings are restricted to bound ports, it is possible to remove ports as long as they are not bound in the architecture. Our definition of the *hotswap* operation is therefore consistent with *contextual substitutability* as defined by Brada [3].

The *hotswap* operation replaces the classical start/stop operations. With this operation, the developer is able to ensure the best continuity of service during a reconfiguration. Indeed, (s)he is able to define a new behavior for the component by providing partial services or all of its services by using other providers for its used services. Notice that this is possible even if the component initial design has not anticipated the situation. Moreover, behavioral changes must consistently reflect in the type of the component, so that any service degradation is explicit in the component type. This makes service degradation controllable.

3.3 Invariants

Coqcots is equipped with a set of invariants to ensure the soundness of the architecture definition:

Correct typing of bindings. This invariant excludes all architectures containing at least two ports bound together having incompatible types.

Existence of bound components. This invariant checks that bound components belong to the architecture.

Unicity of used service bindings. This invariant checks that the architecture does not contain a used port bound to two different provided ports.

Unicity of components characteristics. This invariant ensures that, for each component, the set of ports, constraints, and implementation are defined only once.

Satisfaction of component constraints. This invariant ensures that for each component, its constraint holds.

An architecture is *consistent* if the five previously defined invariants hold. We have proved that any architecture, obtained by applying Coqcots reconfiguration operations starting from the empty architecture, is consistent. It relies on two sub-proofs: (1) the empty architecture is consistent and (2) any of the five proposed reconfiguration operations preserves the invariants and then consistency. These proofs are specified using about 2500 lines of Coq code.

4. THE PYCOTS FRAMEWORK

In order to study practical issues, we have implemented Pycots, a Python-based framework that implements Coqcots. This section contains a brief description of Pycots.

The Pycots framework is composed of (1) a `Component` class, which is used to encapsulate components into black boxes, and (2) functions for reconfiguration operations. A component is basically an object that encapsulates its implementation, which is also an object. Each port is a method of this implementation object, which is either injected by the framework (used port) or coded by the developer (provided port). The provided ports are also exposed as public methods of the component object.

For each used port, we generate a *proxy*, whose role is to redirect method calls to their destinations. The advantage of the DSU approach is that it is easy to perform the *link* and *unlink* operations as they simply consist in hotswapping the proxy implementation of the used port between the two alternative implementations: (1) when the used port is bound, the proxy forwards method calls to the provider; (2) otherwise, the proxy raises an exception.

It is important to notice that the Pycots framework is relieved from runtime verification of constraints, typing and invariants. Indeed, we assume that these issues have been proved with Coq. Furthermore, we split the *hotswap* operation into several more primitive operations that add or remove ports to a component. These operations simply inject or remove proxy methods in the component. In order to hotswap a component implementation, we rely on Pymoult [13], which offers several DSU mechanisms as described in Section 2. The manager, which listens for and executes reconfigurations, is borrowed from Pymoult too.

5. VALIDATION

To validate our approach, we have studied a simple web server whose architecture is depicted in Figure 3. Strips denote the bindings and components that are removed by the reconfiguration, whereas dashes indicate the bindings and components that are added during reconfiguration.

The architecture initially contains four components: (1) the `receiver` wraps an instance of `BaseHTTPServer`, which receives and decodes HTTP requests; (2) the `dispatcher` dispatches requests to handlers according to the requested

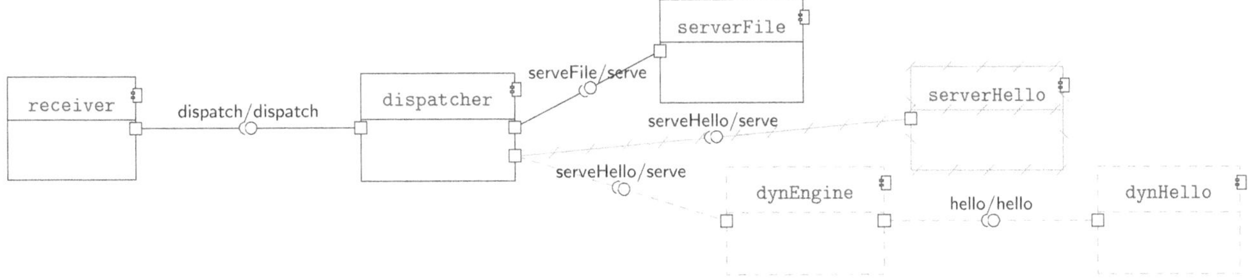

Figure 3: The software architecture of the web server after dynamic reconfiguration.

URL; (3) `serverHello` generates a dynamic web page with a "Hello, world" greeting, and; (4) `serverFile` detects that the given URL is a file name whose content is sent as a response. Its Coqcots model is the conjunction of 44 facts.

The proposed reconfiguration splits the `serverHello` component into two components: `dynEngine`, a generic engine that generates dynamic pages, and `dynHello`, the greetings handler. Since the `serverFile` component is not affected by this reconfiguration, it will continue to handle requests during the reconfiguration. The main idea is to temporarily hotswap the implementation of the `dispatcher` component such that it continues to serve the requests targeting the `serverFile` component while it enqueues those for `serverHello`. The main steps of this reconfiguration are:

1. To modify the implementation of the `receiver` component. As **BaseHTTPServer** handles all the requests by using a single thread, we use **ThreadingMixIn**, a mixin class from the standard library that transforms **BaseHTTPServer** such that it spawns a new thread for each request. Therefore, it will be possible to suspend a thread to delay a request.

2. The implementation of the `dispatcher` component is replaced by the following one: (1) it suspends the current thread (the request-handler thread) by using a global event object, if it receives a request for the `serverHello` component, and (2) it works as before, if a request for the `serverFile` component is received.

3. Once the two previous steps are completed, the serveHello port of `dispatcher` is no longer used: the web server is ready for the architectural changes. The binding between the `dispatcher` and `serverHello` components is removed, the `dynEngine` and `dynHello` components are instantiated and bound, and then `dynEngine` is hotswapped to add its provided port and `dispatcher` is bound to `dynEngine`.

4. Finally, `dispatcher` is hotswapped back to its initial implementation and suspended threads are resumed.

The Coqcots model of this reconfiguration contains about 100 lines of Coq. It proves that the reconfiguration is correct and that requests targeting the `serverFile` component are handled immediately, even during reconfiguration. The corresponding Pycots reconfiguration script contains about 30 lines of Python (without taking into account the code of the new implementation classes).

6. RELATED WORK

OpenCOM [15], Fractal [4] and FraSCAti [17] are well-known component models with similar capabilities for managing and reconfiguring component assemblies at runtime. For each component, controller elements are responsible for managing the reconfiguration operations and ensure their safety and consistency. To achieve these guarantees, components can be stopped such that they are led to a *quiescent state*. A typical reconfiguration scenario is (1) stop affected components, (2) change bindings, and (3) (re)start components. Unaffected components are not stopped hence their services remain available during reconfiguration.

When a component A attempts to use a stopped component B, while the behavior is said undefined in the Fractal textual description, most implementations suspend the calling thread until B is restarted. Even if A is not explicitly stopped, its services are unavailable and unavailability propagates back in the architecture. Alternatively, in the Boyer et al.'s work [2], a consistency invariant requires that mandatory dependencies of started components are bound to started components only: in this case, A must be stopped before B can be. While this approach is better founded, in practice applications are often stopped entirely. OSGi proposes yet another alternative: the framework-provided `getService` method, used by a bundle to resolve a dependency, informs the bundle when the dependency is missing. To some extent, OSGi supports only optional bindings, which is hard to satistify in practice.

The proposal of Bialek and Jul [1] envisions to facilitate the reconfiguration of component-based distributed applications. To take into account the requirement of non-stopping components while reconfiguring, they maintain at the same time the previous and the new versions of a component that needs to be changed. This strategy introduces complexity for managing these elements and may bring up scalability issues. Moreover, the proposal lacks a strong formalism that would ensure important properties throughout the reconfiguration process, such as consistency.

The position paper of La Manna [12] proposes to model the current and new versions of the components using interface automata. These models are then used to automatically generate state transformers, which are functions that map states between the two versions of the interface automata. A state transformer tells when a component can switch from its current version to its new version. This promising approach provides timely, not-disruptive and safe reconfiguration, but the proposal does not consider the implementation aspects.

In summary, although the cited approaches support the

dynamic reconfiguration of component-based applications, most of them do not address the requirement of service continuity while performing the reconfiguration actions. Unlike the proposals discussed in this section, our approach relies on DSU instead of the conventional start/stop operations. Coqcots focuses on maintaining safety and consistency throughout a reconfiguration process and the Coq proof environment allows to alleviate the complexity of performing DSU operations and enforce properties. Thus, correctness properties and service continuity can be proved by using this approach.

7. CONCLUSION

Dynamic reconfiguration provides a solution when stopping a component-based software system is not an option. Unlike previous work, our proposal relies on DSU to avoid the conventional start/stop operations over components. Specific component implementations are used during reconfiguration in order to continuously provide the best possible service. These implementations do not need to be anticipated at design time as DSU let us embed them in the reconfiguration. In this paper, we support verification and validation aspects with Coqcots using the Coq proof assistant. By forcing the reconfiguration developer to explicitly reflect any service degradation in the type of the components, Coqcots makes service continuity controllable and provable. We also describe Pycots, an implementation framework developed using the Python language and the Pymoult library. Our case study demonstrates the advantages of the approach.

Currently, Coqcots and Pycots are still independent as passing from one framework to the other is done by hand. In future work, we plan to better integrate them by generating the Coqcots model of the architecture from the running software system, then translating automatically the Coqcots reconfiguration script to Python. The former will need to add introspection support to Pycots and the Coq's extraction mechanism paves the way to the latter. We also plan to improve the reconfiguration language, which is currently based on Coq, and define specific Coq notations and tactics to hide low-level details of Coqcots such as frame axioms.

8. REFERENCES

[1] R. Bialek and E. Jul. A framework for evolutionary, dynamically updatable, component-based systems. In *Proc. of the Workshops at the 24th International Conference on Distributed Computing Systems*, ICDCS 2004, pages 326–331, USA, 2004. IEEE.

[2] F. Boyer, O. Gruber, and D. Pous. Robust reconfigurations of component assemblies. In *Proc. of the 35th International Conference on Software Engineering*, ICSE'13, pages 13–22, Piscataway, NJ, USA, 2013. IEEE Press.

[3] P. Brada. Enhanced type-based component compatibility using deployment context information. *Electronic Notes in Theoretical Computer Science*, 279(2):17–31, Dec. 2011.

[4] E. Bruneton, T. Coupaye, M. Leclercq, V. Quéma, and J.-B. Stefani. The FRACTAL component model and its support in Java. *Software: Practice and Experience*, 36(11-12):1257–1284, 2006.

[5] J. Buisson and F. Dagnat. ReCaml: Execution state as the cornerstone of reconfigurations. In *Proc. of the 15th ACM SIGPLAN International Conference on Functional Programming*, ICFP'10, pages 27–38, New York, NY, USA, 2010. ACM.

[6] K. Gama, W. Rudametkin, and D. Donsez. Resilience in dynamic component-based applications. In *Proc. of the 26th Brazilian Symposium on Software Engineering*, SBES 2012, pages 191–195, Piscataway, NJ, USA, 2012. IEEE.

[7] M. Ghafari, P. Jamshidi, S. Shahbazi, and H. Haghighi. An architectural approach to ensure globally consistent dynamic reconfiguration of component-based systems. In *Proc. of the 15th ACM SIGSOFT Symposium on Component-Based Software Engineering*, CBSE'12, pages 177–182, New York, NY, USA, 2012. ACM.

[8] P. J. Hayes. The frame problem and related problems in Artificial Intelligence. Technical report, Stanford University, Stanford, CA, USA, 1971.

[9] J. Kramer and J. Magee. The evolving philosophers problem: Dynamic change management. *IEEE Trans. on Software Engineering*, 16(11):1293–1306, Nov. 1990.

[10] W. Li. QoS assurance for dynamic reconfiguration of component-based software systems. *IEEE Trans. on Software Engineering*, 38(3):658–676, 2012.

[11] K. Makris and R. A. Bazzi. Immediate multi-threaded dynamic software updates using stack reconstruction. In *Proc. of the 2009 Conference on USENIX Annual Technical Conference*, USENIX'09, page 31, Berkeley, CA, USA, 2009. USENIX Association.

[12] V. P. L. Manna. Local dynamic update for component-based distributed systems. In *Proc. of the 15th ACM SIGSOFT Symposium on Component-Based Software Engineering*, CBSE'12, pages 167–176, New York, NY, USA, 2012. ACM.

[13] S. Martinez, F. Dagnat, and J. Buisson. Prototyping DSU techniques using Python. In *Proc. of the 5th Workshop on Hot Topics in Software Upgrades*, HotSWUp'13, Berkeley, CA, USA, 2013. USENIX.

[14] E. Miedes and F. D. Muñoz-Escoí. A survey about dynamic software updating. Technical Report ITI-SIDI-2012/003, Instituto Universitario Mixto Tecnológico de Informática, Universitat Politècnica de València, Valencia, Spain, May 2012.

[15] P. Pissias and G. Coulson. Framework for quiescence management in support of reconfigurable multi-threaded component-based systems. *IET Software*, 2(4):348–361, 2008.

[16] H. Seifzadeh, H. Abolhassani, and M. S. Moshkenani. A survey of dynamic software updating. *Journal of Software: Evolution and Process*, 25(5):535–568, Apr. 2012.

[17] L. Seinturier, P. Merle, R. Rouvoy, D. Romero, V. Schiavoni, and J.-B. Stefani. A component-based middleware platform for reconfigurable service-oriented architectures. *Software: Practice & Experience*, 42(5):559–583, May 2012.

[18] Y. Vandewoude, P. Ebraert, Y. Berbers, and T. D'Hondt. Tranquility: A low disruptive alternative to quiescence for ensuring safe dynamic updates. *IEEE Trans. on Software Engineering*, 33(12):856–868, Dec. 2007.

Strengthening Architectures of Smart CPS by Modeling Them as Runtime Product-Lines

Tomas Bures[1,2]
bures@d3s.mff.cuni.cz

Petr Hnetynka[1]
hnetynka@d3s.mff.cuni.cz

Frantisek Plasil[1]
plasil@d3s.mff.cuni.cz

[1]Charles University in Prague
Faculty of Mathematics and Physics
Prague, Czech Republic

[2]Institute of Computer Science
Academy of Sciences of the Czech Republic
Prague, Czech Republic

ABSTRACT

Smart Cyber-Physical Systems (CPS) are complex distributed decentralized systems of cooperating mobile and stationary devices which closely interact with the physical environment. Although Component-Based Development (CBD) might seem as a viable solution to target the complexity of smart CPS, existing component models scarcely cope with the open-ended and very dynamic nature of smart CPS. This is especially true for design-time modeling using hierarchical explicit architectures, which traditionally provide an excellent means of coping with complexity by providing multiple levels of abstractions and explicitly specifying communication links between component instances. In this paper we propose a modeling method (materialized in the SOFA NG component model) which conveys the benefits of explicit architectures of hierarchical components to the design of smart CPS. Specifically, we base our method on modeling systems as reference architectures of Software Product Lines (SPL). Contrary to traditional SPL, which is a fully design-time approach, we create SPL configurations at runtime. We do so in a decentralized way by translating the configuration process to the process of establishing component ensembles (i.e. dynamic cooperation groups of components) of our DEECo component model.

Categories and Subject Descriptors

C.2.4 [**Computer-Communication Networks**]: Distributed Systems—*distributed applications*; D.2.6 [**Software Engineering**]: Programming Environments—*integrated environments*; D.2.11 [**Software Engineering**]: Software Architectures

Keywords

Component-based development; component model; cyber-physical systems; software architecture; software components

CBSE'14, June 30–July 4, 2014, Marcq-en-Baroeul, France.

http://dx.doi.org/10.1145/2602458.2602478.

1. INTRODUCTION

One of the most important advantages of component-based development (CBD) is that it provides powerful and easy to use abstractions for dealing with increasing complexity of today's software systems. This is especially true for component models with explicit architecture and hierarchical composition of, potentially reusable, components. The explicit architecture makes it possible to draw diagrams where components are visibly connected via their provided and required interfaces. The hierarchical composition additionally captures software at multiple levels of granularity and provides a base for reasoning at different levels of abstractions. This includes additional benefits of encapsulation, reuse, and addressing of software complexity.

A significant trend today is the high level of interconnectedness of systems and their mobility. This leads to systems of systems and eventually, when close connection to hardware and physical environment is assumed, to smart Cyber-Physical Systems (as defined by EU framework Horizon 2020). A smart Cyber-Physical System (sCPS) can be seen as a potentially unbounded system of mobile and stationary devices forming an ecosystem in which devices achieve their goals autonomously and cooperatively. Examples of sCPS include smart cities, smart traffic, smart manufacturing, etc. For instance in a smart traffic scenario, cars communicate between each other, with traffic signalization, parking lots, smartphones of passengers to reduce traffic congestion and minimize the time needed for travel and seeking a parking place.

The mobility aspect of sCPS brings about a high level of dynamicity of a system. When modeled using CBD, we get a dynamic architecture that dramatically changes over the runtime – components appear and disappear, connections are formed and dissolved based on the context and current local environment of a component. In addition to dynamicity, sCPS feature important specifics in terms of decentralized and partially disconnected operations. In fact, sCPS have to cope with the situation limited connectivity is available (e.g., only to devices reachable by a short range wireless personal area network or a Mobile Ad-Hoc Network). Similarly, connections may have very limited bandwidth and high frequency of communication error. Such specifics of sCPS render the existing component models (especially those with hierarchical and explicit architectures) inappropriate. This is because component models with explicit architectures rely on static architectures and support only a limited dynamism (e.g. [1, 2, 14, 15, 20]).

Even approaches which resign on the advantages of explicit architectures and rely instead on implicit SOA architectures – such as OSGi [1], iPOJO [9], iPOPO [6] – do not fit well with sCPS. These approaches perceive components as independent units and connect them at runtime based on interface compatibility or on queries to a service registry. This requires a centralized service registry, which is fundamentally opposed to the decentralized nature of sCPS and their operation with limited connectivity.

It turns out that the specifics of sCPS are currently well addressed only by novel component models centered around dynamic ensembles of cooperating components and decentralized and distributed knowledge propagation (e.g., DEECo [4], Helena [13]). These approaches however do not feature explicit architectures (they rely on implicit architectures formed by declarative membership predicate of an ensemble). Additionally, in some cases they do not support synchronous or asynchronous method calls, basing communication on data sharing, a concept unfamiliar to developers.

In this paper, we propose a modeling method which combines the advantages of explicit architectures of hierarchical components with the support for dynamicity and decentralization demanded by sCPS. We materialize the method in a new component model SOFA NG, which we derive as an extension to our existing component model SOFA 2 [2] [5] and its crossover with DEECo, which is our novel component model targeting particularly the specifics of sCPS.

The paper is structured as follows. Section 2 illustrates the issues discussed above on an real-life example. In Section 3 the approach is described from the design point of view while in Section 4 the implementation view is presented and in Section 5, communication aspects are shown. Section 6 discusses related work while Section 7 concludes the paper.

2. CASE STUDY

Compared to traditional systems, sCPS are specific in a number of ways. In addition to mobility, which leads to dynamic architectures and limited connectivity, sCPS feature location awareness and dependence on their environment context. We illustrate these specifics along with the problems discussed in Section 1 on a running example of simplified intelligent vehicle navigation. In this scenario (Figure 1), vehicles are aware of passengers travel itineraries. Vehicles plan optimal routes based on the knowledge of a current traffic situation, which they obtain by communicating with road infrastructure and with other vehicles, and proactively reserve places in parking lots. In addition to this functionality, the navigation system of a vehicle has the capability to remotely communicate with garage doors and garage bars in order to open them when a car is about to pass through.

Note that the scenario contains a "polymorphism", since a single navigation system in a vehicle communicates in the same way with different target systems (parking lots, garage doors and bars). The selection of the particular target system is dynamic. This is based (i) on the state – a parking lot is reserved based on the planned route, and (ii) on the environment context – the garage door/bar in the immediate proximity of a vehicle, through which the vehicle is about to pass through.

[1] http://www.osgi.org/
[2] http://sofa.ow2.org/

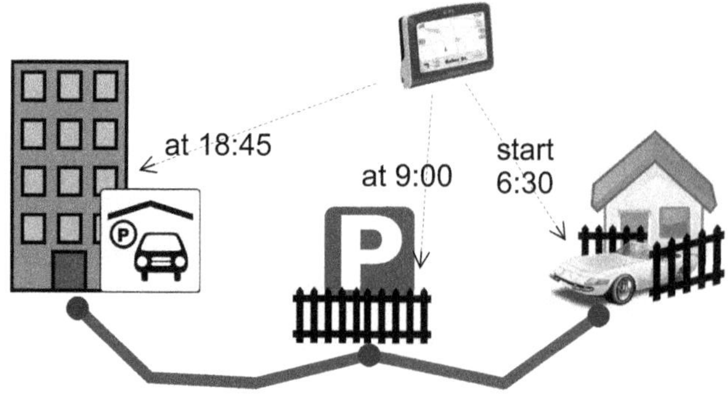

Figure 1: Case study overview

Approaching the case study by CBD yields a runtime architecture, a fragment of which is shown in Figure 2a). The fragment depicts a hierarchical component for intelligent vehicle navigation and the components in its environment that it communicates with. In particular, the navigation component relies on its local subcomponent ParkingManager, which via its required interfaces communicates with a parking lot to manage reservations (using the ParkingReservation interface), and a garage door/bar to enter (using the GateOpener interface). The problem here, though, is the dynamicity, meaning that the figure depicts only a snapshot of the systems architecture at runtime. Later, the architecture may change as for example in Figure 2b) where ParkingReservation is connected to another component (e.g., next parking lot along the route) and the GateOpener interface is left unconnected, as there is no garage door/bar in the proximity to be opened.

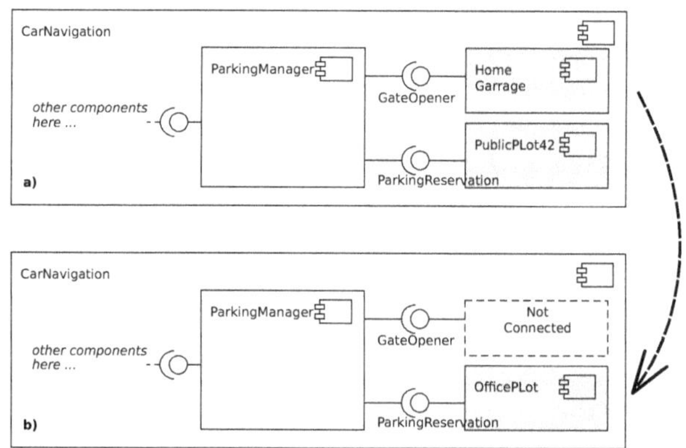

Figure 2: Case study components

The goal is to capture such dynamism at the level of the architecture design. There are of course design approaches that allow for this (as we discuss in Section 6); however all of them fall short when sCPS with high degree of dynamicity and limited connectivity are pursued, and, especially, when aiming at keeping the benefits of explicit architectures and hierarchical composition.

3. INTRODUCING DYNAMICITY

We address the goal of capturing dynamicity in an explicit architecture by employing the idea of software product lines (SPL) [7] and instantiating it at runtime. We explain the fundamentals of the idea below.

SPL is a design time approach which involves two key steps: (1) creation of a reference architecture, and (2) creation of a particular configuration of the reference architecture.

In step (1), the reference architecture is typically described by a hierarchical component composition in which some of the subcomponents are specified as placeholders. A later refinement is normally restricted by a subtype relationship between the type of the placeholder and the type of a component that can be used in that place. Figure 3a exemplifies this concept.

The configuration created in step (2) entails a selection of particular components to substitute the subcomponent placeholders. This selection is done either manually or by using a constraint solver, which given initial requirements (typically high-level product specification) seeks suitable components. The configuration is resolved recursively until there are no placeholders left (Figure 3b).

While SPL are traditionally used at design time, we use them at runtime to address the dynamicity of sCPS. We view a sCPS as a set of software component instances each being bound to a mobile or stationary device (naturally we permit more instances to be hosted on the same device). We assume a known, well-defined (potentially hierarchical) architecture for each of such component instances. A hierarchical architecture is allowed to contain placeholders (as in traditional SPL).

At runtime, each such placeholder is automatically substituted by a component instance available in the sCPS. Technically, this is performed by a runtime component framework. The substitution of the component instance is controlled by constraints associated with the (hierarchical) component architecture. Even though the constraints are initially specified at design time, their modification at runtime is possible. To provide interpretation of the constraints, we assume any component instance to have a set of attributes, which can be dynamically modified by its implementation. Formally, these attributes are free variables in the constraints.

For practical reasons, we permit the situation when a placeholder is not substituted (in case no fitting instance can be found). Similarly, we permit a single component instance to be used in multiple substitutions. This is in a way similar to *shared components* of Fractal model [3]. However, in contrast to Fractal, we make it possible to specify the level of reuse to prevent unwanted reuse of a component instance in an automated composition.

Our approach is exemplified in Figure 4. Here the placeholders are marked by the "«dynamic»" stereotype. Likewise, the constraints are expressed as annotation of connections. For GateOpener, the constraint specifies that there should be placed a component which is "physically close" (its location coordinates being in a defined range). While this constraint is specified at design time, the constraint for ParkReservation is to be specified at runtime (the requested parking lot can be different for each trip). To substitute placeholders, there are component instances available in the scenario that provide the required interface and, based on

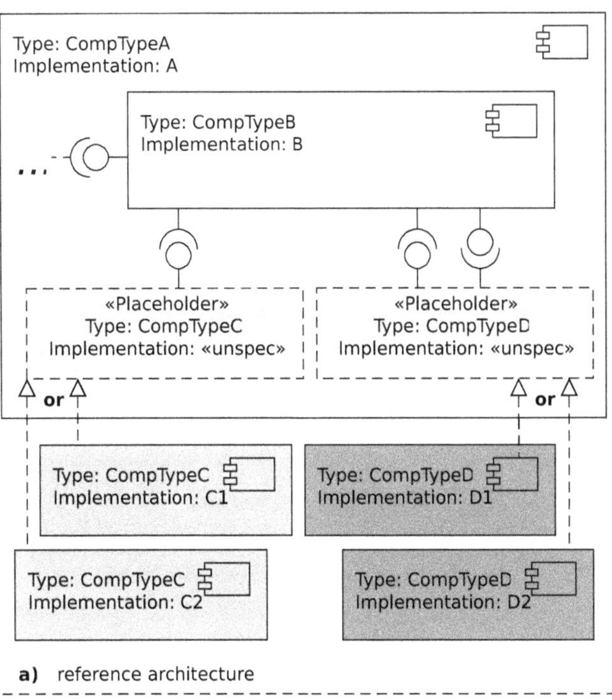

a) reference architecture

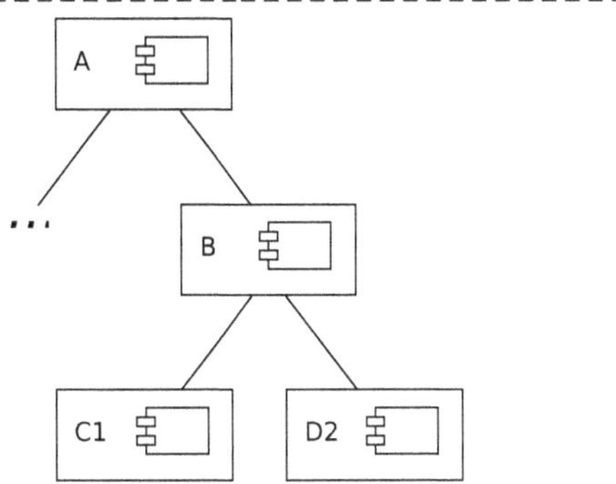

b) a sample configuration of the reference architecture

Figure 3: SPL example

actual values of the attributes and constraints, can substitute the "«dynamic»" component placeholders. These are the Home component instance, which implements a gate opener in a particular house, and ParkingLot1 and ParkingLot2, which are instances corresponding to the two parking lots in the scenario. Also note the limitation of the Home component's level of reuse.

4. RUNTIME SPL CONFIGURATION

Although relatively straightforward from the architectural perspective, our approach brings challenges in terms of dynamic creation and update of a SPL configuration to reflect (a) the component instances available in a given sCPS and (b) the values of their attributes. An additional challenge is that the SPL has to be configured in a decentralized way to reflect the specifics of the given sCPS.

We address these challenges by employing the DEECo component model, a special purpose component model specifically targeting sCPS. It features the concept of component ensembles as dynamically established collaborating groups of components. DEECo comes with a distributed runtime

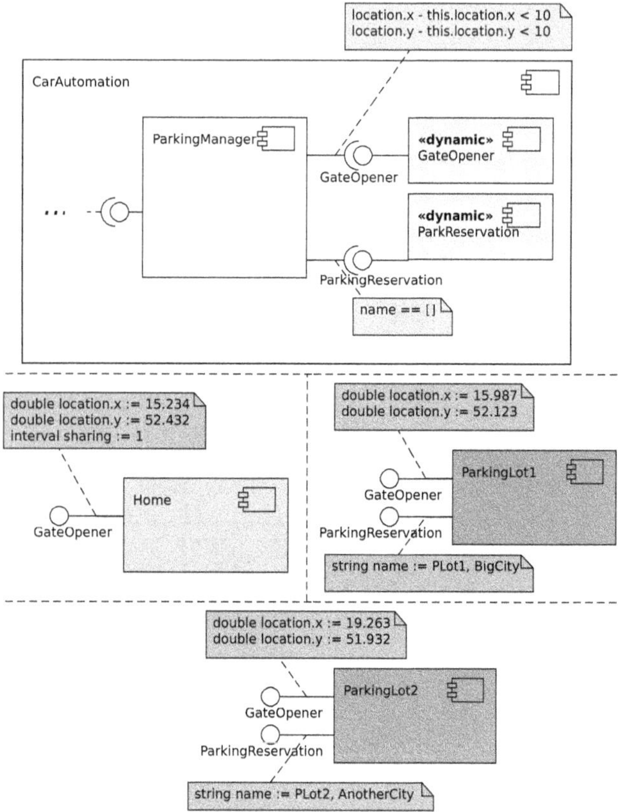

Figure 4: Case study modeled as a runtime SPL

framework, which manages establishing and dissolution of ensembles in a decentralized way.

Technically a component in DEECo is constituted by knowledge (a set of named attributes) and a set of real-time processes, which operate over the component knowledge. An ensemble is a dynamic group of components which satisfy a specific membership condition – a predicate over the knowledge of component instances. This is exemplified in the lower part of Figure 5, where DEECo components are represented as rectangles with name and a list of knowledge fields, and each instance of an ensemble is visualized by an (potentially overlapping) oval shape with its name and membership condition. Namely, there is a component representing the parking manager in a car (plus the car's other components not important for the case study), a component for each parking lot, and a component managing a home gate. For communication of these components, three ensembles are defined. The Parking Reservation ensemble (the red one) manages reservations in parking lots – its membership condition expresses a parking manager's intention to park in a particular parking lot. The Gate Opening ensemble (the orange one) manages opening a gate – its membership condition specifies that a vehicle communicates with a gate being physically close. Finally, the Car ensemble (the grey one) groups together all components in a single car. (Not illustrated in the example is the fact that a single ensemble definition potentially yields a number of ensemble instances, establishing distinct groups of different components, which together satisfy the membership condition.)

In our solution, we exploit the interpretation that ensembles can be viewed as a configuration of a flattened SPL reference architecture. Thus, we create an SPL configuration by (i) transforming the SPL reference architecture to an architecture of DEECo components and ensemble definitions, and (ii) reflecting the establishing and dissolution of DEECo ensembles at the level of the SPL reference architecture. This creates two mutually synchronized layers of (i) hierarchical components at the top layer, and (ii) DEECo components at the bottom layer (Figure 5). In this perspective, hierarchical components reflect the core business logic and structure of an application, whereas DEECo components reflect the physical location and mobility aspects. (Note that, since DEECo establishes the ensembles in a decentralized manner, the creation of the SPL configuration is decentralized as well – thus targeting the key specifics sCPS.)

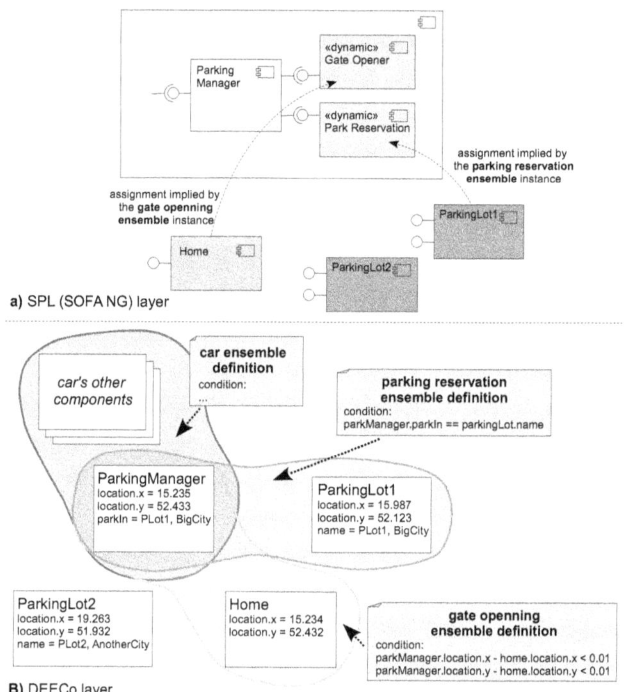

Figure 5: Two-layered architecture

To design application architectures at the upper layer and capture them in the form of SPL, we have created the SOFA NG component model (as an extension of SOFA 2 [5]). The meta-model of SOFA NG is shown in Figure 6. In addition to the traditional concepts of component type, component, interfaces and connections, the meta-model recognizes two types of subcomponents – a static one, which corresponds to a subcomponent in traditional static architectures, and a dynamic one, which corresponds to typed placeholders in SPL architecture (i.e., components marked "«dynamic»" stereotype in Figure 4). Further, we have associated attributes with a component (captured by class Attribute) and constraints with a connection.

Having an application architecture that corresponds to the meta-model, we perform the mapping to DEECo concepts in the following way:

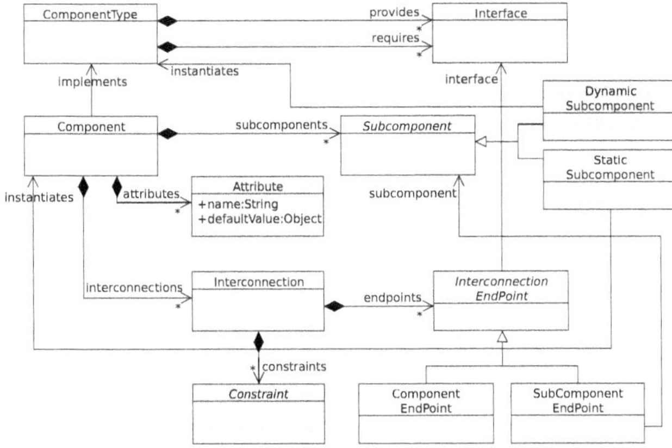

Figure 6: SOFA NG Meta-model

- Every SOFA NG component instance is mapped to a DEECo component instance. Attributes of the SOFA NG component instance are represented as knowledge of the DEECo component instance.
- Every connection that ends at a dynamic subcomponent is mapped to a DEECo ensemble. The constraint associated with the connection is represented as the ensemble's membership condition.

When the DEECo runtime establishes an ensemble, thus effectively selecting a component instance to substitute a dynamic subcomponent placeholder, the runtime architecture at the SOFA NG layer is modified accordingly.

5. DISTRIBUTED COMPONENT COMMUNICATION

So far, we have discussed the way an architecture is dynamically modified. Technically, a reconfiguration of the architecture also implies reconfiguration of the communication channels that components use to interact in a distributed manner (typically via remote procedure call). In our approach, there are two options for distributed communication – it is realized: (a) using knowledge exchange in DEECo, (b) via a standard middleware (e.g., SOAP, CORBA, Java RMI). Each of these options has distinct specifics.

The option (a) depends on the DEECo's native way of communication, which relies on proactive periodic knowledge exchange (via gossip) between components in an ensemble. In this option, we map the synchronous communication at the SOFA NG layer to request/response knowledge structures and use DEECo's knowledge exchange to transmit them among components in an ensamble. This type of communication is highly resilient to disconnections, works seamlessly in an environment with limited connectivity (e.g., in Mobile Ad-Hoc Networks) and is completely decentralized, which makes it highly appealing for sCPS. A penalty for this type of communication is mainly the latency, which may rise to the order of seconds or even tens of seconds.

The option (b) provides a hybrid solution, in which the DEECo knowledge exchange is used only to transmit initial remote references when the architecture is reconfigured. These remote references are used by the standard communication middleware to establish direct links. This mitigates the high latencies and increased communication overhead of the option (a). On the other hand, this solution requires IP connectivity (not always available in sCPS) and relatively stable connections.

6. RELATED WORK

The solution in the paper brings the design with hierarchical components and explicit architectures to the domain of sCPS while respecting the specifics of sCPS. Despite the current intensive research efforts in the area of CPS, there are no approaches that would directly combine the benefits of explicit hierarchical architectures with the high level of dynamicity, decentralized operation, and limited connectivity. Below, we thus overview approaches at least partly related to our goals.

There is already a significant body of knowledge related to general development of CPS, although the dynamicity, decentralization, and limited connectivity are not addressed to a sufficient extent. These works comprise the Helena framework [13] which resembles DEECo by providing the abstraction of ensembles; additionally, it features synchronous and asynchronous message based communication. Compared to our approach, though, Helena does not allow for decentralized operation.

A more traditional approach is [18]. It brings hierarchical components in sCPS by extending the ACME architectural description language [10]. However, compared to our approach, it features only limited dynamism (via special components and connectors) and does not easily allow for decentralization.

The lack of decentralization equally applies also to various SOA-based systems (e.g. OSGi, iPOJO [9] and iPOPO [6]) as they rely on a centralized service/component repository. Another issue of SOA-based systems is that they traditionally rely on implicit architecture. This problem is partially mitigated by using approaches that combine explicit hierarchical architecture with SOA – e.g. Service Component Architecture (SCA)[3]. A representative of this approach in the domain of sCPS is for instance [8], which primarily targets communication fault-tolerance in resilient systems. It is based on FraSCAti [19] framework (a Fractal-based implementation of SCA). Though this approach is viable architecturally, the problem with missing support for decentralization still remains.

Another related research area, although not directly targeting sCPS, are approaches addressing dynamicity in explicit hierarchical component architectures. These approaches typically provide some means of limiting the dynamicity at the architectural level. They include architecture modes, employed in a number of component frameworks (e.g., [2, 15, 17, 20]), and reconfiguration patterns (e.g., [1, 14]). Compared to SOFA NG, these approaches offer only limited dynamicity, which does not fit the open-ended nature of sCPS.

The limitation on dynamicity is lifted for instance by reconfiguration rules in [12]. However, compared to our approach, the reconfiguration rules are firstly complex to specify and, secondly, pollute the architecture by special purpose reconfiguration components. Consequently, this limits comprehensibility of the architecture.

Our approach is also similar to *dynamic software product lines (DSPL)* as proposed in [11]. The main difference is that

[3]`http://oasis-opencsa.org/sca`

DSPL target a primarily evolving system with potentially open runtime variability, while in our approach the system preserves the composition patterns defined in its architecture; this contributes to the predictability of the system's properties.

A common problem of all the approaches discussed above is the lack of decentralized operation. The decentralization has been traditionally addressed in agent based systems. A good representative in the domain of sCPS is [16]. The use of agents additionally makes it easy to tackle dynamicity, however, similar to SOA-based approaches, there is no explicit architecture of a system. Also hierarchical architectures are disregarded.

7. CONCLUSION

In this paper, we have described SOFA NG – an extension of our component model SOFA 2 – combining component-based development with ensemble-based systems (DEECo in particular) and allowing thus for easy development of complex sCPS. In particular, in SOFA NG systems can be modeled as an explicit SPL reference architecture of hierarchical components. Contrary to the traditional use of SPL, we create and update the SPL configuration dynamically at runtime to reflect the overall state of SOFA NG components and their physical environment. This is done by synchronizing the component architecture at the level of SOFA NG with a corresponding dual architecture of DEECo ensembles, which is dynamically maintained in a decentralized manner by DEECo. Thanks to this combination, our solution allows for completely decentralized operation without need for any service repository. Additionally, the use of DEECo makes our approach resilient to network disconnections so that it can be employed even in networks with limited connectivity (e.g., in Mobile Ad-Hoc Networks). As a future work we intend to investigate the security challenges stemming from the open-ended nature of sCPS.

Acknowledgments

This work was partially supported by the EU project ASCENS 257414.

8. REFERENCES

[1] J. Aldrich, C. Chambers, and D. Notkin. ArchJava: connecting software architecture to implementation. In *Proc. of ICSE 2002, Orlando, USA*, pages 187–197. ACM, 2002.

[2] E. Borde, G. Haik, and L. Pautet. Mode-based reconfiguration of critical software component architectures. In *Proc. of DATE '09, Nice, France*, pages 1160–1165, 2009.

[3] E. Bruneton, T. Coupaye, M. Leclercq, V. Quéma, and J.-B. Stefani. The FRACTAL component model and its support in Java. *Software: Practice and Experience*, 36(11-12):1257–1284, 2006.

[4] T. Bures, I. Gerostathopoulos, P. Hnetynka, J. Keznikl, M. Kit, and F. Plasil. DEECO: an ensemble-based component system. In *Proc. of CBSE 2013, Vancouver, Canada*, pages 81–90. ACM, 2013.

[5] T. Bures, P. Hnetynka, and F. Plasil. SOFA 2.0: Balancing advanced features in a hierarchical component model. In *Proc. of SERA 2006, Seattle, USA*, pages 40–48. IEEE, 2006.

[6] T. Calmant, J. C. Americo, O. Gattaz, D. Donsez, and K. Gama. A dynamic and service-oriented component model for python long-lived applications. In *Proc. of CBSE 2012, Bertinoro, Italy*, pages 35–40. ACM, 2012.

[7] P. Clements and L. Northrop. *Software Product Lines: Practices and Patterns*. Addison-Wesley Professional, 3rd edition, 2001.

[8] Q. Enard, M. Stoicescu, E. Balland, C. Consel, L. Duchien, J.-C. Fabre, and M. Roy. Design-driven development methodology for resilient computing. In *Proc. of CBSE 2013, Vancouver, Canada*, pages 59–64. ACM, 2013.

[9] C. Escoffier and R. S. Hall. Dynamically adaptable applications with iPOJO service components. In *Proc. of SC 2007, Braga, Portugal*, volume 4829 of *LNCS*, pages 113–128. Springer, 2007.

[10] D. Garlan, R. T. Monroe, and D. Wile. Acme: architectural description of component-based systems. In *Foundations of Component-based Systems*, pages 47–67. Cambridge Univ. Press, New York, USA, 2000.

[11] S. Hallsteinsen, M. Hinchey, S. Park, and K. Schmid. Dynamic software product lines. In *Systems and Software Variability Management*, pages 253–260. Springer, 2013.

[12] C. Heinzemann and S. Becker. Executing reconfigurations in hierarchical component architectures. In *Proc. of CBSE 2013, Vancouver, Canada*, pages 3–12. ACM, 2013.

[13] R. Hennicker and A. Klarl. Foundations for ensemble modeling – the Helena approach. In *Proc. of SAS 2014 (to appear), Kanazawa, Japan*, LNCS. Springer, 2014.

[14] P. Hnetynka and F. Plasil. Dynamic reconfiguration and access to services in hierarchical component models. In *Proc. of CBSE 2006, Vasteras, Sweden*, volume 4063 of *LNCS*, pages 352–359. Springer, 2006.

[15] J. E. Kim, O. Rogalla, S. Kramer, and A. Hamann. Extracting, specifying and predicting software system properties in component based real-time embedded software development. In *Proc. of ICSE 2009, Vancouver, Canada*, pages 28–38. IEEE, 2009.

[16] J. Lin, S. Sedigh, and A. Miller. Modeling cyber-physical systems with semantic agents. In *Proc. of COMPSACW '10, Seoul, Korea*, pages 13–18, 2010.

[17] T. Pop, J. Keznikl, P. Hosek, M. Malohlava, T. Bures, and P. Hnetynka. Introducing support for embedded and real-time devices into existing hierarchical component system: Lessons learned. In *Proc. of SERA 2011, Baltimore, USA*, pages 3–11. IEEE, 2011.

[18] A. Rajhans, S.-W. Cheng, B. Schmerl, D. Garlan, B. H. Krogh, C. Agbi, and A. Bhave. An architectural approach to the design and analysis of cyber-physical systems. *Electronic Comm. of the EASST*, 21, 2009.

[19] L. Seinturier, P. Merle, R. Rouvoy, D. Romero, V. Schiavoni, and J.-B. Stefani. A component-based middleware platform for reconfigurable service-oriented architectures. *Software: Practice and Experience*, 42(5):559–583, 2012.

[20] H. Yin, H. Qin, J. Carlson, and H. Hansson. Mode switch handling for the ProCom component model. In *Proc. of CBSE 2013, Vancouver, Canada*, pages 13–22. ACM, 2013.

A New Approach to Detect Potential Race Conditions in Component-based Systems

Jean-Yves Didier
IBISC laboratory
40, rue du Pelvoux
91000 Evry, France
Jean-Yves.Didier@ibisc.univ-evry.fr

Malik Mallem
IBISC laboratory
40, rue du Pelvoux
91000 Evry, France
Malik.Mallem@ibisc.univ-evry.fr

ABSTRACT

When programming software applications, developers have to deal with many functional and non-functional requirements. During the last decade, especially in the augmented reality field of research, many frameworks have been developed using a component-based approach in order to fulfil the non-functional requirements. In this paper, we focus on such a specific requirement: race conditions issues in component-based systems. We present a heuristic that analyses data flows and detects components that may be subject to race conditions. A toy example introducing the problem and the solution is developed and implemented under the ARCS (for Augmented Reality Component System) framework. We also show the results of our algorithm on real size applications using up to 70 components and compare those results with some obtained by developers who had to make exactly the same work by hand.

Categories and Subject Descriptors

D.2.11 [**SOFTWARE ENGINEERING**]: Software architectures—*Domain specific architectures*; D.2.13 [**SOFTWARE ENGINEERING**]: Reusable software—*Reusable libraries*; D.2.m [**SOFTWARE ENGINEERING**]: Miscellaneous—*Rapid prototyping*

Keywords

Components; Race conditions; Heuristic; Augmented Reality; Concrete example

1. INTRODUCTION

Augmented Reality (AR) aims at linking virtual entities with real objects through a combination of dedicated hardware and software. Programming such an application requires several skills. Some are purely related to programming techniques and execution environment. They are called non-functional requirements whereas others are related to techniques more specific to the AR field and are therefore called functional requirements (such as image and signal processing, interactions in mixed reality, virtual reality and computer graphics, content authoring, etc).

As a field of research of a growing interest, many researches have been conducted to propose software frameworks tailored to AR needs aiming at reducing the burden for developers to consider non functional requirements when developing. AR is also technology dependent and thus, piece of software piloting these technologies should be as replaceable as the used technologies. The findings of new algorithms and methods are also driving architectures to more and more modularity and genericity. Over the past decade, many software framework for AR [11] have been proposed and they use a component-based scheme. Component based solutions are popular in AR framework since they usually propose software architectures that will address most of the non functional requirements of AR such as modularity, genericity, and reusability. To these requirements we can also add distributed computing which is raised by the current hype in cloud computing and multi-threaded computing which is the target of this paper.

Multi-threading is and has been used in the past to build AR software ([2] is an example of such use) because it can reduce the end-to-end latency of an application in the case several input sensors are needed by the system to extract characteristics from its environment. Moreover it can profit from the multicore processor architectures that were introduced in the consumer market since several years ago. Inexperienced programmers usually have difficulties in mastering thread safety and concurrent access issues. Therefore, furnishing tools that relieves programmers from the burden of managing such issues may be an interesting added value.

The remainder of the paper is organised as followed. First, we will present some related component based systems used in the AR field and introduce our own framework named ARCS (for Augmented Reality Component System). Then, in section 3, we will focus on the problem of concurrent access management in component systems and provide some hints about how to solve the problem. The same section will also introduce some of the general purpose techniques found in the literature to detect where race conditions may occur. We will also propose a heuristic that automatically finds components for which concurrent access is an issue. Section 4 will show how such a heuristic and the associated solution can be implemented in our framework in toy case and we will finish by giving the future road-map on this research and conclude.

2. RELATED AND PREVIOUS WORKS

2.1 Component based AR frameworks

Modular software architectures and frameworks for AR have been addressed during these past years by almost thirty different projects of frameworks. The surveys written by Endres et al. and Huang et al. [11, 18] are quite exhaustive. Therefore, we chose to cite the most prominent component based frameworks.

Amongst these frameworks some are intend to distribute components over a network and thus do not need to manage interference between threads of the same program. This is the case for the StudierStube project led by the Technical University of Vienna [15]. Its main principle is that each user has its own workspace that may be partly shared with other users. Similarly, the DWARF [4] (Distributed Wearable Augmented Reality Framework) project uses decentralised and distributed services. This framework relies on CORBA [24] (Common Object Request Broker Architecture) to provide services. As an example, each input sensor is associated to a service broadcasting data to other services (that could be filters, rendering loops,...). Each service is described by XML data and can be dynamically linked to the current application, which is seen as a distributed data flow. At start-up, applications only need one component manager. This last one discovers step by step other services in order to integrate them at execution. Some other frameworks are following the same guiding precepts such as the AMIRE (Authoring Mixed Reality) project [9] or MORGAN [25].

Another class of component based frameworks for AR do not rely on distribution mechanisms and thus sometimes involves multithreading programming. For example, Tinmith [26] is a library written to develop mobile AR systems. This framework is based on data-flow description and is a library of hierarchical objects. It manages data-flow from sensors, many data filters and rendering components. Objects written in C++ rely on a callback system and data are serialised using XML. Communications between objects are managed through a data-flow graph. Other frameworks from the same category have been proposed such as VHD++ [27], MRSS [19] (Mixed Reality Software Suite) or Avango NG [21].

An AR framework must cope with works in progress and future works built on the present ones. It should be able to integrate technologies of tomorrow in terms of new devices and algorithms. Works in progress would then require flexibility, future works extensibility and future works built on top of current ones reusability. One of the classical answers is to use a component based software architecture because it allows to separate an application into several components, that are, according to Szyperski [35], *"a coherent package of software that can be independently developed and delivered as a unit, and that offers interfaces by which it can be connected, unchanged, with other components to compose a larger system"*. Another benefit associated to reusability is the ability to rapidly prototype applications.

2.2 Previous work: the ARCS framework

ARCS, for Augmented Reality Component System, is a project we started in 2006 [7, 8, 20]. As a framework, it provides several models that should be followed in order to build AR applications. Some choices are made concerning the application model as well as the component model. We describe them in order to introduce later how we will manage concurrent access in such an environment since it is our target framework.

2.2.1 Application model

The ARCS application model describes applications as a set of process (actually a set of threads). Each one of them is controlled by a finite state machine. When the internal state of the state-machine changes, it triggers changes in how components are connected to each other. A set of connections as well as a set of component invocations (in order to initialise them and launch data processing) is called a *sheet*. According to this, each thread is, at a given time, in a given state that corresponds to an active sheet. Sheets are sharing the same components instantiated from a component pool. Therefore, components do not belong to any thread in particular so they may be invoked by different threads.

As we said before, each process maintains one active sheet at a time. A sheet activation cycle follows the following steps:

- The controller (state-machine) receives a token (from a component in the active sheet) that will trigger one of its transitions and then change the controller state;
- All components from the current sheet will be disconnected from each other;
- The controller new state corresponds to another sheet. First, some invocations, called *pre-connection invocations*, are performed on the components to properly initialise them;
- Then connections are established according to the new sheet description;
- Post-connection invocations are finally performed in order to launch the actual processing of data.

2.2.2 Component model

ARCS describes components as entities having signals (outputs) and slots (inputs). The signal/slot mechanism is well known since it is commonly used in graphical user interface libraries such as Qt for instance. It is also deriving from the observer design pattern [16]. Thus, the communication through a signal/slot connection is synchronous. Composition of components can be performed in two different ways: the first one is through *connection composition*, where a component emits a signal that is processed by a slot from another component. The second one is through *invocation composition*: a component is passed as a parameter to a slot of another component.

Amongst its specifics, ARCS provides an abstract component model that allows to introduce new component types or new component behavior as long as they respect the signal/slot scheme.

This abstract model includes the following functionalities:

- Instantiation and destruction of the actual component;
- Signal/slot and connection management;
- Serialisation/deserialisation: this is mainly used at the instantiation of the actual components. Deserialisation allows to configure the component according to string contents passed through an XML description of the application.

In order to complete the integration of other component families, the framework has also abstract type factories that parse XML descriptions and instantiate directly objects of the considered type that can be used as parameters of components invocations in order to initialise the latter ones.

These functionalities are also exposed in the dynamic libraries the ARCS engine can load at runtime by parsing XML descriptions of an application. They usually contain:

- Type factories, in order to extend ARCS with new types when needed and serialise them;
- Native component factories that instantiate components handled by the previous version of the engine and that are the privileged components in the framework;
- Family component factories in order to make ARCS compatible with other component systems.

To finish, in technical terms, ARCS is written in C++ language for performance reasons and depends on the Qt library [30].

2.2.3 *Handling other non-functional requirements*

In ARCS , we decided to develop an engine that is as lightweight as possible. Therefore, the engine in itself does not implement all the non-functional requirements that would be necessary to make all kinds of applications. Nevertheless, it is possible to explore other ways to add non-functional requirements when they are really needed. As an example, we already propose in the framework a mechanism to create distributed applications over a network [6].

As defined here, the ARCS engine is able to create threads and perform different tasks inside these threads but there is no concurrent access management developed in component model. We will now see how it is possible to design and implement such a mechanism in a component based system behaving like ARCS.

3. MANAGING CONCURRENT ACCESS IN COMPONENT BASED SYSTEMS

Managing concurrent access in component based systems depends on the characteristics of components that are used and their environment. For example, in an environment using CORBA components, concurrent access is managed transparently due to the serialisation mechanisms that occur when the CORBA bus is used. Therefore, we will first outline the main characteristics of the component system on which we will work as a basis for our hypotheses.

3.1 Component system main characteristics

We are considering components as stated by Szyperski [35]. To sum it up, component are pieces of software that are reusable and subject to composition in order to produce the final software.

Here, we will restrain the kind of components we are using. We are interested in components having the following characteristics:

- Components have separated inputs and outputs;
- Even if components are black boxes (i.e. we do not know how it is implemented inside), they adhere to the following internal behaviour: if one an input is triggered, it will trigger outputs synchronously (none to all outputs could be triggered). We call this property *internal synchronicity*. However, without a thorough analysis of the behaviour of the black box, we do not known which output is triggered by which input. Therefore, we will consider that when an input is triggered, every output is triggered;
- Components are communicating synchronously: outputs from a component trigger inputs from another component. Outputs then trigger function calls. This property is the *external synchronicity*;
- Communications are supposed unidirectional: data are flowing from outputs to inputs;
- Components are configured by passing arguments to some of their inputs. Inputs may also be used to start processing functions;
- Components are black boxes but communication channels (or *connections*) between components are known and static, that is to say, persistent in time or at least for a known duration.

Such components are also working in a specific execution environment. Concerning this execution environment, we make the following suppositions:

- It is multi-threaded;
- Component configuration and initialisation may be performed by different threads;

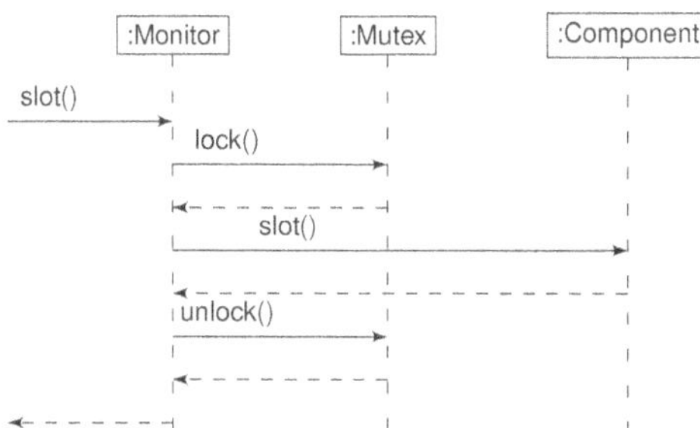

Figure 1: Behaviour of a monitor component wrapping the original component in a mutual exclusion.

3.2 Problem statement: concurrent access

Now that we have described the main characteristics of our component system and its execution environment, we can deduce some problems that will rapidly arise: how can we process issues concerning concurrent access or, more generally, thread-safety ?

There are at least three solutions in order to give a thread-safety property to such a system:

1. We can systematically implement thread safety mechanisms inside components. However, it is generally costly, especially if the component, in its execution context, does not require it;
2. We can implement it by hand in components that may be subject to concurrent access. The weak point here is that a component is a piece of reusable software and therefore it may be put in a situation that was not planned during the design phase of the component;
3. We implement a specific heuristic inside the execution environment that will ensure that components that are subject to concurrent access in their execution context will be guaranteed thread safe. This third way is the one we would like to investigate further in this paper.

Restated in other terms, we would like to give a thread-safe behaviour to components (that do not possess it) by analysing their execution context. We believe it has other strong advantages, one of them being that component developers would not have to worry about thread safety. This is also interesting because inexperienced programmers usually have difficulties in mastering thread safety and concurrent access issues.

3.3 Outline of our solution

The idea we will express here is just an intermediate solution that will give some hints on how the problem could be solved. We intend to give a simple, but practical solution. The main idea is to construct a wrapper component that will regulate concurrent access to the component it shelters. To achieve this, we apply the *monitor object design pattern* [32] as it is done, for instance, in java with the `synchronized` keyword. Components prone to concurrent access are then considered as a resource that will be properly framed inside a mutual exclusion (*mutex*) as represented in figure 1. For each component to protect from concurrent access, a *Monitor* will be generated, associated to an object managing a mutual exclusion (*Mutex*). Therefore, each call performed on *Component* is rerouted to *Monitor*.

Mutual exclusion are known to solve partly the problem of race conditions but they are known to be sensitive to other problems such as deadlocking (where two components are waiting for each other and thus are locking each other, therefore the application cannot perform its intended task) or resource starvation (it occurs when two components are competing for the same resource and one of them is perpetually favoured over the other, thus tasks that were intended to be performed never happen). It would require another detailed analysis that we do not intend to present in this paper.

Our problem is then transformed into how to determine which component should be monitored? Before proposing a heuristic in order to solve it, we will briefly review some techniques used to solve such a problem.

3.4 Concurrent access in literature

In the literature, two complementary problems are addressed: the race detection in itself and the minimal number of places where mutual exclusion should be placed.

Race detections are detected using different approaches. The static approach enforce type systems [1], directly analyse the source code of the application [34, 29, 36] or analyse dataflow [12]. Such approach is not directly usable since we do not have access to the source code of components in every situation. The dynamic approach analyse actual execution traces. Algorithms and tools [31, 3, 28, 14] developed mainly rely on Lamport's happens-before relation [22] or use lockset analysis (a lock set is the set of locks that protect access to a shared variable). The tools have complete access to program context but will also reduce the performances of the program actually analysed and adds to the overhead of running components. Other techniques are also used such as post-mortem analysis but they are not suitable in our case.

Finding the minimal number of places where mutual exclusion should be placed is often called the Minimum Lock Assignment (MLA) problem. Many solutions have been proposed so far to determine where to put mutual exclusions. However, they usually concern parts of the software code (the potential critical sections) and not components as defined by Szyperski as we can see in [33, 17, 10, 38]. In such methods, critical parts of the code are annotated. Then a special compiler will determine where to put mutual exclusion by using special heuristics. MLA is known to be a NP-hard problem so other methods rely on a different approach: the idea is to determine specific use cases and associated use case scenarios and assess the behaviour of the software with respect to this scenario [13, 23]. If an interference is detected, then a mutual exclusion will be put where it occurred. Using use-case scenarios is not a solution that suited our needs since it needs some preparations. Determining MLA is also not our primary concern: the idea is not to be optimal but to relieve the developer from the burden to review his code in order to determine where to put mutual exclusions. The method must also be lightweight, since it should be run on the fly when the description of the application is loaded by our framework's engine. Fortunately, one of the conclusions in [17] is that "high accuracy in program analysis is not always necessary to achieve generally good performance". Therefore, we will provide a heuristic at component level that determines which components might be subject to interference.

3.5 A heuristic to find components subject to race conditions

To determine the solution of our problem, we construct a direct graph. Each vertex of the graph represents a component to which is associated a set of labels (the different threads in the application are also considered as components). Each time components are communicating together, a directed edge between the vertices associated to the components is drawn. The direction of the edge matches the direction of the communication.

We will now expose a heuristic that will determine what are the candidate components subject to monitoring.

3.5.1 *Notations*

- Let $\mathcal{C}$ be the set of components in the system. This set is also the set of vertices in the directed graph;
- Let $\mathcal{M} = \varnothing$ be the set of components that will be candidates to mutual exclusion monitoring;
- Let $\mathcal{L}$ be a set of labels. At initialisation, there are as much labels as threads in our system. $\mathcal{L}$ is very likely to grow, so the easiest way is to define $\mathcal{L}$ as a subset of $\mathbb{N}$ where $\mathcal{L} = [\![1; n]\!]$ where n is the number of threads;
- Let $\mathcal{E}$ be the set of edges of the directed graph;
- Each component c of $\mathcal{C}$ has a property named `labels` which will be noted $c.labels$. It is the set of labels associated to the component c. $c.labels$ is therefore a subset of $\mathcal{L}$;
- Each edge e of $\mathcal{E}$ has two properties: $e.head$ is the head of the edge and $e.tail$ is the tail of the edge. Note that $e.head$ and $e.tail$ are elements of $\mathcal{C}$;
- $|\mathcal{S}|$ is the cardinal number of the set $\mathcal{S}$;

3.5.2 *An algorithm to find components to monitor*

Our heuristic is exposed in algorithm 1. Apart from its initialisation, the heuristic is a loop iterating over three phases:

1. The *propagation* of labels along the edges (lines 14 to 20);
2. The *marking*, where candidate components subject to monitoring are marked (lines 22 to 24);
3. The *pruning and label generation* where some of the components are discarded because they do not need to be monitored with a mutual exclusion. Additional labels are created and labels associated to vertices are reinitialised (lines 25 to 35).

These steps are reiterated until the set of components to monitor is computed.

The initialisation consists in generating the first set of labels (noted $\mathcal{L}$ in the algorithm) and attach them with components considered as threads. Each component that is a thread is initialised with its own label and all other components are associated to an empty set of labels.

The propagation propagates labels along the edges until the label sets associated to each vertex is stabilised. Therefore, we know which thread can access to which component. It corresponds to the *internal* and *external synchronicity* hypothesis: if a thread accesses to an input, therefore it accesses to all corresponding outputs of the same components and inputs that are connected to these outputs.

The marking step creates a temporary set of components (noted $\mathcal{M}_c$) and puts into it components that are very likely to monitor. To find such components, we look at the incoming edges. If the originating component of such an edge is not accessed by the same threads than the target component of the same edge, then it means the component is subject to concurrent accesses and is to be added to the list of components to monitor.

The pruning step removes from study the set of components that are accessed by at most one thread since they are not concerned by concurrent access issues and the edges that come along. Each component that was marked to be monitored is generating a new label (it means we consider the data sent by it thread-safe since it is monitored and therefore it behaves as the data was sent by another thread) and all other components associated labels are reset.

Then we reiterate until there is not any component left to process.

Algorithm 1: Heuristic to determine components to monitor

Data: $\mathcal{C}$ – set of components, $\mathcal{E}$ – set of edges
Result: $\mathcal{M}$ – the set of components to monitor

```
// Initialization
M ← ∅;
L ← ∅;
l ← 1;
foreach c ∈ C do
    if c represents a thread then
        l ← l + 1;
        L ← L ∪ {l};
        c.labels ← {l};
    else c.labels ← ∅;
end
repeat
    // Propagation
    repeat
        applied ← false;
        foreach e ∈ E do
            if e.head.labels ≠ e.head.labels ∪ e.tail.labels then
                e.head.labels ← e.head.labels ∪ e.tail.labels;
                applied ← true;
            end
        end
    until applied = false;
    // Marking
    M_c ← ∅;
    foreach e ∈ E do
        if e.head.labels ≠ e.tail.labels then M_c ← M_c ∪ {e.head};
    end
    // Pruning and label generation
    foreach c ∈ C do
        if |c.labels| ≤ 1 then C ← C \ {c};
        else
            if c ∈ M_c then
                c.labels ← {|L| + 1};
                L ← L ∪ c.labels;
            else c.labels = ∅;
        end
    end
    foreach e ∈ E do if e.head ∉ C or e.tail ∉ C then E ← E \ {e};
    M ← M ∪ M_c;
until C = ∅;
```

3.5.3 *Applying the heuristic: an abstract example*

Figure 2 is illustrating how our heuristic is run. At first, we consider the set of components displayed in 2(a). We introduce in figure 2(b) two new components T_1 and T_2 that are actually the threads that start the application by performing invocations on components A and B. The label set associated to each component is noted between braces. Therefore, components T_1 and T_2 are associated to labels 1 and 2 and other components are associated to an empty label set. According to our heuristic, we then perform a first propagation and marking step (see figure 2(c)). Two components are noted as being subjects to monitoring, here C and D (they are noted with a star $*$). They are marked because preceding components do not share the same set of labels. Then, in the pruning phase (figure 2(d)), the components T_1, T_2, A and B are discarded since they all have only one label associated to them (it means they do not need to be monitored). New labels are generated for C and D that are respectively 3 and 4 whereas other components are associated to empty label sets. We then reiterate through the same steps a second (figure 2(e)) and a third time (figure 2(f)). At the end of the third iteration, since we had a cycle in the graph, all components are associated to empty label sets (figure 2(g)), therefore the algorithm completes in the next step. If we look at the set of components to monitor computed by the algorithm, we will find $\mathcal{M} = \{C, D, E\}$. This result is consistent since components C and D can be accessed through A and B that are invoked by two different threads. The outputs of C and D can come from the first or the second thread, therefore E needs to be monitored too.

Another side effect illustrated in this example is that mutual exclusions should be re-entrant. That is to say, a thread that has locked a mutual exclusion should still be able to enter in the component it has locked a second time. If this condition is not respected, it could lead to a lock in our abstract example since we have a communication cycle between D, E, G and F. Therefore, D can be locked by a thread and the same thread may access to D later through E, G and F.

4. CONCURRENCY MANAGEMENT APPLIED IN ARCS

4.1 A toy case introducing a race condition

In order to understand how it works, we will not consider a real AR application but rather a toy case implementing a race condition. It is organised around three main components: two components (named *loop1* and *loop2*), each in a separate thread, iterate from 0 to 9, and one component (named *sum*) adds all iteration values received from the two other components. The components are, by default, developed without any code that synchronises them (Fig. 3 is showing their pseudo-code). Therefore, our *sum* component, which should reach a total of 90 ($2 \times \sum_{i=0}^{9} i$), does not necessarily reach the right sum in a multi-threading context (the counting slot is called from two different threads and therefore *tmp* and *sum* are in a race condition situation).

The ARCS framework strictly adheres to the component system and environment characteristics we presented in section 3.1. But, as a practical framework, it will require some adjustments and additional components in order to conform to its application model. Figure 4 represents the simplified connection graph of the toy case (as implemented using ARCS – see also figure 5) where we can find the main components as well as thread controllers (state-machines *s*, *s1* and *s2* which are mandatory in the application model[1]. Here

[1]One can notice difference between the abstract data flow and the one presented in the screen capture. This is due to the fact the

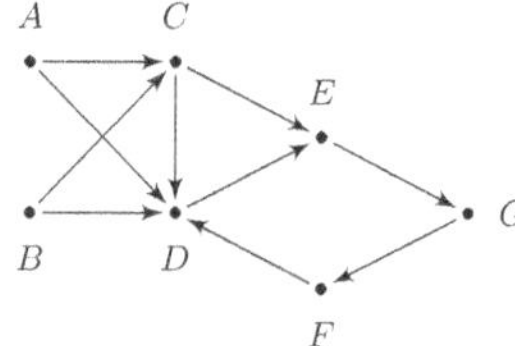

(a) Initial set of components

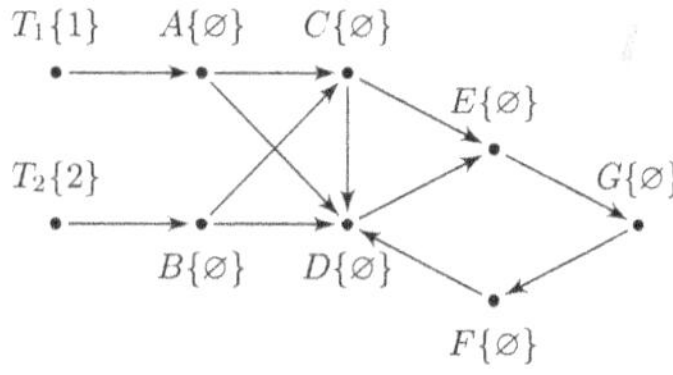

(b) Initialization step of the heuristic

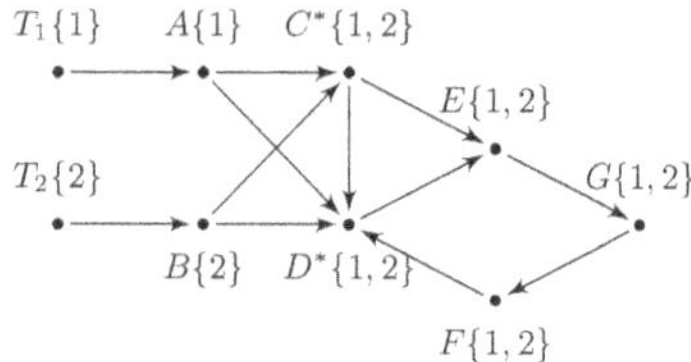

(c) Propagation and marking (1st iteration)

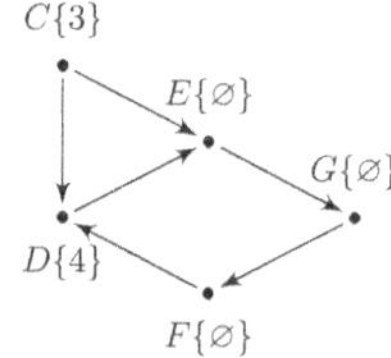

(d) Pruning and label generation (1st iteration)

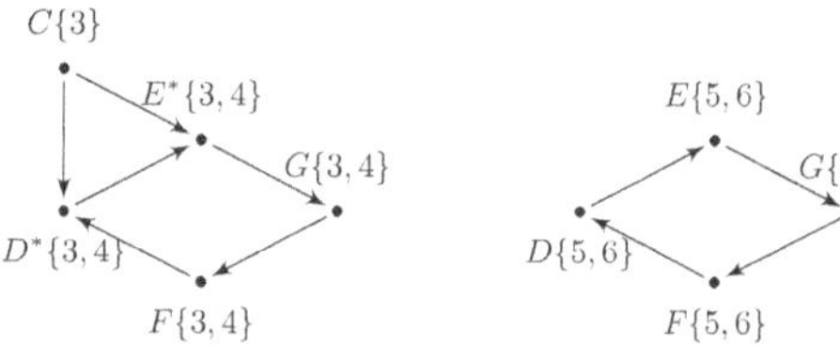

(e) Propagation and marking (2nd iteration)

(f) Propagation and marking (3rd iteration)

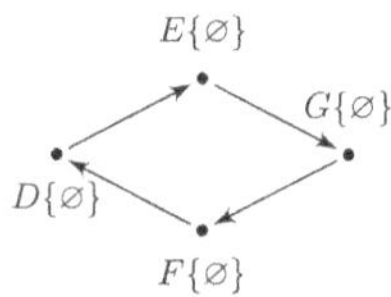

(g) Pruning and label generation (3rd iteration)

Figure 2: Iterations of our heuristic from initialization to the last step before completion

```
For i from 0 to 9
  RandomSleep()
  Emit i
EndFor
Emit "end"
```

(a) *Loop* pseudo-code

```
tmp <- i
RandomSleep()
sum <- sum + tmp
```

(b) *Sum* pseudo-code

Figure 3: ***loop*** **and** ***sum*** **components pseudo-code.**

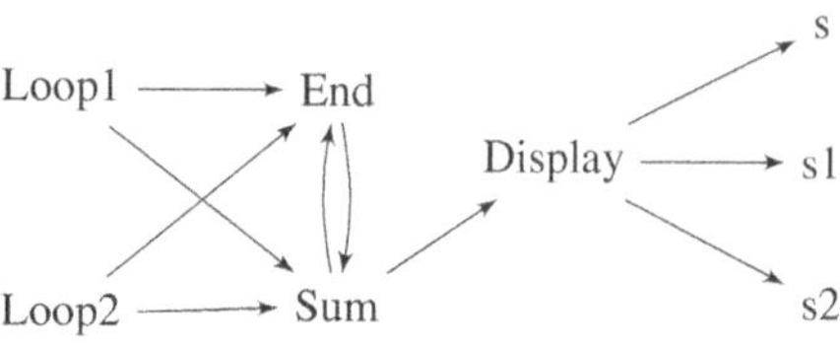

Figure 4: Simplified connection graph of components in the toy case.

s,*s1* and *s2* are only composed of two states: one initial and one final state in order to shut down the application). Some logical glue components are also used: *end* which triggers the end of the application when *loop1* and *loop2* have finished iterating, and *display* which displays the final result. *s*, *s1* and *s2* are controllers that may be accessed by different threads. A first thread triggers *loop1* and a second thread triggers *loop2*. Therefore, if we apply our heuristic, components *end*, *sum* should be monitored. To this set, we will add *s*, *s1* and *s2* since they may be accessed bu different threads.

The result of the implementation of the components without any management of concurrent accesses is shown in figure 6(a). As we can observe, the two threads are sleeping a random duration and wake up in order to send data to the *sum* component. In the end, it displays 92 as a result of the sum whereas it should have been 90 if there was not any race condition.

In order to implement concurrency access management, ARCS also requires some other components that are not shown: a *Monitor component* that acts as a wrapper component for the actual components that have been marked as to be monitored and a *ConcurrencyManager component* that accesses to the application structure, analyses it and compute the set of components to monitor. The application has been modified to import the *ConcurrencyManager* component (it results in modifying one line in the application description file).

We can verify in figure 6(b) that *Monitors* have been put around the right components and that the race condition was suppressed by such modifications. Indeed, the first lines of the screenshot shows the resulting list of components that should be monitored as planned by our heuristic. The last lines indicate that the resulting sum is 90 which means the race condition has been suppressed.

None of the components of the application has specific code for handling mutual exclusion, therefore the *ConcurrencyManager* seems viable in order to manage concurrency on components that were not specifically designed to handle it. We then have built a first step towards automated concurrency management for components in software applications.

heuristic takes into account all connections in all application sheets (in ARCS terms) whereas the screen capture represents one of those sheets, therefore a subset of the connections between components.

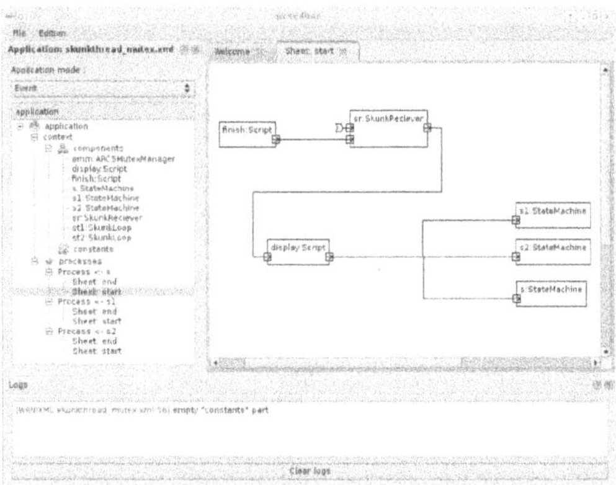

Figure 5: Toy case in development stage using ARCS graphical editor

4.2 Real case study: the RAXENV project

In the past, we developed for the RAXENV project [5, 37] a multisensor system that relied on multi-threading capabilities. This project aimed at demonstrating the practical use of an outdoor AR system for environmental sciences and techniques, both in terms of technology development as well as end-user adoption.

The overall software architecture is depicted in figure 7. The application used data provided by three different sensors: a camera, an inertial unit and a GPS. Data sources were fused to provide a robust localisation of the system in its environment. During the development of such a system, we encountered some difficulties with multi-threading (each sensor provided data in a separate thread) and concurrency management that was implemented by hand. We would like to run our present solution over the RAXENV software in order to assess if concurrency management was implemented at the right place and see if it could eventually be performed in less components than we did and maybe raise some issues we did not see.

The RAXENV software had three nominal states (corresponding to three sheets) where multi-threading capabilities had been enabled. This means our algorithm should then be applied to these three sheets in order to determine which components should be monitored. Moreover, some of the components were composite components (components made of an assembly of components). So we ran our algorithm against two series of tests: one with composite components considered as blackbox components (annotated BB) and another one where composite components are considered as whiteboxes (annotated WB – therefore we consider that we can monitor subcomponents of composite components). The numerical results are gathered in table 1 where we also included our algorithm's result concerning the abstract example and the toy case we presented earlier. The table contains the number of components, the number of edges of the generated graph as well as the final size of the label set, the number of iterations and finally either the size of the component set to monitor or the component set itself. We also represented in Fig. 8 one of the component set (the one annotated MIBB) using the dot utility from graphviz software [2]. It also shows the composite components and components that are to be monitored. One can notice that these first results show that few iterations are in fact needed in order to determine the set of components to be monitored even for datasets containing up to 70 components and 140 edges.

[2]http://www.graphviz.org

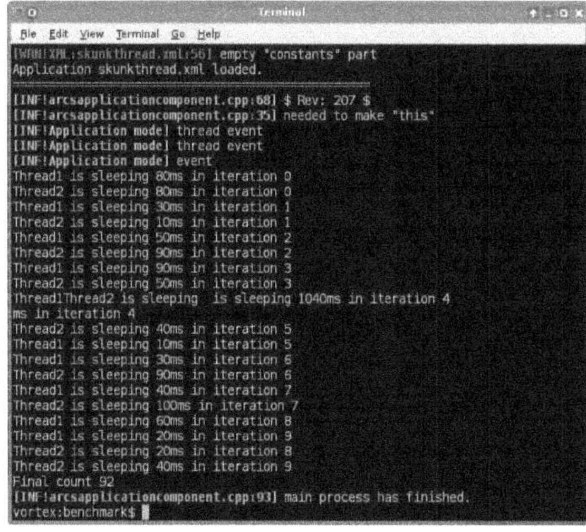

(a) Execution of the toy case without concurrency access management

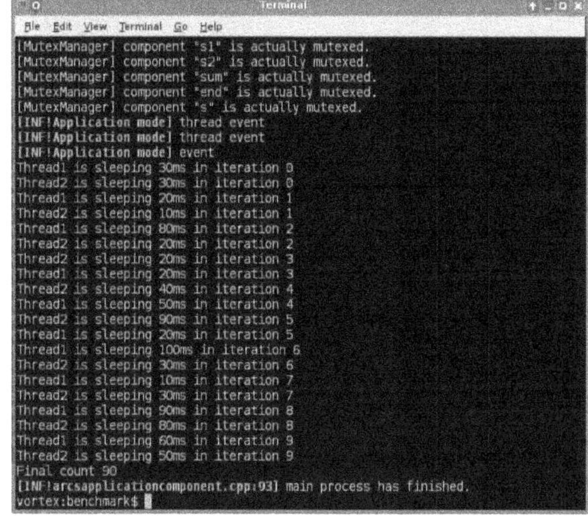

(b) Execution of the toy case with concurrency access management

Figure 6: Toy case implemented and executed using the ARCS framework

In table 2, we regrouped the results obtained from our algorithm, especially the list of components subject to monitoring, for the three datasets RIBB, MIBB and VPBB coming from the actual implementation of the RAXENV software application. For each component, the table states if it should be monitored (*Yes*) or not (*No*) or if it was not used in the dataset (marked with a cross). It exhibits for three components in the list that they should be monitored in some datasets but not in all datasets. It means the very same instance of a component can be subject to monitoring or not depending on the actual state of the application. This is interesting because it is an actual example of a situation where an implementation by hand to make a component thread-safe would lead to a situation where the code written to solve concurrency problems may be useless therefore consuming memory and computation time for nothing.

Interestingly, we compared these results to what was really implemented at that time by developers. Data were only available for the MIBB, RIBB and VPBB dataset and we recorded the differ-

Dataset	Components	Edges	$\|\mathcal{L}\|$	Iterations	Duration	$\mathcal{M}$ / $\|\mathcal{M}\|$
Abstract example	9	12	6	7	3 ms	C, D, E
Toy case	11	15	11	3	3 ms	$End, Sum, s, s1, s2$
Raxenv: reinitialisation (BB) – RIBB	28	34	14	4	4 ms	$ss\_d, widget, iBuf, gm, tc$
Raxenv: manual initialisation (BB) – MIBB	40	62	27	5	4 ms	9
Raxenv: vision predominance (BB) – VPBB	38	53	29	5	4 ms	10
Raxenv: reinitialisation (WB)	35	50	14	4	4 ms	$ss\_d, widget, iBuf, gm, tc$
Raxenv: manual initialisation (WB)	72	145	71	7	20 ms	21
Raxenv: vision predominance (WB)	59	112	44	7	12 ms	19

Table 1: Results gathered from our algorithm ran on different data sets

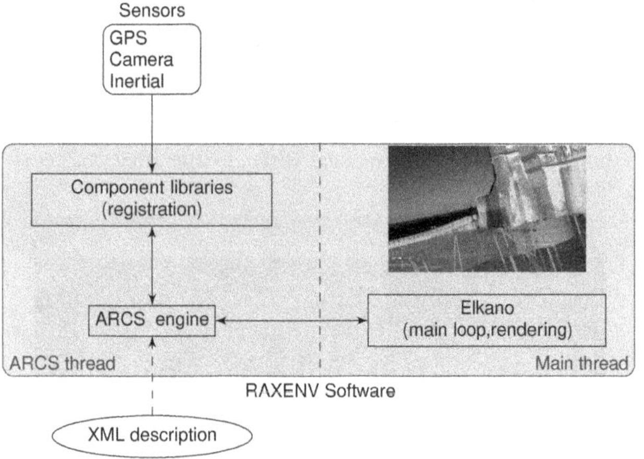

Figure 7: Global interaction between ARCS and RAXENV software modules

Name	In $\mathcal{M}_{\text{RIBB}}$	In $\mathcal{M}_{\text{MIBB}}$	In $\mathcal{M}_{\text{VPBB}}$
ss_d	Yes	Yes	Yes
widget	Yes	Yes	Yes
iBuf	**Yes**	**No**	**Yes**
gm	Yes	Yes	Yes
tc	Yes	Yes	Yes
tmp1	×	Yes	Yes
visP	×	Yes	Yes
isa	×	Yes	×
gm2	×	Yes	×
rinit	**No**	**Yes**	**Yes**
gm3	×	×	Yes
alP	**No**	**No**	**Yes**
chrono	×	×	Yes

Table 2: Recurring components to monitor in RIBB, MIBB and VPBB datasets.

Dataset	RIBB	MIBB	VPBB
Components unprotected	2	5	6
Components overprotected	2	5	2
Differences: total	4	10	8
Differences ratio	14%	25%	21%

Table 3: Comparison with implementation by hand

ences we found out into the implementation and the results provided by our algorithm (see table 3). We counted the number of unprotected components, that is to say components our algorithm marked as subject to be monitored whereas developers did not implemented any thread-safe mechanism, the number of overprotected components (components for which developers have implemented unneeded thread-safe mechanisms) and computed the ratio of the total of such differences to the number of components used in each dataset. One of the most striking result is that we obtained a difference ratio of 25%. This may seem quite high but it does not mean that developers had made mistakes in all situations : one of the prominent problem is that, at that time, mechanisms to monitor composite components were not available whereas it was the kind of components we needed to monitor in this application (It also means that developers did not have, at that time, means to write completely thread safe applications). Another thing to take into consideration is the fact that developers have access to the internals of components and consider them as whiteboxes. Therefore, their analysis may slightly differ than the one from our algorithm because some components may not need to be monitored due to their internal structure. However, overprotected components can be considered as avoidable mistakes.

4.3 Discussion and further work

Concerning our algorithm many things may be subject to discussion. For example, a lot of formal work is still needed in order to assess the complexity of our algorithm as well as proving that it converges in all situations.

Another thing to keep in mind is that our algorithm is only indicating which components are assumed to be monitored. It raises then several other issues. The first one is about the automation of a solution to build monitors at runtime for these components. In some situations, especially if we use the monitor design pattern, we may reach a deadlock situation (when two thread lock components that are needed by each other), therefore a further analysis is needed to detect these situations or we should cast away the monitor paradigm and use another one. However, even if the tool is not fully automated at the execution, the results it produces are interesting for developers since the obtained component set indicates where developers have to focus in order to detect race conditions in their software application.

The last thing we would like to keep in mind is that it may also be interesting to adapt our algorithm in case we may have finer indications of the behaviour of components (i.e. when components are considered as white boxes instead of black boxes). We may then need to write a specific parser and decompose components in several independent vertices in order to build the graph needed by our algorithm.

5. CONCLUSION

We introduced in an actual component based AR framework some automated concurrency management mechanism. To achieve this, we rely on the monitor object design pattern as well as a

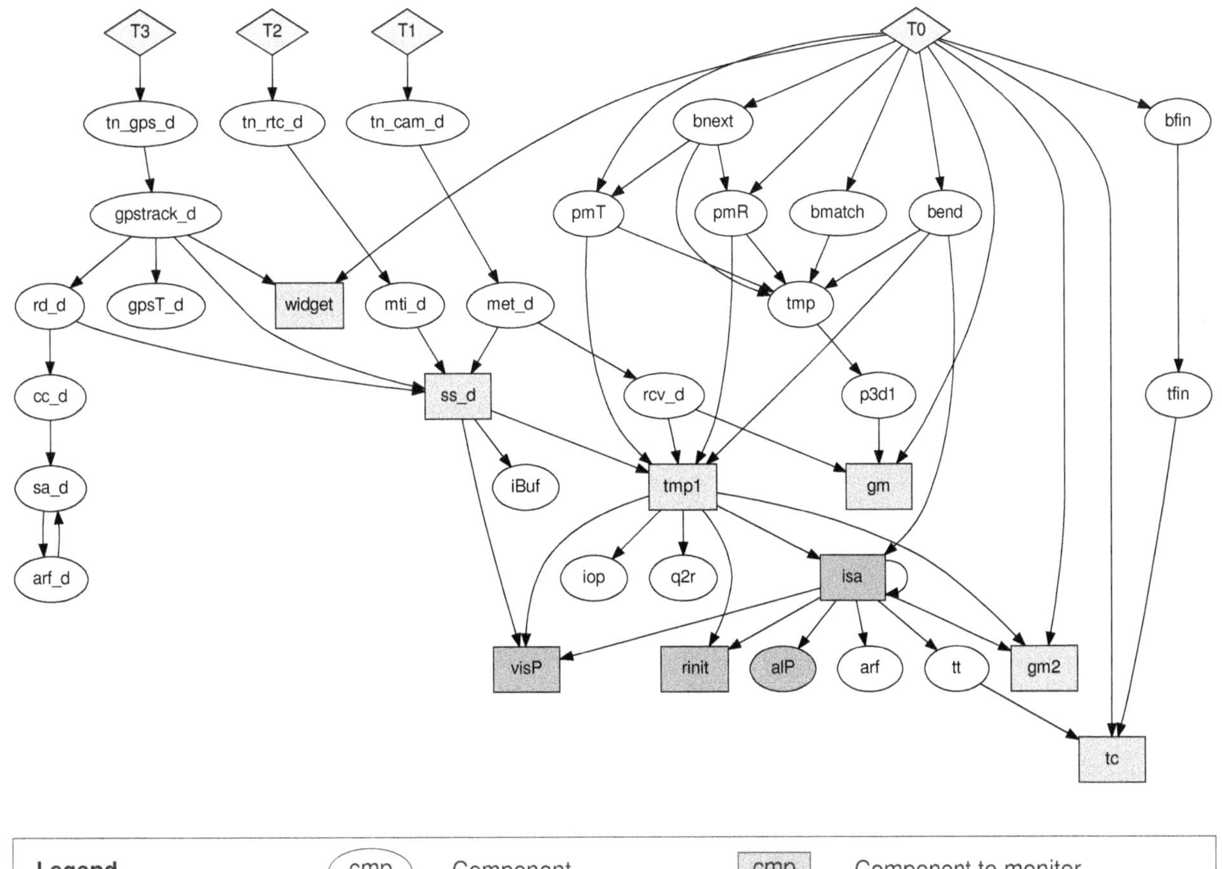

Figure 8: Components configuration in dataset labelled MIBB

heuristic that computesš the components that must be monitored. Applied on a toy case in the ARCS framework, it gave satisfactory result. Therefore we believe that it could be implemented in a larger scale on an actual complex AR application or, more generally, for any component based software using a similar model to the one we presented.

The algorithm was also used on actual data coming from a concrete application and exhibited some differences with the actual implementation made by developers, providing hints about the places where race conditions may occur.

In the future some loose ends associated to concurrency should also be addressed such the problem of deadlock or resource starvation in order to bring out a complete automated concurrency management system that would relieve the developer to determine it and implement it by hand. Therefore, he can focus and spend more time on the functional requirements of software applications.

6. REFERENCES

[1] M. Abadi, C. Flanagan, and S. N. Freund. Types for safe locking: Static race detection for java. *ACM Transactions on Programming Languages and Systems (TOPLAS)*, 28(2):207–255, 2006.

[2] R. Azuma, B. Hoff, H. N. Iii, and R. Sarfaty. A motion-stabilized outdoor augmented reality system. In *Proceedings of the IEEE Virtual Reality*, VR '99, pages 252–, Washington, DC, USA, 1999. IEEE Computer Society.

[3] U. Banerjee, B. Bliss, Z. Ma, and P. Petersen. A theory of data race detection. In *Proceedings of the 2006 workshop on Parallel and distributed systems: testing and debugging*, pages 69–78. ACM, 2006.

[4] M. Bauer, B. Bruegge, G. Klinker, A. MacWilliams, T. Reicher, S. Riss, C. Sandor, and M. Wagner. Design of a component-based augmented reality framework. In *Proceedings of the International Symposium on Augmented Reality (ISAR)*, pages 45–54, octobre 2001.

[5] BRGM. The raxenv project. http://raxenv.brgm.fr/?lang=en.

[6] M. Chouiten, J.-Y. Didier, and M. Mallem. Component-based middleware for distributed augmented reality applications. In *Proceedings of the 5th International Conference on COMmunication System softWAre and MiddlewaRE (COMSWARE 2011)*, page 3, July 1-3 2011.

[7] J.-Y. Didier, S. Otmane, and M. Mallem. A component model for augmented/mixed reality applications with reconfigurable data-flow. In *8th International Conference on*

Virtual Reality (VRIC 2006), pages 243–252, Laval (France), 26-28 avril 2006.

[8] J.-Y. Didier, S. Otmane, and M. Mallem. Arcs : Une architecture logicielle reconfigurable pour la conception des applications de réalité augmentée. *Technique et Science Informatiques (TSI), Réalité Virtuelle - RéalitéAugmentée*, 28(6-7):891–919, Juin-septembre 2009. Numéro spécial.

[9] R. Dörner, C. Geiger, M. Haller, and V. Paelke. Authoring mixed reality. a component and framework-based approach. In *First International Workshop on Entertainment Computing (IWEC 2002)*, pages 405–413, Makuhari, Chiba, Japon, 14-17 mai 2002.

[10] M. Emmi, J. S. Fischer, R. Jhala, and R. Majumdar. Lock allocation. In *ACM SIGPLAN Notices*, volume 42, pages 291–296. ACM, 2007.

[11] C. Endres, A. Butz, and A. MacWilliams. A survey of software infrastructures and frameworks for ubiquitous computing. *Mobile Information Systems Journal*, 1(1):41–80, janvier–mars 2005.

[12] D. Engler and K. Ashcraft. Racerx: effective, static detection of race conditions and deadlocks. In *ACM SIGOPS Operating Systems Review*, volume 37, pages 237–252. ACM, 2003.

[13] Y. Eytani, E. Farchi, and Y. Ben-Asher. Heuristics for finding concurrent bugs. In *Parallel and Distributed Processing Symposium, 2003. Proceedings. International*, pages 8–pp. IEEE, 2003.

[14] C. Flanagan and S. N. Freund. Fasttrack: efficient and precise dynamic race detection. In *ACM Sigplan Notices*, volume 44, pages 121–133. ACM, 2009.

[15] A. Fuhrmann, D. Schmalstieg, and W. Purgathofer. Fast calibration for augmented reality. In *Proceeding of ACM VRST'99*, pages 166–167, Londres, December 1999. ACM.

[16] E. Gamma, R. Helm, R. Johnson, and J. Vlissides. *Design patterns. Elements of reusable object-oriented software*. Addison-Wesley Longman Publishing Co., Inc., Boston, MA, USA, 1995.

[17] R. L. Halpert, C. J. Pickett, and C. Verbrugge. Component-based lock allocation. In *Proceedings of the 16th International Conference on Parallel Architecture and Compilation Techniques*, pages 353–364. IEEE Computer Society, 2007.

[18] Z. Huang, P. Hui, C. Peylo, and D. Chatzopoulos. Mobile augmented reality survey: A bottom-up approach. *arXiv preprint arXiv:1309.4413*, 2013.

[19] C. E. Hughes, C. B. Stapleton, D. E. Hughes, and E. M. Smith. Mixed reality in education, entertainment, and training. *IEEE Comput. Graph. Appl.*, 25:24–30, November 2005.

[20] IBISC. Arcs: Augmented reality component system. http://arcs.ibisc.univ-evry.fr.

[21] R. Kuck, J. Wind, K. Riege, and M. Bogen. Improving the avango vr/ar framework - lessons learned. In M. Schumann, editor, *Virtuelle und Erweiterte Realitat : 5. Workshop der GI-Fachgruppe VR/AR*, pages 209–220, Aachen, 2008.

[22] L. Lamport. Time, clocks, and the ordering of events in a distributed system. *Communications of the ACM*, 21(7):558–565, 1978.

[23] B. Long, P. Strooper, and L. Wildman. A method for verifying concurrent java components based on an analysis of concurrency failures. *Concurrency and Computation: Practice and Experience*, 19(3):281–294, 2007.

[24] ObjectManagementGroup. Omg's corba website. http://www.omg.org/corba/.

[25] J. Ohlenburg, I. Herbst, I. Lindt, T. Fröhlich, and W. Broll. The morgan framework: enabling dynamic multi-user ar and vr projects. In *Proceedings of the ACM Symposium on Virtual Reality Software and Technology, VRST 2004*, pages 166–169, Honk Kong, China, 10-12 novembre 2004.

[26] W. Piekarski and B. Thomas. An object-oriented software architecture for 3d mixed reality applications. In *The Second IEEE and ACM International Symposium on Mixed and Augmented Reality (ISMAR'03)*, pages 247–256, Tokyo, Japan, octobre 2003.

[27] M. Ponder, G. Papagiannakis, T. Molet, N. Magnenat-Thalmann, and D. Thalmann. Vhd++ development framework: Towards extendible, component based vr/ar simulation engine featuring advanced virtual character technologies. *Computer Graphics International Conference*, 0:96–104, 2003.

[28] E. Pozniansky and A. Schuster. Multirace: efficient on-the-fly data race detection in multithreaded c++ programs. *Concurrency and Computation: Practice and Experience*, 19(3):327–340, 2007.

[29] P. Pratikakis, J. S. Foster, and M. Hicks. Locksmith: context-sensitive correlation analysis for race detection. *ACM SIGPLAN Notices*, 41(6):320–331, 2006.

[30] Qt project. Qt web site. http://qt.digia.com/, url.

[31] S. Savage, M. Burrows, G. Nelson, P. Sobalvarro, and T. Anderson. Eraser: A dynamic data race detector for multithreaded programs. *ACM Transactions on Computer Systems (TOCS)*, 15(4):391–411, 1997.

[32] D. C. Schmidt, M. Stal, H. Rohnert, and F. Buschmann. *Pattern-Oriented Software Architecture*, volume 2: Patterns for Concurrent and Networked Objects. John Wiley & Sons, 2000.

[33] V. C. Sreedhar, Y. Zhang, and G. R. Gao. A new framework for analysis and optimization of shared memory parallel programs. Technical report, 2005.

[34] N. Sterling. Warlock-a static data race analysis tool. In *USENIx Winter*, pages 97–106, 1993.

[35] C. Szyperski. *Component Software - Beyond Object-Oriented Programming (Second edition)*. Addison-Wesley, Harlow, England, 2002.

[36] J. W. Voung, R. Jhala, and S. Lerner. Relay: static race detection on millions of lines of code. In *Proceedings of the the 6th joint meeting of the European software engineering conference and the ACM SIGSOFT symposium on The foundations of software engineering*, pages 205–214. ACM, 2007.

[37] I. Zendjebil, F. Ababsa, J.-Y. Didier, and M. Mallem. Large scale localization for mobile outdoor augmented reality applications. In Springer, editor, *International Conference On Computer Vision Theory and Applications*, 2011.

[38] Y. Zhang, V. C. Sreedhar, W. Zhu, V. Sarkar, and G. R. Gao. Minimum lock assignment: A method for exploiting concurrency among critical sections. In *Languages and Compilers for Parallel Computing*, pages 141–155. Springer, 2008.

Memory Monitoring in a Multi-tenant OSGi Execution Environment

Koutheir Attouchi
Orange Labs.
Grenoble, France.
koutheir@gmail.com

Gaël Thomas
Inria & LIP6.
Paris, France.
gael.thomas@lip6.fr

André Bottaro
Orange Labs.
Grenoble, France.
andre.bottaro@orange.com

Gilles Muller
Inria & LIP6.
Paris, France.
gilles.muller@lip6.fr

ABSTRACT

Smart Home market players aim to deploy *component-based* and *service-oriented* applications from *untrusted* third party providers on a single OSGi execution environment. This creates the risk of *resource abuse* by buggy and malicious applications, which raises the need for resource monitoring mechanisms. Existing resource monitoring solutions either are too intrusive or fail to identify the relevant resource consumer in numerous multi-tenant situations. This paper proposes a system to monitor the *memory* consumed by each tenant, while allowing them to continue communicating directly to render services. We propose a solution based on a list of configurable *resource accounting rules* between tenants, which is far less intrusive than existing OSGi monitoring systems. We modified an experimental Java Virtual Machine in order to provide the memory monitoring features for the multi-tenant OSGi environment. Our evaluation of the memory monitoring mechanism on the DaCapo benchmarks shows an overhead below 46%.

Categories and Subject Descriptors

D.2.8 [**Software Engineering**]: Metrics—*Performance measures*; D.2.11 [**Computer Systems Organization**]: Performances of systems—*Measurement techniques, Reliability, and availability*

Keywords

memory monitoring; multitenancy; software platform; smart home; home gateway; OSGi technology

CBSE'14, June 30–July 4, 2014, Marcq-en-Baroeul, France.

ACM 978-1-4503-2577-6/14/06 ...$15.00.
http://dx.doi.org/10.1145/2602458.2602467.

1. INTRODUCTION

A new world of smart home services emerges thanks to the growing variety of sensors and actuators available. Many application domains are involved, e.g., security, energy efficiency, ambient assisted living, multimedia, communication. Consequently, different software editors, called here *tenants*, are developing applications that take advantage of the multitude of devices in the smart home. The smart home ecosystem, as conceived by the Home Gateway Initiative [6], is based on OSGi [14] and Java, in an effort to support the openness of a multi-tenant execution environment hosting component-based applications collaborating to render services. Figure 1 illustrates this component-based and service-oriented architecture [15]. Java and OSGi provide sharing and isolation mechanisms between OSGi components called *bundles*, which are also OSGi deployment units. Components interact via service method calls to each other exported interfaces. Different tenants deploy their components on the same execution environment. This sharing by untrusted competing tenants raises the need to "protect the box against badly written bundles" [16, 4]. Here, a *badly written* bundle is a component that consumes resources, such as CPU usage and memory and network, far above a normal expected level. Therefore, mechanisms that regulate resource consumption at component granularity are necessary, and in particular, *resource monitoring* mechanisms.

Resource monitoring provides essentially two information: (1) *counting*, i.e., how much of the resource is consumed, and (2) *accounting*, i.e., which entity should be charged for using that quantity of the resource. Existing work performed in component-based and service-oriented platforms [11, 3, 10, 8, 4] enable resource accounting at component level in only two cases: (1) when a component calls a service method implemented by a component belonging to the operator platform, or (2) when the opposite happens. Still, there is a third case that occurs when a component from a given tenant calls a service method implemented by a component belonging to another tenant. None of the cited existing work provide a correct way to account for resources consumed during the third case, because such an accounting requires information related to the *business logic* implemented in the components of the tenants. The first approach adopted to deal with the third case is avoiding it entirely, by forbidding interaction between tenants, which is too restrictive, as tenants need to communicate to render integrated services to the end-user. The second solution requires explicit declaration of the component that is accounted for resources consumed during each interaction via a defined API [2]. However, this API cannot be granted to *untrusted* components, because a buggy or malicious component can use this API to declare resource consumption to the wrong entity, causing resource miscounting. A first challenge is implementing a component-level monitoring system that accounts for resources consumed during interactions between tenants.

A second challenge in designing a monitoring system in a multi-tenant environment is the expression of resource accounting rules during interactions between monitored tenants. Declarations of accounting rules should be *precise* and *expressive* enough for all cases, without requiring developers to write and maintain long rules lists.

A third challenge is implementing a *sufficiently accurate* monitoring system with a minimal performance overhead. Previous methods are not accurate enough, mainly because accounting is either (1) *always direct*, i.e., resources consumed during a method call are always accounted to the called entity, or (2) *always indirect*, i.e., resources consumed during a method call are always accounted to the caller entity. This inaccuracy is more *frequent* and more *critical* when untrusted tenants interact via method calls in multi-tenant environments, which are often service-oriented and component-based. For example, Miettinen et al. [11] perform *indirect* monitoring by attaching every thread to a component and accounting resources consumed by that thread to the attached component no matter what code the thread executes. This method produces inaccurate monitoring statistics in some cases, e.g., components managing a thread pool, and components that notify about events by calling event handlers.

In this paper we describe an *OSGi-aware memory monitoring system* that is mostly transparent to application developers, and that allows collaboration between distinct tenants sharing the same OSGi execution environment, therefore preserving the service-oriented nature of OSGi. The system monitors interactions between tenants and provides snapshots of memory usage statistics on demand.

The monitoring subsystem has predefined *implicit* resource accounting rules that describe correctly most interactions between tenants. We purposely focused on the types of interactions that are very common in component-based and service-oriented design, e.g., calls to service methods and event handlers. Because implicit rules cannot accurately account for all cases, the platform operator and each tenant provide configuration files loaded by the monitoring system at start-up, and containing *explicit* rules for resource accounting between tenants. The configuration files are written in a *Domain-Specific Language* (DSL) that we defined, which is tailored to service-oriented applications, as it allows, for example, to specify the *component* implementing the *interface* containing the method called during an interaction. Our prototype requires the resource accounting rules to remain constant during the lifetime of the JVM. Each configuration file lists (1) the components belonging to a specific tenant, and (2) the resource accounting rules, each of which describes which tenant is accounted for resources consumed during a specific interaction. At runtime, the monitoring system applies those rules to correctly account for memory used by components, e.g., local variables, loaded classes, and created objects. In most of the cases, component developers do not need to write accounting rules because implicit rules handle their interactions correctly. Components that need to write explicit accounting rules are mainly those that generate asynchronous activity, such as those that publish events. Examples include the OSGi framework, and components exposing data of home sensors in real time.

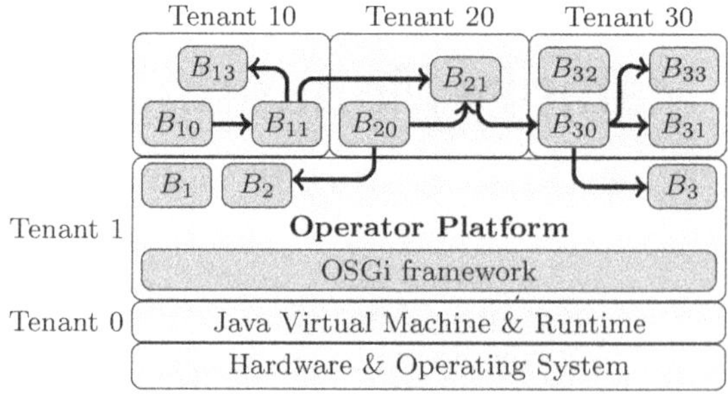

Figure 1: A multi-tenant OSGi execution environment. $B_1 \ldots B_{33}$ are OSGi components, i.e., bundles.

We implemented the monitoring system inside J3, a Java Virtual Machine based on VMKit [5], LLVM [9] and MMTk [1]. Even though we slightly change the native object structure, the changes are invisible to the Java code, which helps preserve the component model of OSGi. We validate our implementation of the monitoring system using a set of micro-tests that mimics common communication patterns in a component-based and service-oriented micro-structure composed of seven tenants. We evaluate the overhead generated by the system based on the real life applications of the DaCapo benchmark, in addition to highly focused micro-benchmarks. The performance overhead of monitoring is always below 46% for DaCapo applications, which is still reasonable for development and testing environment, and tolerable in low-pace production environments.

This paper is organized as follows. We begin by discussing the design of the monitoring mechanism in Section 2. In Section 3, we illustrate our prototype implementation of the design. Section 4 measures the overhead of monitoring and reveals the parts of the system that cause most of it. Previous work related to resource management are described in Section 5. Finally, Section 6 concludes the paper and discusses future directions.

2. DESIGN

In this section, we present the design of a memory monitoring subsystem that is intended to be a part of a more complete system for resource management inside a long running JVM running OSGi. The memory usage information reported by this subsystem would indicate memory leaks and too high memory usage patterns.

Motivating example 1: Service method.

In practice, a tenant would often require the caller of the service it provides to be accounted for resources consumed by that service. For example, a tenant providing a service `playRingTone()` would require the tenant calling that service to be accounted for memory consumed to play the ring tone. No rules should be needed in order to fulfill this accounting, i.e., it should be the default behavior of resource accounting.

Motivating example 2: Event handlers.
Less often, a tenant A provides an interface to notify observers about an event. Another tenant B subscribes to the event and expects to be called when the event occurs. When the event occurs, A calls B as contracted. In this case, implicit rules (see the step 3(d) in Section 2.4) specify that A should be accounted for resources consumed during the call. However, this is unfair given the fact that A calls B only because B asked for that by subscribing to the event. In this case, A needs to write an accounting rule for the notification interface, accounting resources for the called entity (see Section 2.3).

2.1 Assumptions

We assume a number of preconditions on the system where our monitoring subsystem runs.

No need for isolation.
We do not suppose any form of isolation beyond what is provided by OSGi. Therefore, all tenants are able to communicate via service method calls. This enables different tenants to collaborate to create integrated services and user experience, even when the user is using sensors and actuators and applications from different manufacturers and editors.

Constant monitoring, infrequent reporting.
It is typical for a long-running system to have a *resource manager* subsystem that periodically requests memory usage statistics from a memory monitoring subsystem. In the smart home gateway, memory usage statistics would be requested once or twice a day in relatively stable configurations, and the period can be as frequent as every hour when hardware or software configurations change. The memory usage statistics enable detecting *abnormal* memory usage situations, e.g., memory leaks. When such abnormal activity is detected, the resource manager subsystem carries out actions to restore the system to a normal state by making memory available again, such as terminating some applications. The resource manager subsystem can be human driven or autonomous.

Our memory monitoring subsystem runs *continuously*, collecting *raw* memory usage data on running applications. This generates a *persistent* overhead that must be kept to a minimum. Furthermore, in order to report relevant memory statistics, raw data need to be *aggregated* and *filtered*, generating an overhead every time a memory monitoring report is requested. We target systems where memory monitoring reports will be requested *sparingly* in time, in order to check for abnormal resource usage. This is the case of the smart home gateway, where memory monitoring reports would be generated from once per hour to once per day. Therefore, we tolerate the aggregation and filtering overhead needed to generate memory monitoring reports, and we rather focus on the persistent overhead caused by continuous monitoring.

Constant resource accounting configuration.
In order to simplify our prototype and keep performance overhead acceptable, we require that resource accounting rules and tenants list remains *constant* during the JVM lifetime. This allows performing early calculations in order to accelerate inference of accounting rules.

2.2 Goals

We designed our monitoring subsystem in order to fulfill the following goals.

Detailed memory monitoring.
Our prototype monitors memory usage of every tenant in *call stack* space and *heap* space. Call stack space is where most methods variables and parameters are stored. The subsystem reports the number of bytes accounted to each tenant, in the call stacks of all running threads. Heap memory is used to store Java classes and objects, particularly their static fields and object fields. The subsystem reports the number of classes loaded by each tenant and the number of bytes used by those classes. It also reports the number of reachable objects that are accounted to each tenant, in addition to the number of bytes used by those objects.

Expressive resource accounting rules.
The tenants and the platform operator are required to provide accounting rules that describe how accounting should occur when two tenants interact. We designed a Domain-Specific Language (DSL) to enable expression of resource accounting rules.

Only specify special cases.
We want our subsystem to require the smallest configuration possible. The default configuration should work well for most of the cases, and developers and platform administrators should configure and maintain only the special cases of interactions. For this, we armed our subsystem with a list of implicit rules to handle most cases correctly. We also defined a resource accounting algorithm that decides which tenants to account for resources, so that:

- Explicit rules always override implicit rules.
- The order of processing rules is from the most specific, to the most generic.

2.3 Domain-specific language for resource accounting rules

We defined a DSL that enables developers and platform administrators to specify the rules to decide which tenant should be accounted for resources consumed during an interaction. Illustrated in Figure 2, the DSL allows rules of varying levels of precision, which allows factoring the rules, thus writing and maintaining less of them. It also allows correct handling of all possible cases of component interactions.

The DSL describes separately two aspects: a list of tenants, then a list of rules. Each element in the tenants list describes the identifier assigned to a tenant, and the names of components it deploys. Each element in the rules list describes a method call between two tenants, and which tenant should be accounted for resources consumed during that call. We reserve 0 as the tenant ID of the Java runtime and the JVM native code, and we reserve 1 as the tenant ID of the platform operator (see Figure 1). A rule starts with the caller tenant ID (an integer), which can be * to indicate that any caller tenant matches this rule. Then, the called site is specified, followed by the accounting decision. The called site is (1) a method of (2) an interface defined in (3) a tenant and implemented by (4) a component. The four components are optional, and omitting a component matches

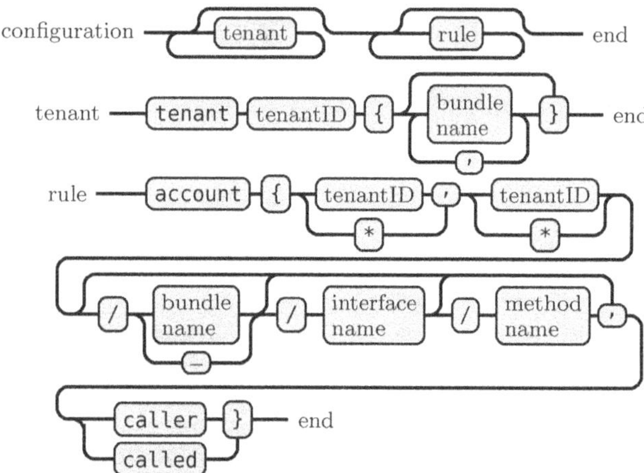

Figure 2: DSL of resource accounting configuration

```
tenant   1 { org.knopflerfish.framework }
tenant  20 { tests.A                    }
tenant 200 { j3mgr                      }

account { 0, 0/_/java.lang.Runnable/run, called }
account { *, 200/j3mgr/j3.J3Mgr,         caller }
account { *, 20/tests.A/tests.A.A,       caller }
```

Figure 3: Sample resource accounting configuration

all possible values, e.g., specifying "_" as the implementation component name matches any components implementing the specified interface or method. Finally, the accounting decision specifies which tenant is accounted for resources consumed during the call. Note that when the called tenant should be accounted for resources, it is the tenant holding the implementation of the called method that is accounted, not the tenant defining the interface.

Figure 3 shows an example of resource accounting configuration. It first associates components with tenants, then it declares rules, each of which specifies which tenant is accounted for resources consumed during a given method call. So, first it declares the platform operator as `tenant 1`, holding the main `framework` component of the Knopflerfish OSGi implementation. It declares two other tenants whose identifiers are 20 and 200, with one component for each tenant. Then it declares that a call from the Java runtime to the method `run` of the `java.lang.Runnable` interface implemented by any component will be accounted to the tenant of the called component, i.e., the tenant of implementation component. Next, a call from any tenant to a method of the interface `j3.J3Mgr` implemented in the component `j3mgr` of the tenant 200 is accounted to the tenant of the caller. Finally, a call from any tenant to a method of the interface `tests.A.A` implemented in the component `tests.A` of the tenant 20 is accounted to the tenant of the caller.

Back to the *Motivating example 2: Event handlers* previously described, all what the developer needs to write is the following accounting rule:
`account(42, 42/_/notify.event/happened, called)`
This rule specifies that a call from the tenant 42 (the tenant ID of A) to the method `happened()` of the interface `notify.event` defined in the tenant 42 (in A) and implemented by any tenant (the _) is accounted to the called tenant implementing the interface, i.e., the tenant subscribed to the event published by A.

2.4 Resource accounting algorithm

This section describes the resource accounting algorithm that decides which tenant is accounted for resources consumed during an interaction.

Algorithm.

The list of tenants described in Section 2.3 is stored in the following data structure associating each tenant ID with the list of components it is responsible of:

$$map = \{..., (\text{TenantID}_i \rightarrow \{..., \text{ComponentName}_j, ...\}), ...\}$$

The list of resource accounting rules is stored in the following data structure associating accounting rules with decisions:

$$\begin{aligned} map =& \{..., (\text{CallConfig}_i \rightarrow \text{caller}|\text{called}), ...\}, \text{where:} \\ \text{CallConfig}_i =& ([\text{CallerTenantID}], \text{CalledSite}), \text{where:} \\ \text{CalledSite} =& (\text{TenantID}, [\text{ComponentName}], \\ & [\text{InterfaceName}], [\text{MethodName}\ ]) \\ & \text{where: } [x] \text{ means } x \text{ is optional} \end{aligned}$$

Given a call configuration λ_i (a.k.a. CallConfig_i in the map expression above) as an input, the algorithm proceeds as follows:

1. The accounting rules map is searched for an exact match for the key λ_i. If that is found, then its associated value indicates explicitly which tenant is accounted for the resource usage, and the process ends.

2. If λ_i is totally generic, i.e., if its method name and interface name and component name are all missing, then continue to 3, otherwise, continue to 4.

3. No rules are defined for this interaction. Apply the following *implicit rules*:

   (a) If the call is an internal operator platform call, then account resource usage to the caller, i.e., the platform operator.

   (b) If the platform operator is calling a tenant, then account resource usage to the called entity, i.e., the tenant.

   (c) If a tenant is calling the platform operator, then account resource usage to the caller, i.e., the tenant.

   (d) Otherwise, account resource usage to the caller.

   And the process ends here.

4. Make λ_i more generic, i.e., remove one non-missing piece on information from it, in the following order: method name, then interface name, then component name.

   Loop to 1.

The illustrated decision algorithm ensures that:

- Accounting rules order is unimportant, i.e., rules are always matched from the most specific, to the most generic.

- Implicit accounting rules account the platform operator only when the interaction is an internal operator platform call.

- Implicit accounting rules between two tenants accounts the caller.

3. IMPLEMENTATION

This section describes our implementation of the design we promote in the previous section. We divided the monitoring subsystem into three major components that run inside the JVM:

- *OSGi state tracker* that acts as a bridge between the JVM subsystems and the OSGi framework.

- *Accounting configuration manager* that parses accounting rules and performs accounting decisions.

- *Monitoring manager* that generates, on-demand, snapshots of detailed memory statistics.

The monitoring subsystem implementation is around 2000 lines of C++ code mostly inside the J3 JVM based on VMKit [5], LLVM [9] and MMTk [1]. The OSGi framework used is Knopflerfish 5.0.

3.1 OSGi state tracker

In resource accounting rules, each component is identified by its name. But, at runtime, each OSGi component instance is identified by a unique framework-assigned ID that is not reused even if that instance is uninstalled. The link between the component name and the component ID enables the monitoring subsystem to know which rule to apply when two components interact. The OSGi state tracker component makes the links between the static component information (e.g., component names) given in the resource accounting rules and the dynamic states of OSGi components at runtime (e.g., component ID, component class loaders). It tracks the OSGi states (e.g., `resolved`, `uninstalled`) of components installed in the OSGi framework running on top of the JVM, by listening to events of component state changes from the JVM and from the OSGi framework.

This component associates component identifiers with their respective component information. The component information includes the component name, and its current and previous class loaders. The association map is expressed as:

$$map = \{..., (\text{CompID}_i \to \text{CompInfo}_i), ...\}, \text{ where:}$$
$$\text{CompInfo}_i = (\text{CompName}, \{..., \text{ClassLoader}_j, ...\})$$

In order to discover component state changes, this component places two hooks in the Knopflerfish 5.0 OSGi framework, which makes it dependent on that particular OSGi implementation. However, those hooks need no more than 10 lines of code inserted into the framework code. Therefore, the dependency is fairly limited.

This component encapsulates all the logic necessary to interact with the OSGi framework. Therefore, porting the monitoring subsystem to another OSGi framework implementation only requires porting this component. This makes the major part of the subsystem independent of any particular OSGi framework implementation.

3.2 Accounting configuration manager

When the JVM starts up, the accounting configuration manager component loads the resource accounting configuration, before loading the OSGi framework code. The configuration is stored in memory in the data structures described in Section 2.4, and it remains constant during the execution of the JVM. We implemented a parser inside this component, in order to load the configuration from any text file (e.g., disk files, names pipes, sockets) that conforms to the DSL described in Section 2.3.

At runtime, each time a component calls a method via direct invocation (i.e., `invoke*`) or object construction (i.e., `new`), this component decides which tenant should be accounted for resources consumed during that call. The decision is based on the algorithm described in Section 2.4, which takes into account the resource accounting configuration, default accounting rules, and runtime information. Some runtime information, e.g., states of components, is provided by the OSGi state tracker component previously described. The accounting decision concerns solely resources consumed in the thread running the called method, and it remains effective until another method is called in that thread.

For each Java thread, we set a thread-local variable γ_i holding the thread's *currently accounted tenant ID*. Initially, γ_i is set to `0`: the special tenant ID reserved to the Java runtime. Before every method call, the resource accounting algorithm decides which tenant is accounted for the resources consumed during the call. If the algorithm decides that the called tenant shall be accounted for resources, then γ_i is set to the tenant ID of the called method. Otherwise, γ_i remains unchanged. In all cases, the tenant identified by γ_i is accounted for resources consumed by the thread. Most changes needed to track method calls and to invoke the decision algorithm are implemented in the Just-In-Time (JIT) subsystem of the JVM.

The monitoring subsystem adds, in every Java object, a hidden field that holds the tenant ID accounted for the object. Every time the JVM creates a new object, i.e., executes a `new` instruction, it reads γ_i to determine which tenant is accounted for the newly created object. The object is consequently tagged with the tenant ID set in of γ_i.

This mode of operation regarding γ_i ensures that resources are accounted to the caller tenant, unless otherwise specified by an implicit or declared accounting rule. The notion of the caller tenant is transitive. Consider the example call sequence:

$$S_1 = ... \to M_1 \to M_2 \to M_3 \to M_4 \to ...$$

where M_i is a method belonging to a tenant T_i, and arrows indicate method calls. In each method call, before entering the called method M_i, the decision algorithm makes the decision D_i, which determines the new value of γ_i. An example of decisions follows:

$D_1 = ... \to M_1$: the **called** tenant is accounted. $\Rightarrow \gamma_i = T_1$

$D_2 = M_1 \to M_2$: the **caller** tenant is accounted. $\Rightarrow \gamma_i = T_1$

$D_3 = M_2 \to M_3$: the **caller** tenant is accounted. $\Rightarrow \gamma_i = T_1$

$D_4 = M_3 \to M_4$: the **called** tenant is accounted. $\Rightarrow \gamma_i = T_4$

This example implies that resources consumed during the execution of M_1, M_2 and M_3 are all accounted to T_1, whereas resources consumed in M_4 are accounted to T_4.

```
tenant 1  { org.knopflerfish.framework }
tenant 50 { tests.A }
tenant 60 { tests.B }
tenant 70 { tests.C }
tenant 80 { tests.D }
tenant 90 { tests.E }
```

Figure 4: Tenants declarations in functional tests.

It is worth noticing that γ_i is restored to its previous value in any scenario that makes the method return to one of its callers, e.g., when a method returns, or when an exception is caught outside the method where it is thrown. The previous values of γ_i are stored in the call stack, as hidden local variables.

This frequent execution of the decision algorithm in every method call is the primary source of the permanent overhead added to the normal execution of Java code.

3.3 Monitoring manager

The monitoring manager component generates, on-demand, snapshots of detailed memory statistics. In order to do so, this component triggers a special garbage collection cycle, during which it scans the object graph and call stacks of running threads, while accumulating statistical counters. This scan is performed by placing hooks in the garbage collector code which scans objects and threads. The counters accumulate the following information, grouped by tenants (see Section 2.2):

- Number of reachable objects and their size.
- Number of loaded classes and their size.
- Amount of used stack space.

It is worth noting that the modifications performed on the garbage collector do not depend on the algorithm used for collection, and do not modify the accessed objects and classes and threads. We only depend on the fact that the garbage collector can perform a collection cycle during which it scans the whole objects graph, and during which all threads are suspended. Otherwise, this component is independent of the garbage collector implementation.

4. EVALUATION

The benchmarks were executed on a computer running the 32-bits version of the Linux 3.12 kernel, on an Intel Xeon CPU running at 2.7 GHz, with 12 megabytes of cache, 12 gigabytes of RAM[1] and 1 terabyte of disk space.

4.1 Functional tests

In order to ensure that the monitoring subsystem works as intended, we performed functional unit tests. To verify correct accounting, we ask the monitoring system to output detailed accounting calculations.

4.1.1 *Operator platform internal accounting*

A part of the detailed accounting calculation is shown in Figure 5, consisting of a thread call stack prefixed with monitoring information, i.e., `T`: identifier of the tenant that is accounted for resources consumed during the method frame, and `Size`: the total size, in bytes, of the method frame. For example, in Figure 5, 1456 bytes of stack space are accounted to the Java runtime (tenant 0), and 1120 bytes of stack space are accounted to the operator platform (tenant 1). The package `java.lang` belongs to the Java runtime. The line `1` in Figure 4 states that the package `org.knopflerfish.framework` belongs to the operator platform.

```
T Size MethodFrameName
1 480  java.lang.VMObject.wait
1 128  java.lang.Object.wait
1 240  org.knopflerfish.framework.Queue.removeWait
1 272  org.knopflerfish.framework.StartLevelController.run
0 96   java.lang.Thread.run
0 304  java.lang.VMThread.run
0 1056 <native>
```

Legend:
`T`: Currently accounted tenant ID, i.e., γ_i.
`Size`: Stack size, in bytes, of the method frame.

Figure 5: Detailed memory accounting calculations on a call stack of a thread internal to the OSGi framework.

The choice of which tenant is accounted for a particular method frame is based on the algorithm described in Section 2.4. As specified in Section 3.2, γ_i denotes the *currently accounted tenant ID*. In fact, γ_i corresponds to `T` in Figures 5 and 6. Initially, $\gamma_i \leftarrow 0$: the tenant ID of the Java runtime. If the algorithm decides that the *called* tenant shall be accounted for resources, then γ_i is set to the tenant ID of the called method. Otherwise, γ_i remains unchanged. In all cases, the tenant identified by γ_i is accounted for resources consumed by the method frame.

In Figure 5, the `<native>` frame is the first code to run in the thread, consisting of operating system thread initialization routine and JVM routines that prepares for Java code execution. Initially, the native frame is accounted to the Java runtime, i.e., the tenant 0 ($\gamma_i \leftarrow 0$). The native code calls the `java.lang.VMThread.run()` method implemented in Java runtime, which makes it an internal Java runtime call. Step 3(a) in the algorithm described in Section 2.4 accounts the call to the caller, i.e., tenant 0 ($\gamma_i = 0$) which is the Java runtime. The same accounting goes for the next method frame.

Next, the Java runtime calls the method `run()` of the class `org.knopflerfish.framework.StartLevelController` defined in the operator platform (tenant 1), and implementing the interface `java.lang.Runnable` defined in the Java runtime (tenant 0). This call matches the predefined explicit rule: `account {0, 0/_/java.lang.Runnable/run, called}`. This is why the called, i.e., the operator platform (tenant 1) is accounted for the call, and $\gamma_i \leftarrow 1$. The next call is internal to the tenant 1, so the caller, i.e., tenant 1 ($\gamma_i = 1$) is accounted for it.

Later, the operator platform calls the Java runtime method `java.lang.Object.wait()`. The step 3(c) in the algorithm implies that the caller, i.e., tenant 1 ($\gamma_i = 1$), is accounted for the call. The rest of the calls are internal Java runtime calls, for which the caller tenant, i.e., the tenant 1 ($\gamma_i = 1$) is accounted for the resources consumed during the calls.

4.1.2 *Implicit and explicit accounting*

To test monitoring of other types of interactions between different tenants, we define five components `tests.A` through `tests.E`, each belonging to a tenant, as declared in Figure 4

[1]The kernel allowed addressing the whole RAM via Physical Address Extensions.

```
T  Size MethodFrameName
50 480  java.lang.VMObject.wait
50 64   java.lang.Object.wait
50 256  java.lang.VMThread.sleep
50 112  java.lang.Thread.sleep
50 224  tests.D.D.sleep
50 160  tests.D.D.handler
50 144  tests.B.C.someProcessing
50 256  tests.B.C.e
50 144  tests.A.Activator.heavyInitialization
50 128  tests.A.Activator.start
1  384  org.knopflerfish.framework.Bundle.start0
1  272  org.knopflerfish.framework.BundleThread.run
0  272  java.lang.VMThread.run
0  1056 <native>

Tenant Stack Objects Classes HeapStatic HeapVirtual
0      14816 7964    129     1600       167336
1      4176  35908   154     1597       1107636
50     1968  55525   16      313        666500
60     0     15      13      104        316
80     0     19      14      104        384
```

(a) Only implicit accounting used.

```
T  Size MethodFrameName
80 480  java.lang.VMObject.wait
80 64   java.lang.Object.wait
80 256  java.lang.VMThread.sleep
80 112  java.lang.Thread.sleep
80 224  tests.D.D.sleep
80 160  tests.D.D.handler
50 144  tests.B.C.someProcessing
50 256  tests.B.C.e
50 144  tests.A.Activator.heavyInitialization
50 128  tests.A.Activator.start
1  384  org.knopflerfish.framework.Bundle.start0
1  272  org.knopflerfish.framework.BundleThread.run
0  272  java.lang.VMThread.run
0  1056 <native>

Tenant Stack Objects Classes HeapStatic HeapVirtual
0      14816 7964    129     1600       167336
1      4176  35906   154     1597       1107592
50     672   5525    16      313        66496
60     0     15      13      104        316
80     1296  50019   15      168        600388
```

(b) Implicit and explicit accounting used.

Legend: `T`: Currently accounted tenant ID, i.e., γ_i. `Size`: Stack size, in bytes, of the method frame.

Figure 6: Detailed memory accounting calculations on a thread call stack.

and illustrated in Figure 7. Then we examine a thread that executes methods from these different components. We execute the thread without defining explicit rules (except a few predefined explicit rules, such as the one shown in the previous subsection), and we show the accounting results in Figure 6a, then we execute it after adding one explicit rule, and we show the accounting results in Figure 6b.

The Figure 6 describes the call stack of a thread that is created by the operator platform in order to start and stop components. A generic description of the thread activity goes as follows. The thread begins running operator platform code in method `org.knopflerfish.framework.BundleThread.run()`. Later, it starts the component `tests.A` by calling the *event handler* `tests.A.Activator.start()` that indirectly calls the method `e()` of the class `tests.B.C` which implements the interface `tests.C.C`, as shown in Figure 7. `tests.B.C` performs some processing before notifying the component `tests.D` of an event by calling the event handler method `handler()` of the class `tests.D.D` which implements the interface `tests.E.E`. Next, `handler()` calls a Java runtime service to sleep.

In Figure 6a, and starting from the first frame executed by the thread, i.e., `<native>`, the three following frames are accounted as previously described for Figure 5. Then, the operator platform (tenant 1) calls method `start()` of the class `tests.A.Activator` (tenant 50) which implements the operator platform interface `org.osgi.framework.BundleActivator`. Step 3(b) of the algorithm described in Section 2.4 states that the called tenant, i.e., tenant 50, is accounted for resources consumed in the method frame, which sets γ_i to 50. In the next five call frames (up to `tests.D.D.sleep()`), step 3(d) of the algorithm states that the caller tenant, i.e., tenant 50 ($\gamma_i = 50$), is accounted for resources consumed in method frames. Then, step 3(c) of the algorithm accounts consumed resources to the caller, i.e., tenant 50 ($\gamma_i = 50$). The remaining method frames are internal Java runtime calls, so step 3(a) of the algorithm accounts consumed resources to the caller, i.e., tenant 50 ($\gamma_i = 50$).

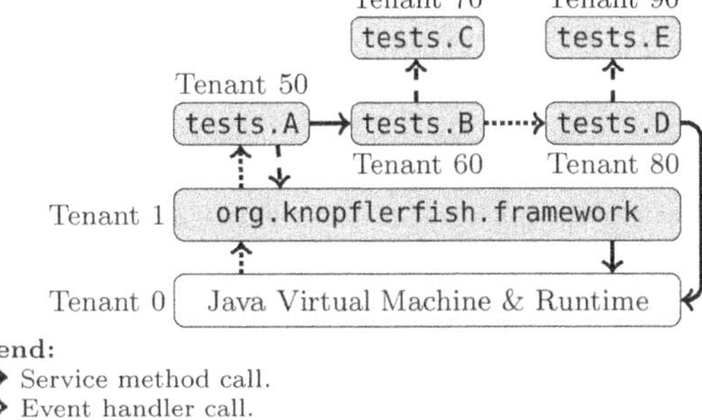

Figure 7: Functional tests components.

The problem observed in Figure 6a is that tenant 50 is held accounted for resources consumed during execution of the event handler method `handler()` and all the methods the latter executes, even though `handler()` is being executed only because the component `tests.D` requested it. Due to this issue, the monitoring system inaccurately accounts to tenant 50 the following amounts of memory: 1296 bytes of stack space, and 50 000 objects totaling 600 004 bytes of heap space, even though that memory was consumed by the event handler. To correct this inaccuracy, we add the following explicit rule: `account {*, 90/_/tests.E.E, called}`, which indicates that `tests.E.E` is an event handling interface (for any caller tenant, for any implementation component, and for any method in the interface).

Figure 6b shows the accounting results after adding the explicit rule and restarting the JVM. Adding the explicit rule effectively solves the problem by accounting the resource consumed by `tests.D.D.handler()` to the called tenant, i.e., tenant 80, which accordingly sets γ_i to 80. This boost in accuracy is also visible in the final statistics, as the monitoring system now accounts tenant 80 for the stack and heap memory that was wrongly accounted to tenant 50.

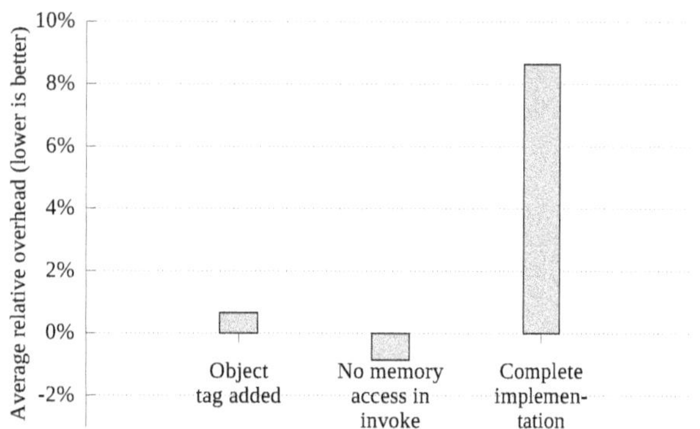

Figure 8: Execution overhead of the method call micro-benchmark when run on partial implementations of the monitoring subsystem, compared to the "Zero implementation". Overhead is an average of 10 runs.

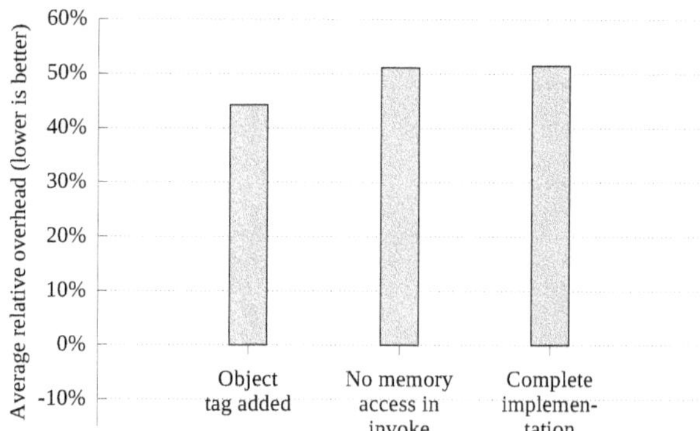

Figure 9: Execution overhead of the small objects micro-benchmark when run on partial implementations of the monitoring subsystem, compared to the "Zero implementation". Overhead is an average of 10 runs.

4.2 Performance micro-benchmarks

In order to show the details of the performance overhead of monitoring, we made four versions of the monitoring subsystem implementation, as follows:

1. *Zero implementation*, i.e., a JVM without monitoring.
2. *Object tag added*, i.e., the only thing modified in the JVM is adding 4 bytes to every Java object to hold the ID of the tenant accounted for the object.
3. *No memory access around* `invoke`, i.e., the whole monitoring subsystem is implemented in the JVM, except that we do not generate code to save and restore the thread's currently accounted tenant ID (6 `store` and 2 `load` instructions, see γ_i in Section 3.2) around the `invoke` bytecode instruction.
4. *Complete implementation* of the monitoring subsystem, i.e., the same as the previous version, in addition to 6 `store` and 2 `load` instructions generated around every `invoke` bytecode instruction.

We also performed some micro-benchmarks that test very specific aspects of execution.

4.2.1 Method call micro-benchmark

This benchmark performs numerous calls to the same Java method. The method itself does nothing special. We are only interested in the overhead of calling a method, with and without the monitoring subsystem.

Figure 8 illustrates the results of this benchmark. A comparison of the results of running this micro-benchmark on the "No memory access around `invoke`" version and the "Complete implementation" version reveals that method invocation performance decreases by 9%. We did not observe a significant additional loss in performance with other versions, i.e., less than 1%. Therefore, method invocation performance is only affected by the additional memory access performed by the monitoring subsystem around every `invoke` instruction.

4.2.2 Object creation micro-benchmark

This benchmark performs numerous creations of objects of the class `java.lang.Integer`. The objects themselves are

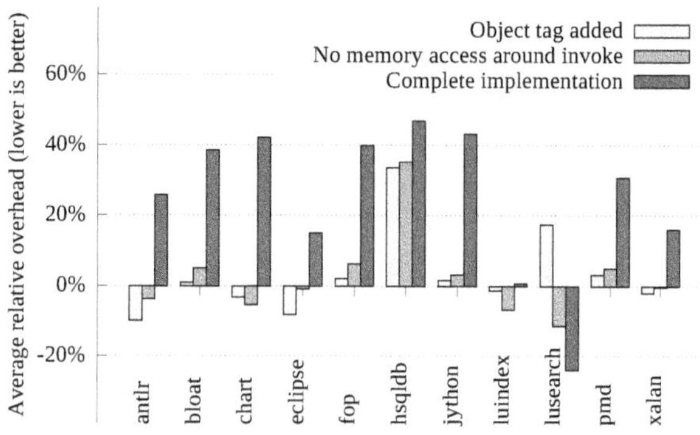

Figure 10: Execution overhead of DaCapo 2006 benchmark applications when run on partial implementations of the monitoring subsystem, compared to the original JVM. Overhead is an average of 10 runs.

relatively small. We are only interested in the overhead of creating an object, with and without the monitoring system.

Figure 9 illustrates the results of this benchmark. A comparison of the results of running this micro-benchmark on the "Zero implementation" version and the "Object tag added" version reveals that object creation performance decreases by 44%. We did not observe a significant additional loss in performance with other versions, i.e., less than 7%. Therefore, object creation performance is mostly affected by the addition of 4 bytes to every Java object.

4.3 DaCapo benchmarks

In order to measure the overhead of the monitoring subsystem on real life Java applications, we performed the DaCapo 2006 benchmarks[2]. Benchmark results in Figure 10 show that the monitoring subsystem overhead is always below 46% for real life DaCapo applications.

It is worth noticing that the monitoring overhead in Figure 10 stays below 6% for all DaCapo applications (except `hsqldb`) when we run DaCapo benchmarks using the "No memory access around `invoke`" version. This suggests that

[2]www.dacapobench.org

accessing memory (`load`, `store`) in every `invoke` bytecode instruction is an expensive operation.

We also notice that the performance of the application `hsqldb` drops by 33% when we run it using the "Object tag added" version. This suggests that this application creates many objects and would suffer from changes to the object structure. The performance of this application drops by another 13% between the "Object tag added" version and the "Complete implementation". This further indicates that `hsqldb` performs much more objects creations than method invocations.

5. RELATED WORK

Thanks to the popularity of Java-based systems, many monitoring tools were developed for them, such as A-OSGi [3], JMX [12], JVM-TI [13], and the method described in [11]. All these solutions are designed to monitor low granularity Java elements, e.g., threads, classes, objects, methods. Taken as is, the information produced by these solutions is of limited interest in OSGi platforms. Thus, we need to raise the abstraction to, at least, the OSGi component, i.e., the OSGi bundle. On a higher level, information about OSGi applications (set of components) and application tenants is also useful in industrial OSGi platform. Furthermore, most of existing tools requires heavy instrumentation, such as the method presented in [7], and often cannot be dynamically activated. However, these tools and methods form a foundation for the techniques described in this paper.

The method presented in [11], and refined in A-OSGi [3] and also in our previous work on *adaptive monitoring* [10] address CPU usage monitoring of components. These solutions show that observing resource consumption at the component granularity can be performed without modifying components. The goal of our previous work was to provide support for runtime activation/deactivation of monitoring of component service bindings, without stopping components and losing states. However, in all the previous work, the authors admitted that, during a service method call between two components, correct resource accounting needed information related to business logic regarding the caller component and the service being called, which is not provided by OSGi and Java. Our current work addresses the remaining challenge.

A rather disruptive approach was presented in the previous work I-JVM [4], where component isolation was achieved while preserving the OSGi component interaction model, relying on direct method calls. Each component runs in a dedicated isolate concept[3], composed of a separate class loader and a private copy of some JVM entities, i.e., static variables, strings and `Java.lang.Class` objects. Isolates run in the same address space, and objects are passed by reference between isolates. Threads migrate between isolates when methods are called/returned and exceptions are thrown/caught. The migration is a context switch to execute in the scope of the target isolate, enabling memory isolation of isolates and direct memory and CPU accounting. This approach enables isolating components and monitoring them. However, it also avoided addressing the challenge of identifying which component should be accounted for the consumed resources.

The standardization work performed at the OSGi Alliance [2], backed by existing OSGi solutions created by Makewave[4] [8] and ProSyst[5], raises the abstraction to the OSGi component. Existing solutions enable the OSGi platform operator to monitor, on a component basis: CPU usage, memory usage, number of threads, number of sockets, and disk usage. However, the ProSyst solution requires the framework developer and every component developer to call an API to indicate which entity is responsible for the resource consumption before any method call. Therefore, access to this API must be granted only to trusted entities, e.g., the OSGi framework and the components provided by the OSGi platform operator. Third party service providers sharing the platform will have no access to the API. This approach is too intrusive and cannot work in an environment where untrusted tenants share the platform. Our paper brings here a first improvement, as it is far *less intrusive* and *does not assume trusted tenants.*

The platform operator uses the standard API to control resource accounting behavior. Five situations can happen:

1. A call between two components in the platform operator is accounted to the platform operator.
2. A call between two components belonging to a given tenant is accounted to the tenant.
3. A call from a component belonging to a given tenant to a service method implemented by the operator platform is accounted to the tenant.
4. A call from a component belonging to the platform operator to a service method implemented by a given tenant is accounted to the tenant.
5. A call from a component belonging to a given tenant to a service method implemented by a different tenant cannot be correctly accounted unless specific information related to business logic is provided.

Often in Smart Home use cases, cases (1) through (4) are adopted, and the last case is completely avoided by disallowing communication between distinct tenants. That is where our paper brings a second improvement by *accounting resources between distinct tenants without requiring any form of isolation* more than the standard OSGi deployment unit.

6. CONCLUSION

OSGi gets increasingly adopted in the smart home as a framework to host service-oriented applications delivered by multiple untrusted tenants. This raises the need for monitoring systems that can provide useful accurate information about OSGi components and applications.

In this paper, we present a monitoring system that monitors memory usage at the component granularity, without requiring isolation of distinct tenants. Our system is far less intrusive than existing systems and methods, and it does not assume trusted tenants. It is based on a list of accounting rules that enable correct resource accounting in all cases. The monitoring system is modular and mostly independent of the implementations of the OSGi framework and the garbage collector.

Based on DaCapo benchmarks, we showed that the overhead of our system was below 46% for real life Java applications. This overhead is acceptable in development and

[3]Not to be confused with Java Isolates (JSR 121)

[4]www.makewave.com

[5]www.prosyst.com

testing time, and it is tolerable in slow pace applications which are frequent in the Smart Home. Our thorough investigation of performance overhead showed the specific aspects of monitoring that caused the most overhead, and the types of applications that would suffer the most from memory monitoring.

We are still searching for ways to make the list of accounting rules *dynamic* while keeping the overhead acceptable. Making the explicit rules further more generic, such as using *regular expressions*, would allow factoring of many explicit rules, but can reduce performance of matching against rules, so we are still unsure if more expressiveness would be worth the performance loss. We also long for monitoring other relevant resources, e.g., CPU usage, disk usage, and network usage. The relevant information reported by the monitoring system can become an accurate input to an *autonomous resource manager*, enabling the latter to automatically detect resource-related threats, such as resource abuse.

References

[1] S. M. Blackburn, P. Cheng, and K. S. McKinley. Oil and water? high performance garbage collection in Java with MMTk. In *Proceedings of the 26th International Conference on Software Engineering*, ICSE '04, pages 137–146, Washington, DC, USA, 2004. IEEE Computer Society.

[2] G. Bonnardel, A. Bottaro, S. Dimov, E. Grigorov, and A. Rinquin. OSGi RFC 200 Resource Management. Request For Comments, OSGi Alliance, December 2013.

[3] J. Ferreira, J. Leitão, and L. Rodrigues. A-OSGi: a framework to support the construction of autonomic OSGi-based applications. *Int. J. Autonomous and Adaptive Communications Systems*, 5(3):292–310, 2012.

[4] N. Geoffray, G. Thomas, G. Muller, P. Parrend, S. Frénot, and B. Folliot. I-JVM: a Java virtual machine for component isolation in OSGi. In *Proceedings of the 2009 IEEE/IFIP International Conference on Dependable Systems and Networks, DSN*, pages 544–553, 2009.

[5] N. Geoffray, G. Thomas, J.Lawall, G. Muller, and B. Folliot. VMKit: a substrate for managed runtime environments. In *Virtual Execution Environment Conference, VEE 2010*, Pittsburgh, USA, March 2010. ACM Press.

[6] Home Gateway initiative. Requirements for Software Modularity on the Home Gateway, version 1.0. Technical Report HGI-RD008-R3, Home Gateway initiative, June 2011.

[7] J. Hulaas and W. Binder. Program transformations for light-weight CPU accounting and control in the Java virtual machine. *Higher Order Symbol. Comput.*, 21: 119–146, June 2008. ISSN 1388-3690.

[8] C. Larsson and C. Gray. Challenges of resource management in an OSGi environment. In *OSGi Community Event 2011, Darmstadt, Germany*, September 2011.

[9] C. Lattner and V. Adve. LLVM: A compilation framework for lifelong program analysis & transformation. In *Proceedings of the 2004 International Symposium on Code Generation and Optimization (CGO'04)*, Palo Alto, California, March 2004.

[10] Y. Maurel, A. Bottaro, R. Kopetz, and K. Attouchi. Adaptive monitoring of end-user OSGi-based home boxes. In *Proceedings of the 15th ACM SIGSOFT Symposium on Component Based Software Engineering, CBSE 2012*, pages 157–166, 2012.

[11] T. Miettinen, D. Pakkala, and M. Hongisto. A method for the resource monitoring of osgi-based software components. In *Proceedings of the 2008 34th Euromicro Conference Software Engineering and Advanced Applications*, SEAA '08, pages 100–107, Washington, DC, USA, 2008. IEEE Computer Society.

[12] Oracle. Java management extensions (JMX) technology, January 2012. URL `http://www.oracle.com/technetwork/java/javase/tech/javamanagement-140525.html`.

[13] Oracle. Java virtual machine tool interface (JVM TI), January 2012. URL `http://docs.oracle.com/javase/6/docs/technotes/guides/jvmti/`.

[14] OSGi Alliance. OSGi service platform core specification release 4 version 4.3. Technical report, OSGi Alliance, April 2011.

[15] M. Papazoglou, P. Traverso, S. Dustdar, and F. Leymann. Service-oriented computing: State of the art and research challenges. *Computer*, 40(11):38–45, Nov. 2007. doi: 10.1109/MC.2007.400.

[16] P. Parrend and S. Frénot. Classification of component vulnerabilities in Java service oriented programming (SOP) platforms. In *Proceedings of the 11th International Symposium on Component-Based Software Engineering*, CBSE '08, pages 80–96, Berlin, Heidelberg, October 2008. Springer-Verlag.

A Memory Isolation Method for OSGi-based Home Gateways

Yushi Kuroda[1], Ikuo Yamasaki[2], Shigekuni Kondo[1], Yukihisa Katayama[1], Osamu Mizuno[1]
[1]NTT Service Evolution Laboratories, [2]Nippon Telegraph and Telephone East Corporation
kuroda.yushi@lab.ntt.co.jp, i.yamasaki@east.ntt.co.jp, {kondo.shigekuni, katayama.yukihisa, mizuno.o}@lab.ntt.co.jp

ABSTRACT
This paper proposes a new memory isolation method for OSGi-based home gateways. The OSGi technology enables embedded gateway devices for smart home services to run multiple software components; "bundles" in OSGi. In OSGi-based smart home platforms, third party service providers' bundles share the limited memory resources of the Java Virtual Machine. If a faulty bundle that is malicious or buggy consumes excessive memory, the platform and other healthy bundles will freeze. To address this issue, we propose a new method that can isolate the memory consumption of bundles without the need to modify bundles or the OSGi framework and has minimal overhead costs. We start by defining the memory consumption of bundles from the new viewpoint of application level "function" for an OSGi-based smart home platform.

Categories and Subject Descriptors
D.2.8 [**Software Engineering**]: Metrics – *Complexity measures*; F.1.3 [**Computation by Abstract Devices**] Complexity Measures and Classes – *Relations among complexity classes*

Keywords
Resource management; isolation; OSGi; smart home; Java Virtual Machine

1. INTRODUCTION
Many home appliances are now being connected to home area networks [1, 8]. These devices have triggered the emergence of a market for smart home services, such as a home surveillance service that controls locks and security cameras via a mobile phone, and a personal healthcare record service that collects weight or blood pressure data periodically [18]. To implement these services cost-effectively while ensuring for quality, it is a great challenge to open the home gateways (HGWs) for third party applications supplied by service providers (SPs). For this purpose, we launched the "Home ICT Platform", a software management platform on which multiple service providers can deliver such services, as shown in Figure 1. This platform is currently available as the commercial service "FLET'S Joint" in Japan [19]. There are two kinds of providers on this platform: the platform provider runs the platform itself, while SPs deliver their services via this platform. This platform provides the shared functions among multiple SPs to supply smart home services. Therefore, by using this platform, the shared environment offers advantages to the SPs in terms of cost; developing and maintaining their own system, such as gateway devices and a management server, is much more expensive. As a result, end users receive the benefit of lower service fees and rapid service introduction.

Because an HGW's programmability is important to ensure ease of updating and separation of services [16], we have adopted an OSGi framework [15] on an HGW as the platform's software execution environment. This framework ensures that multiple Java software components, called "OSGi bundles" or "bundles", can run on a single embedded gateway device, which means multiple service providers share the embedded HGW hardware resources. The HGW architecture in Figure 2 shows that all bundles share the hardware resources of a Java Virtual Machine (JVM) [9]. Therefore, if one bundle is faulty or malicious, other bundles may be unable to reserve enough hardware resources to provide their

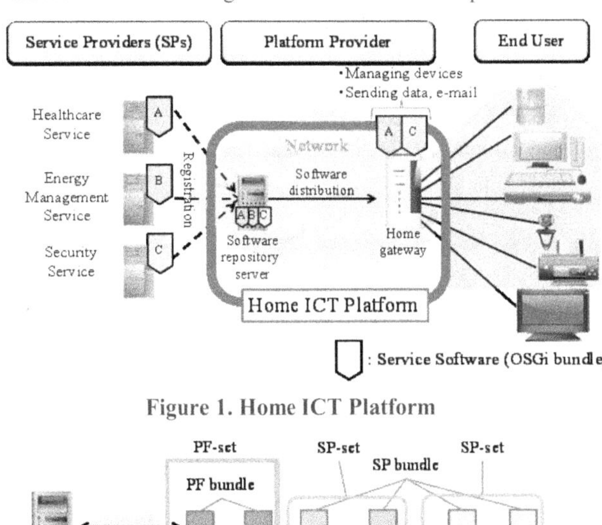

Figure 1. Home ICT Platform

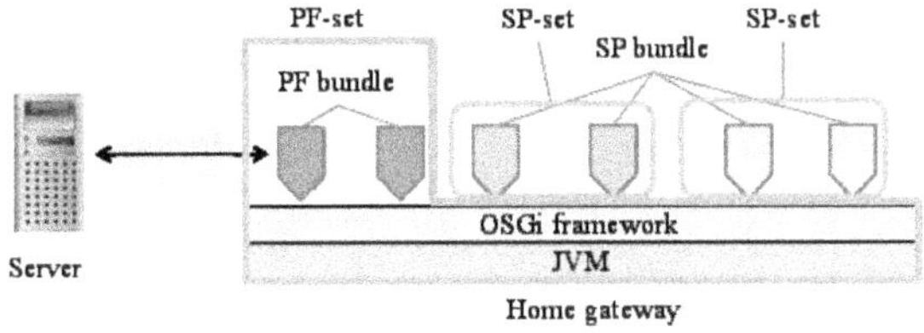

Figure 2. Home gateway structure

CBSE'14, June 30–July 4, 2014, Marcq-en-Baroeul, France.

services [6]. Some studies try to monitor bundle resources [13, 14], but this does not resolve the problem. Even though isolating an OSGi-based platform is a challenging task [12], it makes this platform more reliable.

To achieve this goal and achieve stable platform operation, we present a new resource isolation method. This paper focuses on memory resources such as heap memory in the JVM, as the shared hardware resources to be isolated. It is a well-known issue in Java programming that programming errors often trigger memory leaks leading to failure of the JVM. While our goal is to design an isolation method, we must define a metric for memory consumption. The reason is that since bundles can invoke each other in OSGi, memories are consumed when a bundle is called. This memory usage is counted to either the caller bundle or the callee, but general consensus regarding exists this definition [14]. This issue is important because when a platform bundle (PF bundle) provides a function to a service provider bundle (SP bundle), the PF bundle is the callee at one time and the caller at another. In this paper, we discuss definitions of "memory consumption" and propose an appropriate one for multi-SP platforms such as the Home ICT Platform.

The rest of the paper is organized as follows. Section 2 discusses the issues in detail. Section 3 defines the memory consumption of bundles and introduces basic use cases for multi-SP platforms. In Section 4, we propose a method to cope with the problem on the basis of the "bundle memory consumption" definition given in Section 3. Section 5 presents an evaluation of the proposed method and Section 6 describes related studies. Section 7 summarizes the present study and discusses future studies.

2. ISSUES AND APPROACH

This section shows the Home ICT Platform as an example of OSGi-based multi-SP platform and clarifies how the memory is used in OSGi. Then, we define issues and requirements relevant to the usage.

2.1 Home ICT Platform

The Home ICT Platform which provides functions for SPs, includes the following components (shown in Figure 2). Bundles that the platform provider provides, "PF bundles", provide shared functions for SPs. One smart home service is usually provided by more than one SP bundle (SP-set). "PF-set" comprises the JVM, the OSGi framework, and PF bundles.

In this platform, bundles run on a single process and so share JVM resources such as memory, CPU, and network bandwidth. Since the HGW is an embedded device, its resources are finite. This paper focuses on memory usage of bundles, especially Java heap memory, because the memory leak is a common bug and OutOfMemoryErrors (OOMEs) are fatal errors. Once a bundle raises an OOME and does not release the memory resource, other bundles may not be able to allocate sufficient memory for themselves. As a result, some services will not execute correctly. In other words, the platform provider cannot guarantee that the SP bundles will run their bundles successfully. However, since this platform is a commercial platform that supports SP bundles, the platform provider has a responsibility to run SP bundles without errors of this kind. In particular, the platform provider should not stop essential services like security services that must run continually. Therefore, the problem addressed in this paper is as follows: "The Home ICT Platform cannot guarantee the amount of memory that the SP bundles require". The platform has a restriction not to require any special implementations for SP bundles only for addressing this issue. This is because a platform provider cannot modify SP bundles or validate whether or not SP bundles' source codes meet the stipulated requirements. In other words, the components of the PF-set can be modified for isolation purpose.

2.2 Invocation Mechanism among Bundles

In Java, each thread has a call chain of instruction, which is called the "stack". This stack has the Last In, First Out (LIFO) structure, where the called "stack frame" is pushed onto the calling "stack frame". This paper refers to these as "callee" and "caller". The JVM loads each class from the classloader, and bundles have their own user classloader in OSGi. In Java, heap memory consumption means allocating memory to a Java heap. In other words, the caller triggers the creation of the callee stack frame during a method call, and the JVM allocates the memory to the heap during the processing of the callee stack frame.

A bundle is a group of classes and bundles can invoke each other for realizing services. In other words, Bundle A can invoke an implementation class method provided by Bundle B. This means Bundle A is the caller bundle and Bundle B is the callee bundle. This raises the question of who is consuming the memory when Bundle A invokes Bundle B. When the providers of caller and callee bundles are different (SP-set or PF-set), we must define which bundle should be responsible for the amount of memory used. There is no general definition for this in the OSGi specification [15]. Thus, we must settle on an appropriate definition before discussing memory isolation methods. Although there have been some previous studies on memory isolation method of OSGi, none considered a definition of memory consumption for this kind of platform [6, 7, 12, 13, 17]. They defined a certain memory consumption but did not examine how exact the metric was. In this paper, we discuss what the most appropriate metric for memory consumption is.

2.3 Issues & Requirements

As described above, this paper resolves two issues. This paper defines "isolating" as "limiting memory consumption".

- Defining "memory consumption" appropriately for a multi-SP platform
- Developing a system and method for isolating the memory consumption of bundles

The implementation requirements (R1 – R4) are as follows.

R1. The amount of memory used per SP-set must be limited.

R2. The definition of a memory consumption of bundles must be appropriate for a multi-SP platform.

R3. SP bundles must require no special code to guarantee isolation of memory consumption. This is because the platform cannot check the implementation of SP bundles and cannot modify the source code of SP bundles

R4. Overhead costs should be minimized as much as possible in terms of memory consumption and processing speed.

We deliver R1, memory consumption definitions appropriate for a multi-SP platform, in the next section.

3. DEFINITIONS OF THE MEMORY CONSUMPTION OF BUNDLES

In this section, we first consider use cases for the multi-SP platform in general Home ICT Platform, and then raise definitions of the memory consumption of bundles. Second, we subject the definitions to a preliminary assessment from the viewpoint of practical use. Finally, we select the most appropriate definition for the Home ICT Platform.

3.1 Callee & Caller

In OSGi, bundles mainly communicate thorough OSGi services. In other words, a bundle can invoke the implementation class method provided by another bundle mainly through OSGi services. For example, if Bundle A creates an object and registers it as OSGi service S, Bundle B can get this object and invoke its class method. The memory consumption of the called class can be charged in two ways.

- direct accounting (callee): the memory is charged to the bundle providing the class.
- indirect accounting (caller): the memory is charged to the call side.

In general, from the view of direct accounting (callee), since the caller does not know how the class is implemented, the callee should be responsible for the memory consumed. From the view of indirect accounting (caller), the memory is consumed because the class is invoked, so the caller has responsibility for the memory consumed. The OSGi framework and JVM can be callers and callees as well as bundles. Thus, considering the PF-set and the SP-set, four combinations of caller and callee are possible as shown in Figure 3. The charging of memory consumed can be assessed by examining each of the four quadrants a-d. a) caller: PF-set, callee: PF-set; b) caller: SP-set, callee: PF-set; c) caller: PF-set, callee: SP-set; d) caller: SP-set, callee: SP-set.

3.2 Function Providers and Function Users

Now, let us look at calling at the application level. For most OSGi services, Bundle B (callee) registers service S to provide a "function" to Bundle A (caller). For example, Bundle B provides the HttpService, which follows the OSGi specification as an OSGi service (B has the implemented class). Other bundles can use the Java Servlet registration function for an HTTP server. In this case, the callee is the "function provider" and the caller is the "function user". We introduce another, converse case. The prime example is a listener program. For instance, Bundle B (callee) registers an event listener service L that listens for an event from Bundle A (caller). When Bundle A fires the event, Bundle A gets the service L from the service repository, and calls the method for notification of Bundle B class. This is a common case in OSGi known as the White-Board Pattern[1]. In this case, the caller is the function provider and the callee is the function user.

3.3 Definitions of Memory Consumption of Bundles in Home ICT Platform

This section presents three definitions as follows.

Definition 1: The callee is charged with the amount of memory consumption in all quadrants, a-d (direct accounting).

Definition 2: The caller is charged with the amount of memory consumption in all quadrants, a-d (indirect accounting).

Definition 3: This definition considers "function" in calling. In quadrants b and c, the SP-set is charged with the amount of memory. That is, the SP-set is the caller in quadrant b and the callee in quadrant c; the PF-set is always the function provider in this platform. In quadrant d, the function user is charged with the amount of memory. In quadrant a, the caller is charged with the amount of memory. This is convenient because the caller must be identified to discern the function user in quadrants b to d.

Section 3.1 describes the validity of definitions 1 and 2. Definition 3 has validity from the viewpoint of fairness. We discuss this in next section in detail.

3.4 Assessment of Definitions

In this section, we assess the adequacy of each definition with respect to determining the most appropriate memory isolation method for the Home ICT Platform. We make the following premises for this assessment.

Premise 1: The SP notifies the platform provider of each bundle's memory consumption as determined by a tool provided by the platform provider. This notification is necessary because the platform provider cannot predict the precise behavior of the SP bundles.

Premise 2: The platform provider gives the SP an incentive to minimize the SP bundles' memory consumption. For example, the platform usage fees can be proportional to the expected memory consumption of the SP bundles. This incentive is necessary because HGW resources are limited.

The viewpoints and assessments are as follows. These viewpoints are suitable for reusable component based software and multi-SP platforms.

Viewpoint 1: The fairness of function use and provision

From this viewpoint, we assess the adequacy of each definition with respect to the provision and utilization of functions as described in Section 3.2. We consider whether the memory consumption of the bundle using the function can be charged to the responsible bundle that uses the function appropriately. In Definition 1, the bundle using the function cannot be charged with the memory consumed in quadrants b and d. An SP bundle invokes the PF-set as quadrant b while an SP bundle offers the function; this definition considers that the memory is consumed by the caller. In quadrant d, it cannot charge the memory consumption appropriately when the SP bundle that provides the class is invoked from a different SP-set. In this case, although the caller performing a callback operation provides the function, the definition charges the caller with the memory consumed. Therefore, Definition 1 cannot be accepted from this viewpoint. In Definition 2, the bundle using the function cannot be charged with the memory consumed in quadrants c and d. In quadrant c, when the PF-set callbacks a SP bundle, the memory consumption is charged to PF-set. Quadrant d is similar to Definition 1. Therefore, Definition 2 cannot be accepted from this viewpoint. In Definition 3, the bundle using the function is charged with the memory consumed in every case. Definition 3 suits this viewpoint.

Viewpoint 2: The platform provider's readiness to provide a class for SP use

This viewpoint considers that the PF-set is providing a class as the callee. If the SP-set is charged with the memory consumed

callee \ caller	PF-set	SP-set
PF-set	a	b
SP-set	c	d

Figure 3. Quadrant of the callee and the caller

[1]www.osgi.org/wiki/uploads/Links/whiteboard.pdf

when it invokes the PF-set, the PF-set should be responsible for disclosing the amount of memory consumed by the call to a SP-set. Once a PF-set's class is provided, the SP measures the maximum memory consumed by the class. As described in Premise 2 above, the SP pays fees set by the platform on the basis of the amount of memory consumed. Therefore, it is difficult for the platform provider to modify the class, because the SP-set's memory consumption will change if the PF-set changes the class. As a result, it is difficult for the platform provider to provide classes if we adopt Definitions 2 and 3. This difficulty is not an issue with Definition 1. However, in Definition 1, if the PF-set is invoked many times, there is a concern that the resulting memory consumption will be excessive. For this reason, it is difficult for the platform provider to provide classes under Definition 1.

Viewpoint 3: The ease with which the SP-set can call the class provided by the PF-set

This viewpoint is opposite to Viewpoint 2. In Definition 1, since there is no disadvantage for the SP, the SP considers that calling the PF-set's class is easy. In Definitions 2 and 3, the advantage is that the SP can eliminate the cost of developing the class itself. On the other hand, the class provided by the PF-set may consume more memory than the equivalent developed by the SP. The exact determination depends on the SP, but Definition 1 is advantageous in general.

In this study, since Viewpoint 1 is most important for the Home ICT Platform, we chose Definition 3. This is because a multi-SP platform provides functions for the SP-sets and multiple bundles, which have the roles of not only "caller and callee" but also "function provider" or "function user" running on the same JVM. Likewise, if an SP-set provides functions to other SP-set, Definition 3 is the most appropriate approach. The next section proposes a system that realizes memory isolation for bundles according to Definition 3.

4. MEMORY ISOLATION SYSTEM

We modified only the JVM for our purpose because the JVM manages the heap memory in Java. In addition, we implemented a memory management bundle that sets the SP bundle's information in the JVM. The OSGi framework, the PF bundles, and the SP bundles do not need to be modified.

4.1 JVM modifications

4.1.1 Features of the JVM

The modified JVM has the following features. A new field is added to the all object data structure to hold GroupID which indicate a PF-set's object or an SP bundles' object. In OSGi, bundles have their own classloader object which is created at the time of bundle instantiation. Thus, each bundle has only one GroupID but each SP-set has the same GroupID. Every SP-set has its own limit value that is declared by the SP, thus the JVM has thresholds in each GroupID. The class object has a Class Type Flag (CTF) that can distinguish whether or not the class provides a function when an SP-set invokes other SP-set. A class in a bundle has one of roles: "function user" or "function provider". This cannot be done via the GroupID in the classloader object. Therefore, the JVM needs the CTF to distinguish the classes that provide a function from others. For this, the CTF has the value of "0" or "1" as a flag. The JVM updates the amount of memory consumed by the referenced object with the GroupIDs in the full garbage collection.

4.1.2 Memory Allocation Method

The JVM limits the memory consumption of bundles with the processes shown below, which are executed every time an object is created. Figure 4 shows the flow chart that determines GroupID. These processes and affirmations are as follows.

P1: When an object is created, a GroupID is given to the object through the algorithm shown in Section 4.1.3. The GroupID is GroupID[x].

P2: The memory allocation succeeds.

P3: The JVM replaces the total memory consumption of GroupID[x] with "the memory total consumption + the object size".

P4: The JVM executes full garbage collection, and then updates the amount of memory consumed.

P5: The JVM throws OOME. The memory allocation fails.

A1: The total memory consumption of GroupID[x] < the memory limit value of the GroupID[x]

A2: The total memory consumption of GroupID[x] + the memory consumption of created object <= the memory limit value of the GroupID[x]

The OOME in P5 is a common OOME, because an OOME causes a thread failure rather than a JVM failure.

4.1.3 Algorithm for Determining GroupID

This section proposes an algorithm that determines GroupIDs according to Definition 3. When an object is created, the JVM runs this algorithm by tracing the stack to discriminate which bundle uses the function. An object is created from a class that is loaded by a classloader. The JVM determines the GroupID from the GroupID of the classloader objects and the CTF of the class objects. The JVM can trace the classloader objects and the class objects from a stack by pointers. This enables the algorithm to reduce the calculation cost.

Figure 5 shows the flow chart that determines the GroupID. We define that only the PF-set has a GroupID of "0" and define CTF "0" as a "function using" class and "1" as a "function providing" class. The PF-set's classes are always "function-providing" classes, so the class of GroupID "0" is always CTF "1". In the figure, constants are in capital letters and variables are in lower

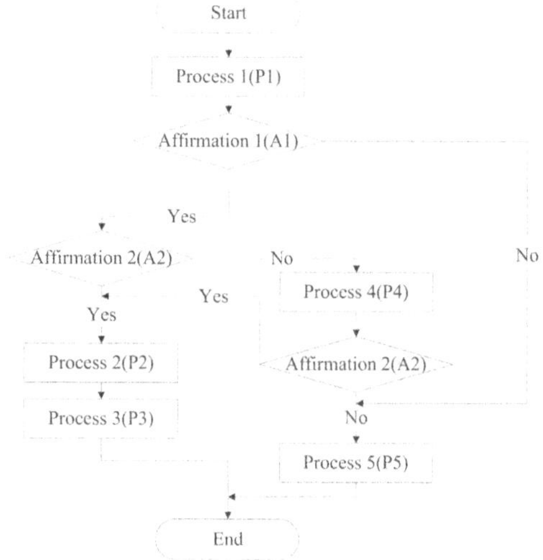

Figure 4. Flow chart of memory allocation method

case letters. This algorithm traces the stack frame from the top of the stack ("TOP_STACK"). The stack frame that is currently being traced is named "currentStackFrame". The stack frame below "currentStackFrame" is "next stack frame". The stack frame under the bottom of the stack has a "NULL" value. The GroupID of the classloader of the class that generates the stack frame is "STACK_FRAME_GROUPID". The CTF of the class that generates the stack frame is "STACK_FRAME_CTF". The "lastCTF" is the CTF that is set to the class called by the "currentStackFrame".

4.2 Memory Management Bundle Implementation

The memory management bundle has the following features.

1. The memory management bundle gets SP bundles' information, the limit value and the CTF from the PF server. The PF server contains the information declared by the SPs.
2. The memory management bundle requests the JVM to create a new GroupID when new SP-set is installed, and then configures the GroupID and CTF to the classloader and the class objects. Then, the memory management bundle configures the limit value to the JVM.

4.3 Overall Processing Flow

The processing flow of our proposed system is as follows. Before this system runs, the platform provider adjusts the amount of the SP-sets' total memory limit value so as not to exceed the amount of an HGW's memory.

Process 1: The memory management bundle acquires data such as SP bundle's information.

Process 2: The memory management bundle requests the creation of a GroupID when new SP-set is installed.

Process 3: After the SP-set is installed, the memory management bundle acquires their classloader objects through an OSGi specified API.

Process 4: The memory management bundle configures the CTF, GroupID, and the SP-set's memory limit value to the JVM.

Process 5: The JVM runs as described in Section 4.1.2.

5. PROTOTYPE EVALUATION

This section presents an evaluation of the functionality, performance, and memory consumption of the proposed system. We implemented the proposed memory isolation method on a virtual machine, Android (DalvikVM) [3], running on the x86 architecture. The computer environment is an Intel Core i5-2500 3.30GHz processor with 2GB of RAM. This environment is faster than the targeted one but well adapted to first application prototyping. Prototype tests showed our method satisfies R1 to R4 described in Section 2.3. That is, the system isolates bundles without bundle modification, and the definition of memory consumption is Definition 3, which is suitable for the Home ICT Platform. The following evaluation targets the JVM in terms of satisfying R4, because our method modifies only the JVM.

Performance: The proposed method only requires modification of the JVM, and so we measured the performance of the JVM without the OSGi framework. For this evaluation, we used the Embedded CaffeineMark [4] benchmark suite. This is a popular benchmark suite for embedded systems such as HGWs and cell phones. This benchmark is a black box test that indicates performance per unit time. Figure 6 shows the score of comparing the original JVM (not modified) to the proposed JVM (modified to include our proposed method). The proposed JVM showed 10% lower performance than the original JVM as regards the "String" score. This is because our method raises cost when an object is created, and "String" creates a lot of objects. However, there was no statistically significant difference between the scores (without "Overall") the proposed JVM and the original JVM (t test, p=.95 >.05).

Memory consumption: We measured the memory consumption in two ways. TABLE I. shows the results. The VM option of "–Xmx 20MB" was set to evaluate memory consumption; it can limit maximum heap memory size. First, we measured the memory usage of the JVM process in the OS by using the "ps" command. On the JVM, we ran a Java program that consumes 10 MB by array allocation. The proposed JVM consumed around 50

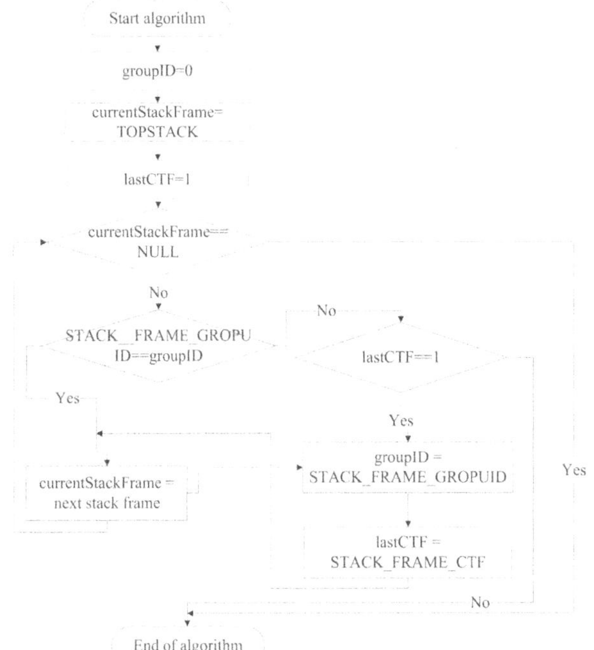

Figure 5. Algorithm for determining GroupID

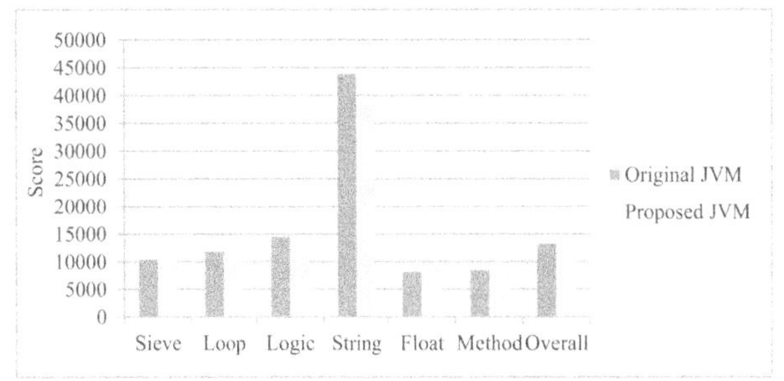

Figure 6. Embedded Caffeinemark score

TABLE I. Memory consumption result

Test	Original JVM	Proposed JVM
memory consumption of process(KB)	18900	18952
available memory when objects are allocated(KB)	10958	10957

KB more memory than the original JVM. In other words, its overhead memory cost was only 1%. Second, we measured the heap memory when many objects were allocated on the JVM. In this case, the memory limit value of the program was set to 10 MB. We observed the memory consumption of the objects using the Runtime#freeMemory method. In this case, the proposed JVM consumed about 1 KB more memory than the original JVM.

The above results showed that the proposed method satisfies R1-R3 with only 1% higher memory consumption and slight difference in total performance though 10% degradation in the "String" score. Since these levels of degradation are not especially critical for the Home ICT Platform, we can consider that the result satisfies R4.

6. RELATED STUDIES

Related studies on isolating or managing resources in OSGi include those given below.

Maurels' [14] target platform is similar to ours; it is also an OSGi-based smart home platform. Their objective is to reduce overhead for monitoring CPU usage. The callee and the caller are dynamically exchangeable in counting CPU usage.

All the following studies used Definition 1 for the metric of a bundle's memory consumption. Thus, they do not satisfy R1 described in Section 2.3. The method reported by Miettinen et al. [13] is similar to ours in terms of purpose, but it achieves only monitoring. They use the JVM Tool Interface [11] and bytecode instrumentation to monitor the memory consumption and CPU utilization of bundles. Unfortunately, their method significantly degrades system performance; the processing speed was reduced by 40%. Ferreira et al. [5] also studied a modified OSGi framework for monitoring. They use JVM TI and Java Management Extensions (JMX) [10], which are Java technologies that supply tools for monitoring Java systems. Their definition of the memory consumption is Definition 1 due to using these tools. Similar approach can be found in Larssons' study [12]. Geoffray et al. [7] studied how to isolate memory and CPU consumption with a modified JVM, "I-JVM". Their method measures the memory consumption of bundles when GC runs. If a bundle exceeds its memory consumption limit value, the system stops the bundle. However, their method requires modification of the bundles' source code. Moreover, its memory consumption overhead is 20%. Gama et al. [6] studied a sandbox method for CPU usage and memory consumption by using Multi-tasking Virtual Machine [2]. Their study shows the feasibility of providing autonomic management for an OSGi platform through completely autonomic managers implementing complete loops. However, their definition of the memory consumption is Definition 1 and so does not satisfy R1. Richardson et al. [17] studied the resource isolation of real-time systems; they used the real-time specification for Java to isolate resources. Their method requires modification of the bundles' source code.

7. CONCLUSION AND FUTURE WORK

We discussed definitions of the memory consumption metric and proposed a memory isolation method for multiple bundles that share finite Java Virtual Machine (JVM) memory resources. First, we introduced three definitions that take the requirements of OSGi-based smart home platforms into account. The first charges the amount of memory consumed to the callee, the second charges it to the caller, and the third take into account the relationship between the roles of function provider and function user. We assessed the definitions from three viewpoints and determined that the third was the most advantageous from the viewpoint of fairness. Second, on the basis of this definition, we proposed a memory isolation method that assigns a GroupID to each object when the object is allocated. A key advantage of the method is that only the JVM needs to be modified; the bundles and the OSGi framework are used as is. The method achieves memory isolation with only slight degradation in total performance and only 1% more memory consumption.

In future work, we intend to investigate technologies to isolate the usage of other resources such as CPU and network bandwidth.

8. REFERENCES

[1] AT&T Smart Controls. http://www.att.net/smartcontrols

[2] G. Czajkowski and L. Daynès. Multitasking without Compromise: a Virtual Machine Evolution. In *16th Proc. on Object-Oriented Programming, Systems, Languages, and Applications*, pp. 125–138, 2001.

[3] Dalvik Virtual Machine. https://code.google.com/p/dalvik/

[4] The Embedded CaffeineMark 3.0. http://www.benchmarkhq.ru/cm30/info.html

[5] J. Ferreira, J. Leitao, and L. Rodrigues. A-OSGi: a framework to support the construction of autonomic OSGi-based applications. In *Autonomic Computing and Communications Systems*, pp.1-16, 2012.

[6] K. Gama and D. Donsez. A self-healing component sandbox for untrustworthy third party code execution. *In Component-Based Software Engineering*, pp. 130-149, 2010.

[7] N. Geoffray, G. Thomas, G.Muller, P. Parrend, S. Fr´enot, and B. Folliot. I-JVM: a Java virtual machine for component isolation in OSGi. In *Dependable Systems & Networks, 2009. DSN'09*, pp. 544-553, 2009.

[8] D. M. Han, J. H. Lim. Smart home energy management systemusing IEEE 802.15.4 and zigbee. In *IEEE Trans. on Consumer Electronics*, vol. 56, pp. 1403-1410, 2010.

[9] Java Language and Virtual Machine Specifications. Technical report, Oracle. http://docs.oracle.com/javase/specs/

[10] Java management extensions (JMX)technology. http://www.oracle.com/technetwork/java/javase/tech/

[11] JVM Tool Interface. http://docs.oracle.com/javase/1.5.0/docs/guide/jvmti/

[12] C. Larsson and C. Gray. Challenges of resource management in an OSGi environment. In *OSGi Community Event 2011*, 2011.

[13] T. Miettinen, D. Pakkala, and M. Hongisto. A Method for the resource monitoring of OSGi-based software components. In *SEAA'08. 34th Euromicro Conference, Software Engineering and Advanced Applications*, pp. 100–107, 2008.

[14] Y. Maurel, A. Bottaro, R. Kopetz, and K. Attouchi. Adaptive monitoring of end-user OSGi-based home boxes. In *Proceedings of the 15th ACM SIGSOFT symposium on Component Based Software Engineering*, CBSE '12 ACM, pp. 157-166, 2012.

[15] OSGi service platform specification release 5. Technical report, OSGi Alliance, 2012.

[16] Requirements for Software Modularity on the HomeGateway, version 1.0. HGI-RD008-R3, Home Gateway initiative, 2011.

[17] T. Richardson, J. A. Wellings, J. A. Dianes, and M. Díaz. Providing temporal isolation in the OSGi framework,. In *Proceedings of the 7th International Workshop on Java Technologies for Real-Time and Embedded Systems*, pp1-10, 2009.

[18] T. Tamura, I. Mizukura, M. Sekine, and Y. Kimura. Monitoring and Evaluation of Blood Pressure Changes With a Home Healthcare System. *IEEE Trans. Information Technology in Biomedicine*, vol. 15, pp. 602–607, 2011.

[19] T. Yamazaki. Home ICT Services with OSGi-HGW at NTT. In *OSGi Community Event* 2011, 2011.

Execution Cost Estimation for Software Deployment in Component-based Embedded Systems*

Michael Pressler[1], Alexander Viehl[1], Oliver Bringmann[1,2], Wolfgang Rosenstiel[1,2]

[1]FZI Forschungszentrum Informatik
Haid-und-Neu-Str. 10-14
76131 Karlsruhe, Germany
pressler,viehl@fzi.de

[2]Universität Tübingen
Sand 13
72076 Tübingen
bringman,rosenstiel@informatik.uni-tübingen.de

ABSTRACT

We present an approach for the determination of initial mapping configurations for embedded software components on modern embedded heterogeneous processor architectures. The presented work combines the advantages of component-based design and properties obtained from source-code analysis. The goal is a very fast estimation of execution costs for multiple hardware/software component pairs even before the hardware is physically available.

Categories and Subject Descriptors

B.8 [**Performance and Reliability**]: Performance Analysis and Design Aids; D.2.8 [**Software Engineering**]: Metrics—*Performance measures*; C.4 [**Performance of Systems**]: Design studies, Modeling techniques, Performance attributes

Keywords

Component-based design; execution cost estimation; initial mapping determination; performance prediction; system architecture

1. INTRODUCTION

Emerging embedded system hardware platforms utilize heterogeneous architectures to enable the next generation applications like advanced driver assistant systems in the automotive domain. The increasing complexity of embedded systems impedes the manageability of configuration and efficient system integration. For instance in the automotive domain the integration of additional functions classically results in a rising numbers of dedicated electronic control units (ECU) with isolated functionality. The progress achieved in semiconductor industry during the past decades results in high-performance, energy-efficient and reliable embedded multi-core processor architectures which are ready to be integrated into automotive ECUs. This leads to the ability to realize a major share of the core functionality as software on only a few high-performance ECUs. The system integration process needs to be evolved for further assessing the high potential of architectures with few, powerful, multi-application ECUs.

Component-based design has proven high applicability and maturity in making components reusable and available for composition of new functionality. The components to be composed, configured and mapped typically differ in terms of functional dependencies, performance, availability, or specific safety-related constraints which all need to be considered during the design and integration process. In the automotive domain the AUTOSAR methodology aims at reducing the number of ECUs and obtaining better resource efficiency by making automotive embedded software components independent of the underlying hardware platform.

The deployment decisions for software systems are nowadays made rather manually. With growing degrees of freedom and numbers of components and deployment targets, implicitly resulting from component-based frameworks, a manual determination of an optimal or at least suitable configuration is infeasible. The mapping of functionality to a given interconnected hardware platform and the automated determination of configuration issues like scheduling strategies and priorities as well as bus access schedules should be derived automatically or at least supported by tools.

The pursued idea aims at closing the gap between component-based design and the fast determination of execution costs for heterogeneous embedded hardware architectures. Our scenario covers an early stage in the design process where the developer needs a fast determination of execution costs and suitability of software components for heterogeneous hardware components rather than exact timing information. This leads to the tackled challenges:

- Using bottom-up source code analysis in component-based design to extract the computational demand
- Fast execution cost determination of software components on heterogeneous embedded hardware processors even before binary tools and physical targets are available
- Automatic generation of an initial mapping configuration based on the extracted execution costs

These execution costs indicate if whether hardware platform is suitable with respect to the execution characteristics of a software component before a physical target is available. Due to the high reuse of implementations in the automotive domain we extract the computation demand of software components from existing source code. The analysis calculates the execution costs in a subsequent step using a fast transition for each possible hardware/software pair. The cost figures are then used to determine an initial mapping configuration for high number of software components that need

*This work was supported by the ITEA2/BMBF Project MACH - MAssive Calculations on Hybrid systems under grant 01IS13016B

CBSE'14, June 30–July 4, 2014, Marcq-en-Baroeul, France.
Copyright is held by the owner/author(s). Publication rights licensed to ACM.
ACM 978-1-4503-2577-6/14/06 ...$15.00.
http://dx.doi.org/10.1145/2602458.26024622.

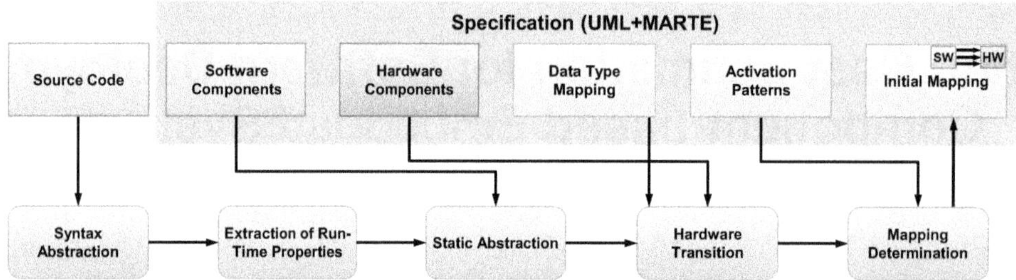

Figure 1: Development Steps

to be mapped to a given hardware platform with heterogeneous hardware processors connected via on-chip or field-busses.

This procedure can be easily adopted for new hardware components since the extracted information is fixed and the hardware characteristics for the analysis can be extracted from data sheets and fed into the templates of the proposed framework. Based on the calculated execution costs for each mapping alternative, the framework connects further analysis steps for an initial determination, a refinement or an optimization of deployment parameters.

2. RELATED WORK

Many approaches in pertinent and recent literature tackle the issue of execution cost estimation. They can be categorized in static and dynamic approaches. Static approaches include, for example, WCET analyzers like aiT [1]. Dynamic approaches are simulation-based using techniques like virtual prototypes in SystemC or ISS like SimpleScalar. Virtual prototypes executing binary code and cycle accurate ISS need a lot of simulation time because every software process needs to be compiled and executed on every hardware model to determine performance properties. Interesting approaches that are directly integrated in the component based design approach were presented in [6] and [7]. But none of these approaches determine the execution costs from given implementations for feeding their analysis. Especially in the automotive domain new functionality is generated by the interconnection of existing functionality and integration of external software IP.

Many approaches tried to speed up the estimation process while limiting the loss of accuracy. In [4] an abstract virtual platform model is simulated in parallel to the application to gain performance metrics for the simulated application. This speeds up the estimation processes but still needs adaption towards different hardware architectures. All hardware models must be available and the simulation for every platform needs time which could be unacceptable in early design phases.

In [5] a component-based design space exploration was presented. It shows the tool-guided design of multiple mapping alternatives. The approach enables an early exploration of system configurations including the impact of resource scheduling and requirement validation. The determination of execution costs requires the actual hardware model or a reference model in order to scale the execution costs of the software component to different architectures. Each software component must be executed on this reference hardware. Finding one reference model for all available embedded hardware components is quite challenging because of the variety of architectural features. Including heterogeneous hardware component can be very time consuming, because each software component must be executed on each reference hardware component. The simulation on embedded hardware is normally slow and all of these hardware components must be available during the design process.

In [11] a component-based approach was presented that allows a fast prediction of execution costs of Java applications. This approach reuses hardware-specific results of byte code benchmarking to transform hardware-independent resource demands into execution costs. This approach seems promising but focusses on Java applications which could not be easily adapted properly to C/C++ applications. Additionally, every hardware component must be benchmarked and therefore be available at design time including its binary tools. This is most likely for the standard systems presented in this approach but difficult for expensive embedded hardware.

The approach in [10] is based on source-code annotations at basic block level. Each basic block is compared to an abstract hardware models annotated into the source code and then executed to gain overall performance values. While this approach is really fast estimating the execution time of many software components running on different hardware components, it is still time consuming and the designer must model each hardware component. [8] describes a quite similar approach to handle fast estimations of execution costs. But the approach is quite simple and does not consider architectural features like caches and branch prediction.

Other approaches, like [16] and [17], compile the source code to binaries, gain static execution times of basic blocks and back-annotate them into the source code. The data-dependent simulation can then be executed without any architectural model to estimate timing properties. But still, the code has to be compiled and analyzed for every processing unit and the entire tool chain with target compilers and binary tools must be available. Some approaches use estimation techniques based on linear regression [12] or neural nets [15] to determine the execution cost of applications. These approaches always need training sets to generate reference models for each processing unit. While these approaches can determine the execution time faster than simulation and would fit well in the modern system design approaches, the training of the reference models takes a lot of time and the analysis accuracy strongly depends on the quality of the training set.

3. ANALYSIS FRAMEWORK

The steps of our analysis are illustrated in **Figure 1**. The grey box in the upper part of the figure shows the specification of our system. We use the UML tool Papyrus enriched with stereotypes from the UML profile Modeling and Analysis of Real-Time and Embedded Systems (MARTE). Additionally, we use profile extensions to capture needed inputs for the analysis. The model includes the structural description of the software components, the hardware components and a data type mapping configurations. The behavior of the software component is implemented in C/C++ and linked to the corresponding software component in the model.

Our approach aims at extracting and quantifying ***hardware-independent computational demand*** **(HIC)** from source code and defines a transition to gain ***hardware-specific execution costs***

(HSE). The main advantage of our approach is the extraction of computational demand in a ***static abstraction*** from source code. This has to be done only once. Target compilers or binary tools are not needed. We additionally execute the application on the development platform to obtain data dependent but hardware-independent ***run-time properties*** of the application. If the developer changes components of the hardware platform or their configuration only the transition to the HSE needs to be recalculated.

The ***hardware transition*** calculates the HSE for each possible hardware/software pair. This estimation requires an abstract hardware specification that can be extracted from the data sheets of the hardware platforms. This means much less effort than implementing virtual models or using target compilers and binary tools for instruction-set simulators (ISS) or worst-case execution time (WCET) analyzers . The transition only takes seconds which makes the approach much faster and can speed up the design process in complex software systems on heterogeneous hardware platforms before the initial mapping configuration is available. The results are then used for the ***mapping determination*** approach.

4. SYSTEM SPECIFICATION

This section describes our system modelling approach. It includes every aspect that is needed for the analysis.

4.1 Functional Specification

The functional modeling focusses on the structural composition and complies with standard component-based modelling approaches. We do not model the behavior of the component since the source code is linked to it. To include communication volumes in the analysis the interfaces of the model must be identical to the interfaces implemented in the source code. The activation patterns for the software components must also be modeled. For each provided port the periodic or sporadic pattern is annotated using the MARTE stereotype «RtFeature». We consider activation patterns to determine the utilization of software components and different hardware components. We address periodic and sporadic release patterns. Operations with a periodic release are activated every multiple of the period. Sporadic operations are executed in a dedicated thread in response to an explicit call. The analysis needs the minimum separation time between two subsequent releases of a sporadic operation, the minimum inter-arrival time (MIAT).

4.2 Hardware Specification

For our approach we need a specification of the target hardware-platform. For the determination of HSE numbers we need a characterization of the hardware components which are possible target for the software components. We enrich the hardware components with stereotypes in order to model their computational capabilities. To describe a computation unit and its architecture we use the MARTE stereotype «HwProcessor» and the following properties:

- *Clock-Frequency*
- Branch prediction model *HwBranchPredictor* specifying the type and the penalty of a branch prediction miss
- Cache models using the stereotype *caches* specifying the cache replacement strategy and the penalty for a cache miss
- Superscalar factor using the attribute number of pipelines *nbPipelines*

Additionally, hardware data types are modeled to specify the execution cycles for different arithmetic operation classes and data types. To capture the hardware data types we extended the MARTE stereotype «HwProcessor» with the attribute *dataType : HSE_HWDataType [0..*]* to assign hardware data types to the hardware processor.

We defined a stereotype named *«HSE_HwDataType»* to describe the characteristics of hardware data types in terms of bit length, whether it is a signed/unsigned variable or whether it is a floating point variable. This stereotype has the following attributes:

- *bitLength <Integer>*
- *signed <Boolean>*
- *fixedPoint <Boolean>*
- *float<Boolean>*
- *execution_type [0..*] <DataTypeExecution>*

These parameters can have an influence on the number of execution cycles. Additionally, the attribute $execution\_type$ is introduced to represent the classification of the computation capabilities of CPUs. The stereotype *«DataTypeExecution»* describes the execution properties of a data type with the following attributes:

- *Operation [1..*]<String>*
- *executionCycles <Integer>*
- *superscalar <Integer>*

The specification contains an enumeration of different operations (e.g. add, mul, div, mod, shift, etc.), their executed cycles, and possible superscalar operations. This must be specified because they can have different execution times depending on the hardware platform. The superscalarity factor is optional if the architecture of the hardware component provides superscalar capabilities for special operations (e.g. an additional multiplier unit) and not general superscalar execution with parallel pipelines. The latter is captured in the general hardware component specification. If more than one operation needs the same amount of execution cycles, a list of operations can be provided using the stereotype. If an operation is not defined the analysis reports back to the designer and asks for further specification. To take the communication infrastructure into account we use the stereotype «HwBus» from MARTE and specify the bandwidth of the used bus system. A more detailed description for modelling the hardware platform is given in [18].

4.3 Preliminary Deployment Configurations

To enhance the analysis results the mapping between software data types and data representation at hardware level must be specified. The data type has a large impact on the execution time due to the possible availability of e.g. floating point units. The data type mapping is dependent on the hardware architecture, compiler and possible specifications in the software (like typedefs in C/C++). This means that the user has to specify the hardware representation of each data type for the implementation language. This step is not mandatory for simple assignments like integer mappings since there will be an automatic mapping between standard data types and the modeled hardware data types. If the mapping is not obvious because of the complexity of the hardware component this needs to be modeled. Obvious mappings are, for example, integer to integer and float to float mappings. We use the MARTE stereotype «Assign» to map software data types to the hardware data types and therefore create a link for each data type and the execution cycles needed for different operations on different hardware platforms. This is modeled for each hardware component or, if this detail is necessary, for each software/hardware pair.

The mapping determination analysis considers constraints dealing with mapping restrictions and enforcement. This can be the prohibition of mapping software components to FPGAs or a fixed

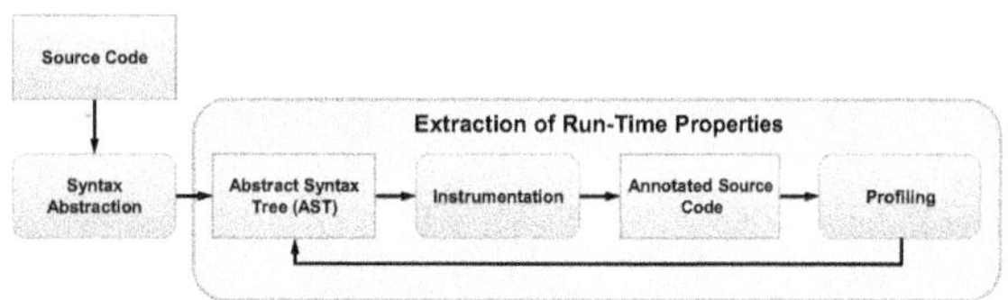

Figure 2: Profiling Process to Extract Execution Counts, Cache Misses, and Branch Prediction Penality of Basic Blocks

mapping decision that is unchangeable. To achieve this we also use the MARTE stereotype «Assign». The main requirements as input for the mapping determination analysis are the maximum resource usage and the optimization goal of the analysis. This can be an average usage of all resources or an exploration of minimizing the number of computation resources by maximizing the resource usage of high-performance hardware components.

4.4 Back-Annotation

The framework offers a variety of back-annotation options to maximize the use. The information is automatically extracted from the UML model using QVT-o transformations into the ecore models of the framework to feed the analysis. First of all, the resulting hardware-independent internal process graph (iPG) is back-annotated to the software component. As long as the profiled data input for the component or the run-time specific hardware properties (new branch prediction models or cache replacement strategies) do not change, the iPG can be reused for new hardware components enabling a fast evaluation of the execution costs. Even when reusing the software component in new designs with new hardware architectures this can be the starting point for further deployment configuration decisions. Furthermore the matrices representing the utilization and execution cost figures for each hardware/software component pair are visible for the designer.

Additionally, the designer can specify in the analysis context using the MARTE stereotype «GaAnalysisContext» whether he wants to generate a mapping decision and/or whether the resulting execution costs are back-annotated to software components. The designer can reuse the annotated matrices to model the deployment manually. If generating the mapping configuration is chosen we add the configuration to a specified package using the MARTE stereotype «Assign». The calculated execution costs are broken down to execution costs for each provided interface of the software component. This is necessary if a software component has multiple remote method calls or threads that handle different provided interfaces. The resulting execution costs can then be annotated to the provided interfaces of the software component using the «RtFeature» stereotype of MARTE.

5. ANALYSIS

The approach depicted in **Figure 1** extracts behavioral and computational complexity directly from the source code. The initial abstraction is provided by a framework [19] that abstracts C/C++ source code to an Abstract Syntax Tree (AST). These models form the input for the analysis approach. In the following sections each subsequent transformation step is described.

5.1 Extraction of Run-Time Properties

To enhance the determination of the HSE we capture run-time specific properties. The AST is instrumented for a profiling approach depicted in **Figure 2**. The framework allows transformations that analyze the AST and detect conditional operations and loops. The transformation inserts a count statement for each basic block. Our analysis considers static and dynamic branch prediction strategies. The static approach is often used in simple embedded CPUs. The designer can decide whether a branch was taken by setting a special compiler flag. The compiler itself optimizes the code to make static assumptions about the branch behavior. This can reduce the number of wrong branch predictions. As a dynamic approach we consider a common 2-bit saturation counter. We simulate the branch prediction model in parallel to the application to gain the number of wrong branch predictions. A cache model is also runs in parallel to the application to improve the results. We use the source code variables as addresses and only support full-associative caches. Since the target compiler optimizes the code and e.g. changes the order of the instructions this procedure is not fully accurate but still provides an indication in order to incorporate the impact of cache misses in the calculation of the HSE.

The AST is then transformed into source code using Xtext. With a test bench provided by the developer dynamic behavioral properties during execution are captured and back-annotated into the AST model. Additionally, a heap/stack analysis using *valgrind* [13] is performed to determine the required memory of each software component.

5.2 Static Abstration

The AST and the description of the software components form the input for the static abstraction illustrated in **Figure 3**. The static abstraction generates a graph-based representation of the software composition model in UML. The approach extracts the communication interfaces from the model and determines the control-flow of the software component enriched with HIC information. To determine the inter-component communication dependencies the source code is examined to identify communication endpoints corresponding to the interfaces in the UML model. The communication data sizes are extracted from the model interfaces. The specified or extracted interfaces are detected in the source code and linked to the basic blocks in the order of their occurrence.

In order to add HIC information to the graph-based representation we extract computational characteristics from the source code. The characteristics of interest are arithmetic operations and the data types of the operands. This information has an impact on the execution costs. The data types are responsible for result accuracy, cache and memory consumption and duration of an executed operation. Examples are low-cost embedded hardware components that execute one 8bit integer add operation in one cycle while a 16 bit float multiplication takes multiple cycles to execute. Modern high performance processors can execute both operations in one cycle. In Section 5.3, this information is used to calculate the influence on the execution time for different hardware components.

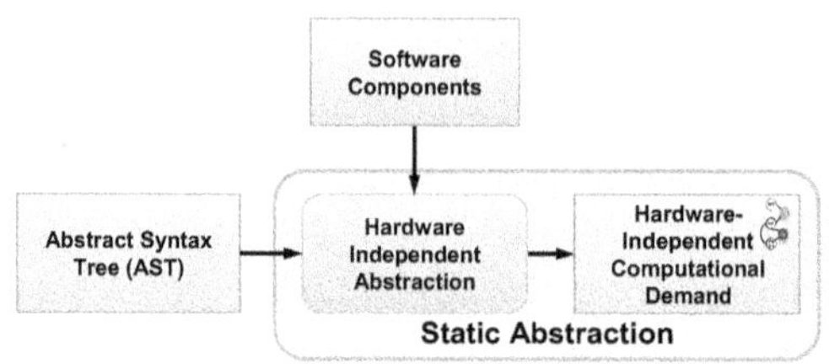

Figure 3: Abstraction

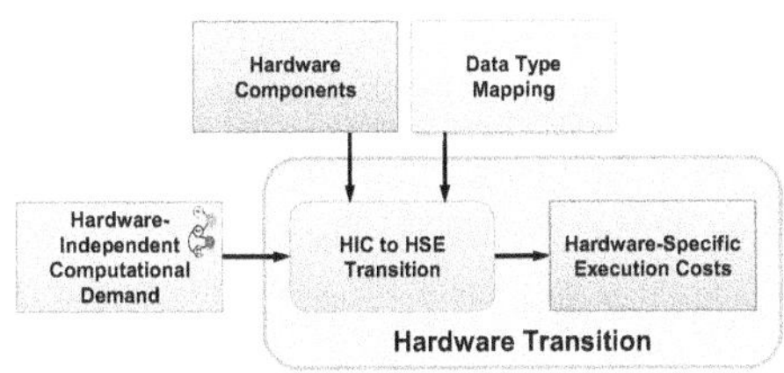

Figure 4: Transition

To represent the abstract control flow the iPG is used. The graph represents the control flow of the software component including the communication endpoints. The HIC information is annotated to the control-flow edges. The computational blocks of an annotated iPG contains executed operations, data types of the operation as well as execution counts of this basic block, cache misses and false branch predictions captured during the profiling approach. To incorporate the influence of communicating software components on the communication infrastructure edges between the communication endpoints are created and annotated with the obtained data volumes.

5.3 Hardware Transition

The iPG with the annotated HIC is used to determine hardware-specific execution costs. The specification of hardware components and the data type mapping are necessary information to estimate the HSE values for each possible hardware/software pair. The transition step is illustrated in **Figure 4**. The analysis considers the influence of heterogeneous CPUs on the execution costs of software as well as the impact on the communication network.

The properties of the hardware models are extracted from the MARTE stereotypes. HSE of a basic block is then calculated multiplying the annotated execution cycles for each operation and software data type pair multiplied with the execution count. We calculate the HSE for the complete software component using the HSE for each basic block as well as the penalties for false branch prediction and cache misses. The penalty for each cache miss and false branch prediction is extracted from the hardware specification in the MARTE model.

5.4 Mapping Determination

The goal of the presented approach to help designers making deployment decisions. The focus is to determine the initial mapping configuration. The procedure is illustrated in **Figure 5**. To achieve this, the designer needs the utilization of software on every hardware component. With the calculated HSE for each software component, the clock-frequency of the hardware component and the activation patterns from the model we are able to determine the utilization for every software/hardware pair. The HSE for each software component is divided by the clock-frequency of the hardware component and by its activation period or, in case of sporadic release patterns, by the minimum inter-arrival time (MIAT). The utilization is calculated for every mapping pair. This approach gives the designer additional information regarding the communication between software components. This improves the system design because not only execution costs are included in the initial mapping configuration approach but also the interconnection between the software components and their impact on the communication infrastructure. Therefore, we determine the communication volumes between all software components.

With the activation pattern of the software component we can determine its bandwidth demand on a specific communication infrastructure. The bandwidth of the bus system is extracted from the infrastructure specification to determine the utilization of the bus system that is generated by one communication endpoint.

For the mapping determination we calculate all utilization numbers of communication endpoints between all software component pairs. With this kind of information we automatically generate an ILP formulation that determines an initial mapping configuration if the designer wants automated support for this decision. An additional constraint is used which enforces that all software components mapped to one hardware component do not exceed the available memory. We do not explain the ILP formulation in detail since there exist many approaches for an ILP approach to solve this problem [14].

6. EXPERIMENTAL RESULTS

In this section we would like to demonstrate the results for the HSE determination in our design flow. As reference platforms we used ARM7TDMI, ARM9, ARM11 and the Infineon Tricore 1767 from a state-of-the-art commercial instruction-set simulator based on embedded JIT compilation (ISS-JIT) and the PPC604 processor of the SimpleScalar ISS [3]. Additionally, we used the Cortex-M and Leon3 processor as real hardware references. We executed different algorithms an these platforms, to be specific a JPEG encoder and decoder, a DES and Triple DES implementation, a Synthetic Aperture Radar (SAR), a set of benchmarks from the Mälardalen University [9], and a Viterbi decoder. The DES and Triple DES implementation are executed with both modes of operation, CBC and ECB, and with different block sizes (100, 1000, 10000). Extensive testing showed that using hardware-independent compiler optimizations improved our analysis. Therefore, we used the back-end of the ACE CoSy compiler tools [2] before executing our analysis. Instead of the CoSy compiler suits any other framework that produces optimized code can be used to enhance results. We normalize the HSE and the execution time to a clock rate of 100 MHz.

Table 1 displays the results for the transition process for each application and the hardware component. We used up to five different input data samples for each application and estimated the HSE as well as the simulation time on each platform. The percentages show the divergence between our analysis results and the reference execution time from the ISS-JIT, ISS, and real hardware. The goal of this approach is to gain helpful hints for the designer indicating suitable initial mapping configurations. Therefore more important than accuracy is the linearity of the results. Our estimation costs are always lower the simulation timing. The reason for this is that we do not assume all factors that have an influence on the execution time and just consider an optimal execution.

The minimal discrepancy is 42.18% for the SAR application on the ARM7 processor while the maximum is 50.59% for the JPEG on the ARM9. The worse results for the JPEG in combination

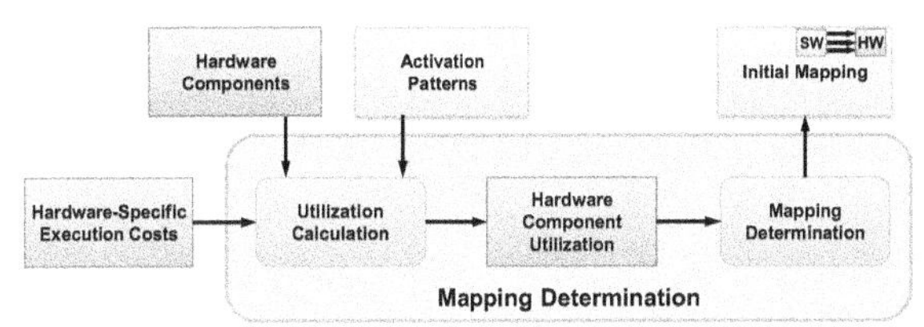

Figure 5: Initial Mapping Configuration

	DES	Viberbi	JPEG	SAR	Bench
ARM7	44.49	48.79	49.02	42.18	49.15
ARM9	49.56	46.24	50.59	46.58	49.63
ARM11	49.60	47.23	49.12	46.62	49.27
Tricore	45.79	47.91	44.95	47.37	48.62
PPC604	48.56	47.38	47.52	-	-
Cortex-M	-	-	-	-	42.25
Leon3	-	-	-	-	48.07

Table 1: Deviation of HSE from Execution Time

with the ARM processors is due to the divide operations of the *quant* process in the JPEG encoder. The ARM processors have no hardware division unit and the operations are executed in software. This cannot be estimated at our abstraction level.

While the numbers seam quite high we detect linearity in the results. Therefore we introduce a linearity factor χ to scale the results representing execution costs that are closer to real execution times and are more helpful for the designer and the initial mapping determination. Our experience show, that a $\chi = 1.9$ is a factor that significantly improves the results. The new calculated HSE are presented in **Table 2**. The new minimal discrepancy is 0.002% for the SAR application executed on the Tricore processor. The maximum is -9.88% for the SAR executed on the ARM7 platform. In this case negative values means that the estimated HSE from our analysis are higher than the actual execution time from simulation. This shows that with a linearization factor we are at maximum 10% off.

The cache simulation results shows, that the number of cache misses resulting from our analysis is within the same order of magnitude as the results from the ISS-JIT. For example, an execution of the DES with the parameters des, cbc and 10000 resulted in a cache miss ratio of 1.35%. Our analysis calculated a miss ratio of 1.41%.

If we compare the time effort needed to determine the results of our analysis compared to the reference values the benefit of our approach is quite obvious. We needed about three hours to generate all presented results. The instrumentation needs about 30 seconds, the profiling approach, which depends on the algorithm and the input data, takes 2 minutes for the biggest data input, about 20 seconds for the extraction of the HIC and less than one minute to calculate the HSE for each hardware platform. To complete all simulation runs on the ISS for comparison it took two weeks not mentioning the adaption of the source code to the different platforms and the use of the target compilers. The adaption for the commercial ISS-JIT consumed most the time.

Considering the abstraction level of the analysis and the fast calculation of the HSE the estimation is accurate enough to feed automated deployment configuration approaches or provide the developer with helpful hints for making design decisions. At the current development stage of the framework, data dependencies and the resulting pipeline stalls are not considered. An incorporation of this will lead to a more precise assumption of the speed-up due to parallelism. We want to achieve this in generating execution traces during profiling. This will also help us to perform the analysis of cache misses and branch prediction penalty during the transition process. This will decouple the HSE completely from the HIC determination. The estimation approach does not yet consider all architectural features but even at this stage it shows potential to enable a fast and early determination of execution costs.

	DES	Viberbi	JPEG	SAR	Bench
ARM7	-5.45	2.72	3.15	-9.88	3.38
ARM9	4.12	-2.14	6.14	-1.50	4.30
ARM11	4.24	-0.15	3.33	-1.42	3.61
Tricore	-3.94	1.04	-4.58	0.00	2.42
PPC604	-	0.02	0.29	-	-
Cortex-M3	-	-	-	-	-9.72
Leon3	-	-	-	-	1.32

Table 2: Deviation of HSE from Execution Time with linearization factor

7. REFERENCES

[1] AbsInt GmbH. `http://www.absint.com/`.

[2] Associated Compiler Experts ACE: CoSy compiler platform. www.ace.nl, 2012.

[3] T. Austin, E. Larson, and D. Ernst. Simplescalar: An infrastructure for computer system modeling. *IEEE Computer*, 2002.

[4] J. R. Bammi, W. Kruijtzer, L. Lavagno, E. Harcourt, and M. T. Lazarescu. Software performance estimation strategies in a system-level design tool. In *Proceedings of the eighth international workshop on Hardware/software codesign*, CODES '00, pages 82–86, New York, NY, USA, 2000. ACM.

[5] E. Bondarev, M. R. V. Chaudron, and E. A. de Kock. Exploring performance trade-offs of a jpeg decoder using the deepcompass framework. In *Proceedings of the 6th International Workshop on Software and Performance*, WOSP '07, pages 153–163, New York, NY, USA, 2007. ACM.

[6] F. Brüseke, G. Engels, and S. Becker. Decision support via automated metric comparison for the palladio-based performance blame analysis. In *Proceedings of the 4th ACM/SPEC International Conference on Performance Engineering*, ICPE '13, pages 77–88, New York, NY, USA, 2013. ACM.

[7] T. Bures, J. Carlson, I. Crnkovic, S. Sentilles, and A. Vulgarakis. Procom - the progress component model reference manual, version 1.0. Technical Report ISSN 1404-3041 ISRN MDH-MRTC-230/2008-1-SE, June 2008.

[8] L. Cai, A. Gerstlauer, and D. Gajski. Retargetable profiling for rapid, early system-level design space exploration. In *Proceedings of the 41st annual Design Automation Conference*, DAC '04, pages 281–286, New York, NY, USA, 2004. ACM.

[9] J. Gustafsson, A. Betts, A. Ermedahl, and B. Lisper. The Mälardalen WCET benchmarks – past, present and future. In B. Lisper, editor, *WCET2010*, pages 137–147, Brussels, Belgium, July 2010. OCG.

[10] Y. Hwang, S. Abdi, and D. Gajski. Cycle-approximate retargetable performance estimation at the transaction level. In *Proceedings of the conference on Design, automation and test in Europe*, DATE '08, pages 3–8, New York, NY, USA, 2008. ACM.

[11] M. Kuperberg, K. Krogmann, and R. Reussner. Performance prediction for black-box components using reengineered parametric behaviour models. In *Proceedings of the 11th International Symposium on Component-Based Software Engineering*, CBSE '08, pages 48–63, Berlin, Heidelberg, 2008. Springer-Verlag.

[12] M. Lattuada and F. Ferrandi. Performance modeling of embedded applications with zero architectural knowledge. In *Proceedings of the eighth IEEE/ACM/IFIP international conference on Hardware/software codesign and system synthesis*, CODES/ISSS '10, pages 277–286, New York, NY, USA, 2010. ACM.

[13] N. Nethercote and J. Seward. Valgrind: a framework for heavyweight dynamic binary instrumentation. In *Proceedings of the 2007 ACM SIGPLAN conference on Programming language design and implementation*, PLDI '07, pages 89–100, New York, NY, USA, 2007. ACM.

[14] R. Niemann and P. Marwedel. An algorithm for hardware/software partitioning using mixed integer linear programming. In *Proceedings of the ED and TC*, pages 165–193. Kluwer Academic Publishers, 1996.

[15] M. Oyamada, F. Wagner, M. Bonaciu, W. Cesario, and A. Jerraya. Software performance estimation in MPSoC design. *Asia and South Pacific Design Automation Conference*, 0:38–43, 2007.

[16] J. Schnerr, O. Bringmann, A. Viehl, and W. Rosenstiel. High-performance timing simulation of embedded software. In *Proceedings of the 45th annual Design Automation Conference*, DAC '08, pages 290–295, New York, NY, USA, 2008. ACM.

[17] S. Stattelmann, O. Bringmann, and W. Rosenstiel. Fast and accurate source-level simulation of software timing considering complex code optimizations. In *DAC*, pages 486–491. ACM, 2011.

[18] J. Zimmermann, M. Pressler, A. Viehl, O. Bringmann, and W. Rosenstiel. Model-based virtual prototyping for early automotive software systems evaluation. 2010.

[19] J. Zimmermann, S. Stattelmann, A. Viehl, O. Bringmann, and W. Rosenstiel. Model-driven virtual prototyping for real-time simulation of distributed embedded systems. In *SIES*, pages 201–210. IEEE, 2012.

Design-by-Contract for Reusable Components and Realizable Architectures

Mert Ozkaya
City University London
School of Informatics
London EC1V 0HB, U.K.
mert.ozkaya.1@city.ac.uk

Christos Kloukinas
City University London
School of Informatics
London EC1V 0HB, U.K.
c.kloukinas@city.ac.uk

ABSTRACT

Architectural connectors can increase the modularity and reusability benefits of Component-based Software Engineering, as they allow one to specify the *general* case of an interaction pattern and reuse it from then on. At the same time they enable components to be *protocol-independent* – components do not need to know under which interaction patterns they will be used, as long as their minimal, local interaction constraints are satisfied. Without connectors one can specify only *specific* instances of such patterns and components need to specify themselves the interaction protocols that they will follow, thus reducing their reusability.

Connector frameworks so far allow designers to specify systems that are unrealizable in a decentralized manner, as they allow designers to impose global interaction constraints. These frameworks either ignore the realizability problem altogether, ignore connector behaviour when generating code, or introduce a centralized controller that enforces these global constraints but does so at the price of invalidating any decentralized properties of the architecture.

We show how the XCD ADL extends Design-by-Contract (DbC) for specifying *(i)* protocol-independent components, and *(ii)* arbitrary connectors that are always realizable in a decentralized manner as specified by an architecture – XCD connectors impose local constraints only. Use of DbC will hopefully make it easier for practitioners to use the language, compared to languages using process algebras. We show how XCD specifications can be translated to ProMeLa so as to verify that *(i)* provided services local interaction constraints are satisfied, *(ii)* provided services functional pre-conditions are complete, *(iii)* there are no race-conditions, *(iv)* event buffer sizes suffice, and *(v)* there is no global deadlock. Without formally analyzable architectures errors can remain undiscovered for a long time and cost too much to repair.

Categories and Subject Descriptors

D.2.11 [**Software Engineering**]: Software Architectures—*Languages*; D.2.4 [**Software Engineering**]: Software/Program Verification—*Programming by contract*; F.3.1 [**Logics and Meanings of Programs**]: Specifying and Verifying and Reasoning about Programs—*Pre- and post-conditions*

CBSE'14, June 30–July 4, 2014, Marcq-en-Baroeul, France.

ACM 978-1-4503-2577-6/14/06 ...$15.00.
http://dx.doi.org/10.1145/2602458.2602463.

Keywords

Modular specifications; Separation of functional and interaction behaviours; Connector realizability.

1. INTRODUCTION

Component-based Software Engineering helps develop software systems out of largely reusable components, thus reducing development time and cost, and leading to a higher system quality. Reusable components end up having fewer design and implementation errors, as these are identified and corrected through their use by different systems. Researchers in software architectures [36, 19] have identified connectors as another important element for increasing modularity and reusability even further. Connectors allow the specification of arbitrary interaction patterns, thus allowing such patterns to be reused. At the same time, components no longer need to specify instances of such patterns themselves, thus increasing component reusability too. Indeed, designers can more easily explore alternative designs/protocols to meet the requirements of their specific system when components are separated from the possible interaction patterns (i.e., connectors) that they can be used with. This is similar to how we program in languages such as C++. We define a vector class (re-sizable array), specifying its basic operations and the minimal, local constraints on its use, e.g., that the vector should not be empty when retrieving an element. The vector does not specify anything about reverse, sort, etc. to be more reusable. These are instead specified by independent algorithms, among which one selects the most appropriate to their context, e.g., bubble or merge sort. Keeping the two separate increases the code modularity and reusability. Our data-structures/classes stay independent of specific usage patterns, which are described separately as algorithms. Indeed, the reusability of the algorithms themselves increases as well, as they can usually be applied at different classes. Specifying component becomes harder without support for connectors and sometimes specifiers avoid specifying the interaction patterns altogether, which leads to the architectural mismatch problem [17, 18].

1.1 Connector Realizability

A formal framework for specifying connectors in the Wright language was presented in the seminal work of Allen and Garlan [4] and has been followed by almost all approaches that support connectors – a set of protocol role behaviours, that component participants should implement, and a "glue" element that choreographs them. However, connectors are not supported in the main languages used by practitioners [26], who complain about the complexity of ADLs (an orthogonal issue). This may have been a blessing in disguise, since the ADLs supporting connectors do so in a manner that is somewhat dangerous for general usage. This is because, following Wright [4], these languages allow architects to specify connectors that are potentially *unrealizable* in a distributed manner

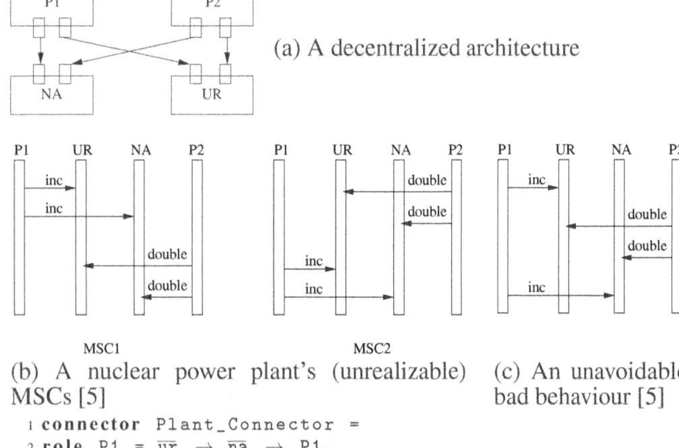

(b) A nuclear power plant's (unrealizable) MSCs [5]

(c) An unavoidable bad behaviour [5]

```
connector Plant_Connector =
role P1 = u̅r̅ → n̅a̅ → P1.
role P2 = u̅r̅ → n̅a̅ → P2.
role UR = inc → UR □ double → UR.
role NA = inc → NA □ double → NA.
glue = P1.ur→UR.i̅n̅c̅ → P1.na→NA.i̅n̅c̅
        → P2.ur→UR.d̅o̅u̅b̅l̅e̅ → P2.na→NA.d̅o̅u̅b̅l̅e̅ → glue
     ⊓ P2.ur→UR.d̅o̅u̅b̅l̅e̅ → P2.na→NA.d̅o̅u̅b̅l̅e̅
        → P1.ur→UR.i̅n̅c̅ → P1.na→NA.i̅n̅c̅ → glue.
```

(d) Wright's *(unrealizable)* connector for Alur's plant of (b)
Note: barred actions are initiated by the current process, → is the action sequence operator, and □/⊓ are external/internal choice.

Figure 1: An unrealizable protocol/connector

[33]. Realizability is defined as: "a set of MSCs *[i.e., a glue]* [is] realizable if there exist concurrent automata *[the connector roles]* which implement precisely the MSCs it *[the glue]* contains." [5]

Consider the nuclear power plant case study [5], shown in Figure 1a. In the plant, the quantities of Uranium (UR) and Nitric Acid (NA) need to be the same at all times. Two processes P1 and P2 respectively increase and double these quantities and to ensure the plant's safety they need to strictly follow the protocol described by the message sequence charts of Figure 1b. However the protocol in Figure 1b was proved to be unrealizable in a decentralized manner, since bad behaviours like in Figure 1c cannot be avoided [5].

One can check conditions implying a protocol's realizability [6, 9], attempt to identify implied scenarios from the protocol [43], or even attempt to repair it [23] by multi-casting messages to more recipients. However, there will always be cases where the protocol cannot be realized. Worse yet, there are cases where it cannot be decided whether a protocol is realizable in a distributed manner with only the specified roles or not – the general problem is undecidable [6] and relates to the undecidability of decentralized observation and control [41]. Connectors can use their "glue" to impose non-local interaction constraints on the participating components, just like service choreographies do. Such global interaction constraints cannot be realized always by the participating components, since the global system state is not always known. Nevertheless, such unrealizable protocols are very easy to specify in existing ADLs. Indeed, Figure 1d shows the Wright [4] connector specification of the unrealizable protocol of Figure 1b. It shows the four participating roles (`P1`, `P2`, `UR`, and `NA`), and the `glue` part of the connector. The glue element links role actions together (e.g., `P1.ur->UR.i̅n̅c̅`), establishing the communication channels between component ports. Unfortunately, the glue also imposes global interaction constraints – here that roles `UR` and `NA` follow the behaviour `inc→inc→double→double ⊓ double→double→inc→inc`. While linking component actions together does not create any realizability problems, global interaction constraints allow architects to present unrealizable specifications as architectural solutions. While a requirements language needs to be able to express something potentially unrealizable (as it is a wish), we believe that an ADL needs to be able to specify only realizable designs, as these are supposed to be solutions for the requirements: wishing for a building that is suspended in the air is acceptable but presenting a drawing of such a building as an architectural solution is not, unless it is made explicit how this can be achieved (builders cannot "refine" the architecture).

Some approaches follow Wright [4] in supporting connectors with a glue element but ignore the connector behavioural specification when generating code. This is for example the case with SOFA [13] and its code generation ConGen [16, 12]: "we are rather interested in rich functionality than formal proving that a connector has specific properties; thus, at this point we do not associate any formal behavior with a connector." [12, p. 14]. Without associated behaviour one cannot generate code for arbitrary, user-defined protocols. Only simple connectors like procedure call can be supported, which forces one to specify protocols inside components.

Finally, a third approach implements arbitrary, user-defined connectors by introducing additional centralized controllers for connectors. In Exogenous Connectors [22] these controllers are explicit and clearly visible – while this centralizes all behaviour, it avoids surprises. In BIP [8], an underlying distributed consensus protocol is employed instead, so that connector participants can know the exact global system state – essentially adding an implicit centralized controller. However, network overhead, reliability, scalability, etc. analyses (what practitioners *really* care about [26]) based on the decentralized architectural design are now invalid. BIP's implicit centralization changes the system structure and its behaviour with respect to these properties – it breaks what ArchJava calls "communication integrity" [1]. After all, if the architect wished for a centralized solution they should have specified it explicitly by introducing a controller component in the system in Figure 1d – that is the solution at the architectural level for the requirement. If they did not do so it was probably because they desired a decentralized solution, so as to get its benefits. But such a decentralized solution must be shown to satisfy the requirement, not simply repeat it, as the glue does in this specification.

1.2 Paper Contribution and Structure

Herein we present XCD, a formal ADL that, following Wright [4], supports arbitrary, user-defined, connectors. Unlike Wright and all other ADLs following it, XCD allows only local constraints to be defined in connectors, so as to ensure realizability by definition. Non-local interaction constraints are now only expressible as properties the architecture should satisfy. Our work builds on our earlier attempts at such an ADL [21, 32], and using FSP [25] to specify and verify architectures [35]. The differences from these are the following: *(i)* We have simplified the main notions, no longer having "control strategies"; strategies are connectors. *(ii)* We have extended the language to better support architects with: data arrays, enumerated types, interval values, helper functions, asynchronous interaction, and composite components that were not supported in our initial FSP encoding and tool. *(iii)* We have also replaced FSP with Spin's ProMeLa language [20], as encoding asynchronous interaction and method/event parameters in FSP required too much effort. Spin's code availability also helped us in better understanding the use of some constructs and optimizing our models.

XCD tries to resemble a programming language and follows a Design-by-Contract (DbC) based approach, as practitioners find process algebra-based ADLs to have a "steep learning curve" [26].

A brief, high-level introduction of the current version of the XCD language was presented in an earlier short position paper [34]. This

```
1 SimpleCType:component ID^CTypeName ( [DataType ID^ParamName]* )
2   { Variable* Port+ } ;
3
4 Port: RequiredPort | ProvidedPort ;
5 ProvidedPort: provided ID^PortName
6   { ProvidedPortMethod+ } ;
7 RequiredPort: required ID^PortName
8   { RequiredPortMethod+ } ;
9 ProvidedPortMethod:
10   [ ProtocolAwaits | ProtocolAccepts ]?
11       FunctionalReqEns? MethodSignature ;
12 RequiredPortMethod:
13   ProtocolAwaits?
14       FunctionalPromReqEns? MethodSignature ;
15
16 ProtocolAwaits:  @interaction { waits   Expression } ;
17 ProtocolAccepts: @interaction { accepts Expression } ;
18
19 FunctionalReqEns:
20   @functional { ReqEns [ otherwise ReqEns ]* };
21 ReqEns: [ requires Expression ]? ensures Assignments
22       | requires Expression ;
23 FunctionalPromReqEns:
24   @functional { PromReqEns [otherwise PromReqEns]* };
25 PromReqEns: [ promises Assignments ]? ReqEns
26           | promises Assignments ;
27
28 Variable: DataType ID^VarName := Expression ;
29 DataType: bool | byte | short | int | ID^DataTypeName ;
30 Assignments: Assignment [ Assignment ]* ;
31 Assignment: ID^VarName := Expression ;
32       | ID^VarName in '[' Expression , Expression ']' ;
```

Note: Rules are of the form `symbol: expression;`. Keywords are in bold, "`(){}=,`" are part of the input, "`[]`" are used for grouping (unless quoted), and "`?+*`" stand for optional, at least once, and zero or more repetitions respectively. Superscripts refer to the meaning of an `ID`, e.g., $\texttt{ID}^{\texttt{CTypeName}}$ is a component type name.

Figure 2: Simple components (`SimpleCType`) grammar

paper describes in detail the XCD notions, its grammar, and the language mappings to Spin's ProMeLa language, so as to enable formal verification of architectural designs. It identifies the five properties that can be verified without any further input from designers, and shows how designers can modify the ProMeLa models to verify more properties. It demonstrates most of the new features (enums in Figure 6 line 1, helper functions in Figure 8 lines 55-58) and discusses others (intervals in section 2.1). It shows how global constraints can be supported by an *explicit* centralized controller component when decentralized control is impossible. The paper also includes an extensive experimental evaluation using a number of well-known architectural case studies (all available at [40]), and some further related work before the final discussion.

2. CONTRACTS FOR ARCHITECTURES

In XCD we follow a Design-by-Contract (DbC) [28] approach to specify the behaviours of components, extending it in two ways so as to support software component frameworks like CORBA [30] and OSGi [31] better. We extend DbC so as to be able to specify contracts not only for the component provided services but for its required services too. This is because, unlike object classes for which DbC was initially designed, components also have required services in their public interfaces. At the same time, we propose a different contract structure so as to better distinguish between the functional and interaction component constraints, which are usually mixed together in most DbC approaches. Finally, we use DbC to specify connectors/protocols as well as components.

2.1 Structure of Simple Components

A simple (non-composite) component has data variables and a set of ports for interacting with its environment. We ignore ports supporting events due to lack of space. Each port can be either a provided one, offering a number of methods to the environment, or a required one, which uses methods provided by the environment. XCD component ports execute concurrently to each other and operate as a monitor, i.e., at most one method of a port can be active at any time. Interaction between ports is asynchronous, as we target mainstream software components. Figure 2 shows the high-level grammar for simple components, abstracting over a number of language details, e.g., helper functions, for simplicity. Figure 3 shows a small component example, described in more detail later.

```
component Thread {
  bool started := false; // component data.
  bool died := false;

  provided p {
    @interaction   { accepts: ! started; }
    @functional { ensures: started := true;}
    void start();

    @functional {
      ensures: \result := started && ! died; }
    bool isAlive();

    @interaction { waits: died; }
    void join();
    // ... other methods
  };
};
```

Figure 3: Java Thread as an XCD component

As aforementioned, provided port methods (`ProvidedPortMethod`, at line 9) resemble object methods and their constraints can essentially be described through classic DbC. Ignoring the interaction contract, whenever a method is called and the method pre-condition (**requires** of `FunctionalReqEns`, at line 21) on the parameter and component data values is satisfied, the method post-condition (**ensures**) should be satisfied as well. It should be noted that while pre-conditions are expressions, post-conditions in XCD are in fact assignments. In assignments (lines 31-32) we also allow a variable to be set to a value within a range, for non-deterministic specifications. The use of assignments instead of post-conditions is to make our models easier to formally analyze. Trying to ensure a post-condition like $0 \leq x+y+z \leq n$ means that we need to consider all possible combinations of x, y, z within the range $[0,n]$, i.e., $(n+1)^3$ states. Instead, architects write this as $x \in [0,n]; y \in [0,n-x]; z \in [0,n-x-y];$, which has $(n+1)(n^2+5n+6)/6$ states [1]. For $n = 255$, i.e., a byte, we need explore 2.8 M instead of 16.7 M states. A provided port method is atomic – testing its required pre-condition and performing its ensured assignment is done as one action.

Required port methods (`RequiredPortMethod`, at lines 12-14) do not have an equivalent in object class definitions and, as such, classic DbC does not consider them. These are actions that the component enacts itself, instead of actions that it reacts to (in its provided ports). A restaurant may provide a service between 7pm and 11pm (protocol) and offer an Italian menu (functional). Symmetrically, a customer may require a service between 9pm and 10pm (protocol) and desire to have a pizza (functional). A required port method is non-atomic (race-conditions are considered later). At the first state it selects parameter values (i.e., affects its **promises** at lines 25-26) and makes the method call. At the second state it receives the method call results and updates the component data, according to the required/ensures pair establishing appropriate assignments given conditions on the component data and the method results.

2.1.1 Functional and Interaction Contracts

As shown in Figure 2, along with functional contracts methods in XCD can have protocol contracts too. The latter can be of a

[1] Wolfram Alpha: `https://www.wolframalpha.com/input/?i=sum_x=0^n+sum_y=0^(n-x)+sum_z=0^(n-x-y)+1,n=255`

waits (line 16) or an **accepts** type (line 17). Provided port methods can use either type. The former indicates that the action will be delayed until some predicate on the component data and the method parameters is satisfied. The latter indicates that the action will be processed immediately when received and either it will be accepted or it will be rejected – whereby rejection leads to chaotic behaviour (caught as a violated assertion in our models). So a data queue may use a waits constraint to specify that a request for an element will be delayed till the queue is not empty. Alternatively, an object lock can use an accepts constraint to specify that attempts to unlock it cause undefined behaviour when it is already unlocked.

Examples of such protocol contracts abound in everyday life. A washing machine manufacturer can warn users against opening the door while the machine is operating (**accepts**: `! operating`) or add a safety mechanism that delays the door opening (**waits**: `! operating`). The former protocol contract makes no guarantees whatsoever if someone attempts to open the door during operation – water may be spilt outside and the user can even be electrocuted because of it. In fact, such bad behaviour due to a component's protocol contract violation appears in the standard libraries of mainstream languages already. In Java, `RuntimeExceptions` are used extensively to represent such situations. Unlike other exceptions, they are not supposed to be caught by code. In fact, they are not even supposed to be declared by the methods that may throw them – Java calls them "unchecked exceptions". The method `Thread.start()` can throw such an exception when called on a thread that has already started. Using XCD protocol contracts this can be specified as in line 6 of Figure 3. Note that a method may have no protocol contract, e.g., `isAlive` (lines 10-12). Sometimes it may have no functional contract instead, like `join` that can be specified entirely through a protocol contract (lines 14-15).

Another example of protocol contract violations in Java is `SocketException`, thrown when a socket's `setSocketFactory` is called more than once. Exception `InternalError` as well, thrown by `wait/notify` when the thread is not the current owner of the object's monitor. And of course, a `NullPointerException`, which is thrown when an object reference has not been initialized properly. All these are examples of erroneous protocol usage. All of them terminate a program immediately. By introducing the separate protocol contract (**@interaction**) construct, such interface protocols become easier to express and their importance is highlighted. Functional contracts also become easier to express. Indeed, in the functional contract of method `start` at lines 6-8 of Figure 3, the requires clause does not consider the state of variable `started`. It assumes that the call has already been accepted, at which point it has no functional constraint to impose. It should be noted that component protocol contracts do not modify the component state – there is no ensures clause in them. State updates in XCD components are instead the sole responsibility of functional contracts, so as to keep contracts simpler.

User obligations. When a required port `r` makes a request on a provided port `p`, it needs to ensure that `p.`**accepts** is satisfied, if the provided method has an accepts protocol (so `p.`**waits** is **true**), otherwise (`p.`**accepts** being **true**) that `p.`**waits** is satisfied. So in general:

$$(\ \texttt{r}.\mathbf{waits} \rightarrow \texttt{r}.\mathbf{promises}\ ) \rightarrow (\ \texttt{p}.\mathbf{waits} \rightarrow \texttt{p}.\mathbf{accepts}\ )$$

Interestingly, the user does not need to satisfy the functional requirements of the provided service (`p.`**requires**), since these must be complete when the service's interaction constraint is satisfied – the call has been accepted already, so it must be honoured.

Simple component types define the data a component has and its ports with their methods and protocol/functional contracts. However in order to produce formal models of the component *instances* we need to consider also the protocol/connector roles these are assuming within an architecture, as roles constrain their behaviour.

```
1 XType:connector ID^XTypeName ( XTypeParam+ )
2   { Role+ XInstance+ } ;
3 XTypeParam: ID^RoleName { ID^PortVarName+ }
4             | DataType ID^ParamName;
5
6 Role:role ID^RoleName
7   { Variable+ [[required|provided] PortVar]+ } ;
8
9 PortVar: ID^PortVarName
10   { [ [XProtocol]? MethodSignature]+ } ;
11 XProtocol: @interaction {
12    [ waits Expression ]? ensures Assignments
13    | waits Expression } ;
14
15 XInstance: ID^XTypeName ID^XInstanceName ( XInstanceArg+ );
16 XInstanceArg: ID^RoleName { ID^PortVarName+ } | Expression ;
```

Figure 4: High-level XCD grammar – Connectors (`XType`)

While a component type may have just accepts conditions, its instances may also get waits conditions from their roles.

2.2 Connector/Protocol Structure

As shown in Figure 4, XCD connectors have a set of roles (each assumed by some component) and instances of other connectors that they are using. A basic connector is provided by the language to specify a simple asynchronous method call, linking the required port of one component to the provided port of another, without imposing any further constraints on their actions. There is no glue element in XCD connectors, nor any other way to specify global state or constraints – everything is *local* and so *directly realizable*. Each role consists of role data, that keep track of the protocol's local state, and a set of provided/required port variables, to be assumed by the role component's ports. Role port variables have actions like component ports do. These are the actions that the role requires its component to have and that the role will constrain. The behaviour of port variable actions is again specified through contracts, only now all contracts have the same form, i.e., a pair of a **waits** precondition and an **ensures** assignment, as shown in lines 11-13. This is because roles can only delay some component port action, until the point where it is acceptable by the protocol/connector they are a part of. Role actions have no functional contracts, as they cannot influence the component's action parameters, or its result or the manipulation of the component's private data. Instead, the protocol contracts of role actions use their **ensures** assignments, to update the role's local protocol state after the action.

A component instance is provided with all the roles it assumes in an architecture, just like actors are provided with the roles and corresponding scripts they play in a movie. Component instances use the role(s) port method contracts to further constrain their own contracts and are responsible for updating the role variables along with their own. Here again we diverge from Wright [4]. In Wright, components should refine/implement the roles they assume; the final system is the composition of components and connector glues only – roles are ignored. This restricts the reusability of components – they need to know beforehand all protocols under which they may be used, something that one would never require of actors. Instead, in XCD components do not need to refine their roles. On the contrary, their behaviour can be much richer. For this to work, XCD components need to be presented with their role constraints – XCD components are *interpreters* of connector roles.

2.2.1 A Centralized Nuclear Plant Xcd Connector

Figures 6–9 specify a centralized XCD connector that ensures the required glue property of the nuclear plant example in Figure 1 – the architecture is shown in Figure 5. The glue property states that UR and NA should always increase and double their quantities in tandem: `UR.i->NA.i->UR.d->NA.d|UR.d->NA.d->UR.i->NA.i`, where `i`

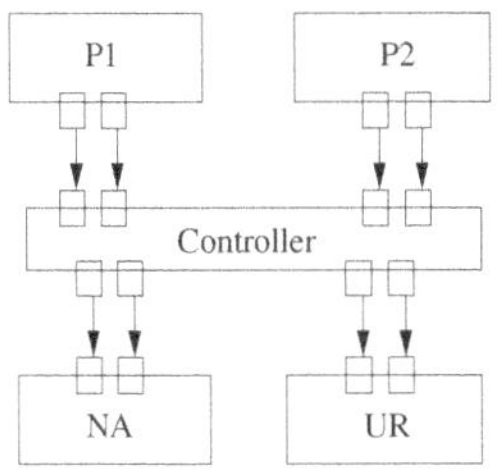

Figure 5: A centralized architecture

```
1 enum order := {none, incFirst, dblFirst}; // New type.
2
3 connector centralised(roleP1{toUR, toNA},
4                       roleP2{toUR, toNA},
5                       roleUR{inc, double},
6                       roleNA{inc, double},
7 /*extra role*/  roleController{P1toUR,  P1toNA,
8                                P2toUR,  P2toNA,
9                                CtoURinc, CtoURdouble,
10                               CtoNAinc, CtoNAdouble}) {
// P1/UR/NA/P2 and Controller from Fig. 7 and Fig.8-9 respectively.

134   // Controller appears to P1 & P2 as UR & NA.
135   connector async link1(roleP1{toUR},
136                         roleController{P1toUR});
137   connector async link2(roleP1{toNA},
138                         roleController{P1toNA});
139   connector async link3(roleP2{toUR},
140                         roleController{P2toUR});
141   connector async link4(roleP2{toNA},
142                         roleController{P2toNA});
143   // Controller appears to UR & NA as P1 & P2.
144   connector async link5(roleUR{inc},
145                         roleController{CtoURinc});
146   connector async link6(roleUR{double},
147                         roleController{CtoURdouble});
148   connector async link7(roleNA{inc},
149                         roleController{CtoNAinc});
150   connector async link8(roleNA{double},
151                         roleController{CtoNAdouble});
152 }
```

Figure 6: Centralized nuclear plant connector in XCD

```
12   role roleP1 {
13     bool urFirst:=false;
14     required port_variable toUR {
15       @interaction{ waits: !urFirst;
16             ensures: urFirst := true; }
17       void incUR(); }
18     required port_variable toNA {
19       @interaction{ waits: urFirst;
20             ensures: urFirst := false; }
21       void incNA(); }
22   }
23   role roleUR {
24     provided port_variable inc { void incUR(); }
25     provided port_variable double { void doubleUR(); }
26   }
```

Figure 7: Original nuclear plant roles in XCD (part of Figure 6)

and d are the increase and double actions. The connector employs five roles instead of the four roles in the decentralized connector, as it has an explicit centralized controller (lines 7-10). Without a controller it is impossible to ensure the glue property (indeed, the decentralized connector violates it). Figure 7 shows the P1 and UR roles of the decentralized connector (omitted roles P2 and NA are similar). These roles behave as in the Wright specification of Figure 1d. Roles UR (lines 23-26) and NA have no constraints, as they can receive requests to increase or double their amount of fuel anytime. Roles P1 (lines 12-22) and P2 impose that increase/doubling requests are sent first to UR and then to NA. The controller role, shown in Figure 8 and Figure 9, presents itself as UR and NA to P1 and P2 using its provided ports (lines 60-71 for

```
43   role roleController {
44     order corder := none;
45     bool p1_incNARcvd :=false;
46     bool p1_incURRcvd :=false;
47     bool p2_dblNARcvd :=false;
48     bool p2_dblURRcvd :=false;
49
50     bool ur_incUREmtd := false;
51     bool na_incNAEmtd := false;
52     bool ur_dblUREmtd := false;
53     bool na_dblNAEmtd := false;
54
55 all_received(){return p1_incURRcvd && p1_incNARcvd
56 /*helper functions*/ && p2_dblURRcvd && p2_dblNARcvd;}
57 inc_emitted(){return ur_incUREmtd && na_incNAEmtd;}
58 dbl_emitted(){return ur_dblUREmtd && na_dblNAEmtd;}
59
60     provided port_variable P1toUR {
61       @interaction{
62       waits: !p1_incURRcvd;
63       ensures: p1_incURRcvd :=true;
64         corder := pre(corder) == none
65           ? incFirst : pre(corder); }
66       void incUR(); }
67     provided port_variable P1toNA {
68       @interaction{
69       waits: !p1_incNARcvd;
70       ensures: p1_incNARcvd :=true; }
71       void incNA(); }
```

Figure 8: Nuclear plant controller role in XCD – provided ports

```
85     required port_variable CtoURinc {
86       @interaction{
87       waits: all_received() && !ur_incUREmtd
88         && ( (corder==incFirst)
89         || (corder==dblFirst && dbl_emitted()) );
90       ensures: ur_incUREmtd := true; }
91       void incUR(); }
92     required port_variable CtoNAinc {
93       @interaction{
94       waits: ur_incUREmtd && !na_incNAEmtd;
95       ensures: // clear flags if dblFirst
96         p1_incURRcvd := !(pre(corder) == dblFirst);
97         p1_incNARcvd := !(pre(corder) == dblFirst);
98         ur_incUREmtd := !(pre(corder) == dblFirst);
99         na_incNAEmtd := !(pre(corder) == dblFirst);
100        p2_dblURRcvd := !(pre(corder) == dblFirst);
101        p2_dblNARcvd := !(pre(corder) == dblFirst);
102        ur_dblUREmtd := pre(corder) == dblFirst
103          ? false : pre(ur_dblUREmtd);
104        na_dblNAEmtd := pre(corder) == dblFirst
105          ? false : pre(na_dblNAEmtd);
106        corder := pre(corder) == dblFirst
107          ? none : pre(corder); }
108      void incNA(); }
```

Figure 9: Nuclear plant controller role in XCD – required ports

ports related to increase). Using its required ports, it presents itself as P1 and P2 to UR and NA (lines 85-108 for ports related to increase). The provided ports note which commands have been received by P1 and P2, and which of increase or double was received first in each round, using the `corder` variable (an enumerated type). The expression on lines 64-65 uses the *if-then-else* operator "`guard ? exp1 : exp2`", and the operator `pre` to access the value of variable `corder` when the action started. Once all commands have been received, the required ports in Figure 9 start requesting from UR and NA to update their fuel amounts. This behaviour uses helper functions `all_received`, `inc_emitted`, and `dbl_emitted` (defined in Figure 8, lines 55-58). Depending on whether it was the increments or the doubles that were received last, action `incNA` (or `doubleNA` respectively) reset all role variables, to enable the next round. The full models for both the decentralized and centralized protocols are available at the XCD website [40].

Compared to the Wright connector in Figure 1d, the XCD connector is longer – much more so. This is for two main reasons.

```
CompositeCType:component ID^CTypeName (
                         [DataType ID^ParName]* )
           { [ CInstance | XInstance ]+ } ;
CInstance: ID^CTypeName ID^CInstanceName ( Expression* ) ;
```

Figure 10: High-level XCD grammar – Composite components (CompositeCType)

```
component NuclearPlant() {
  component P1 p1inst();  component P2 p2inst();
  component NA nainst();  component UR urinst();
  component controller controllerinst();

  connector centralised  centrins(
        p1inst{incUR,    incNA},
        p2inst{doubleUR, doubleNA},
        urinst{incUR,    doubleUR},
        nainst{incNA,    doubleNA},
        controllerinst{P1_incUR,    P1_incNA,
                       P2_doubleUR, P2_doubleNA,
                       UR_incUR,    UR_doubleUR,
                       NA_incNA,    NA_doubleNA}
        );
}
```

Figure 11: Nuclear plant composite component in XCD

Firstly, it does not employ a process algebra but uses a language similar to a programming one, e.g., Java, which is more verbose but also more familiar. Secondly, and more importantly, the XCD connector specifies a *solution*. Indeed, it does not simply repeat the requirement about the behaviour of the UR and NA roles but it guarantees it. It should be noted that this solution increases the number of messages per round, from four to eight. It also changes the structure of the system – if one of P1 or P2 fails, no interactions are possible any more, unlike in the original architecture. Both the number of messages and system structure are crucial for a proper architectural system analysis. Lower-level designs should not modify them, since then the architecture is compromised – what ArchJava calls (lack of) "communication integrity" [1]. XCD aims at facilitating the expression of architectures that can be realized without compromising their communication integrity. If a Wright connector is realizable then XCD can also represent it.

2.3 Structure of Composite Xcd Components

The grammar for specifying composite components is shown in Figure 10. A composite component declares a set of component instances (which can be either simple or composite) and a set of connector instances. The connector instances are initialized with the component instances that will assume their roles. In this way, a composite component defines the configuration of its sub-components. The ports of sub-components that are not connected through the connectors employed in the composite component become ports of the composite component. An architecture is a composite component where all the ports of the sub-components are connected, as the composite component in Figure 11.

3. TRANSLATING XCD INTO PROMELA

We translate XCD models into Spin's ProMeLa [20], in order to formally verify architectures. Each component *instance* becomes a separate ProMeLa process. The number of component instances is fixed in each architecture (we consider only static architectures). ProMeLa processes are concurrent automata that are composed together through synchronous or buffered asynchronous channels. We use asynchronous channels in our models, as we target software systems, where asynchronous interaction is the mainstream. For each simple component (c) instance's (i) provided port (p) we introduce one asynchronous channel ($ch_p^{c_i}$), with a buffer size equal to the number $N = \text{connectedTo}(c_i, p)$ of required ports that are

```
1 SimpleComponent2Promela(SimpleCInstance comp)
2
3 FORALL port ∈ comp.SimpleCType.ProvidedPortSet
4   // Requests
5   chan cReq.comp.port = [port.Connections] ...
6   // Responses
7   chan cRes.comp.port = [1] ...
8
9 proctype comp.InstanceID (params...) {
10  LET
11    RoleVars = { role.VarSet | role ∈ comp.RoleSet };
12      VarSet = RoleVars ⋃ comp.SimpleCType.VarSet;
13    RoleReqPorts = { r ∈ role.RequiredPortSet
14        | role ∈ comp.RoleSet };
15    RoleReqMethods = { m ∈ r.Methods
16        | r ∈ RoleReqPorts };
17    RoleVarsRace = { v ∈ m.Methods.Ensures.VarSet
18        | m ∈ RoleReqMethods };
19    compReqPorts = { r
20        | r ∈ comp.SimpleCType.RequiredPortSet};
21    compReqMethods = { m ∈ r.Methods
22        | r ∈ compReqPorts };
23    compVarsRace = { v ∈ m.Methods.Ensures.VarSet
24        | m ∈ compReqMethods };
25      VarSetRace = RoleVarsRace ⋃ compVarsRace;
26  IN
27  FORALL var ∈ VarSet
28    var.DataType var.Pre_State  = var.InitialValue;
29    var.DataType var.Post_State = var.InitialValue;
30  FORALL var ∈ VarSetRace
31    var.DataType var.Pre_State_Copy=var.InitialValue;
32  FORALL port ∈ comp.SimpleCType.RequiredPortSet
33    short port.Lock=0; // One lock per required port.
34
35  Start:
36  do
37   FORALL port ∈ comp.SimpleCType.ProvidedPortSet
38     Port2Promela_Provided(comp, port);
39   FORALL port ∈ comp.SimpleCType.RequiredPortSet
40     Port2Promela_Required(comp, port);
41  od
42 }
```

Figure 12: Translating a simple component instance to ProMeLa

connected to port p of component instance c_i, as in lines 4-5 of Figure 12. This is because in the worst case there will be N concurrent service requests to port p from these N required ports. No more service requests can be initiated by them, as required component ports, just like provided ports, act as a monitor and therefore allow at most one method request to be active each time. We also introduce a channel to carry the response back to the required port (lines 6-7). Due to lack of space we omit here the discussion of XCD support for events (emitter and consumer ports) or for non-atomic provided methods, which are needed when a provided method has to call another method to obtain partial results.

3.1 Translating Simple Component Instances

Figure 12 shows the top-structure of the ProMeLa translation for a simple XCD component instance. The translation goes through the instance's assumed roles, collecting their variables and noting which ones of them are used in **ensures** clauses in methods of required port variables (to check for race-conditions later). It declares corresponding variables for each variable of the component and its roles. It then translates the provided and required ports themselves. All port actions are inside a `do/od` loop of guarded actions [14].

Each component and role data `var` is mapped to two variables (lines 27-29 of Figure 12). The first one (`var.Pre_State` on line 28) is the current data value, i.e., the value right before a call, used to evaluate the protocol constraints and the pre-conditions. The second one (`var.Post_State`) is the data value immediately after a call, i.e., where we have just established the post-conditions. The two variables are needed because an assignment of some $\texttt{var}_i\texttt{.Post\_State}$ may refer to some $\texttt{var}_j\texttt{.Pre\_State}$ values.

```
1 Port2Promela_Provided(SimpleCInstance comp, Port port)
2  FORALL method ∈ port.MethodSet
3  LET
4   roles = { method.roleMethod(r) | r ∈ port.RoleSet };
5   roleAwaits = { r.method.Awaits | r ∈ roles };
6   rolePostEnsures = { r.method.Ensures | r ∈ roles };
7
8   compPos = roleAwaits ⋀ method.Awaits
9             ⋀ method.Accepts;
10  compNeg = roleAwaits ⋀ ¬ method.Accepts;
11
12  compFCReq = method.FCRequiresEnsures.Requires ;
13  compFCEns = {method.FCRequiresEnsures.Ensures}
14              ⋃ rolePostEnsures;
15 IN
16 ::atomic {
17   port.Channel_req ? method.Args : compPos ->
18      assert(compFCReq); // Ensure functional completeness
19      calcData(comp.SimpleCType.VarSet, compFCReq,
20               compFCEns);
21      port.Channel_res ! method.Args;
22   }
23 ::atomic {
24   port.Channel_req ? method.Args : compNeg ->
25      assert(! compNeg); // Request rejected - CHAOS
26   }
```

Figure 13: Translating a provided port to ProMeLa

In order to identify race-conditions that may arise due to the non-atomicity of required method requests, we also introduce another variable `var.Pre_State_Copy` for each data `var` appearing in an **ensures** clause (lines 30-31). This variable keeps a copy of the data's pre-value (`var.Pre_State`) at the point the request was started at the port. For required port methods, we have that `var.Pre_State` $=$ `var.Pre_State_Copy` before and immediately after enacting the method request. But when the response is received we may find that `var.Pre_State` $\neq$ `var.Pre_State_Copy`, because some other component port has modified `var.Pre_State` (the current variable value) in between. This is a write-read race when a post-condition attempts to use the value var_i`.Pre_State` to establish the value of some var_j`.Post_State` and a write-write race when a post-condition attempts to establish a new value for var_i`.Post_State` itself. We check for such conflicts separately, as architects may be interested in the particular type of race-conditions in their system.

3.2 Translating Provided Ports

Figure 13 shows the translation to ProMeLa of provided ports. Their methods are translated as a pair of mutually exclusive atomic actions (lines 16–22 and 23-26). Both are guarded by the delaying guards of the role port variables that have been assumed by the port (`roleAwaits` in line 5, which is part of both `compPos` and `compNeg` defined in lines 8-10). When both role and method protocol guards are satisfied, service requests are processed by the first atomic block of actions (lines 16-22), which computes the next values of the component and role variables and sends back a response to the caller. On line 18 we check the completeness of the required conditions, when the interaction constraints (`compPos`) are satisfied. If the role guards are satisfied and the negation of the method's accepts guard is also satisfied, then the service request is rejected (lines 23-26) and the model fails explicitly, so as to indicate that a service user has violated the protocol constraints of the provided service. Both atomic blocks use the extended (non-)ProMeLa expression `chanX ? msg : pred` to receive `msg` from `chanX` only when `msg` satisfies `pred` – we have implemented this ourselves.

As can be seen, the role constraints are *injected* in the corresponding port (see usage of `roleAwaits` in lines 8-10 of Figure 13). The same behaviour could have been achieved by using a wrapper around provided ports, in which case ports would not need to know about their role constraints. Wrappers however cannot constrain required ports, as these can make requests whenever their protocol constraints allow them to do so. A wrapper of a required port could only delay such a request but it could not undo it – the request would still exist. For this reason we have opted for the injection of the role constraints directly into the components. This is similar to how human actors work – they are given the script of their roles to read, as, unlike marionettes, they are active entities which need to know when they should perform an action. Directors do not attempt to delay actions initiated by actors during a play.

```
1 Port2Promela_Required(SimpleCInstance comp, Port port)
2  FORALL method ∈ port.MethodSet
3   LET
4   roles = { method.roleMethod(r) | r ∈ port.RoleSet };
5   roleAwaits = { r.method.Awaits | r ∈ roles };
6   rolePostEnsures = { r.method.Ensures | r ∈ roles };
7
8   compPos = rAwaits ⋀ method.Awaits;
9
10  compFCProm =
11   {method.FCPromisesRequiresEnsures.Promises} ;
12  compFCReq = method.FCPromisesRequiresEnsures.Requires;
13  compFCEns = {method.FCPromisesRequiresEnsures.Ensures}
14              ⋃ rolePostEnsures;
15
16  RoleVarsRace = { v ∈ e.VarSet | e ∈ rolePostEnsures };
17  compVarsRace = { v ∈ method.Ensures.VarSet };
18    VarSetRace = RoleVarsRace ⋃ compVarsRace;
19 IN
20 ::atomic { // sending a request
21   selectParams(method.Args,
22                comPos ⋀ !port.Lock,compFCProm)→
23     port.Lock = method;
24     FORALL var ∈ VarSetRace
25        var.Pre_State_Copy = var.Pre_State;
26     port.Channel_req
27         ! method.Args;
28   }
29 ::atomic { // receiving a response
30   port.Channel_res ? method.Args
31                       : port.Lock == method →
32      raceCheck(compVarsRace,compFCEns); // Check race-conditions
33     calcData(comp.SimpleCType.VarSet,compFCReq,
34              compFCEns);
35     port.Lock = 0;
36   }
```

Figure 14: Translating a required port to ProMeLa

3.3 Translating Required Ports

Required ports are translated to ProMeLa as shown in Figure 14. Now actions are translated into a pair of co-dependent atomic actions (lines 20-28 and 29-36). The first block initiates a service request to a provided port; the second treats the response.

If each port was a separate process then they would be specified as two sequential (non-atomic) steps – the port process would block after sending a request, until it would receive the response. In our translation however all ports are part of the same component process, so as to decrease the overall number of active processes (Spin has an upper limit). This is why we use a lock (**port**.`Lock`) per each required port, to hold the currently active method. When none is active, a request can be made, as long as we can also select appropriate method parameter values that meet the promise of the method and satisfy its protocol constraints (lines 21-22). In this case we keep copies of the variables that might suffer a race-condition, so as to identify these later, and emit the request message, updating the lock to indicate which method made the request.

Once a response can be received (line 29-31), we check for race-conditions among the variables (line 32), use the ensures clause of the method contract to compute new values for the component data (lines 33-34), and free the lock on this required port.

Table 1: Memory and time required for verifying architectural specifications

Case Study		Issues ‡	State-vector (Bytes)	States Stored	States Matched	Memory (MB)	Time (sec)
[5]	Centralized Nuclear Plant		424	168349	407776	186	1.21
	Decentralized Nuclear Plant	1	240	137	73	130	0.00
[39, 7, 27]	Lunar Lander v. 1	4	372	118	78	131	0.01
	Lunar Lander v. 2		392	4223125	8072166	3793	15.50
[29]	Gas Station (1 customer)		188	1003	1401	130	0.00
	Gas Station (2 customers)		288	1136214	2793961	382	3.23
	Gas Station (3 customers)		368	25056808	89254880	7024†	78.00
	BITSTATE Gas Station (3 customers)		368	62792292	207452380	24	242.00
	BITSTATE Gas Station (4 customers)		456	66989014	289982810	25	321.00
	BITSTATE Gas Station (5 customers)		544	69607515	356984080	26	365.00
[3]	Aegis v. 1	2	620	13834057	71301546	7024†	52.00
	BITSTATE Aegis v. 1	2	620	64408848	266469200	37	330.00
	BITSTATE Aegis v. 2		548	63568962	268078040	35	304.00
[15]	English auction v. 1 (1 participant)	3, 4	140	296	295	130	0.00
	English auction v. 2 (1 participant)	4	144	776	1642	130	0.00
	English auction v. 2 (2 participants)	4	232	1293488	3732650	367	5.00
	English auction v. 2 (3 participants)	4	312	27315867	96797687	7024†	134.00
	BITSTATE English auction v. 2 (3 participants)	4	312	57105380	189090640	20	310.00

‡ Issues: The model fails to satisfy a property. 1: glue, 2: local deadlock, 3: global deadlock, 4: buffer overflow.
Column "States Stored" shows the number of unique global system states stored in the state-space, while column "States Matched" the number of states that were revisited during the search – see: `spinroot.com/spin/Man/Pan.html#L10`
† Cases marked with † in the Memory column run out of memory.
Using a 64bit Intel Xeon CPU (W3503 @ 2.40GHz × 2), 11.7GB of RAM, and Linux version 3.5.0-39-generic.
Spin (version 6.2.4) and gcc (version 4.7.2) used, with up to 7024MB of RAM and a search depth of 50,000:

```
spin -a configuration.pml
gcc -DMEMLIM=7024 -O2 -DXUSAFE -DSAFETY -DNOCLAIM -w -o pan pan.c
./pan -m50000 -c1
```

For bit-state verification, the `-DBITSTATE` option needs to be passed to gcc. All case studies available at the XCD web site [40].

4. TOOL EVALUATION

We have evaluated our language and translation tool by considering a number of well-known case studies, apart from the nuclear plant used so far. The Lunar Lander [39, 7, 27] has been considered extensively in the software architecture community. A number of sensors and actuators are controlled by a single controller that attempts to safely land a spacecraft on the moon. The Gas Station [29], another classic case study in software architectures, consists of a number of gas pumps and customers that need to pay a cashier before a pump is released for them. The Aegis Weapons System [3] is a Command-and-Control system developed by the US Navy using a client-server approach, containing a number of sensors to establish the environment a ship is in and components that analyze this context in order to react to potential threats. Finally, FIPA's English Auction [15], describes a marketplace with an auctioneer who uses the English auction variant to sell an item.

The XCD models of these systems (available at the XCD web site [40]) were translated into ProMeLa so as to verify various properties that are encoded in our translation. First, we verify that users respect the protocol constraints of provided services, i.e., no chaotic behaviours are possible. Second, we verify that provided services functional pre-conditions are complete when their protocol constraints are satisfied. Third, we verify against race-conditions, write-read and write-write ones. Fourth, we verify that when using events, then the finite size of the asynchronous channel buffers suffices. Finally, Spin itself verifies deadlock-freedom.

Currently our language and tool do not allow the specification in XCD of other, more general properties, e.g., like the nuclear plant glue property. For these one needs to edit the produced ProMeLa model. We added an extra ProMeLa process (`glueP`), which receives messages through an additional channel from the `UR` and `NA` processes whenever they act on a request and checks if the glue property sequence is respected. Most importantly, we had to modify the produced ProMeLa models of `UR` and `NA`, so that they notify `glueP`. These modifications added another message emission (to `glueP`) in their code, right before they emit the `inc/double` method response in the atomic block, i.e., between lines 20 and 21 of Figure 13. This should be done carefully and only after having verified the general properties, as these message emissions render provided methods non-atomic – they terminate the atomic block in Spin (since emission is blocked by a full channel buffer). This is how we verified that while the decentralized version of the plant does not satisfy the property, the centralized version of it (in Figure 6-9) satisfies it.

Table 1 shows the obtained experimental results. These case studies can be analyzed extremely quickly in most cases, with a reasonable amount of memory. When memory is insufficient (marked with a †), one can use Spin's bit-state hashing mode, which reduces memory drastically through Bloom filters [10].

We view these results as extremely promising – they indicate that a formal architectural analysis of systems is far from unrealistic, even when these are described with such detailed models (e.g., modelling method parameters). We believe that having widespread support for this is something that can improve software systems quality substantially, as architectural errors that are not identified early are extremely costly to correct at later development stages and can easily lead to project failure. At the same time, powerful architectural analysis greatly facilitates architectural design exploration, thus helping designers to consider many more alternatives when designing their systems, without increasing their workload or the overall cost unreasonably.

The downside of our approach is that components and connectors cannot be analyzed in isolation, as Spin requires a closed system. For each component one wishes to analyze, a corresponding testing component is needed. Similarly, for each connector one wishes to analyze, a testing component is needed for each role.

5. RELATED WORK

All the ADLs supporting connectors that we have studied permit the specification of unrealizable connectors [33], since they all support an element like Wright's glue. Of the ADLs we studied that do not support connectors, all of them are realizable apart from Rapide [24], which allows the specification of global constraints.

ArchJava [1, 2] supports connectors but targets code generation, not formal analysis. It uses reflection to type-check that connector roles are associated with appropriate component ports but this considers just their interfaces. Connector roles function as wrappers to component ports, thus we cannot see how required port methods can be (temporarily or permanently) deactivated (not just delayed), as XCD can do by strengthening their protocol constraints.

Trust-By-Contract [38] uses DbC to describe component port protocols but does not support connectors. XCD also follows a more programming-like approach in the description of interfaces and contracts, like JML [11, 37], so that it looks more familiar to practitioners than the usual formal notations used in ADLs. Unlike JML that allows it but does not insist on it, XCD imposes the separation of protocol and functional constraints – we believe that this can make both easier to understand. XCD also extends DbC to support required methods too, that JML does not consider (as they are not part of a class's interface – only provided methods are).

Archface [42] is geared more towards code generation and design/code bidirectional traceability. In Archface connector roles are specified through interfaces (called component interfaces) that also contain predicates on aspect-oriented "pointcuts", such as "call (method call), execution (method execution), and cflow (control flow)". These seem to be able to describe a local role behaviour like in XCD, though the use of interfaces means that Archface cannot have as fine control as XCD – one cannot declare role variables. The connector element itself specifies how some role interface ports (i.e., methods) are connected to each other, adding further interaction constraints. These constraints can only be applied at the provided method side "A connector interface represents connections among ports. The types of advice that can be applied to [a provided port] are declared in an in statement." [42, p. 80]. We could not see any global constraints in the provided examples, so it seems that Archface specifications are realizable. The formal ProMeLa models produced are far simpler than those for XCD, not modelling component data, method parameters, race-conditions, etc. Indeed, constraints on these cannot be specified in Archface. Its input language requires that users know AOP, while XCD does not require so. We failed to understand how connector usage integrity is achieved – consider the following architecture [42, List 3, lines 01-04, p. 79]:

```
1 architecture aObserverPattern {
2  class Subject  implements cSubject;
3  class Observer implements cObserver;}
```

Types `cSubject` and `cObserver` are role interfaces used by a connector called `cObserverPattern`. But the latter does not appear in the architecture (nor did we find a rule that makes it impossible for another connector to use the same role interfaces). We cannot see what would happen if designers forgot to instantiate one of the roles or added an `Observer` component instance without stating that it implements `cObserver`. In XCD a connector is instantiated explicitly and the components that use it are passed as parameters to the connector constructor, so there is no doubt of which connector is being used or which component has assumed which role.

6. DISCUSSION AND CONCLUSIONS

The XCD formal architectural description language (ADL) supports arbitrary, user-defined connectors/protocols that are guaranteed to be realizable. It does so without requiring underlying mechanisms that introduce extra, unspecified information flows, e.g., distributed consensus protocols, which break communication integrity. XCD guarantees connector realizability by not allowing the expression of any global interaction constraints. All constraints in XCD are expressed using local state and therefore each interacting party in a protocol knows at any time what it needs to do. All other ADLs we have studied [33] fail in this respect because they allow architects to impose any kind of global constraint through what they call connector glue – XCD has no connector glue.

We believe that support for user-defined connectors is crucial if we are ever to achieve the goal of CBSE for modular, reusable component specifications that we can easily adapt through our connectors when exploring different architectural solutions. Without support for connectors, one needs to restrict component specifications to specific protocol interactions, thus reducing their reusability, while substantially increasing their complexity at the same time.

XCD also attempts to increase the uptake of formal ADLs by practitioners, through a programming language-like syntax and use of Design-by-Contract (DbC) concepts. As reported recently [26], practitioners find that formal ADLs have a "steep-learning curve", as these require the use of process algebras. Compared to languages like π-Calculus or CSP, we believe that XCD specifications are easier to understand. We have extended DbC to better support components (and connectors), by splitting contracts into their protocol and functional parts and by providing contractual support for required services, along with that already existing for provided services.

Our experience so far with the tool [40] that translates XCD into ProMeLa models is quite encouraging. We can verify that *(i)* users of provided services respect their local protocol constraints, *(ii)* functional pre-conditions of provided services are complete (modulo their protocol constraints), *(iii)* there are no race-conditions, *(iv)* event buffer sizes suffice, and *(v)* there is no global deadlock.

We are working on improving the support for component/role arrays and recursive definitions, as well as the efficiency of our models. A user-friendly (sub-)language for expressing general properties, e.g., a glue, is an open issue.

7. REFERENCES

[1] J. Aldrich, C. Chambers, and D. Notkin. ArchJava: Connecting software architecture to implementation. In W. Tracz, M. Young, and J. Magee, editors, *ICSE*, pages 187–197. ACM, 2002.

[2] J. Aldrich, V. Sazawal, C. Chambers, and D. Notkin. Language support for connector abstractions. In L. Cardelli, editor, *ECOOP*, volume 2743 of *LNCS*, pages 74–102, Darmstadt, Germany, July 2003. Springer-Verlag.

[3] R. Allen and D. Garlan. A case study in architectural modelling: The Aegis system. In *IWSSD-8*, pages 6–15, Paderborn, Germany, Mar. 1996.

[4] R. Allen and D. Garlan. A formal basis for architectural connection. *ACM TOSEM*, 6(3):213–249, July 1997.

[5] R. Alur, K. Etessami, and M. Yannakakis. Inference of message sequence charts. *IEEE TSE*, 29(7):623–633, 2003.

[6] R. Alur, K. Etessami, and M. Yannakakis. Realizability and verification of MSC graphs. *Theor. Comput. Sci.*, 331(1):97–114, 2005.

[7] H. Bagheri and K. J. Sullivan. Monarch: Model-based development of software architectures. In D. C. Petriu, N. Rouquette, and Ø. Haugen, editors, *MoDELS (2)*, volume 6395 of *LNCS*, pages 376–390. Springer, 2010.

[8] A. Basu, S. Bensalem, M. Bozga, J. Combaz, M. Jaber, T.-H. Nguyen, and J. Sifakis. Rigorous component-based system design using the BIP framework. *IEEE Software*, 28(3):41–48, 2011.

[9] S. Basu, T. Bultan, and M. Ouederni. Deciding choreography realizability. In J. Field and M. Hicks, editors, *POPL*, pages 191–202. ACM, 2012.

[10] B. H. Bloom. Space/time trade-offs in hash coding with allowable errors. *Commun. ACM*, 13(7):422–426, 1970.

[11] L. Burdy, Y. Cheon, D. R. Cok, M. D. Ernst, J. R. Kiniry, G. T. Leavens, K. R. M. Leino, and E. Poll. An overview of JML tools and applications. *STTT*, 7(3):212–232, 2005.

[12] T. Bures. Automated synthesis of connectors for heterogeneous deployment. Tech. report no. 2005/4, Dep. of SW Engineering, Charles University, Prague, Aug. 2005.

[13] T. Bures, P. Hnetynka, and F. Plasil. Sofa 2.0: Balancing advanced features in a hierarchical component model. In *SERA*, pages 40–48. IEEE Computer Society, 2006.

[14] E. W. Dijkstra. Guarded commands, nondeterminacy and formal derivation of programs. *Commun. ACM*, 18(8):453–457, 1975.

[15] FIPA TC C. FIPA English auction interaction protocol specification. Technical Report XC00031F (Experimental), FIPA, Aug. 2001. `www.fipa.org/specs/fipa00031/`.

[16] O. Galik and T. Bures. Generating connectors for heterogeneous deployment. In E. D. Nitto and A. L. Murphy, editors, *SEM*, pages 54–61. ACM, 2005.

[17] D. Garlan, R. Allen, and J. Ockerbloom. Architectural mismatch or why it's hard to build systems out of existing parts. In *ICSE*, pages 179–185, Apr. 1995.

[18] D. Garlan, R. Allen, and J. Ockerbloom. Architectural mismatch: Why reuse is still so hard. *IEEE Software*, 26(4):66–69, 2009.

[19] D. Garlan and M. Shaw. An introduction to software architecture. In *Adv. in SW Eng. and Knowledge Eng.*, pages 1–39, Singapore, 1993. World Scientific Publishing Company.

[20] G. J. Holzmann. The Spin model checker. *IEEE TSE*, 23(5):279–295, May 1997.

[21] C. Kloukinas and M. Ozkaya. XCD - Modular, realizable software architectures. In C. S. Pasareanu and G. Salaün, editors, *FACS*, volume 7684 of *LNCS*, pages 152–169. Springer, 2012.

[22] K.-K. Lau, P. V. Elizondo, and Z. Wang. Exogenous connectors for software components. In G. T. Heineman, I. Crnkovic, H. W. Schmidt, J. A. Stafford, C. A. Szyperski, and K. C. Wallnau, editors, *CBSE*, volume 3489 of *LNCS*, pages 90–106. Springer, 2005.

[23] G. Lekeas, C. Kloukinas, and K. Stathis. Producing enactable protocols in artificial agent societies. In D. Kinny, J. Y. jen Hsu, G. Governatori, and A. K. Ghose, editors, *PRIMA*, volume 7047 of *LNCS*, pages 311–322. Springer, 2011.

[24] D. C. Luckham, J. Kenney, L. Augustin, J. Verra, D. Bryan, and W. Mann. Specification and Analysis of System Architecture Using Rapide. *IEEE TSE*, 21(4):336–355, Apr. 1995.

[25] J. Magee and J. Kramer. *Concurrency – state models and Java programs*. Wiley, 2 edition, 2006.

[26] I. Malavolta, P. Lago, H. Muccini, P. Pelliccione, and A. Tang. What industry needs from architectural languages: A survey. *IEEE TSE*, 39(6):869–891, 2013.

[27] S. Maoz, J. O. Ringert, and B. Rumpe. Synthesis of component and connector models from crosscutting structural views. In B. Meyer, L. Baresi, and M. Mezini, editors, *ESEC/SIGSOFT FSE*, pages 444–454. ACM, 2013.

[28] B. Meyer. Applying "Design by Contract". *IEEE Computer*, 25(10):40–51, 1992.

[29] G. Naumovich, G. S. Avrunin, L. A. Clarke, and L. J. Osterweil. Applying static analysis to software architectures. In M. Jazayeri and H. Schauer, editors, *ESEC / SIGSOFT FSE*, volume 1301 of *LNCS*, pages 77–93. Springer, 1997.

[30] OMG. Common object request broker architecture (CORBA) specification, version 3.3 – Part 3: CORBA component model. Specification formal/2012-11-16, OMG, Nov. 2012. `omg.org/spec/CORBA/3.3/`.

[31] OSGi Alliance. OSGi core release 5. Specification, Mar. 2012. `osgi.org`.

[32] M. Ozkaya and C. Kloukinas. Highly analysable, reusable, and realisable architectural designs with XCD. In T.-h. Kim, C. Ramos, H.-k. Kim, A. Kiumi, S. Mohammed, and D. Slezak, editors, *Computer Applications for Software Engineering, Disaster Recovery, and Business Continuity*, volume 340 of *CCIS*, pages 72–79. Springer Berlin Heidelberg, 2012.

[33] M. Ozkaya and C. Kloukinas. Are we there yet? Analyzing architecture description languages for formal analysis, usability, and realizability. In O. Demirors and O. Turetken, editors, *SEAA*, pages 177–184, Santander, Spain, Sept. 2013. IEEE.

[34] M. Ozkaya and C. Kloukinas. Towards a design-by-contract based approach for realizable connector-centric software architectures. In J. Cordeiro, D. A. Marca, and M. van Sinderen, editors, *ICSOFT*, pages 555–562. SciTePress, 2013.

[35] M. Ozkaya and C. Kloukinas. Towards design-by-contract based software architecture design. In *SoMeT*, pages 157–164. IEEE, 2013.

[36] D. E. Perry and A. L. Wolf. Foundations for the study of software architecture. *SIGSOFT Softw. Eng. Notes*, 17(4):40–52, Oct. 1992.

[37] E. Rodríguez, M. B. Dwyer, C. Flanagan, J. Hatcliff, G. T. Leavens, and Robby. Extending JML for modular specification and verification of multi-threaded programs. In A. P. Black, editor, *ECOOP*, volume 3586 of *LNCS*, pages 551–576. Springer, 2005.

[38] H. W. Schmidt, I. Poernomo, and R. H. Reussner. Trust-by-contract: Modelling, analysing and predicting behaviour in software architectures. *Journal of Integrated Design and Process Science*, 5(3):25–51, September 2001.

[39] R. N. Taylor, N. Medvidovic, and E. M. Dashofy. *Software Architecture: Foundations, Theory, and Practice*. Wiley, 2010.

[40] XCD. Website, 2013. Maintained by Mert Ozkaya. URL: www.staff.city.ac.uk/c.kloukinas/Xcd/.

[41] S. Tripakis. Undecidable problems of decentralized observation and control on regular languages. *Inf. Process. Lett.*, 90(1):21–28, 2004.

[42] N. Ubayashi, J. Nomura, and T. Tamai. Archface: A contract place where architectural design and code meet together. In J. Kramer, J. Bishop, P. T. Devanbu, and S. Uchitel, editors, *ICSE*, pages 75–84. ACM, 2010.

[43] S. Uchitel, J. Kramer, and J. Magee. Incremental elaboration of scenario-based specifications and behavior models using implied scenarios. *ACM TOSEM*, 13(1):37–85, 2004.

A Specification Schema for Software Connectors

Thomas Slotos
Leuphana University of Lueneburg
Scharnhorststr. 1
21335 Lüneburg, Germany
++49 4131 677 2196
slotos@leuphana.de

ABSTRACT

Since the invention of the connectors that serve as one of the building blocks of software architecture, various researchers have described the characteristics of connectors that they have discovered in given software systems. These characteristics have frequently been revealed by employing a bottom-up approach to different disciplines of software engineering. As a consequence, numerous attributes of connectors have been introduced at a rather technical level, and the vocabulary regarding specific aspects of connectors is highly heterogeneous. This eclectic list of attributes is not an appropriate abstraction level for an architect when developing connectors for application software. Instead, it would be more helpful to have a framework that begins from a conceptual perspective and guides the software architect in identifying the attributes required for a specific connector. To this end, a hierarchical schema for specifying software connectors is proposed in this paper. In contrast to existing schemas in which either the attributes considered are few in number and ungrouped or the attribute specification and grouping was not the main focus of the research, this paper presents a homogenous specification schema at different levels of abstraction and is based on logical perspectives rather than technical features. The schema can support architects in various situations—such as connector selection and documentation—and can aid in implementing or generating concrete software connectors. The application of the schema will be demonstrated by specifying a software connector between Twitter and an application.

Categories and Subject Descriptors

D.2.11 [**Software Architectures**]

Keywords

Connector; specification; software architecture.

1. INTRODUCTION

After realising that software products were becoming increasingly complex, there was a need to address this phenomenon. One common approach is to investigate systems and extract commonalities found in different types of software. These structural commonalities are called "architectural styles or patterns" and are based on components and connectors. As one of the results of defining architectural styles, connectors were introduced as "first class citizens" by Shaw [33]. There are diverse definitions of software connectors that describe their different features [34][2]. One of the most succinct among these is that "Connectors are functional bindings between components enabling their controlled interoperability" [26]. Since the introduction of connectors to software architecture, several research questions regarding their description, categorisation and development have arisen. As a basis for answering these questions, studies from different areas of software engineering have explored existing systems that employ these considerations. In the absence of a general concept, a common approach has been to characterise the qualities of software connectors primarily at a technical level. Insights from given technical instances of connectors are abstracted to a technology-independent level using a "bottom-up" approach. Step by step, characteristic properties of connectors have thus been revealed. However, these properties are distributed over numerous research papers in diverse scientific fields and at a variety of levels of software engineering. A heterogeneous vocabulary has thus emerged; as a consequence, efforts have been made to collect and group these properties in schemas that are based primarily on the technical origins of connectors found in existing systems [34][13]. For an architect who must map architectural constraints in the form of high-level requirements for concrete connector attributes, there is a mismatch of different abstraction levels. To overcome this mismatch, I argue that a specification schema is required that integrates these opposing views into a unified form.

The need for such a view has also been noted by Hirsch et al.: "If connectors could be characterised by means of high level properties, descriptions would be much more declarative and adequate for architectural analysis" [13]. The need to distinguish "what" should be generally supported by a connector from "how" these described attributes should be accomplished with a certain implementation at a (technically) lower level stands behind the idea of a high-level specification schema for software connectors. Hirsch et al. [13] state that "... working with high level properties can deliver architectural mechanisms that are not bound by language features". This concept of different types of views is not new to software architecture [27]. For example, Hofmeister et al. distinguish among four different views: conceptual, module, code and execution [14].

In this paper, a high-level view of connector attributes is presented that can be assigned to the conceptual view of software architecture. The schema collects characteristic attributes of software connectors from various research areas and groups these attributes into categories at different levels of abstraction, forming a unifying specification structure that considers not only research papers from the component-and-connector approach but also results from such areas as distributed systems [37], middleware [17], architecture description languages [28] and enterprise application integration [15].

CBSE'14, June 30–July 4, 2014, Marcq-en-Baroeul, France.

http://dx.doi.org/10.1145/2602458.2602464

The remainder of the paper is organised as follows. Section 2 consists of a brief review of the literature. Section 3 addresses the unified specification schema for software connectors. Section 4 describes how the specification schema can aid a software architect and the purposes for which it can be used, which thereby illustrate the benefits of such a schema. In Section 5, the specification schema is applied to a concrete example to illustrate its use in practice. Section 6 concludes.

2. RELATED WORK

Since the introduction of the concept of a "software connector", researchers have worked on describing the characteristics of connectors by establishing different types of specification dimensions and attributes. The study from Shaw and Clements [34] was one of the first to introduce the dimensions of data and control flow. In their research, they examined the characteristics of connectors and stated that "The major axes of classification are the control and data interactions among components". Certain other attributes of data and control flow were also mentioned, but the main focus of their study was to establish a *"uniform descriptive standard* for architectural styles".

One of the next important contributions was the idea to formulate a "canonical set of primitives [that] would provide a framework for comparing, refining and reusing connectors" [13]. The first step towards such an organisation of attributes was a tabular schema presented by Hirsch et al. [13] that included a list of connector properties that are applied to differentiate connector types. Because connector classification was the focus, the schema lacks any grouping of attributes at different levels of abstraction and the collection of attributes is rudimentary. A similarly organised specification schema is presented in [10].

The most important improvement towards a unifying specification schema was achieved by Mehta et al. [29], whose main contribution was to distinguish four general services (communication, conversion, coordination and facilitation service) and to differentiate among eight connector types for interaction (procedure call, event, data access, linkage, stream, arbitrator, adaptor and distributor). Characterisation criteria at different levels are used to define specific connector types. Because Metha et al. aimed to provide a taxonomy for connectors, the classification begins with connector types at the root and results in connector properties that are assigned more than once to a connector type. Their intentional decision for that type of entry point into the specification structure leads to a classification that "does not result in a strict hierarchy, but rather in a directed acyclic graph (DAG)" [29]. The specification schema presented in this paper is a strict hierarchy that is completely independent of any technically motivated entry point at the beginning; this decision was taken because of a broader view about connectors that incorporates more than the interaction mechanisms of connector types that were the formative force for Mehta et al. To achieve such a broader view, it is necessary to address connectors at the conceptual level and to be guided by general principles that are not technically driven. In contrast to Mehta et al., the approach to specifying software connectors in the present paper has narrowed its focus to the design phase of software development. The subsequent phases of coding, compilation, linkage, deployment and runtime—in which connectors are also relevant—are not covered because the schema is designed for software architects and not for application programmers differentiating "what" should be specified from "how" these attributes could be realised.

The two approaches do not conflict but complement one another. In principle, combining the two schemas is possible over the described dimensions with respect to the attributes they have in common.

3. THE SPECIFICATION SCHEMA

There are different types of structuring possibilities for specifying software connectors depending on the task and background of the creator. Assuming that such a specification schema is used by architects who must map the non-functional requirements of a future system to the concrete attributes of connectors within that system, beginning from a conceptual level would minimise the complexity of the specification process. Therefore, in this paper, an elaborated specification schema is presented that describes software connectors from both an external view and an internal view.

From an outside perspective on the connector, the internals within the connector are hidden, and only essential attributes that are required by the components that the connector interconnects with are to be considered. This type of perspective will be called the "external view" (Figure 1). For example, two distributed components in a software system lead to the construction of a connector that supports remote communication. Or, a uni-directional connector between two components is only necessary if one component is dependent on the functions of the other component, but not the reverse. After describing the attributes that are enforced by the components, the inner properties of the connector that are mostly independent of the components should be specified in the "internal view" (Figure 2). The inner set-up of a connector is based on decisions that relate to the tasks of the connector (e.g., transformation and filtering) or control flow considerations (e.g., pull vs. push mechanism).

Both the external and the internal views are successively refined such that similar attributes are grouped together at different levels, which are called "dimensions" and "criteria". At the end of this specification hierarchy, "attributes" or "sub-attributes" terminate the description structure. For each attribute, concrete values are given from which an architect can choose characteristics for a connector type or instance. These values are suggestions that are extracted from various research papers and integrated in the schema. The proposed values neither form a complete set nor constitute the only possibilities for specifying software connectors. Other specification forms, such as diagrams, can also support the description of connector aspects (e.g., the composition of a connector might be described by a class diagram).

3.1 External View – dimensions, attributes and values

To describe a connector from the external view, several criteria for the dimensions *space* and *time* should be specified.

3.1.1 Space dimension

The *space* dimension consists of the criteria *location*, *cardinality* and *directionality*.

A connector can be either *local* or *remote*, depending on the location of the connecting components [15].

One of the basic tasks of a connector is coordination among components. How many components are the subject of coordination is indicated by the cardinality at each end of the connector. Only three types (1:1, 1:N and M:N) of quantifying relations between components are necessary to characterise a connector. In software architecture, a 1:1-relationship is known as

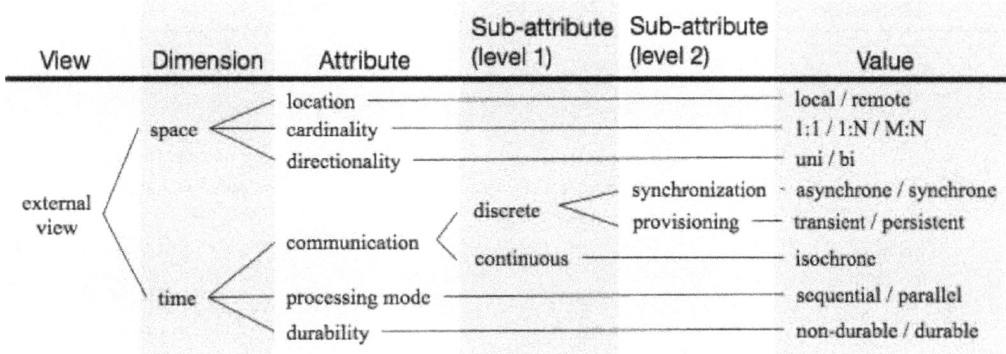

Figure 1. External view

a unicast connection and a 1:M-relation as a multicast or broadcast communication [34], [5].

The directionality of a connector indicates whether components at both ends are invoked (*bi-directional*) or if it is only necessary to call the functions of a component at one end of the connector (*uni-directional)* [34], [24].

3.1.2 Time dimension

An external perspective on the *time* dimension of the connector includes criteria such as *communication*, *processing mode* and *durability*.

Selecting one of the values of the communication criterion for a connector determines how data will be transferred with regard to time considerations. In general, it is possible to differentiate between a *time independent* (*discrete*) and a *time dependent* (*continuous*) mode of data transmission. Using time independent communication indicates that there are no constraints from the receiver regarding the transmission time for data. For time dependent communication, the target component has a communication constraint on the connector to deliver the data continuously (e.g., a video data stream) [37]. The continuous transmission of data is specified by the *isochronous* value.

Discrete communication can be further subdivided into the two attributes *synchronisation* and *provisioning*. Synchronisation is coordinating data between a sending and a receiving component by a connector. The strength of the coupling (loose or strong) between components after one component has initiated a call to the other component via a connector determines whether there is a *synchronous* or an *asynchronous* invocation [15]. A call is considered synchronous if it blocks the caller until the caller receives a response. By contrast, if the caller is not blocked after sending data to the target component, there is an asynchronous communication between the sending and receiving components. A synchronous call can be understood as a strong coupling between the sending and receiving component because the execution of the sender is blocked until the response is delivered. Using asynchronous communication allows the sending component to execute further statements (non-blocking behaviour) and to receive the response to the call later in time.

A determination of the *provisioning* of the data in the connector is required when the data cannot be delivered immediately because the receiving component is not accessible. In using *persistent communication,* the connector stores the data as long as necessary to deliver it to the target component. By contrast, *transient* communication is applied when the connector discards the data because the receiving components are not online [37].

Connecting at least two components is one of the main tasks of a connector. In specifying the durability of a connector, the software architect selects either *connectionless* (non-durable) or a *connection-oriented* (durable) communication between components [13].

Depending on the sending or receiving time constraints of the components, the architect must design a connector that uses either *sequential* or *parallel* communication paths [34]. In sequential communication, the data are transported one after another. Using parallel communication for data transportation instead is faster because several pathways for data delivery are available.

3.2 Internal view – dimensions, criteria, attributes and values

Mehta et al. indicate that a "connector can also have an internal architecture ...." [29]. The internal view of a connector can be differentiated according to the dimensions *structure*, *behaviour* and *information*. Clements et al. [9] offer the following definition: "A software architecture for a system is the structure or structures of the system, which comprise elements, their externally visible behaviour, and the relationships among them." Because software systems manipulate and transport information within the system and to neighbouring systems, the third important dimension of a connector is information.

3.2.1 Structure dimension

Two criteria comprise the *structure* dimension: *horizontal* and *vertical*. The horizontal perspective describes the component set-up that sketches how many inner functional units there are and how they are arranged "At the architecture level ... capturing connectors as a composition of connector elements, which can be primitive or composed" [7] A connector is called *atomic* if it consists of a single building block that is sufficient to satisfy the constraints on the connector. For example, Shaw and Clements [34] indicate that procedure calls might be understood as a type of undividable connector. More common are *composed* connectors, which are made up of several chained functional units that represent the connector architecture [36], [25], [23].

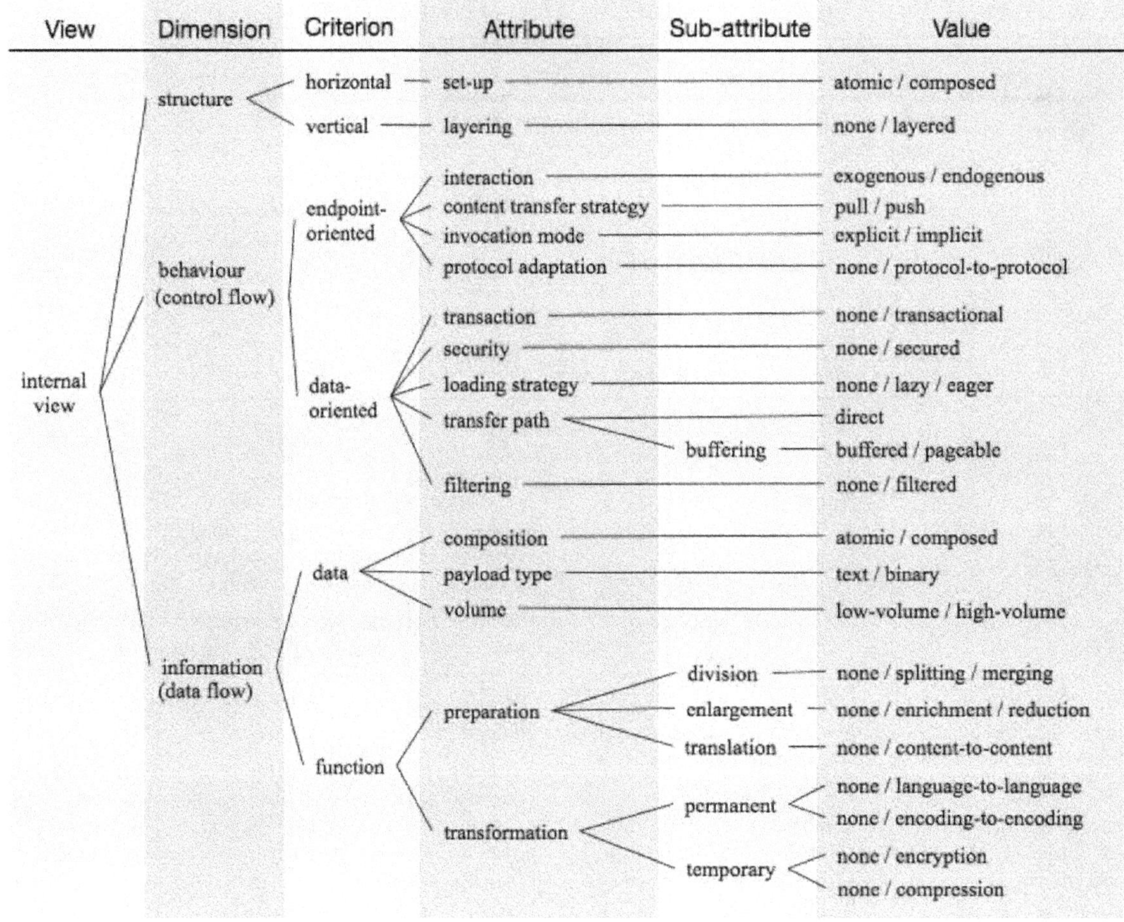

Figure 2. Internal view

The vertical perspective on the structure of a connector describes how the functionality inside the connector is based on other services that are provided by lower layers. As with the ISO/OSI [39] model for specifying interconnection among physical/logical computation units depicted in a layered design, the architecture of a software connector can also be based on layers of different abstractions. Instead of implementing required functionality (e.g., protocol adaptation) on its own, a software connector can utilise a service provided by the platform. Middleware as a common interconnection platform facilitates several general services, which can be included in the connector design leading to a layered connector architecture [17]. If *layered* is selected, a more detailed description of the underlying services within a specification is often necessary.

3.2.2 *Behaviour dimension*

In the *behaviour* dimension of the internal view of a connector, the order of the data transmission, often called *control flow*, is considered. It is important to note that data, which are transferred according to a control flow definition, are not changed by the connector [34], [29].

To specify the control flow of a connector, several attributes are necessary to guarantee the correct ordering of the data. To group these attributes, two criteria are established for the schema, called *endpoint-oriented* and *data-oriented* behaviour. Whereas the endpoint-oriented criterion represents attributes for handling the connection to the components, the data-oriented criterion includes attributes that add functionality while data are transferred through the connector. *Interaction*, *content transfer strategy*, *invocation mode* and *protocol adaptation* are the attributes that belong to the *endpoint-oriented* criterion. The *data-oriented* criterion encompasses the *transaction, security, loading strategy, buffering, paging* and *filtering* attributes.

Next, the attributes of the endpoint-oriented criterion are described. For interaction requirements, the software architect chooses between an "*exogenous*" and an "*endogenous*" connector (see [22]). An exogenous connector controls the coordination between components, whereas this task is assigned to the interconnecting components with an endogenous connector.

The content transfer strategy of a connector indicates how data are received from or sent to a component and can be chosen from two different strategies. In using the *pull* strategy, the connector fetches data from the component, which indicates that the connector determines the point in time when data are required. A connector uses the other mechanism (*push*) when it initiates data delivery to a component [7].

The manner in which a source component delivers data is determined by the invocation mode. A connector uses an *implicit* or event-based mechanism if the target components are anonymous for the source component. By contrast, *explicit* method-invocation is used when the concrete type of the target components must be known by the source component [12].

Sometimes a connector must support different protocols at its endpoints, such as when the connecting components provide different protocols, which is known in the connector community by the term "*protocol adaptation*" (see [2]).

Next, the data-oriented criterion and its attributes are considered. The attributes of this criterion regulate which data are transferred through the connector and how rapidly, securely and consistently this transfer is. These attributes can be added between the endpoint-oriented attributes. This added functionality is called the "aspect" or "crosscutting concerns" in aspect-oriented programming (AOP) [19], and Batista et al. call a connector that uses aspects "aspectual" [3]. These authors state that "the presence of crosscutting concerns in an architecture design leads to new aspectual connectors, but interfaces and components remain the same" [4].

One of the crosscutting concerns regarding data is the notion of *transaction*. Adding a transaction to the connector leads to the opening of a transaction after data enter the connector and the completion of the transaction after the data is delivered to the target component [7]. If *transactional* is defined, then more refined transactional properties (e.g., whether the same transaction or a new transaction is used) can be described in the extended specification for that attribute.

Similarly, a *secured* connector can be achieved by adding a *security* mechanism such as authentication to the transmission functionality of the connector [32].

During the flow of data through the connector, *filtering* operations for the data can be applied. Whether and what type of filtering is enabled should be part of the functional specification of the connector.

The next three attributes address how data are provisioned within the connector. Provisioning is required because of the different memory sizes and processing speeds of the interconnecting components. If a *loading strategy* inside a connector is applied, it can be differentiated between *eager* and *lazy* loading. Eager loading is used if data dependent on the requested data are loaded simultaneously. Lazy loading is enabled when the dependent data are loaded by a later request [20], [21]. When data can be transferred depends on the availability of the components and its processing speed. If the initiating component delivers the data faster than it can be received from the target components, some type of *buffering* is required [15], [25]. If both components are available and have established a synchronised processing speed, *direct* data transport occurs. A specialised strategy for data buffering is *paging*. The paging attribute indicates that a subset of a result set will be organised in blocks and held by the connector [6]. When the requesting component requires the next block of data (page), the paging mechanism determines the appropriate range of data within the subset, which is then delivered by the connector. This type of provisioning facility is often called pre-fetching [8].

3.2.3 Information dimension

The *information* dimension of the connector describes the attributes for the data that must be transferred to and from a component and the functions that will be executed on the data while they are transported through the connector. These attributes are often called *data flow* [34], [29].

The *composition, payload type* and *volume* attributes are relevant for the "*data*" criterion.

How the data are structured is defined by the *composition* attribute, which is represented by the two values, "*atomic*" and "*composed*" [15]. Data consisting of many parts are considered "composed", whereas logically undividable data are "atomic".

There are two alternatives for data representation for a payload type: *textual* and *binary*. In a textual representation, the content is readable by humans as well as by machines. Binary representation is used for data when the content must be in a format on which machines can operate (e.g., transferring objects).

The volume attribute indicates how much information is conducted through the connector. There are two possible extremes for this attribute: *low-volume* and *high-volume* [34]. These values represent a rather general description, and leave specifying the concrete amount of the data volume to the architect.

The specification of the *function* criterion describes what type of processes operates on the transferring data. *Preparation* and *representation transformation* are the attributes that should be considered. In contrast to the data-oriented criterion in the behaviour (control flow) dimension, whose attributes do not change the data while they are transferred through the connector, the functions of the information (data flow) dimension manipulate data while transmitting them from component to component.

If the preparation of data is active, then the attribute values "*splitting*" or "*merging*", "*enrichment*" or "*reduction*" and "*content-to-content translation*" must be considered at minimum as modifying functions on the data [36], [15]. Splitting occurs when the original data are divided into smaller parts due to the properties of the content or meta information. The opposite operation occurs when two or more data parts are merged according to a criterion. Data that are transferred through the connector can be enriched by additional attributes (e.g., time stamps and state information) or reduced by applying predefined rules to decrease the number of attributes of the original data. Another operation that changes the data during transportation is content translation. Spitznagel states: "When two components agree on the semantics of a communication protocol but disagree on details such as the format or unit of the data to be communicated, a data translation may be used to resolve the mismatch" [36].

For the representation transformation of data, the two disjoint facets *permanent* and *temporary transformation* are relevant.

A *language-to-language* translation takes place when data that are described in one language must be transformed into another language without altering content. If the character set in which the data are encoded is changed while it is transferred through the connector, an *encoding-to-encoding* translation occurs. Both are permanent transformations because the change in data representation extends beyond the transportation of data through the connector.

If the data rather than the connector are secured, an *encryption* of the content is required. After entering the connector, the data are translated into a secured intermediate format and will be decrypted before reaching the target endpoint [24]. An identical temporary transformation occurs when the data are *compressed* at one endpoint of the connector and will be uncompressed before leaving at the other endpoint [11], [25], [2].

4. BENEFITS OF THE SPECIFICATION SCHEMA

Using the specification schema for software connectors is helpful for several purposes that range from evaluation of modelling to documentation. In particular, the schema offers advantages in performing the following tasks:

- comparing connectors (evaluation)
- choosing connectors (selection)

- designing connectors (modelling)
- describing connectors (documentation)
- creating connectors (synthesising)
- establishing connectors (generative)

For a set of given connectors, it is frequently difficult to decide which connector best fulfils the requirements and is most appropriate for a particular envisioned architecture. Thus, the specification schema helps compare connectors according to their attributes and leads to the selection of the connector that fits best.

The specification schema is reasonable not only when connectors exist but also under circumstances when connectors have yet to be developed. At least four situations can be addressed and supported by the schema. First, for an architect, the descriptive structure of the schema can act as a checklist to reconcile system requirements with connector attributes at different levels. The different views and levels of the specification schema ensure that the relevant connector properties are not omitted. Second, the specification schema supports the documentation of connector attributes after design decisions have been made. The specification schema forms a standardised documentation template for fixing connector features during or after design and development and presents a clear and unified structure for discovering the characteristics of existing connectors in the case of connector adaptation. Third, by combining reasonable attributes of different dimensions, new connector types can be synthesised that represent previously unknown connector aspects [29]. Fourth, because the specification schema describes "what" are the attributes of a connector and not "how" a connector is implemented in a certain technology, this high-level description can act as the starting point for a generative approach. The schema can be related to model-driven architecture [31] such that it represents a platform-independent model (PIM) for connector generation. Based on this PIM, a translator for a targeting technology can be described that generates concrete connectors for a specific runtime platform, thus realising a platform-specific model.

5. EXAMPLE SPECIFICATION OF A CONNECTOR

To illustrate the use and feasibility of the proposed specification schema, the schema will be applied to the design of a connector between Twitter and a fictitious application.

Today, micro-blogs of companies and private users are a widely used type of service to stay informed of events in both business and private areas. One big player in the micro-blogging domain is Twitter [38], known for its simple use of spreading short text information (aka tweets) to interested users, called followers. To provide its services, Twitter offers an application programming interface (API) that covers four main use cases [16]. First, a user can send a tweet to its micro-blog to update its current status. Second, interested followers who have subscribed to the blog can retrieve tweets when they are online. Third, users can search for tweets using predefined topics called hashtags. Fourth, before using these services, the user must authenticate itself.

A software connector that coordinates and communicates between the Twitter API and an application must integrate these four services. A design that incorporates all four use cases can either interconnect the application and Twitter by establishing a separate connector for each service or by integrating them into a complex connector. For the following discussion, a complex connector is assumed that is separately developed for an individual application and is not provided by Twitter as a standard connector but can be instantiated for various applications.

Figure 3 depicts the design of this connector and shows the services that the connector mediates between Twitter and the application and the internal structuring of this connector.

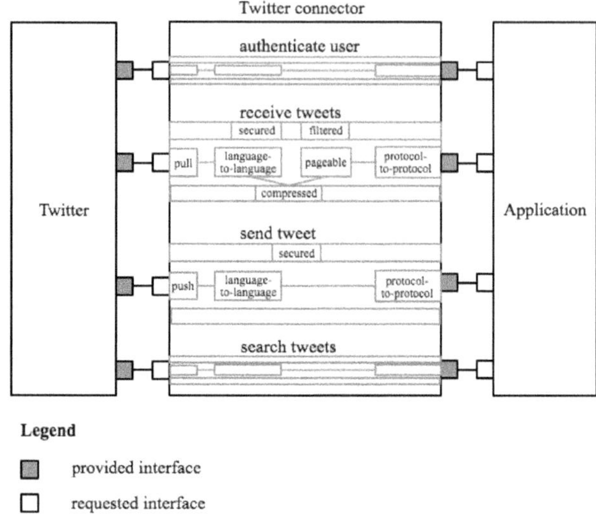

Figure 3. Architecture of Twitter connector

For reasons of clarity, only the attributes of the specification schema and their selected values are listed in Tables 1 and 2, and a detailed discussion of other aspects of the schema is left to the subsequent textual description. For the same reason, only the use cases "send tweet" and "receive tweets" are selected to apply the specification schema to the Twitter connector.

5.1 External view

From the outside, the attributes of the connector that are required by the interconnecting components are in view. The space and time considerations of the connector must be considered to fulfil the given requirements. The space dimension of the external view can be described by the attributes location, cardinality and directionality. Because Twitter and the fictitious application are distributed in different runtime environments, a remote connector is required. Because the connector is separately designed for an interconnection between an individual application and Twitter, a one-to-one relationship between them can be assumed. This connection thus forms a uni-directional communication that is initiated by the application.

How the communication takes place, what type of processing mode is required and how durable the connection should be are discussed in the time dimension of the external view. Different communication types are required for selected use cases. To add a tweet to the micro-blog, a discrete message of limited length is asynchronously sent to Twitter, whereas to retrieve tweets, a continuous connection in which several tweets are sent by Twitter to the application must be opened. For the user of the application, it is faster if messages can be sent while new tweets are retrieved at the same time (parallel processing). Maintaining a durable connection between Twitter and the application enables the user to use the services provided one after another without creating a connection every time a service is invoked.

Table 1. External view of Twitter connector

Attribute	Value	
	Send tweet	Receive tweets
location	remote	remote
cardinality	1:1	1:1
directionality	uni	uni
communication	discrete (asynchronous)	continuous (isochronous)
processing mode	parallel	parallel
durability	durable	durable

5.2 Internal view

The attributes of the connector that are essentially independent of the components are the focus of the internal view. Because of the many attributes that can be assigned to internal connector properties, the internal view consists of more levels. To group the view at a high level, the dimensions of structure, behaviour (control flow) and information (data flow) have been introduced.

The structure dimension indicates how a connector is set up (horizontal criterion) and whether technically lower-level services are used (vertical criterion). The structural organisation of the Twitter connector is depicted in Figure 3. This complex connector consists of four simpler connectors, each mediating a service between Twitter and the application. These functional units are horizontally arranged between the endpoints of the connector. Instead of creating these interconnection services from scratch, platform services (e.g., the Spring framework and its social media subproject) at technically lower levels may reasonably be utilised.

The behaviour dimension describes how the control flow is managed between the components. The endpoint-oriented criterion groups attributes that can be assigned to both ends of the connector. Here, the interaction, content transfer strategy invocation mode and protocol adaptation are important to specify. Because there is no superordinate component that integrates Twitter and the application as a starting point for coordination in the exogenous connector, an endogenous connector is assumed to be invoked by the application. To add a message to the micro-blog at Twitter, a "push" content transfer strategy is used at the endpoint towards Twitter, initiating the transmission of a short message. The opposite is true when tweets from Twitter are received using a "pull" transfer strategy. It can be assumed that the Twitter API provides an explicit method invocation mode for sending tweets to Twitter, whereas spreading tweets to followers is reasonably accomplished by using an implicit mechanism such as event-delegation. Coordinating components is forced by protocol considerations. At the endpoint towards Twitter, the connector must use an advanced protocol over http (e.g., WebService), whereas the application expects to use a protocol incorporated in the programming language (e.g., Java). Therefore, the Twitter connector must manage protocol-to-protocol conversion for all four use cases. The data-oriented criterion focuses on the control flow within the connector that is neither influenced by the endpoint of the connector nor the information to be transmitted. Attributes such as transaction, security, loading strategy, the type of data transfer path and filtering are defined. There is no need for a transactional mechanism inside the connector because every action can be considered atomic in nature. Tweets, which go to and from Twitter, are generally for public use, but a secured connection from the application to Twitter is reasonable to guarantee privacy concerns. Different design decisions are necessary for sending and retrieving tweets, depending on their delivery. To send a tweet, no buffering is required, and an exception is raised if a message cannot be added. Paging is mandatory for fetching tweets from Twitter. The number of tweets assigned to a hashtag and later retrieved from Twitter can be enormous and can only be reasonably handled by a paging mechanism, but no such mechanism is required when sending messages to Twitter. Adding a message to the micro-blog at Twitter via the connector normally requires no filter to check messages against predefined criteria. For retrieving tweets from Twitter, such a filtering mechanism sometimes makes sense if a follower has subscribed to a large number of micro-blogs, and a filter using certain keywords might eliminate uninteresting tweets.

The information dimension comprises the criteria "data" and "function" and answers the questions of how information is made up and what functions can be applied to information. To differentiate the data criterion, attributes such as composition, payload type and volume are important. Twitter allows the sending and retrieving not only of short text messages but also of photos. If both media types are included in a message, the tweet represents "complex" data that the connector transmits. In such a complex message, there are two different types of payload. The plain text of the message belongs to the "text" payload type category, whereas a photo represents "binary" data. It can be assumed that the data volume to be transferred to Twitter is at a lower level, whereas receiving tweets from Twitter is in the range of low to mid-volume. The type of functions that operate on the data interchanged by the connector is the focus of the function criterion and is detailed by the preparation and transformation attributes. Data can be manipulated by division, enlargement or translation, as indicated by the preparation attribute. The three sub-attributes of the preparation attribute are not applied to the Twitter connector because it is assumed that the application sends and receives messages without manipulation. No division of a tweet makes sense; no extra values have to be added to the tweet, and the same defined content format for text messages is processed in both applications. The last function to be considered is content transformation. The permanent sub-attribute indicates that the change in data representation lasts longer than the transportation of data through the connector. For the Twitter connector, it can be assumed that a tweet, represented in plain text like XML or JSON, must be transformed to a Java object for the fictitious application. However, no encoding is required because the content of the tweets can be supposed to be in a frequently used type of code (e.g., UTF-8). Temporary transformations are functions such as encryption and compression, which translate the data in an intermediate format while it is transported through the connector. The tweets need not be encrypted because the Twitter connector is secured. However, because tweets can contain not only plain text but also photos, they will be compressed inside the connector after they are received from Twitter and will be uncompressed before delivery to the application.

Table 2. Internal view of Twitter connector

Attribute	Value	
	Send tweet	Receive tweets
connector set-up	composed	composed
layering	layered	layered
interaction	endogenous	endogenous
content transfer strategy	push	pull
invocation mode	explicit	implicit
protocol adaptation	protocol-to-protocol	protocol-to-protocol
transaction	none	none
security	secured	secured
loading strategy	none	none
transfer path	direct	pageable
filtering	none	filtered
data composition	composed	composed
payload type	text and binary	text and binary
volume	low	low-mid
preparation	division (none) enlargement (none) translation (none)	division (none) enlargement (none) translation (none)
transformation	permanent (language-to-language, none) temporary (none, none)	permanent (language-to-language, none) temporary (compression, none)

6. CONCLUSION AND FUTURE WORK

This paper has presented a hierarchical specification schema for software connectors. The major difference between this schema and other proposals is that it differentiates between external and internal views of connectors and guides the architect so that the specification process of a connector begins at a conceptual level. The external view allows a rather coarse-grained description of a connector, focusing on attributes required by the interconnecting components. Detailed characterisations of attributes that are realised inside the connector are mostly independent of component constraints and are described by the internal view. Both views of the presented schema begin at a conceptual level and proceed through a stepwise refinement of characterising connector attributes that are described independently of technical considerations, until concrete attribute values are reached. The benefits resulting from the new specification schema have been identified and described. Finally, the schema was successfully applied to the design of a Twitter connector, which interconnects a fictitious application and Twitter.

The intended focus of the proposed specification schema is to describe connectors at the conceptual level, ignoring technical considerations. Nonetheless, within a software project, concrete connectors must be derived from architectural design to be realised in a given software environment. How the specification schema might be used in conjunction with a collection of existing connectors in a concrete software platform (e.g., the JEE platform specification) is a question for a future research paper.

7. ACKNOWLEDGMENTS

I would like to thank Stefan Kleine Stegemann for his scrutiny of the approach and for proposing Twitter as an example for applying the specification schema.

8. REFERENCES

[1] Amirat, A., & Oussalah, M. (2009). First-class connectors to support systematic construction of hierarchical software architecture. *Journal of Object Technology*, *8*(7), 107-130.

[2] Bálek, D., & Plasil, F. (2000). Software connectors: A hierarchical model. *Charles University, Prague, Tech. Report*, *2*

[3] Batista, T., Chavez, C., Garcia, A., Rashid, A., Sant'Anna, C., & Kulesza, U. (2006). Reflections on architectural connection: seven issues on aspects and ADLs. In *Proceedings of the 2006 international workshop on Early aspects at ICSE* (pp. 3-10). ACM.

[4] Batista, T., Chavez, C., Garcia, A., Kulesza, U., Sant'Anna, C., & Lucena, C. (2006). Aspectual connectors: supporting the seamless integration of aspects and ADLs. In *Proceedings of the ACM SIGSoft XX Brazilian Symposium on Software Engineering (SBES'06), Florianopolis, Brazil.*

[5] Bhattacharya, S., & Perry, D. E. (2007). Predicting Emergent Properties of Component Based Systems. In *Commercial-off-the-Shelf (COTS)-Based Software Systems, 2007. ICCBSS'07. Sixth International IEEE Conference on* (pp. 41-50). IEEE.

[6] Breslauer, D. (1996). *On competitive on-line paging with lookahead* (pp. 593-603). Springer Berlin Heidelberg.

[7] Bures, T., & Plasil, F. (2004). Communication style driven connector configurations. In *Software Engineering Research and Applications* (pp. 102-116). *Springer Berlin Heidelberg.*

[8] Byna, S., Chen, Y., & Sun, X. H. (2008). A taxonomy of data prefetching mechanisms. In *Parallel Architectures, Algorithms, and Networks, 2008. I-SPAN 2008. International Symposium on* (pp. 19-24). IEEE.

[9] Clements, P., Garlan, D., Bass, L., Stafford, J., Nord, R., Ivers, J., & Little, R. (2002). Documenting software architectures: views and beyond. *Pearson Education.*

[10] Fairbanks, G. (2010). Just enough Software Architecture – A Risk-Driven Approach. *Marshall & Brainerd*

[11] Garlan, D. (1998). Higher Order Connectors. *Workshop on Compositional Software Architecture, Monterey, CA*

[12] Garlan, D., and Shaw, M. (1994). An Introduction to Software Architecture. *Computer Science Department, Carnegie Mellon University. Paper 724.*

[13] Hirsch, D., Uchitel, S., & Yankelevich, D. (1999). Towards a periodic table of connectors. In *COORDINATION* (p. 418).

[14] Hofmeister, C.; North, R., Soni, D. (1999). Applied software architecture. *Addison-Wesley Professional.*

[15] Hohpe, G., & Woolf, B. A. (2004). Enterprise integration patterns: Designing, building, and deploying messaging solutions. *Addison-Wesley Professional.*

[16] Honey, C., & Herring, S. C. (2009, January). Beyond microblogging: Conversation and collaboration via Twitter. In *System Sciences, 2009. HICSS'09. 42nd Hawaii International Conference on* (pp. 1-10). IEEE.

[17] Issarny, V., Bennaceur, A., & Bromberg, Y. D. (2011). Middleware-layer connector synthesis: Beyond state of the art in middleware interoperability. In *Formal Methods for Eternal Networked Software Systems* (pp. 217-255). Springer Berlin Heidelberg.

[18] Kazman, R., Clements, P., Bass, L., & Abowd, G. (1997). Classifying architectural elements as a foundation for mechanism matching. In *Computer Software and Applications Conference, 1997. COMPSAC'97. Proceedings. The Twenty-First Annual International* (pp. 14-17). *IEEE.*

[19] Kiczales, G., Lamping, J., Mendhekar, A., Maeda, C., Lopes, C., Loingtier, J. M., & Irwin, J. (1997). *Aspect-oriented programming* (pp. 220-242). Springer Berlin Heidelberg.

[20] Kircher, M. (2001). Lazy Acquisition. In *EuroPLoP* (pp. 151-164).

[21] Kircher, M., & Jain, P. (2002). Eager Acquisition. In EuroPLoP (pp. 511-520).

[22] Lau, K. K., Elizondo, P. V., & Wang, Z. (2005). Exogenous connectors for software components. In *Component-Based Software Engineering* (pp. 90-106). *Springer Berlin Heidelberg.*

[23] Lau, K. K., Ling, L., Ukis, V., & Elizondo, P. V. (2007). Composite connectors for composing software components. In *Software Composition* (pp. 266-280). Springer Berlin Heidelberg.

[24] Lopes, A., Wermelinger, M., & Fiadeiro, J. L. (2001). A compositional approach to connector construction. In *Recent Trends in Algebraic Development Techniques* (pp. 201-220). Springer Berlin Heidelberg.

[25] Lopes, A., Wermelinger, M., & Fiadeiro, J. L. (2003). Higher-order architectural connectors. *ACM Transactions on Software Engineering and Methodology (TOSEM)*, *12*(1), 64-104.

[26] Marangozov, V., Bellissard, L., Vion-Dury, J. Y., & Riveill, M. (1997). Connectors: a Key Feature For Building Distributed Component-based Architectures. *interfaces*, *1*(r2), r2.

[27] May, N. (2005, March). A survey of software architecture viewpoint models. In *Proceedings of the Sixth Australasian Workshop on Software and System Architectures* (pp. 13-24).

[28] Medvidovic, N., & Taylor, R. N. (2000). A classification and comparison framework for software architecture description languages. *Software Engineering, IEEE Transactions on*, *26*(1), 70-93.

[29] Mehta, N. R., Medvidovic, N., & Phadke, S. (2000). Towards a taxonomy of software connectors. In *Proceedings of the 22nd international conference on Software engineering* (pp. 178-187). *ACM.*

[30] Mehta, N. R., & Medvidovic, N. (2003). Composing architectural styles from architectural primitives. In *ACM SIGSOFT Software Engineering Notes* (Vol. 28, No. 5, pp. 347-350). ACM.

[31] Mellor, S. J., Scott, K., Uhl, A., & Weise, D. (2002). Model-driven architecture. In *Advances in Object-Oriented Information Systems* (pp. 290-297). Springer Berlin Heidelberg.

[32] Ren, J; Taylor, R., Dourish, P., & Redmiles, D. (2005). Towards an architectural treatment of software security: a connector-centric approach. In *Proceedings of the 2005 workshop on Software engineering for secure systems—building trustworthy applications* (SESS '05). ACM, New York, NY, USA, 1-7. DOI=10.1145/1082983.1083203 http://doi.acm.org/10.1145/1082983.1083203

[33] Shaw, M. (1994). Procedure Calls Are the Assembly Language of Software Interconnection: Connectors Deserve First-Class Status. *Software Engineering Institute. Paper 234.*

[34] Shaw, M., & Clements, P. (1997). A field guide to boxology: Preliminary classification of architectural styles for software systems. In *Computer Software and Applications Conference, 1997. COMPSAC'97. Proceedings, The Twenty-First Annual International* (pp. 6-13). *IEEE.*

[35] Spitznagel, B., & Garlan, D. (2001). A compositional approach for constructing connectors. In *Software Architecture, 2001. Proceedings. Working IEEE/IFIP Conference on* (pp. 148-157). IEEE.

[36] Spitznagel, B. (2005). Compositional transformation of software connectors. PhD thesis, *Carnegie Mellon University School of Computer Science Technical Report CMU-CS-04-128*

[37] Tanenbaum, A. S., & Van Steen, M. (2006). Distributed systems, 2nd ed. *Prentice Hall*

[38] Zhao, D., & Rosson, M. B. (2009, May). How and why people Twitter: the role that micro-blogging plays in informal communication at work. In *Proceedings of the ACM 2009 international conference on Supporting group work* (pp. 243-252). ACM.

[39] Zimmermann, H. (1980). OSI reference model--The ISO model of architecture for open systems interconnection. *Communications, IEEE Transactions on*, *28*(4), 425-432.

Ensuring Application Integrity in Shared Sensing Environments

Pedro Javier del Cid
iMinds-DistriNet
Katholieke Universiteit Leuven
Leuven, Belgium

Danny Hughes,
Sam Michiels, Wouter Joosen
iMinds-DistriNet
Katholieke Universiteit Leuven
Leuven, Belgium

ABSTRACT

Smart Environments, such as smart offices, must support multiple applications that are deployed and managed by different parties. Smart Environments are 'always on' and application software must therefore be deployed, configured and reconfigured while the system is running. Re-configurable component models provide the basic mechanisms necessary to achieve runtime reconfiguration. However, in cases with shared component instances, ensuring application integrity during 3rd party reconfiguration leads to high developer effort and disruption. This paper addresses this problem through *Composition-Swapping*, an extension of re-configurable component models wherein state management delegation and extended component meta-data are used to support component-sharing and ensure application integrity. We demonstrate that Composition-Swapping reduces reconfiguration effort and disruption for four concurrently running applications on a real-world smart office environment.

Categories and Subject Descriptors

C.3 [**Special purpose and application based systems**]: Real time and embedded systems

Keywords

wireless sensor networks, software reconfiguration, sharing

1. INTRODUCTION

Smart environments embed intelligence and enable context-awareness using resource constrained Wireless Sensor and Actuator Networks (WSANs). As multi-purpose sensing infrastructures, emerging smart environments will host a range of applications that may be managed, deployed and used by different parties [15]. As it is critical to reduce deployment and administrative costs of sensing infrastructures [15, 24], smart environments should be designed to maximize the number of concurrent applications they can support. This makes effectively sharing WSAN resources between concurrent applications of paramount importance. Smart environments are 'always-on' and application software must therefore be deployed, configured and reconfigured while the system is running. To address the need for runtime reconfiguration of WSANs, several runtime re-configurable component models have been proposed, such as: RUNES [5], LooCI [11] and Lorien [21]. In addition, lightweight generic re-configurable component models such as OpenCOM [6], Fractal [4] and OSGi [19] have also been used in WSAN scenarios. These models offer the basic mechanisms to achieve runtime reconfiguration, but lack appropriate mechanisms to support shared sensing environments.

Our real-world shared sensing environment, a smart office WSAN, provides a shared and re-usable platform to sense environmental conditions and actuate appliances in our research facility. The core of the smart office is a network of AVR Raven sensor nodes [1], which offer an 8 bit 16MHz microcontroller and 16KB of RAM. To enable sharing in such a resource constrained environment, every processor cycle, byte of memory and radio transmission must be carefully considered. Four distinct sensing applications (elaborated further in Section 2.2) were incrementally deployed on the shared infrastructure. This was a process which led to disruptions and considerable overhead in reconfiguration effort.

One of the main challenges of shared sensing is to allow new applications to be deployed on the infrastructure without compromising existing applications [15, 24]. In our work we focus on the integrity of existing applications as a new application is added to a shared infrastructure. We have analyzed the adverse effects the reconfiguration of an application may have on co-executing applications. Where we quantified the disruption, reconfiguration effort and resource efficiency incurred in the process of ensuring application integrity. We define application integrity as the consistent functioning of an application. Consistent functioning requires that applications execute in accordance with their specification, without faults due to resource competition or disruptions due to software reconfiguration. During reconfiguration we assume no pre-deployment coordination, thus the deploying party has no a-priori knowledge about existing applications and needs to gather information about existing software compositions using reflective mechanisms.

Two primary classes of approaches have been proposed which are designed to allow for the safe co-execution of component based applications in pervasive environments. The first, focuses on offering virtually separated networks leveraging system Virtual Machine (VM) type of concurrency. As in SenShare [15], where they use the capabilities offered in the embedded Linux OS to provide the required isolation between applications. However, this requires of multiple orders of magnitude more resource than available in the nodes we target. The second, are those that leverage code-

CBSE'14, June 30–July 4, 2014, Marcq-en-Baroeul, France.
Copyright 2014 ACM 978-1-4503-2577-6/14/06 ...$15.00.
http://dx.doi.org/10.1145/2602458.2602474 .

recompilation based optimization techniques. As in [12], where at compilation time, application specifications are parsed to find conflicts. However, this entails a disruptive reconfiguration process that requires that all potential configuration conflicts be identified at development time. Furthermore, it requires considerably more resource than available in the nodes we target.

Based on our experiences with our smart office, we have distilled three key requirements for resource sharing in WSAN environments:

1. *Minimize disruption* caused during 3rd party reconfiguration while not restricting component interactions.
2. *Minimize reconfiguration overhead* in terms of developer effort (decisions required, commands issued).
3. *Minimize runtime resource consumption* due to concurrently executing applications (i.e. CPU, RAM, flash memory, # of nodes required) by effectively sharing resources between applications.

To address these requirements, we propose **Composition- Swapping**, wherein a running instance of a software component is shared and reconfigured at runtime to support multiple concurrent applications with different configuration requirements while ensuring application integrity. During Composition-Swapping, isolation between applications is achieved by executing one composition per time period. To support component-sharing and enable Composition-Swapping two key extensions are made to re-configurable component models. First, *state management delegation*, allows our software framework to isolate and manage component configuration and coordination on a per-application basis. Second, *we extended component meta-data*, to describe performance restrictions and application constraints. The former as component annotations and the latter as configuration meta-data. We demonstrate the benefits of Composition-Swapping in a real-world smart office infrastructure, where it (i) eliminates disruption during reconfiguration, (ii) reduces reconfiguration effort, and (iii) makes more efficient use of resources.

2. SHARING IN COMPONENT BASED APPLICATIONS

This section first provides basic insight into Component Based Development (CBD), followed by details on ensuring application integrity and then a summarized description of common reconfiguration challenges. Finally, it highlights the two main causes of this overhead and disruption. CBD is based on the concept of providing generic and reusable software building blocks, i.e. components[1], that can be composed together by third parties into software compositions in order to form distributed applications. The support offered by the component runtime is usually limited to the assembly, introspection (i.e. retrieve information) and reconfiguration of components. Component runtime refers to middleware implemented to provide an execution environment based on a model.

2.1 Ensuring Application integrity

In order to manually ensure the integrity of applications, the deploying party must check three primary issues:

1. There must be no conflicts, between the component configurations of the applications involved, that may lead to faults. Faults are generated when component output does not comply with the expected data accuracy and timeliness. Accuracy refers to the degree in which the reported data corresponds to the observed phenomena. Timeliness refers to the extent in which the age of the reported data is appropriate for the task at hand.
2. Given the combined resource demands and the performance restrictions of the execution environment, applications must execute in accordance with their constraints. Delay is an example of a performance restriction. Delay refers to the time required, by the different parts of the execution environment, to complete data acquisition or processing. The execution environment refers to the software components and hardware elements invoked during the execution of a software composition. Application constraints describe the different factors which may bound resource allocation and component configuration. For example, data accuracy and timeliness.
3. During the reconfiguration process, disruption must not occur. Disruption refers to application down time created by the interruption of its data-flow.

[1]Component refers to the reusable code base, while component instance refers to the runtime entity instantiated from the code base.

2.2 Reconfiguration challenges

The objective of this subsection is to highlight some reconfiguration challenges commonly encountered in shared WSANs. Challenges that often lead to increased effort, disruption and faults. Before we present theses challenges, we will briefly introduce the four applications deployed in our smart office. As they will aid in the exemplification of these challenges and will also provide the reader with insight into the applications that were used during the evaluation.

2.2.1 *Deployed applications*

The application deployed were: HVAC, workplace safety, comfort and security. We describe each in the following enumeration:

1. The HVAC application was designed to control ventilation and illumination appliances independently for each desk in our offices. Actuation is controlled based on personalized temperature (temp) and light thresholds. Sensing happens stochastically, i.e. unpredictably, only when the Radio Frequency IDentification (RFID) card of the corresponding employee is detected.
2. The safety application was designed to identify potential health risks based upon the filtered and correlated readings from temp, Carbon Monoxide (CO), methane (CH4) and humidity (RH) sensors (see Fig. 1A). Sensing in this application is periodic and happens every 7 minutes when a timer expires.
3. The comfort application was designed to determine office comfort levels based on averaged readings from temp, light, CO, CH4, RH and sound (dB) in each office. Application for which sensing should happen every 4 minutes.
4. Finally, the security application is designed to provide access control and motion detection, based on RFID and Passive InfraRed (PIR) motion detection. Application for which motion detection is only activated if no employees are in the office.

2.2.2 *Reconfiguration challenges*

During the deployment of a new application onto a shared WSAN, there are some challenges that are particularly notable. Primarily because of the effort, disruption or faults they commonly create. In the following enumeration we describe these challenges:

1. *Identifying potential configuration conflicts under the coexistence of periodic and stochastic interactions.* This co-existence

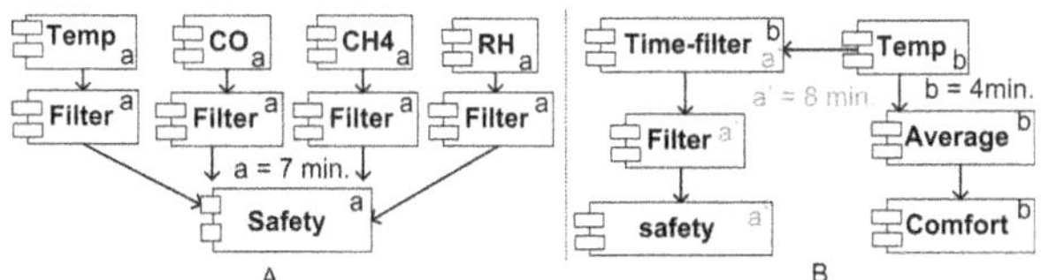

Figure 1: (A) Safety app. (B) Disruption caused during reconfiguration.

creates a degree of uncertainty in the verification of integrity. This is the case because the deploying party is not able to identify nor resolve potential resource contention, as it is unknown when and if concurrent invocation will happen. Thus leaving behind the potential for faults and disruption. For example: in the case of the temperature sensing components for the HVAC and safety applications.

2. *Modifying any running component instance.* Modification made to instances being used, affects all compositions connected to them. An action that potentially leads to disruption and faults. More so if the strategy of filter insertion is used to reconcile different configuration requirements. For example: in the case of our safety and comfort applications, which share temp, CO, CH4 and RH sensors. Reconciliation is needed because one app. requires 4 min. sampling intervals and the other 7 min.. Thus, filter insertion is used to down sample readings and allow components to be shared between applications (see Fig. 1B). Disruption is unavoidably caused during the insertion of filters into the composition and the loss of sensing precision is caused to the safety application as the new sampling interval is 8 min..
3. *Establishing if the planned modifications will adversely affect the integrity of existing applications.* There is usually no explicit and machine parse-able information pertaining to each application's constraints. Therefore, detailed software specifications and in some cases even inter-party coordination is needed to realize this task.
4. *Establishing if the WSAN will support the combined resource demand.* There is usually no explicit and machine parse-able information pertaining to the performance of both: the applications involved, and of the execution environment. Therefore, detailed hardware specification and in some cases even the component's source code is needed to complete this task.

2.3 Causes for the reconfiguration overhead

We have described the need to manually ensure application integrity in order to be able to deploy new applications on a shared WSAN without compromising existing ones. We have also provided a summarized description of challenges that commonly arise during reconfiguration; challenges which often lead to additional reconfiguration overhead, disruption and faults. To conclude we enumerate the two primary causes of the reconfiguration effort, faults and disruption illustrated:

1. Due to a lack of per-application isolation of component configuration and coordination information, any change in configuration or coordination on a shared component instance affects all compositions using that instance. It is thus necessary to *manually* ensure application integrity.
2. Due to a lack of application constraint and performance meta-data, additional documentation (e.g. hardware and software specifications) and in some cases, inter-party coordination is needed in order to ensure integrity.

3. RELATED WORK

This section first provides an overview of alternatives for sharing a WSAN. Second, reviews component models applicable in WSANs, and finally, discusses ensuring application integrity for component based systems.

3.1 Sharing a WSAN

Research approaches that allow the sharing of sensing infrastructures can be broadly classified by the sharing strategy they utilize. These are: network partitioning, virtual WSANs, data-centric and node-level. In network partitioning, a part of the network is assigned to each application, e.g. TinyCubus [17]. Virtual WSANs offer virtually separated networks on top of shared nodes (using system VM type support for concurrency), e.g. SenShare [15]. Data-centric approaches present the WSAN as a database, e.g. TinydB [16]. Node-based approaches leverage node-level concurrency models, as those offered by threading libraries or process VMs, e.g. [2, 12, 13]. These broad categories vary primarily in the resource efficiency and isolation they provide. Network partitioning requires node redundancy therefore it is not adequate for smart environments. Virtual WSANs offer a high degree of isolation and allow node sharing but the per node resources required are considerably above those offered by embedded nodes (e..g [15] requires Linux based nodes with 32MB RAM whereas embedded nodes commonly have at most 16KB). Data-centric approaches implicitly support multi-application scenarios, but they do not support the dynamics of smart environments [15, 24].

Node-level approaches can be further classified into coarse-grained and component based (CBD) approaches. Coarse-grained approaches as Umade [2] support multiple applications by implementing each application separately as a dedicated coarse grained module. This leads to a high degree of redundant functionality, which is resource inefficient (e.g. [2] with 7 KB of RAM runs on average only 2 apps. per node). Furthermore, they do not ensure application integrity. Approaches based on CBD, as GatorTech [10], due to componentization, offer the possibility of a higher degree of reuse. However these offer very limited support for isolation, lack the meta-data required to ensure integrity and are resource inefficient (due to redundant component instances). Note: these are all limitations intrinsic to the underlying component model. In the pervasive space, stream processing frameworks [13] and code-based optimization [12], have leveraged component sharing to improve resource efficiency. However, they do not offer the required isolation or meta-data. Furthermore, they require over 10 times more resources than available in embedded nodes and only support periodic interactions.

3.2 Re-configurable component models applicable in WSAN

Existing re-configurable models [4–6, 11, 19, 21] have three major shortcomings, which we elaborate on below.

3.2.1 Resource inefficiency

Stems from the need to rely on multiple instances of functionally equivalent and thus redundant component instances to support concurrent applications. In contemporary models [4–6, 11, 19, 21] it is assumed that each application will be assembled from dedicated instances. An assumption which is not appropriate in embedded WSANs for of two reasons: First, sharing of sensor hardware is a necessity. As it is cost prohibitive and technically unfeasible to have dedicated sensors for each application [13, 24]. Second, improved resource control is obtained by mediating concurrent access to a shared resource using a *Singleton* instance [9]. Furthermore, in these models, it is assumed that sensor contention will be properly managed by the OS. Which is not the case, as WSAN OSes [22] offer no support to resolve contention over sensors. Instead, these only provide support to read values at each analog or digital IO port [1].

3.2.2 *Lack of isolation*

In current models [4–6, 11, 19, 21] configuration is part of the internal state of each component instance (in form of parameters) and coordination (i.e. interconnections and interactions) is part of the state managed by the component runtime. However, component configuration and coordination information is not isolated in a per-application basis, thus any change will affect all connected compositions. These models are not concerned with per-application isolation because they do not foresee the need to support component-sharing, which as elaborated in Sec. 3.2.1 is not an appropriate assumption. Fractal [4] and Ernie [20] provide *limited* component-sharing support, as they only allow the sharing of single-configuration components. This is useful to keep state consistent in cases of concurrent access to actuation components (e.g. controlling a fan). However, it does not improve reconfiguration or resource efficiency.

3.2.3 *Lack of application constraint and performance restriction meta-data.*

In these model [4–6, 11, 19, 21], application constraints are only implicitly represented through the values assigned to component configuration parameters and performance restrictions are not represented at all. Therefore, application developers need access to hardware and software specifications, and in some cases even inter-party coordination is needed to ensure application integrity.

3.3 Ensuring application integrity

In mainstream computing, similar integrity requirements, are present in the dynamic change management, e.g. [14] and adaptive software domains, e.g. [25]. However, there are two key differences between our perspective on integrity and the perspective these approaches commonly adopt. The first, in our work we focus on the integrity of existing applications as new applications are added to a shared infrastructure. Therefore, we consider the adverse effects the reconfiguration of an application may have on co-executing applications. Existing approaches commonly focus more on the safety of transitions as an application moves from one steady-state to another [25]. Therefore, the focus lies solely on a single application and its adaptations. Second, in our work we consider resource constraints and the issues of resource competition, and existing approaches generally do not [14, 25]. Component frameworks, e.g. [6], ease configuration effort due to the reuse of known configurations, but do not ensure application integrity. In embedded WSANs a simplified approach is used where only structural integrity is verified, e.g. [18, 21]. This generally only involves a light-weight mechanism to verify that mandatory component interconnections are satisfied before a component can be activated.

4. RESOURCE SHARING FRAMEWORK

The Resource Sharing Framework (*RSF*) extends re-configurable component models in order to support concurrently running applications in shared sensing environments through a process we refer to as **Composition-Swapping**. Composition-Swapping, allows application developers to deploy applications which share component instances with existing applications, but treat them as if they are dedicated instances. Therefore, developers are relieved from the complexity of ensuring application integrity. As discussed in Section 2, with existing models any modification to the configuration or coordination of a shared component instance affects all associated compositions (see Fig 1B). On the other hand, now consider Fig. 2A and B, where due to their per-application isolation, the temp component can have a unique configuration for each composition without affecting other applications. This isolation is achieved by executing one composition per time-period[2] and swapping composition configurations in and out as required, hence Composition-Swapping. To achieve this, each time a composition is triggered for execution, the RSF configures the corresponding component instances and prepares the composition's structure. In order to obtain higher resource efficiency gains, the RSF supports the sharing of sensing and data-processing component instances.

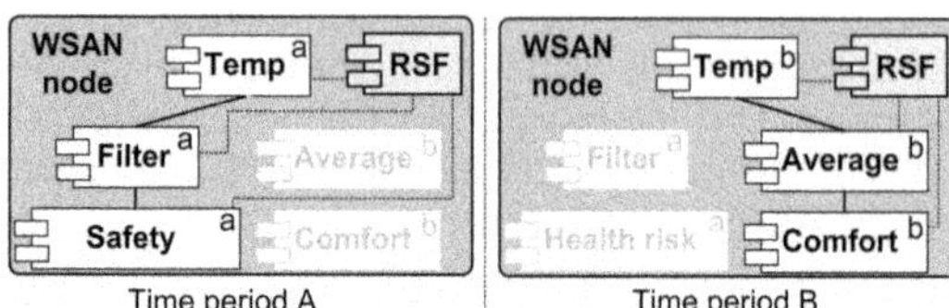

Figure 2: Per-application isolation is achieved by Composition-Swapping.

To elaborate on Composition-Swapping, we discuss its involvement in three phases of the software life cycle:

(A) *Development time:* The component developer follows a patterned component implementation to enforce state management delegation and annotates components with performance meta-data.

(B) *Configuration time:* The application developer makes application constraints explicit and assembles the application using the standard mechanisms offered by the component runtime.

(C) *Runtime:* The RSF realizes Composition-Swapping and ensures application integrity.

We delve further into each of these in Sections 4.1 to 4.3 respectively and end with a note on modifiability in Sec. 4.4.

4.1 Development time

The RSF is designed as a modular add-on for existing component runtimes and is itself implemented as a standard component. It is not a programming approach, therefore, applications are still designed according to the chosen component model. However, there are two core extensions needed in the implementation of each shared component: State management delegation and the annotation of component meta-data.

4.1.1 *State management delegation*

State management delegation allows the RSF to isolate and manage component configuration and coordination on a per-application basis. This idea is inspired by state management in multi-tenant middleware, e.g. [23]. State management delegation is achieved by enforcing a patterned component implementation, as shown in Listing 1. Each component instance interacts with the RSF through `Idelegate`and `Iexecute`.`Idelegate` allows component instances to delegate their state to the RSF. In turn, `Iexecute` allows the RSF to return their state and control their execution. To achieve delegation, the developer must implement three things:
(i) A call to the `delegateToRSF()` method (Line 9) from within

[2] A notion similar to time-slotting, commonly used in OSes [22] to support the execution of concurrent threads.

the `setProperties()` method. In this way, every time the application developer submits application data through the `setProperties()` interface (Line 6), it will be immediately delegated to the RSF.
(ii) The `submitContext()` method (Line 10), which handles context occurrences (e.g. detection of an RFID card). For instance in cases where a component should sense when an RFID card is detected. It must then be delegated with the `delegateContextToRSF()` call in Line 11.
(iii) The `execute()` method (Line 12) contains the component's functional code, its configuration and control. In the case of sensing components, a `copy()` method must also be provided, which allows the RSF to request a copy of the latest reading.

```
1  componentType = type; // e.g. sensing, data processing
2  mutexIds; // IDs for applicable mutex locks
3  outputType;// to select algorithm to check accuracy
4  performanceDelay1 = time1;//device specific
5  performanceDelay2 = time2;//peripherals
6  setProperties(configuration){
7      // Delegation call for submitted configuration
8      // and the annotated meta-data.
9      delegateToRSF(configuration,componentMetaData);}
10 submitContext(occurrence){
11     delegateContextToRSF(occurrence);}
12 execute(parameters){
13     // Configure how functionality should execute.
14     // Execute functionality.}
15 copy(parameters){ }
```

Listing 1: RSF-shared component implementation template

4.1.2 *Component meta-data*

The component developer must specify the component type, applicable mutex locks, output type and the corresponding delays, i.e. performance restrictions. The component type identifies the type of functionality implemented by the component (Line 1 in Listing 1), e.g. sensing, data processing. Mutex locks mediate access to contentious resources which are not externalized through component instances. For example, as there is only one ADC, it must be shared by all analog sensors. At runtime, the RSF locks and releases them when the execution of the corresponding component terminates, to ensure consistent sharing. The component developer must identify where locks are necessary from hardware specifications. The ID of each applicable lock is included in an array (Line 2). She is responsible for using these IDs consistently, i.e. in all components, the same ID refers to the same resource.

Output type is used to select the appropriate algorithm to verify data accuracy and it specifies the characteristics of the data output for each component. For example, temp, light, RH sensors generally have noiseless measurements which are steady, thus are type 1, and use a simple exponential smoothing function for accuracy [3]. For noisy moving values, as those expected from proximity sensors, a type 2 would be used, which uses a double exponential smoothing function [3].

Performance meta-data in the form of delay, allows the RSF to account for the time it takes, each of the involved parts of the execution environment, to complete data acquisition or processing. The component developer, must, through the use of technical hardware specifications ascertain applicable delays caused by hardware elements and measure component execution time to quantify software delays. These measurements must cover the total scope of initialization and computation of each component. For example, analog sensing components must account not only for the initialization of the sensing hardware but also for peripheral resources used. Peripheral resource refer to the secondary resources that are used during the invocation of a sensor (e.g. the ADC circuitry). These delays are measured in time and normally in the order of milliseconds. However, radical variations exist as, chemical sensors with a 24hr. heatup time (due to chemical substrate) and PIR sensors with a 2 sec. capture time. See a sample implementation of a Temp sensing component in Listing 2.

```
int cT = 1; // 1= sensing
int [] mIds = {3}; // 3 = mutex for ADC
int outputType = 1 // 1 = steady noiseless measurement
int R_device = 20;//millisec. sensing time
int R_peripheral = 10;//millisec. ADC reset-time
int copy;
void setProperties(char[] configuration){
    delegateToRSF(configuration,R_device,R_peripheral,cT,mIds);}
void submitContext(char[] occurrence){
    delegateContextToRSF(occurrence);}
int execute(){
        int value = ReadADC(TEMP_ADC_CHANNEL);
        copy = value;
        return value }
int copy(){
         return copy;}
```

Listing 2: Example implementation of shared temp component

4.1.3 *The differences to non-shared component implementation*

The standard (i.e. non-shared) implementation lacks performance annotations and does not delegate its configuration, control or context occurrences. Therefore, it is responsible for persisting its own configuration (Line 3 in Listing 3) and controlling its own execution (Line 4).

```
1 char[] configProperties;
2 void setProperties(char[] configurationProperties){
3     // persist config. properties
4 main control loop {
5     // Implement occurrence handlers and timers.
6     // configure functionality from persisted state.
7     // Execute functionality.}
```

Listing 3: non-shared component implementation template

4.2 Configuration time

At configuration time, the application developer is responsible for two things. The first, quantifying application constraints, and the second, the assembly of the application.

4.2.1 *Application constraint meta-data*

The application developer must, based on application requirements, identify and quantify applicable application constraints. This meta-data is added to the usual component configuration information submitted during application assembly. Application constraint meta-data allows developers to specify additional constraints that inform the RSF's allocation and verification processes. In this way the RSF is able to ascertain the validity of a given configuration under current system conditions. In our smart office we accounted for accuracy and timeliness. Data accuracy is considered in two ways: The first is designed to determine the 'safe' or appropriate time for a component to acquire or process data. This procedure, which is enabled by default for all components, verifies that component computation is done in accordance with the limitations of the execution environment. The second, is designed to account for faulty or noisy sensors. This is an optional verification procedure which can be activated per application. In our current implementation, this verification is done using either simple or double exponential smoothing [3]. For which, the developer needs to submit the alpha and delta to be used. Alpha indicates how responsive to change the verification function should be ($0 \geq \alpha \leq 1$). Delta is a percentage which indicates how close an output value must be to the expected value, in order for it to be considered accurate (e.g. safety has `ApC_3 = [`α` =.5,`δ` = 10%])`. Timeliness, is expressed either with the time-drift (e.g. comfort has `ApC_1 = 5%`) or response-time constraint (e.g. HVAC has `ApC_2 = 3 minutes`).

4.2.2 *Application assembly*

The application developer must submit two commands per component instance: First, the configuration of each instance is sent directly to the instance using its `setProperties(configuration)` interface (see Fig. 3B step 1). This configuration data is then automatically delegated to the RSF (step 2). Second, coordination information (i.e. composition structure) for each instance is submitted to the RSF directly using its `setProperties(coordination)` interface (step 3). We elaborate further on each step:

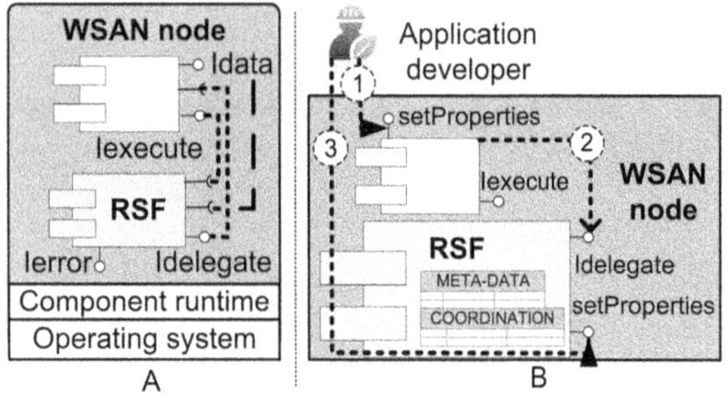

Figure 3: (A) RSF node view, (B) Application assembly

Step 1: Configure component The command used is: `setProperties(Set-ID, interaction, interval, duration,` $ApC_n[\,], P_n[\,]$`)`
The submitted data is: (i) Set-ID is a unique meta-data set identifier, (ii) interaction type: 1 for periodic or 2 for stochastic, (iii) interval, in the case of periodic interactions it specifies the sample interval for computation. For stochastic interactions, it specifies the type of occurrence that will trigger computation, (iv) duration specifies for how long a configuration is valid, (v) application constraints, (vi) Parameters[], which inform computation (e.g. high or low pass filtering). For example:
`setProperties(001,1,7 min.,31 days, [5%,0,.5, 10%], 0)` This commands configures the temp component for composition 001 (i.e. safety app), in a periodic interaction with a sample interval of 7 minutes, during the next 31 days. The RSF should allow for a time-drift of 5%, and check accuracy using an alpha of .5 and a delta of 10%.
Step 2: Delegate configuration and meta-data Each submission triggers the component instance to delegate all the meta-data to the RSF. This data is persisted in the RSF as a new record in the meta-data table. Each record represents a software composition an instance is part of. Each instance can delegate multiple meta-data sets, one for each application where it is being used in. The RSF then checks for compliance with performance restrictions and application constraints (see Alg. 1). First, it establishes if a response-time constraint has been submitted. Then the RSF checks two things. First, the submitted configuration against performance restrictions. Second, compliance of the response-time constraint. This ensures that erroneous data will not be generated from invoking components in an unready state or non-compliance to app. constraints.
Step 3: Configure composition structure The command used is: `setProperties(set-ID, thisInstanceID, otherInstance, otherAddress, interfaceType, interactionType)`

Algorithm 1 Initial configuration check

Meta-data is delegated → check R_j,ApC_2
Establish if there is a response-time constraint.$\{ApC_2 \neq 0\}$
for each restriction **do** $\{\forall i[1..n]$ and $\forall j[1..t]\}$
  Check every parameter. $\{check(P_i, R_j)\}$
for response-time **do**
  Check that interval meets response time.$\{interval \leq ApC_2\}$

This data becomes another record in the coordination table. The data is structured as follows: (i) Set-ID: associates this data to the component instance configuration, (ii) thisIntanceID: the instance in question, (iii) otherInstance: in the case of pull interaction, the other instance is the data-producer and in push interaction, it is the data-consumer, (iii) otherAddress: network address of the node where the other instance is instantiated, (iv) type of the interfaces to connect and (v) interactionType: pull or push. Note that this submission is made directly to the RSF, in a traditional assembly, this would have been submitted directly to the component runtime. For example:
`setProperties(001, temp, filter, IP2, Itemp, push).`
This command connects the `Itemp` interface from the temp to the filter component for composition 001 (i.e. safety app). The filter is running in node with address IP2 and a push interaction is used.

4.3 Runtime

Composition-Swapping is comprised of three primary steps: composition triggered, composition verified and composition swapped. We describe each of them in Sections 4.3.1 to 4.3.3 respectively.

4.3.1 *Composition triggered*

As execution is signaled, either by the expiration of a timer (Step 1a in Fig. 4) or a context occurrence (step 1b in Fig. 4), the corresponding composition is selected and its configuration is verified on-the-fly. As we follow a reactive on-the-fly approach, there is no need to statistically model each possible interaction (as is needed in preemptive scheduling). E.g. In our deployment RFID cards are detected following a normal bell shaped distribution, and employees walking in an office, follow a Poisson distribution.

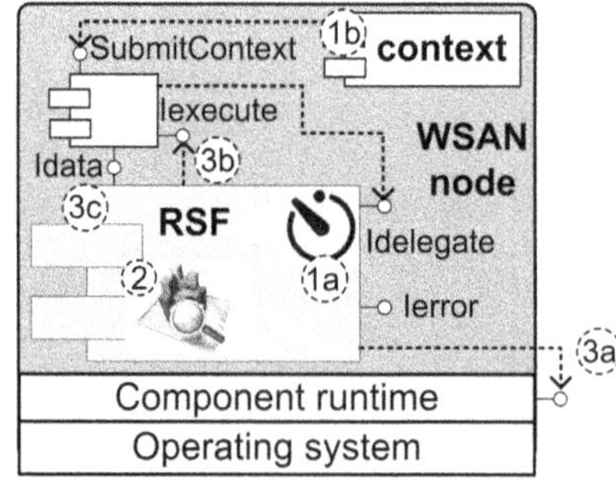

Figure 4: Application integrity is ensured during Composition-Swapping

4.3.2 *Composition verified*

When a composition is triggered, its meta-data is retrieved and passed to the runtime configuration verification process (see Alg. 2). If all required component instances are available and mutex locks are free, computation is scheduled and application constraints are checked ($\forall i[1..RA]$, $(min\{ApC_i\} \leq t_{allowed} \leq max\{ApC_i\})$). If constraints are met the Composition-Swap is authorized. If the constraints are not satisfied, a *composition-drop* is executed. Where the contending composition is no longer considered for a Composition-Swap and an error event is generated (using `Ierror`). This composition will be reconsidered when it is triggered for execution again. This verification ensures that erroneous data is not generated from the invocation of a sensor or peripheral resource in an unready state or due to violations of application constraints.

Algorithm 2 Runtime configuration verification

```
Composition is triggered → retrieve meta-Data.
if instances are avail. and mutexes are free then
    Schedule execution. {t_expected = t_now}
    if time-drift ApC_1 is respected then
        Authorize Composition swap.
    else
        Composition-drop.
else
    Invoke contention management strategy.
```

In the cases where an instance is busy, the contention management strategy is used. The RSF calculates the time when these instances will be released based on the time each instance started execution and the total time arising from its performance restrictions ($t_{release} = |R_i - (|t_{now} - t_{start}|)|$).

Sensing components: If allowable time-drift specified allows for the latest reading to be reused ($t_{release} \leq A_{td}$). Then a copy is provided for the contending composition (by invoking `Iexecute.copy()`). This not only resolves contention but also reduces energy expenditure from additional invocation of sensors [15, 16]. If not, a *composition-drop* is executed.

Data processing components: The contending composition is queued if its constraints will still be satisfied even after waiting for the release of busy instances ($\forall i[1..RA]$, $(min\{ApC_i\} \leq t_{allowed} \leq max\{ApC_i\})$). If its constraints are violated, a *composition-drop* is done. Delving further into contention management strategies is outside the scope of this paper. The reader is directed to [8], where we discussed alternative strategies, as SLA based prioritization.

Algorithm 3 Contention management strategy

```
for each busy instance i do
    Calculate release time. {t_release = t_release + |R_i − (|t_now − t_start_i|)|}
Schedule execution. {t_expected = t_now + t_release}
if instance is a sensing component and time-drift is respected then
    Request a copy of latest reading.
else if instance is a processing component and time-drift is respected then
    Queue composition to execute later. {t_expected}
else
    Composition-drop.
```

4.3.3 *Composition swapped*

The swap is comprised of three steps. First, the RSF removes all previous interconnections to the affected component instances and then submits the coordination information to the component runtime in order to assemble the expected composition (Step 3a in Fig. 4). Second, the RSF completes the Composition-Swap by configuring each component, applying corresponding mutual exclusion (mutex) locks and finally signaling the instance for execution (Step 3b in Fig. 4). Third, the RSF monitors the execution of the composition and removes the corresponding mutex locks as each component's delay time expires. In the cases where an accuracy constraint is present, the RSF monitors component output to check data accuracy. This is achieved by connecting the RSF to `Idata` of the component being monitored (Step 3c in Fig. 4). In this way, every time the component produces data, the RSF, receives a copy, which it then uses to perform an accuracy check (see Alg. 4). `Idata` represents a standard interface used to expose the component's functionality. `Ierror` is used to notify of any violations to accuracy constraints. The Composition-Swapping process occurs every time a composition is triggered for execution in the RSF.

Algorithm 4 Accuracy verification strategy

```
Data value is received → retrieve accuracy constraint ApC_3.
Set alpha and delta based on the submitted constraints
if outputType = 1 then
    Run simple exponential smoothing
    if data value is NOT within acceptable delta then
        raise corresponding accuracy constraint violation
else if outputType = 2 then
    Run double exponential smoothing
    if data value is NOT within acceptable delta then
        raise corresponding accuracy constraint violation
```

4.4 Modifiability

Although we consider a performance restriction expressed as delay, and quality of data based application constraints, generic enough to be broadly applicable, we did foresee their extension or modification. Their definitions and corresponding verification processes (see Sec. 4.2.1 and 4.3.2), are isolated and contained in pre-defined modifiable locations. As these locations have been designed as adaptability points in the framework, the scope of change is limited to the interpretation of each restriction or constraint and the check function used. We refer the reader to [8] for further details.

5. EVALUATION ENVIRONMENT AND RESULTS

We now describe the environment used for evaluation of the RSF and its results. We present our evaluation in two parts: reconfiguration efficiency and runtime resource consumption.

5.1 Evaluation environment

Our smart office has been running for over one year, during which time five reconfiguration scenarios were enacted to deploy/extended four distinct concurrently running sensing applications (described in Sec. 2). Each reconfiguration case is comprised of the deployment of a new application. The exception lies in cases one and two, which comprise the initial deployment and extension of the HVAC application. The infrastructure consists of two different platforms: 25 AVR raven nodes [1] and 2 Alix gateways. The raven nodes, have a 20 Mhz CPU, 16Kb of RAM and 128Kb of FLASH memory. They run Contiki 2.5 OS (consumes 40Kb FLASH and 5Kb RAM) [22] and the LooCI middleware (consumes 25Kb FLASH and 5Kb RAM) [11], both programmed with C. Contiki provides support for concurrency, networking and dynamic loading of code, and LooCI provides the component runtime and handles distribution concerns. Alixes have 500 MHz CPUs, Linux and OSGi [19].

5.1.1 The benchmark configuration

The smart office design and benchmark implementation was initially completed using a standard component model, i.e. LooCI. Detailed logs and records were kept as applications were deployed and reconfigured on the 25 Raven embedded nodes [1], keeping track of disruption, developer effort, and resource consumption. All reconfiguration actions, i.e. commands issued to the LooCI API, as well as all events generated by the system and runtime performance metrics for each node were logged. Performance metrics include: dynamic use of stack, heap, CPU[3], and MMEM[4] memory. Access to the smart office's code, configuration files and architectural views used for the benchmark implementation and RSF evaluation can be found at the RSF website (https://code.google.com/p/r-s-f/wiki/smartOffice) .

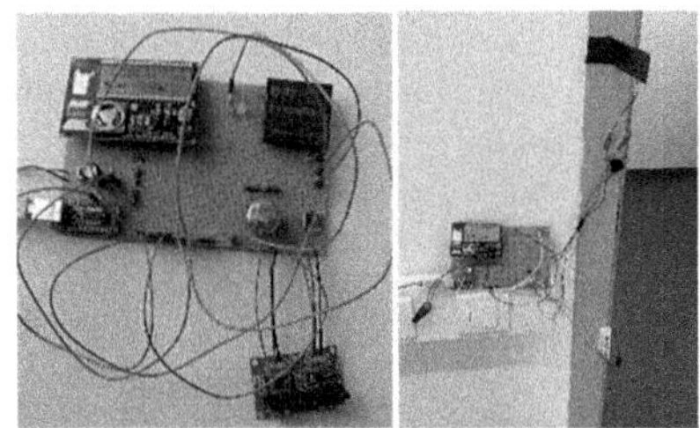

Figure 5: Raven nodes equipped w RFID, CH4, actuators, etc.

5.1.2 RSF implementation and evaluation procedure

We replicated the benchmark configuration using the RSF. The applications deployed for evaluation are functionally identical. We re-enacted all of the reconfiguration scenarios undergone by the benchmark deployment: Case 1, temperature control for the HVAC application is deployed. Case 2, HVAC application is extended with illumination control. Case 3, workplace safety application is deployed. Case 4, comfort application is deployed. Case 5, security application is deployed. We have recorded: disruption, developer effort, resource consumption, reconfiguration actions and node performance metrics just as we did during the benchmark.

5.2 Reconfiguration efficiency

Reconfiguration efficiency includes developer effort, disruption and data transmission experienced during reconfiguration. Developer effort is quantified in terms of the number of decisions required and commands issued during reconfiguration activities.

5.2.1 Quantifying each evaluation metric

All reconfiguration processes (containing over 1,000 actions), commands issued and time elapsed, where recorded and averaged. We quantified disruption in terms of down time, due to interrupted data-flow, experienced by each application during reconfiguration. Additionally a set of experiments where prepared in order to further refine these averaged results, from which we derived a set of equations that describe the observed behavior. The number of decisions required is directly dependent on the possible Configuration Conflicts CC which need to be identified by considering: for each S shared instance, if any of the configuration parameters P and any of the performance restrictions R have conflicts with any application constraint ApC from the RA Running Applications. $CC_S = \sum_{l=1}^{S}(\sum_{q=1}^{RA} ApC_q(R_l + P_l))$, thus the number of Decisions D required to reconcile conflicts in the simplest case is $D = CC_S$. In cases where the entire component graph needs to be understood, e.g. case 4, one must transverse and check all potential configuration conflicts CC for the entire affected component graph, not only the shared component instances.

5.2.2 Developer effort and disruption

As can be seen in Fig. 6, there is a considerable decrease in developer effort and disruption with the use of the RSF after the 5 reconfiguration scenarios. The # of decisions required decreased by over 79%, and the # of commands needed decreased by over 24%. Zero disruption was experienced with the RSF. While with plain LooCI, applications experienced 38 minutes of downtime.

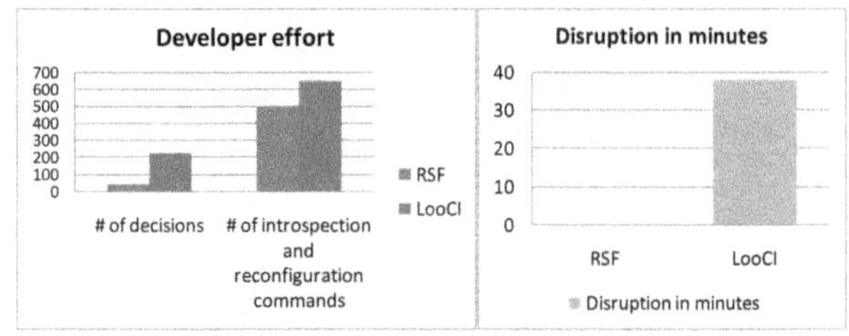

Figure 6: RSF decreases effort and disruption.

RSF case:	1	2	3	4	5	Total
# decisions	28	4	5	5	4	46
# commands	156	96	107	107	29	495
disruption(minutes)	0	0	0	0	0	0
ave. deg. sharing	1	2	2	3	1	NA
% shared components	0	25%	21%	39%	31%	NA
LooCI case:	1	2	3	4	5	Total
# decisions	24	20	25	153	4	226
# commands	148	108	131	239	29	655
disruption(minutes)	0	9	11	18	0	38
ave. deg. sharing	1	2	2	3	1	NA
% shared components	0	11%	7%	11%	9%	NA

Table 1: RSF incurs less reconfiguration effort and disruption.

Breakdown of results for each office per case: Table 1 lists the results obtained for developer effort, and disruption in each office. We also list: (i) The averaged degree of sharing, which represent the number of compositions an instance is shared in, and (ii) the % of shared instances.

In Case 1, there is no component sharing, the worst case scenario for the RSF, there is an increase of 14% # decisions, and 5% # commands.

In Case 2, benefits in all dimensions are noticed for the RSF with a reduction of: 80% in decisions, 11% in commands, and 100% in disruption. The RSF is sharing 1 sensing and 1 processing components per node.

In Case 3, bigger benefits occur across the board because the RSF shares 2 sensing and 2 processing components per node.

In Case 4, even greater benefits are obtained because this reconfiguration requires full introspection scope (see Sec. 2).

In Case 5, there are no measurable benefits as there is no sharing on either system. The RSF imposes no overhead for effort in the cases where no sharing is required, once the overhead of the initial deployment has incurred.

5.2.3 Amount of bytes transmitted

We have measured the amount of bytes transmitted in each office per case during reconfiguration activities (see Fig. 7). The

[3]CPU measurements with Contiki's energest module.

[4]Contiki's managed dynamic memory module.

RSF achieves a reduction of over 33% (i.e. 87Kb) on the averaged amount of bytes transmitted. This is primarily due to component instance sharing in RSF, as no redundant components need to be deployed.

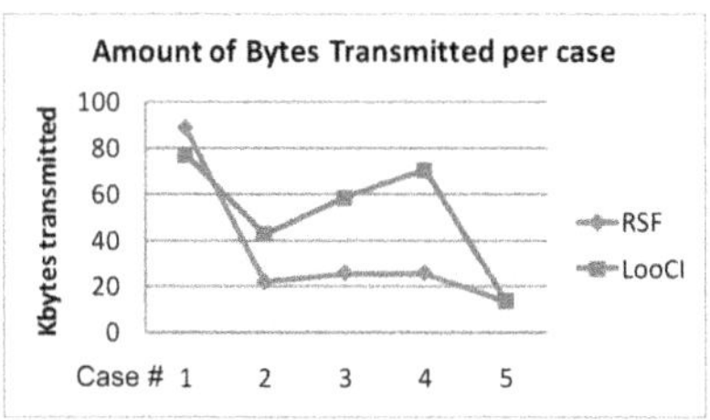

Figure 7: Fewer bytes transmitted with the RSF

5.3 Runtime resource consumption

Runtime resource consumption is quantified in terms of: footprint, performance, processing overhead of the RSF, and the number of nodes required per office.

5.3.1 Footprint and performance of the RSF

We have measured static footprint and evaluated performance, in terms of RAM, and FLASH memory usage at runtime:
Footprint: The RSF consumes about 11Kb of FLASH (17% overhead over OS) and 400b RAM (4% overhead over OS).
Memory: We instrumented our code to provide real-time monitoring traces at 5 min. intervals throughout the deployment. As one can see in Fig. 8A and B we plotted the averaged results per node. RAM overhead is compensated for when 25% of the instances are shared and FLASH overhead is compensated for when 39% of instances are shared. Thereafter maintaining a lower per application overhead in the use of memory.

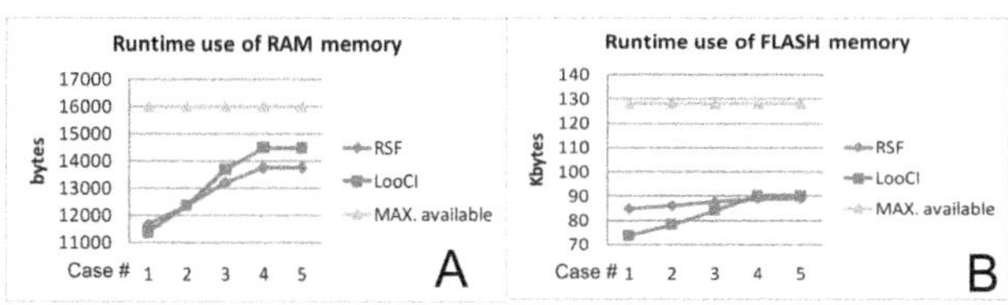

Figure 8: RSF proves resource efficiency.

5.3.2 Processing overhead of the RSF

We have measured processing overhead in terms of CPU usage and the time delay created by RSF interactions with the MCU configured at a speed of 8 MHz:
CPU: We have measured CPU usage using the Energest module from Contiki (see Fig. 9). The graph plots averaged CPU usage for all running processes (i.e. Contiki, LooCI, and the RSF) and also illustrates the portion of this CPU usage that is attributable to LooCI and to the RSF. This plot was made based on averaged CPU usage across all nodes at configuration time and runtime. At configuration time, component deployment required 80% of the CPU, for which LooCI accounts for about 50% and the RSF has no noticeable usage. During component instance configuration, 60% of the CPU was used, from which LooCI consumes about 18% and RSF has no noticeable usage. At runtime every time a composition is triggered for execution, on average 55% of the CPU is used, from which LooCI has no noticeable usage and RSF consumes under 5% of the CPU (these are the RSF's peak processes).

Time delay: The RSF imposes time delays due to the exchange of two messages between the RSF and each component (each takes 0.07977 milliseconds) and the time incurred during verification processes (on average 0.159 milliseconds). We have added and averaged these delays taking into account the variations of composition size and complexity of computation. The RSF imposes an averaged delay of .249 ms. A delay which causes no noticeable decrease in the data accuracy or timeliness for any application.

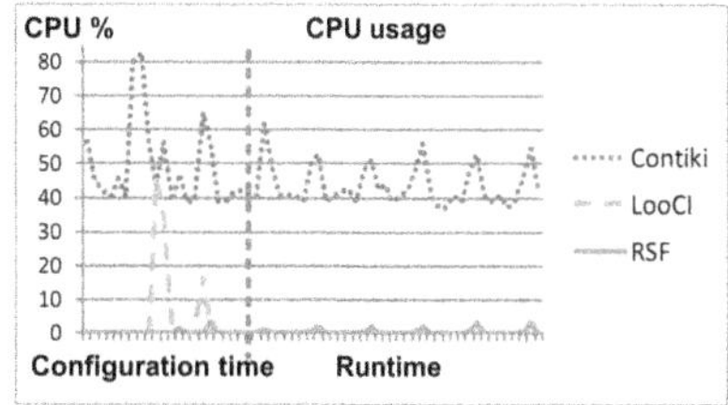

Figure 9: Low CPU overhead with the RSF.

5.3.3 Fewer nodes required with the RSF

The RSF requires 30% (i.e. 4) fewer nodes per office. In Fig. 10A, one can see the LooCI component graph, which is functionally equivalent to one of the RSF component graphs shown in Fig. 10B. In Fig. 10B, each graph denotes the triggered composition, during one time period, for one node after case 4 (it takes six time periods to activate all six compositions). The criteria used to modularize functionality is identical for LooCI and the RSF. As a result of composition-swapping, the RSF requires only 10 components to achieve what in a standard model requires 17 components. Furthermore, as each Raven node can support a max. of 12 components, due to limitations intrinsic to the code deployment infrastructure and EEPROM size, more nodes are required to support the same functionality. ID-F implements a string matcher used to identify a user. TrH-F is a threshold filter. TimeF is a down-sampler. AVE is an averager. FAN and LAMP are actuator controls for ventilation and illumination.

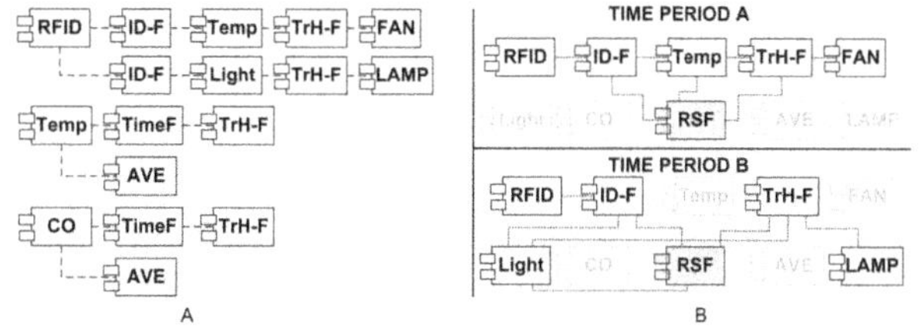

Figure 10: Component graph for (A) LooCI (B) RSF in 2 time periods.

6. DISCUSSION

We have demonstrated two extensions to embedded re-configurable component models, which ensure application integrity and provide resource efficient co-execution. A fundamental primitive in our design was to offer 'add-on' unintrusive extensions. Thus, two key features of the RSF design are particularly notable. First, the RSF itself is implemented as a standard software component and therefore can be integrated with existing models without changes to their supporting middleware. Second, the approach embodied in the RSF can be applied to any re-configurable component model [4–6, 11, 19, 21]. The RSF only requires that component instances are: persistent, have explicit interfaces and are runtime re-configurable. In our prior work [7] we have demonstrated RSF implementations for various interaction models including: synchronous pull, request-reply interactions using Runes [5], and with asynchronous push, publish-subscribe interactions using LooCI [11].

Achieving lower processing overheads, with comparable features, might have been achieved through the use of more intrusive modifications to the component runtime, OS and system drivers. However, this would lead to cross-cutting code insertions that would have been hard to maintain. Furthermore, making the extensions mandatory, even in the cases when component-sharing is not required by the deployment scenario.

7. CONCLUSION

We have shown that during the deployment of applications on shared environments, the need to *manually* ensure application integrity, causes significant disruption and reconfiguration effort. We identified the two primary limitations that cause this. First, the lack of per-application isolation of component configuration and coordination. Second, the lack of application constraint and component performance meta-data. To address these, we proposed two extensions to re-configurable component models. Mainly, state management delegation and extended component meta-data. These extensions enable component-sharing, which in turn supports Composition - Swapping. Finally, we have shown that for our smart office, Composition - Swapping has: eliminated disruption, lowered reconfiguration overhead and lowered resource consumption. Specifically by reducing, the required decisions by 79%, the commands issued by 24%, and bytes transmitted by 33%. The resource efficiency of our approach can be seen in terms of the lower per-app overhead and fewer nodes required. Its runtime use of RAM is compensated when 25% of the running components are shared. The RSF consumes at most 5% of CPU and its FLASH memory overhead is compensated for when 39% of the components are shared.

Acknowledgment

This research is partially funded by the Interuniversity Attraction Poles Programme Belgian State, Belgian Science Policy, IMEC and by the Research Fund KU Leuven.

8. REFERENCES

[1] Atmel, Corp. AVR RZ Raven.

[2] S. Bhattacharya, A. Saifullah, C. Lu, and G. Roman. Multi-application deployment in shared sensor networks based on quality of monitoring. In *IEEE RTAS*, 2010.

[3] R. G. Brown. *Smoothing, forecasting and prediction of discrete time series*. Courier Dover Publications, 2004.

[4] E. Bruneton, T. Coupaye, M. Leclercq, V. Quéma, and J.-B. Stefani. The Fractal component model and its support in Java. *Software: Practice and Experience*, 36(11-12):1257–1284, 2006.

[5] Costa P, Coulson G, Gold R, Lad M, Mascolo C, Mottola L, Picco GP, Sivaharan T, Weerasinghe N, Zachariadis,S. The RUNES middleware for networked embedded systems and its application in a disaster management scenario. In *Percom07*, pages 69–78. IEEE, 2007.

[6] Coulson G, Blair G, Grace P, Taiani F, Joolia A, Lee K, Ueyama J, Sivaharan T. A generic component model for building systems software. In *ACM Transactions on Computer Systems*, volume 26, pages 1–42. ACM, 2008.

[7] P. del Cid, D. Hughes, S. Michiels, and W. Joosen. Applying a metadata level for concurrency in wireless sensor networks. *Concurrency and Computation: Practice and Experience*, 24(16), 2012.

[8] P. J. del Cid, D. Hughes, S. Michiels, and W. Joosen. Evolving wireless sensor network behavior through adaptability points in middleware architectures. *IJDATICS*, 2(1):1–13, 08 2011.

[9] E. Gamma, R. Helm, R. Johnson, and J. Vlissides. *Design Patterns: Elements of Reusable Object-Oriented Software*. Addison-Wesley, Boston, MA, 1995.

[10] S. Helal, W. Mann, H. El-Zabadani, J. King, Y. Kaddoura, and E. Jansen. The gator tech smart house: a programmable pervasive space. *Computer*, 38(3):50 – 60, march 2005.

[11] D. Hughes, K. Thoelen, J. Maerien, N. Matthys, P. J. del Cid, W. Horre, C. Huygens, S. Michiels, and W. Joosen. Looci: the loosely-coupled component infrastructure. In *IEEE NCA12*, 08 2012.

[12] M. Iqbal, M. Handte, S. Wagner, W. Apolinarski, and P. Marron. Enabling energy-efficient context recognition with configuration folding. In *PerCom, 2012 IEEE*, pages 198 –205, 03 2012.

[13] Y. Ju, Y. Lee, J. Yu, C. Min, I. Shin, and J. Song. Symphoney: A coordinated sensing flow execution engine for concurrent mobile sensing applications. In *SenSys, 2012 ACM*, pages 211–224, 11 2012.

[14] J. Kramer and J. Magee. Analysing dynamic change in distributed software architectures. *IEEE Software*, 145(5), oct 1998.

[15] I. Leontiadis, C. Efstratiou, C. Mascolo, and J. Crowcroft. Senshare: transforming sensor networks into multi-application sensing infrastructures. In *EWSN*. Springer-Verlag, 2012.

[16] S. Madden and W. Hong. TinyDB: an acquisitional query processing system for sensor networks. *ACM TODS*, 30(1), 2005.

[17] Marron P, Lachenman A, Minder D, Hahner J, Sauter R, Rothermel K. TinyCubus a flexible and adaptive framework for sensor networks. In *EWSN05*, pages 278–289. IEEE, 2005.

[18] Mottola L, Picco GP, Sheikh S. FiGaRo: fine-grained software reconfiguration for wireless sensor networks. In *LNCS*, volume 2008, pages 286–304. Springer, 2008.

[19] OSGi Alliance, Org. OSGi - The Dynamic Module System for Java. `http://www.osgi.org/`.

[20] G. Outhred and J. Potter. A model for component composition with sharing. In W. Weck, J. Bosch, and C. Szyperski, editors, *Proc. component-Oriented Programming (WCOP âĂŹ98)*, 1998.

[21] B. Porter, G. Coulson, and U. Roedig. Managing software evolution in large-scale wireless sensor and actuator networks. *ACM Transactions on Sensor Networks*, 9(4):1–28, 2013.

[22] Swedish Institute of Computer Science (SICS). The Contiki OS. `http://www.contiki-os.org/`.

[23] S. Walraven, E. Truyen, and W. Joosen. A Middleware Layer for Flexible and Cost-Efficient Multi-tenant Applications. In *Middleware*, volume 7049, 2011.

[24] Yu, Y. Rittle, L. Bhandari, V. LeBrun, J. Supporting concurrent applications in wireless sensor networks. In *ACM Sensys*, 2006.

[25] J. Zhang and B. H. C. Cheng. Model-based development of dynamically adaptive software. In *ICSE06*, pages 371–380. ACM, 2006.

Quantifying the Parallelism in BPMN Processes using Model Checking

Radu Mateescu
Inria, University of Grenoble Alpes, LIG, CNRS, France
Radu.Mateescu@inria.fr

Gwen Salaün
University of Grenoble Alpes, Inria, LIG, CNRS, France
Gwen.Salaun@imag.fr

Lina Ye
Inria, University of Grenoble Alpes, LIG, CNRS, France
Lina.Ye@inria.fr

ABSTRACT

A business process is a set of structured, related activities that aims at fulfilling a specific organizational goal for a customer or market. An important metric when developing a business process is its degree of parallelism, *i.e.*, the maximum number of tasks that are executable in parallel in that process. The degree of parallelism determines the peak demand on tasks, providing a valuable guide for the problem of resource allocation in business processes. In this paper, we investigate how to automatically measure the degree of parallelism for business processes, described using the BPMN standard notation. We first present a formal model for BPMN processes in terms of Labelled Transition Systems, which are obtained through process algebra encodings. We then propose an approach for automatically computing the degree of parallelism by using model checking techniques and dichotomic search. We implemented a tool for automating this check and we applied it successfully to more than one hundred BPMN processes.

Categories and Subject Descriptors

D.2.4 [**Software Engineering**]: Software/Program Verification—*Model checking*; D.2.8 [**Software Engineering**]: Metrics—*Process metrics*

General Terms

Design, Languages, Verification

Keywords

BPMN Process, Degree of Parallelism, Process Algebra, Labelled Transition System, Model Checking

1. INTRODUCTION

A business process is a set of structured, related activities or tasks designed to produce a specific output for a customer or market. It defines a specific ordering of activities across time and space, with a beginning and an end [5]. Business process modelling is an important area in software engineering. The idea is to represent processes so that they can be analyzed in order to improve process efficiency and quality. More precisely, it is a stage to model activities, their causal and temporal relationships, and specific business rules that process executions have to comply with.

An important metric when modelling and developing a business process is its degree of parallelism, which is the maximum number of tasks that are executable in parallel in the process. Parallel job processing is known as a solution for improving the efficiency of business processes [5]. Hence, when the performance of a process is an important criterion, one may seek to augment the parallelism degree as much as possible. However, the number of parallel branches in a process also complicates process design, development, and maintenance. This means that when performance is not crucial, one may prefer to reduce the parallelism degree. Note that these design tradeoffs between high performance and simplified development, and the refactorings they impose on the corresponding process, can be both guided by the degree of parallelism.

Furthermore, the degree of parallelism, which determines the peak demand on tasks, provides a valuable guide for the problem of resource allocation in business processes [25]. Examples of such resources include physical objects, time, budget as well as human beings. A typical example of resource allocation constraint is that a same agent cannot be assigned to parallel branches of the same workflow and execute different tasks simultaneously.

In this paper, we study how to compute the degree of parallelism, simply also called degree in the sequel, for business processes modelled in Business Process Modelling Notation 2.0 (BPMN for short in the rest of the paper), which is now published as ISO/IEC standard [13]. This is not a trivial task because a BPMN process may be large and may involve intricate structures, such as infinite loops or nested gateways, which impede its degree computation.

In this context, we propose a new framework to automatically compute this degree. We first present a formal model in terms of Labelled Transition Systems (LTSs) for BPMN processes. This model is obtained by encoding a BPMN process into process algebra and then using classical enumerative exploration techniques for generating the corresponding LTS. Such a low-level formal model makes much easier the definition of formal analysis techniques and algorithms, what would have been more complicated if defined directly at the BPMN level. We describe how to extend

CBSE '14 Lille, France
Copyright 2014 ACM 978-1-4503-2577-6/14/06 ...$15.00.
http://dx.doi.org/10.1145/2602458.2602473.

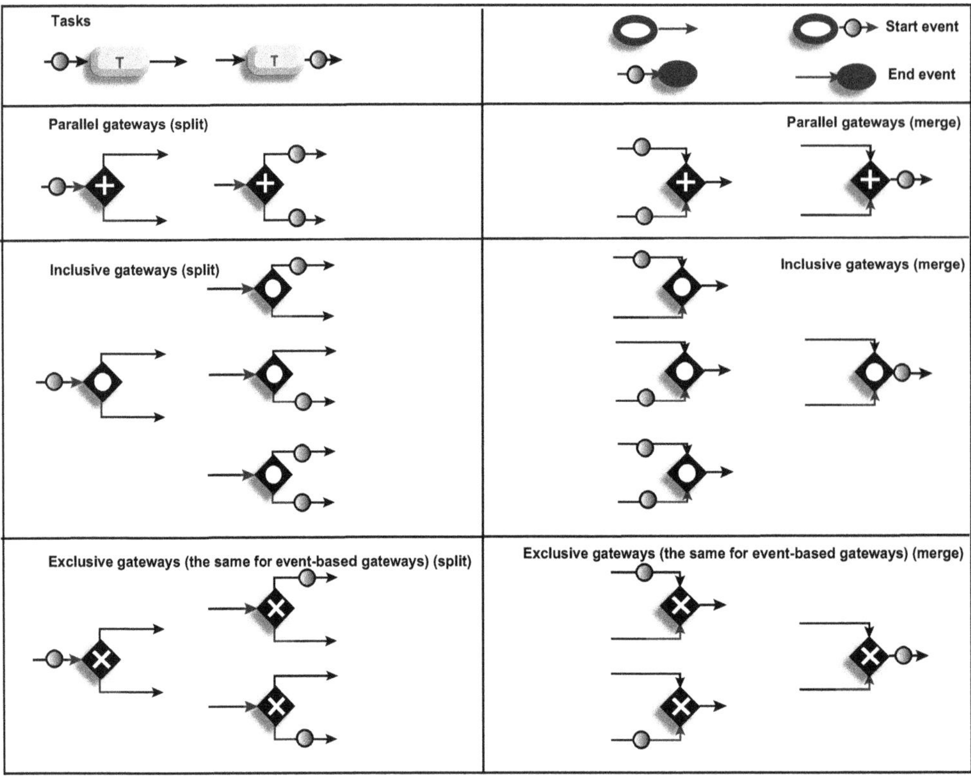

Figure 1: Execution semantics for BPMN elements.

such LTSs with special transitions whose labels contain the information about the number of parallel branches present in the initial BPMN process. These extended LTSs are used in a next step for computing the degree of parallelism. To do so, we propose an algorithm that encodes the degree computation as a model checking problem and applies this verification following a dichotomic search until obtaining the final result. We chose model checking because it is a well-established technique, supported by powerful tools.

To evaluate our approach, we implemented and applied it on more than one hundred BPMN processes that contain combinations of different BPMN gateways as well as cycles. Let us note that even if the degree measurement is illustrated with BPMN, the approach can be applied to other kinds of notations that can be expressed by control flows with parallel tasks, such as UML activity diagrams [14] or YAWL workflows [26].

To sum up, the four major contributions of this work with respect to existing results are as follows:

- We present an (extended) LTS formal model obtained via process algebra encodings for a representative subset of BPMN processes including typical gateways.
- We propose an approach relying on model checking techniques and dichotomic search to measure the degree of parallelism for BPMN processes.
- We implemented our approach as a tool that efficiently automates the degree computation.
- We applied our tool on more than one hundred BPMN processes, in particular on some real-world ones borrowed from the literature on the subject.

The rest of the paper is organized as follows. Section 2 briefly introduces BPMN and formally defines the degree of parallelism for BPMN processes. In Section 3, we present formal models for BPMN using process algebra and LTSs. Section 4 shows how to compute the degree of parallelism on such LTSs. We introduce tool support and experimental results in Section 5. Section 6 reviews related work and Section 7 concludes the paper.

2. DEGREE OF PARALLELISM FOR BPMN PROCESSES

BPMN [13] is a graphical notation for modeling business processes, which can be defined as a collection of related tasks that produce specific services or products for particular clients. BPMN is now an ISO/IEC standard [13]. Its semantics is only described informally in official documents [20, 13], but some attempts have been made for giving a formal semantics to BPMN, see *e.g.*, [8, 27, 22].

2.1 BPMN Processes

In this paper, we focus on the BPMN elements related to control-flow modelling that have an impact on the degree of parallelism [25], and we do not take data objects into account. Hence, three types of nodes named *event*, *task*, and *gateway*, are considered, as well as one type of edges called *sequence flow*. More precisely, we consider start and end

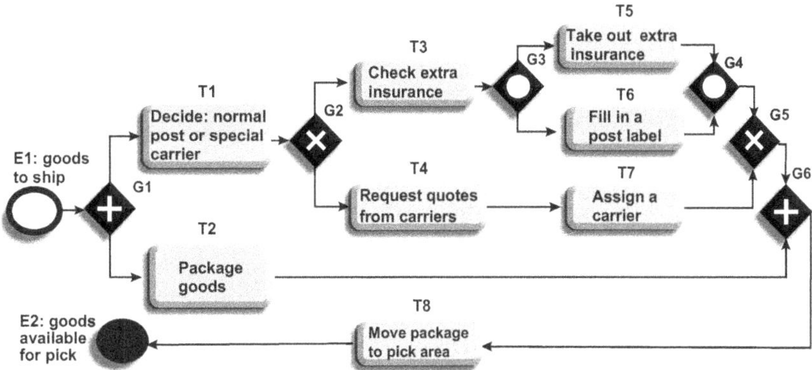

Figure 2: An example of BPMN process: Shipment Process of a Hardware Retailer.

events that are used to initialize and to terminate a process, respectively. A task represents an atomic activity that has exactly one incoming and one outgoing branch. A gateway is used to control the divergence and convergence of execution flow. A sequence flow describes two nodes executed one after the other, *i.e.*, imposing the execution order. We denote $n \rightarrow m$ when there is a sequence flow from node n to m in a BPMN process.

Gateways are crucial since they are used to model control flow branching in BPMN and therefore influence the parallelism degree. There are five types of gateways in BPMN: *exclusive, inclusive, parallel, event-based* and *complex gateways*. We take into account all of them except complex gateways, which are used to model complex synchronization behaviors especially based on data control.

For each type of gateways, if it has one incoming branch and multiple outgoing branches, we call it a *split*, *e.g.*, split inclusive gateway. Otherwise, if it has one outgoing branch and multiple incoming branches, we call it a *merge*, *e.g.*, merge inclusive gateway. An exclusive gateway chooses one out of a set of mutually exclusive alternative incoming or outgoing branches. For an inclusive gateway, any number of branches among all its incoming or outgoing branches may be taken. A parallel gateway creates concurrent flows for all its outgoing branches or synchronizes concurrent flows for all its incoming branches. For an event-based gateway, it takes one of its outgoing branches or accepts one of its incoming branches based on events. From the parallelism point of view, it can be handled in the same way as an exclusive gateway. In the following, we call the branches that can be taken by a gateway during an execution as *active* branches.

The execution semantics of BPMN elements under our consideration is depicted in Figure 1, where the execution order is from left to right. If a token is on one sequence flow, then the destination node for this sequence flow is ready to be triggered. Besides this, there is no time constraint on when it should start. Particularly, the start event node can be triggered at any moment, which creates a token on its outgoing sequence flow. As for an end event node, whenever a token arrives on its incoming sequence flow, this process can be terminated by firing it.

Now we present and explain the following BPMN process, which serves as an illustrative example in one of the standard documents for BPMN [21].

Example 1. A BPMN process called Shipment Process of a Hardware Retailer is shown in Figure 2. It begins from the start event, *i.e.*, goods are ready to ship ($E1$), and immediately splits into two parallel branches with the parallel gateway $G1$. Thus, two tasks after $G1$ are executable in parallel: deciding normal post or special carrier ($T1$) and packaging goods ($T2$). The split exclusive gateway $G2$ after $T1$ means that only one of its outgoing branches is taken, *i.e.*, either normal post or special carrier is selected. In the former case, the task of checking if extra insurance is necessary ($T3$) is carried out. In the latter case, requesting quotes from carriers ($T4$) is executed. After completing $T3$, two tasks are independently executable due to the split inclusive gateway $G3$: taking out extra insurance ($T5$) and filling in a post label ($T6$). The corresponding merge inclusive gateway for $T5$ and $T6$ is $G4$. The merge exclusive gateway $G5$ has two incoming branches: either the completion of assigning a carrier ($T7$) or the outgoing flow of $G4$. To execute the final task that moves package to pick area ($T8$), one has to wait for both incoming branches of the merge parallel gateway $G6$, *i.e.*, the completion of $T2$ and the branch outgoing from $G5$.

2.2 Parallelism Definition for BPMN Processes

In our BPMN processes, gateways are the only constructs that can change the number of parallel branches, and thus have an impact on the degree of parallelism. To facilitate the computation of this degree, we define the parallel impact of the different gateways on BPMN processes. Precisely, if the number of parallel branches is increased (decreased, resp.) by m after a gateway n_g, then the parallel impact of n_g is m ($-m$, resp.). Particularly, an exclusive (event-based, resp.) gateway does not influence the parallelism since it only takes one of the incoming or outgoing branches. Hence, its parallel impact is 0. We formally define such parallel impacts as follows.

Definition 1. (Parallel Impact of Gateways) Given a gateway n_g, we denote its impact on the maximum number of parallel branches by $\Lambda(n_g)$, which is defined for each gateway as follows:

- if n_g is a split parallel (inclusive, resp.) gateway with $m+1$ outgoing branches, then $\Lambda(n_g) = m$;
- if n_g is a merge parallel (inclusive, resp.) gateway with $m+1$ incoming branches, then $\Lambda(n_g) = -m$;

- if n_g is a split or merge exclusive (event-based, resp.) gateway, then $\Lambda(n_g) = 0$.

Given a BPMN process B, we call an *enactment* of B a set of nodes involved in one actual execution, whose ordering should respect the execution semantics defined by B. For example, $p = E1.G1.T1.T2.G2.T4.T7.G5.G6.T8.E2$ is one enactment for Example 1 but $p\prime = E1.G1.T1.T2.G2.T3.G3.T5.G4.T4.T7.G5.G6.T8.E2$ is not since $T3.G3.T5.G4$ and $T4.T7$ are exclusive alternatives due to exclusive gateway $G2$. We denote the set of all enactments for a BPMN process B by $\Phi(B)$, simply Φ if there is no ambiguity. Note that any non-empty prefix of an enactment is also considered as an enactment.

Definition 2. (Degree of parallelism for enactments) Given an enactment $e \in \Phi$ of a BPMN process, let $\{n_g^1, ..., n_g^n\}$ be the set of all gateways involved in e. The degree of parallelism for e is $D(e) = 1 + \sum_{i=1}^{n} \Lambda(n_g^i)$.

The degree of parallelism for an enactment denotes the maximum number of active parallel branches at the end of this enactment.

Definition 3. (Degree of parallelism for BPMN processes) Given a BPMN process B and its set of all enactments Φ, the degree of parallelism for B is the maximum degree of its enactments, *i.e.*, $D(B) = Max_{e \in \Phi} D(e)$.

Given a BPMN process B, if $\forall k > 0$, we have $D(B) > k$, then B has an infinite degree of parallelism. Since BPMN processes have a finite number of nodes, this situation can be caused only by a cycle containing more added parallel branches than reduced ones. In a BPMN process, if we have a sequence $n_0 \twoheadrightarrow n_1 ... \twoheadrightarrow n_m$ such that $n_0 = n_m$, then we say that it is a process cycle. Only such cycles can generate infinite enactments considering that a BPMN process has a finite set of nodes.

Definition 4. (Parallel Augmented Cycle). Given a cycle ϕ in a BPMN process, $\phi = n_0 \twoheadrightarrow n_1 \twoheadrightarrow ...n_m \twoheadrightarrow n_0$, where $n_i, i \in \{0, ..., m\}$ are BPMN nodes, let $\{n_g^1, ..., n_g^k\}$ be the set of all gateways involved in ϕ. Then ϕ is called a Parallel Augmented Cycle (PAC) if $\sum_{i=1}^{k} \Lambda(n_g^i) > 0$.

LEMMA 1. *Given a BPMN process, its degree is infinite iff it contains a PAC.*

PROOF. Suppose that the degree of a BPMN process B is infinite and that it does not contain a PAC. Non existence of PAC implies that if B has cycles, for each cycle ϕ, we have $\sum_{i=1}^{n} \Lambda(n_g^i) \leq 0$, where n_g^i is a gateway in ϕ. Any possible infinite enactments in B can only come from such cycles, *i.e.*, ϕ executes infinitely. Since the impact of ϕ on the parallelism is not positive, it follows that $\exists k \in N, k \geq D(B)$, which contradicts the assumption of infinite degree for B. Now suppose that the degree of B is finite and it contains a PAC. This means that $\exists k \in N, k \geq D(B)$ and there exists a cycle for which we have $\sum_{i=1}^{n} \Lambda(n_g^i) > 0$, where n_g^i is a gateway in ϕ. From the latter, we know that for each $k \in N$, we can always find a number p such that the cycle is executed p times, leading to an enactment e with $D(e) > k$, which contradicts the assumption that $D(B)$ is finite. □

Our approach for computing the degree of parallelism described in the following sections only concerns the BPMN processes with finite degree, *i.e.*, processes without PAC. The presence of PAC in BPMN processes can be detected by static analysis, as it is done in our tool chain described in Section 5.

3. FORMAL MODELS FOR BPMN

In this section, we show how to transform BPMN processes into LTS models. This is achieved through process algebra encodings and enumerative state space exploration. These models are equipped with model checking features, which facilitate the computation of parallelism degree.

3.1 Process Algebra Encoding

Process algebras are used to formally model concurrent systems, which include a family of related approaches, *e.g.*, CSP, CCS, or ACP. We chose LNT [2] for three reasons. First, it is a value-passing process algebra that provides expressive operators for translating rather complex BPMN constructs, *e.g.*, nested gateways can be modeled by nested choice and/or parallel compositions. Second, a translation between two high-level languages is much simpler since both share similar operators, *e.g.*, sequence, choice, or interleaving. Third, LNT is supported by CADP, a state-of-the-art verification toolbox [10], that can be used to compile the LNT specification into an LTS, enumerating all the possible behaviors. Furthermore, CADP provides various analysis techniques and tools such as model checking, compositional verification, or performance evaluation.

We suppose that BPMN processes are syntactically correct. This can be achieved using existing tools (*e.g.*, the Bonita studio [7]). Now we briefly describe the principles for translating BPMN to LNT (more details are available in [11, 22]). For each BPMN process node, we generate an LNT process as follows.

- Start/End event node: for the start event node n, suppose $n \twoheadrightarrow m$, *i.e.*, m is the next node of n. The process for n calls the process for m. For an end event node, its process does nothing but terminates by using the empty statement (**null**).
- Split: we have three types of gateways relative to split structure.
    1. split parallel gateway n: suppose that n has k outgoing branches, *i.e.*, $n \twoheadrightarrow m_i, i \in \{1, ..., k\}$. The LNT process models the parallel execution of all outgoing branches using the LNT parallel operator (**par**). Each branch $m_i, i \in \{1, ..., k\}$ is translated by a call to the LNT process encoding the node m_i. In addition, if there exists a corresponding merge parallel gateway node mp, we need to generate an additional parallel branch to realize the synchronization point among the different branches. To do so, for this merge, we create a synchronization action *sync* at the beginning of the additional branch and at the end of all other branches. In this way, the additional branch synchronizes with all other branches on *sync* before calling the process for the next node after mp.

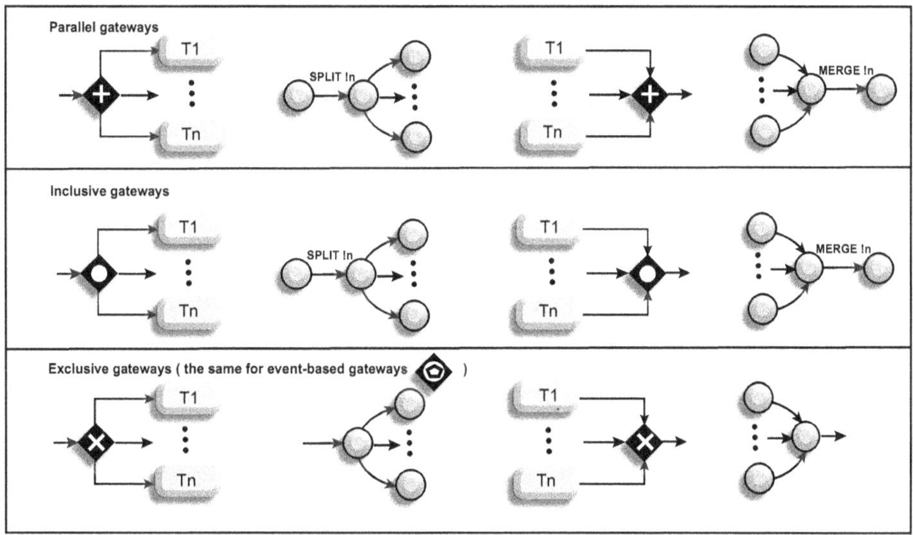

Figure 3: Extra transitions with parallelism information for each gateway considered.

2. split inclusive gateway n: suppose $n \twoheadrightarrow m_i, i \in \{1, ..., k\}$. Any combination of the branches m_i can be executed. For each subset $\{m_{i_1}, ..., m_{i_n}\}, 1 \leq n \leq k, \forall j \in \{1, ..., n\}, i_j \in \{1, ..., k\}$, we obtain all combinations of this subset by using the LNT parallel operator between $m_{i_j}, j \in \{1, ..., n\}$. Then the LNT choice operator (**select**) is used between all combinations of all subsets. If there exists a corresponding merge inclusive gateway, we generate an additional branch for synchronization purpose as above.

3. split exclusive gateway n: suppose $n \twoheadrightarrow m_i, i \in \{1, ..., k\}$. The process models the choice execution of all outgoing branches m_i using the LNT choice operator (**select**). Each branch calls the LNT process encoding the corresponding node.

- Merge: We have three types of merge gateways. A merge gateway has only one outgoing branch.

  1. merge parallel (inclusive, resp.) gateway n: suppose $n \twoheadrightarrow m$. The process for n first synchronizes with all corresponding incoming active branches on the synchronization action *sync* before calling the process for m, *i.e.*, it corresponds to the additional parallel branch produced by translating the split (parallel or inclusive) gateway.

  2. merge exclusive gateway n: suppose $n \twoheadrightarrow m$, then the process for n calls the process for m. Recall that there is no synchronization point for this gateway.

- Sequence: only task nodes are considered as sequential structure since they have exactly one incoming and one outgoing branch. For a task node n, if $n \twoheadrightarrow m$, its process first executes this task that is defined as an action. If m is not a merge (parallel or inclusive) gateway, the process for n calls the process for m. Otherwise, we synchronize the corresponding branch with merge gateway on the synchronization action *sync*, as described in split (parallel or inclusive) gateway.

Given a BPMN process B, the LNT specification obtained using the encoding sketched in this section preserves its execution semantics [11, 22]. Hence, by using classical enumerative exploration techniques, *e.g.*, the LNT compilers of CADP, the LTS generated from this LNT specification corresponds to all possible enactments of B.

3.2 LTS Models

LTS is a low-level formal model, which is defined as follows:

Definition 5. (LTS) An LTS is a tuple $L = (S, s^0, \Sigma, T)$ where S is a finite set of states; $s^0 \in S$ is the initial state; Σ is a finite set of labels; $T \subseteq S \times \Sigma \times S$ is a finite set of transitions.

In an LTS, we denote $s \xrightarrow{\sigma} s\prime$ for $(s, \sigma, s\prime) \in T$. A finite sequence $s_0 \xrightarrow{\sigma_0} s_1 \xrightarrow{\sigma_1} ...s_{n-1} \xrightarrow{\sigma_{n-1}} s_n$ is called a *path*, and the sequence of labels $\sigma_0\sigma_1...\sigma_{n-1}$ is called a *trace*. The LTS obtained from the LNT specification encoded from a given BPMN process represents exactly its execution semantics. We call such an LTS a BPMN LTS or simply LTS if there is no ambiguity.

LEMMA 2. *Each enactment of a BPMN process is represented by a trace in the corresponding LTS. Each trace of a BPMN LTS describes an enactment of its corresponding process.*

PROOF. Suppose that one enactment of a BPMN process is not represented by a trace in its BPMN LTS or one trace in the BPMN LTS does not describe an enactment of the process. This means that either the BPMN LTS does not represent the total execution semantics of the process or it encodes more than the execution semantics. It follows that the LNT specification does not strictly preserve the execution semantics of its BPMN process. However, this is not true according to [11, 22], and thus we get a contradiction. □

3.3 Extended LTS Models

In a BPMN LTS, parallelism is flattened into sequential interleaved executions, which casts away the parallelism information. To compute the degree of parallelism, it is necessary to retrieve such information from the corresponding BPMN process. More precisely, we have to know the number of active split or merge branches for all gateways. In the following, a state s in a BPMN LTS is called an *enabling* state for a BPMN gateway n_g if n_g is ready to be launched from s. Now we show how to extend a BPMN LTS by adding extra transitions with parallelism information for each type of gateways, as shown in Figure 3. This is done by adding extra transitions with corresponding parallelism labels in the LNT specification.

- For a split parallel gateway, its *enabling* state in the LTS is s, suppose $(s\prime \xrightarrow{\sigma})$ s. One extra transition with label *SPLIT* $!n$ is added before s, *i.e.*, $(s\prime \xrightarrow{\sigma})$ $s1 \xrightarrow{SPLIT\ !n} s$, where n represents the number of split branches from this parallel gateway. In a similar way, consider a merge parallel gateway whose *enabling* state is s, suppose s $(\xrightarrow{\sigma} s\prime)$. We add one transition with label *MERGE* $!n$ after s, *i.e.*, $s \xrightarrow{MERGE\ !n} s1$ $(\xrightarrow{\sigma} s\prime)$, where n is the number of merge branches to this parallel gateway.
- For split and merge inclusive gateways, we add extra transitions in the same way as parallel gateways. The difference is that in the label *SPLIT* $!n$ or *MERGE* $!n$, the value n represents the maximum number of split branches or merge branches taken by the gateways. This is because we aim at computing the maximum number of parallel branches.
- For split and merge exclusive gateways, only one branch is active at a time. Thus, we keep the corresponding LTS the same without adding any extra transition. Event-based gateways are treated exactly in the same way as exclusive gateways since they also execute only one branch.

4. DEGREE COMPUTATION

In this section, we show how to compute the degree of parallelism for a given BPMN process B directly on its corresponding Extended LTS, which is called ELTS in the following. We formally define the degree of ELTS, prove that it is equal to that of B, and propose model checking techniques to compute this degree.

4.1 Degree of ELTS

Given a trace π in a BPMN ELTS, the maximum number of active parallel branches at the end of π is called its degree of parallelism. Recall that in the ELTS, the labels of extra transitions contain the information about the maximum number of active split and merge branches for all gateways. Such information can be used to compute the degree of a trace. We consider the default trace degree as 1. After each transition whose label is *SPLIT* $!n$, we will have $n-1$ more parallel branches. In a similar way, for a transition label *MERGE* $!n$, the number of parallel branches will be reduced by $n-1$. In the following, the transition labels added for control flow are called control flow labels.

Definition 6. (Trace degree) Given a trace in an ELTS, denoted $\pi = \sigma_0\sigma_1...\sigma_t$, suppose the set of control flow labels in π is $\{SPLIT\ !i_1,\ SPLIT\ !i_2, ...,\ SPLIT\ !i_m,\ MERGE\ !j_1,\ MERGE\ !j_2, ...,\ MERGE\ !j_n\} \subseteq \{\sigma_0,\ \sigma_1, ..., \sigma_t\}$, the degree of parallelism for the trace π is

$$D(\pi) = 1 + \sum_{k=1}^{m}(i_k - 1) - \sum_{k=1}^{n}(j_k - 1).$$

Definition 7. (ELTS degree) Given a BPMN ELTS L, the set of all traces beginning from the initial state in L is denoted by $\Psi(L)$. The degree of parallelism for this ELTS is the maximum trace degree, $D(L) = Max_{\pi\in\Psi(L)}D(\pi)$.

THEOREM 1. *The degree of parallelism for a BPMN ELTS is equal to the degree of parallelism for the corresponding BPMN process.*

PROOF. Suppose that the degree for a BPMN ELTS, denoted by $D\prime$, does not equal to that for its corresponding BPMN process, denoted by D, *i.e.*, $D\prime \neq D$. Recall that $D\prime$ denotes the maximum trace degree in the ELTS and D equals to the maximum enactment degree in the process. Hence, the inequality of $D\prime$ and D implies that either the trace with maximum degree in ELTS does not represent an enactment of the process or the enactment with maximum degree in the process is not described by a trace in the ELTS. Both cases contradict with Lemma 2. □

Example 2. Consider the trace in Figure 4, which is contained in the ELTS for Example 1. In this trace, we have four control flow labels: two *SPLIT* $!2$ and two *MERGE* $!2$. From Definition 6, the degree for this trace is $1+(2*(2-1))-(2*(2-1)) = 1$. In other words, at the end of this trace, the number of active parallel branches is 1. Now consider its (sub) trace from beginning until $T5$, we have two control flow labels, both being *SPLIT* $!2$. The degree for this (sub) trace is $1+((2-1)+(2-1)) = 3$. This means that at the end of $T5$, the maximum number of active parallel branches is 3. To calculate the degree of the BPMN process, *i.e.*, the maximum trace degree from Theorem 1 and Definition 7, we must explore all traces of the corresponding ELTS.

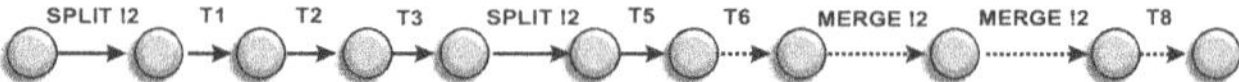

Figure 4: One trace of the ELTS for the BPMN example given in Figure 2.

4.2 Degree Computation by Model Checking

Given a BPMN process with finite degree, we propose model checking techniques to compute this degree on its corresponding ELTS. Recall that this degree is the maximum trace degree in the ELTS. Formula 1, written in MCL (*Model Checking Language*) [17], defines the property *SPLIT_MERGE(N)*, which expresses the existence of a trace whose degree is greater than or equal to N:

Formula 1.

$$SPLIT\_MERGE(N) = \quad (1)$$
$$mu\ X\ (c : Nat := 1). \quad (2)$$
$$((c >= N)\ or \quad (3)$$
$$< SPLIT\ ?\ fan\_out : Nat > X(c + (fan\_out - 1))\ or \quad (4)$$
$$< MERGE\ ?\ fan\_in : Nat > X(c - (fan\_in - 1))\ or \quad (5)$$
$$< not(SPLIT...\ or\ MERGE...) > X(c)) \quad (6)$$

More precisely, given a natural number N, there are two stop conditions for Formula 1. One is that after exploring all traces, there is no trace whose degree is greater than or equal to N, which means that the degree of the corresponding process is smaller than N. In this case, the returned value is false. The other one is that the degree of the trace currently explored becomes greater than or equal to N, in which case the process degree must be greater than or equal to N. Under this condition, the formula returns true. The functions used in Formula 1 are described as follows:

- Line 2 creates a parameter c of type natural number representing the degree of the currently explored trace. It is initialized as 1 because we consider the default degree for any trace as 1.
- Line 3 gives the positive stop condition, under which the value true is returned, *i.e.*, the degree is not smaller than N.
- Line 4 indicates how to deal with a transition with label *SPLIT !fan_out*, where *fan_out* is the number of active outgoing branches from the corresponding gateway. During the exploration of an ELTS, when arriving at such a transition, the degree of the current trace should be increased by *fan_out* − *1*.
- In a similar way, line 5 shows how to handle a transition with label *MERGE !fan_in*, where *fan_in* is the maximum number of active incoming branches to the corresponding gateway. Whenever reaching such a transition, the degree of the current trace should be subtracted by *fan_in* − *1*.
- Line 6 means that when meeting a transition whose label is not a control flow one, we continue to explore the ELTS without changing the degree.

COROLLARY 1. *Given a BPMN ELTS, if the value returned for SPLIT_MERGE(N) is true, then the degree of the corresponding process is greater than or equal to the number N. Otherwise, the degree is smaller than N.*

For the sake of efficiency, we apply Formula 1 to compute the degree for a given BPMN ELTS by adopting a dichotomic search. More precisely, we check the degree by verifying *SPLIT_MERGE*(2^1) for the first time since the default degree is 1. If the returned value is true, the degree is not smaller than 2. We continue to check the next number, denoted by *numFuture*, which is 2^2 for the second time and 2^m for the mth time until the returned value is false. We keep the last checked number for which the formula returns false, denoted by *negRecent*, as well as that for which the formula returns true, denoted by *posRecent*. The next number to be checked is in the middle of *negRecent* and *posRecent*, *i.e.*, *numFuture* = (*negRecent* + *posRecent*)/2. The stop condition is that *negRecent* is greater than *posRecent* by only 1. Algorithm 1 shows the pseudo code for this dichotomic search procedure, which is a variant of the classic binary search algorithm existing in the literature [24].

THEOREM 2. *If the value of (negRecent−posRecent) is 1, then the number posRecent is exactly the degree of parallelism for the given process.*

Algorithm 1 Computing the degree of parallelism using a dichotomic search

```
Input: BPMN ELTS
Initializations: posRecent:=1; negRecent:=1;
  numFuture:=2
while ((negRecent-posRecent) ≠ 1) do
  if SPLIT_MERGE(numFuture) then
    posRecent:=numFuture
    if negRecent=1 then
      numFuture:=posRecent * 2
    else
      numFuture:=(posRecent+negRecent)/2
  else
    negRecent:=numFuture
    numFuture:=(posRecent+negRecent)/2
return posRecent
```

PROOF. We know that *posRecent* denotes the last checked number that is smaller than or equal to the degree of the given process and *negRecent* represents the last checked number that is greater than this degree. If the value of (*negRecent* − *posRecent*) is equal to 1, then *posRecent* must be equal to the degree since there is no other natural number between *negRecent* and *posRecent*. □

As for the complexity of the degree computation on the ELTS, since we adopt a dichotomic search strategy, the number of times the formula is verified is proportional to the base 2 logarithm of the degree. Furthermore, the complexity of checking Formula 1 (alternation-free) with parameter N is linear *w.r.t.* the size of the formula (proportional to N) and the size of the ELTS (number of states and transitions). Note that the degree is bounded by the total number of outgoing branches for all split parallel and inclusive gateways, which is denoted by N^{out}_{p+i}.

THEOREM 3. *Given a BPMN ELTS L, its degree of parallelism can be computed in* $O((|S| + |T|) \cdot N^{out}_{p+i} \cdot log(N^{out}_{p+i}))$ *time, where |S| (|T|, resp.) is the number of states (transitions, resp.) of L.*

5. EVALUATION

In this section, we first present the architecture of our tool, which is integrated with the CADP toolbox [10]. CADP is a verification toolbox dedicated to the design, analysis, and verification of asynchronous systems consisting of concurrent processes interacting via message passing. Then, we present our experimental results obtained by applying it to a set of BPMN processes.

5.1 Tool Support

To evaluate our approach, we implemented a prototype tool (DeCa) connected to CADP. Figure 5 shows our tool architecture. Given a BPMN process, our tool first encodes it into the LNT value-passing process algebra, one of the input languages accepted by CADP, to capture the behavioral semantics of the process. This LNT encoding is an extension of the VerChor platform [11, 12, 22]. VerChor uses Eclipse Indigo and the BPMN 2.0 modeler as front-end for BPMN, and transforms BPMN into the LNT process algebra by using several intermediate translation steps. Afterwards, the CADP compilers are invoked on the corresponding LNT specification. Recall that a process with

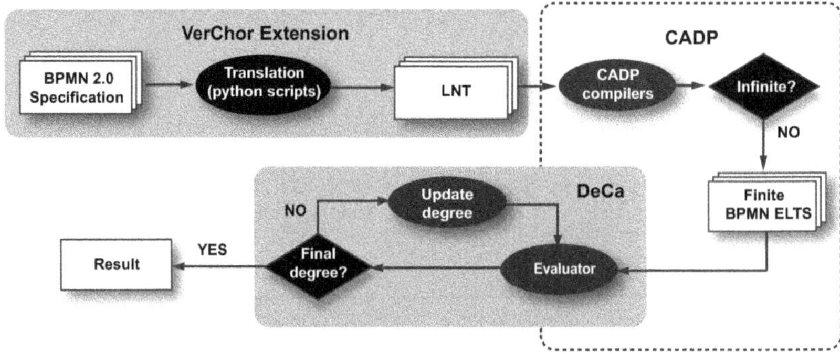

Figure 5: Tool architecture.

infinite degree corresponds to the existence of PAC, which is detected by CADP compilers by checking the finite control property [4]. Hence, only ELTSs for the processes with finite degree are generated. Then, the tool DeCa takes a BPMN ELTS as input and repeatedly invokes the Evaluator 4.0 model checker [16, 17] of CADP to verify Formula 1 encoded in MCL, until the final degree is obtained. This is done by adopting a dichotomic search to minimize the number of model checking invocations. It is worth noticing that, since the LTSs obtained by our tool encode the semantics of the initial BPMN processes, they can be analyzed using other tools available in CADP, such as interactive simulators or testing tools.

5.2 Experimental Results

All our experiments were conducted by using a (server) machine that has six 3.07 GHz processors and 11.7 GB of RAM. Our DeCa tool is implemented in C, using gcc with version 3.4.3. The version of CADP used in our evaluation is BETA-VERSION 2014-a "Amsterdam".

In our approach, one costly computation is the ELTS construction, which includes two phases. The first one is the transformation from BPMN to LNT specification, which has only linear complexity since the specification is generated directly from each node of the BPMN process (see Section 3.1). The second is about the ELTS generation from the LNT specification, which may suffer from state explosion. This can be greatly improved through abstraction.

From Formula 1 and Algorithm 1, we know that the only necessary information to compute the degree is contained in the control flow labels. To reduce the size of BPMN ELTSs without affecting the computation of the degree, we replace all LNT actions representing BPMN tasks by the empty statement (**null**), which keeps the same branching structure with only control flow labels. In the following, we call such an ELTS *abstracted* ELTS and the original ELTS containing all tasks *raw* ELTS. The complexity of degree computation, which depends on the size of the input ELTS (Theorem 3), is greatly reduced if the dichotomic search is applied on the abstracted ELTS instead of the raw one. This improvement becomes clearer for the BPMN processes with a larger number of tasks, and is also demonstrated by the analysis of our experimental results.

We applied our tool on more than one hundred BPMN processes, 90% of which being handcrafted. The experimental results of some examples are shown in Table 1, including several ones extracted from the literature. For instance, Shipment is the example depicted in Figure 1. ChoreOs1 is a variant used in the ChoreOs project [1] and ChoreOs2 is the one obtained from ChoreOs1 by replacing parallel gateways with inclusive gateways. We also present in the second part of the table a few handcrafted examples to show the scalability of our approach considering that those from the literature are quite small.

In this table, for each BPMN process, we give its size (number of tasks and gateways), the size of raw and abstracted ELTS (number of states and transitions), its degree of parallelism as well as the total required time, including the generation of abstracted ELTS from LNT specification as well as the degree computation on the abstracted ELTS. The number of each type of gateways includes split and merge ones.

BPMN processes may correspond to very large raw ELTSs because the parallel operators from parallel and inclusive gateways are expanded in all the possible interleaved behaviors. However, their abstracted ELTSs have very small size, which only depend on the structure of gateways. For example, P111 has more tasks than P110. Hence, the size of the raw ELTS for P111 is much bigger than that for P110. However, they have exactly the same structure in terms of gateways. This is why they have the same abstracted ELTS and total computation time. In our experiments, calculating the degree on abstracted ELTSs reduces drastically the required time, both for ELTS generation and degree computation, especially for the processes whose raw ELTS has large size. For example, if we compute the degree directly on the raw ELTS for P111, it requires about 36 minutes, whereas it takes only 8 seconds on the abstracted ELTS.

With Formula 1 and the ELTS, we can also obtain some important information about the enactment(s) of the BPMN process whose degree is the maximum one. To do this, we add gateway identifiers to all control labels of extra transitions in ELTS, *i.e.*, $MERGE\,!n$ becomes now $MERGE\,!n\,!id_g$, where id_g is the identifier of the gateway associated to this extra transition. The Evaluator 4.0 model checker of CADP provides diagnostics (witnesses and counterexamples) ex-

Table 1: Experimental results for computing the degree of parallelism, where |TS|, |P|, |I|, |E|, and |D| are the number of tasks, parallel, inclusive, exclusive gateways, and the degree of parallelism, respectively.

BPMN	|TS|	|P|	|I|	|E|	raw ELTS($\|S\|/\|T\|$)	abs. ELTS($\|S\|/\|T\|$)	|D|	time
Shipment [21]	8	2	2	2	56/96	9/11	3	2s01
PizzaOrder [21]	9	2	0	0	30/51	3/2	3	1s53
ChoreOs1 [1]	6	4	0	0	20/26	6/5	3	1s56
ChoreOs2	6	0	4	0	22/37	7/8	3	2s03
BookingSystem [22]	6	1	0	1	12/12	2/1	2	1s23
P010	4		4	2	134/275	30/63	3	3s05
P050	5	6			95/220	8/7	4	2s21
P060	8	4	2		576/1596	40/68	5	3s31
P070	30	2		4	20,745/100,234	3/2	6	3s27
P080	40	2			746,505/4,852,234	3/2	8	3s58
P110	25	4	2	2	32,849/245,932	24/36	15	8s15
P111	45	4	2	2	33,554,513/335,544,492	24/36	15	8s18
P120	31	3	2	4	983,188/9,847,132	14/19	17	7s72

plaining the verification result. Precisely, if the verdict is true, then the diagnostic generated is the shortest trace corresponding to the enactment of the BPMN process whose degree is equal to or greater than the input number N. Otherwise, if the verdict is false, then the diagnostic is the whole BPMN LTS to explain that it is impossible to find a trace whose degree is equal to or greater than N. Suppose that the degree of parallelism for a BPMN process is computed as D. If we apply Formula 1 on the number D, then the diagnostic returned actually corresponds to the shortest enactment(s) with the maximum number of parallel branches, which provides valuable information for resource allocation planning.

6. RELATED WORK

First of all, some metrics have been developed for business processes that are regarded as predictors in terms of errors estimation, such as McCabe cyclomatic, CFC and CC metrics [15, 19]. All these complexity metrics were analyzed from an empirical point of view. Differently, the degree of parallelism is a metric that represents the peak demand on tasks to be performed. It can be considered as a worst case metric for business processes, that is a valuable guidance on process modelling and execution.

Several works have focused on providing formal semantics and verification techniques for BPMN, *e.g.*, [23, 27, 28, 8, 6, 22]. The authors of [27] present a formal semantics for BPMN by encoding it into the CSP process algebra. Thus, formal verifications can be carried out against some properties like consistency and compatibility [28]. Decker and Weske present in [6] an extension of BPMN 1.0 (iBPMN) in the direction of interaction modeling. They also propose a formal semantics for iBPMN in terms of interaction Petri nets. [8] presents a mapping from BPMN to Petri nets that enables the static analysis of BPMN models. [23] presents a double transformation from BPMN to Petri nets and from Petri nets to mCRL2. This allows one to use both Petri nets based tools and the mCRL2 toolset for searching deadlocks, livelocks, or checking temporal properties. Our solution, based on a direct translation from BPMN to the LNT process algebra, allows the analysis of business processes using model checking and equivalence checking.

As far as the degree of parallelism for BPMN is concerned, theoretically, it can also be computed by reasoning on Petri net models and determining the bound of a Petri net, which is the maximum number of tokens in a marking of the net. However, to do so, the reachability graph for the net should be constructed entirely. The reachability problem for some specific Petri nets, such as conflict-free Petri nets and 1 safe live free-choice nets [9], is NP-complete. Note that for arbitrary Petri nets, this problem is much harder [18]. This is probably one reason why there is no work on degree computation with Petri nets in the literature. In our paper, we present a very efficient solution for computing the degree of parallelism since we handle LTSs containing only control flow labels by replacing tasks with empty statement.

[25] proposes several algorithms for directly calculating the degree of parallelism of a BPMN process without establishing its behavior model. In this work, a duration constraint is associated to each task, *i.e.*, a task is obliged to be completed within a certain period of time. Furthermore, a task must begin immediately after the completion of its precedent task. Without considering inclusive gateways, they deal with three special cases of BPMN processes: with only one type of gateways; without split exclusive gateway nor cycles; with only two types of gateways. Each case is treated with a different algorithm. Our work focuses on BPMN processes without time constraints because it is not always possible to associate duration to tasks and ensure they can start upon demand, *e.g.*, one task may not start immediately after the precedent one. In this context, we propose a uniform approach, which can automatically analyze the degree of parallelism using model checking techniques for complex BPMN structures, *i.e.*, combining different gateways and cycles.

7. CONCLUSION

In this paper, we show how to represent BPMN processes in terms of ELTSs that contain the information about the maximum number of split and merge branches. This is achieved by an encoding into the LNT value-passing process algebra. It is worth noting that BPMN processes handled by our approach are general enough to be able to contain nested gateways as well as infinite loops. The control-flow information is then used for computing the degree of parallelism with model checking techniques. Our approach is fully supported by a chain of tools, including the encoding of BPMN into process algebra, the ELTS generator, and the degree computation. Furthermore, we show how to construct an abstracted ELTS by keeping only control flow labels and replacing tasks with empty statements, which greatly improves performance, as shown in our experimental results. Finally, with the CADP model checker, we produce the enactments of BPMN processes that possess the maximum number of parallel branches, which is a valuable guide for resource allocation planning.

As far as future work is concerned, we first plan to consider a larger subset of BPMN including data objects. Indeed, we currently compute an upper bound of the parallelism degree, which may be actually lower if gateway decisions are controlled by data. Such an extension would allow us to compute (by reusing the same tool chain) the exact degree for a given BPMN process with data control. A second perspective is to investigate other forms of quantitative analysis, such as the throughput and latency of tasks in a BPMN process, which can be computed by extending LTS models with Markovian information and carrying out steady-state analysis [3].

Acknowledgements. This work has been partially supported by the OpenCloudware project (2012-2015), which is funded by the French "*Fonds national pour la Société Numérique*" (FSN), and is supported by *Pôles* Minalogic, Systematic, and SCS.

8. REFERENCES

[1] M. Autili, P. Inverardi, and M. Tivoli. CHOREOS: Large Scale Choreographies for the Future Internet. In *Proc. of CSMR-WCRE'14*, pages 391–394. IEEE, 2014.

[2] D. Champelovier, X. Clerc, H. Garavel, Y. Guerte, C. McKinty, V. Powazny, F. Lang, W. Serwe, and G. Smeding. Reference Manual of the LOTOS NT to LOTOS Translator, Version 5.4. INRIA/VASY, 2011.

[3] N. Coste, H. Garavel, H. Hermanns, F. Lang, R. Mateescu, and W. Serwe. Ten Years of Performance Evaluation for Concurrent Systems using CADP. In *Proc. of ISoLA'10*, volume 6416 of *LNCS*, pages 128–142. Springer, 2010.

[4] M. Dam. Model Checking Mobile Processes. *Information and Computation*, 129(1):35–51, 1996.

[5] T.H. Davenport. *Process Innovation: Reengineering Work Through Information Technology*. Harvard Business School Press, 1993.

[6] G. Decker and M. Weske. Interaction-centric Modeling of Process Choreographies. *Information Systems*, 36(2):292–312, 2011.

[7] Bonita designer (online). Available: http://www.bonitasoft.com/.

[8] R.M. Dijkman, M. Dumas, and C. Ouyang. Semantics and Analysis of Business Process Models in BPMN. *Inf. Softw. Technol.*, 50(12):1281–1294, 2008.

[9] J. Esparza. Reachability in Live and Safe Free-choice Petri Nets is NP-complete . *Theoretical Computer Science*, 198:211–224, 1998.

[10] H. Garavel, F. Lang, R. Mateescu, and W. Serwe. CADP 2011: A Toolbox for the Construction and Analysis of Distributed Processes. *STTT*, 2(15):89–107, 2013.

[11] M. Güdemann, P. Poizat, G. Salaün, and A. Dumont. VerChor: A Framework for Verifying Choreographies. In *Proc. of FASE'13*, volume 7793 of *LNCS*, pages 226–230. Springer, 2013.

[12] M. Güdemann, G. Salaün, and M. Ouederni. Counterexample Guided Synthesis of Monitors for Realizability Enforcement. In *Proc. of ATVA'12*, volume 7561 of *LNCS*, pages 238–253. Springer, 2012.

[13] ISO/IEC. International Standard 19510, Information technology – Business Process Model and Notation. 2013.

[14] C. Larman. *Applying UML And Patterns: An Introduction To Object-Oriented Analysis And Design And Iterative Development*. Prentice Hall, 2005.

[15] K. Bisgaard Lassen and W. Van der Aalst. Complexity Metrics for Workflow Nets. *Inf. Softw. Technol.*, 51(3):610–626, 2009.

[16] R. Mateescu and M. Sighireanu. Efficient On-the-Fly Model-Checking for Regular Alternation-Free Mu-Calculus. *Sci. Comput. Program.*, 46(3):255–281, 2003.

[17] R. Mateescu and D. Thivolle. A Model Checking Language for Concurrent Value-Passing Systems. In *Proc. of FM'08*, volume 5014 of *LNCS*, pages 148–164. Springer, 2008.

[18] E.W. Mayr. An Algorithm for the General Petri Net Reachability Problem. *SIAM J. Comput.*, 13(3):441–460, 1984.

[19] T. McCabe. A Complexity Measure. In *IEEE Transactions on Software Engineering*, volume 2, pages 308–320. IEEE, 1976.

[20] OMG. *Business Process Model and Notation (BPMN) – Version 2.0*. January 2011.

[21] OMG. BPMN 2.0 by Example. 2010.

[22] P. Poizat and G. Salaün. Checking the Realizability of BPMN 2.0 Choreographies. In *Proc. of SAC'12*, pages 1927–1934. ACM Press, 2012.

[23] I. Raedts, M. Petkovic, Y. S. Usenko, J. M. van der Werf, J. F. Groote, and L. Somers. Transformation of BPMN Models for Behaviour Analysis. In *Proc. of MSVVEIS'07*, pages 126–137, 2007.

[24] T. J. Rolfe. Analytic Derivation of Comparisons in Binary Search. *SIGNUM Newsletter*, 32(4):15–19, 1997.

[25] Y. Sun and J. Su. Computing Degree of Parallelism for BPMN Processes. In *Proc. of ICSOC'11*, volume 7084 of *LNCS*, pages 1–15. Springer, 2011.

[26] W. M. P. van der Aalst and A. H. M. Ter Hofstede. YAWL: Yet Another Workflow Language. *Information Systems*, 30:245–275, 2003.

[27] P.Y.H. Wong and J. Gibbons. A Process Semantics for BPMN. In *Proc. of ICFEM'08*, volume 5256 of *LNCS*, pages 355–374. Springer, 2008.

[28] P.Y.H. Wong and J. Gibbons. Verifying Business Process Compatibility. In *Proc. of QSIC'08*, pages 126–131. IEEE, 2008.

Architecture Internalisation in BIP

Simon Bliudze, Joseph Sifakis
EPFL, Station 14
CH-1015 Lausanne,
Switzerland
firstname.lastname@epfl.ch

Marius Bozga
UJF-Grenoble 1 / CNRS
VERIMAG UMR 5104
F-38041 Grenoble, France
marius.bozga@imag.fr

Mohamad Jaber
American University of Beirut
Lebanon
mj54@aub.edu.lb

ABSTRACT

We consider two approaches for building component-based systems, which we call respectively *architecture-based* and *architecture-agnostic*. The former consists in describing coordination constraints in a purely declarative manner through parametrizable glue operators; it provides higher abstraction level and, consequently, stronger correctness by construction. The latter uses simple fixed coordination primitives, which are spread across component behaviour; it is more error-prone, but allows performance optimisation. We study architecture internalisation leading from an architecture-based system to an equivalent architecture-agnostic one, focusing, in particular, on component-based systems described in BIP. BIP uses connectors for hierarchical composition of components. We study connector internalisation in three steps. 1) We introduce and study the properties of interaction expressions, which represent the combined information about all the effects of an interaction. We show that they are a very powerful tool for specifying and analysing structured interaction. 2) We formalize the connector semantics of BIP by using interaction expressions. The formalization proves to be mathematically rigorous and concise. 3) We introduce the T/B component model and provide a semantics preserving translation of BIP into this model. The translation is compositional that is, it preserves the structure of the source models. The results are illustrated by simple examples. A Java implementation is evaluated on two case studies.

Categories and Subject Descriptors

D.3.1 [**Programming Languages**]: Formal Definitions and Theory; D.3.2 [**Programming Languages**]: Language Classifications—*Concurrent, distributed and parallel languages*

Keywords

BIP; interaction expressions; connectors; data transfer; architecture internalisation; Top/Bottom component model

CBSE'14, June 30–July 4, 2014, Marcq-en-Baroeul, France.
Copyright 2014 ACM 978-1-4503-2577-6/14/06 ...$15.00.
http://dx.doi.org/10.1145/2602458.2602477.

1. INTRODUCTION

Architectures depict design principles, paradigms that can be understood by all, allow thinking on a higher plane and avoiding low-level mistakes. They are a means for ensuring correctness by construction by enforcing global properties characterizing the coordination between components.

Using architectures largely accounts for our ability to master complexity and develop systems cost-effectively. System developers extensively use libraries of reference architectures ensuring both functional and non-functional properties, for example fault-tolerant architectures, architectures for resource management and QoS control, time-triggered architectures and security architectures.

Using architectures allows shifting the focus of developers from low-level code to high-level structures ensuring coordination in a component-based system. These structures are constraints between the coordinated components expressed in terms of communication mechanisms such as multiparty interaction, message passing, broadcast etc. Formally they can be understood as the assembly of coordination mechanisms which restrict the behavior of the coordinated components so as to satisfy a global characteristic property.

There exists an abundant literature on software architectures. Most papers study Architecture Description Languages (ADLs) for representing and analyzing architectural designs [15]. ADLs provide both conceptual frameworks and concrete syntax for characterizing software architectures. They also provide tools for parsing, compiling, analyzing, or simulating architectural descriptions written in their associated language. While all ADLs are concerned with architectural design, there is no agreement on what is an ADL, what aspects of architecture should be modeled in an ADL, and which of several possible ADLs is best suited for a particular problem. The borders between the realm of the ADLs and that of programming languages are blurring.

Despite the considerable diversity in the capabilities of different ADLs, they all share a common paradigm: software can be designed as the hierarchical composition of components by application of architectures. Components are computational elements characterized by their behavior and their interface. The latter defines points of interaction between a component and its environment.

ADLs specify the "glue" of architectural designs, usually expressed as the combination of connections between components. Connections may denote simple interaction mechanisms such as rendezvous, broadcast and function call. But they also may represent more complex ones such as protocols, buses and schedulers. In both cases, they are intended to specify two main aspects of interaction: 1) *control-flow* that is synchronization constraints; 2) *data-flow* that is how data of each component are transformed upon interaction.

If the ADL is expressive enough, it is possible to describe architectures in a purely declarative manner. Architectures can be understood as constraints that adequately restrict the behavior of the coordinated components so as to achieve a desired coordination property. They are defined to a large extent, independently from the components that make up the system. We speak then of an *architecture-based* approach for building component-based systems. Another approach considers irrelevant the distinction between atomic components and their associated coordination mechanisms: a system consists of a set of components—some providing basic functionality and some ensuring coordination. Dependencies between components are explicitly described by their behavior (code) via import clauses, function calls and read/write instructions. We call this approach *architecture-agnostic.*

The distinction between architecture-based and architecture-agnostic approaches appears very early in process algebra theories. CCS proposes a single parallel composition operator based on matching between input and output actions occurring in the description of processes. On the contrary, CSP, proposes a parallel composition operator *parameterized* by a set of actions that must synchronize. The dichotomy illustrated by this example is further accentuated in practice. Architecture-based approaches adopted by ADLs are CSP-like. They consider coordination as external and independent from the evolution of components. Architectures are, to a large extent, entities distinct from behavior. They are combinations of operators parameterized by the allowed interactions. Architecture-agnostic designs are based on a single composition operator. Coordination is described in terms of communication primitives appearing in their code. This approach is taken by most programming languages and by the various process algebras cloned from CCS.

In this paper, we study architecture internalisation leading from an architecture-based system to an equivalent architecture-agnostic one. Two main reasons motivate this study. One is the exploration of relationships between architecture-based and architecture-agnostic approaches. The other is more practically oriented and deals with the possibility to compile declarative-style architectural constraints into executable code. Is it possible to generate from an architecture-based system an equivalent architecture-agnostic one, where architecture glue is cast in dependencies between components explicitly described in their code?

We study the internalisation problem for component-based systems described in BIP [5]. BIP (Behaviour, Interaction, Priority) is a component-based framework that allows hierarchical composition of components by using connectors. Components can be considered as transition systems. A component interface consists of ports that label its transitions with associated exported variables. From some state, a port p can participate in an interaction if the component has a transition labeled by p which is enabled at this state.

In BIP, a connector is composed of two distinct parts:

Control-flow part specifies a relation between a set of bottom ports and a set of top ports. The interaction requires synchronization of all the ports. The top ports can be used to export the results of the interaction.

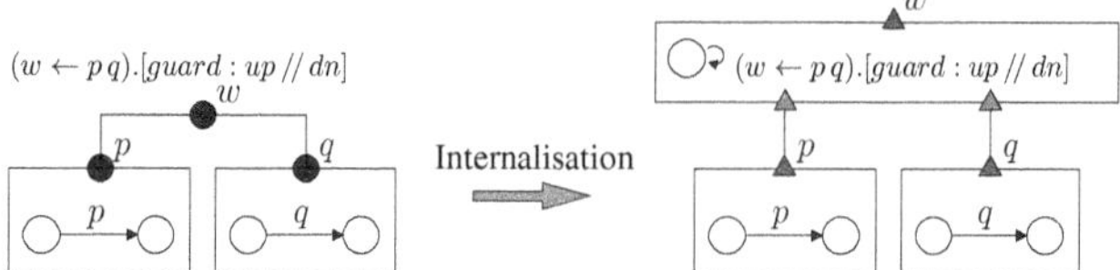

Figure 2: A BIP and the corresponding T/B component

Data-flow part specifies the computation associated with the interaction. The computation can affect local variables and those associated with the ports.

In Fig. 1a, we provide the specification of the connector describing the interaction between two ports p and q. The control flow part is described by the relation $w \leftarrow pq$ meaning that for the interaction w to take place both p and q should participate—$\{p, q\}$ is the set of bottom ports and $\{w\}$ is the set of top ports. The data-flow part consists of an upward computation followed by a downward computation separated by "//". The execution of an interaction is atomic. For the considered example, the interaction between p and q consists in computing $\max(x_p, x_q)$ and assigning this value to the variables x_p and x_q. Fig. 1b depicts a hierarchical connector r enforcing the interaction between ports p, q and s. The execution of this interaction results in an upward computation of $\max(\max(x_p, x_q), x_s)$ followed by a downward computation assigning this value to the port variables of the atomic components. As shown in [10], hierarchical connectors can be flattened into equivalent connectors. Fig. 1c shows a connector equivalent to the hierarchical connector by eliminating the interaction w.

Internalization of connectors in BIP models, consists in replacing them by a set of coordinators that directly implement their semantics. Coordinators play the role of an Engine that handles each interaction atomically. The internalised BIP model is the plain composition of the atomic BIP components with a set of coordinators, in bijection with the BIP connectors. To describe coordinators, we extend the BIP component model. The behavior of the components of the extended model is a set of transitions labeled with interaction expressions. Their interface is composed of sets of top and bottom ports and associated variables. As all the interaction capabilities of components are specified in their behavior, they can be composed without any additional external information. We show that component composition in the new model, called Top/Bottom (T/B) model, can be expressed by using a single associative partial operator $\|$.

The correspondence between a connector and the associated coordinator is straightforward. The latter is a T/B component that has the same interface as the connector (same set of top and bottom ports and associated variables). It exhibits a cyclic behavior by computing the data transfer functions of the connector. Fig. 2 illustrates the principle of connector internalisation on a simple example. The corresponding coordinator is a stateless automaton that can perform a transition labeled by the interaction expression. Top and bottom ports are shown by blue outward- and red inward-facing triangles, respectively.

We study the connector internalisation problem for BIP in three steps. First, we study interaction expressions and their properties. We show in particular that they are a very powerful tool for specifying and analyzing structured interaction. Second, we formalize the connector semantics of BIP by using interaction expressions. The formalization proves

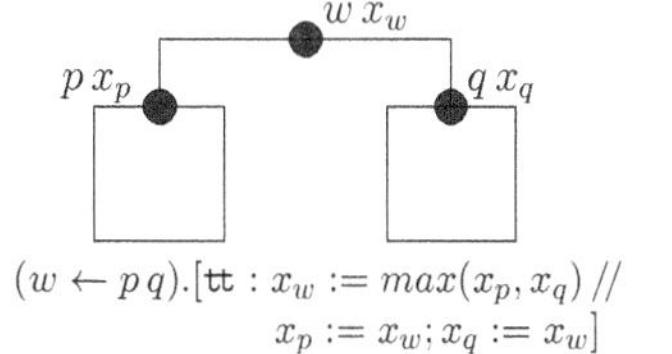

$(w \leftarrow p\,q).[\mathtt{tt} : x_w := max(x_p, x_q)\,//\, x_p := x_w; x_q := x_w]$

(a) Simple BIP connector

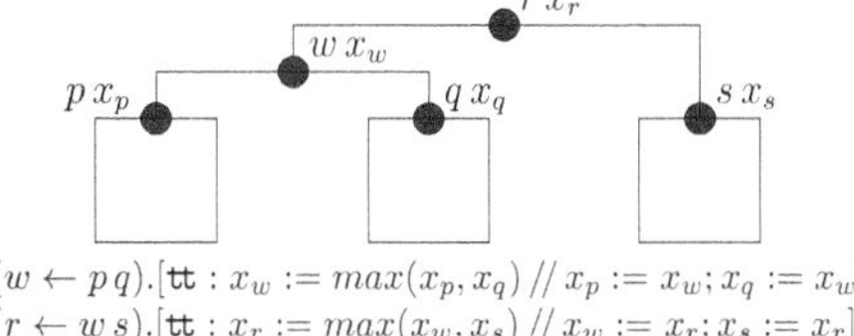

$(w \leftarrow p\,q).[\mathtt{tt} : x_w := max(x_p, x_q)\,//\, x_p := x_w; x_q := x_w]$
$(r \leftarrow w\,s).[\mathtt{tt} : x_r := max(x_w, x_s)\,//\, x_w := x_r; x_s := x_r]$

(b) Hierarchical BIP connector

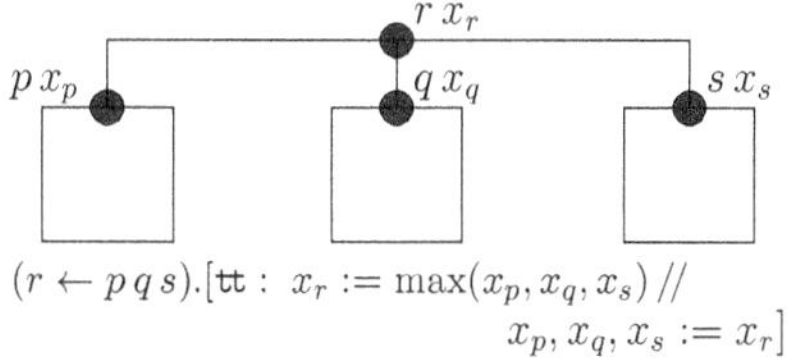

$(r \leftarrow p\,q\,s).[\mathtt{tt} :\ x_r := \max(x_p, x_q, x_s)\,//\, x_p, x_q, x_s := x_r]$

(c) Simple equivalent of Fig. 1b

Figure 1: BIP connectors

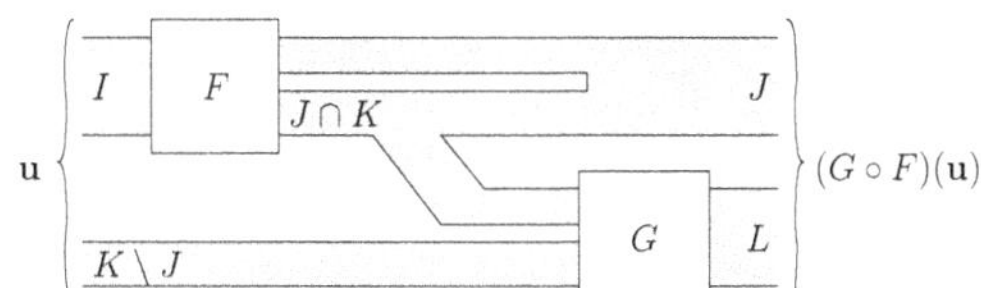

Figure 3: Composition of structured functions

to be mathematically rigorous and concise. It treats on an equal footing control and data flow aspects. It differs from previous formalizations that were focusing mainly on control flow. Third, we introduce the T/B component model and provide a semantics preserving translation of BIP into this model. The translation is compositional: it preserves the structure of the source models.

We discuss an implementation of the T/B components and provide an algorithm for their execution. The implementation can be used for the execution of BIP components after internalisation of their connectors. Furthermore, it can be used for the execution of general T/B models.

The paper is structured as follows. In Sect. 2, we introduce the notion of interaction expressions, shared by all the models in the subsequent sections. In Sect. 3, we provide a formalization of connectors in BIP and present their properties. In Sect. 4, we present the T/B component model, study its properties and present a structured encoding of BIP models. In Sect. 5, we provide experimental results about a Java-based implementation.

2. INTERACTIONS

2.1 Structured Partial Functions

Let $(\mathsf{D}_i)_{i\in\mathcal{I}}$ be data domains, $\mathcal{I}$ a universal index set. For each $I \subseteq \mathcal{I}$, denote by $\mathsf{D}[I] \triangleq \prod_{i\in I} \mathsf{D}_i$ the set of unordered tuples $\mathbf{u} = (u_i)_{i\in I}$, such that $u_i \in \mathsf{D}_i$, for all $i \in I$. For $I = \emptyset$, we have $\mathsf{D}[\emptyset] = \mathbf{1} \triangleq \{*\}$. For each $\mathbf{u} = (u_i)_{i\in I} \in \mathsf{D}[I]$ and $I' \subseteq I$ define the *projection* $\mathbf{u}_{I'} = (u_i)_{i\in I'} \in \mathsf{D}[I']$. We also denote $\mathbf{u}_{\overline{I'}} \triangleq \mathbf{u}_{I\setminus I'}$ the complementary projection. For $I, J \subseteq \mathcal{I}$, the *merge* of tuples is the partial operation $\sqcup : \mathsf{D}[I]\times\mathsf{D}[J] \to \mathsf{D}[I\cup J]$ defined only if $\nexists i \in I\cap J : u_i \neq v_i$, by putting, for $\mathbf{u} \in \mathsf{D}[I], \mathbf{v} \in \mathsf{D}[J]$, $\mathbf{u} \sqcup \mathbf{v} \triangleq (w_i)_{i\in I\cup J}$, with $\forall i \in I,\ w_i = u_i$ and $\forall j \in J,\ w_j = v_j$.

Consider structured partial functions $F : \mathsf{D}[I] \to \mathsf{D}[J]$. For each $J' \subseteq J$ the *projection* $F_{J'} : \mathsf{D}[I] \to \mathsf{D}[J']$ is defined by putting $F_{J'}(\mathbf{u}) \triangleq F(\mathbf{u})_{J'}$, for all $\mathbf{u} \in \mathsf{D}[I]$. The complementary projection notation is extended analogously: $F_{\overline{J'}} \triangleq F_{J\setminus J'}$. The *composition* of two structured partial functions $F : \mathsf{D}[I] \to \mathsf{D}[J]$ and $G : \mathsf{D}[K] \to \mathsf{D}[L]$ is the structured partial function $G \circ F : \mathsf{D}[I \cup (K \setminus J)] \to \mathsf{D}[J \cup L]$ defined, when all sub-terms are defined, by putting $(G \circ F)(\mathbf{u}) \triangleq F(\mathbf{u}_I) \sqcup G(F_{K\cap J}(\mathbf{u}_I) \sqcup \mathbf{u}_{K\setminus J})$ (see Fig. 3).

Proposition 2.1 *Composition of structured partial functions is associative. It is commutative whenever $J\cap K = I\cap L = \emptyset$.*

For any $I \subseteq \mathcal{I}$, let $X_I = \{x_i{:}\mathsf{D}_i \mid i \in I\}$ be a set of typed variables x_i with corresponding domains D_i. We write $X_I : \mathsf{D}[I]$ to denote the product domain of the variables in X_I.

Let $F : \mathsf{D}[I] \to \mathsf{D}[J]$ be a structured partial function, such that $I \cap J \neq \emptyset$ and consider a non-empty set of variables $X_L : \mathsf{D}[L]$ with $L \subseteq I \cap J$. The variables X_L can be used with F as *local* variables to compute values in $\mathsf{D}[J \setminus L]$ based on values in $\mathsf{D}[I \setminus L]$; the variables X_L are updated by *side effect*. We write $F[\![X_L]\!] : \mathsf{D}[I \setminus L] \to \mathsf{D}[J \setminus L]$.

Let $\mathbf{v} \in \mathsf{D}[L]$ be the valuation of X_L and let $\mathbf{u} \in \mathsf{D}[I\setminus L]$. If F is defined on $(\mathbf{u}, \mathbf{v})$, an application of $F[\![X_L]\!]$ to $\mathbf{u}$ produces the values $\mathbf{w} \in \mathsf{D}[J \setminus L]$ and the new valuation $\mathbf{v}' \in \mathsf{D}[L]$ of X_L, such that $(\mathbf{w}, \mathbf{v}') = F(\mathbf{u}, \mathbf{v})$.

Lemma 2.2 *Let $F_1[\![X_{L_1}]\!]$ and $F_2[\![X_{L_2}]\!]$ be two structured partial functions and assume $L_1 \cap L_2 = X_{L_1} \cap X_{L_2} = \emptyset$. Then holds $F_1[\![X_{L_1}]\!] \circ F_2[\![X_{L_2}]\!] = (F_1 \circ F_2)[\![X_{L_1} \cup X_{L_2}]\!]$.*

Structured partial functions with local variables are particularly useful for the definition of the semantics of *assignment expressions* of the form $(X_J, X_L) := e(X_I, X_L)$, where e is an expression on variables X_I and X_L. Indeed, the expression defines a structured partial function $e : \mathsf{D}[I \cup L] \to \mathsf{D}[J\cup L]$ and the fact that variables X_L appear on both sides of the assignment is reflected by considering $e[\![X_L]\!]$.

2.2 Interaction Expressions

Interaction expressions defined below represent the combined information about all the effects of an interaction involving several ports. We show that they are the basic and general concept for expressing coordination in both architecture-based and architecture agnostic models.

Let $\mathcal{P} \subseteq \mathcal{I}$ be a set of ports. For each $p \in \mathcal{P}$, let $x_p : \mathsf{D}_p$ be a typed variable. The interaction expressions represent the combined information about the effects of an *interaction* involving several ports.

Definition 2.3 *An* interaction *is an expression of the form $\alpha(X_L) = (P \leftarrow Q).[g(X_Q, X_L) :\ (X_P, X_L) := up(X_Q, X_L)\,//\,(X_Q, X_L) := dn(X_P, X_L)]$, where $P, Q \subseteq \mathcal{P}$ are the* top *and* bottom *sets of ports; $X_L : \mathsf{D}[L]$ is the set of* local variables*; $g(X_Q, X_L)$ is the boolean* guard*; $up(X_Q, X_L)$ and $dn(X_P, X_L)$ are respectively the* up- *and* downward data transfer *expressions.*

For an interaction expression $\alpha(X_L)$ as above, we denote by $top(\alpha) \triangleq P$, $bot(\alpha) \triangleq Q$ and $supp(\alpha) \triangleq P\cup Q$ the sets of top, bottom and by all ports in α, respectively. We denote g_α, up_α and dn_α the corresponding expressions in α.

The first part, $(P \leftarrow Q)$, of an interaction expression describes the control flow, that is the dependency relation between the bottom and the top ports. The expression in the brackets describes the data flow. The guard $g(X_Q, X_L)$ gives the dependency between the two parts: interaction is only enabled when the values of the local variables together with those of variables associated to the bottom ports satisfy a boolean condition. As a side effect, the firing of an interaction expression can modify the local variables X_L.

Notice that an interaction expression can be understood as a generalized synchronous function call involving a set of callees P and a set of callers Q. When the callers Q are enabled, they offer a set of parameter values X_Q that are used to compute sequentially the two functions *up* and *dn*. The computation is possible only if the guard g is true depending on the values of the exported parameters and the local variables. The *up* function updates the variables of the callees and the local variables. The returned values of the caller variables are computed by the *dn* function that also updates the local variables. As explained in Section 3, when interactions are structured hierarchically, the callees at one level may become callers for the upper levels.

Formally, the *data transfer semantics* of α is defined by two parameterised structured partial functions $\alpha^{\uparrow}[\![X_L]\!] : \mathsf{D}[Q] \to \mathsf{D}[P]$ and $\alpha^{\downarrow}[\![X_L]\!] : \mathsf{D}[P] \to \mathsf{D}[Q]$:

$$\alpha^{\uparrow}[\![X_L]\!](\mathbf{u}) = up[\![X_L]\!](\mathbf{u}) \text{ if } g(\mathbf{u}, \mathbf{v}) = \mathtt{tt}\,, \quad \text{for all } \mathbf{u} \in \mathsf{D}[Q]\,,$$

$$\alpha^{\downarrow}[\![X_L]\!](\mathbf{u}) = dn[\![X_L]\!](\mathbf{u})\,, \quad \text{for all } \mathbf{u} \in \mathsf{D}[P]\,,$$

where $\mathbf{v}$ is the current valuation of variables X_L. The *top-level semantics* of α is $\widehat{\alpha}\,[\![X_L]\!] : \mathsf{D}[Q] \to \mathsf{D}[Q]$, with $\widehat{\alpha}\,[\![X_L]\!] = \alpha^{\downarrow}[\![X_L]\!] \circ \alpha^{\uparrow}[\![X_L]\!]$.

Example 2.4 The interaction expression $\alpha_{io}(\emptyset) = (w \leftarrow out\ in_1\ in_2).[\mathtt{tt} :\ x_w := x_{out} \,/\!/\, x_{in_1}, x_{in_2} := x_w]$ represents the coordination between an port *out* that delivers simultaneously its value to two ports in_1 and in_2. To avoid synchronization when the data at ports *in* have the same value as at *out*, we add a guard: $(w \leftarrow out\ in_1\ in_2).[(x_{out} \neq x_{in_1}) \vee (x_{out} \neq x_{in_2}) :\ x_w := x_{out} \,/\!/\, x_{in_1}, x_{in_2} := x_w]$. The interaction expression $Max(\emptyset) = (w \leftarrow pqr).[\mathtt{tt} :\ x_w := \max(x_p, x_q, x_r) \,/\!/\, x_p, x_q, x_r := x_w]$ allows the synchronization between ports p, q and r and returns the maximum of the values associated to these ports.

Definition 2.5 *The* composition *of interaction expressions is a partial operation ';' defined, for two interaction expressions α_1, α_2, with $X_{L_1} \cap X_{L_2} = \emptyset$, $X_L = X_{L_1} \cup X_{L_2}$ and $\alpha_i(X_{L_i}) = (P_i \leftarrow Q_i).[g_i(X_{Q_i}, X_{L_i}) :\ (X_{P_i}, X_{L_i}) := up_i(X_{Q_i}, X_{L_i}) \,/\!/\, (X_{Q_i}, X_{L_i}) := dn_i(X_{P_i}, X_{L_i})]$, for $i = 1, 2$, by putting*

$$(\alpha_1; \alpha_2)(X_L) \triangleq (P \leftarrow Q).[g(X_Q, X_L) :$$
$$(X_P, X_L) := up(X_Q, X_L) \,/\!/\, (X_Q, X_L) := dn(X_P, X_L)]\,,$$

where $P = P_1 \cup P_2$ and $Q = Q_1 \cup Q_2$, $up(X_Q, X_L) = up_2(X_{Q_2}, X_{L_2}) \circ up_1(X_{Q_1}, X_{L_1})$, $dn(X_P, X_L) = dn_1(X_{P_1}, X_{L_1}) \circ dn_2(X_{P_2}, X_{L_2})$, $g(X_Q, X_L) =$

$$g_1(X_{Q_1}, X_{L_1}) \wedge \Big[g_2(X_{Q_2}, X_{L_2}) \circ up_1(X_{Q_1}, X_{L_1})\Big]_{\overline{P_1 \cup L_1}}$$

(the projection in the second conjunct removes the outputs of up_1, keeping only the boolean value of g_2—cf. Fig. 3).

Notice that three expressions $g(X_Q, X_L)$, $up(X_Q, X_L)$ and $dn(X_P, X_L)$ do not involve variables in $X_{P_1 \cap Q_2}$.

Example 2.6 We continue Ex. 2.4. The composition of two interaction expressions, $Max_1(\emptyset)$ and $Max_2(\emptyset)$, respectively

$$(w \leftarrow pqr).[\mathtt{tt} :\ x_w := \max(x_p, x_q, x_r) \,/\!/\, x_p, x_q, x_r := x_w]$$
$$(z \leftarrow uvw).[\mathtt{tt} :\ x_z := \max(x_u, x_v, x_w) \,/\!/\, x_u, x_v, x_w := x_z]$$

is the new interaction expression:

$$(Max_1; Max_2)(\emptyset) = (wz \leftarrow pqruvw).[\mathtt{tt} :$$
$$x_w := \max(x_p, x_q, x_r), x_z := \max(x_u, x_v, \max(x_p, x_q, x_r) \,/\!/$$
$$x_p, x_q, x_r, x_u, x_v, x_w := x_z]$$

Proposition 2.7 *The operator ';' is associative. When $P_1 \cap Q_2 = P_2 \cap Q_1 = X_{L_1} \cap X_{L_2} = \emptyset$, it is also commutative.*

Under this disjointness condition, we write $\alpha_1 | \alpha_2 \triangleq \alpha_1; \alpha_2 = \alpha_2; \alpha_1$ and speak of interaction *synchronisation*.

3. ARCHITECTURE-BASED MODEL

This section provides a brief overview of BIP and a formalisation for simple and hierarchical connectors in BIP. The latter formalisation comprises abstract syntax and denotational semantics in terms of partial functions operating on structured domains. In addition, it formalises the flattening as a rewriting rule on hierarchical connectors and proves its soundness as a semantics-preserving transformation.

3.1 Simple Connectors in BIP

In BIP, systems are build by composing *atomic components* with *interactions* defined using connectors. As in Sect. 2, let $\mathcal{P} \subseteq \mathcal{I}$ be a set of ports and assume that a variable $x_p : \mathsf{D}_p$ is associated with each port $p \in \mathcal{P}$.

Definition 3.1 *An atomic component B is a tuple $B = (\Sigma, P, X_L : \mathsf{D}[L], \to)$ where Σ is a finite set of control locations; $P \subseteq \mathcal{P}$ is a finite set of ports—the* interface *of B; $X_L : \mathsf{D}[L]$ is a set of local variables, with $X_L \cap X_P = \emptyset$; $\to \subseteq \Sigma \times \mathcal{E} \times \Sigma$ is a finite transition relation, with $\mathcal{E}$ the set of interaction expressions of the form $p(X) = (p \leftarrow \emptyset).[g(X) : x_p := up(X) \,/\!/\, X := dn(x_p, X)]$, for $p \in P$ and $X \subseteq X_L$.*

Henceforth, we call interaction expressions of this form actions. *We use p for both the port and the action.*

Definition 3.2 *The operational semantics of an atomic component $B = (\Sigma, P, X_L : \mathsf{D}[L], \to)$ is given by an LTS $\sigma(B) = (\Sigma \times \mathsf{D}[L], 2^P \times (\bigcup_{p \in P} \mathsf{D}_p)^2, \to)$, where a state (q, v) consists of a control state of B and the valuation $v \in \mathsf{D}[L]$ of local variables; $\to$ is the minimal transition relation defined by the following rule:*

$$\frac{\begin{array}{c} p(X) = (p \leftarrow \emptyset).[g(X) :\ x_p := up(X) \,/\!/\, X := dn(x_p, X))] \\ q \xrightarrow{p(X)} q',\ g(v) = \mathtt{tt}\,,\ v^p_{up} = up_p(v)\,,\ v' = dn(v^p_{dn}, up_X(v)) \end{array}}{(q, v) \xrightarrow[v^p_{up} : v^p_{dn}]{p} (q', v')}\,,$$

where up_p and up_X are the corresponding components of the up expression; $v^p_{up}, v^p_{dn} \in \mathsf{D}_p$ are the data values associated to the port p at the upward and downward data transfer.

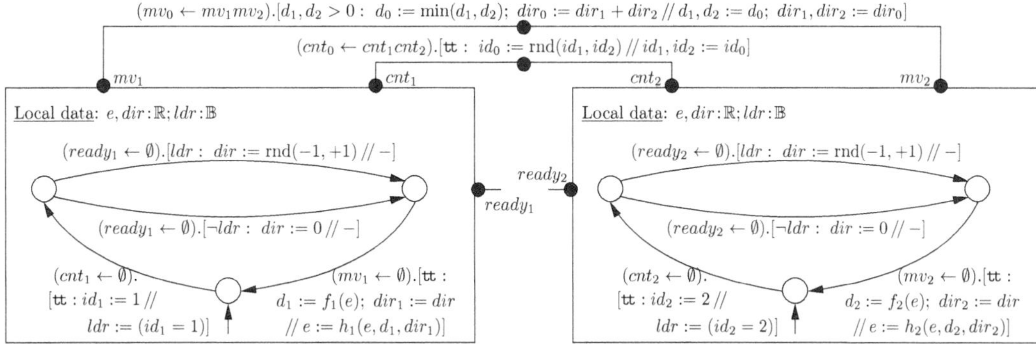

Figure 4: Leader/Follower example

Example 3.3 The system shown in Fig. 4 consists of two identical atomic components that can toghether move in one of two opposite directions. They have to agree on the distance, based on their respective energy levels. Each component has two real local variables: e to store its energy level and dir to store its opinion on the direction to follow, as well as a boolean variable ldr to remember whether it is a leader or not. In each operation cycle the i-th component performs the following three steps:

First, the component performs the *connect* action $cnt_i(ldr) = (cnt_i \leftarrow \emptyset).[\mathtt{tt}: \; id_i := i \,//\, ldr := (id_i = i)]$, where i is the constant component id (see Fig. 4) and id_i is the variable associated to the port cnt_i. In the upward transfer, the component proposes itself as a candidate for the leadership. In the downward transfer, the updated value of id_i is compared to the component id. The result of this comparison is stored in the local variable ldr.

In the second step, the component performs its corresponding action $ready_i(dir, ldr)$. The leader randomly picks the direction and stores it in the local variable dir: $(ready_i \leftarrow \emptyset).[ldr: \; dir := \mathrm{rnd}(-1, +1) \,//\, -]$. The follower stores zero: $(ready_i \leftarrow \emptyset).[\neg ldr: \; dir := 0 \,//\, -]$. These actions do not have any downward data transfer, but only update the local data in the upward transfer.

In the last step, the leader and the direction of the movement are chosen. The component performs the action *move*: $(mv_i \leftarrow \emptyset).[\mathtt{tt}: \; d_i := f_i(e); \; dir_i := dir \,//\, e := h_i(e, d_i, dir_i)]$. In the upward transfer, the component exposes the distance it can cover based on its available energy stored in the local variable e, as well as its direction suggestion stored in the local variable dir from the previous step. In the downward transfer, the move is materialised by updating the energy level of the component, based on the new values of the direction and distance of the move.

Definition 3.4 *A* simple connector *is an interaction expression $\alpha(X_L)$, such that $top(\alpha) = \{w\}$ is a single port $w \in \mathcal{P}$, $bot(\alpha) = a \subseteq \mathcal{P}$, such that $w \notin a$, and both up and g expressions do not involve local variables, i.e. $\alpha(X_L) = (w \leftarrow a).[g(X_a): \; (x_w, X_L) := up(X_a) \,//\, X_a := dn(x_w, X_L)]$.*

Example 3.5 Consider the connector (without local variables) shown in Fig. 4:

$$(cnt_0 \leftarrow cnt_1cnt_2).[\mathtt{tt}: \; id_0 := \mathrm{rnd}(id_1, id_2) \,//\, id_1, id_2 := id_0].$$

On every cnt_i port the value id_i represents the id of a component interacting through this port. The guard of the interaction expression is a constant true, hence no additional restrictions are imposed on the interaction. As part of the upward data transfer the connector randomly picks and propagates one of the proposed id's. At the downward data transfer, the updated value is communicated to both participating ports.

Definition 3.6 *Let $\mathcal{B} = \{B_1, \dots, B_n\}$ be a finite set of atomic components with $B_i = (\Sigma_i, P_i, X_{L_i} : \mathsf{D}[L_i], \rightarrow)$ such that their respective sets of ports and variables are pairwise disjoint. Let Γ be a set of simple connectors such that, for every $\alpha \in \Gamma$, $top(\alpha) \notin \bigcup_{i=1}^n P_i$, $bot(\alpha) \subseteq \bigcup_{i=1}^n P_i$ and $|supp(\alpha) \cap P_i| \leq 1$ for all $i \in [1, n]$. The operational semantics of the* parallel composition *$\Gamma(\mathcal{B})$ is defined as the LTS $(\Sigma, P, \rightarrow)$ where $\Sigma = \prod_{i=1}^n (\Sigma_i \times \mathsf{D}[L_i])$, $P = \{top(\alpha) \mid \alpha \in \Gamma\}$, $\rightarrow$ is the minimal transition relation defined by the rule*

$$\frac{\begin{array}{ccc} \alpha(X_L) \in \Gamma & top(\alpha) = w & bot(\alpha) = a = \{p_i \mid i \in I\} \\ \forall i \in I, q_i \xrightarrow{p_i(X_i)} q_i' & & \forall i \notin I, (q_i = q_i' \wedge \mathbf{u}_i = \mathbf{u}_i') \\ \alpha_\star = (|a); \alpha & (\mathbf{u}_i')_{i \in I} = \left[\widehat{\alpha}_\star \, [\![X_L]\!]((\mathbf{u}_i)_{i \in I}) \right]_{\bigcup_{i \in I} L_i} & \end{array}}{(q_1, \mathbf{u}_1), \dots, (q_n, \mathbf{u}_n) \xrightarrow{w} (q_1', \mathbf{u}_1'), \dots, (q_n', \mathbf{u}_n')},$$

where $|a$ is the synchronisation of all $p_i(X_i)$ with $p_i \in a$.

Notice that the involved interaction expressions are partial. Hence, for instance, when the guard of one of the actions is not satisfied, the values $(\mathbf{u}_i')_{i \in I}$ are undefined and, thus, the rule is not applicable.

Intuitively, an interaction can be fired only if its guard and all guards associated to the corresponding component actions are true. When an interaction is fired, its upward transfer is computed first using the exposed values offered by the participating components. Then, the downward transfer modifies back all the port variables followed by execution of the update functions associated to component actions.

Example 3.7 The first synchronisation among the atomic components of Ex. 3.3 is performed through the connector $(cnt_0 \leftarrow cnt_1cnt_2).[\mathtt{tt}: \; id_0 := \mathrm{rnd}(id_1, id_2) \,//\, id_1, id_2 := id_0]$. The id of the leader is randomly selected in the connector and transferred downward through both participating ports. In the next step each component idependently performs its corresponding step $ready_i$ (see Ex. 3.3). Finally, components synchronise again through the connector

$$\begin{aligned} (mv_0 \leftarrow mv_1mv_2).[d_1, d_2 > 0: & \\ d_0 := \min(d_1, d_2); \; dir_0 &:= dir_1 + dir_2 \,// \\ & d_1, d_2 := d_0; \; dir_1, dir_2 := dir_0)]. \end{aligned}$$

The distances each component can cover and their direction suggestions are combined in the connector to compute the global distance and direction (variables d_0 and dir_0), which are propagated further, updated and then distributed down to components.

3.2 Hierarchical Connectors in BIP

Definition 3.8 *A hierarchical connector $h\alpha$ is a term generated by the grammar $h\alpha ::= \alpha \mid \alpha\langle h\alpha_1, \dots, h\alpha_n\rangle$, where α denotes an arbitrary simple connector. We extend the top(), bot() and supp() to hierarchical connectors:*

$$top(\alpha\langle h\alpha_1, \dots, h\alpha_n\rangle) = top(\alpha)\,,$$
$$bot(\alpha\langle h\alpha_1, \dots, h\alpha_n\rangle) = \bigcup_{i=1}^n bot(\alpha_i)\,,$$
$$supp(\alpha\langle h\alpha_1, \dots, h\alpha_n\rangle) = supp(\alpha) \cup \bigcup_{i=1}^n supp(h\alpha_i)\,.$$

$h\alpha = \alpha\langle h\alpha_1, \dots, h\alpha_n\rangle$ is valid *iff all sets $supp(h\alpha_i)$, for $i \in [1,n]$, are pairwise disjoint; for all $i \in [1,n]$, holds $supp(h\alpha_i) \cap supp(\alpha) = \{top(h\alpha_i)\}$ and $top(h\alpha_i) \in bot(\alpha)$; and all hierarchical sub-connectors $h\alpha_1, \dots, h\alpha_n$ are valid.*

We tacitly restrict ourselves to valid hierarchical connectors. Their data transfer semantics is defined structurally:

$$\alpha\langle h\alpha_1, \dots, h\alpha_n\rangle^\uparrow = \alpha^\uparrow \circ (h\alpha_1{}^\uparrow \circ \cdots \circ h\alpha_n{}^\uparrow)$$
$$\alpha\langle h\alpha_1, \dots, h\alpha_n\rangle^\downarrow = (h\alpha_1{}^\downarrow \circ \cdots \circ h\alpha_n{}^\downarrow) \circ \alpha^\downarrow$$

Notice that the order of composition for sub-connector functions is irrelevant as they operate on disjoint sets of ports.

Example 3.9 We continue the running example of this section. Consider a system shown in Fig. 5, combining that of Fig. 4 with a third atomic component of exactly the same type as the other two. The behaviour of the systems is generalised by a hierarchical application of the same (up to port renaming) connectors mv and cnt. Composing the interaction expressions for simple connectors cnt_0 and cnt gives $(cnt_0\, cnt \leftarrow cnt_0\, cnt_1\, cnt_2\, cnt_3).[\mathtt{tt} : id_0 := rnd(id_1, id_2);\ id := rnd(id_1, id_2, id_3) \mathbin{//} id_0, id_1, id_2, id_3 := id]$. Notice that, by discarding the port cnt_0 and the associated variable id_0, we obtain an equivalent simple connector $(cnt \leftarrow cnt_1\, cnt_2\, cnt_3).[\mathtt{tt} : id := rnd(id_1, id_2, id_3) \mathbin{//} id_1, id_2, id_3 := id]$.

Similarly, any hierarchical connector can be *flattened* into a simple one [10], allowing us to extend BIP operational semantics (Def. 3.6) to hierarchical connectors. This is done formally in the extended version of this paper [6].

4. ARCHITECTURE AGNOSTIC MODEL

4.1 T/B Component Model

Architecture-agnostic models are obtained from BIP models as the plain composition of *Top/Bottom (T/B) components*. In the translation, BIP connectors are replaced by T/B components that play the role of *coordinators*. These are extensions of the BIP components whose transitions are labeled with interaction expressions. The parallel composition mechanism relies on the matching between bottom and top ports (as for hierarchical connectors).

Interaction execution exhibits a cyclic pattern. In each cycle, the data of interacting atomic components are propagated upwards through top ports towards all relevant coordinators. At each stage, the computation can influence the decision as to what transitions of atomic components are enabled. Finally, once a global interaction has been choosen at the top level, the updated data is propagated back to atomic components. As above, we assume a universal set of ports $\mathcal{P}$ and, for each port $p \in \mathcal{P}$, a typed variable $x_p : \mathsf{D}_p$.

Definition 4.1 *A* T/B component *is a tuple $T = (\Sigma, P^{bot}, P^{top}, X_L : \mathsf{D}[L], \rightarrow)$, where Σ is a set of states, $P^{bot}, P^{top} \subseteq \mathcal{P}$ are finite sets of* bottom *and* top *ports; $X_L : \mathsf{D}[L]$ is a set of* local data variables*; $\rightarrow \subseteq \Sigma \times \mathcal{E} \times \Sigma$ is a transition relation, with $\mathcal{E}$ being the set of action expressions $\alpha(X)$, such that $X \subseteq X_L$, $top(\alpha) \subseteq P^{top}$, $bot(\alpha) \subseteq P^{bot}$. We write $q \xrightarrow{\alpha(X)} q'$ for $(q, \alpha(X), q') \in \rightarrow$.*

A T/B component $(\Sigma, P^{bot}, P^{top}, X_L : \mathsf{D}[L], \rightarrow)$ is an atomic component*, if $P^{bot} = \emptyset$; it is a* coordinator *if $P^{bot} \neq \emptyset$, but $P^{bot} \cap P^{top} = \emptyset$. Finally, if $P^{bot} \cap P^{top} \neq \emptyset$, the T/B component is* compound *(obtained by hierarchically composing atomic components and coordinators).*

Definition 4.2 *The* operational semantics of a T/B component *$T = (\Sigma, P^{bot}, P^{top}, X_L : \mathsf{D}[L], \rightarrow)$ is given by an LTS $\sigma(T) = (\Sigma \times \mathsf{D}[L], 2^P \times \mathsf{D}[P]^2, \rightarrow)$, where a state (q, v) consists of a control state of T and the value $v \in \mathsf{D}[L]$; $\rightarrow$ is the minimal transition relation defined by the following rule:*

$$\frac{\begin{array}{c}\alpha(X) = (a^{top} \leftarrow a^{bot}).[g(X_{a^{bot}}, X) : \\ (X_{a^{top}}, X) := up(X_{a^{bot}}, X) \mathbin{//} (X_{a^{bot}}, X) := dn(X_{a^{top}}, X)] \\ q \xrightarrow{\alpha(X)} q' \qquad g(\mathbf{v}_{up}^{bot}, v) = \mathtt{tt} \qquad \mathbf{v}_{up}^{top} = up_{a^{top}}(\mathbf{v}_{up}^{bot}, v) \\ (\mathbf{v}_{dn}^{bot}, v') = dn(\mathbf{v}_{dn}^{top}, up_X(\mathbf{v}_{up}^{bot}, v))\end{array}}{(q, v) \xrightarrow[\mathbf{v}_{up} : \mathbf{v}_{dn}]{a} (q', v')}\,,$$

where $a = a^{top} \cup a^{bot}$; $up_{a^{top}}$ and up_X are the corresponding components of the up expression; $\mathbf{v}_{up}, \mathbf{v}_{dn} \in \mathsf{D}[P]$ are partial data valuations associated to ports at the upward and downward data transfer phases *respectively (the values of variables assocaited to ports that do not participate in the interaction are undefined).*

Notice that T/B components and their operational semantics generalise atomic BIP components (Def. 3.2). In particular, all components in the examples of Sect. 3 are T/B components without bottom ports.

Note 4.3 Notice that the values $\mathbf{v}_{up}$ and $\mathbf{v}_{dn}$ do not directly correspond to inputs and outputs. Indeed, in terms of the transferred data, the component *input* is the pair $(\mathbf{v}_{up}^{bot}, \mathbf{v}_{dn}^{top})$, whereas its *output* is the pair $(\mathbf{v}_{up}^{top}, \mathbf{v}_{dn}^{bot})$.

Recall the generalised function call metaphor (see the discussion after Def. 2.3). When a transition labelled by $\alpha(X)$ is called, it is provided the values $\mathbf{v}_{up}^{bot}$. If these values satisfy the guard g, they are used by the function up to compute the values $\mathbf{v}_{up}^{top}$, which are provided to the subsequent callees. In return, the latter provide the updated values $\mathbf{v}_{dn}^{top}$, which are, finally, used by the function dn to compute $\mathbf{v}_{dn}^{bot}$.

4.2 Systems and Composition

Definition 4.4 *Let $S = \{(\Sigma_i, P_i^{bot}, P_i^{top}, X_{L_i} : \mathsf{D}[L_i], \rightarrow)\}_{i=1}^n$ be a finite set of T/B components and denote $P^{bot} \triangleq \bigcup_{i=1}^n P_i^{bot}$ and $P^{top} \triangleq \bigcup_{i=1}^n P_i^{top}$. Here and below, we skip the index on $\rightarrow$ since it is always clear from the context. S is a* system *iff*

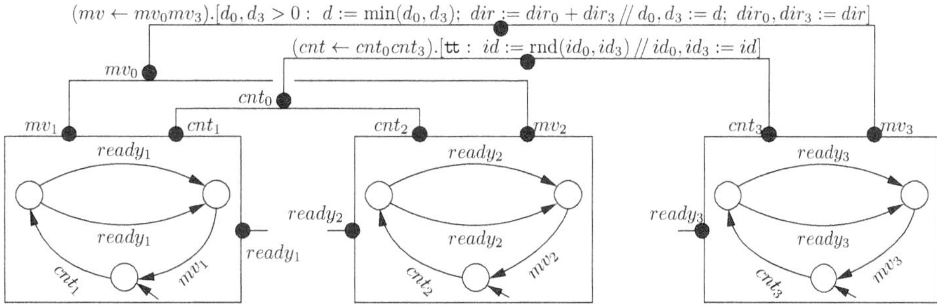

Figure 5: Leader/follower example with three atomic components

the sets of local variables and top ports of all the components are pairwise disjoint, i.e. $\forall i \neq j,\ X_i \cap X_j = P_i^{top} \cap P_j^{top} = \emptyset$. *A system is* closed *if* $P^{bot} = P^{top}$.

Definition 4.5 *Let* $T_i = (\Sigma_i, P_i^{bot}, P_i^{top}, X_{L_i} : \mathsf{D}[L_i], \rightarrow)$, *for* $i = 1, 2$, *be two T/B components, such that* $P_2^{top} \cap P_1^{bot} = \emptyset$ *(cf. Def. 4.8 below). Their* parallel composition *is a compound T/B component* $T_1 \parallel T_2 \triangleq (\Sigma, P^{bot}, P^{top}, X_L : \mathsf{D}[L], \rightarrow)$, *where* $\Sigma = \Sigma_1 \times \Sigma_2$, $P^{bot} = P_1^{bot} \cup P_2^{bot}$, $P^{top} = P_1^{top} \cup P_2^{top}$, $X_L = X_{L_1} \cup X_{L_2}$ *and* $\rightarrow$ *is the minimal transition relation defined by the following rules* ($i \neq j \in \{1, 2\}$)*:*

$$\frac{q_i \xrightarrow{\alpha_i(X_i)} q_i'}{q_i q_j \xrightarrow{\alpha_i(X_i)} q_i' q_j}\ , \qquad \frac{q_1 \xrightarrow{\alpha_1(X_1)} q_1' \quad q_2 \xrightarrow{\alpha_2(X_2)} q_2'}{q_1 q_2 \xrightarrow{(\alpha_1;\alpha_2)(X)} q_1' q_2'}\ .$$

When $P_1^{top} \cap P_2^{bot} = \emptyset$, we put $T_1 \parallel T_2 \triangleq T_2 \parallel T_1$. Thus, $\parallel$ is a commutative partial operator defined when $P_2^{top} \cap P_1^{bot} = \emptyset$ or $P_1^{top} \cap P_2^{bot} = \emptyset$. When both equalities hold, the transition in the conclusion of the second rule is labelled by $\alpha_1 \parallel \alpha_2$, which is symmetric in the order of its operands. When both $P_2^{top} \cap P_1^{bot} \neq \emptyset$ and $P_1^{top} \cap P_2^{bot} \neq \emptyset$, this means that there is a data-flow causality loop among the two components (as in I/O models [11, 14]) and the composition is undefined.

Example 4.6 Fig. 6a shows a simple model consisting of two T/B components R_0 and R_1 without data variables and transfer, identical up to port renaming. Each models a Mod-2 counter, which produces one event on its top port (shown by blue outward-facing triangles) for every second event on its bottom port (shown by red inward-facing triangles). R_0 and R_1 share port t_1. Fig. 6b shows the T/B component $R_0 \parallel R_1$ (for clarity we omit two transitions indicated by the dotted green arrow).

Proposition 4.7 *Composition operator* $\parallel$ *is associative.*

Definition 4.8 *Let* S *be a system and consider the directed graph* $\tau(S) = (S, E)$, *having the components of the system as vertices and the set of edges* $E = \{(T_i, T_j) \mid P_i^{top} \cap P_j^{bot} \neq \emptyset\}$. *In other words, there is an edge from* T_i *to* T_j *if some of the top ports of the former are bottom ports of the latter.* S *is* composable *iff* $\tau(S)$ *is a directed acyclic graph.*

In a composable system S, any pair of components can be ordered so as to satisfy the requirement of Def. 4.5. Thus, by Prop. 4.7, the composed T/B component $\|S$ is well-defined.

As in process calculi like CCS [16], in order for the composition operator $\parallel$ to be associative, it must allow interleaving (i.e. independent firing) of transitions involving matchable ports (compare first and third rules in Def. 4.5 with the second rule). The meaning of a complete system is defined as the largest closed sub-system obtained by pruning out all the non-matching transitions; thus the following definition.

Definition 4.9 *Let* $S = \{(\Sigma_i, P_i^{bot}, P_i^{top}, X_{L_i} : \mathsf{D}[L_i], \rightarrow)\}_{i=1}^n$ *be a closed composable system and let* $\|S = (\Sigma, P^{bot}, P^{top}, X_L : \mathsf{D}[L], \underset{par}{\longrightarrow})$. *The* restriction *of* S *is given by a T/B component* $\rho(S) = (\Sigma, P^{bot}, P^{top}, X_L : \mathsf{D}[L], \underset{pr}{\longrightarrow})$, *where* $\underset{pr}{\longrightarrow}$ *is the minimal transition relation defined by the rule*

$$\frac{q \xrightarrow[par]{\alpha(X)} q' \quad bot(\alpha) = top(\alpha)}{q \xrightarrow[pr]{\alpha(X)} q'}\ .$$

The second premise means that, for every bottom (resp. top) port, α must also contain the corresponding top (resp. bottom) port. Restriction, in our context, is the generalisation of the CCS restriction operator.

Example 4.10 Fig. 6c shows a system comprising T/B components R_0 and R_1 as in Ex. 4.6 and closed with two additional components: an atomic T/B component that generates events t_0 and a top-level T/B component that consumes t_2. One can easily see that the restriction of this system, shown in Fig. 6d is, indeed, a Mod-4 counter.

Lemma 4.11 *For any transition in the restriction of a closed composable system, the data transfer coincides with the top-level semantics of the composition of the corresponding interaction expressions.*

4.3 T/B Component Encoding of BIP Models

Any atomic BIP component $B = (\Sigma, P, X_L : \mathsf{D}[L], \rightarrow)$ can be trivially encoded as a T/B component by making all ports of B top ports, i.e. $\tau(B) = (\Sigma, \emptyset, P, X_L : \mathsf{D}[L], \rightarrow)$. Thus, we only have to provide the encoding for connectors. Let $\alpha(X) = (w \leftarrow a).[g(X_a) : (x_w, X) := up(X_a) \,/\!/\, X_a := dn(x_w, X)]$ be a simple connector with a set of local variables $X : \mathsf{D}$. The T/B component encoding of α is given by $\tau(\alpha) \triangleq (\{*\}, P, \{w\}, X : \mathsf{D}, \{* \xrightarrow{\alpha(X)} *\})$.

Hierarchical connectors are encoded component-wise: $\tau\big(\alpha\langle h\alpha_1, \ldots, h\alpha_n\rangle\big) \triangleq \{\tau(\alpha)\} \cup \bigcup_{i=1}^n \tau(h\alpha_i)$.

In the BIP operational semantics Def. 3.6, only one connector $\alpha \in \Gamma$ can be fired at a time. On the contrary, parallel composition of T/B components allows any number of component transitions to synchronise. To enforce BIP semantics, for a set of connectors Γ, we add an *arbiter*: $\tau(\Gamma) = \big(\{*\}, P_\Gamma, \emptyset, \{y_w : \mathsf{D}_w \mid w \in P_\Gamma\}\{* \xrightarrow{\tilde{\alpha}} * \mid \alpha \in \Gamma\}\big)$,

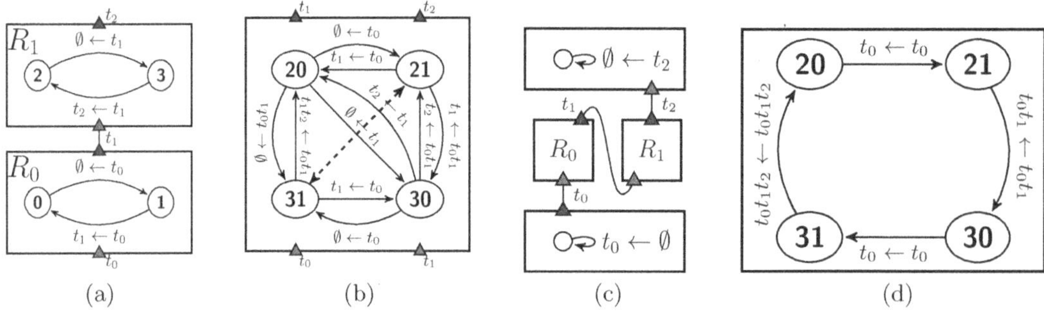
Figure 6: T/B component model for the Mod-4 Counter

where $P_\Gamma = \bigcup_{\alpha\in\Gamma} top(\alpha)$, y_w are fresh variables and, for each $\alpha \in \Gamma$ and $\{w\} = top(\alpha)$, we put $\tilde{\alpha}(y_w) = (\emptyset \leftarrow w).[\mathtt{tt} : y_w := x_w \,//\, x_w := y_w]$, that is the data provided by α in the upward data transfer is reinjected back into the downward data transfer by $\tilde{\alpha}$.

Theorem 4.12 *Let $\mathcal{B}$ be a set of atomic BIP components and Γ be a set of hierarchical connectors and put $S = \{\tau(\Gamma)\} \cup \bigcup_{B\in\mathcal{B}}\{\tau(B)\} \cup \bigcup_{\alpha\in\Gamma} \tau(\alpha)$. The LTS $\sigma(\rho(S))$ and $\Gamma(\mathcal{B})$ are isomorphic: there exist agreeing bijections between their sets of states and transitions.*

5. EXPERIMENTAL RESULTS

5.1 Java Implementation

The implementation consists mainly of: 1) atomic components; 2) coordinators; and 3) connections. Recall that, atomic components have no bottom ports. Connections connect top ports to bottom ports. For composable system they define a hierarchy on T/B components. We assume that a bottom port is connected to exactly one top port; a top port may be connected to more than one bottom port (cf. Def. 4.4). In [6], we provide the Java implementation of the Mod-4 counter from Ex. 4.6.

At runtime, we create a Java thread for each atomic component and a thread that plays the role of an *arbiter* for all the coordinators. The implementation of the execution engine can be drastically optimized in case where the coordinators are deterministic, i.e. if from any state: 1) there exists only one outgoing transition; or 2) the guards of all the outgoing transitions are mutually exclusive. Non-deterministic coordinators may contain a state with more than one outgoing transitions that could be enabled at the same time. That is, more than one *up* function may be executed. For the sake of clarity, we first provide the algorithm for deterministic coordinators. Atomic component threads cyclically execute the following protocol: 1) Notify the top ports of the current outgoing transitions, whereof the guards are satisfied; 2) Notify the arbiter thread; 3) Wait for a notification from the arbiter; 4) Upon the notification from the arbiter, execute the action that corresponds to the received top port; 5) Modify the current state according to transition labeled by the received top port. Below is the algorithm of the atomic component thread.

```
// atomic component's thread
run() {
  while(true) {
    for all current outgoing transitions t {
       if guard of t is true {
          t.sendPort.notify();
    } }
    notify arbiter thread;
    wait for arbiter thread;
    port = notification received from arbiter thread;
    performTransition(port);
} }
```

Notification of the top ports is executed by the threads of the atomic components. It is propagated upward by the atomic component thread until it reaches a top-level coordinator component (i.e. a coordinator whereof current outgoing transition does not have a top port).

```
topPort.notify() {
  notify bottom ports that are connected to topPort;
  for each coordinator component c that has a
  bottom port notified {
    if exists a current outgoing transition t in c
    where all its bottom ports have been notified
    and its guard is true {
      store the values of the variables of c;
      execute its corresponding up function;
        if t is labeled by a top port {
          t.topPort.notify();
}  }  } }
```

Note that, upward propagation is done in parallel by the atomic components' threads. Arbiter thread resumes its execution when the upward propagation is completed by all the atomic components' threads. Arbiter's thread cyclically executes the following:

1. Select non-deterministically an enabled top-level coordinator component, i.e. such that its the current outgoing transition has no top ports and all its bottom ports have been notified. (If such a component does not exist, a deadlock has occurred.)

2. Execute the *dn* function of the selected transition and update the state of the coordinator accordingly.

3. Notify all the top ports that are connected to the bottom ports of the selected transition until we reach atomic components. Execute the *dn* function of the transition that has a top port notified.

4. When the downward propagation is completed, notify all the atomic components to execute their corresponding transitions. Moreover, recover the values of the variables of all the coordinators that have been notified during the upward propagation without being modified during the downward propagation.

Notice that arbiter selects only one top-level coordinator even though there exits more than one top-level coordinator that are non conflicting. Two top-level coordinators are conflicting if the downward propagation will lead to notify the same atomic component but with two different top ports. Obviously, selecting two top-level coordinators that are conflicting will lead to the violation of the semantics presented in Sect. 4. Thread arbiter is parameterized to support the two implementations (one top-level selection, or multiple non-conflicting top level selection).

For non-deterministic coordinators, the upward propagation has to be modified as follows. First the up function does not modify the actual data of a coordinator but it creates a copy of its variables. If a transition has a top port, we notify that port with an index which represents the values of the data that make this transition enabled. Recall that, the guard of a given transition depends on the value of the variables of the coordinator and the variables of the top ports that are connected to the bottom ports of that transition. So that, before evaluating the guard of a given transition of a coordinator component, we should first set the indices of the bottom coordinators. As the upward propagation is done in parallel, we should also lock those bottom coordinators to avoid the evaluation of other guards that depend on those coordinators but with different indices.

5.2 Case Studies

5.2.1 Network Sorting Algorithm (NSA)

NSA [2] can be considered as the coordinated product of 2^n atomic components, each containing an array of N items. The goal is to sort the items, so that all the items in the first component are smaller than those of the second component and so on. In [10], we have provided a BIP application implementing this algorithm. In order to evaluate the results of the present paper, we have implemented an internalised version using T/B components. We have also implemented a modified version of this model, where we merge some coordinators, which might improve the performance. Detailed descriptions are available in [6].

Figures 7a and 7b provide benchmarks for NSA by considering the initial and merged models for the two implementations (deterministic and non-deterministic). Fig. 7a shows that the non-deterministic implementation introduces some overhead. We also study the efficiency of selecting all non-conflicting top-level coordinators versus selecting only one top-level coordinator. Fig. 7b shows that the former implies slightly better performance.

5.2.2 Plain Old Telephone Service (POTS)

We have implemented a T/B component model for POTS [12], which provides voice connections between pairs of clients. We distinguish between clients and coordinators. Clients are atomic components with three states. Initially a client can start a new call by dialing the callee id, or it can receive a call from another caller. Then, a voice connection is established between the two clients. When a client hangs up the call is disconnected. We have two-level hierarchy of coordinators. The first level includes coordinators that collect requests coming from the clients as follows: 1) *CallerAgregration* collects dialing requests, 2) *CalleeAgregation* collects waiting requests, 3) $VoiceAgregation_1$ and $VoiceAgregation_2$ collect voice requests, 4) $DiscAgregation_1$ and $DiscAgregation_2$ collect disconnect requests. The second level includes coordinators that synchronize requests of bottom coordinators. More precisely, *DialWaitSync* synchronizes a dialing request (from *CallerAgregation*) with its corresponding waiting request (from *CalleeAgregation*). *VoiceSync* synchronizes voice request (from $VoiceAgregation_1$) with its corresponding voice request (from $VoiceAgregation_2$). *DiscSync* synchronizes a disconnect request (from $DiscAgregation_1$) with its corresponding disconnect request (from $DiscAgregation_2$). More detailed description is available in [6]. The proposed model is very concise and can be modified incrementally, e.g. by adding new clients.

Fig. 7c shows the performance of POTS for three different values of the number of calls to be satisfied.

6. RELATED WORK

Coordination [13] as a means to alleviate complexity in complex system design by distinguishing between a computing part comprising components involved in manipulating data and a coordination part responsible for the harmonious cooperation between the components. The paper points out two main approaches to coordination and studies their relationship. The key concept relating the two approaches is internalisation meaning that external architectural constraints applied to a set of components are cast into their code. To the best of our knowledge, there is no work clearly addressing the problem. In [17], a survey of coordination models and languages is presented and their classification as either "data-driven" or "control-driven". Data-driven coordination languages offer coordination primitives which are mixed within the purely computational part of the code. In the control-driven category, there is a complete separation of coordination from computational concerns. The state of the computation at any moment in time is defined in terms of only the coordinated patterns that the components involved in some computation adhere to. There exists a broad literature on bridging the gap between the design level, as this is expressed by some ADL, and the implementation level, as this is realized by some computational model. ArchJava [1, 3] is a small, backwards-compatible extension to Java that smoothly integrates software architecture specifications into Java implementation code. It seamlessly unifies architectural structure and implementation in one language, allowing flexible implementation techniques, ensuring traceability between architecture and code, and supporting the co-evolution of architecture and implementation. In [18], is presented a methodology for mapping architectural representations written in ACME a generic language for describing software architectures, down to executable code. The mapping process involves the use of the coordination paradigm. All these works lack formal foundation and do not allow a deep understanding of the differences between architecture-based and architecture-agnostic approaches. The T/B-component model has some similarities with formalisms using an input/output interaction mechanism for the description of hierarchically structured automata such as Argos [14] and Statecharts [11]. Our model extends the interaction mechanism with data transfer. To avoid causality anomalies [14], we restrict composition to composable systems where hierarchical structure of interaction eliminates by construction cyclic dependencies.

7. CONCLUSION AND FUTURE WORK

We study a formal framework bridging the gap between architecture description languages and their implementation. The framework clearly distinguishes between two main

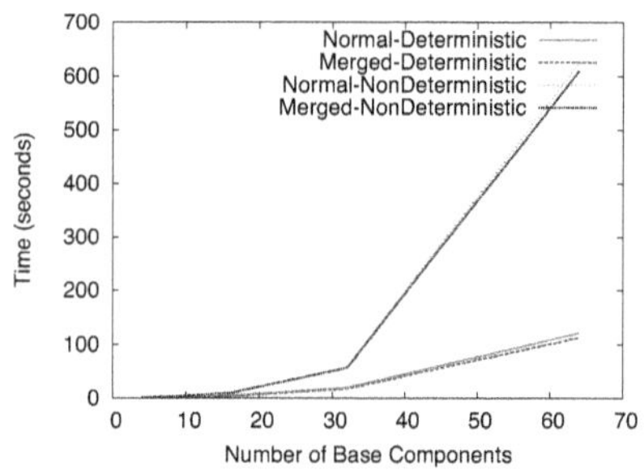

(a) Deterministic/Non-Deterministic

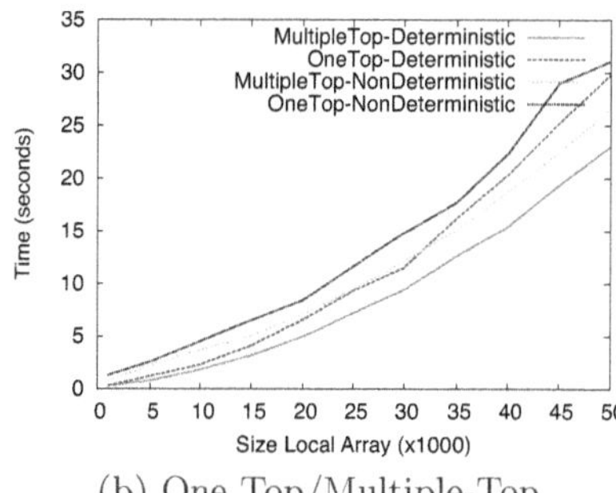

(b) One Top/Multiple-Top

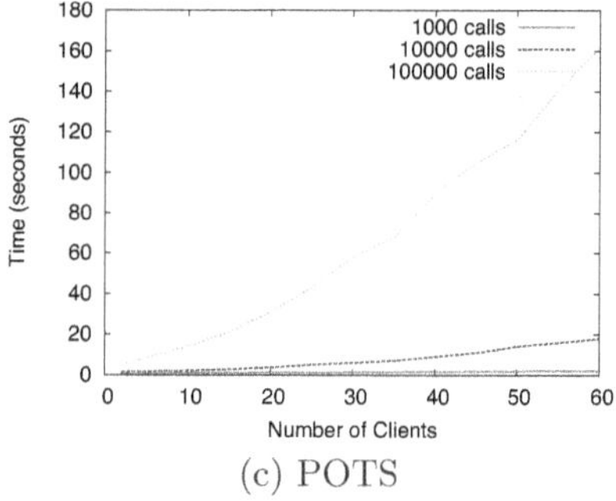

(c) POTS

Figure 7: Performance (execution time in seconds) of the case-study examples: (a),(b) NSA; (c) POTS

approaches for tackling the coordination paradigm. One approach is based on the separation between computational and coordination mechanisms; the latter are described as constraints that are independent from the internal behavior of the coordinated components. The other approach consists in internalising the constraints by generating a set of coordinators that play the role of an execution engine. Formally relating the two approaches opens the way for consistent code generation and guarantees that important architectural properties are guaranteed to hold in the implementation.

Interaction expressions are a key concept, fully describing the control- and data-flow involved in an interaction. They are used both to specify connectors, i.e. architectural constraints, and executable code in the coordinators. They directly express multiparty interactions and have features for hierarchical structuring. They can be assimilated to synchronous function calls from the bottom ports, that return values computed when the interaction occurs. The proposed coordination mechanism is general enough to directly encompass existing mechanisms. In particular it can express data-driven and event-driven interaction. Usually, ADLs use connectors that do not involve computation. For example, data-flow is defined by distinguishing between input and output ports. When an interaction occurs the value of an output is copied into possibly many inputs. For such languages, the expression of interactions involving computation requires the use of additional components.

We have already published formal operational semantics for BIP and developed implementations in the form of various execution engines [4]. Nonetheless, so far the relation between semantics and the corresponding implementation was not fully formalized. The proposed translation provides a full formalization of the execution engine as a set of interacting coordinators and an arbiter. It preserves the structure of the BIP models: each connector is implemented by a coordinator. Furthermore, by applying the T/B component composition rule the executable model can be flattened in different possible ways. As shown in [10] flattening allows the generation of more efficient code.

The implementation of T/B component models can be used either for the execution of BIP models after internalisation of their connectors or for the execution of such models written independently of BIP.

We see two main directions for future work. One is to study extensions of interaction expressions to encompass dynamic coordination. This can be achieved by including in the set of local variables X_L, port and component variables as in the Dy-BIP coordination language [9]. These could be used in the guards and affected by the *up* and *dn* functions, making possible dynamic configuration of a model.

The second direction is to study techniques for distributing the generated engine in the form of a T/B component model. So far, we have studied code generation techniques for BIP, that generate distributed implementations for flattened models [7, 8]. This limits the possibility of physically distributing coordinators by preserving the architecture hierarchy. The new techniques will allow full preservation of the coordination structure and enhanced freedom for discovering optimal implementations.

8. REFERENCES

[1] Marwan Abi-Antoun et al. Modeling and implementing software architecture with ACME and ArchJava. In *ICSE*, pages 676–677. ACM, 2005.

[2] Miklós Ajtai, János Komlós, and Endre Szemerédi. Sorting in $c \log n$ parallel steps. *Combinatorica*, 3(1):1–19, 1983.

[3] Jonathan Aldrich, Craig Chambers, and David Notkin. ArchJava: connecting software architecture to implementation. In *ICSE*, pages 187–197. ACM, 2002.

[4] Ananda Basu et al. Distributed semantics and implementation for systems with interaction and priority. In *FORTE*, volume 5048 of *LNCS*, pages 116–133. Springer, 2008.

[5] Ananda Basu, Marius Bozga, and Joseph Sifakis. Modeling heterogeneous real-time components in BIP. In *SEFM06*, pages 3–12, September 2006. Invited talk.

[6] Simon Bliudze et al. Architecture internalisation in BIP. Technical Report EPFL-REPORT-196997, February 2014. http://infoscience.epfl.ch/record/196997.

[7] Borzoo Bonakdarpour et al. From high-level component-based models to distributed implementations. In *EMSOFT*, pages 209–218, 2010.

[8] Borzoo Bonakdarpour et al. A framework for automated distributed implementation of component-based models. *Distributed Computing*, 25(5):383–409, 2012.

[9] Marius Bozga et al. Modeling dynamic architectures using Dy-BIP. In *SC, LNCS 7306*, pages 1–16. Springer, 2012.

[10] Marius Bozga, Mohamad Jaber, and Joseph Sifakis. Source-to-source architecture transformation for performance optimization in BIP. *IEEE Trans. Industrial Informatics*, 6(4):708–718, 2010.

[11] David Harel. Statecharts: A visual formalism for complex systems. *Sci. Comput. Program.*, 8(3):231–274, 1987.

[12] Jonathan D. Hay and Joanne M. Atlee. Composing features and resolving interactions. In *FSE*, pages 110–119. ACM, 2000.

[13] Thomas W. Malone and Kevin Crowston. The interdisciplinary study of coordination. *ACM Comp. Surv.*, 26(1):87–119, 1994.

[14] Florence Maraninchi and Yann Rémond. Argos: an automaton-based synchronous language. *Comput. Lang.*, 27(1/3):61–92, 2001.

[15] Nenad Medvidovic and Richard N. Taylor. A framework for classifying and comparing architecture description languages. In *ESEC/FSE, LNCS 1301*, pages 60–76. Springer, 1997.

[16] Robin Milner. *Communication and Concurrency*. PHI Series in Computer Science. Prentice Hall, 1989.

[17] George A. Papadopoulos and Farhad Arbab. Coordination models and languages. *Adv. in Computers*, 46:329–400, 1998.

[18] George A. Papadopoulos, Aristos Stavrou, and Odysseas Papapetrou. An implementation framework for software architectures based on the coordination paradigm. *Sci. Comput. Program.*, 60(1):27–67, March 2006.

Robust Reconfiguration of Cloud Applications

Francisco Durán
University of Málaga, Spain
duran@uma.es

Gwen Salaün
University of Grenoble Alpes,
Inria, LIG, CNRS, France
gwen.salaun@imag.fr

ABSTRACT

Cloud applications involve a set of interconnected software components running on remote virtual machines. Once cloud applications are deployed, one may need to reconfigure them by adding/removing virtual machines or components hosted on these machines. These tasks are error-prone since they must preserve the application consistency and respect important architectural invariants related to software dependencies. We present in this paper a protocol for automating these reconfiguration tasks.

Categories and Subject Descriptors

D.2.11 [**Software Engineering**]: Software Architectures—*Languages*; D.2.2 [**Software Engineering**]: Design Tools and Techniques—*Modules and Interfaces*

General Terms

Algorithms, Reliability

Keywords

Cloud Computing, Component-based Systems, Dynamic Reconfiguration

1. INTRODUCTION

Cloud computing aims at delivering resources and software applications on demand over a network, leveraging hosting platforms based on virtualization, and promoting a new software licensing and billing model based on the *pay-per-use* concept. For service providers, this means the opportunity to develop, deploy, and possibly sell cloud applications everywhere on earth without investing in expensive IT infrastructure. Cloud computing is at the crossroads of several recent computing paradigms such as grid computing, peer-to-peer architectures, autonomic computing, or utility computing. It allows users to benefit from all these technologies without requiring a deep expertise in each of them. In particular, autonomic computing is convenient for automating specific tasks such as the provisioning of resources on-demand or facing peak-load capacity surge. Automation reduces user involvement, which speeds up the process and minimizes the possibility of human errors.

Cloud applications are distributed applications composed of a set of virtual machines running a set of interconnected software components. Such applications benefit from several services provided in the cloud such as database storage, virtual machine cloning, or memory ballooning. To deploy their applications, cloud users need first to provision and instantiate some virtual machines (VMs) and indicate the software components to be run on them. Once these applications are deployed, some reconfiguration operations may be required, such as instantiating new VMs, dynamically replicating some of them for load balancing purposes (elasticity), destroying or replacing VMs, etc. However, setting up, monitoring, and reconfiguring distributed applications in the cloud are complicated tasks because software involves many dependencies that oblige any change to be made in a certain order for preserving application consistency. Moreover, some of these tasks can be executed in parallel for execution time and performance optimization, but this cannot easily be achieved manually. Thus, there is a need for robust protocols that fully automate reconfiguration tasks on running applications distributed across several VMs. The design of these reconfiguration mechanisms is complicated not only due to the high level of parallelism inherent to such applications, but also because they must preserve important architectural invariants at each step of the protocol application, *e.g.*, a started component cannot be connected to (and then possibly using) a stopped component.

In this paper, we present a new protocol, which aims at reconfiguring at runtime cloud applications consisting of a set of interconnected components hosted on remote VMs. We consider several kinds of reconfiguration operations, namely addition and suppression of bindings, components, and VMs. When configuring an application (up phase), the protocol is able to instantiate VMs, effectively connect the components as required, and start these components respecting their functional dependencies. When removing parts of an application (down phase), the protocol needs to stop and disconnect components in a certain order for preserving the architecture consistency. For instance, since we never want a started component to be connected to a stopped component, in order to stop a component, we must previously ask their client components (components bound to that component) to unbind, and we can stop the

CBSE'14, June 30–July 4, 2014, Marcq-en-Baroeul, France.
Copyright 2014 ACM 978-1-4503-2577-6/14/06 ...$15.00.
http://dx.doi.org/10.1145/2602458.2602479.

component only when they have all done so. This supposes a backward-then-forward propagation of messages across VMs composing the application, along bindings connecting components on mandatory required services.

The paper is structured as follows. We present the reconfiguration mechanisms in Section 2. We review related work in Section 3 and we conclude in Section 4.

2. RECONFIGURATION PROTOCOL

2.1 Application Model

For the sake of comprehension, we abstract away from several implementation details such as IP addresses or configuration parameters. Thus, an application model consists of a set of VMs. These VMs do not play any role *per se*, from a functional point of view, but each of them hosts a set of components, where resides the functional part of the application. A component can be in one of these two states: *started* and *stopped*. A component can either provide or require services. This is symbolized using ports: an *import* represents a service required by a component and an *export* represents a service provided by a component. An import can be *optional* or *mandatory*. An import is *satisfied* when it is connected to a matching export and the component offering that export is started. Such a connection is called a *binding*. A component can import a service from a component hosted on the same VM (local binding) or hosted on another VM (remote binding). A component can be started, and then be fully operational, when all its mandatory imports are satisfied. A component can be fully operational even if its optional imports are not satisfied.

We will use as running example a three-tier Web application (Fig. 1). Although this is a simple example, it shows several kinds of dependencies and allows us to illustrate our algorithm on interesting cases. VM1, hosts two components: a front-end Web server (Apache) and a profiling component. VM2 hosts an application server (Tomcat) and an object cache component. VM3 corresponds to the database management system (MySQL). These components are connected using local or remote bindings. These bindings can involve optional imports (o in the figure) or mandatory imports (m).

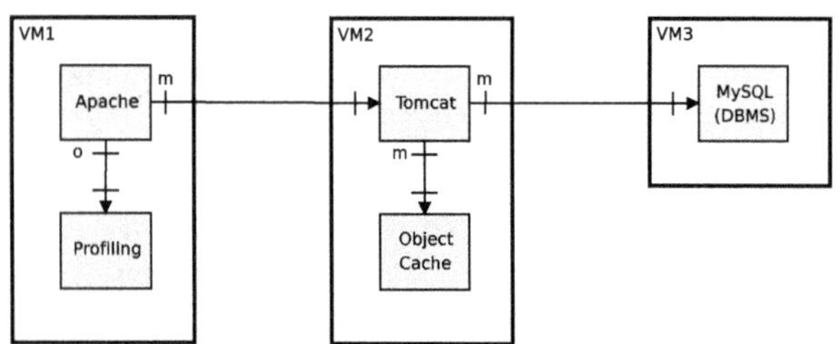

Figure 1: Example: A Web Application Model

2.2 Protocol Features

Our reconfiguration protocol exhibits three main important design features, namely, it is fully automated, decentralized, and robust.

Each VM is equipped with a VM manager in charge of automating the reconfiguration tasks at the VM level.[1] All VM managers work without any human intervention. The cloud manager posts reconfiguration operations that can be given by a cloud user or encoded into a scripting language. Thus, the cloud manager does not necessarily require the presence of a human being for interacting with the running system and application.

VM managers are in charge of starting/stopping their own components and no centralized manager is used for that purpose. The protocol is also loosely-coupled because each VM manager does not have a global view of the current state of the application and particularly of the other VMs. Yet the VM managers need to exchange information in order to connect bindings on remote components or to let certain components know that other (partner) components have started or stopped. The only way to exchange necessary information for the component start-up/shutdown is to interact via asynchronous message passing. Each VM is equipped with two FIFO buffers, one for incoming messages and one for outgoing messages. VMs interact together in a point-to-point fashion (no broadcast or multi-way communication). This solution is standard in distributed systems, and avoids the use of bottleneck centralized servers or communication media (*e.g.*, a publish-subscribe messaging system [2]), which limit the parallelism induced in the distributed system by transforming it somehow into a centralized one.

The protocol is robust in the sense that, during its application, some important architectural invariants are preserved, *e.g.*, all mandatory imports of a started component are satisfied (*i.e.*, bound to started components). These invariants are crucial because they ensure that component assemblies are well-formed. Therefore, they must be preserved during the whole lifetime of the application and at any step of the reconfiguration protocol execution.

2.3 Participants

The reconfiguration protocol involves a cloud manager and a set of VM managers. The cloud manager (CM) guides the application reconfiguration by instantiating/destroying VMs and adding/removing components/bindings. Each VM in the distributed application is equipped with a VM manager that is in charge of (dis)connecting bindings and starting/stopping components upon VM instantiation/destruction operations posted by the CM. Communications between participants (CMs and VM managers) are achieved asynchronously via FIFO buffers. When a participant needs to post a message, it puts that message in its output buffer. When it wants to read a message, it takes the oldest one in its input buffer. Messages are transferred at any time from an output buffer to its addressee's input buffer. Buffers are unbounded, but the protocol does not involve looping tasks that would make the system infinitely send messages to buffers.

Fig. 2 depicts a sample system with a CM and two VMs, and shows how they exchange messages through their buffers (dashed lines). More precisely, when the CM, for instance, needs to send an output message to VM1, it first adds it to its output buffer. The message is then transferred from CM's output buffer to VM1's input buffer. The VM1 manager can finally consume this message from its input buffer.

[1] We distinguish in the rest of this paper a VM, which is a software implementation of a physical machine, and a VM manager, which is the piece of software embedded on a VM in charge of applying the reconfiguration tasks on that VM.

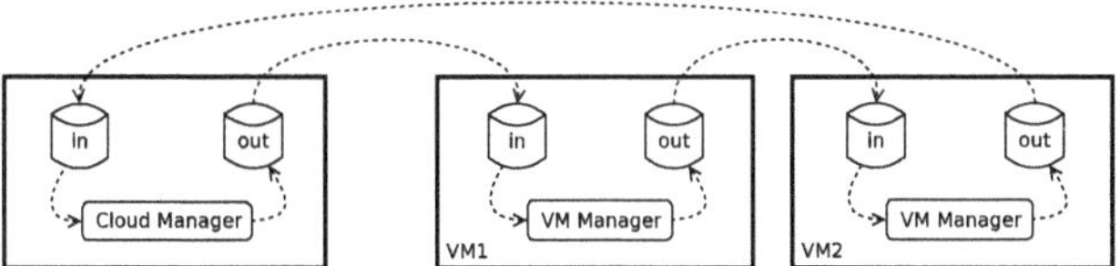

Figure 2: Participants and Communication Model

2.4 Cloud Manager

The CM submits reconfiguration operations to the running application and keeps track of the state of the deployed VMs. We consider the following reconfiguration operations: instantiation/destruction of a VM, addition/removal of a component on/from an existing VM, and addition/suppression of bindings.

In order to ensure a correct execution of the protocol, the CM validates the operations before applying them, *e.g.*, a VM is destroyed only if instantiated before, a new binding is added only if both ports exist in the application, or a binding is added only if it does not form a cycle along mandatory imports. Our reconfiguration mechanisms are triggered by the execution of a sequence of such operations posted by the CM for, *e.g.*, maintenance or elasticity purposes [20].

The protocol works applying *up* and *down* phases. A phase has a coarse-grained granularity compared to atomic reconfiguration operations introduced above. An *up* phase corresponds to a set of reconfiguration operations dedicated to start-up operations (*e.g.*, VM instantiation or binding addition). When the CM instantiates a VM, it creates an image of this VM and the VM starts executing itself. When a CM adds a set of required bindings to the running application, it submits messages to all VMs impacted by these changes, that is, all VMs hosting components involved in those bindings. These messages come with some configuration information necessary to the VM manager for binding purposes. In contrast, a *down* phase involves shutdown operations only (*e.g.*, VM destruction or binding removal). When the CM decides to destroy a VM, it sends a message to that VM. A VM destruction message implies the destruction of all bindings on components hosted on that VM. These two kinds of phases are applied alternatively in sequence and each phase is initiated by the CM. The CM also keeps track of the current state of all VMs running in the system (instantiated VMs and whether they are started or not). A VM is declared *started* when all components on that VM are started. A VM is declared *stopped* otherwise. Fig. 3 summarizes the CM lifecycle where we distinguish reconfiguration operations posted by the CM (solid lines) and messages received from the VM managers (dashed lines).

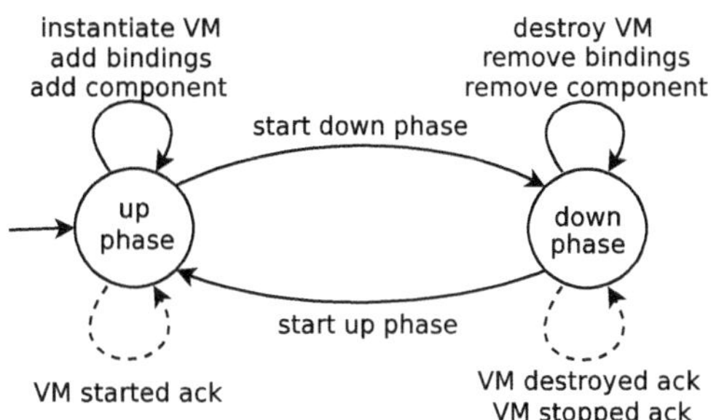

Figure 3: Cloud Manager Lifecyle

We give in Fig. 4 a scenario with successive up/down phases for our running example. In a first up phase, we instantiate all VMs and add a set of required bindings (Bds corresponds to the set of bindings in Fig. 1). Then, we decide to remove the MySQL component for replacing it by a new version (down phase). Finally, we add this new component (MySQL') on VM3 and add a binding (Bd') connecting the Tomcat component to the new MySQL component.

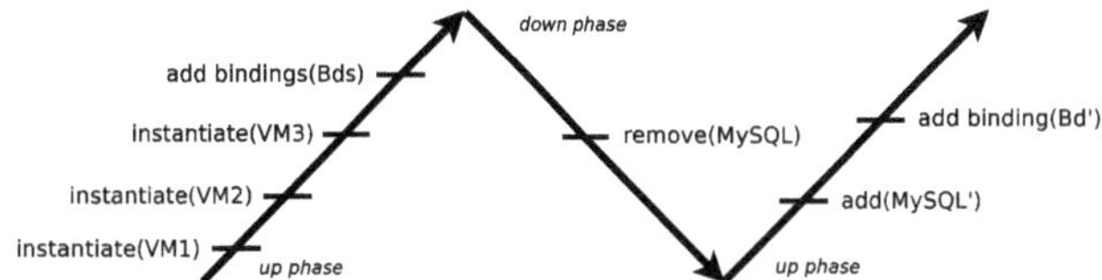

Figure 4: Running Example: Up/Down Scenario

2.5 VM Manager

Each VM is equipped with a VM manager, which starts its activity when the CM instantiates its VM. A VM manager is in charge of binding, unbinding, starting, and stopping components. In the rest of this section, we present the two most general reconfiguration operations, which are the instantiation and the destruction of a VM, resp.

Binding and start-up. Fig. 5 shows how a newly instantiated VM proceeds in order to bind its ports and start its components. After instantiation (❶), the VM manager can immediately start a component without imports or with optional imports only (❷). If a component involves mandatory imports, that component can only be started when all its mandatory imports are satisfied, *i.e.*, when all these imports are bound to started components. When a component is started, its VM manager informs the VM managers of all remote components using it by sending *component started* messages (❸). If all components of a VM are started, its VM manager sends a message to inform the CM (❹), otherwise it starts reading messages from its input buffer (❺):

- If a VM receives from the CM some binding information (for both local and remote bindings), the manager first connects local bindings (❼). As for remote bindings, when an export of one of its components is involved in a binding, the VM manager sends a message (❽) with its export connection information (*e.g.*, IP address) to the VM hosting the other component (import side).
- If the VM receives a remote binding message, this means that an import of one of its components is involved in a binding. Upon reception of that message, the VM manager makes the binding effective (❻).
- Every time a *component started* message is received, the VM manager checks if the corresponding components can be started (❷). Each VM manager keeps the states of its partner components.

Note that the start-up process implies a propagation of *started* messages along bindings across several VMs. Local bindings are handled directly by VM managers and there is no need of exchanging messages with other VMs. The algorithm checks for cycles of bindings over mandatory ports, thus ensuring the termination of the start-up process.

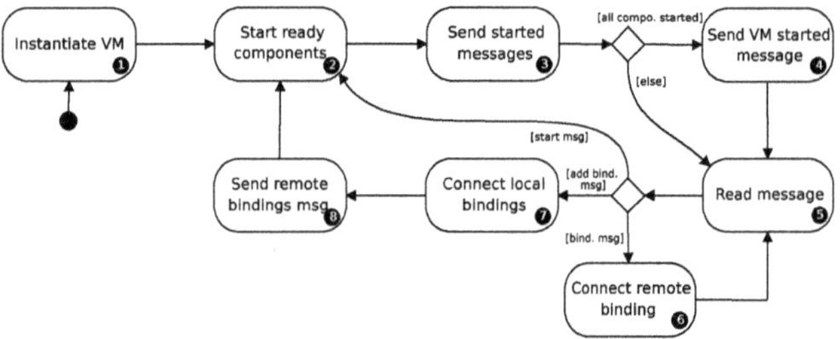

Figure 5: VM Manager Activity Diagram: Up Phase

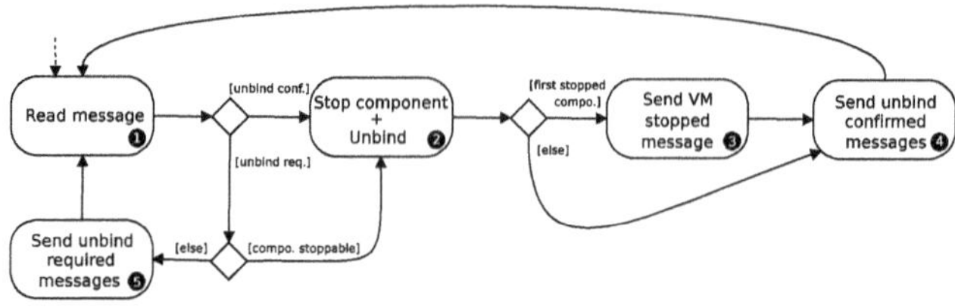

Figure 7: VM Manager Activity Diagram: Down Phase (Side Effect)

Unbinding and shutdown. A VM manager is in charge of stopping some local components, or all its components when the VM is to be destroyed (Fig. 6, ❶), *i.e.*, removed from the running application. In this case, all the components hosted on that VM need to be stopped and all bindings on these components (connected to imports or exports) need to be removed. If a component involved in the shutdown process does not provide any service (there is no component connected to it), it can immediately stop, and all outgoing bindings can be removed for these components (❷). Otherwise, it cannot stop before all partner components connected to it on mandatory imports have unbound themselves. To do so, the VM manager of the VM under destruction first sends *unbind required* messages to all VMs hosting components connected to those VM's components (❸). The VM manager of the VM to be destroyed then collects *unbind confirmed* messages (❹) and stops the corresponding components when all components using that component on mandatory imports have stopped and unbound (❺). Whenever a component stops, an *unbind confirmed* message is sent (❻). The VM is destroyed and the CM informed when all components are stopped (❼).

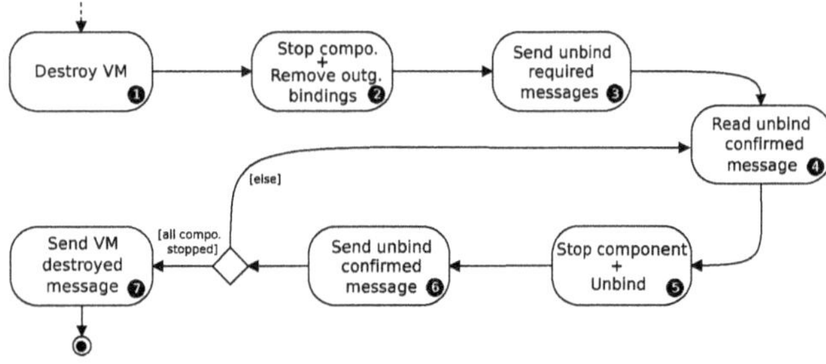

Figure 6: VM Manager Activity Diagram: Down Phase (Destruction)

As a side effect to a VM destruction, the other VM managers can receive messages (Fig. 7, ❶) from their partner VMs. Upon reception of an *unbind required* message, the VM manager either stops and unbinds some components (❷) if possible (no bindings on them or bindings on remote optional imports only), or sends similar messages for all remote components bound on mandatory imports to its components (❺). When a VM manager stops (and unbinds) a component (❷), it may send a message to the CM indicating that the VM is not fully operational (❸). It also sends messages to all remote partner components formerly providing a service to that component, to let them know that this component has been stopped/unbound (❹). Upon reception of an *unbind confirmed* message, the VM manager goes to step ❷.

Components bound on optional imports just need to unbind themselves, but do not need to stop. Local bindings are handled locally by the VM manager, but these changes can impact other remote components, and in that case additional *unbind required* messages may be emitted. The component shutdown implies a backward propagation of *unbind required* messages and, when this first propagation ends (on components without exports or with optional imports only), a second forward propagation of *unbind confirmed* messages starts to let the components know that the disconnection has been actually achieved. These propagations terminate because there is no cycle of bindings over mandatory imports.

2.6 Examples of Reconfiguration Scenarios

We show in this section how the protocol works on simple reconfiguration scenarios for the Web application presented in Fig. 1. Let us assume that the application is fully operational and all components on all VMs are started (end of the first *up* phase in Fig. 4). A new version of the MySQL database management system is available and we decide to upgrade that component to this new version. Accordingly, the whole system initiates a *down* phase (middle part of Fig. 4) characterized by an emission of a *remove* message to VM3. We show in Fig. 8 a Message Sequence Chart (MSC) overviewing the interactions and behaviors of all participants (CM and VM managers) for this specific scenario.

Upon reception of the *remove* message, VM3 sends an *unbind required* message to VM2 requesting to unbind the Tomcat component from the MySQL component. When VM2 receives this message, it cannot unbind immediately because Tomcat is used by a remote component (Apache), therefore it sends too an *unbind required* message to VM1. Upon reception of that message, the VM1 manager stops the Apache component, because no other component is connected to it, and then unbinds the Apache component from the Tomcat component. VM1 sends a confirmation message to VM2 indicating that the disconnection has been achieved. VM1 also sends a *VM stopped* message to the CM indicating that all its components are not started anymore. When VM2 receives the *unbind confirmed* message, its manager stops Tomcat and unbinds it from MySQL. A confirmation is sent from VM2 to VM3 and a *VM stopped* message is sent to the CM. Once VM3 receives the confirmation message, its manager stops the MySQL component, and sends an acknowledgement message to the CM indicating that the VM is stopped too. Stopping Tomcat and Apache is required to preserve architectural invariants, here a started component cannot be connected to a stop component.

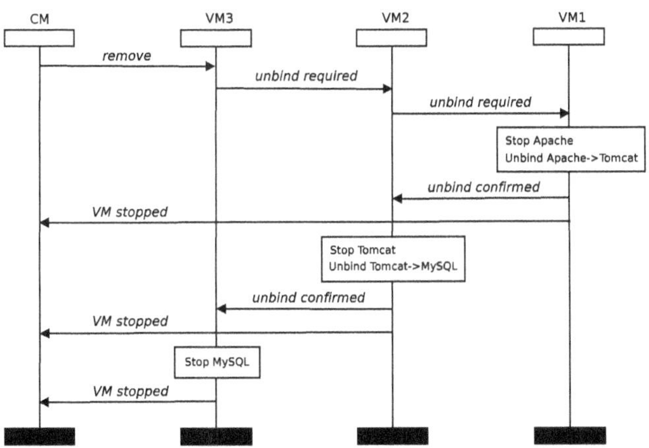

Figure 8: MySQL Removal Scenario

After the removal of MySQL, the application is in a situation where components Apache and Tomcat are off and components Profiling and Object Cache are on.

In order to restore a fully operational application, let us now consider an *up* scenario (right-hand side of Fig. 4) where the CM manager adds a new version of the MySQL component on VM3 (*add* message) and a new binding between the Tomcat component and the new MySQL component. We show in Fig. 9 the interactions and actions involved in this scenario. VM3 can start the MySQL' component immediately because this component does not require any service from other components (no imports). VM3 knows that VM2 needs to connect its component to the MySQL' component, therefore the VM3 manager posts a *send export* message with the connection information to VM2. Upon reception, the VM2 manager can connect both components. The VM3 manager also indicates to VM2 that its MySQL' component has started and to the CM that VM3 is started. Upon reception of the *send export* message, the VM2 manager starts the Tomcat component. VM2 sends a *send export* message and a *started* message to VM1, because the VM2 manager knows the dependency between the Apache component and the Tomcat component. VM2 also informs the CM that VM2 is started. The VM1 manager finally binds Apache to Tomcat, starts the Apache component, and informs the CM that VM1 is started too. Note that acknowledgement messages are not systematically required. They are useful in some specific cases, *e.g.*, when a component (import side) expects its partner (export side) to start.

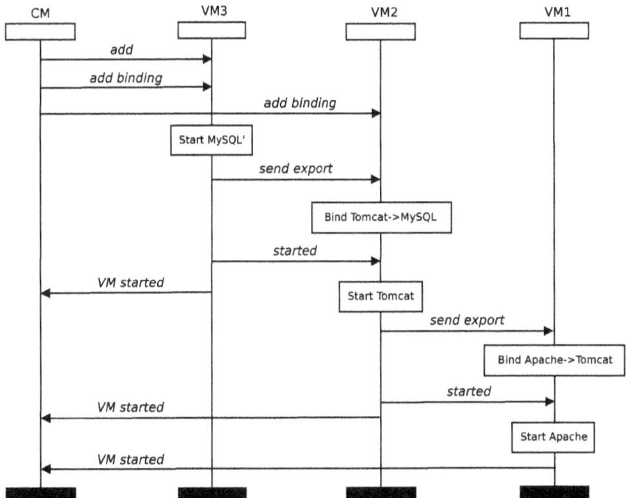

Figure 9: MySQL' Addition Scenario

3. RELATED WORK

Dynamic reconfiguration has been extensively studied in the last 20 years in the context of, *e.g.*, software architectures [16, 19, 15, 4, 17], graph transformation [3, 24], software adaptation [22, 21, 8], metamodelling [14, 18], or reconfiguration patterns [7]. In software architectures, for example, the authors proposed various formal models, such as Darwin [16] or Wright [4], in order to specify dynamic reconfiguration of component-based systems whose architectures can evolve (adding or removing components and connections) at run-time. In the cloud computing area, some existing environments already provide some mechanisms to automatically scale deployed applications based on monitoring data (see, *e.g.*, the Elastic Beanstalk from Amazon Web Services). However, these approaches typically work at the application level (Platform-as-a-Service, PaaS). Moreover, changes are triggered with respect to the individual performance of each tier, although there are attempts to decide elasticity actions from entire application performance models, see, *e.g.*, the Reservoir [9] or ConPaaS projects [20]. In [11, 23, 12], the authors present a protocol that automates the deployment of distributed applications in cloud environments in a decentralized way. Each VM is in charge of starting its own components and to do so needs to interact with the other VMs in order to exchange binding information. Another related work [13] presents a system that manages application stack configuration. It provides techniques to configure services across machines according to their dependencies, to deploy components, and to manage the life cycle of installed resources. This work presents some similarities with ours, but [13] does not focus on composition consistency, architectural invariants preservation, or robustness of the reconfiguration protocol. [6, 5] present a reconfiguration protocol applying changes to a set of connected components for transforming a current assembly to a target one given as input. Reconfigurations steps aim at (dis)connecting ports and changing component states. The protocol is robust in the sense that all the steps of this protocol preserve a number of architectural invariants. This protocol does not easily scale to cloud applications because the authors assume that all components are hosted on a same VM and a unique centralized manager is in charge of the reconfiguration steps. In contrast, our protocol is fully parallel (all VMs evolve independently one from another, at different speeds). In [2], the authors present a management protocol for instantiating and removing VMs from a running cloud application, but the protocol is quite different because it relies on another communication model, namely a publish-subscribe messaging system.

4. CONCLUDING REMARKS

In this paper, we have presented a new protocol for automatically reconfiguring cloud applications consisting of interconnected components distributed over several VMs. The protocol does not only support VM instantiation and component start-up, but also VM destruction and component shutdown. These management tasks are guided by reconfiguration operations posted through a cloud manager. All VMs work in a fully decentralized and loosely-coupled way in order to apply these reconfiguration tasks, exchanging messages when necessary via FIFO buffers. The protocol is robust in the sense that it preserves composition consistency and well-formedness architectural invariants at any step of its application.

Due to the high degree of parallelism inherent to the applications to be reconfigured, the design of these reconfiguration mechanisms was very complicated and would have been impossible without the support of formal techniques and tools. Therefore, we specified the reconfiguration protocol using the rewriting-logic-based Maude language [10]. This results in a formal model of the protocol that we analyzed using Maude verification tools for chasing subtle bugs in boundary cases and therefore ensuring that our implementation satisfies some key properties and invariants. All Maude sources for our specification and its verification are available online [1]. It is worth noting that a Java implementation of the protocol is under development at Orange Labs in the context of the OpenCloudware funded project.[2]

A first perspective aims at improving the protocol to avoid using up/down phases. This is a non-trivial change since start and stop messages may be unwillingly mixed up. We also plan to extend the protocol to support VM failures.

Acknowledgements. This work has been partially supported by the Spanish project TIN2011-23795, the SeaClouds EU project, Universidad de Málaga (Campus de Excelencia Internacional Andalucía Tech), and the OpenCloudware project, which is funded by the French *Fonds national pour la Société Numérique* (FSN), by *Pôles* Minalogic, Systematic, and SCS.

5. REFERENCES

[1] http://maude.lcc.uma.es/HRfCA.

[2] R. Abid, G. Salaün, F. Bongiovanni, and N. De Palma. Verification of a Dynamic Management Protocol for Cloud Applications. In *Proc. of ATVA'13*, vol. 8172 of *LNCS*, pages 178–192. Springer, 2013.

[3] N. Aguirre and T. Maibaum. A Logical Basis for the Specification of Reconfigurable Component-Based Systems. In *Proc. of FASE'03*, vol. 2621 of *LNCS*, pages 37–51. Springer, 2003.

[4] R. Allen, R. Douence, and D. Garlan. Specifying and Analyzing Dynamic Software Architectures. In *Proc. of FASE'98*, vol. 1382 of *LNCS*, pages 21–37. Springer, 1998.

[5] F. Boyer, O. Gruber, and D. Pous. Robust Reconfigurations of Component Assemblies. In *Proc. of ICSE'13*, pages 13–22. IEEE/ACM, 2013.

[6] F. Boyer, O. Gruber, and G. Salaün. Specifying and Verifying the Synergy Reconfiguration Protocol with LOTOS NT and CADP. In *Proc. of FM'11*, vol. 6664 of *LNCS*, pages 103–117. Springer, 2011.

[7] T. Bures, P. Hnetynka, and F. Plasil. SOFA 2.0: Balancing Advanced Features in a Hierarchical Component Model. In *Proc. of SERA'06*, pages 40–48. IEEE Computer Society, 2006.

[8] C. Canal, J. Cámara, and G. Salaün. Structural Reconfiguration of Systems under Behavioral Adaptation. *Science of Computer Programming*, 78(1):46–64, 2012.

[9] C. Chapman, W. Emmerich, F. G. Márquez, S. Clayman, and A. Galis. Software Architecture Definition for On-demand Cloud Provisioning. *Cluster Computing*, 15(2):79–100, 2012.

[10] M. Clavel, F. Durán, S. Eker, P. Lincoln, N. Martí-Oliet, J. Meseguer, and C. Talcott. *All About Maude - A High-Performance Logical Framework* , vol. 4350 of *LNCS*. Springer, 2007.

[11] X. Etchevers, T. Coupaye, F. Boyer, N. de Palma, and G. Salaün. Automated Configuration of Legacy Applications in the Cloud. In *Proc. of UCC'11*, pages 170–177. IEEE Computer Society, 2011.

[12] X. Etchevers, G. Salaün, F. Boyer, T. Coupaye, and N. D. Palma. Reliable Self-Deployment of Cloud Applications. In *Proc. of SAC'14*, pages 1331–1338. ACM Press, 2014.

[13] J. Fischer, R. Majumdar, and S. Esmaeilsabzali. Engage: A Deployment Management System. In *Proc. of PLDI'12*, pages 263–274. ACM, 2012.

[14] A. Ketfi and N. Belkhatir. A Metamodel-Based Approach for the Dynamic Reconfiguration of Component-Based Software. In *Proc. of ICSR'04*, vol. 3107 of *LNCS*, pages 264–273. Springer, 2004.

[15] J. Kramer and J. Magee. Analysing Dynamic Change in Distributed Software Architectures. *IEE Proceedings - Software*, 145(5):146–154, 1998.

[16] J. Magee and J. Kramer. Dynamic Structure in Software Architectures. In *Proc. of SIGSOFT FSE'96*, pages 3–14, 1996.

[17] J. Magee, J. Kramer, and D. Giannakopoulou. Behaviour Analysis of Software Architectures. In *Proc. of WICSA'99*, vol. 140 of *IFIP Conference Proceedings*, pages 35–50. Kluwer, 1999.

[18] J. Matevska-Meyer, W. Hasselbring, and R. Reussner. Software Architecture Description Supporting Component Deployment and System Runtime Reconfiguration. In *Proc. of WCOP'04*, 2004.

[19] N. Medvidovic. ADLs and Dynamic Architecture Changes. In *SIGSOFT 96 Workshop*, pages 24–27. ACM, 1996.

[20] G. Pierre and C. Stratan. ConPaaS: A Platform for Hosting Elastic Cloud Applications. *IEEE Internet Computing*, 16(5):88–92, 2012.

[21] P. Poizat and G. Salaün. Adaptation of Open Component-Based Systems. In *Proc. of FMOODS'07*, vol. 4468, pages 141–156. Springer, 2007.

[22] P. Poizat, G. Salaün, and M. Tivoli. On Dynamic Reconfiguration of Behavioural Adaptation. In *Proc. of WCAT'06*, pages 61–69, 2006.

[23] G. Salaün, X. Etchevers, N. D. Palma, F. Boyer, and T. Coupaye. Verification of a Self-configuration Protocol for Distributed Applications in the Cloud. In *Proc. of SAC'12*, pages 1278–1283. ACM Press, 2012.

[24] M. Wermelinger, A. Lopes, and J. L. Fiadeiro. A Graph Based Architectural (Re)configuration Language. In *Proc. of ESEC / SIGSOFT FSE'01*, pages 21–32. ACM Press, 2001.

[2] http://opencloudware.org

Software Component Models: Past, Present and Future

Kung-Kiu Lau
School of Computer Science
The University of Manchester, UK
kung-kiu@cs.man.ac.uk

ABSTRACT

In the early years of the CBSE Symposium, much research was focused on identifying the desiderata of CBSE [3] and developing different approaches to CBSE. However, a common framework for defining and analysing CBSE approaches with respect to these desiderata was only introduced later: this was provided by the notion of *component models* [9, 12, 13, 6]. Every CBSE approach is underpinned by a component model, and therefore the study of component models, in particular how to define ones that can potentially meet the desiderata of CBSE, is pivotal to the success of CBSE.

We have surveyed and studied existing CBSE approaches and their corresponding component models [12, 13], and as a result we have: (i) shown that early approaches/models do not fully meet the CBSE desiderata; (ii) identified criteria for designing component models that can better meet the CBSE desiderata; (iii) defined a new component model according to (ii); (iv) defined a taxonomy of existing component models based on the desiderata.

In addition to the classic desiderata described in [3], nowadays CBSE has to address new challenges posed by an unprecedented increase in the scale and complexity of software applications, in particular safety-critical ones. As a result, there are new CBSE desiderata for which we need to define new models.

In this tutorial, we will: (i) present a taxonomy of existing component models, both old and new; (ii) discuss how well they meet the classic desiderata; (iii) discuss criteria that new models must meet in order to address future CBSE challenges.

The CBSE Symposium celebrated its fifteenth anniversary in 2012 [14]. For the next 15 years, the study of component models will continue to play a pivotal role in future CBSE success. This tutorial aims to contribute to this effort.

CBSE'14, June 30–July 4, 2014, Marcq-en-Baroeul, France.
ACM 978-1-4503-2577-6/14/06.
http://dx.doi.org/10.1145/2602458.2611456 .

Categories and Subject Descriptors

H.4 [**Information Systems Applications**]: Miscellaneous; D.2.8 [**Software Engineering**]: [component-based software engineering]

General Terms

Software Component Models

Keywords

Software Components; Composition

1. SOFTWARE COMPONENT MODELS

The cornerstone of any CBSE methodology [16] is its underlying component model [9, 12, 13, 6], which defines what components are, how they can be constructed and represented, how they can be composed or assembled, how they can be deployed; and how to reason about all these operations on components in terms of the usual accompanying quality metrics.

The tutorial will look at the past, present and future of component models.

1.1 The Past

Early CBSE research focused on identifying desiderata and on defining different approaches to CBSE.

Classic CBSE Desiderata. Components should pre-exist; what components are; components should be produced and deployed independently; composites should be possible; components should be copiable and instantiable, etc. Widely accepted, 'classic', desiderata are described in [3].

Idealized Component and System Life Cycles. An idealised component life cycle is one that meets the CBSE desiderata. An idealised system life cycle uses pre-existing components developed during the component life cycle; it thus intersects the idealised component life cycle at the point at which components have been built.

Early Component Models. Early component models are based on: (i) object-oriented frameworks, e.g. CCM [15] and EJB [7], where components are objects and composition is by object delegation; and (ii) first-generation ADLs (architecture description languages), e.g. ACME [8] and ArchJava [1], where components are architectural units (with ports) and composition is by port linking.

Early Component and System Life Cycles. Early component life cycles deviate from the idealized one. Early system life cycles often subsume component life cycles, i.e. they do not use pre-existing components but rather identify and develop components afresh for each system.

1.2 The Present

Currently, the majority of component models in use are based on second-generation ADLs, e.g. Fractal [4] and SOFA [5]. Whereas first-generation ADLs generally lack tool support, in particular for component repositories and for connector generation, second-generation ADLs provide much more tool support.

Current Component and System Life Cycles. Current component life cycles also deviate from the idealized one somewhat, mainly in the use of repositories.

New Component Models. New component models have been defined that are not based ADLs: web services [2] and X-MAN [11]. These models use coordination as a composition mechanism, and better meet the CBSE desiderata than earlier models.

A Taxonomy of Component Models. The result of our study of component models, old and new, is summarised in a taxonomy based on the classic desiderata. This taxonomy has five categories, and include the following component models:

ACME-like ADLs, CCM, COM, EJB, Fractal, JavaBeans, Koala, KobrA, .NET, OSGi, Palladio, Pin, ProCom, SOFA, UML 2.0, PECOS, X-MAN, and Web Services.

1.3 The Future

The classic CBSE desiderata alone are not sufficient for meeting new challenges for the future.

Scale and Complexity. An unprecedented increase in the scale and complexity of software applications poses new challenges. CBSE is well-placed to meet these challenges, but to do so it must meet additional desiderata.

Safety. Safety is another challenge. An increase in scale and complexity makes it more difficult to ensure safety. Again, CBSE is well-placed to meet this challenge, but has to meet additional desiderata to do so. For V&V, adapting the V model [17] for CBSE needs to be done correctly.

Future Component Models. Future component models must have compositionality in all aspects relevant to scale, complexity and safety. Compositionality to ensure scale and complexity entails hierarchical system construction; whereas compositionality to ensure safety entails compositional V&V.

Future Component and System Life Cycles. To support compositionality, new life cycles like the W Model [10] have to be developed.

2. REFERENCES

[1] J. Aldrich, C. Chambers, and D. Notkin. Component-oriented programming in ArchJava. In *First OOPSLA Workshop on Language Mechanisms for Programming Software Components*, pages 1–8, 2001.

[2] G. Alonso, F. Casati, H. Kuno, and V. Machiraju. *Web Services: Concepts, Architectures and Applications*. Springer-Verlag, 2004.

[3] M. Broy, A. Deimel, J. Henn, K. Koskimies, F. Plasil, G. Pomberger, W. Pree, M. Stal, and C. Szyperski. What characterizes a software component? *Software – Concepts and Tools*, 19(1):49–56, 1998.

[4] E. Bruneton, T. Coupaye, and M. Leclercq. An open component model and its support in Java. In *Proc. 7th CBSE, LNCS 3054*, pages 7–22. Springer -Verlag, 2004.

[5] T. Bures, P. Hnetynka, and F. Plasil. SOFA 2.0: Balancing Advanced Features in a Hierarchical Component Model. In *Proc. SERA 2006*, pages 40–48. IEEE, 2006.

[6] I. Crnkovic, S. Sentilles, A. Vulgarakis, and M. Chaudron. A classification framework for software component models. *IEEE Transactions on Software Engineering*, 37(5):593–615, Oct. 2011.

[7] L. DeMichiel, L. Yalçinalp, and S. Krishnan. *Enterprise JavaBeans Specification Version 2.0*, 2001.

[8] D. Garlan, R. Monroe, and D. Wile. ACME: An architectural interconnection language. In *Proc. CASCON'97*, pages 169–183, 1997.

[9] G. Heineman and W. Councill, editors. *Component-Based Software Engineering: Putting the Pieces Together*. Addison-Wesley, 2001.

[10] K.-K. Lau, F. Taweel, and C. Tran. The W Model for component-based software development. In *Proc. 37th EUROMICRO Conference on Software Engineering and Advanced Applications (SEAA)*, pages 47–50. IEEE, 2011.

[11] K.-K. Lau and C. Tran. X-MAN: An MDE tool for component-based system development. In *Proc. 38th SEAA*, pages 158–165. IEEE, 2012.

[12] K.-K. Lau and Z. Wang. A taxonomy of software component models. In *Proc. 31st SEAA*, pages 88–95. IEEE Computer Society Press, 2005.

[13] K.-K. Lau and Z. Wang. Software component models. *IEEE Transactions on Software Engineering*, 33(10):709–724, October 2007.

[14] J. Maras, L. Lednicki, and I. Crnkovic. 15 years of CBSE Symposium – impact on the research community. In *Proc. 15th CBSE*, pages 61–70. ACM, 2012.

[15] OMG. *CORBA Component Model, V3.0*, 2002. `http://www.omg.org/technology/documents/formal/components.htm`.

[16] C. Szyperski, D. Gruntz, and S. Murer. *Component Software: Beyond Object-Oriented Programming*. Addison-Wesley, second edition, 2002.

[17] The V-model. Development standard for IT-systems of the Federal Republic of Germany, IABG. `http://www.v-modell.iabg.de`.

Rigorous Component-Based Design in BIP

Half-Day Tutorial

Simon Bliudze
Ecole polytechnique fédérale de Lausanne
Rigorous System Design Laboratory
Station 14, CH-1015 Lausanne, Switzerland
simon.bliudze@epfl.ch

ABSTRACT

This tutorial presents the BIP component-based design and analysis framework, primarily focusing on the control software for (real-time) embedded systems. We provide the participants with an overview of the research and some practical hands-on experience of application design in BIP. After a short motivation, we discuss the BIP component model, then move directly to the demonstration of the BIP language, design process, code generation and simulation.

Categories and Subject Descriptors

D.3.1 [**Programming Languages**]: Formal Definitions and Theory; D.3.2 [**Programming Languages**]: Language Classifications—*Concurrent, distributed and parallel languages*

Keywords

Component-based design; rigorous design flow; BIP

1. INTRODUCTION

The tutorial comprises an overview of the research activities around the BIP component framework as well as a tool demonstration. Thus, it is intended for a mixed audience comprising students, researchers and practitioners in the field of component-based design of concurrent software and systems.

BIP is a component-based design and analysis framework, primarily focusing on the control software for (real-time) embedded systems. It has been successfully used for modelling and analysis of a variety of case studies and applications, such as performance evaluation, modelling and analysis of TinyOS-based wireless sensor network applications, construction and verification of a robotic system. In the latter, the code generated by the tool-chain along with the BIP engine is used as a controller for the robot. The BIP model also offers validation techniques for checking essential safety properties.

CBSE'14, June 30–July 4, 2014, Marcq-en-Baroeul, France.
ACM 978-1-4503-2577-6/14/06.
http://dx.doi.org/10.1145/2602458.2611457.

Component-based design relies on the separation between coordination and computation. Systems are built from units processing sequential code insulated from concurrent execution issues. BIP [1] is a component framework for constructing systems by superposing three layers of modelling: *Behaviour*, *Interaction*, and *Priority*. The first layer consists of a set of atomic components represented by transition systems. The second layer models Interaction between components. Interactions are sets of ports specified by connectors. Priority, given by a strict partial order on interactions, is used to enforce scheduling policies applied to interactions of the second layer. Atomic components are communicating automata with transitions labelled by sets of communication ports. Compound components are obtained from subcomponents by application of glue operators (connectors and priorities). The BIP component framework has a formal operational semantics given in terms of Labelled Transition Systems (LTS) and Structural Operational Semantics derivation rules [3].

The execution of a BIP system is driven by a dedicated *engine*, which has access to the set of connectors and the priority model of the system. In a given global state, each atomic component waits for an interaction through a set of active ports (i.e. ports labelling active transitions) communicated to the engine. The engine computes from the connectors of the BIP program and the set of all active ports, the set of maximal interactions (involving active ports). It chooses one of these interactions, computes the associated data transfer functions and notifies the involved components.

Several engines are available for execution of BIP models on various architectures. For execution on distributed platforms, BIP models are transformed into Send-Receive BIP [4], where components communicate by sending messages and the choice of the interaction to be executed is distributed across the platform. In Send-Receive BIP models, this choice is realised by additional automatically generated components, which are replaced by appropriate communication protocols in the generated code.

The BIP design methodology [2] is illustrated in Figure 1. First, a taxonomy of architectural components specific to the case-study application domain is identified (not shown in the figure). Template BIP models are then designed for various component types of this taxonomy, which are used to assemble the application model. Deadlock analysis with DFinder is performed on the obtained model to verify safety properties. The system model is then generated combining the application model with the BIP model of the hardware platform, taking into account architectural constraints, such

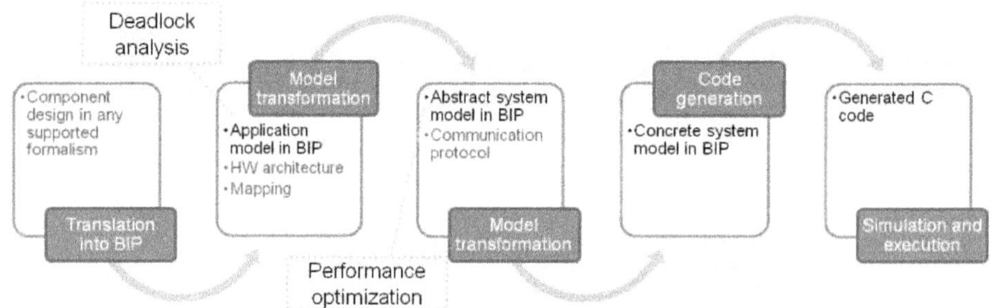

Figure 1: Rigorous design flow

as mutual exclusion, execution times of atomic actions and scheduling policies for optimal resource utilisation. The obtained system model can be used for performance analysis and optimisation, in particular using the Statistical Model Checking technique developed at Verimag. This model is then transformed into a platform-specific model (distributed model in the figure), by expressing high-level BIP coordination mechanisms with execution platform primitives, e.g. asynchronous message passing in the Send-Receive BIP for distributed platforms.

Although most of the tools implementing the above design flow[1] are research prototypes, the C++ code generator and several engines[2] can be used for the design of real-life applications. Therefore, the tutorial focuses primarily on the application design targeting C++ code generation and an overview of the research activities and results driving the development of the BIP framework.

2. TUTORIAL OUTLINE

The structure of the tutorial reflects its goal of providing the participants with some practical hands-on experience of application design in BIP. After a short motivation, we discuss the BIP component model, then move directly to the demonstration of the BIP language, design process, code generation and simulation. The breadth and detail of the overview of the BIP research depends on the time left after the demonstration. We address the following topics:

1. *Motivation*: The neccesity of formalising the system design discipline; heterogeneity of the underlying computing models and architectures; separation of concerns and raising the abstraction level.

2. *BIP component model*: basic component model (LTS, Interactions, Priorities); formal semantics; engine-driven execution; extension with variables and data transfer.

3. *Application design in BIP*: language introduction by examples; code generation and simulation; interface with the environment.

4. *Overview of the BIP research*: existing results and future research directions.

3. ADDITIONAL MATERIALS

This tutorial includes some elements that have appeared in talks given by Prof. Joseph Sifakis, in particular:

- At the Microsoft Research Asia conference "Computing in the 21st Century", which took place in Heifei, Anhui, China on November 1st, 2013.[3] The video recording of the talk is available from the RiSD website: `http://risd.epfl.ch`.

- During the Nano-Tera/Artist International Summer School on Embedded System Design, which was held in Aix-les-Bains, France on September 17th–21st, 2012. The recording of the lecture is available from the summer school web-site: `http://artist-summer-school.epfl.ch/sifakis`

4. PRESENTER BIO

Simon Bliudze (`http://people.epfl.ch/simon.bliudze`) holds an MSc in Mathematics from the St. Petersburg State University (Russia, 1998), an MSc in Computer Science from the University Pierre et Marie Curie (Paris 6, France, 2001) and a PhD in Computer Science from École Polytechnique (Paris, France, 2006). He has spent two years at Verimag (Grenoble, France) as a post-doc with Joseph Sifakis working on formal semantics for the BIP component framework. After three years as a research engineer at CEA Saclay, France, he has joined the newly created Rigorous System Design Laboratory (RiSD) at École Polytechnique Fédérale de Lausanne (Switzerland).

5. REFERENCES

[1] Ananda Basu, Saddek Bensalem, Marius Bozga, Jacques Combaz, Mohamad Jaber, Thanh-Hung Nguyen, and Joseph Sifakis. Rigorous Component-Based System Design Using the BIP Framework. *IEEE Software*, 28(3):41–48, 2011.

[2] Ananda Basu, Saddek Bensalem, Marius Bozga, Jacques Combaz, Mohamad Jaber, Thanh-Hung Nguyen, and Joseph Sifakis. Rigorous Component-Based System Design Using the BIP Framework. *IEEE Software*, 28(3):41–48, 2011.

[3] Simon Bliudze and Joseph Sifakis. The algebra of connectors — Structuring interaction in BIP. In *Proceedings of the EMSOFT'07*, pages 11–20, Salzburg, Austria, October 2007. ACM SigBED.

[4] Borzoo Bonakdarpour, Marius Bozga, Mohamad Jaber, Jean Quilbeuf, and Joseph Sifakis. From high-level component-based models to distributed implementations. In *Proceedings of the 10th ACM International Conference on Embedded Software*, pages 209–218, New York, NY, USA, 2010. ACM.

[1] `http://www-verimag.imag.fr/BIP-Tools,93.html`
[2] `http://www-verimag.imag.fr/New-BIP-tools.html`
[3] `http://www.msra.cn/21ccc`

Development of Smart Cyber-Physical Systems

Tomas Bures
Faculty of Mathematics and Physics, Charles University
Malostranske namesti 25, Prague
Czech Republic
bures@d3s.mff.cuni.cz

ABSTRACT

The recent increase in the ubiquity and connectivity of computing devices allows forming large-scale distributed systems that respond to and influence activities in the real world (typically called *smart Cyber-Physical Systems* – sCPS). Examples of such systems include intelligent vehicle navigation, autonomous operation of smart buildings and civil infrastructure, emergency coordination in case of disaster, and even interactive distributed games. Engineering sCPS is typically very challenging because of their inherent dynamicity, open-endedness, autonomicity, and close relation to the real world. The goal of this tutorial is to acquaint the participants with the challenges of engineering sCPS and to explain and demonstrate a novel approach based on autonomic component ensembles that provides means (methods and tools) for relatively seamless design and development of sCPS.

Categories and Subject Descriptors

C.2.4 [**Computer-Communication Networks**]: Distributed Systems – *distributed applications*; D.2.6 [**Software Engineering**]: Programming Environments – *integrated environments*; D.2.9 [**Software Engineering**]: Management – *life cycle*; D.2.11 [**Software Engineering**]: Software Architectures.

General Terms

Design, Experimentation, Verification.

Keywords

Smart cyber-physical systems; component-based software engineering; emergent architectures; component ensembles; autonomic systems; runtime framework

1. INTRODUCTION

The recent advancement in hardware and network infrastructures and the resulting increase in the ubiquity and connectivity of computing devices has opened new possibilities for addressing societal and environmental challenges such as ambient assisted living, smart city infrastructures, emergency coordination, environmental monitoring, etc. It is now technologically possible (at least from the hardware perspective) to build large-scale distributed systems that respond to and influence activities in the real world and mutually coordinate to provide globally optimal solutions. These systems are typically referred to as *smart Cyber-Physical Systems* (sCPS).

CBSE'14, Jun 30–July 04, 2014, Marcq-en-Bareul, France.
ACM 978-1-4503-2577-6/14/06.
http://dx.doi.org/10.1145/2602458.2611458

As sCPS become increasingly important and seemingly feasible to create and operate, their efficient development has been recognized as a priority by a number of research and innovation frameworks – for instance, efficient development of sCPS constitutes one of EU's research priorities in the funding frameworks H2020 and ECSEL.

By their nature, sCPS have to combine control of the physical world with large-scale coordination, and opportunistic distributed communication with autonomic and adaptive operation. They have to cope with dynamic and open-ended environments; they themselves also become architecturally very dynamic. The open-endedness and dynamicity of sCPS further typically causes emergent behavior – i.e. behavior of the sCPS as a whole that cannot be accredited to any of its individual constituents alone. Consequently, software engineering for sCPS becomes a significant challenge: a sCPS practitioner has to have working knowledge of multiple (and usually not well-related) areas – software architectures, real-time and embedded systems, distributed systems, autonomic agents, and control systems. This calls for suitable architectural, computation and process models that would simplify the development of sCPS by offering tailored abstractions that address the complexity and specifics of sCPS. Such models should directly address the requirements of scalability, distribution, and well-defined architecture, while, at the same time, deal with the requirements of dynamicity, open-endedness, robustness, and autonomicity.

In the last years, such novel software engineering approaches have emerged. They view sCPS as dynamic ensembles of autonomic components and enable their development using component-based software engineering methods. These approaches have been referred to as *ensemble-based component systems* (EBCS). EBCS view a component as an autonomic entity which is in close relation to the real world (embodying the aspects of feedback-based control loops and real-time operation). At the same time, the component is capable of high-level interaction and coordination with other components in the system. This happens via goal-driven groups of components called *ensembles*. An ensemble defines an interaction frame in which different components take well-defined roles to achieve a particular goal (e.g. a car in the front takes the role of convoy leader while cars in the rear take the roles of followers and adjust their driving based on information from the leader). An important feature of ensembles is that they are highly dynamic – they get formed based on the actual state and location of the components (e.g.

when a car reaches a convoy) and dissolved whenever the conditions for forming the ensemble cease to hold (e.g. when a car needs to pull off). The concept of ensembles thus allows capturing highly dynamic architectures and achieving self-organization of the system (responding to the dynamicity and open-endedness of sCPS environments), while still preserving certain well-defined structural and interaction patterns in the system (important for dependable operation). The ad-hoc opportunistic formation of ensembles and the component interaction within them brings about also the important aspects of autonomous agents and (mobile) peer-to-peer ad-hoc communication. The concepts of autonomic components and ensembles are typically backed by a dedicated component runtime and communication middleware, which transparently addresses a number of related technical challenges (e.g. real-time scheduling, communication in ad-hoc networks with limited connectivity and reliability, distributed coordination), thus allowing a developer to focus on the business functionality and high-level architecture. Practical examples of EBCS are showcased in particular in the FP7 project ASCENS [1]. They include SCEL/jRESP [5], Helena [4], and DEECo [2] models.

The tutorial will provide theoretical and practical insight into the problematics of software engineering for sCPS, together with practical hands-on experience. On the technical side, to give concrete examples, the tutorial will make use of DEECo – possibly, as of now, the most mature framework for architecting sCPS by ensembles of autonomic components. It will explain how DEECo concretizes the idea of autonomic component ensembles in an operational and communication semantics which combines real-time execution with opportunistic communication (in both IP and mobile ad-hoc networks). It will show a Java-based realization of DEECo (called jDEECo [3]) and use it for practical experiments with autonomic component ensembles. Further, the tutorial will touch the topic of experimentation with large-scale deployment of sCPS using a simulation-based approach by showing examples combining (i) simulation of execution of DEECo components, (ii) simulation of realistic properties of component communication in mobile ad-hoc networks, and (iii) simulation of component mobility.

2. TUTORIAL DESCRIPTION

The tutorial is delivered in two parts in total amounting to three hours. The first part includes a brief introduction to sCPS and the specific challenges they introduce to software engineering practices and an overview of the suitable methods for architecting them, focusing specifically on EBCS and the related concept of autonomic component ensembles. The second part goes into the more technical aspects and provides a hands-on experience in EBCS development by means of DEECo/jDEECo. The following subsections detail on each of these two parts.

2.1 Part 1: sCPS and Component Ensembles

The goal of this part is to acquaint the participants with the underlying ideas of sCPS and their architecting practices. We will demonstrate the challenges that arise when developing a system characterized by a dynamic architecture and discuss how commonly used approaches to engineering distributed software-intensive systems (e.g. component-based, service-oriented, agent-based) scale with respect to the distinct challenges imposed by sCPS.

Based on a simple use case taken from the ASCENS project, we will introduce the novel concept of EBCS, which specifically targets the development of sCPS. We will explain how the EBCS approach addresses the challenges of dynamic architecture, open-endedness, and self-adaptivity imposed by sCPS. The provided examples will be based on the DEECo component model, which is a publicly available instantiation of EBCS.

2.2 Part 2: Hands-on experience

The second half of the tutorial will focus on the practical aspects and will provide a hands-on experience to the participants. For this purpose, we will introduce the jDEECo framework, which is a Java reification of the DEECo component model. Providing both programming abstractions and a runtime environment, jDEECo eases the development and deployment of DEECo applications. In this context the tutorial will showcase the implementation of a simple demonstrator of the use case introduced in the previous part. Further, it will show how the implemented sCPS can be simulated using jDEECo in order to assess its behavior in large-scale deployment while taking into account the aspects of mobility and network communication in mobile ad-hoc networks. Being realized purely in Java, the implementation of the demonstrator will be easy to be tried out by the participants on their own laptops. The required software and libraries will be made available to the participants along with ready-made examples.

3. INTENDED AUDIENCE

The tutorial is intended for researchers and practitioners interested in novel approaches in the development of architecturally dynamic distributed systems (in particular sCPS). Basic previous acquaintance with the concepts of component models and architecture modeling is recommended but not necessary for following the tutorial. Basic knowledge of Java is needed for anyone interested in practically trying out the provided examples.

4. ACKNOWLEDGMENTS

This work was supported by the EU project ASCENS 257414.

5. REFERENCES

[1] *ASCENS Project*. Accessed April 29, 2014. http://www.ascens-ist.eu/, 2010.

[2] Bures, T., Gerostathopoulos, I., Hnetynka, P., Keznikl, J., Kit, M. and Plasil, F. 2013. DEECo – an Ensemble-Based Component System. In *Proc. of CBSE'13*, ACM.

[3] D3S, Charles University in Prague. *jDEECo website*. Accessed April 29, 2014. https://github.com/d3scomp/JDEECo, 2013.

[4] Hennicker R., Klarl A. 2014. Foundations for Ensemble Modeling - The Helena Approach. In *Proc. of SAS'14*, Springer.

[5] Nicola R.D., Ferrari G., Loreti M., Pugliese R. 2013. A Language-Based Approach to Autonomic Computing. In *Formal Methods for Components and Objects*. Springer.

Author Index

www.ingramcontent.com/pod-product-compliance
Lightning Source LLC
Chambersburg PA
CBHW081525220326
41598CB00036B/6329

* 9 7 8 1 4 5 0 3 3 1 1 6 6 *